D1271499

# Grade 5

# Addison-Wesley Mathematics

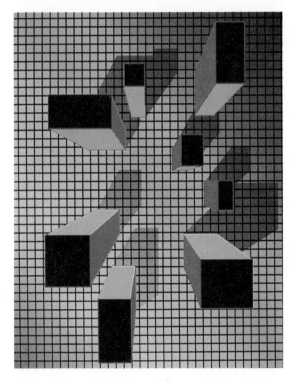

**Robert E. Eicholz**
**Sharon L. Young**

**Phares G. O'Daffer**
**Carne S. Barnett**

**Randall I. Charles**
**Charles R. Fleenor**

**Stanley R. Clemens**
**Freddie L. Renfro**
**Joan E. Westley**

**Gloria F. Gilmer**
**Mary M. Thompson**

**Andy Reeves**
**Carol A. Thornton**

## ▲ Addison-Wesley Publishing Company

Menlo Park, California ■ Reading, Massachusetts ■ New York
Don Mills, Ontario ■ Wokingham, England ■ Amsterdam ■ Bonn
Sydney ■ Singapore ■ Tokyo ■ Madrid ■ San Juan ■ Paris
Seoul, Korea ■ Milan ■ Mexico City ■ Taipei, Taiwan

## PROGRAM ADVISORS

**John A. Dossey**  Professor of Mathematics
Illinois State University, Normal, Illinois

**Bonnie Armbruster**  Associate Professor, Center for the Study of Reading
University of Illinois, Champaign, Illinois

**Karen L. Ostlund**  Associate Professor of Science Education
Southwest Texas State University, San Marcos, Texas

**Betty C. Lee**  Assistant Principal
Ferry Elementary School, Detroit, Michigan

**William J. Driscoll**  Chairman, Department of Mathematical Sciences
Central Connecticut State University, New Britain, Connecticut

**David C. Brummett**  Educational Consultant
Palo Alto, California

## MULTICULTURAL ADVISORS

| | | | |
|---|---|---|---|
| Bill Bray | Moyra Contreras | Barbara Fong | Jeanette Haseyama |
| James Hopkins | Carol Artiga MacKenzie | Gloria Maldonado | Mattie McCloud |
| Marsha Muhammad | Margarita Perez | | |

## CONTRIBUTING WRITERS

| | | | |
|---|---|---|---|
| Betsy Franco | Mary Heinrich | Penny Holland | Marilyn Jacobson |
| Ann Muench | Gini Shimabukuro | Marny Sorgen | Connie Thorpe |
| Sandra Ward | Judith K. Wells | | |

## EXECUTIVE EDITOR

Diane H. Fernández

Cover Photo Credit: Digital Art/West Light

TI-12 Math Explorer™ is a trademark of Texas Instruments.

ISBN: 0-201-44550-6

1 2 3 4 5 6 7 8 9 10 11 12 -DO- 96 95 94 93 92

# Contents

**1**    Letter to the Student

## 1

### NUMBERS AND OPERATIONS

**4**    Understanding Numbers

**6**    Number Properties

**7**    **Mixed Review**

**8**    Mental Math: Using Compatible Numbers

**10**    Problem Solving: Understanding the Operations

**12**    Exploring Algebra: Understanding Variables

**13**    **Power Practice / Quiz**

**14**    Using Critcal Thinking

**15**    **Mixed Review**

**16**    Problem Solving: Introduction

**18**    Problem Solving: Deciding When to Estimate

**20**    Group Decision Making

**22**    **Wrap Up**

**23**    **Power Practice / Test**

**24**    **Enrichment: Triangular and Square Numbers**

**25**    **Cumulative Review**

## 2

### PLACE VALUE: WHOLE NUMBERS AND DECIMALS

**28**    Place Value Through Thousands

**30**    Millions and Billions

**31**    **Mixed Review**

**32**    Comparing and Ordering Whole Numbers

**34**    Rounding Whole Numbers

**36**    Problem Solving: Draw a Picture

**38**    Exploring Algebra: Variables and Expressions

■ **39**     **Power Practice / Quiz**

**40**     Decimal Place Value: Tenths and Hundredths

**42**     Thousandths

**44**     Comparing and Ordering Decimals

**46**     Rounding Decimals

■ **47**     **Mixed Review**

**48**     Problem Solving: Understanding the Question

**50**     Data Collection and Analysis: Group Decision Making

■ **52**     **Wrap Up**

■ **53**     **Power Practice / Test**

**54**     **Enrichment: Roman Numerals**

■ **55**     **Cumulative Review**

## 3

### ADDITION AND SUBTRACTION: WHOLE NUMBERS AND DECIMALS

**58**     Estimation: Using Rounding

■ **59**     **Mixed Review**

**60**     Reviewing Whole Number Addition and Subtraction

**62**     Front-End Estimation

**64**     Problem Solving: Guess and Check

**66**     Adding Decimals: Making the Connection

**68**     Adding Decimals

**70**     Using Critical Thinking

■ **71**     **Power Practice / Quiz**

**72**     Problem Solving: Choosing a Calculation Method

**74**     Subtracting Decimals: Making the Connection

**76**     Subtracting Decimals

**78**     Mental Math: Using Compensation

■ **79**     **Mixed Review**

**80**     Problem Solving: Using a Calculator

**82**     Applied Problem Solving: Group Decision Making

■ **84**     **Wrap Up**

■ **85**     **Power Practice / Test**

**86**     **Enrichment: Finding and Using Patterns**

■ **87**     **Cumulative Review**

# 4

## DATA AND GRAPHS

90    Thinking About Graphs
92    Reading and Interpreting Line Graphs
94    Making Line Graphs
95      **Mixed Review**
96    Double Bar Graphs
98    Using Critical Thinking
100    Running Totals with a Calculator
101    **Power Practice / Quiz**
102    Range, Mean, Median, and Mode
103      **Mixed Review**
104    Making a Questionnaire
106    Problem Solving: Make a Table
108    Estimation: Substituting Compatible Numbers
110    Problem Solving: Extra Data
112    Data Collection and Analysis:
         Group Decision Making
114    **Wrap Up**
115    **Power Practice / Test**
116    **Enrichment: Organizing Data to
         Make Comparisons**
117    **Cumulative Review**

# 5

## MULTIPLICATION: WHOLE NUMBERS AND DECIMALS

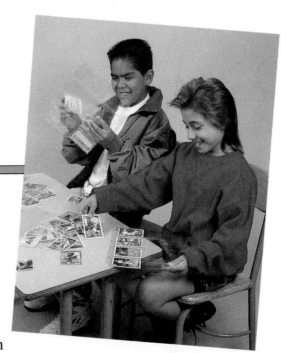

120    Mental Math: Special Products
122    Estimating Products Using Rounding
123      **Mixed Review**
124    Reviewing Whole Number Multiplication
126    Problem Solving: Multiple-Step Problems
128    Problem Solving: Solve a Simpler Problem
130    Mental Math: Breaking Apart Numbers
131    **Power Practice / Quiz**
132    Multiplying Decimals: Making the Connection
134    Multiplying Decimals
136    Estimating with Decimals

**138** More About Multiplying Decimals
■ **139**     **Mixed Review**
**140** Problem Solving: Using a Calculator
**142** Mental Math: Multiplying Decimals
    by 10, 100, and 1,000
**144** Applied Problem Solving:
    Group Decision Making
■ **146** **Wrap Up**
■ **147** **Power Practice / Test**
**148** **Enrichment: Exponents**
■ **149** **Cumulative Review**

## 6

### METRIC MEASUREMENT

**152** Estimating Length
**154** Meters and Centimeters
**156** Centimeters and Millimeters
■ **157**     **Mixed Review**
**158** Area of a Rectangle
**160** Kilometers
■ **161** **Power Practice / Quiz**
**162** Capacity and Volume
■ **163**     **Mixed Review**
**164** Kilograms and Grams
**166** Problem Solving: Make an Organized List
**168** Time
**170** Problem Solving: Using Data from a Thermometer
**172** Data Collection and Analysis:
    Group Decision Making
■ **174** **Wrap Up**
■ **175** **Power Practice / Test**
**176** **Enrichment: Time Zones**
■ **177** **Cumulative Review**

## 7

### DIVISION: WHOLE NUMBERS AND DECIMALS

**180** Mental Math: Special Quotients
**182** Estimating Quotients:
    Rounding and Compatible Numbers

■ **183** **Mixed Review**
184 Dividing Whole Numbers: Making the Connection
186 Dividing: 2- and 3-Digit Quotients
188 Dividing: Deciding Where to Start
190 Dividing: Special Cases
192 Finding Averages
■ **193** **Power Practice / Quiz**
194 Problem Solving: Interpreting Remainders
196 Problem Solving: Work Backward
198 Dividing Decimals: Making the Connection
200 Dividing Decimals
■ **201** **Mixed Review**
202 Problem Solving: Determining Reasonable Answers
204 Applied Problem Solving:
    Group Decision Making
■ **206** **Wrap Up**
■ **207** **Power Practice / Test**
208 **Enrichment: Short Division**
■ **209** **Cumulative Review**

## 8

### MORE DIVISION:
### WHOLE NUMBERS AND DECIMALS

212 Mental Math: Special Quotients
214 Estimating Quotient Digits
216 Dividing: 1-Digit Quotients
218 Changing Estimates
220 Finding Larger Quotients
■ **221** **Mixed Review**
222 Problem Solving: Choosing a Calculation Method
■ **223** **Power Practice / Quiz**
224 Dividing: Special Cases
226 Problem Solving: Look for a Pattern
228 Mental Math: Dividing Decimals by
    10, 100, and 1,000
■ **229** **Mixed Review**
230 Problem Solving: Estimating the Answer

**232** Data Collection and Analysis:
  Group Decision Making
■ **234** **Wrap Up**
■ **235** **Power Practice / Test**
  **236** **Enrichment: Divisibility**
■ **237** **Cumulative Review**

9

## UNDERSTANDING FRACTIONS AND MIXED NUMBERS

**240** Reviewing the Meaning of Fractions
**242** Equivalent Fractions
■ **243** **Mixed Review**
**244** Finding Equivalent Fractions
**246** Greatest Common Factor
**248** Lowest-Terms Fractions
**250** Exploring Algebra: More About Variables
■ **251** **Power Practice / Quiz**
**252** Problem Solving: Use Logical Reasoning
**254** Comparing and Ordering Fractions
**256** Improper Fractions and Mixed Numbers:
  Using Manipulatives
**258** More Improper Fractions and Mixed Numbers
■ **259** **Mixed Review**
**260** Problem Solving: Using Data from a Table
**262** Applied Problem Solving:
  Group Decision Making
■ **264** **Wrap Up**
■ **265** **Power Practice / Test**
  **266** **Enrichment: Finding Prime Factors**
■ **267** **Cumulative Review**

10

## ADDITION AND SUBTRACTION: FRACTIONS AND MIXED NUMBERS

**270** Adding and Subtracting Fractions:
  Like Denominators
**272** Least Common Multiple

**274** Adding and Subtracting Fractions:
   Making the Connection

**276** Adding and Subtracting Fractions:
   Unlike Denominators

■**277** **Mixed Review**

**278** Problem Solving: Problems Without Solutions

**280** Estimating Fraction Sums and Differences

■**281** **Power Practice / Quiz**

**282** Adding and Subtracting Mixed Numbers:
   Making the Connection

**284** Adding Mixed Numbers

**286** Subtracting Mixed Numbers

■**287** **Mixed Review**

**288** More Adding and Subtracting:
   Whole Numbers, Fractions, and
   Mixed Numbers

**290** Problem Solving: Choosing A Calculation Method

**292** Data Collection and Analysis:
   Group Decision Making

■**294** **Wrap Up**

■**295** **Power Practice / Test**

**296** **Enrichment: Fractions Between Fractions**

■**297** **Cumulative Review**

11

## CUSTOMARY MEASUREMENT

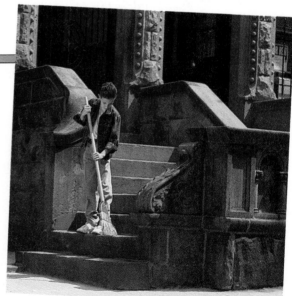

**300** Customary Units of Length

**302** Length: Parts of an Inch

**304** Length: Feet, Yards, and Miles

■**305** **Mixed Review**

**306** Problem Solving: Problems with More
   Than One Answer

**308** Temperature: Degrees Fahrenheit

■**309** **Power Practice / Quiz**

**310** Customary Units of Capacity

**312** Customary Units of Weight

■**313** **Mixed Review**

**314** Problem Solving: Deciding When to Estimate

316 Applied Problem Solving:
   Group Decision Making
318 **Wrap Up**
319 **Power Practice / Test**
320 **Enrichment: Estimating Length**
321 **Cumulative Review**

## 12

### MULTIPLICATION AND DIVISION OF FRACTIONS

324 Multiplying a Fraction and a Whole Number
326 Estimating a Fraction of a Number
328 Multiplying Fractions: Making the Connection
330 Multiplying Fractions
331 **Mixed Review**
332 Exploring Algebra:
   Informal Algebra in Problem Solving
333 **Power Practice / Quiz**
334 Problem Solving: Multiple-Step Problems
336 Multiplying Mixed Numbers
338 Problem Solving: Using a Calculator
340 Dividing Fractions: Using Objects and Pictures
342 Data Collection and Analysis:
   Group Decision Making
344 **Wrap Up**
345 **Power Practice / Test**
346 **Enrichment: Following Flowchart Directions**
347 **Cumulative Review**

## 13

### GEOMETRY

350 Analyzing Solid Figures
352 Exploring Triangles
354 Measuring Angles
356 Quadrilaterals
358 More about Quadrilaterals
359 **Mixed Review**
360 Using Critical Thinking

■ 361 **Power Practice / Quiz**
362 Congruent Figures and Motions
364 Problem Solving: Using Data from a Picture
366 Other Polygons: Tessellations
■ 367 **Mixed Review**
368 Circles
370 Circumference
372 Coordinate Geometry
374 Applied Problem Solving:
Group Decision Making
■ 376 **Wrap Up**
■ 377 **Power Practice / Test**
378 **Enrichment: Top, Bottom, Front,
and Side Views**
■ 379 **Cumulative Review**

## 14

### RATIO AND PERCENT

382 Ratio
384 Ratio Tables
386 Proportions
388 Problem Solving:
Using Data from a Scale Drawing
390 Understanding Percent
■ 391 **Mixed Review**
392 Percents as Decimals or Fractions
394 Percents and Lowest-terms Fractions
■ 395 **Power Practice / Quiz**
396 Mental Math and Estimation with Percents
■ 397 **Mixed Review**
398 Finding a Percent of a Number
400 Problem Solving: Finding Related Problems
402 Data Collection and Analysis:
Group Decision Making
■ 404 **Wrap Up**
■ 405 **Power Practice / Test**
406 **Enrichment: Percent Patterns**
■ 407 **Cumulative Review**

## 15

### PROBABILITY

410    Fair and Unfair Games

412    Equally Likely Outcomes

414    Probability of Outcomes

■ 415    **Mixed Review**

416    Experimental and Mathematical Probabilities

418    Using Critical Thinking

■ 419    **Power Practice / Quiz**

420    Problem Solving: Using Data from an Order Form

422    Making Estimates by Sampling

424    Simulations

■ 425    **Mixed Review**

426    Applied Problem Solving:
       Group Decision Making

■ 428    **Wrap Up**

■ 429    **Power Practice / Test**

430    **Enrichment: Combinations**

■ 431    **Cumulative Review**

## 16

### PERIMETER, AREA, AND VOLUME

434    Perimeter

■ 435    **Mixed Review**

436    Problem Solving: Estimating the Answer

438    Area of Figures with Irregular Shapes

440    Using Critical Thinking

■ 441    **Power Practice / Quiz**

442    Area of Right Triangles

444    More About Area of Triangles

446    Area of Parallelograms

■ 447    **Mixed Review**

448    Volume

450    Surface Area

452    Data Collection and Analysis:
       Group Decision Making

■ 454    **Wrap Up**

**455** Power Practice / Test

**456** Enrichment: Estimating Area

**457** Cumulative Review


**458** RESOURCE BANK AND APPENDIX

**460** Skills Review Bank

**468** Data Bank

**484** Calculator Bank

**492** Computer Bank

**500** More Practice Bank

**528** Table of Measures

**529** Glossary

**537** Index

**545** Acknowledgments

Dear Student:

Get ready for an exciting year in mathematics. By the end of the year you'll be a whiz at math! It's going to be fun!

This year, you'll be using what you already know in interesting new ways. For example, you'll be working with huge numbers in the millions and billions — that's a lot of zeros! You'll also learn more about fractions, decimals and calculating averages. You'll become a super problem solver and learn about problems with more than one answer!

Puzzles are fun and some math problems are like puzzles. For example, you'll learn how to figure out the size of the space inside a triangle or a circle.

You'll have opportunities to work in groups and use the Resource Bank in the back of the book which is filled with fascinating facts and ways to help you develop your new math skills.

We know that you will enjoy this exciting year in mathematics.

From your friends at Addison-Wesley.

# 1

# NUMBERS
# AND
# OPERATIONS

**THEME: WORDS AND SYMBOLS**

**M**ATH AND LANGUAGE ARTS

**DATA BANK**

Use the Language Arts Data Bank on page 468 to answer the questions.

1 If you wanted to do some research on the number system we use, you would be most likely to find the information in books within which group of Dewey Decimal Numbers?

**2** In Braille some symbols are used for both numbers and letters. What number in Braille would be written the same as the word "cab"?

**3** Write the problem 8 + 12 in Egyptian hieroglyphics. Then write the solution to the problem in Egyptian hieroglyphics.

**4** **Using Critical Thinking** Compare the Egyptian hieroglyphic number symbols with those we use. Describe what you observe to be the main difference between their system and ours.

Picture symbols carved thousands of years ago tell fascinating stories about ancient Egyptians and their culture.

3

# Understanding Numbers

Many math words and symbols appear in newspapers, in magazines, and on television. The language of mathematics is an important part of what you learn in this book.

**EXPLORE** **Study the Information**

Find at least eight math words and symbols in the article below.

---

### MathMasters Winners Announced

The winner of the 1992 Tri-city MathMasters Contest is eleven-year-old Mai Binh. A fifth grade student at Keller Elementary, Mai correctly solved 49 of the 50 problems on the test for a record score of 98%. Tied for second place with scores of 96% were Ray Parish and Linda Kress of Fairview Elementary.

More than 300 students from the city's twelve elementary schools took part in this year's contest. The average score for all contestants was 80%—another all-time high for this annual contest.

---

## TALK ABOUT IT

**1.** What are some math words in the article?

**2.** What are some math symbols in the article?

Numbers can be expressed in different forms. For example, each of the following **numerical expressions** is another name for 24.

| Using Symbols | Using Words |
|---|---|
| $3 \times 8$ | three times eight *or* three multiplied by eight |
| $15 + 9$ | fifteen plus nine *or* nine more than fifteen |
| $40 - 16$ | forty minus sixteen *or* sixteen less than forty |

Express the mathematical symbols in words.

**1.** $7 + 5$    **2.** $8 \times 32$    **3.** $48 \div 6$    **4.** $12 - 6$    **5.** $\frac{1}{2}$

4

Express the mathematical symbols in words.

**1.** $4 + 34$   **2.** $63 \times 4$   **3.** $42 \div 7$   **4.** $16 - 9$   **5.** $\frac{3}{4}$

Choose the correct symbols for the math words. More than one choice may be correct.

**6.** sixty-five divided by five

    **A.** $\frac{5}{65}$   **B.** $\frac{65}{5}$   **C.** $65 \div 5$

**7.** five less than eight

    **A.** $5 - 8$   **B.** $5 < 8$   **C.** $8 - 5$

**8.** twenty more than sixty

    **A.** $20 > 60$   **B.** $60 + 20$   **C.** $20 + 60$

**9.** one fourth

    **A.** $\frac{1}{4}$   **B.** $1 \times 4$   **C.** $\frac{4}{1}$

Write each numerical expression using symbols.

**10.** thirty divided by five

**11.** the product of ten and nine

**12.** the difference of nine and seven

**13.** the sum of nine and five

**MATH REASONING**

Write **true** or **false** for each statement.

**14.** The numerical expression $\frac{1}{3}$ means both *one third* and *one divided by three.*

**15.** *Thirty-five divided by seven* has the same meaning as both $35 \div 7$ and $\frac{7}{35}$.

**PROBLEM SOLVING**

**16.** This year 21 more students entered the contest than entered last year. Last year 298 entered the contest. Write the numerical expression for the number who entered this year.

**17. Language Arts Data Bank** How would you write the following numbers using Egyptian hieroglyphic numerals? See page 468.

    **A.** 13   **B.** 121   **C.** 110,000

▶ **ESTIMATION**

**18.** Each dot represents one person in a section of the stands in a football stadium. Use the colored lines to help you estimate the total number of people in this section.

*More Practice, page 500, set A*

# Number Properties

**EXPLORE** **Solve to Understand**

Kyle and Dana want to know how many students named neon yellow, rainbow stripes, or apple green as their favorite kind of shoelace. Which child's numerical expression will give the correct total?

Kyle: $(5 + 4) + 3$
Dana: $5 + (4 + 3)$

> Do operations inside parentheses ( ) first.

| Survey of Students' Favorite Kinds of Shoelaces | |
| --- | --- |
| color | number of students |
| neon yellow . . . . . . . . . . . . . . . | 5 |
| rainbow stripes . . . . . . . . . . . . | 4 |
| apple green . . . . . . . . . . . . . . | 3 |
| candy cane . . . . . . . . . . . . . . | 7 |

**TALK ABOUT IT**

1. Does the position of the parentheses in Kyle's and Dana's expressions change the value? Explain.

2. Give a numerical expression whose value changes when the position of the parentheses changes. (Hint: You may have to use two operations.)

These **number properties** help us evaluate expressions.

| **Commutative (Order) Property** |
| --- |
| Changing the order of addends or factors does not change the sum or product. |

$9 + 3 = 12$
$3 + 9 = 12$

$5 \times 3 = 15$
$3 \times 5 = 15$

| **Associative (Grouping) Property** |
| --- |
| Changing the grouping of addends or factors does not change the sum or product. |

$3 + (7 + 8) = 18$
$(3 + 7) + 8 = 18$

$5 \times (1 \times 3) = 15$
$(5 \times 1) \times 3 = 15$

Give the property that tells you that both expressions name the same number.

1. $42 + 10 = 10 + 42$
2. $(20 + 8) + 4 = 20 + (8 + 4)$
3. $2 \times (4 \times 6) = (2 \times 4) \times 6$
4. $4 \times 5 = 5 \times 4$

6

Give the property that tells you that each expression names the same number.

1. $25 + 12 = 12 + 25$
2. $(6 \times 1) \times 5 = 6 \times (1 \times 5)$
3. $3 + (4 + 6) = (3 + 4) + 6$
4. $16 + (7 + 9) = (16 + 7) + 9$
5. $8 \times 2 = 2 \times 8$
6. $3 \times (4 \times 2) = (3 \times 4) \times 2$
7. $(17 + 11) + 5 = 17 + (11 + 5)$
8. $15 + (5 + 9) = (15 + 5) + 9$

Find the value of each expression.

9. $6 + (8 + 1)$
10. $(36 \div 4) + 5$
11. $(3 + 4) \times 6$
12. $(13 - 7) \times 8$
13. $(7 + 1) + 8$
14. $(6 + 8) - 9$
15. $(24 \div 3) \times 4$
16. $13 - (45 \div 9)$
17. $9 + (4 \times 2)$

## APPLY

### MATH REASONING

Copy the equations and put in parentheses to show which operation was done first.

18. $4 \times 2 + 5 = 13$
19. $3 \times 4 - 3 = 9$
20. $8 \times 5 + 2 = 56$
21. $2 \times 4 + 3 = 14$
22. $3 + 4 \times 5 = 35$
23. $24 \div 6 + 2 = 3$

### PROBLEM SOLVING

Use the table on page 6.

24. How many students named rainbow stripes, apple green, or neon yellow as their favorite?

25. How many more students named candy cane than named apple green as their favorite?

## MIXED REVIEW

Add, subtract, multiply, or divide.

26. $5 + 8$
27. $6 + 7$
28. $4 + 6$
29. $3 + 9$
30. $6 + 8$
31. $12 - 5$
32. $15 - 9$
33. $11 - 3$
34. $17 - 9$
35. $10 - 6$
36. $8 \times 3$
37. $6 \times 6$
38. $4 \times 7$
39. $5 \times 8$
40. $7 \times 2$
41. $24 \div 4$
42. $18 \div 6$
43. $15 \div 5$
44. $28 \div 7$
45. $30 \div 6$

*More Practice, page 500, set B*

# Mental Math
## Using Compatible Numbers

**LEARN ABOUT IT**

**EXPLORE** **Examine the Data**

The Eager Readers Club made a table to show how many and what kinds of books the members read during summer vacation. Ray and Wanda wanted to find out how many books the members read in all.

| Kind of Book | Number Read |
|---|---|
| Mystery | 90 |
| Adventure | 75 |
| Sports | 38 |
| Famous People | 10 |
| Others | 25 |

Ray used his calculator to solve the problem this way:

ON/AC  90  +  75  +  38  +  10  +  25  =  ?

Wanda used **mental math** to solve the problem this way: $(90 + 10) + (75 + 25) + 38 = ?$

**TALK ABOUT IT**

**1.** Do you think that Ray and Wanda got the same answer?

**2.** What do the parentheses ( ) tell about what Wanda did?

When there are three or more addends or factors in a problem involving addition or multiplication, look for **compatible numbers.** Compatible numbers are numbers that are easy to compute mentally. Here is how.

Find: $25 + 19 + 75 + 1$ Think: 25 and 75 are easy to add mentally.
19 and 1 are easy to add mentally.

The commutative and associative properties let you rearrange and regroup addends.

$(25 + 75) + (19 + 1) = 100 + 20 = 120$

**TRY IT OUT**

Order and group the addends and factors to make it easy to compute mentally. Then give the sums and products.

**1.** $39 + 60 + 17 + 1$ **2.** $4 \times 13 \times 25$ **3.** $120 + 57 + 80$

**4.** $50 \times 25 \times 2 \times 4$ **5.** $530 + 290 + 70 + 8$ **6.** $5 \times 18 \times 20$

Show how you would change the order and grouping. Then solve using mental math.

1. $9 + 23 + 1$

2. $5 \times 19 \times 2$

3. $75 + 16 + 25$

4. $3 + 40 + 7 + 50$

5. $20 \times 37 \times 5$

6. $60 + 36 + 40$

7. $50 \times 18 \times 2$

8. $25 + 9 + 25$

9. $15 + 190 + 2 + 10$

10. $4 \times 8 \times 25$

11. $6 + 9 + 94 + 1$

12. $87 \times 2 \times 10 \times 5$

13. $95 + 113 + 5$

14. $2 \times 160 \times 5$

15. $50 + 8 + 3 + 50$

16. $2 \times 31 \times 50$

17. $170 + 17 + 30$

18. $50 \times 9 \times 2$

19. $125 + 36 + 75$

20. $5 \times 4 \times 3 \times 5$

## APPLY

### MATH REASONING

Name the property (commutative or associative) used to complete steps B and C.

21. **A.** $25 + (38 + 25)$
    **B.** $25 + (25 + 38)$
    **C.** $(25 + 25) + 38$

22. **A.** $(14 + 28) + 16$
    **B.** $16 + (14 + 28)$
    **C.** $(16 + 14) + 28$

### PROBLEM SOLVING

23. Use the table on page 8. What is the total number of these kinds of books that were read during the summer by the club members: sports, mystery, and famous people?

**DATA BANK**

24. **Language Arts Data Bank** Lamont was looking in the library for a book about the life of Albert Einstein. In which group of Dewey Decimal System numbers would he find the book he wanted? See page 468.

### ▶ MENTAL MATH

When adding or subtracting a 1, 2, or 3, you can count on or count back to find the sum or difference mentally. For example, to find $49 + 3$, start with 49 and count on: 49.....50, 51, 52. $49 + 3 = 52$

Solve mentally by counting on or counting back.

25. $19 + 2$

26. $298 + 3$

27. $30 - 1$

28. $51 - 2$

29. $3 + 679$

*More Practice, page 500, set C*

# Problem Solving
## Understanding the Operations

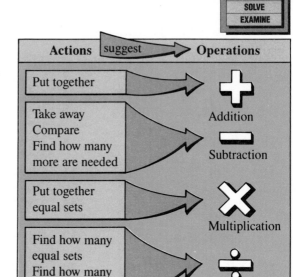

UNDERSTAND
ANALYZE DATA
PLAN
ESTIMATE
SOLVE
EXAMINE

**LEARN ABOUT IT**

The action in a problem suggests the operation needed to solve the problem. The diagram at the right reviews the actions you learned about in earlier grades.

Sometimes the actions in problems are not easy to recognize. You need to think carefully to decide which of the operations they suggest. Study the examples below.

| Actions | suggest → Operations |
|---|---|
| Put together | + Addition |
| Take away, Compare, Find how many more are needed | − Subtraction |
| Put together equal sets | × Multiplication |
| Find how many equal sets, Find how many in each set | ÷ Division |

Tammy had some old coins. She gave 5 of them to Lita and has 4 coins left. How many coins did she have before she gave some away?

> Since I want to find how many coins she had to begin with, I need to find the total of the coins she gave away and the coins she still has.

$$4 + 5 = 9$$

Tim had some Presidents buttons. A friend gave him 5 more buttons. Now he has 13. How many buttons did he have before his friend gave him some more?

> I want to find how many he already had, so I need to find the difference in the amount he has now and the amount he was given.

$$13 - 5 = 8$$

**TRY IT OUT**

Name the operation you need to use for each problem. Then solve the problem.

1. Joanna shows 14 different baseball caps in this year's hobby show. Last year she showed only 8. How many more caps did she show this year?

2. Skip has 18 national parks posters. He has 3 from each park he visited. How many parks did he visit?

3. School posters cost $9 each last year. This year they cost $4 more than last year. How much does a school poster cost this year?

4. Brenda bought 3 Save-the-Seals T-shirts. They cost $8 each. How much did Brenda spend for all 3?

Name the operation you need to use. Then solve.

1. Chris had some glass bears. He was given 8 more for his birthday. Now he has 15. How many glass bears did he have before his birthday?

2. Renaldo has 9 famous player baseball cards and 7 famous player football cards. How many famous player cards does he have altogether?

3. Each school T-shirt costs the same amount. Anita paid $15 for 3 T-shirts. What was the cost of each T-shirt?

4. Janis had 12 boxes of greeting cards to sell for a school fund-raising project. She has sold all but 3 boxes of cards. How many boxes has she sold?

5. Anita bought 6 Big Bend National Park arm patches for her friends at home. Each patch costs $3. How much did she spend for the patches?

6. Russ wants to buy a stamp album that costs $18. He has $9. How much more money does he need to buy the album?

7. The Woo family takes a 7-mile bicycle trip together every Saturday in good weather. How far would they ride during 5 trips?

8. Barbara has 48 coins in her coin book. Each page has 8 coins on it. How many pages of her book are filled with coins?

9. Judy now has 9 lava rocks in her rocks box. She did have more, but she gave 8 of them to Ernie yesterday. How many lava rocks did Judy have before she gave some to Ernie?

10. **Write Your Own Problem** Write a question that you could answer by using the data in this story. Then answer your question.

In 1987 Kari had 9 full books of stamps. In 1990 she had 14 full books of stamps.

# Exploring Algebra
## Understanding Variables

Riddle: *What do* MATH *and* READING *have in common?*

To solve the riddle, follow these steps:

- Find the number each letter in the equations stands for. Each letter stands for **0, 1, 2, 3, 4,** or **5** and stands for the same number in each equation.

- Copy the Riddle Answer Key.

- Write each letter above the number it stands for in the equations.

Riddle Answer Key

$$\overline{0} \;\; \overline{1} \;\; \overline{2} \;\;\; \overline{3} \;\; \overline{2} \;\; \overline{0} \;\; \overline{0} \;\; \overline{2} \;\; \overline{4} \;\;\; \overline{5}$$

**Equations**

$L \times H = L$      $E + E = R$

$E + T = E$      $A - H = R$

**Zero Property of Addition**
The sum of a number and zero is that number.

**Zero Property of Subtraction**
When zero is subtracted from a number, the difference is that number.

**One Property of Multiplication**
The product of a number and one is that number.

**Zero Property of Multiplication**
The product of a number and zero is zero.

## TALK ABOUT IT

1. Which number property did you use to find the number that $H$ stands for in the equation $L \times H = L$?

2. Which number property did you use to find the number that $T$ stands for in the equation $E + T = E$?

This book introduces you to several topics from algebra. One of the most important of these topics is the idea of a **variable.** A variable is a letter that stands for a single number or a range of numbers.

In the boxed equations each variable stands for one of these numbers: 1, 2, 5, 6, or 7. The same variable stands for the same number in each equation. Find the number each variable stands for.

$$C \times C = 36 \qquad H \times T = H$$
$$E + H = 9 \qquad C + E = 8$$
$$H - A = E$$

Express the math symbols in words.

**1.** $9 + 11$    **2.** $6 \times 45$    **3.** $63 \div 9$    **4.** $22 - 7$    **5.** $\frac{1}{3}$

Choose the correct symbols for the math words. More than one choice may be correct.

**6.** thirty-five divided by seven

    **A.** $35 \div 7$  **B.** $\frac{35}{7}$  **C.** $7 \div 35$

**7.** seven less than fifteen

    **A.** $7 < 15$ **B.** $15 - 7$ **C.** $7 - 15$

**8.** the sum of nine and eight

    **A.** $8 + 9$ **B.** $8 \times 9$ **C.** $9 + 8$

**9.** the product of four and six

    **A.** $6 \div 4$  **B.** $4 + 6$  **C.** $4 \times 6$

Use the properties to help you find the missing numbers.

**10.** $15 \times 1 = $ ▥

**11.** $4 + (5 + 6) = ($ ▥ $+ 5) + 6$

**12.** $12 + 0 = $ ▥ $+ 12$

**13.** $8 + $ ▥ $= 8$

**14.** $(3 \times 5) \times 7 = ($ ▥ $\times 3) \times 7$

**15.** $(4 \times 1) \times 5 = $ ▥ $\times ($ ▥ $\times 5)$

**16.** $(8 \times 5) \times 2 = (2 \times 5) \times $ ▥

**17.** ▥ $+ (8 + 4) = (4 + 6) + 8$

Solve using mental math.

**18.** $5 \times 17 \times 2$

**19.** $8 + 127 + 2$

**20.** $12 + 25 + 8$

**21.** $147 \times 5 \times 2$

**22.** $60 + 87 + 40$

**23.** $96 \times 5 \times 20$

**24.** $16 + 8 + 4 + 19 + 2$

**25.** $25 \times 7 \times 3 \times 4$

**26.** $17 + 46 + 23 + 4$

## PROBLEM SOLVING

Name the operation that you need to use for each problem. Then solve the problem.

**27.** Greg has 1 homework assignment for each of the 6 classes he takes. How many homework assignments does he have?

**28.** Loni plans to read 6 pages in her language arts book and 2 pages in her science book. How many pages does she plan to read?

**29.** Mary has 2 crossword puzzle books and 5 number puzzle books. How many more number puzzle books than crossword puzzle books does she have?

**30.** Bill must read 12 pages in his social studies textbook. He will read 4 pages each day. How many days will it take him to finish his reading?

# Using Critical Thinking

LEARN ABOUT IT

When Carlos saw his friend Holly, he showed her this record of tips he had made during his first two days of work at the diner. He wondered how much money he would make in tips after six days. "Wow," Carlos exclaimed, "if I can keep this pattern going, I'll have made $126 in tips in my first six days!" "Something's wrong with your calculations," Holly said. "At most you'd make $42 in tips." When they asked Patty to settle the argument, she exclaimed, "Sorry, but you're both wrong! Carlos would make exactly $62 in tips this week."

Who do you think was correct, if anyone?

**TALK ABOUT IT**

1. What was Carlos trying to do?

2. How did Carlos, Holly, and Patty get their answers?

3. Who, if anyone, is correct—Carlos, Holly, or Patty?

4. Using Carlos' pattern, what would be the total amount of money he would have made in tips at the end of ten days?

5. Can you determine a pattern for certain with just two numbers? with three numbers? Explain.

| TIP RECORD | |
|---|---|
| Day Number | Amount of Tips |
| 1 | 2 |
| 2 | 4 |
| 3 | |
| 4 | |
| 5 | |
| 6 | |

**TRY IT OUT**

Look for a pattern. Give the next three numbers.

1. 1, 2, 2, 3, 3, 3, 4, 4, 4, 4, 5, 5, 5, 5, ▓ , ▓ , ▓ , ...

2. 1, 2, 3, 2, 4, 6, 4, 5, 6, 8, 10, 12, 7, 8, 9, ▓ , ▓ , ▓ , ...

Look for a pattern in the tables below. Suppose it continues.
Give the next 2 numbers.

| | Weeks | New Employees | | Months | Hamburger Sales (1000s) | | Years | Savings ($1000) |
|---|---|---|---|---|---|---|---|---|
| | 1 | 1 | | 1 | 2 | | 1 | 2 |
| | 2 | 3 | | 2 | 5 | | 2 | 4 |
| | 3 | 5 | | 3 | 8 | | 3 | 6 |
| **3.** | 4 | ▦ | **5.** | 4 | ▦ | **7.** | 4 | ▦ |
| **4.** | 5 | ▦ | **6.** | 5 | ▦ | **8.** | 5 | ▦ |

Give the next three numbers in each pattern.

**9.** 1, 3, 5, 7, 9, ▦, ▦, ▦, …

**10.** 2, 6, 10, 14, 18, ▦, ▦, ▦, …

**11.** 1, 2, 4, 7, 11, ▦, ▦, ▦, …

**12.** 1, 4, 9, 16, 25, ▦, ▦, ▦, …

**13.** 5, 15, 25, 35, ▦, ▦, ▦, …

**14.** 50, 43, 36, 29, 22, ▦, ▦, ▦, ..

**15.** 5, 5, 10, 6, 6, 12, ▦, ▦, ▦, …

**16.** 1, 1, 2, 3, 5, 8, ▦, ▦, ▦, …

**17.** What patterns do you see in the graph at the right?

**18.** What would you predict would be the numbers of band members and chorus members in 1990 and 1991?

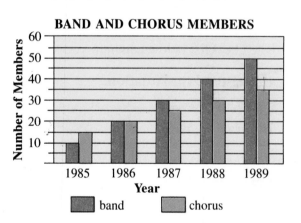

BAND AND CHORUS MEMBERS

MIXED REVIEW

Give the property that tells you that each expression names the same number.

**19.** 12 + 15 = 15 + 12

**20.** 3 + (8 + 6) = (3 + 8) + 6

**21.** 7 + 0 = 7

**22.** (1 × 5) × 7 = (5 × 1) × 7

Choose compatible numbers and find the sum or product.

**23.** 75 + 18 + 25 + 12

**24.** 4 × 2 × 6 × 50

**25.** 150 + 17 + 50 + 3

**26.** 25 × 2 × 2 × 9

**27.** 4 × 8 × 25 × 2

**28.** 125 + 27 + 3 + 75

# Problem Solving
## Introduction

UNDERSTAND
ANALYZE DATA
PLAN
ESTIMATE
SOLVE
EXAMINE

**LEARN ABOUT IT**

Some problems can be solved by using one of the operations—addition, subtraction, multiplication, or division. These are called **one-step** problems. One-step problems can be solved using the strategy **Choose the Operation.**

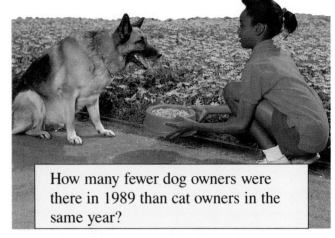

How many fewer dog owners were there in 1989 than cat owners in the same year?

| Pets Owned (1,400 people surveyed) | | |
| --- | --- | --- |
| Pet | 1989 | 1990 |
| Cat | 621 | 560 |
| Dog | 582 | 601 |
| Birds | 89 | 93 |
| Fish | 61 | 52 |
| Other | 43 | 94 |

The checklist below can help you solve problems.

**Understand the situation.**

I want to compare the number of dog owners to the number of cat owners in 1989.

**Analyze the data.**

Dogs in 1989: 582    Cats in 1989: 621

**Plan what to do.**

Since I want to **compare** the two numbers, I should subtract.

**Estimate the answer.**

582 is about 580. 621 is about 620.
$620 - 580 = 40$    The answer should be about 40.

**Solve the problem.**

$621 - 582 = 39$    There were 39 fewer dog owners than cat owners in 1989.

**Examine the answer.**

39 is close to the estimate of 40, so 39 is a reasonable answer.

**TRY IT OUT**

Choose the numerical expression you would use to solve the problem.

1. How many more dog owners were there in 1990 than in 1989?

   **A.** $582 + 601$    **B.** $601 - 582$

2. What was the total number of cat owners and dog owners in 1990?

   **A.** $621 + 582$    **B.** $560 + 601$

16

Pick the numerical expression you would use to solve the problem.

1. The number of fish owners in 1991 is expected to be twice as great as it was in 1989. How many fish owners are there expected to be in 1991?

   **A.** 61 + 2
   **B.** 2 × 61

2. The number of bird owners in 1990 was three times the number of bird owners in 1980. How many bird owners were there in 1980?

   **A.** 93 ÷ 3
   **B.** 93 × 3

3. An average dog eats $250 worth of dog food in a year. How much was spent on dog food by the people surveyed in 1990?

   **A.** $250 + 601
   **B.** $250 × 601

Solve.

5. One kind of dry dog food sells for $5 a bag. Each bag lasts a week. How much would it cost to buy this dog food for 1 month (4 weeks)?

6. Ali bought collars for her 4 puppies. The collars cost $16 in all. Each collar cost the same. What was the cost for each collar?

4. The people surveyed came from 5 regions of the U.S. Each region had the same number of people. How many were from each region?

   **A.** 1,400 × 5
   **B.** 1,400 ÷ 5

7. Muffin had two litters of kittens. There were 6 kittens in her first litter. There were 5 kittens in her second litter. How many kittens did Muffin have?

8. **Data Hunt** Make a survey of 10 of your friends. Find out how many have dogs or cats as pets. Find how many more there are of one kind of pet than there are of the other.

**Write Your Own Problem**

Write questions that can be answered using the data given in the table on page 16 and the numerical expressions given below.

9. 93 − 52

10. 560 + 601

11. 601 − 560

# Problem Solving
## Deciding When to Estimate

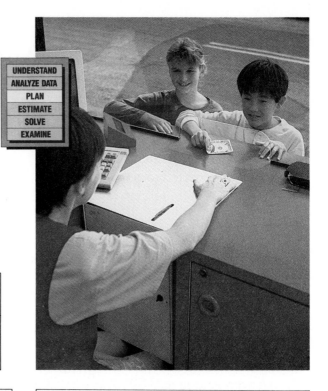

UNDERSTAND
ANALYZE DATA
PLAN
ESTIMATE
SOLVE
EXAMINE

### LEARN ABOUT IT

When you solve problems, you must decide whether you need an **estimate** or an **exact answer:** When you make an estimate, you are finding *about how much* or *about how many.*

| Movie Prices | |
|---|---|
| Student:  $2.50 | Adult:  $4.75 |
| Popcorn | Drinks |
| Large:  $1.50 | Small (8 oz):  $1.25 |
| Small:  $0.95 | Large (12 oz):  $1.95 |

Suppose you have $5. Do you have enough money for a ticket, a small box of popcorn, and a small drink?

How much change should a student get from $5 for a ticket and a large box of popcorn?

*All I need to know is whether I have enough money. I can estimate the total cost.*

*A clerk must give the exact amount. I need to find the exact answer.*

These examples show that the person who needs the answer and the real-world situation help you decide whether an exact answer or an estimate is needed.

### TRY IT OUT

Explain whether you should estimate the answer or whether you need an exact answer.

1. You have $2.00. Can you afford to buy a small drink and a large popcorn?

2. What is the total cost of 3 adult tickets?

3. You have a $10 bill. Can you buy a large drink for each of your 4 friends and yourself?

Explain whether you can estimate the answer or whether you need an exact answer.

1. The show will start at 1:56 p.m. It will last 1 hour and 49 minutes. What time should you tell your parents they should meet you outside the theater at the end of the show?

2. Fulton School has 317 girls and 289 boys. If a family friend asks you how many students are in the school, what kind of answer would you give?

3. Fruit drinks cost 75¢ each and apples cost 45¢ each. Jered had $3. Did he have enough money to buy 2 soft drinks and 1 apple?

4. There are 34 red gym shirts and 28 green gym shirts in a box. How many more shirts are needed for the 100 students who take gym?

5. Suppose you saved $15. How much more money do you need to buy a school jacket that costs $29.95?

6. A school bus can hold 65 students. This morning there were 12 empty seats. How many students were on the bus?

7. Maria bought 12 stamps for the invitations to her birthday party. Each stamp cost 29¢. How much did she pay altogether for the stamps?

8. Karla sold posters for the student council. Each poster sells for $8.95. Will she reach her goal of $100 if she sells 10 posters?

9. The 5th-6th grade band has 35 members. Last year there were 47 members. How many more were in the band last year?

10. Each student will drink about 2 cans of juice at the school picnic. How many cans of juice should be bought if there are 78 students coming to the picnic?

11. **Determining Reasonable Answers**  Tell whether the calculator answer is reasonable. If it is not, explain why not.

    Each section of the bleachers holds 125 students. How many students can sit in 5 sections?

# Group Decision Making

UNDERSTAND
ANALYZE DATA
PLAN
ESTIMATE
SOLVE
EXAMINE

**Group Skills**
Listen to Others
Encourage and Respect Others
Explain and Summarize
Check for Understanding
Disagree in an Agreeable Way

You will be asked to work with other students for many lessons in this book. To make a good team, all members of your group need to feel that their ideas and questions are important. Building a good team spirit is one of the keys to working successfully in cooperative groups.

Suppose someone in your group suggests an idea that the rest of you think will not work. What could you say to the person that would show that you respect his or her opinion even though you disagree with the idea? What might you do or say to make sure that the person will feel free to offer suggestions in the future?

## Cooperative Activity

For this activity your group will need 8 blue blocks, 4 yellow blocks, and 4 red blocks and a grid like the one below. Use the rules that follow to place the blocks in the grid.

Rule 1    There are at least 2 blues in the first row.

Rule 2    There are no reds in row 2.

Rule 3    There are exactly 2 yellows in either row 2 or row 3, but not in both rows.

Rule 4    Each blue touches at least 1 other blue at corners. No blues are next to each other in a row or column.

1. How many different ways did you find to arrange the blocks?

2. Have each person in your group talk about whether or not they thought they were able to contribute their fair share of ideas.

3. Was it difficult to do this activity together? Explain why or why not.

**Check Your Group Skills**

4. Think about how your group worked together. Give two or three examples of how someone gave encouragement or treated another group member with respect.

# WRAP UP

## Vocabulary Match

Match each phrase on the left with the correct word(s) on the right. Some words will not be used.

1. a way of naming a number

2. computing in your head

3. find about how many or how much

4. a property that states that you can change the order of numbers

5. a property that states that you can change the grouping of numbers

A. parentheses

B. mental math

C. associative property

D. commutative property

E. estimate

F. numerical expression

## Sometimes, Always, Never

Complete each statement by writing **sometimes, always,** or **never.** Explain your choice.

6. Thirty-six divided by nine is __?__ written in symbols as $36 \div 9$.

7. When you evaluate an expression that includes parentheses ( ), you should __?__ do the operations inside parentheses last.

8. If $B = 3$, $C = 1$, and $D = 4$, then $B + C$ will __?__ equal $D$ and $D - C$ will __?__ equal $B$.

## Project

All whole numbers except 0 can be written as sums of other whole numbers in different ways. For example, $8 = 3 + 5$, $8 = 6 + 2$, $8 = 1 + 3 + 4$, and so on. Some whole numbers can be written as the sum of consecutive numbers. For example, $3 = 0 + 1 + 2$, $6 = 0 + 1 + 2 + 3$, and so on. For each whole number from 1 through 15, find all possible ways to write the number as a sum of consecutive numbers.

# POWER PRACTICE/TEST

## Part 1  Understanding

Write the numerical expression using symbols.

1. the product of four and six

2. forty-five divided by five

3. one less than nineteen

Give an example of each property.

4. commutative property, addition

5. commutative property, multiplication

6. associative property, addition

7. associative property, multiplication

## Part 2  Skills

Find the value of these expressions using mental math.

8. $75 + 87 + 25$

9. $20 \times 47 \times 5$

10. $16 \times 4 \times 25$

11. $60 + 93 + 2 + 40$

Find the value of each variable in the following equations. Each variable stands for one and only one of these numbers: 2, 3, 4, 5, and 7.

12. $M + P = R$      $P + P = T$      $R - T = S$      $P + S = M$

## Part 3  Applications

13. Name the operation. Then solve. At the bookstore, paperbook books cost $5 and hardback books cost $9. What is the cost of 6 paperbacks?

14. Tell whether you need an exact answer or an estimate. Then solve.
Jim wants to buy a book for $6.95 and a globe for $18.25. He has $22. Does he have enough money?

15. **Challenge.** Carla asked students who had pets to tell her what kind of pets they had. She made a table.

| | Kind of pet | | | |
|---|---|---|---|---|
| | Dog | Cat | Bird | Fish |
| Number of Students | 5 | 4 | 3 | 7 |

Four students had 2 kinds of pets each. One student had 3 kinds. All the rest had 1 kind of pet each. How many students had at least 1 kind of pet?

23

Early Greek mathematicians related numbers to shapes. Look at the arrangements of dots shown at right. Can you see why 6 is an example of a triangular number and why 9 is an example of a square number?

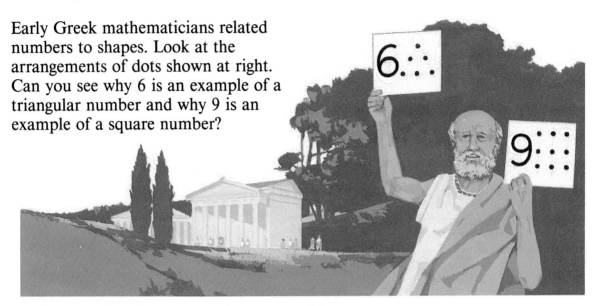

The chart below shows several patterns with triangular numbers.

| Dot Arrangement | Triangular Number | Difference | Equation |
|---|---|---|---|
| • | 1 | | 1 = 1 |
| | | 2 | |
| •• | 3 | | 1 + 2 = 3 |
| | | 3 | |
| •••| 6 | | 1 + 2 + 3 = 6 |
| | | 4 | |
| ••••| 10 | | 1 + 2 + 3 + 4 = 10 |

1. Describe the pattern you see between triangular numbers and their differences.

2. Describe the pattern you see in the number sentences.

3. There are 15 triangular numbers from 1 through 120. Use the patterns in the chart to find and list them.

4. Make a similar chart for square numbers. The first four square numbers are 1, 4, 9, and 16. What patterns do you find?

# CUMULATIVE REVIEW

Add, subtract, multiply, or divide.

**1.** 7 × 9

   A. 72   B. 54   C. 56   D. 63

**2.** 80 + 320 + 6

   A. 386   B. 326   C. 406   D. 460

**3.** 447 − 20

   A. 227   B. 220   C. 427   D. 467

**4.** 32 ÷ 4

   A. 9   B. 8   C. 7R4  D. 8R2

Name each figure.

**5.**
   A. angle
   B. perpendicular lines
   C. segment
   D. parallel lines

**6.**
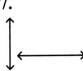
   A. circle
   B. cube
   C. square
   D. trapezoid

**7.**
   A. congruent segments
   B. perpendicular lines
   C. parallel lines
   D. skew lines

**8.** How would you group these factors to find the product of 45 × 4 × 10 × 25 mentally?

   A. (4 × 10) × (25 × 45)

   B. (4 × 25) × (45 × 10)

   C. (45 × 4) × (10 × 25)

   D. (10 × 25) × (45 × 4)

Choose the correct symbols.

**9.** twenty-four more than eighty-two

   A. 24 × 82   B. 82 ÷ 24

   C. 82 − 24   D. 82 + 24

**10.** fifty divided by five

   A. $\frac{5}{50}$   B. 5 ÷ 50

   C. 50 − 5   D. $\frac{50}{5}$

Choose the operation or symbol you need to solve each problem.

**11.** Barbara has invited 6 girls to her birthday party. She wants to give each girl 3 small gifts. How many gifts should she buy?

   A. addition   B. multiplication

   C. subtraction   D. division

**12.** Erik wants to buy a school jacket that costs $24. If he saves $4 a week, how many weeks will it take him to save enough money to buy the jacket?

   A. +   B. ×

   C. −   D. ÷

# 2

## PLACE VALUE: WHOLE NUMBERS AND DECIMALS

**THEME: COLONIAL HISTORY**

**M**ATH AND
SOCIAL STUDIES

**DATA BANK**

Use the Social Studies
Data Bank on page 480
to answer the questions.

1 How many more states
entered the Union in
1788 than in 1787? How
many states had entered the
Union by the end of 1788?

**2** How many decades old must a state be before it can celebrate its 100th birthday? before it can celebrate its 200th birthday?

**3** How many of the original 13 states had been part of the Union for two centuries by the end of 1987?

**4** Using Critical Thinking
What will the next century be called? In what year will that century begin? In what year will that century end? Use the data to justify your answers.

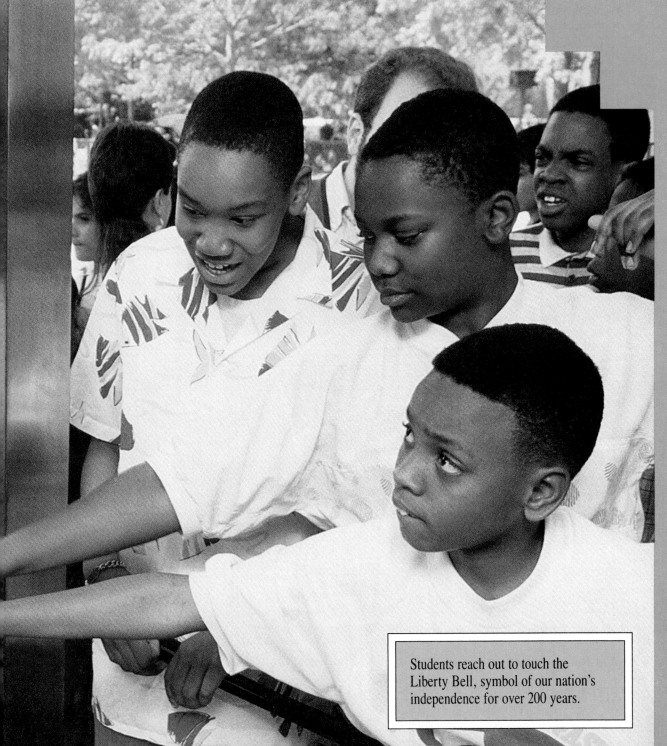

Students reach out to touch the Liberty Bell, symbol of our nation's independence for over 200 years.

27

# Place Value Through Thousands

**LEARN ABOUT IT**

**EXPLORE  Use Play Money**

Work in groups. Imagine that you are a bank teller. Use play money to show $1,256 in 3 different ways. Use only $1,000, $100, $10, and $1 bills.

**TALK ABOUT IT**

1. Can you show $1,256 without using any $1,000 bills? Explain.

2. Describe how you can show $1,256 using the fewest pieces of play money.

All whole numbers can be written using only the **digits** 0, 1, 2, 3, 4, 5, 6, 7, 8, and 9. Large numbers are separated by commas into groups with three digits, called **periods.** The value of a digit is shown by its **place** in a number.

| Periods → | Thousands Period | | | Ones Period | | |
|---|---|---|---|---|---|---|
| Place values → | hundred thousands | ten thousands | thousands | hundreds | tens | ones |
| | 2 | 3 | 8 | 4 | 7 | 5 |
| | 200,000 | 30,000 | 8,000 | 400 | 70 | 5 |

We write, in **expanded form:** 200,000 + 30,000 + 8,000 + 400 + 70 + 5
We write, in **standard form:** 238,475
We read: "two hundred thirty-eight thousand, four hundred seventy-five"

**TRY IT OUT**

Write each in standard form and in expanded form.

1. two thousand, five hundred forty

2. nine hundred sixty-five

3. seven hundred ninety-one thousand, six hundred twenty-one

Read each number. Then use place value to tell what the red digit means.

4. 213,546

5. 19,798

6. 3,725

7. 638,407

28

Write the number for each amount in standard form.

**1.**

2 thousands, 3 hundreds, 4 tens, 1 one

**2.**

4 thousands, 4 hundreds, 4 ones

Use place value to tell what the red digit in each number means.

**3.** 37,649      **4.** 213,765      **5.** 347,821      **6.** 792,463

Write in standard form.

**7.** 500,000 + 80,000 + 3,000 + 70 + 2      **8.** 800,000 + 70,000 + 400 + 60 + 5

**9.** 400,000 + 3,000 + 70 + 8      **10.** 90,000 + 10 + 7

Write in standard form and in expanded form.

**11.** forty-five thousand, six hundred      **12.** two hundred forty-eight thousand

**13.** seven hundred twenty-five thousand, sixty      **14.** seven hundred thirty thousand, one

Write each number in words.

**15.** 39,405      **16.** 61,824      **17.** 135,400      **18.** 794,608

**MATH REASONING**

The beads on the number frame show the number 314,412.

Draw number frames that show: **19.** 421,304   **20.** 204,213

**PROBLEM SOLVING**

**21.** Karla cashed a check for a customer and gave him these bills: 6 tens, 2 thousands, 4 ones, and 7 hundreds. What was the amount of the check that she cashed?

▶ **USING CRITICAL THINKING   Support Your Conclusion**

**22.** Mary claimed that the value of each place on a place-value chart is 10 times the value of the place to its right. Is she correct? Give examples to explain.

*More Practice, page 500, set D*

# Millions and Billions

**EXPLORE** **Make a Decision**

- 1 thousand tennis balls would fill a box about 1 foot deep and 3 feet on each side.
- 1 million (1,000 thousand or 1,000,000) tennis balls would fill a space the size of a classroom.

Do you think your entire school is big enough to hold 1 billion (1,000 million or 1,000,000,000) tennis balls?

**TALK ABOUT IT**

1. About how many classrooms would be needed to hold 10 million (10,000,000) tennis balls?
2. About how many classrooms would be needed to hold 100 million (100,000,000) tennis balls?
3. How does thinking of 1 billion as 1,000 million help to think about the number of classrooms needed for 1 billion tennis balls?

The table below shows how the smaller periods relate to the larger periods.

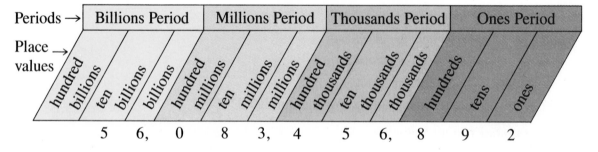

| | Billions Period | | | Millions Period | | | Thousands Period | | | Ones Period | | |
|---|---|---|---|---|---|---|---|---|---|---|---|---|
| Periods → | hundred billions | ten billions | billions | hundred millions | ten millions | millions | hundred thousands | ten thousands | thousands | hundreds | tens | ones |
| | 5 | 6, | 0 | 8 | 3, | 4 | 5 | 6, | 8 | 9 | 2 | |

We read: "fifty-six billion, eighty-three million, four hundred fifty-six thousand, eight hundred ninety-two"

## TRY IT OUT

Read each number. Then use place value to tell what the red digit means.

**1.** 5,937,862     **2.** 935,467,854     **3.** 836,975,123,468     **4.** 9,367,800,672

30

Use place value to tell what each red digit means.

**1.** 14,753,000   **2.** 368,571,000,000   **3.** 35,296,417   **4.** 73,550,221

Give the letter for the number in the list in which the digit 4
has a value of

**5.** 400,000   **6.** 4,000,000,000

**7.** 4,000,000   **8.** 400,000,000

| A 354,782,631,983 | B 782,629,480,115 |
|---|---|
| C 356,487,215,009 | D 209,364,080,296 |

Write in standard form.

**9.** 700,000,000 + 30,000,000 + 2,000,000 + 500,000 + 4,000

**10.** 800,000,000,000 + 5,000,000,000 + 600,000,000 + 2,000,000

**11.** three hundred forty-five million, eight hundred two
thousand, six hundred

**12.** fifty-four billion, two hundred fifteen million, one
thousand, three hundred

Write each number in words.

**13.** 510,431,200          **14.** 650,215,400,020

## APPLY

### MATH REASONING

**15.** How much greater is A than B?
   **A.** 718,425,319,250          **B.** 717,425,319,250

### PROBLEM SOLVING

**16.** A company said it made 1,000,000 tennis balls in 1 year.
The same year it made 10 times as many table tennis balls
as tennis balls. How many table tennis balls was that?

## MIXED REVIEW

Use the number properties to help you find the missing numbers.

**17.** $27 + \text{▥} = 27$   **18.** $8 + \text{▥} = 12 + 8$   **19.** $2 \times (5 \times 7) = (2 \times \text{▥}) \times 7$

**20.** $32 \times 1 = \text{▥}$   **21.** $\text{▥} \times 17 = 17 \times 23$   **22.** $(6 + 5) + 4 = (\text{▥} + 6) + 5$

# Comparing and Ordering Whole Numbers

LEARN ABOUT IT

**EXPLORE** Examine the Data

Susan found her state in an alphabetical listing of states by area in square miles. She wanted to make a list of these states in order from smallest to largest.

| State | Area (square miles) |
|---|---|
| Florida | 58,560 |
| Georgia | 58,876 |
| Hawaii | 6,450 |
| Idaho | 83,557 |
| Illinois | 56,400 |

**TALK ABOUT IT**

1. Which number in the list above has the greatest digit in the ten thousands place?
2. Which two numbers in her list have the same digits in the thousands place but different digits in the hundreds place?

Here is one way to **compare** two numbers:
Compare 56,131 and 57,598.

- Line up the numbers by place value.
- Start at the left and find the first place where the digits are different.
- Compare those digits. The numbers compare the same way.

Example:  56,131
          57,598

> The digits in the thousands place are different.

6 < 7   so 56,131 < 57,598
        or 57,598 > 56,131

Here is one way to **order** numbers:

- Compare the numbers two at a time.
- List the numbers from greatest to least or from least to greatest.

Order     23,578     2,354     23,592
23,578 > 2,354 and 23,592 > 23,578
        In order: 23,592 ← greatest
                  23,578
                  2,354 ← least

**TRY IT OUT**

Write >, <, or = for each ▦ .

1. 2,135 ▦ 2,136

2. 382 ▦ 467

3. 1,000 tens ▦ 10,000

4. 5,008 ▦ 5,080

5. 543,817 ▦ 540,298

6. 38,417 ▦ 38,409

7. Order these numbers from least to greatest: 543,890   542,760   54,817   535,300

8. Order these numbers from greatest to least: 101,999   99,990   110,000   109,990

32

Write $>$, $<$, or $=$ for each .

**1.** 743  758

**2.** 3,976  3,980

**3.** 9,999  10,000

**4.** 16,878  16,783

**5.** 54,079  54,079

**6.** 786,300  786,099

**7.** 365 thousand  356,000

**8.** 979,000,000  236 billion

**9.** 34 thousand  34,000

**10.** 49 billion  490,000,000

Which numbers in the box are

**11.** greater than 480,823?
**12.** less than 50,000?
**13.** between 295,000 and 405,000?
**14.** greater than 45,000 and less than 68,500?

| 382,417 | 416,950 | 38,245 |
| 376,892 | 405,887 | 40,590 |
| 281,045 | 683,215 | 68,322 |
| 473,819 | 517,325 | 51,735 |

Write each group of numbers in order from least to greatest.

**15.** 3,574; 3,618; 358; 3,592
**17.** 5,389; 5,840; 589; 5,390
**19.** 456,800; 453,400; 45,418; 456,512

**16.** 24,327; 25,782; 24,315; 2,579
**18.** 87,400; 78,400; 84,562; 87,399
**20.** 1,000,000; 909,000; 1,100,000

APPLY

**MATH REASONING**

Write three numbers that are

**21.** a little more than 250,000.

**22.** a little more than 250.

**23.** a little less than 250,000.

**24.** a little less than 250.

**PROBLEM SOLVING**

**25.** Which state is smaller, Iowa or Wisconsin?

**26. Social Studies Data Bank** Which of the original 13 states have areas greater than 50,000 square miles? See page 480.

DATA BANK

| State | Area (mi²) |
| --- | --- |
| Alabama | 51,609 |
| Iowa | 56,290 |
| Michigan | 58,216 |
| Wisconsin | 56,154 |

▶ **ALGEBRA**

Find the number represented by each variable. Each variable represents one unknown number.

**27.** $b - a = a$
$b + c = 20$
$a + a = 14$

**28.** $d + e = f$
$f - d = 6$
$d + d = 10$

# Rounding Whole Numbers

## LEARN ABOUT IT

**EXPLORE  Think About the Situation**
Kristi and Dave made a poster about
their city. According to the 1980 census
the population was 61,902. They
decided that for their poster it would
make sense to round that number.

GALVESTON

Population: 62,000
Metropolitan area population: 196,000
City charter Date: 1839
Great Hurricane: 1900

**TALK ABOUT IT**

1. Explain how this number line can be used to show that
   61,902 is closer to 62,000 than to 61,000.

61,000  61,100  61,200  61,300  61,400  61,500  61,600  61,700  61,800  61,900  62,000

2. Why does it make sense to use a rounded number on
   the poster?

To **round** to any place:

- First underline the digit in the place to
  which you want to round.

- Look at the digit one place to its right.
  If the digit is less than 5, round **down.**

- If the digit is 5 or more, round **up.**

**Examples:**  Round 52,434 to the nearest
thousand.

5$\underline{2}$,434

5$\underline{2}$,434
52,000

Round 52,534 to the nearest thousand.

5$\underline{2}$,534 → 53,000

## Other Examples

**A** Round to the nearest **ten thousand:**  1$\underline{5}$7,843 → 160,000
**B** Round to the nearest **hundred thousand:**  1$\underline{5}$0,000 → 200,000
**C** Round to the nearest **million:**  4$\underline{2}$,300,000 → 42,000,000

## TRY IT OUT

Round to the nearest thousand.       **1.** 4,817        **2.** 27,294
Round to the nearest ten thousand.   **3.** 27,294       **4.** 380,467
Round to the nearest million.        **5.** 7,824,315    **6.** 43,500,000

Round to the nearest thousand.

**1.** 12,346     **2.** 74,652     **3.** 35,350     **4.** 10,238     **5.** 98,500

Round to the nearest ten thousand.

**6.** 174,825     **7.** 356,219     **8.** 473,532     **9.** 789,613     **10.** 999,850

Round each number to the greatest place possible.

**11.** 845,750     **12.** 98,945     **13.** 283,002     **14.** 9,543,918

**15.** 4,723,800     **16.** 30,345,604     **17.** 42,500,750     **18.** 99,635,400

When rounded to the nearest hundred thousand, which populations

**19.** round to 100,000?
**20.** round to 200,000?
**21.** round to 300,000?

| City Populations | |
| --- | --- |
| Abilene, TX | 96,573 |
| Akron, OH | 239,229 |
| Birmingham, AL | 280, 413 |
| Gary, IN | 156,056 |
| Greensboro, NC | 163,493 |
| Louisville, KY | 317,503 |
| Orlando, FL | 120,181 |
| Tulsa, OK | 328,684 |

APPLY

**MATH REASONING**

**22.** Give the greatest number and the smallest number that round to 20,000 when rounded to the nearest thousand.

**23.** Give the greatest number and the smallest number that round to 1,000 when rounded to the nearest thousand.

**PROBLEM SOLVING**

**24.** A newspaper article said that the Mountain City airport took in about $4,000,000 in parking fees. What year was the article most likely discussing?

**25.** The average attendance at Mountain College football games last year was 37,845. What rounded number would a newspaper be apt to use to report this data?

| Airport Parking Earnings | |
| --- | --- |
| 1989 | $3,384,217 |
| 1990 | $4,228,350 |
| 1991 | $4,965,272 |

▶ **USING CRITICAL THINKING**   Give a Counterexample

Decide whether the statement below is correct or incorrect. If you think it is incorrect, give an example to show why.

**26.** A three-digit number rounded to the nearest hundred will always have exactly two zeros.

*More Practice, page 501, set C*

# Problem Solving
## Draw a Picture

UNDERSTAND
ANALYZE DATA
PLAN
ESTIMATE
SOLVE
EXAMINE

## LEARN ABOUT IT

You can use a problem-solving strategy called **Draw a Picture** to help you solve many problems.

To get ready for the Flying Disc Games, George started mowing at one end of the football field. He mowed up to the 30 yard line. Rosa started at the other end of the field. She mowed up to the 40 yard line. The football field is 100 yards long. How many yards were not yet mowed?

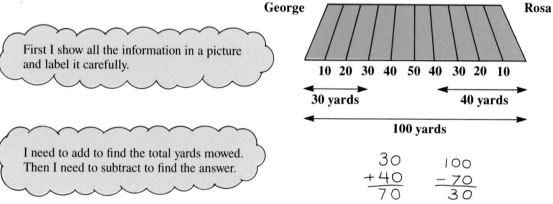

George                                                    Rosa

10  20  30  40  50  40  30  20  10

30 yards              40 yards

100 yards

First I show all the information in a picture and label it carefully.

I need to add to find the total yards mowed. Then I need to subtract to find the answer.

$$\begin{array}{r} 30 \\ +40 \\ \hline 70 \end{array} \qquad \begin{array}{r} 100 \\ -70 \\ \hline 30 \end{array}$$

There were 30 yards that were not yet mowed.

## TRY IT OUT

In the distance throwing event at the Flying Disc Games, Katie made four throws. Each of her throws was longer than the one before it. The distance between the first throw and the fourth was 15 feet. The distance between the second throw and the third was 2 feet. The distance between the third throw and the fourth was 7 feet. How much longer was the second throw than the first?

- Which throws were the longest and the shortest?
- How far apart were the first throw and the fourth throw?
- How far apart were the third throw and the fourth throw?
- Copy and complete the drawing below to solve the problem.

First          Fourth
throw          throw

15 ft

36

Draw a picture to help you solve the following problems.

**1.** Jim and Ingrid were throwing flying discs directly toward each other. They were 18 yards apart. Jim threw his disc 5 yards between his legs. Ingrid threw hers 4 yards using a behind-the-back throw. How far apart were the two flying discs after they landed on the ground?

**2.** On the way to the Flying Disc Games, Ozzie will pass 4 towns. Kingston is between Montclare and Bedford. Kingston is 3 miles from Montclare. Bedford is between Kingston and Dublin. Bedford and Dublin are 6 miles apart. The distance from Montclare to Dublin is 17 miles. How far is it from Kingston to Bedford?

## MIXED PRACTICE

Solve. Choose a strategy from the list or use other strategies that you know.

**3.** Darla has a large flying disc that is 13 inches across the middle. She also has a small disc that measures 6 inches across the middle. How much wider across the middle is the larger disc?

13″

| Some Strategies |
|---|
| Act Out |
| Use Objects |
| Choose an Operation |
| Draw a Picture |

**4.** At camp, a rectangular field was marked off for a flying disc competition. Starting at one of the corners, a cone marker was set up at every 5 yards around the field. The field is 40 yards long and 20 yards wide. How many cones were needed?

**5.** The first day Flora tried to spin the disc on her fingertip, she could do it for only 5 seconds. The next day, she could do it for 9 seconds longer. How long could she do it the second day?

**6.** Larry and Dave were 16 yards apart. They threw their flying discs toward each other with their left hands. Each threw his disc 9 yards. How far apart were the discs when they landed on the ground?

**7.** James divided 28 campers into 4 teams to play flying disc football. There were the same number of campers on each team. How many were there on each team?

**8.** Small flying discs were on sale for $4 each. How much would 6 discs cost?

# Exploring Algebra
## Variables and Expressions

You learned in Chapter 1 that a numerical expression is a name for a number. You also learned that a variable can be used to stand for a single number. In this lesson you will explore how variables are used in expressions like $n + 8$.

**EXPLORE** **Think About the Situation**

Todd's teacher drew these figures on the chalkboard and asked, "What numerical expression could you write to show the length of the whole board?" When a student responded "8 + 4," the teacher said, "Very good! Now, suppose you know the length of only the first part of the board? What expression could you write to give the total length?"

**TALK ABOUT IT**

1. What is the value of the expression $8 + 4$?
2. Which of these expressions could you write to show the total length of the second board?
   **A.** $8 + n$    **B.** $8 - n$    **C.** $8 + y$    **D.** $8 \times y$

An expression like $n + 8$ that contains a variable is called an **algebraic expression.**

To evaluate an algebraic expression, you replace the variable with a number and perform the operation. Here is how to do it.

Evaluate $n + 8$ when $n = 9$.

Replace $n$ with 9 and add.    $9 + 8 = 17$

Evaluate $18 \div y$ when $y = 6$.

Replace $y$ with 6 and divide.    $18 \div 6 = 3$

**TRY IT OUT**

Find the value of each expression.

1. $y - 7$ when $y = 15$
2. $8 + m$ when $m = 6$
3. $7 \times t$ when $t = 3$
4. $n \div 8$ when $n = 32$
5. $13 - g$ when $g = 5$
6. $h \times 9$ when $h = 5$

## POWER PRACTICE/QUIZ

Use the number in the box. Give the digit that is in the **place** named.

**1.** hundreds
**2.** billions
**3.** ten thousands
**4.** hundred millions

| 358,140,239,607 |
|---|

Give the digits that are in the **period** named.

**5.** thousands      **6.** billions      **7.** ones      **8.** millions

Write the number from the box in which the digit 7 has the given value.

| | |
|---|---|
| 5,723,019 | 175,222,951 |
| 43,837,636 | 247,186,665,290 |
| 304,239,931 | 25,938,463 |
| 429,694,531,684 | 472,145,954,266 |

**9.** 7,000
**10.** 7,000,000,000
**11.** 700,000
**12.** 70,000,000,000

Write the number in standard form.

**13.** 6 thousands, 5 ones, 7 tens, and 2 hundreds
**14.** 40,000,000 + 3,000,000 + 9,000 + 800 + 6
**15.** ten thousand, forty-one
**16.** five hundred million, sixty-seven thousand, four hundred eight

Write >, <, or = for each ▦.

**17.** 2,375 ▦ 2,368      **18.** 59,075 ▦ 58,986      **19.** 10 thousand ▦ 100 hundred
**20.** Order from least to greatest: 101,900   109,100   101,899   101,690

Round to the **nearest thousand:**    **21.** 89,560      **22.** 8,050      **23.** 116,495

Round to the **nearest million:**     **24.** 15,495,999    **25.** 9,501,001

### PROBLEM SOLVING

**26.** Della wants to make a rectangular fence in her backyard. She needs to use 6 posts on each long side and 4 posts on each short side of the fence. How many posts does she need to use in all?

**27.** Five girls ran in the 12-mile marathon. Alicia came in last. Barbara finished ahead of Cindy. If Cindy was ahead of Debra and JoAnn was just behind Debra, who came in third?

**28.** Tom made 2 stops during his 50-mile bike trip. He first stopped after 20 miles. His second stop was 15 miles before the end of the trip. How many miles did he travel between his first and second stops?

39

# Decimal Place Value
## Tenths and Hundredths

| | ones | | tenths | | hundredths |

**LEARN ABOUT IT**

**EXPLORE** **Use Place Value Blocks**

Work in groups. You need blocks for ones, tenths, and hundredths. Use at least one but no more than two blocks of each value. How many decimal numbers can you make using some or all of those blocks? Make a table like this to show the numbers. One possibility is shown for you.

| ones | tenths | hundredths |
|------|--------|------------|
| 1 | 2 | 1 |
| | | |
| | | |
| | | |
| | | |
| | | |
| | | |
| | | |

**TALK ABOUT IT**

1. How many numbers can you show using exactly 2 ones and 1 or 2 of each of the other pieces?
2. How many different numbers could you show without using any hundredths pieces?
3. How many different numbers did you find altogether? Do you think you found them all? Explain.

Here is how you can show, write, and read decimals.

We see:

We think:

| hundreds | tens | ones | tenths | hundredths |
|----------|------|------|--------|------------|
| | | 2 | 6 | 5 |

6 tenths is the same as 60 hundredths.

We write:   2.65

We read:   "two and sixty-five hundredths"

**TRY IT OUT**

Use place value materials. Show, write, and read each number.

1. 1 one, 5 tenths, 6 hundredths
2. 0 ones, 7 tenths
3. 3 ones, 5 hundredths

4. 2 ones, 3 tenths, 1 hundredth
5. 4 ones, 1 tenth
6. 5 ones, 2 hundredths

**40**

Write the decimal for each picture.

**1.**     **2.**     **3.**

Write all the numbers from the box

**4.** where the digit 6 has a value of 60.
**5.** where the digit 7 has a value of 7.
**6.** where the digit 2 has a value of 0.2.
**7.** where the digit 9 has a value of 0.09.

| 76.92 | 96.72 | 27.96 |
| 68.19 | 29.67 | 76.27 |
| 79.27 | 27.62 | 62.79 |

Match each food item to the decimal word name.

**8.** twelve hundredths kg (kilogram)
**9.** one and two hundredths kg
**10.** one and two tenths kg

1.2 kg
A

1.02 kg
B

0.12 kg
C

**MATH REASONING**

Which expression does not belong in each group? Tell why.

**11.** 2.4; 2 + 0.40; 2.40; two and four hundredths
**12.** 8.09; 8 + 0.90; eight and nine hundredths

**PROBLEM SOLVING**

**13. Talk About Your Solution**  Solve the problem below.
Then compare your solution with that of a classmate.
   What is the smallest number of thumbtacks needed
to attach 4 rectangular pieces of paper to a board? Each
corner of each piece of paper must be tacked.

▶ **CALCULATOR**

Count by hundredths on your calculator using this key code:
[ON/AC] [+] 0.01 [=] [=] [=]. Stop when the display
shows each of the numbers below. How many times would
you have to press [=] to show each number?

**14.** 0.09        **15.** 0.29        **16.** 0.1        **17.** 0.15

*More Practice, page 501, set D*

# Thousandths

**EXPLORE** **Use Models**   Cut out a ten-by-ten square from graph paper. Label the whole square 1 unit. Lightly shade one row of the small squares. Label the row 0.1. Lightly shade just one of the small squares and label it 0.01.

   If you could divide the small square into ten parts, each of these parts would be one thousandth. How would you label one of these parts?

## TALK ABOUT IT

1. If 0.1 is "one tenth" and 0.01 is "one hundredth," what is "one thousandth"?
2. Which has a greater value, one hundredth or one thousandth? Explain.
3. How many thousandths are in one hundredth? in the whole unit?

Here is how to write and read decimals with thousandths.

We see:

We think:

| ones | tenths | hundredths | thousandths |
|------|--------|------------|-------------|
| 3 | 1 | 2 | 5 |

We write:       3.125

We read:        "three and one hundred twenty-five thousandths"

## TRY IT OUT

Write the decimal and the word name for each.

1.

2 ones
3 tenths
0 hundredths
4 thousandths

2.

0 ones
0 tenths
4 hundredths
2 thousandths

Write the decimal and the word name for each.

1.    3 ones
   2 tenths
   4 hundredths
   5 thousandths

2.   0 ones
   6 tenths
   5 hundredths
   3 thousandths

Give the numbers from the box in which the digit 8 has a value of

| | | |
|---|---|---|
| 0.876 | 75.482 | 238.056 |
| 1.84 | 43.82 | 250.132 |
| 2.378 | 78.334 | 4.328 |

3. 0.08          4. 0.8

5. 0.008          6. 8

Write in standard form.

7. eleven and thirty-four hundredths          8. forty and four thousandths

9. two and three hundred seventy-one thousandths

10. seven hundred twenty-one and thirty-nine thousandths

Write the word name for each decimal.

11. 3.254          12. 42.305          13. 0.248          14. 6.004

**APPLY**

**MATH REASONING**

Use mental math and place value to find how much less A is than B.

15. A. 0.372          16. A. 3.857          17. A. 29.379          18. A. 0.9
    B. 0.373              B. 3.867              B. 29.380              B. 0.91

**PROBLEM SOLVING**

19. Carla's time for the bicycle race was 45.538 seconds. The winning time was 45.528 seconds. By how many seconds did Carla lose the race?

20. Benji needs to weigh 40.4 kg to wrestle in the grade 5 wrestling meet. He weighs 40 kg. How much weight does he need to gain?

► **ESTIMATION**

Match each decimal with its point on the number line.

21. 0.45   22. 0.719   23. 0.204   24. 0.102   25. 0.77   26. 0.29

# Comparing and Ordering Decimals

**EXPLORE** **Examine the Data**

Kerry found his state on a list of state populations per square mile. He looked at other states on the list and said, "It's easy to see that Nebraska has the fewest people per square mile."

| State | Population per square mile |
|---|---|
| Colorado | 29.2 |
| Kansas | 29.27 |
| Nebraska | 20.54 |
| Oregon | 27.31 |
| Arizona | 25.11 |

**TALK ABOUT IT**

1. At what place in the numbers did Kerry look to make the statement he made?

2. Which state on the list has the greatest number of people per square mile? How did you decide?

The steps you use to **compare** decimals are like those for whole numbers.

Compare 0.845 and 0.85.

- Line up the numbers by place value.

- Start at the left and find the first place where the digits are different.

- Compare those digits. The numbers compare the same way.

Example: 0.845
0.85

The digits in the hundredths place are different.

$4 < 5$ so $0.845 < 0.85$ or $0.85 > 0.845$

Here is one way to **order** decimals:

- Compare the numbers two at a time.

- List them from greatest to least or least to greatest.

Order 2.143, 0.214, and 2.14.
$2.143 > 2.14$ and $2.14 > 0.214$
In order: 2.143 ← greatest
2.14
0.214 ← least

**TRY IT OUT**

Write $>$, $<$, or $=$ for each ▥.

1. 4.35 ▥ 4.36     2. 0.82 ▥ 0.67     3. 0.27 ▥ 0.270     4. 1.099 ▥ 1.99

5. Order these numbers from smallest to largest: 6.73   6.783   0.673   6.7

## PRACTICE

Write >, <, or = for each ▦.

**1.** 7.30 ▦ 7.03
**2.** 12.6 ▦ 12.60
**3.** 0.95 ▦ 0.89

**4.** 14.8 ▦ 14.48
**5.** 0.069 ▦ 0.690
**6.** 39.6 ▦ 36.9

**7.** 3.47 ▦ 3.49
**8.** 27.15 ▦ 27.150
**9.** 1.295 ▦ 12.96

**10.** 4.510 ▦ 4.49
**11.** 0.790 ▦ 0.791
**12.** 50.19 ▦ 50.2

Use the number list to answer these questions.

Which numbers are

**13.** greater than 1.5?
**14.** less than 0.075
**15.** between 0.5 and 1?

| 1.438 | 0.75 | 0.07 |
|-------|-------|-------|
| 0.567 | 0.055 | 1.63 |
| 1.003 | 1.501 | 0.078 |
| 0.3 | 0.47 | 1.295 |

## APPLY

### MATH REASONING

Copy the numbers. Place a decimal point in the middle number so that the numbers are in order from least to greatest.

**16.** 3   345   4
**17.** 0.3   573   1
**18.** 0.34   406   0.43

### PROBLEM SOLVING

**19.** Use all three of the digits 0, 3, and 5 to make decimals less than 1. In each decimal use each digit only once. (Do not count the zero left of the decimal point.) How many can you write? Arrange the ones you write in order from least to greatest.

 **20.** **Social Studies Data Bank**   Which state had the most people per square mile in 1980? See page 480.

### ▶ MENTAL MATH

You can count on by tenths, hundredths, or thousandths to mentally add or subtract some decimal numbers.

Examples   4.25 + 0.3   → Think: 4.25, 4.35, 4.45, 4.55
0.718 + 0.003 → Think: 0.718, 0.719, 0.720, 0.721

Count on to find these sums mentally.

**21.** 2.38 + 0.3
**22.** 3.465 + 0.002
**23.** 0.667 + 0.04

# Rounding Decimals

ANIMAL BIRTH WEIGHTS
AT THE CITY ZOO

Gorilla....2.134 kg
Panda.... 0.096 kg
Lion..... 1.262 kg

## LEARN ABOUT IT

You can apply what you know about rounding whole numbers to help you round decimals.

### EXPLORE  Examine the Data

Rosita rounded the birth weights when she wrote this part of her report about baby animals.

The gorilla weighed about 2 kg at birth, but the lion weighed only about 1 kg.

### TALK ABOUT IT

1. Use this number line to explain why the gorilla's weight was closer to 2 kg than to 3 kg.

| 2 | 2.1 | 2.2 | 2.3 | 2.4 | 2.5 | 2.6 | 2.7 | 2.8 | 2.9 | 3 |

2. Would it make sense to round the panda's weight to the nearest kilogram? Explain.

You round decimal numbers using steps similar to those you use for whole numbers.

- First underline the digit in the place to which you want to round.
- Look at the digit one place to its right.
- If the digit is less than 5, round **down.**
- If the digit is 5 or more, round **up.**

Round 4.324 to the nearest tenth.

4.3̲24

4.3̲24
4.3

Round 4.364 to the nearest tenth.
4.3̲64 → 4.4

## Other Examples

Round to the nearest hundredth.     0.45̲63 → 0.46
Round to the nearest whole number.  2.5̲39 → 3

## TRY IT OUT

Round each number to the place of the underlined digit. For example: 2.15̲8 (round to the nearest hundredth) → 2.16

**1.** 5.2̲3     **2.** 2̲.51     **3.** 78.34̲5     **4.** 0.8̲27     **5.** 14.09̲9     **6.** 20.4̲5

Round each number to the place of the underlined digit.

| | | | | |
|---|---|---|---|---|
| **1.** 8.4̲3 | **2.** 15.7̲6 | **3.** 66.0̲6 | **4.** 49.5̲5 | **5.** 52.̲63 |
| **6.** 21.7̲5 | **7.** 0.̲58 | **8.** 1.4̲2 | **9.** 56.2̲9 | **10.** 0.7̲4 |
| **11.** 1.28̲8 | **12.** 7.0̲52 | **13.** 0.̲934 | **14.** 1.5̲37 | **15.** 9.6̲73 |
| **16.** 8.̲624 | **17.** 39.8̲51 | **18.** 21.38̲1 | **19.** 1.9̲64 | **20.** 99.9̲91 |

Give the names of the animals whose weights

**21.** round to 1 kg.

**22.** round to 2 kg.

**23.** round to 3 kg.

| Weights of Young Animals in Zoo Hospitals | |
|---|---|
| anteater | 1.945 kg |
| ostrich | 1.468 kg |
| wild turkey | 2.3 kg |
| kangaroo | 2.86 kg |
| python | 1.497 kg |
| turtle | 2.5 kg |

**APPLY**

### MATH REASONING

**24.** Give two different decimal numbers with digits in the thousandths place that round to 5.2 when the numbers are rounded to the nearest tenth.

### PROBLEM SOLVING

**25.** A report said Hillston spent $4.25 million on feeding and caring for animals in the zoo last year. Hillston spent $13.8 million on road repairs. Round each number to the nearest million. Then find about how much more money was spent on road repairs.

**26. Data Hunt** Look through some newspapers and find 2 examples where numbers have been rounded. Explain why you think the numbers are rounded rather than exact.

### MIXED REVIEW

Add or subtract.

**27.** $12 - 12$ **28.** $18 + 0$ **29.** $11 - 4$ **30.** $2 + 108$ **31.** $10 - 7$ **32.** $2 + 3 + 5$

Multiply or divide.

**33.** $10 \times 4$ **34.** $36 \div 6$ **35.** $12 \div 4$ **36.** $124 \times 0$ **37.** $24 \div 8$ **38.** $6 \times 7$

**39.** $9 \times 3$ **40.** $7 \times 8$ **41.** $45 \div 9$ **42.** $25 \times 4$ **43.** $21 \div 21$ **44.** $5 \times 2 \times 0$

*More Practice, page 502, set B*

# Problem Solving
## Understanding the Question

| UNDERSTAND |
| ANALYZE DATA |
| PLAN |
| ESTIMATE |
| SOLVE |
| EXAMINE |

### LEARN ABOUT IT

One of the first things you should do when you solve a problem is to make sure you understand the question. Sometimes it helps to put the question in your own words.

> The distance traveled in one early gas balloon race was 673 miles. The distance in another race was 1,315 miles. How much greater was the distance traveled in the second race?

First I'll read the question.

Then I'll ask the question in a different way.

How much greater was the distance traveled in the second race?

What is the difference in the distances traveled in the races?

### TRY IT OUT

Read each problem. Which question asks the same thing?

1. The Big Sky Ballooning Company gave 25 hot-air balloon rides last week. There were 5 people aboard for each ride. How many people went on rides?

   A. What was the total number of people who went on rides?

   B. How many people were aboard each balloon?

2. The weight of a balloon is 335 pounds. The people aboard the balloon weigh 481 pounds altogether. What is the total weight?

   A. How much more do the people weigh than the balloon?

   B. How much do the people and the balloon weigh together?

Write a question for each statement. Then solve the problem.

3. To become a private ballooning pilot, you need 10 hours of training. Jan has 6 hours of training already.

4. One balloon can hold 6 people. There are 4 balloons in all.

5. There are 30 ground crew workers at the balloon race. Each balloon has 6 ground crew workers.

6. One gas balloon race lasted 17 hours. Another race lasted 8 hours less.

Solve. Use any problem solving strategy.

1. Joey is 4 years old. When he is 4 times as old as he is now, he can get a license to be a ballooning pilot. How old will he be when he can get the license?

2. The balloon has 36 pounds of propane gas left. Each gallon of gas weighs 4 pounds. How many gallons are left?

3. Two balloons were 17 miles apart. The red balloon flew 6 miles toward the blue one. The blue balloon flew 3 miles toward the red one. How many miles apart were they then?

Use the Balloon Race table for problems 4–8.

| | Gordon Bennett Balloon Race (Gas Balloons) | | |
|---|---|---|---|
| Date | Number of Participants | Launch Site and Destination | Winner |
| 1906 | 16 | France to England | U.S.A. |
| 1907 | 9 | Missouri to New Jersey | Germany |
| 1908 | 23 | Germany to Norway | Switzerland |
| 1909 | 17 | Switzerland to Poland | U.S.A. |
| 1910 | 10 | Missouri to Quebec, Canada | U.S.A. |
| 1911 | 7 | Missouri to Wisconsin | Germany |
| 1912 | 22 | Germany to U.S.S.R. | France |
| 1913 | 18 | France to England | U.S.A. |

4. Which of the races listed in the table had twice as many participants as the race in 1907?

5. How many more participants did the race in 1906 have than the race in 1911?

6. The U.S.A. won two times as many races as which other country?

7. Which race had 8 fewer participants than the race in 1909?

8. Order the numbers of participants in the races from least to greatest.

9. **Suppose** A class of 32 students signed up to go ballooning. There is 1 balloon and it holds up to 8 students at a time. How many balloon rides are needed?

Suppose the facts were changed. Which of these facts would change the solution to the problem?
A. The balloon holds only 6 students.
B. The trip cost $75 for the class.
C. 2 students are absent on the day of the trip.
D. 8 students are absent on the day of the trip.

# Data Collection and Analysis
## Group Decision Making

UNDERSTAND
ANALYZE DATA
PLAN
ESTIMATE
SOLVE
EXAMINE

**Doing a Survey**
**Group Skill:**
Listen to Others

The numbers of elephants, rhinos, gorillas, and many other kinds of animals have grown much smaller over recent years. Many animals are on the endangered species list. Do you and other people know which animals are or are not classified as endangered? Conduct a survey to find out.

### Collecting Data

1. Look in an almanac or other reference book to find some lists of endangered animals. Look under *animals* in the index.

2. Work with your group to make a list of 5 animals that are endangered and 5 animals that are not endangered. Mix the listings so that the endangered and not endangered are not grouped together.

3. Show the list to 20 people. Ask them to tell whether they think that each animal on the list is or is not endangered. Make tallies on your list to record the answers of the people you survey, as in the example below.

| Do you think each of the following animals is or is not an endangered species? | | |
|---|---|---|
| | Yes | No |
| 1. Gorilla | | |
| 2. Giraffe | | |
| 3. Panda | | |
| 4. | | |

**4.** Make a bar graph to show the data collected in your survey. For each endangered animal, draw a bar to show how many of those surveyed knew that it is endangered. Be sure to choose a scale for your graph that will give you enough space to record the greatest number of tallies for any endangered animal on your list.

Here is how you might start your graph.

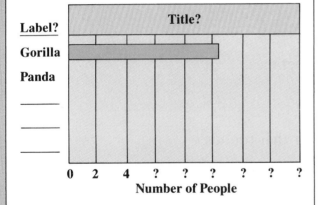

**5.** Check your graph. Did you give it a title and appropriate labels?

**6.** Write a paragraph to tell what your group found out. Which endangered animal was correctly identified as endangered by the greatest number of the people you surveyed? Were you surprised by the results?

51

# WRAP UP

## Place Value Words

Choose the word from the box that completes each sentence correctly. Not all words will be used.

| | | | |
|---|---|---|---|
| ones | hundredth | billions | place |
| millions | thousand | hundreds | periods |

1. The number 460,254,178 has three __?__.

2. To find the value of a digit, look at its __?__ in a number.

3. There are ten thousandths in one __?__.

4. A number in the __?__ has four periods.

5. Ten __?__ is the same as one thousand.

## Sometimes, Always, Never

Complete each statement by writing **sometimes, always,** or **never.** Explain your choice.

6. 54.821 __?__ rounds to 55.

7. 349 is __?__ the greatest whole number that rounds down to 300.

8. The value of a place in a number is __?__ greater than the value of any place to its left.

## Project

Estimate the number of days it would take you to count by ones to 1 million. Assume that you count for 8 hours a day. Begin by estimating how many numbers per second or per minute you can count.

HINT: Start at 1. Count for 10 seconds. How many numbers did you count? Do it again, starting at 325. Do it again, starting at 124,578. How many numbers did you count in all? How many seconds did you count in all? About how many numbers per second is that?

# POWER PRACTICE/TEST

## Part 1   Understanding

Write each number in words.

**1.** 4,329,607          **2.** 7,000,158,000          **3.** 3.05          **4.** 12.071

**5.** Give the greatest whole number and the smallest whole number that round to 10,000 when rounded to the nearest thousand.

**6.** Give the greatest two-place decimal number and the smallest two-place decimal number that round to 7 when rounded to the nearest tenth.

## Part 2   Skills

Find the value of each expression.

**7.** $x + 7$ when $x = 12$

**8.** $13 - y$ when $y = 11$

Write >, <, or = for each ⦀.

**9.** 28,374 ⦀ 28,376

**10.** 150,420 ⦀ 150,320

**11.** 8.116 ⦀ 8.126

Round to the place value of the underlined digit.

**12.** 8,4<u>7</u>6,325          **13.** 50<u>6</u>,328          **14.** 4.<u>1</u>25          **15.** <u>6</u>.832

## Part 3   Applications

**16.** Write a question for the statements. Then solve the problem.
Bruce has filled 8 pages of his photo album. Each page of the album holds 4 photos.

**17.** Rita and Mark live 18 miles from each other. They plan to meet halfway between their homes, in Midtown. Rita has gone 7 miles toward Midtown. Mark has gone 6 miles toward Midtown. How far apart are Rita and Mark?

**18. Challenge.** Write as a number in standard form: fifteen thousand, fifteen hundred fifteen and fifteen hundredths.

# ENRICHMENT
## Roman Numerals

The Ancient Romans developed a numeral system that was used throughout most of Europe until Arabic numerals came into popular use in the sixteenth century. The Romans wrote their numbers using these letters or symbols.

| I | V | X | L | C | D | M |
|---|---|---|---|---|---|---|
| 1 | 5 | 10 | 50 | 100 | 500 | 1,000 |

The Romans combined these symbols to write other numerals. Roman numerals do not have place value. Instead, the Romans added the value of a symbol when they wrote it to the right of a symbol that was of equal or greater value.

| | |
|---|---|
| II means 1 + 1, or 2. | CLV means 100 + 50 + 5, or 155. |
| XXI means 10 + 10 + 1, or 21. | MDC means 1,000 + 500 + 100, or 1,600. |

When the Romans wrote I, X, or C to the left of a symbol of greater value, they subtracted.

| | |
|---|---|
| IV means 5 − 1, or 4. | XC means 100 − 10, or 90. |
| XL means 50 − 10, or 40. | CM means 1,000 − 100, or 900. |

Write the standard number for these Roman numerals.

**1.** VII   **2.** XIII   **3.** LV   **4.** CLX   **5.** LIX   **6.** MCMLXXI   **7.** DCIV

Write the Roman numerals for these standard numbers.

**8.** 25   **9.** 8   **10.** 109   **11.** 54   **12.** 19   **13.** 1,550   **14.** 206

**54**

# CUMULATIVE REVIEW

**1.** Subtract.

$$504$$
$$-\ 276$$

A. 372  B. 880
C. 238  D. 228

**2.** Multiply.

$327 \times 4$

A. 1,288  B. 1,308
C. 1,228  D. 1,302

Identify each figure.

**3.**

A. cone
B. cylinder
C. sphere
D. pyramid

**4.**

A. equilateral triangle
B. right triangle
C. scalene triangle
D. obtuse triangle

**5.** In the equation $G \times H = G$, $G$ is a whole number greater than 0. What number does the $H$ stand for?

A. 0  B. 1  C. 2  D. 3

**6.** In the equation $L - M = L$, what number does the $M$ stand for?

A. 0  B. 1  C. 2  D. 3

**7.** Which three digits are in the millions period in the number 475,680,321,419?

A. 475  B. 680  C. 321  D. 419

**8.** If $N$, $P$, and $Q$ stand for numbers, which property tells you that $(N + P) + Q = N + (P + Q)$?

A. zero property of addition
B. commutative property of addition
C. zero property of multiplication
D. associative property of addition

**9.** Choose the next three numbers in the pattern.

5, 11, 17, 23, 29, —, —, —

A. 31, 37, 41  B. 33, 35, 37
C. 25, 21, 17  D. 35, 41, 47

**10.** Use mental math. How would you group the numbers to find 36 + 240 + 2 + 60?

A. (36 + 60) + 240 + 2
B. (36 + 60) + 240 + 2
C. (240 + 60) + 36 + 2
D. (60 + 2 + 36) + 240

**11.** Trisha and her father are building a fence around a rectangular area 20 feet wide and 30 feet long. They want to put a post every 5 feet. How many posts will they need?

A. 24  B. 22  C. 20  D. 18

# 3

## ADDITION AND SUBTRACTION: DECIMALS AND WHOLE NUMBERS

**THEME: KEEPING FIT**

**M**ATH AND
HEALTH AND FITNESS

DATA BANK

Use the Health and Fitness Data Bank on page 474 to answer the questions.

1 What is the minimum number of hours of sleep per day needed by the 10-year-old? How many more hours is this than the minimum needed by the average person over 60?

**2** How much greater is the maximum number of hours of sleep needed by the average 4-year-old than the maximum number needed by the average person over 60?

**3** Would you get more iron from eating one serving of cooked beef or from eating two slices of roast pork and a cup of raw carrots?

**4** **Using Critical Thinking** Find a pattern in the data about hours of sleep needed by humans. Give some reasons that you think may explain why the pattern occurs.

People of widely varying abilities can enjoy the challenges and rewards of athletic competition.

# Estimation
## Using Rounding

You can use what you know about rounding to estimate sums and differences.

### EXPLORE  Examine the Data

A newspaper reported that about 1,000 people attended the Madison Middle School's Fitness Fair. Use the data in the graph to decide whether you think the newspaper's report was justified.

Fitness Fair Attendance

### TALK ABOUT IT

1. Is the Thursday attendance closer to 200 or to 300 when it is rounded?
2. Is the Friday attendance closer to 400 or to 500?
3. What is the Saturday attendance rounded to the nearest hundred?

One way to estimate is to round numbers and use mental math to find the sum or difference. We can do this with decimals as well as with whole numbers. Here is how.

Find the sums.

| nearest hundred | nearest dollar |
|---|---|
| 219 → 200 | $3.19 → 3 |
| 298 → 300 | + 5.72 → 6 |
| +389 → 400 | $9 |
| 900 | |

Find the differences.

| nearest hundred | nearest whole number |
|---|---|
| 1,679 → 1,700 | 14.8 → 15 |
| −1,226 → 1,200 | − 7.2 → 7 |
| 500 | 8 |

We can also round to other places when appropriate, such as tens, tenths, and thousands.

Estimate by rounding. Round so that you can use mental math.

| 1. 368 | 2. 1,295 | 3. 8.26 | 4. $8.79 | 5. 3,984 |
|---|---|---|---|---|
| +529 | − 887 | −4.93 | +9.07 | +9,156 |

Estimate by rounding. Round so you can use mental math.

| | | | | | | | | | |
|---|---|---|---|---|---|---|---|---|---|
| **1.** | 92<br>+28 | **2.** | 73<br>+68 | **3.** | 123<br>− 57 | **4.** | 16.6<br>− 7.8 | **5.** | 617<br>+376 |
| **6.** | 3.4<br>+5.9 | **7.** | 1,486<br>− 626 | **8.** | 6.81<br>−3.2 | **9.** | 3,456<br>+6,790 | **10.** | 15,987<br>− 8,584 |
| **11.** | $5.89<br>+ 6.13 | **12.** | $9.89<br>−2.19 | **13.** | $8.56<br>+ 4.65 | **14.** | $6.75<br>+ 3.49 | **15.** | $4.58<br>− 1.90 |

## APPLY

### MATH REASONING

**16.** Use estimation. Pick two numbers that have a difference close to 500. Try 5 pairs of numbers. Then find the actual differences. Which is closest to 500?

| | | |
|---|---|---|
| 257 | 1,275 | 749 |
| 798 | 698 | 1,203 |
| 136 | 1,657 | 612 |
| 1,098 | 1,409 | 1,894 |
| 897 | 937 | 384 |
| 419 | 1,386 | 1,562 |
| 1,805 | 809 | 1,184 |

### PROBLEM SOLVING

**17.** Thursday 117 people had their blood pressure checked. Friday 192 people had their blood pressure checked. Estimate how many people in all had their blood pressure checked on Thursday and Friday.

**18. Health and Fitness Data Bank** The average cat sleeps about 16 hours per day. How many hours more per day does the cat sleep than a 10 year-old human who sleeps the minimum number of hours for that age? See page 474.

## MIXED REVIEW

Write each numerical expression using words.

**19.** $56 \div 8$    **20.** $36 - 6$    **21.** $9 \times 9$    **22.** $\frac{2}{3}$

Write each numerical expression using symbols.

**23.** fifteen divided by three    **24.** one fifth    **25.** seventy-two less nine

*More Practice, page 503, set C*

# Reviewing Whole Number Addition and Subtraction

## LEARN ABOUT IT

The examples below will help you review adding and subtracting whole numbers.

**A**

$$
\begin{array}{r}
{\scriptstyle 1} \\
637 \\
+\ \ 835 \\
\hline
1,472
\end{array}
$$

12

12 ones =
1 ten
and
2 ones

**B**  $69 + 108 + 125 + 6$

Line up addends so digits with the same place value are in the same column.

$$
\begin{array}{r}
{\scriptstyle 1\ 2} \\
69 \\
125 \\
+\ \ \ \ 6 \\
\hline
200
\end{array}
$$

**C**

$$
\begin{array}{r}
{\scriptstyle 6\ 13} \\
7\not3 8 \\
-275 \\
\hline
463
\end{array}
$$

1 less hundred gives 10 more tens.

**D**

$$
\begin{array}{r}
{\scriptstyle 5\ 9\ 14} \\
\not6\not0\not4 \\
-286 \\
\hline
318
\end{array}
$$

60 tens =
59 tens
and
10 ones

## TRY IT OUT

Add or subtract.

1. $\begin{array}{r} 506 \\ +853 \\ \hline \end{array}$  
2. $\begin{array}{r} 527 \\ -454 \\ \hline \end{array}$  
3. $\begin{array}{r} 385 \\ +207 \\ \hline \end{array}$  
4. $\begin{array}{r} 7,645 \\ +8,397 \\ \hline \end{array}$  
5. $\begin{array}{r} 853 \\ -317 \\ \hline \end{array}$

6. $\begin{array}{r} 704 \\ -628 \\ \hline \end{array}$  
7. $\begin{array}{r} 4,263 \\ -1,896 \\ \hline \end{array}$  
8. $\begin{array}{r} 9,156 \\ +8,375 \\ \hline \end{array}$  
9. $\begin{array}{r} 57,364 \\ +18,906 \\ \hline \end{array}$  
10. $\begin{array}{r} 54,375 \\ -17,682 \\ \hline \end{array}$

11. $175 - 84$  
12. $305 - 196$  
13. $274 + 3,866 + 95$

14. $1,519 - 915$  
15. $2,176 + 897$  
16. $328 + 97 + 205 + 88$

**60**

Add or subtract.

| | | | | |
|---|---|---|---|---|
| **1.** 69 <br> +46 | **2.** 247 <br> −136 | **3.** 495 <br> +230 | **4.** 1,578 <br> − 391 | **5.** 5,038 <br> +2,847 |
| **6.** 467 <br> +548 | **7.** 5,289 <br> + 76 | **8.** 4,364 <br> − 867 | **9.** 6,034 <br> −2,993 | **10.** 51,764 <br> +27,896 |
| **11.** 45 <br> 58 <br> +75 | **12.** 594 <br> 385 <br> +257 | **13.** 65 <br> 93 <br> +451 | **14.** 6,576 <br> 937 <br> +8,142 | **15.** 47,836 <br> 4,927 <br> + 398 |

**16.** 74 + 85    **17.** 365 + 278    **18.** 186 − 27    **19.** 9,634 − 5,798

**20.** Subtract 376 from 704.    **21.** Find the sum of 78, 156, and 732.

**MATH REASONING**    Without calculating, tell which sum is greater.

**22.** 724 + 88 + 165   OR   524 + 488 + 165

**23.** 453 + 325 + 210   OR   385 + 299 + 195

**PROBLEM SOLVING**

**24.** Jack started driving in Bloomington. Now he is between Milford and Rockford and is 45 miles from Rockford. How far is he from Bloomington?

| | |
|---|---|
| Bloomington to Milford | 85 mi |
| Milford to Rockford | 196 mi |

**25.** Verna flew 2,500 miles on Sunday, 485 miles on Monday, and 1,265 miles on Tuesday. How many miles altogether did she fly in three days?

▶ **ESTIMATION**

Choose numbers from the cards to make subtraction problems.

**26.**
393

**27.**
231

**28.**
663

| | |
|---|---|
| 529 | 49 |
| 417 | 186 |
| 712 | 136 |

# Front-End Estimation

You can use mental math to estimate sums.

**EXPLORE  Solve to Understand**

- How many pairs of numbers can you find on the bulletin board that have a sum within 10 of the target number 100?

- List the target pairs and tell whether each sum is more or less than 100.

**TALK ABOUT IT**

1. How would you find a number that forms a target pair with 32?

2. How can you see that 55 and 59 do not form a target pair?

3. Can you look only at the tens digits to find target pairs? Explain.

**Front-end estimation** is a method of estimation where we add the digits with the greatest place value (the front-end digits) to get a rough estimate. Then we use the rest of the numbers to adjust the estimate.

**Add the front-end digits. → Adjust using the other digits.**

$$\begin{array}{r} 396 \\ 263 \\ +537 \end{array}$$

1,000 +

$$\begin{array}{r} 396 \\ 263 \\ +537 \end{array}$$

about 200 more

**Estimate: 1,200**

**TRY IT OUT**

Use the front-end digits to estimate. Tell whether the exact sum or difference is more than or less than your estimate.

| 1. | 2. | 3. | 4. |
|---|---|---|---|
| 475 | 934 | 508 | 820 |
| +420 | −306 | −259 | 470 |
| | | | +381 |

Use front-end digits to estimate. Tell whether the exact sum or difference is more than or less than your estimate.

| | | | | |
|---|---|---|---|---|
| **1.** 449<br>+246 | **2.** 978<br>−536 | **3.** 987<br>+875 | **4.** 862<br>−358 | **5.** 629<br>+308 |
| **6.** 384<br>625<br>+824 | **7.** 486<br>589<br>+795 | **8.** 678<br>329<br>+598 | **9.** 456<br>749<br>+804 | **10.** 987<br>243<br>+548 |

**APPLY**

## MATH REASONING

Estimate to find the best missing number for each ▨ .

**11.** 46 + ▨ is close to 80

**12.** 29 + ▨ is close to 50

**13.** 67 − ▨ is close to 30

## PROBLEM SOLVING

**14.** Pedro earned $256 one week and $369 the next. Then he spent $417 dollars for a television set. Estimate the amount of money he then had left to put in the bank.

**15.** **Determining Reasonable Answers**  In a telephone poll, Ted made 398 calls the first week and 476 the second. Use estimation to decide whether or not Ted's computed total is reasonable. If it is not reasonable, find the correct answer.

▶ **USING CRITICAL THINKING**  **Support Your Conclusions**

Study the examples shown. Make up some other examples. Then complete these statements with the word **odd** or **even.**

**16.** The sum of any two odd numbers is always ___?___ .

**17.** The sum of an odd and an even number is always ___?___ .

**18.** The sum of any two even numbers is always ___?___ .

| |
|---|
| 0 + 1 = 1 |
| 1 + 1 = 2 |
| 2 + 1 = 3 |
| 2 + 2 = 4 |
| 2 + 3 = 5 |

*More Practice, page 503, set E*

# Problem Solving
## Guess and Check

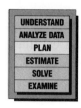

UNDERSTAND
ANALYZE DATA
PLAN
ESTIMATE
SOLVE
EXAMINE

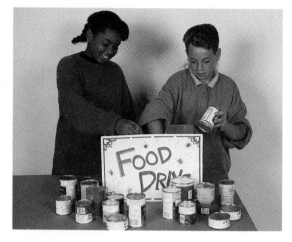

To solve some problems you need to do more than just choose an operation. You can often use a problem solving strategy called **Guess and Check.**

> Vic's school had a yearly food drive. Vic won a movie pass for bringing in a total of 56 cans of food in two days. He brought in 12 more cans the second day than the first. How many cans did he bring in each day?

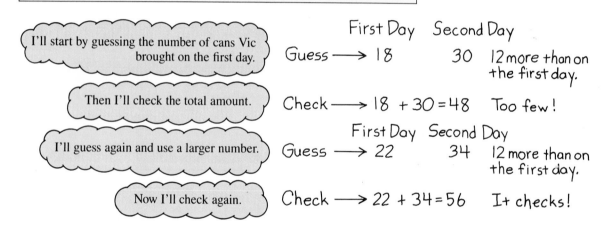

*I'll start by guessing the number of cans Vic brought on the first day.*

First Day   Second Day

Guess ⟶ 18      30      12 more than on the first day.

*Then I'll check the total amount.*

Check ⟶ 18 + 30 = 48      Too few!

*I'll guess again and use a larger number.*

First Day   Second Day

Guess ⟶ 22      34      12 more than on the first day.

*Now I'll check again.*

Check ⟶ 22 + 34 = 56      It checks!

Vic brought in 22 cans the first day and 34 the second day.

**TRY IT OUT**

Judith helped pack up the games and stuffed animals collected for the Toys for Children Project. She packed 97 toys in all. There were 23 fewer stuffed animals than games. How many stuffed animals were there?

| | Animals | Games |
|---|---|---|
| Guess 1 | 25 | 48 |
| Check | 25 + 48 = 73 | |
| Guess 2 | | |
| Check | | |
| Guess 3 | | |
| Check | | |

- What was the total number of toys Judith packed?
- How many fewer stuffed animals were there than games?
- Copy and complete the table to solve the problem.

**64**

Use the strategy Guess and Check to help you solve each problem.

1. Eban and Clint Lemon each have a box of cans to donate to the food drive. Eban said, "If you give me 4 cans, we'll each have the same number." Together they have 32 cans. How many cans does Eban have?

2. Sandy and Rosa together gave a total of 88 hours of service at the Senior Retirement Home last year. Rosa gave 24 fewer hours than Sandy. How many hours of service did each girl give?

## MIXED PRACTICE

Choose a strategy from the strategies list or use other strategies you know to solve these problems.

| Some Strategies | |
| --- | --- |
| Act Out | Choose an Operation |
| Use Objects | Draw a Picture |
| Guess and Check | |

3. Judith could fit 6 games in each box for the Toys for Children Project. She packed 6 boxes. How many games did she pack?

4. Mrs. Grand, the principal, said she would jump into a pool with her clothes on if the students at Lincoln collected 350 cans of food for charity. How many cans more than that did they collect?

School District Food Drive
Top Three Schools

| School | Number of Cans |
| --- | --- |
| King | 784 |
| Lincoln | 429 |
| Washington | 417 |

5. About how many cans did the top three schools bring in for the food drive?

6. Altogether, 7,679 cans were brought in for the food drive. How many cans were donated by all the schools not counting those from King School?

7. George rode in a bike-a-thon to raise money to fight heart disease. He collected a total of $40 from 8 different people. Each person gave the same amount of money. How much did each person give?

8. Naomi saved $79. She gave $11 less to charity than she kept. How much did she give to charity?

9. The newspaper in Bo's town gave $5,676 to charity last year. A bank gave $8,598. How much did the two give altogether?

10. A truck delivered cans from the food drive to 4 different towns. The trip is 1,012 miles long, starting in Bay and ending in Dodge. The towns between Bay and Dodge are Ross and then Statton. The distance between Bay and Ross is 347 miles. The distance between Ross and Statton is 126 miles. How far is it between Ross and Dodge?

# Adding Decimals
## Making the Connection

The picture at the right shows how we can use place-value blocks to show decimals.

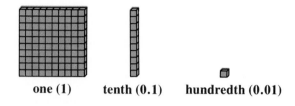

one (1)        tenth (0.1)        hundredth (0.01)

**EXPLORE** Use Place Value Blocks

Work with a partner.

- Spin a spinner three times to get a number of hundredths, tenths, and ones. Record the numbers in a table like the one at the right. Use blocks to show how many.

- Repeat this for a second number.

- Push the two groups of blocks together. Make all possible trades. Make a table to record how many blocks in all.

- Repeat this activity two times.

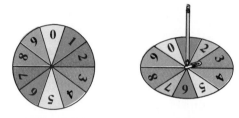

| ones | tenths | hundredths |
|------|--------|------------|
|      |        |            |

**TALK ABOUT IT**

1. Describe any trades you made in the activity above.

2. Why is it possible that you did not make any trades?

3. What is the greatest number of trades that you could have to make?

You have used blocks to find how many in all when you add two decimal numbers. The example below shows that recording this is like recording what you do when adding whole numbers, except for lining up the decimal points. Here is how you find the sum 2.35 + 3.28.

| **What You Do** | **What You Record** |

**1.** Are there enough hundredths to make a trade?

Put together and trade.

Line up the decimal points to add.

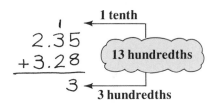

$$\begin{array}{r} \overset{1}{2.35} \\ +3.28 \\ \hline 3 \end{array}$$

1 tenth

13 hundredths

3 hundredths

**2.** Are there enough tenths to make a trade?

Put together.
No trade

$$\begin{array}{r} \overset{1}{2.35} \\ +3.28 \\ \hline 63 \end{array}$$

**3.** How many ones are there?

Put together.
No trade

$$\begin{array}{r} 2.35 \\ +3.28 \\ \hline 5.63 \end{array}$$

Be sure to place the decimal point.

**TRY IT OUT**

Use place value blocks to add. Record your work.

**1.**   0.45
       +0.34

**2.**   1.06
       +2.32

**3.**   0.78
       +0.46

**4.**   2.54
       +1.08

67

# Adding Decimals

**EXPLORE  Analyze the Process**

Suppose you chose chicken, a sliced tomato, and corn for a meal. How many milligrams (mg) of vitamin C would they provide?

To solve this problem add 8.75, 28.39 and 12.7.

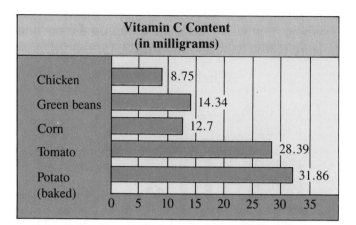

**Vitamin C Content (in milligrams)**

| Line up the decimal points. | Add the hundredths. Trade if necessary. | Add the tenths. Trade if necessary. | Add the whole numbers. Write the decimal point. |
|---|---|---|---|
| 8.75<br>28.39<br>+12.7 | $\overset{1}{}$<br>8.75<br>38.39<br>+12.7<br>————<br>4 | $\overset{1\ \ 1}{}$<br>8.75<br>28.39<br>+12.7<br>————<br>84 | $\overset{1\ 1\ \ 1}{}$<br>8.75<br>28.39<br>+12.7<br>————<br>49.84 |

## TALK ABOUT IT

1. Why do we line up decimal points?

2. Use estimation to show that the answer is reasonable.

3. Give the answer to the Explore problem in a complete sentence.

**Other Examples**

**A**
$$\begin{array}{r} \$7.80 \\ +\ 9.65 \\ \hline \$17.45 \end{array}$$

**B**
$$\begin{array}{r} 9.576 \\ +0.489 \\ \hline 10.065 \end{array}$$

**C**
$$\begin{array}{r} 0.763 \\ 4.69 \\ +1.8 \\ \hline 7.253 \end{array}$$

Add.

**1.**
$$\begin{array}{r} \$0.76 \\ +\ 1.34 \end{array}$$

**2.**
$$\begin{array}{r} 1.746 \\ +0.205 \end{array}$$

**3.**
$$\begin{array}{r} 1.6 \\ +0.753 \end{array}$$

**4.**
$$\begin{array}{r} 7.864 \\ +0.189 \end{array}$$

**5.**
$$\begin{array}{r} 6.478 \\ 0.7 \\ +2.85 \end{array}$$

Add.

| | | | | |
|---|---|---|---|---|
| **1.** 46.8 <br> +59.7 | **2.** 37.8 <br> + 9.6 | **3.** 6.27 <br> +2.88 | **4.** 0.85 <br> +4.36 | **5.** 3.7 <br> +2.46 |
| **6.** 7.386 <br> +0.049 | **7.** 36.35 <br> +19.2 | **8.** 4.180 <br> +3.675 | **9.** $5.63 <br> + 2.48 | **10.** 8.985 <br> +4.69 |
| **11.** 36.8 <br> 19.3 <br> +26.4 | **12.** 128.7 <br> 36.480 <br> + 9.867 | **13.** 1.869 <br> 2.088 <br> +3.548 | **14.** 0.687 <br> 0.975 <br> 0.836 <br> +0.548 | **15.** $124.73 <br> 642.80 <br> 376.57 <br> +290.17 |

**16.** 26.6 + 42.9    **17.** $16.37 + $17.96    **18.** 6.478 + 0.7 + 2.85

**Estimate** each sum to the place value of the underlined digit.

**19.** 0.3$\underline{4}$ + 0.6$\underline{7}$    **20.** $\underline{7}$.6 + $\underline{6}$.9    **21.** 43.$\underline{6}$2 + $\underline{9}$.47    **22.** 2$\underline{1}$.97 + 3$\underline{7}$.41

**APPLY**

### MATH REASONING

Without adding, tell whether each sum is greater than or less than 2.

**23.** 0.875 + 1.105    **24.** 1.086 + 0.92    **25.** 1.006 + 0.999

### PROBLEM SOLVING

**26.** Ian had 46.2 mg of vitamin C. Which two items from the chart did he have?

**27.** Loran had beans, corn, and a tomato. How much vitamin C did she get?

**28. Health and Fitness Data Bank** Find the number of milligrams of vitamin C in three things you like to eat What is the total amount of vitamin C you would get from one serving of each? See page 474. **DATA BANK**

### ▶ CALCULATOR

Use a calculator to change the first number into the second number.
Use the addition or subtraction key only once for each problem.

**29.** first: 6.78 → second: 6.38    **30.** first: 43.5 → second: 73.5

**31.** first: 0.545 → second: 0.245    **32.** first: 2.37 → second: 2.49

# Using Critical Thinking

**Function Machine**

| In | Out |
|----|-----|
| 57 | 1 |

| In | Out |
|----|-----|
| 100 | 0 |

| In | Out |
|----|-----|
| 3 | 1 |

| In | Out |
|----|-----|
| 6 | 0 |

| In | Out |
|----|-----|
| 9 | 1 |

## LEARN ABOUT IT

Dr. Awesome was showing Nathan and Stephanie the function machine he made. When he put an input number in the machine, it used a rule and produced an output number. Then it printed an input-output card to show the results.

Nathan said, "I see. If my input number was 6 and my rule was add 3, my output number would be 9." "Right!" said Dr. Awesome.

Stephanie turned on the machine and put in different input numbers. The machine used another rule to print the cards shown above. "I think the machine is broken," said the doctor. "I'm not so sure," said Nathan. "I think I know the rule."

## TALK ABOUT IT

1. What does the function machine do?
2. Why do you think Dr. Awesome thought the machine was broken?
3. Do you think the machine is broken? If not, what is the rule?
4. What would the output be for these inputs: 5, 10, 17?

## TRY IT OUT

Suppose each set of cards was produced by a function machine. Give the function rule for each. Then give 3 more pairs that the rule might produce.

**1.**

| In | Out |
|----|-----|
| 1 | 1 |
| 2 | 4 |
| 3 | 9 |
| 4 | 16 |
| 5 | 25 |

**2.**

| In | Out |
|----|-----|
| 1 | 3 |
| 2 | 5 |
| 3 | 7 |
| 4 | 9 |
| 5 | 11 |

**3.**

| In | Out |
|----|-----|
| 1 | 6 |
| 2 | 11 |
| 3 | 16 |
| 4 | 21 |
| 5 | 26 |

# POWER PRACTICE/QUIZ

Round so you can estimate using mental math.

1. $\begin{array}{r} 27 \\ + 46 \\ \hline \end{array}$    2. $\begin{array}{r} 89 \\ - 33 \\ \hline \end{array}$    3. $\begin{array}{r} 621 \\ - 82 \\ \hline \end{array}$    4. $\begin{array}{r} 418 \\ + 168 \\ \hline \end{array}$    5. $\begin{array}{r} \$19.57 \\ - 3.98 \\ \hline \end{array}$

Add or subtract.

6. $\begin{array}{r} \$127.24 \\ + 83.27 \\ \hline \end{array}$    7. $\begin{array}{r} 43{,}188 \\ + 86{,}832 \\ \hline \end{array}$    8. $\begin{array}{r} 462 \\ - 385 \\ \hline \end{array}$    9. $\begin{array}{r} 23{,}040 \\ + 37{,}625 \\ \hline \end{array}$    10. $\begin{array}{r} 7{,}207 \\ - 4{,}308 \\ \hline \end{array}$

Estimate the sum or difference.

11. $\begin{array}{r} 378 \\ + 455 \\ \hline \end{array}$    12. $\begin{array}{r} 3{,}149 \\ + 465 \\ \hline \end{array}$    13. $\begin{array}{r} 317 \\ - 222 \\ \hline \end{array}$    14. $\begin{array}{r} 527 \\ - 350 \\ \hline \end{array}$    15. $\begin{array}{r} 285 \\ 464 \\ + 677 \\ \hline \end{array}$

Tell which expressions give the same answer as the first.
More than one may be correct.

16. 87 + 24
    A. 80 + 20 + 11       B. 87 + 20 + 4       C. 87 + 20 + 11

17. 153 − 86
    A. (150 − 80) + (6 − 3)  B. (140 − 80) + (13 − 6)  C. (100 − 80) + (53 − 6)

Add.

18. $\begin{array}{r} \$6.29 \\ + 5.07 \\ \hline \end{array}$    19. $\begin{array}{r} 23.4 \\ + 61.6 \\ \hline \end{array}$    20. $\begin{array}{r} 3.005 \\ + 2.12 \\ \hline \end{array}$    21. $\begin{array}{r} 0.036 \\ 1.208 \\ + 29.1 \\ \hline \end{array}$    22. $\begin{array}{r} \$316.07 \\ 412.10 \\ + 628.86 \\ \hline \end{array}$

23. 0.994 + 0.123       24. 1.1 + 0.3 + 6.06       25. 12.3 + 104.027 + 6.1354

## PROBLEM SOLVING

Solve by guessing and checking.

26. Emilia is two years older than Nicholas. The sum of their ages is 20. How old is each child?

27. Ryan has 5 coins that total 65¢. What coins does he have?

28. Tracey collected 21 shells in 3 days. Each day she collected 4 more shells than she collected the day before. How many shells did she collect each of the 3 days?

29. Ms. Chou has twice as many children in her class as Mr. James has in his. There are a total of 48 children in the two classes. How many children are in each class?

# Problem Solving
## Choosing a Calculation Method

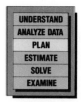

UNDERSTAND
ANALYZE DATA
PLAN
ESTIMATE
SOLVE
EXAMINE

One of the decisions you must make when you solve problems is which calculation method you should use.

**Calculation Methods**
- Paper and Pencil
- Mental Math
- Calculator

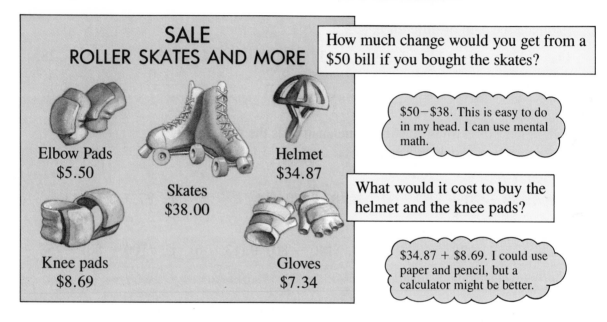

**SALE**
**ROLLER SKATES AND MORE**

Elbow Pads
$5.50

Skates
$38.00

Helmet
$34.87

Knee pads
$8.69

Gloves
$7.34

How much change would you get from a $50 bill if you bought the skates?

$50−$38. This is easy to do in my head. I can use mental math.

What would it cost to buy the helmet and the knee pads?

$34.87 + $8.69. I could use paper and pencil, but a calculator might be better.

When you have to choose a calculation method, you may find it helpful to:
- *First try mental math.* Look for numbers that can be computed easily in your head.
- *If mental math would be difficult, choose between paper and pencil and a calculator.* Problems that require many steps and trades are often more quickly solved using a calculator.

Choose an appropriate calculation method and tell why.
Then solve.

**1.** $365 - 43$

**2.** $28 \times 20$

**3.** $134 \times 24$

**4.** $1075 - 289$

**5.** $\$40.50 \times 2$

**6.** $150 \div 25$

**7.** $30 \times 40 \times 5$

**8.** $\$95.85 - \$14.75$

Choose an appropriate calculation method and tell why.
Then solve.

**1.** $28.74 + $24.95       **2.** 5 × 127       **3.** 41 + 12 + 19

**4.** 49 + 19 + 32 + 166    **5.** $75 − $62.50  **6.** $320 × 20

**7.** 4 × 3 × 30            **8.** 3,000 − 299   **9.** 700 − 438

**10.** 400 ÷ 20            **11.** $35 − $12.75  **12.** $8.75 × 8 × 12

Solve. Choose the calculation method that seems best for
you. Use data on page 72 when needed.

**13.** The cost of two books about roller
skating is $11.50. One costs $2.50
more than the other. What is the cost
of each book?

**14.** Some new skates and other items you
want cost $55 including tax. You have
saved $33.45. How much more
money do you need to buy the things
you want?

**15.** How much less do the gloves cost
than the helmet?

**16.** About how much would it cost to
buy all of the equipment that is
on sale?

**17.** The entry fee for a skating contest is
$15. For entering, you get a free
T-shirt worth $8.95. How much more
is the entry fee than the amount the
T-shirt is worth?

**18.** A subscription to a skating magazine
costs $27 a year. There are 9 issues a
year. What is the cost of each issue?

**19.** How much difference is there in the special prices
between the most expensive and the least expensive
skating shirt?

> **Great Shirts for Skating**
> Regular prices $13.79 to $21.95
> Special prices $8.89 to $15.89

▶ **COMMUNICATION   Writing to Learn**

**20.** Suppose you have a friend who said, "I always use my
calculator to do computations." Write a letter to this
friend giving some examples that would show that it is
sometimes better not to use a calculator.

*More Practice, page 523, set A*

# Subtracting Decimals
## Making the Connection

You have used place value blocks to add decimals. You can also use them to show how to subtract decimals.

one (1)        tenth (0.1)        hundredth (0.01)

### EXPLORE  Use Place Value Blocks

Work with a partner.

■ Spin a spinner three times to get a number of hundredths, tenths, and ones. Record the number in a table, and use blocks to show how many.

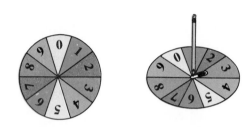

■ Repeat the spins until you get a number smaller than your first number. Record the number in your table.

| ones | tenths | hundredths |
|------|--------|------------|
|      |        |            |

■ Take away this number from the blocks that show your first number. Trade when you need to. Record how many blocks are left.

■ Repeat this activity two times.

### TALK ABOUT IT

1. Describe any trades that you made in the activity above.
2. What is the smallest number of trades you might have to make? the greatest number?
3. How does the number for the blocks that were left compare to the number for the blocks in the first group?

You have used blocks to find how many are left when you take away a decimal number. The example below shows that recording this is like recording what you do when subtracting whole numbers, except for lining up decimal points. Here is how you subtract 1.25 from 3.62.

| **What You Do** | **What You Record** |

**1.** Can you take away 5 hundredths without trading? How many tenths and hundredths are there after the trade?

**Not enough hundredths to take away 5. Regroup.**

Line up the decimal points to subtract.

$$
\begin{array}{r}
{}^{5\ 12} \\
3.\cancel{6}\cancel{2} \\
-1.25 \\
\hline
\end{array}
$$

**2.** How many hundredths are left after you take away 5 hundredths?

$$
\begin{array}{r}
{}^{5\ 12} \\
3.\cancel{6}\cancel{2} \\
-1.25 \\
\hline
7
\end{array}
$$

**3.** How many tenths do you take away? how many ones?

Be sure to place the decimal point.

$$
\begin{array}{r}
{}^{5\ 12} \\
3.\cancel{6}\cancel{2} \\
-1.25 \\
\hline
2.37
\end{array}
$$

**TRY IT OUT**

Use place-value blocks to subtract. Record your work.

**1.**  0.65
  −0.24

**2.**  1.24
  −0.17

**3.**  3.08
  −0.46

**4.**  3.14
  −1.38

75

# Subtracting Decimals

**EXPLORE  Analyze the Process**

The width of the rectangular swimming pool is 5.94 m (meter) less than the length. What is the width of the swimming pool?

16.31 m

Since you are taking away a certain amount from another, use subtraction.

To solve this problem, subtract 5.94 from 16.31.

| Line up the decimal points. | Subtract the hundredths. Trade if necessary. | Subtract the tenths. Trade if necessary. | Subtract the whole numbers. Place the decimal point. |
|---|---|---|---|
| 16.31<br>− 5.94 | 2 11<br>16.3̶1̶<br>− 5.94<br>7 | 5 12 11<br>1̶6̶.3̶1̶<br>− 5.94<br>37 | 5 12 11<br>1̶6̶.3̶1̶<br>− 5.94<br>10 37 |

**TALK ABOUT IT**

1. Where did the 11 above the 1 in the second step come from?
2. Why did you have to trade from ones to tenths?
3. Give an estimate for 16.31 − 5.94.
4. Give an answer to the Explore problem in a complete sentence.

## Other Examples

**A**
$$\begin{array}{r} {\scriptstyle 3\ \ 16} \\ \$4.\!\!\not6\!0 \\ -\ 1.80 \\ \hline \$2.80 \end{array}$$

**B**
$$\begin{array}{r} {\scriptstyle 8\ 9\ 14} \\ 0.9\!\!\not0\!\not4 \\ -0.478 \\ \hline 0.426 \end{array}$$

**C**
$$\begin{array}{r} 856.7 \\ -534.16 \end{array}$$

Write 856.7 as 856.70.

→

$$\begin{array}{r} {\scriptstyle 6\ 10} \\ 856.7\!\!\not0 \\ -534.16 \\ \hline 322.54 \end{array}$$

1.  0.803
   −0.369

2.  $47.60
   − 24.15

3.  58.3
   −23.76

4.  6.75
   −3.84

5.  50.18
   −30.09

Subtract.

1.     8.4
     −3.6

2.     8.34
     −4.65

3.    57.82
    −18.97

4.    304.26
    −  96.56

5.     7.064
     −1.244

6.    596.74
    −258.68

7.    9,743
    −  862.6

8.    $89.42
    −  64.86

9.    $102.51
    −    84.38

10.   $547.23
    −  268.59

11. 4.3 − 0.9

12. 3.85 − 1.596

13. $547.34 − $98.67

14. 81.05 − 4.3

Use rounding to estimate each difference to the place value
of the underlined digit.

15. 8̲.78 − 1̲.92

16. 5̲.3 − 2̲.7

17. 18̲9.75 − 3̲2.26

18. 37̲.2 − 26̲.8

**MATH REASONING**

19. Use each of the given digits one time.
Write a problem with a difference
greater than 3 and less than 3.5. Can
you find more than one problem?

1   2   3

4   5   6

**PROBLEM SOLVING**

20. The distance around a triangular
exercise field is 34.25 m. Each of two
of the sides is 13.6 m long. What is
the length of the third side?

21. The distance around a rectangular
playground is 54.31 m. The total
length of three of the sides is 36.01 m.
What is the length of the other side?

▶ **ESTIMATION**

Estimate each sum or difference using
one of the estimation techniques you
have learned.

| **Estimation Techniques** |
| :--- |
| ■  Front-end |
| ■  Rounding |
| ■  Compatible Numbers |

22. 390 − 94

23. 1,395 − 215

24. 4.9 + 5.02

25. 13.82 − 9.4

26. 926 − 387

27. 3.92 + 4.09

*More Practice, page 503, set B*

**77**

# Mental Math
## Using Compensation

**LEARN ABOUT IT**

### EXPLORE  Solve to Understand

Can you think of a mental shortcut to find the total number of pictures students had paid for by the end of Wednesday?

| Student Payments for Class Pictures | | |
|---|---|---|
| **Day** | **Number Paid** | **Total Number Paid** |
| Mon. | 135 | 135 |
| Tues. | 212 | 347 |
| Wed. | 198 | ? |

### TALK ABOUT IT

1. What numbers were added to get the total for Tuesday?

2. What numbers would you add to find the total for Wednesday?

3. Suppose you added 200 + 347. Would this sum be greater than or less than 198 + 347? How much more or less?

**Compensation** is a mental math technique we can use to help us add or subtract. When one of the numbers involved in a problem is close to another number that is easier to work with mentally, we use the easier number to find an answer. Then we adjust that answer by adding to it or subtracting from it.

■ Find 347 + 198.

> Add 2 too much and find 347 + 200.

> Subtract 2 from 547.

347 + 200 = 547; 547 − 2 = 545

■ Find 463 − 198.

> Subtract 2 too much and find 463 − 200.

> Add 2 to 263.

463 − 200 = 263; 263 + 2 = 265

In the first example, when 2 was added to 198 to make the addition easier, we had to **compensate** by subtracting 2. In the second example, when 200 rather than 198 was subtracted, 2 had to be added to **compensate.**

**TRY IT OUT**

Use compensation to find the sum or difference.

1. 97 + 538        2. 253 − 99        3. 101 + 657        4. 403 − 95

Find the sums or differences mentally. Use compensation.

**1.** 29 + 37     **2.** 48 + 27     **3.** 99 + 17     **4.** 483 + 298     **5.** 397 + 456

**6.** 43 − 9     **7.** 51 − 9     **8.** 62 − 8     **9.** 684 − 196     **10.** 571 − 295

**11.** 4,588 + 298    **12.** 685 − 396    **13.** 567 + 297    **14.** 2,778 − 98    **15.** 3,998 + 547

APPLY

### MATH REASONING

Complete each statement.

**16.** Adding 8 is like adding 10 and then subtracting  _?_  .

**17.** Subtracting 9 is like subtracting 10 and then  _?_  (adding or subtracting) 1.

**18.** Adding 9 is like adding 10 and then subtracting  _?_  .

### PROBLEM SOLVING

**19.** Cynthia collected $197 for yearbooks and $79 for class pennants. How much did she collect in all?

**20. Missing Data**   Make up reasonable data so you can find the answer mentally.
Problem: Daniel bought 3 T-shirts and an $8 yearbook. How much change should he receive from a $50 bill?

 MIXED REVIEW

Find the value of each expression.

**21.** (9 + 15) − 6     **22.** (36 ÷ 6) × 5     **23.** 22 − (33 ÷ 3)     **24.** (4 × 8) − 12

Write in standard form.

**25.** 7,000,000,000 + 500,000,000 + 2,000,000 + 800,000 + 40,000 + 1,000 + 500 + 90 + 6

**26.** seventy-two billion, one hundred fifty-seven million, eight hundred sixty-three thousand, two

**27.** sixty-five million, seventy thousand, fifty-eight

# Problem Solving
## Using a Calculator

| UNDERSTAND |
| ANALYZE DATA |
| PLAN |
| ESTIMATE |
| SOLVE |
| EXAMINE |

When you want to add the same amount to, or subtract the same amount from, many different numbers, it is helpful to use the addition and subtraction **constants** on your calculator.

The Special package is $879 more than the Basic package for each tour. What will be the total cost for each Special tour?

| | ECONOMY | BASIC | SPECIAL | DELUXE |
|---|---|---|---|---|
| Tour A: South to Brazil | | $3476.— | | |
| Tour B: Experience the Orient | | $2875.— | | |
| Tour C: Touring the Congo | | $2498.— | | |
| Tour D: Australia down under | | $3319.— | | |

There is no special key on your calculator for the addition and subtraction constants. It is a hidden calculator feature. The second number is held in the calculator memory and can be added or subtracted again and again. This key code will give the amounts for the four Special tours.

[ON/AC] 3476 [+] 879 [=] ↓    2875 [=] ↓    2498 [=] ↓    3319 [=] ↓

Use the constant feature on your calculator to complete the following.

**1.** Copy the table above. Use the key code given above and write in the amounts for each Special tour.

**2.** Each Economy tour is $468 less than a Basic tour. Find the total cost for each Economy tour. Write each amount in your table. (The subtraction constant is like the addition constant, but uses the [−] key instead of the [+] key.)

**3.** The cost of a Deluxe tour is $1,329 more than a Basic tour. Find the total cost for each Deluxe tour and write it in your table.

**4.** Next year the cost of all Basic tours will increase by $178. How much will each Basic tour cost next year?

80

Solve. Use any problem solving strategy.

1. Sam is flying from San Francisco to Tokyo. The distance from San Francisco to Honolulu is 2,398 miles in the air. The distance from Honolulu to Tokyo is 3,859 miles. How far will Sam fly?

2. When Miko's tour group arrived in India, their suitcases were in 7 piles. There were the same number of suitcases in each pile. The group had a total of 49 suitcases. How many suitcases were in each pile?

3. Nick and his dad paid a total of $96 for their train fare to Boston. Nick's fare was $32 less than his dad's. How much was his dad's fare?

4. The River Rhine tour costs $2,797 for one person and $4,129 for two people traveling together. How much more does it cost for two people?

5. Before packing any items for his China trip, Ray weighed them on a scale. Each pair of socks weighed 6 ounces. How many ounces would 7 pairs of socks weigh?

Use the table below for problems 6 and 7.

| Safari Prices | | | |
|---|---|---|---|
| | Rough-It | Basic | Luxury |
| One week | | $2,345 | |
| Two weeks | | $3,195 | |
| Three weeks | | $3,976 | |

6. The Rough-It Safari package costs $547 less than the Basic package. How much does each Rough-It package cost? Copy the table and write in the amount for each Rough-It package.

7. The Luxury Safari package costs $926 more than the Basic package. What is the cost of each Luxury package? Write the amounts in the table.

8. **Talk About Your Solution** Solve the problem below. Then explain your solution to a classmate. Compare your solutions.

In Tokyo, Jan ordered an American breakfast on Monday and a Japanese breakfast on Tuesday. The total cost of the breakfasts was $46. The American breakfast was $22 more than the Japanese breakfast. How much was the American breakfast?

# Applied Problem Solving
## Group Decision Making

UNDERSTAND
ANALYZE DATA
PLAN
ESTIMATE
SOLVE
EXAMINE

**Group Skill:**
Check for Understanding

You and your mother are hiking through the Bitteroot Mountains with a donkey carrying your gear. One night you tie the donkey too loosely, and it strays away. It may take you as long as 3 days to reach help. Since you need to carry your own supplies now, you cannot take all you have with you. What will you leave behind?

### Facts to Consider

- The temperatures have been as low as 34 degrees at night and as high as 75 degrees during the day.

- It has rained one night out of four.

- You and your mother are both wearing hiking boots, jeans, and a short-sleeved shirt.

- You will probably be able to go back later to get the things you leave behind.

- You and your mother each can carry 5 more kilograms of items from the lists that follow:

| Equipment (for both) | |
|---|---|
| cooking stove | 1.0 kg |
| sleeping bags | 1.6 kg |
| foam pad for sleeping bag | 0.3 kg |
| tube tent | 0.6 kg |
| camera | 0.7 kg |
| tripod to hold camera | 1.4 kg |
| radio (for weather information) | 0.2 kg |
| flashlight | 0.6 kg |
| **TOTAL** | **6.4 kg** |

## Clothing (for each)

| | |
|---|---|
| rainsuit | 0.5 kg |
| heavy sweater | 0.3 kg |
| down jacket | 0.8 kg |
| warm shirt | 0.6 kg |
| wool pants | 0.6 kg |
| jeans | 1.0 kg |
| shorts | 0.5 kg |
| **TOTAL** | **4.3 kg** |

## Food

| | |
|---|---|
| 4 liter bottles of water | 4.0 kg |
| 20 granola bars | 0.5 kg |
| peanut butter and jelly in a tube | 0.2 kg |
| 6 packages instant cocoa powder | 0.1 kg |
| crackers and hard bread | 0.1 kg |
| two big hunks of cheese | 1.8 kg |
| bag of dried fruit | 0.2 kg |
| 6 candy bars | 0.1 kg |
| 2 cans tuna | 0.5 kg |
| 4 cans chicken | 1.0 kg |
| **TOTAL** | **8.5 kg** |

## Some Questions to Answer

1. What is the total weight of the items on the lists?

2. Which three items of equipment are the heaviest?

3. If you left behind the radio and tripod, how many kilograms is that altogether? How many more kilograms would you need to get rid of?

4. Would a calculator be helpful for answering questions 1–3? Explain why.

## What Is Your Decision?

Make a list showing which items you are going to take with you and a list showing which you will leave behind. Include the total weight on each list. Give reasons for your decision.

83

# WRAP UP

## Matching Descriptions and Examples

Match the mental math and estimation techniques
with the examples.

1. counting back

2. using compatible numbers

3. using compensation

4. estimating by rounding

5. front-end estimating

A. $82 - 4$   81, 80, 79, 78

B. $517 - 98 = (517 - 100) + 2$

C. $90 + 37 + 10 + 13 = 100 + 50$

D.
$$\begin{array}{rr} 378 & 400 \\ + 234 & + 200 \\ \hline & 600 \end{array}$$

E.
$$\begin{array}{rr} 756 & 700 \\ - 439 & - 400 \\ \hline & 300 \end{array}$$

## Sometimes, Always, Never

Complete each statement by writing **sometimes**,
**always**, or **never**. Explain your choice.

6. The sum of two odd numbers is __?__ an even
number.

7. The sum of an even number and an odd number
is __?__ an even number.

8. When you add a 3-digit whole number and a
2-digit whole number you __?__ get a 4-digit whole
number.

9. When you add hundredths to hundredths, you
__?__ get thousandths.

## Project

Do an estimation experiment. Fill a jar with small
objects of different colors (colored chips, play coins,
colored paper clips, or mixed dry beans). One person
estimates the number of each color or type of object
and another estimates the number of other objects.
Then estimate the total number of objects in the jar.

Discuss the ways you estimated. Decide which you
think may be most accurate. Check your estimates.

# POWER PRACTICE/TEST

## Part 1 Understanding

For each problem, tell the places in which you would need to trade.

1.  2,480
   + 3,075

2.  4,516
   − 2,345

3.  5.76
   + 2.93

4.  7.96
   − 5.78

Would you choose calculator, paper and pencil, or mental math to do each? Why?

5. $14.24 × 3 × 15

6. 5 × 4 × 20

## Part 2 Skills

Add or subtract.

7.  38,023
   +  9,148

8.  6,016
   − 2,948

9.  5.973
   + 4.82

10.  $304.26
    −   87.39

Use rounding to estimate.

11.  326
    + 459

12.  5,077
    −  959

Use front-end estimation and adjust.

13.  541
    + 869

14.  574
    − 136

Use compensation and mental math for each.

15. 142 + 298

16. 349 + 120

17. 74 − 25

18. 560 − 199

## Part 3 Applications

19. Mr. Peary met his daughter in Troy. It took him 48 minutes longer to drive there than it took his daughter. If the total driving time for both together was 120 minutes, how long did each drive?

20. **Challenge.** Scott's class entered a charity race. Mr. Riley said he would pay $1.25 for each mile the class ran. Mrs. Sanchez said she would pay twice as much for each mile run. Scott's class collected $93.75 from them. How much did each pay?

# ENRICHMENT
## Finding and Using Patterns

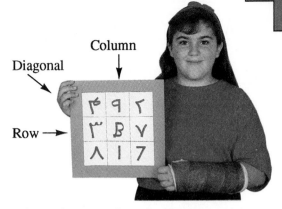

The sum of the numbers in each row, column, and diagonal of a **magic square** is the same. According to a Chinese myth, the first magic square appeared over 4,000 years ago. It was on the shell of a turtle.

The magic square shown in this picture uses East Arabic numbers. It was found in a book written by a Muslim African mathematician.

The following steps will help you make your own magic square. The magic sum is 15.

1. Draw a 3-by-3 square like the one in the picture (but without the numerals).

2. List the 8 ways you can name 15 by using three different addends from the numbers 1 through 9. One way is $1 + 5 + 9$ (with the addends in any order).

3. Use the list you made for step 2 to complete a table like this one.

| Number | 1 | 2 | 3 | 4 | 5 | 6 | 7 | 8 | 9 |
|---|---|---|---|---|---|---|---|---|---|
| How many times number appears in list of addends | 2 | | | | | | | | |

4. Find how many times the number in the magic square's center box will be used to get the magic sum of 15. (Hint: 1 column, 1 row, 2 diagonals) Find the number in the table that appears that many times in your list. Write that number in your magic square's center box.

5. Find how many times a number in your square's corner boxes will be used to get the magic sum. Find how many times a center number in each outside row or column will be used to get the magic sum. Now complete your magic square!

Use the digits 0 through 8 to make another 3-by-3 magic square. This time the magic sum is 12.

# CUMULATIVE REVIEW

Add.

**1.** 326 + 84 + 125

    A. 425   B. 535   C. 445   D. 545

**2.** 27 + 44 + 13 + 86

    A. 170   B. 169   C. 150   D. 179

**3.** 125 + 49 + 175

    A. 249   B. 339   C. 349   D. 319

**4.** Which number has six fewer hundredths than tenths?

    A. 1.46   B. 5.84   C. 4.93   D. 6.39

**5.** Which is another way to say 58 − 24?

    A. fifty-eight plus twenty-four

    B. twenty-four less than fifty-eight

    C. fifty-eight divided by twenty-four

    D. twenty-four more than fifty-eight

**6.** Which operation would you use? Paula counted 16 red cars on her way to school and 14 red cars on her way home. How many more red cars did she see on her way to school?

    A. addition     B. multiplication

    C. subtraction    D. division

**7.** Use place value to tell what the 4 means in 1,654,671,583.

    A. 4 hundreds    B. 4 millions

    C. 4 thousands   D. 4 billions

Use front-end estimation to estimate the sum.

**8.**
$$\begin{array}{r} 527 \\ 853 \\ + 721 \\ \hline \end{array}$$

    A. 2,000    B. 1,900

    C. 2,100    D. 2,200

**9.**
$$\begin{array}{r} 945 \\ 258 \\ + 799 \\ \hline \end{array}$$

    A. 1,800    B. 2,100

    C. 1,900    D. 2,000

Add.

**10.** 6.214 + 5.87 + 6.49

    A. 7.450          B. 17.474

    C. 12.733        D. 18.574

**11.**
$$\begin{array}{r} \$345.16 \\ 894.78 \\ + \phantom{0}776.27 \\ \hline \end{array}$$

    A. \$1,805.01    B. \$2,016.21

    C. \$2,016.00    D. \$1,805.21

**12.** Sean drove 321 miles in two days. He drove 57 miles more on the first day than on the second day. How many miles did he drive on the second day?

    A. 167   B. 189   C. 128   D. 132

**13.** Which calculation method might you use to solve this problem? Terri bought 20 memo books at 49¢ each. Can she pay for them with a ten dollar bill?

    A. mental math    B. calculator

    C. estimation    D. paper and pencil

# 4

**M**ATH AND
SOCIAL STUDIES

DATA BANK

Use the Social Studies
Data Bank on page 481
to answer the questions.

1 Which was invented first,
the telephone or the telegraph? Which was in-
vented later, the ballpoint pen or
the McCormick reaper?

# DATA
# AND
# GRAPHS

**THEME: INVENTIONS**

**2** List the years of the following inventions in order, from most recent to oldest: steamboat, telegraph, telephone, electric washer, typewriter.

**3** Benjamin Franklin invented the lightning rod 124 years before Alexander Graham Bell invented the telephone. When did Franklin invent the lightning rod?

**4** **Using Critical Thinking** Connie made a list of the years these items were invented: steamboat, telegraph, typewriter, car starter. Then she added one more year to the list. What do you think it was? Why?

A visitor to the Black American West Museum and Heritage Center admires a 19th century riding saddle.

# Thinking About Graphs

### EXPLORE  Analyze a Graph

Study the bar graph, line graph, and pictograph.

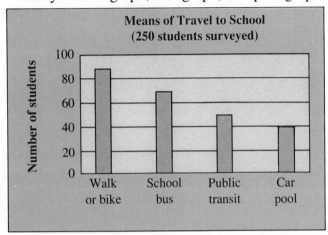

Means of Travel to School
(250 students surveyed)

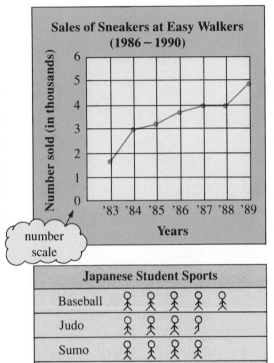

Sales of Sneakers at Easy Walkers
(1986 – 1990)

number scale

| Japanese Student Sports | |
|---|---|
| Baseball | 人 人 人 人 人 |
| Judo | 人 人 人 人 |
| Sumo | 人 人 人 人 |
| Kendo | 人 人 人 人 人 人 |
| 人 = 20 students | 人 = 10 students |

key

### TALK ABOUT IT

1. How do the greatest number of students get to school?

2. In what year were the sales of sneakers the greatest? the least? How did you decide?

3. Which Japanese sport has the greatest number of student participants? Explain.

All graphs should have a **title,** each part of a graph should have a **label,** and bar and line graphs should have a **number scale.** A pictograph should have a **key** that tells what number each symbol represents.

Use the graphs above to answer these questions.

1. What is the title of each graph?

2. What are the labels for the sides of the bar graph?

3. How many students does each half picture represent in the pictograph?

| Languages Spoken in India (2,000 people surveyed) | |
|---|---|
| Hindi | 웃 웃 웃 웃 웃 웃 |
| Oriya | 웃 웃 웃 ᶳ |
| Telugu | 웃 웃 웃 웃 웃 |
| English | 웃 웃 웃 웃 웃 웃 |
| 웃 = 100 people | ᶳ = 50 people |

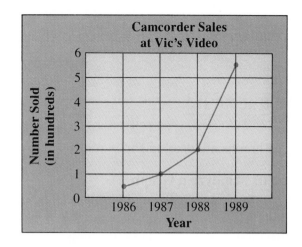

1. Give the title of the pictograph.

2. Give the title of the line graph.

3. What do the numbers 1, 2, 3, 4, 5, and 6 represent in the line graph?

4. What is the key for the pictograph?

APPLY

**MATH REASONING**

5. Can you tell from the pictograph above whether Hindi and English are spoken by *exactly* the same number of people who were surveyed?

6. Between which two years was the growth in Camcorder sales the greatest? How did you decide?

**PROBLEM SOLVING**

Use the data in the graphs on page 90 to solve.

7. About how many more students walk or bike to school than go by car pool?

8. By about how much did sneaker sales increase from 1983 to 1989?

▶ **ESTIMATION**

9. Predict the number of aerobics classes there will be in the year 2000.

10. About how many aerobics classes will there be in the year 2020 if the rate of increase in classes continues?

# Reading and Interpreting Line Graphs

Line graphs are used to show trends in data.

**EXPLORE** **Analyze a Graph**
When do you usually buy a swimsuit? The graph at the right shows swimsuit sales at a particular store for March through August.

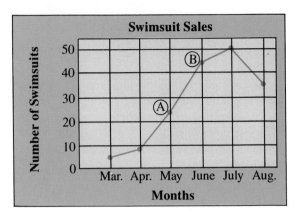

**TALK ABOUT IT**

1. As you go up the vertical number scale, each mark represents how many swimsuits?
2. Point A on the graph lies on the line for what month?
3. Which month had the highest sales? How did you decide?

- The horizontal and vertical number scales on a line graph are sometimes called the **horizontal axis** and **vertical axis.**
- The **slope** of the line tells whether there is an increase, a decrease, or no change.
- Each point on a line graph stands for two values. Point B on the graph above stands for June on the horizontal scale and for about 45 on the vertical scale. About 45 swimsuits were sold in June.

**TRY IT OUT**

Use the temperature graph at the right.

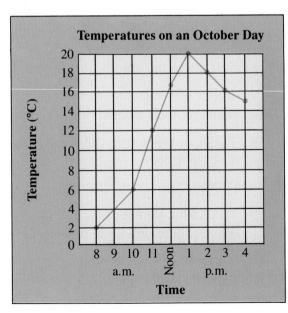

1. For which hours during the day did the students collect data?

2. What was the high temperature of the day according to the graph?

3. Do you predict the temperature at 5 p.m. will be higher or lower than 16° C?

92

Use the sports graph.

1. As you go up the vertical number scale, each mark represents how many students?

2. What year had the smallest number of men participants? women?

3. In which years did the number of male participants drop from the previous year?

4. About how many more women were participating in 1990 than in 1983?

5. Are the two lines about the same distance apart for each year?

6. Did the number of women participants increase more or less than the number of men participants from 1983 to 1990?

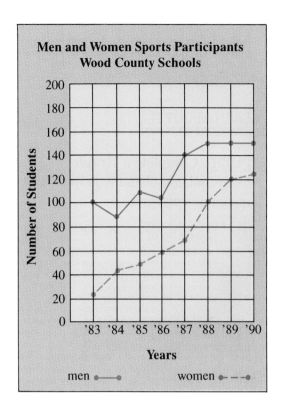

**Men and Women Sports Participants Wood County Schools**

### MATH REASONING

7. Make a prediction based on the sports graph above. How many men and women participants do you predict there will be in 1991? in 1995?

### PROBLEM SOLVING

8. Estimate how many more men were participating in sports in 1990 than in 1983. Then do this for the women. By how much more did the number of women increase?

▶ **USING CRITICAL THINKING   Interpret a Graph**

Tanya rides her bicycle to school. It takes her 20 minutes. Here is a graph showing the time she travels and her speed on her bike. Write an explanation of why her speeds change during her trip.

93

# Making Line Graphs

## LEARN ABOUT IT

### EXPLORE  Complete a Graph

Copy and complete the graph about inventions patented.

| Year | Number of Inventions Patented in the U.S. |
|------|-------------------------------------------|
| 1836 | 103 |
| 1837 | 426 |
| 1838 | 514 |
| 1839 | 404 |
| 1840 | 458 |

## TALK ABOUT IT

1. What is the largest number you need for the vertical axis? the horizontal axis? How did you decide?
2. Why would an interval of 100 rather than 50 not be as good a choice for the vertical number scale?
3. Did the number of inventions patented increase each year? Explain.

To make a line graph:

- Draw each axis. Select a scale for each.
- Label the parts of the graph. Title the graph.
- Plot the points for the data. Connect the points with line segments.

## TRY IT OUT

Copy and complete the line graph. Use data from the table.

| Year | Population per square mile |
|------|----------------------------|
| 1790 | 4.5 |
| 1800 | 6.1 |
| 1810 | 4.3 |
| 1820 | 5.5 |
| 1830 | 7.4 |

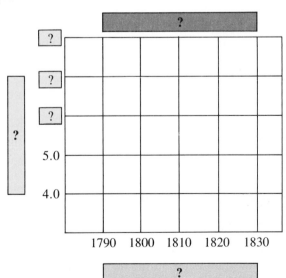

94

Use the given data to make line graphs.

**1.**

| Day of the Week | Number of Minutes of Homework |
|---|---|
| Day 1 | 20 |
| Day 2 | 45 |
| Day 3 | 20 |
| Day 4 | 60 |
| Day 5 | 45 |

**2.**

| Year | Number of Vans Sold by One Dealer |
|---|---|
| 1985 | 8 |
| 1986 | 12 |
| 1987 | 18 |
| 1988 | 28 |
| 1989 | 35 |

APPLY

**MATH REASONING**

**3.** Decide whether the data below would best be graphed using a bar graph, a line graph, or a pictograph. Explain why.

| Kilowatt Hours of Electricity Used by Five Families in One Year | | | | | |
|---|---|---|---|---|---|
| Family | Davis | Lee | Conrad | Jacobs | Grasso |
| Kwh | 27,000 | 46,000 | 49,000 | 24,000 | 35,000 |

DATA BANK

**PROBLEM SOLVING**

**4.** Use the table on page 94. Estimate how many more inventions were patented in 1838 than in 1836.

**5. Social Studies Data Bank** Make a line graph that shows how many patents on inventions were requested in the years 1836–1840. See page 481.

MIXED REVIEW

Write $<$, $>$, or $=$ for each ▐.

**6.** 8.04 ▐ 8.40      **7.** 2.362 ▐ 2.326      **8.** 6.41 ▐ 4.41      **9.** 20.01 ▐ 20.010

Find the sums.

**10.** 41.92 + 67.98      **11.** 0.009 + 0.009      **12.** 7.8 + 9.098

# Double Bar Graphs

A double bar graph compares two sets of data using the same units.

**EXPLORE  Analyze a Graph**

This graph compares the costs of renting and buying a masquerade costume. What parts of the costume would you consider buying and what parts would you rent?

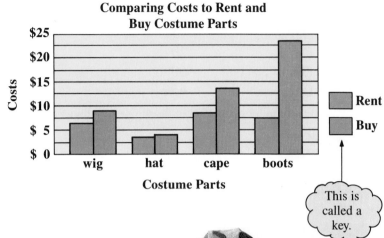

**Comparing Costs to Rent and Buy Costume Parts**

Costs / Costume Parts: wig, hat, cape, boots

Rent / Buy (key)

This is called a key.

**TALK ABOUT IT**

1. What do the darker bars represent?
2. Which item costs almost as much to rent as to buy?
3. If you were to rent only one item, which would you rent and why?

To make a double bar graph:
- Select a scale that fits the data.
- Make a key for the graph.
- Draw the axes and label the parts of the graph.
- Draw the bars.
- Title the graph.

Use the graph above to answer these questions.

1. About how much does it cost to rent a cape?
2. Estimate the cost of buying a wig.
3. Estimate the cost of buying boots.
4. About how much more does it cost to buy boots than to rent boots?

1. Copy and complete the double bar graph.
   **Survey Question and Results**
   Which one of these people would you
   most like to have known?

   |  | Adults | Children |
   |---|---|---|
   | Susan B. Anthony | 16 | 12 |
   | Albert Einstein | 22 | 18 |
   | Martin Luther King | 24 | 31 |
   | Helen Keller | 9 | 15 |

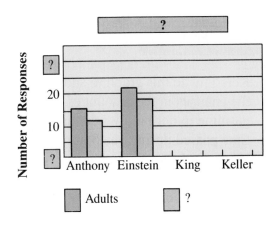

**MATH REASONING**

Could each set of data be graphed using a double bar
graph? Write **yes** or **no.**

2. | Plant Height | |
   |---|---|
   | 2 days | 1 cm |
   | 4 days | 1.5 cm |
   | 6 days | 21.5 cm |

3. | Scores: | Game 1 | Game 2 |
   |---|---|---|
   | Wildcats | 57 | 64 |
   | Tigers | 34 | 45 |
   | Bears | 56 | 40 |

4. | | Fall City | Twin Peaks |
   |---|---|---|
   | Rainfall | 13 in. | 9 in. |
   | Temp. | 72° | 53° |
   | Altitude | 1,200 ft | 3,200 ft |

**PROBLEM SOLVING**

5. **Data Hunt**   Make a double bar graph to show the daily
   high and low temperatures for your city for one week.

▶ **USING CRITICAL THINKING**   Comparing Graphs

Some graphs can be misleading. Study these graphs.

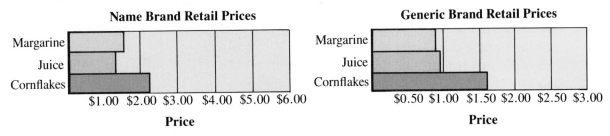

6. What is the interval on the scale at the left? on the scale
   at the right?
7. If you did not look at the horizontal scales, which prices
   would you think are higher, name brand or generic? Explain.

# Using Critical Thinking

Keiko made this graph to show the changes in the amount of gasoline in her family's car as time passed during one Saturday. When Carl saw the graph, he said, "That graph has no numbers. It doesn't tell me a thing!" Berti smiled, and said, "It tells me just what happened to the car during that day!" What story does the graph tell you about what happened to the car on Saturday?

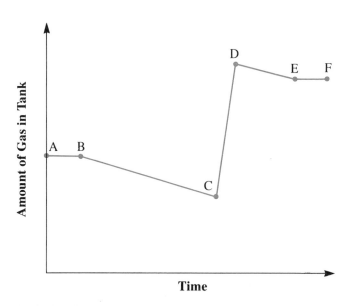

**TALK ABOUT IT**

1. What could a downward sloping line mean on the graph? an upward sloping line?

2. How would the line on the graph look if the car was parked in the garage for a couple of hours?

3. Is the line from A to B earlier in the day or later in the day than the line from E to F?

4. Tell a story about what happened. Compare your story with the stories of other students.

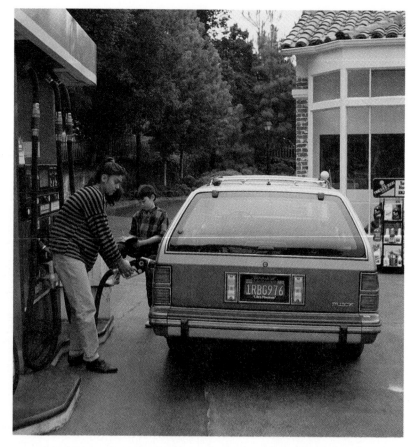

98

Use the graph at the right for exercises 1−3.

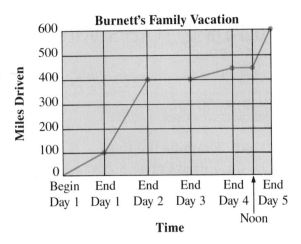

**Burnett's Family Vacation**

1. On which day did the Burnetts do the most driving?

2. They stayed at their grandmother's house one day and did not drive at all. What day did they stay at their grandmother's?

3. Give an explanation for what could have happened during day 5.

Use the graph at the right for exercises 4−6.

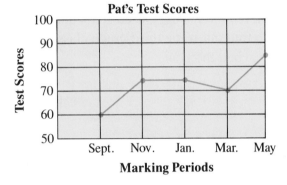

**Pat's Test Scores**

4. Were Pat's scores at the end of the school year better or worse than at the beginning of the year?

5. For which marking periods were the scores the same?

6. Did this student's scores ever drop? If so, when?

7. Draw a graph like the ones above. Make the graph tell a story about someone's pulse rate while doing some kind of an activity (for example, riding a bike). Write a short story that goes with your graph.

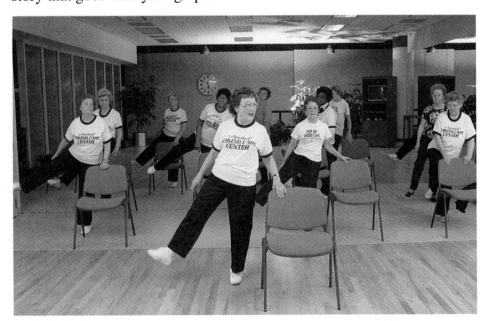

# Running Totals with a Calculator

## EXPLORE  Examine the Data

The students at Carver School had a drive to collect used toys and games. The goal was for each grade to collect a total of 100 toys and games in 5 weeks. The results for each week are shown in the table.

Here is how Peggy used a calculator to find out if the third grade class reached the goal.

| Toys and Games Collected | | |
|---|---|---|
| | Grade 3 | Grade 4 | Grade 5 |
| Week 1 | 18 | 32 | 39 |
| Week 2 | 34 | 29 | 18 |
| Week 3 | 27 | 25 | 44 |
| Week 4 | 26 | 19 | 23 |
| Week 5 | 17 | 31 | 19 |

| Keys | Display |
|---|---|
| [ON/AC] 18 [+] 34 [+] | <u>52</u> |
| 27 [+] | <u>79</u> |
| 26 [+] | <u>105</u> |

> Not enough. Add week 3.

> Still not enough. Add week 4.

> That's enough!

### TALK ABOUT IT

1. Why did Peggy stop and look at the total display each time?

2. Peggy did not press the [ = ] key. Why?

Use your calculator to solve each problem.

1. Which grade reached the collection goal first?

2. Suppose the goal had been 60 toys and games rather than 100. Which grade would have reached that goal first?

3. Which grade collected the most toys and games altogether?

100

# POWER PRACTICE/QUIZ

For items 1–4, use the graph at the right.

1. What is this kind of graph called?

2. What is the title of the graph?

3. What do the numbers on the vertical axis show?

4. Between what two hours did the greatest temperature change occur?

5. What kinds of graphs could you use to compare two sets of data using the same units?

6. What number of units are shown by the portion of the pictograph at the right?

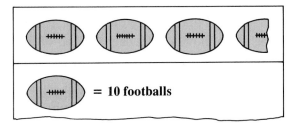

## PROBLEM SOLVING

The table at the right shows the results of a newspaper collection drive that two fifth grade classes took part in. Use the data for items 7–10.

| Pounds of Newspapers Collected | | | | |
|---|---|---|---|---|
| | Week 1 | Week 2 | Week 3 | Week 4 |
| Class A | 30 | 26 | 17 | 15 |
| Class B | 40 | 42 | 55 | 60 |

7. Make a line graph to show the data for Class B. Use a scale with 5-pound intervals to show the amount collected each week.

8. Make a double bar graph to show the data for both classes. Choose a scale with some interval other than 5 pounds to show the amounts collected each week.

9. Which class showed an increase in amount collected each week?
Which class showed a decrease?

10. Suppose Bobby Brownlee was the top collector in his class and then he moved to the other class. Which class do you think he left? When do you think he left?

# Range, Mean, Median, and Mode

## LEARN ABOUT IT

The difference between the greatest and least numbers in a set of numerical data is called the **range** of the data.

**EXPLORE** **Analyze Some Data**
Find the range for the ages at which the presidents listed in the table took office.

**TALK ABOUT IT**

| Presidents' Ages When Inaugurated | |
| --- | --- |
| George Washington | 57 |
| William Henry Harrison | 68 |
| John Tyler | 51 |
| Franklin Pierce | 48 |
| James Buchanan | 65 |
| Abraham Lincoln | 52 |
| William Howard Taft | 51 |

1. How did you find the range for the ages?
2. Suppose Lincoln's age had been 50 rather than 52. Would that change the range? Explain.
3. What number between 48 and 68 is about in the middle of the list of ages? How did you decide?

The **mean** or **average** of a set of numbers can be found by finding the sum of all of the numbers and then dividing by the number of addends. Here is how to find the mean of the presidents' ages.

$$\text{Mean} = (57 + 68 + 51 + 48 + 65 + 52 + 51) \div 7$$
$$= 392 \div 7 = 56 \qquad 392 \div 7 \quad \boxed{56}$$

The **median** is the middle number when the data are arranged in order. If there are two middle numbers, the median is the mean of the two middle numbers.

48   51   51   52   57   65   68
                  ↑
              Median

The **mode** is the number that appears most often in a set of data. For the presidents' ages the mode is 51. Sometimes no one number appears more often than any others. In such cases there is no mode.

## TRY IT OUT

Find the range, mean, median, and mode for each set.

**1.** 45, 76, 88, 99, 104, 56

**2.** 78, 88, 85, 90, 78, 71, 63

Find the range, mean, median, and mode for each set of data.

**1.** 17, 24, 24, 30, 20    **2.** 17, 24, 34, 27, 18    **3.** 43, 29, 29, 38, 26, 15

**4.** 103, 113, 97, 89, 98    **5.** 125, 146, 140, 159, 140    **6.** 215, 219, 202, 219, 225

**7.** $3.75, $8.25, $5.50, $3.75, $4.00    **8.** $20, $12, $28, $12, $35, $91

APPLY

**MATH REASONING**

**9.** Change one number in the following data so that the range is 20. 7, 5, 18, 21, 6, 24, 17

**10.** Change one number in the following data so that the mode is 12. 15, 13, 18, 12, 16, 25

**11.** Without computing, tell which set of data has the greater mean.
**A.** 46, 56, 82, 91, 75, 81   **B.** 56, 82, 91, 46, 120, 81

**PROBLEM SOLVING**

**12.** When becoming President of the U.S., Millard Fillmore was 50 years old, Theodore Roosevelt was 42, Woodrow Wilson was 56, and Harry Truman was 60. What is the mean for the ages at which these men became President?

**13.** **Social Studies Data Bank**   What is the range for the set of ages at which Presidents Washington through Harrison were inaugurated? What is the mode? What is the median? See page 481.

MIXED REVIEW

Write the word name for each decimal number.

**14.** 0.09          **15.** 1.002          **16.** 0.32          **17.** 2.061

Subtract.

**18.**    37.88          **19.**    2.543          **20.**    34.6          **21.**    7.803
        − 21.46                  − 0.697                  − 16.7                  − 4.637

# Making a Questionnaire

Pottery made by a skilled artist
of Acoma Pueblo, New Mexico

**EXPLORE**  **Complete a Questionnaire**
Work in groups. Write your answers to the questionnaire.

1. Your grade? _____
2. What item or items could you bring to be shown at your school's Small World Arts and Crafts Fair? _____
3. How would you rate the following kinds of entertainment for the fair? (**1** means "would enjoy very much" and **5** means "would not enjoy at all.")

| | | | | | | |
|---|---|---|---|---|---|---|
| **A.** | Native costumes parade | 1 | 2 | 3 | 4 | 5 |
| **B.** | "Guess the Culture" contest | 1 | 2 | 3 | 4 | 5 |
| **C.** | Dances of many lands | 1 | 2 | 3 | 4 | 5 |
| **D.** | "How to . . ." demonstrations (origami, weaving, beadwork, . . .) | 1 | 2 | 3 | 4 | 5 |

**TALK ABOUT IT**

1. Is each question clear? Do you think everyone would interpret each question the same way?
2. Do you think every student would clearly understand what each activity is?

To make a questionnaire:
- Decide on the subject you want information about.
- Brainstorm ideas you want to cover in the questionnaire.
- Write questions for the questionnaire.
- Give your questionnaire to a few people to find out whether all questions are clearly stated.
- Revise the questionnaire if necessary.

Hand-decorated gourd from
Kenya, eastern Africa

Suppose you have been asked to decide what games and food booths to have at a school carnival.

1. Brainstorm ideas you might put on your questionnaire.
2. Give reasons why it might or might not make sense to have a student's name on the questionnaire.
3. Write four questions you might include on your questionnaire.

Statue of a Chinese Imperial
Palace guard (Han Dynasty)

**104**

**1.** Copy and complete the questionnaire.

Name_____

**A.** What grade are you in? Circle one.

K−2          2−4          4−6          6−8

**B.** Which of these foods is your favorite? Circle it.

Spinach          Eggs          Carrots

**C.** Circle the price you would be most willing to pay for a ticket to the fair.

$0.50          $1.00          $2.00          $3.00

**D.** Circle the number of brothers and sisters you have.

1          2          3          4

Use the questionnaire above for exercises 2−7.

**2.** Why would a fourth-grader have difficulty answering item A?

**3.** Rewrite question A so that the grade levels do not overlap.

**4.** What is wrong with item B?

**5.** What is wrong with Question C?

**6.** Rewrite item C so that you can find out the most someone would pay.

**7.** Rewrite item D so that everyone can answer.

**APPLY**

**MATH REASONING**

**8.** How could you fairly select 25 students in your school to be given a questionnaire about choosing a new name for your school?

**PROBLEM SOLVING**

**9.** Lanny gave out a questionnaire to 9 girls and 7 boys. He got back completed questionnaires from 6 girls and 5 boys. How many completed questionnaires has he not yet gotten back?

▶ **ESTIMATION**

**10.** Cut out some 1 ft² paper "tiles." Use them to estimate the area of your classroom floor. Explain how you made your estimate.

# Problem Solving
## Make a Table

| UNDERSTAND |
| ANALYZE DATA |
| PLAN |
| ESTIMATE |
| SOLVE |
| EXAMINE |

### LEARN ABOUT IT

To solve some problems you may find it helpful to use the given data and a strategy called **Make a Table.**

Helga's after school service club set up an assembly line to make stuffed brown bears. The furry fabric needed to make 3 bears cost $11. How much does the fabric for 18 bears cost?

I'll make a table using the data in the problem.

Now I'll complete the table to find the solution.

This data was given in the problem.

| bears | 3 | | | | | |
|---|---|---|---|---|---|---|
| fabric | $11 | | | | | |

| | | 2×3 | 3×3 | 4×3 | 5×3 | 6×3 |
|---|---|---|---|---|---|---|
| bears | 3 | 6 | 9 | 12 | 15 | 18 |
| fabric | $11 | $22 | $33 | $44 | $55 | $66 |
| | | 2×11 | 3×11 | 4×11 | 5×11 | 6×11 |

The fabric for 18 bears costs $66.

### TRY IT OUT

Jim and Juan are the quality control inspectors at the end of the assembly line. Out of every 5 completed bears, 4 bears pass their inspection. The class has completed 25 bears. How many of them would you expect to pass the inspection by Jim and Juan?

- Out of 5 completed bears, how many usually pass inspection?

- How many bears has the class completed?

- Copy and complete the table below to solve the problem.

| Completed bears | 5 | 10 | 15 | 20 | 25 |
|---|---|---|---|---|---|
| Bears that pass | 4 | | | | |

Make a table to help you solve each problem.

1. The class needs 10 ounces of stuffing for every 4 bears. How much stuffing does the class need in order to make 20 bears?

| stuffing | | | | |
|---|---|---|---|---|
| bears | | | | |

2. The first week, the class made bears at a rate of 3 every 20 minutes. How many did they make in 120 minutes (2 hours)?

| bears | | | | |
|---|---|---|---|---|
| minutes | | | | |

## MIXED PRACTICE

Choose a strategy from the strategies list or use other strategies you know to solve these problems.

| Some Strategies | |
|---|---|
| Act Out | Draw a Picture |
| Use Objects | Guess and Check |
| Choose an Operation | Make a Table |

3. The bear's eyes cost 9¢ each. How much would 8 eyes cost?

4. During the week that the bear-mascots were on sale, the class also made and sold lemonade. They used 5 lemons for every 8 cups of lemonade. How many lemons did they need for 48 cups of lemonade? Make a table like the one below to help you.

| lemons | | | | | |
|---|---|---|---|---|---|
| cups | | | | | |

Use this graph for problems 7 and 8.

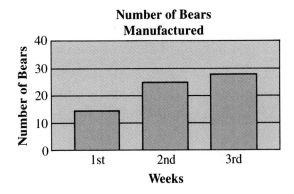

**Number of Bears Manufactured**

5. It cost the class $146.75 to make all the bears. They made a total of $191.54 in sales. How much profit did they make?

6. The class sold 98 bears. 12 more students from the upper grades bought a bear than students from the lower grades. How many customers were from the upper grades?

7. The class worked 5 days the second week of the assembly line. They made the same number of bears each day. How many bears did they make each day?

8. About how many bears did the class make altogether in the second and third weeks?

# Estimation
## Substituting Compatible Numbers

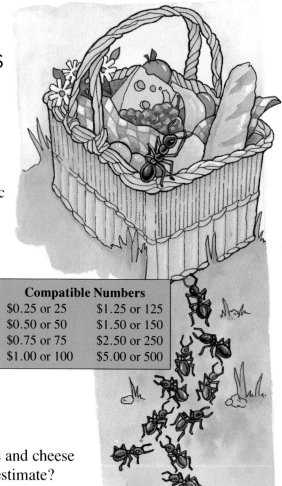

**EXPLORE  Make Some Estimates**

The costs of the items Patty bought for a picnic
are shown below. Estimate the total cost of
Patty's items. Replace numbers in the list
with compatible numbers.

| Picnic Items and Costs | | | |
|---|---|---|---|
| paper cups | $1.59 | buns | $3.49 |
| paper plates | $2.19 | ketchup | $1.19 |
| cheese slices | $2.64 | pickles | $1.67 |
| soft drinks | $7.54 | mustard | $0.98 |
| charcoal | $2.58 | ice | $1.63 |
| ground beef | $8.70 | chips | $2.59 |

| Compatible Numbers | |
|---|---|
| $0.25 or 25 | $1.25 or 125 |
| $0.50 or 50 | $1.50 or 150 |
| $0.75 or 75 | $2.50 or 250 |
| $1.00 or 100 | $5.00 or 500 |

**TALK ABOUT IT**

1. Suppose you rounded amounts for the cups and cheese
   to the nearest dollar. Do you get the same estimate?
2. Does this way of estimating always give the same answer
   as rounding? Think of an example to show why or why not.

To estimate Patty's total, you can use a technique called
**substituting compatible numbers.** Replace some or all of
the numbers with numbers that are easy to compute with
mentally. Then add or subtract.

Here are some examples of how to estimate by substituting
compatible numbers.

| 29.4 + 72.6 | $3.89 + $4.58 | 553 − 229 |
|---|---|---|
| Estimate: 25 + 75 = 100 | Estimate: $4.00 + $4.58 = $8.58 | Estimate: 550 − 225 = 325 |

Substitute compatible numbers to estimate each cost.

1. paper plates and charcoal

2. soft drinks and ground beef

3. mustard and ice

4. buns and ketchup

Substitute compatible numbers to estimate each sum or difference.

**1.** $143 - 54$     **2.** $79 + 123$     **3.** $193 + 261$     **4.** $874 - 196$

**5.** $597 + 324$     **6.** $158 - 78$     **7.** $989 - 496$     **8.** $354 + 78$

**9.** $\$6.06 - \$3.95$    **10.** $\$2.49 + \$6.03$    **11.** $\$248.99 + \$97.88$   **12.** $\$553 - \$103.49$

**13.** $\$174 + \$245 + \$25 + \$150$      **14.** $\$429 + \$128 + \$564 + \$459 + \$79 + \$298$

## APPLY

### MATH REASONING

Use estimation to find the approximate value of the variable.

**15.** $227 + x$ is about 475.        **16.** $y + 668$ is about 1,000.

### PROBLEM SOLVING

Use the data list about camping gear.

**17.** Zina is going on a fishing trip with her best friend. She needs a sleeping bag and a fishing pole. Estimate the cost for these items.

**18.** Terry's family is going on a camping trip this summer. They bought 4 items whose total cost was a little less than $300. What could they have bought?

**19.** Sandy bought a sleeping bag and paid for it with a hundred dollar bill. About how much change did she get back?

| Camping Gear Costs | |
|---|---|
| Back pack | $229.99 |
| Tent | $179.97 |
| Fishing pole | $ 29.95 |
| Pots and pans | $ 22.99 |
| Sleeping bag | $ 76.95 |
| First aid kit | $ 27.50 |
| Camp stove | $135.75 |
| Raft | $ 55.95 |

### ▶ MENTAL MATH

You can break apart a decimal and use mental math to add a whole number to it. For example, $3.4 + 2$ is $3 + 2 + 0.4$, or $5.4$.

Use mental math to find these sums.

**20.** $8 + 9.4$     **21.** $12.8 + 4$     **22.** $2.5 + 7$     **23.** $7 + 6.8$

**24.** $7.9 + 3$     **25.** $8 + 12.5$     **26.** $10.8 + 9$     **27.** $13 + 2.7$

*More Practice, page 504, set A*

# Problem Solving
## Extra Data

UNDERSTAND
ANALYZE DATA
PLAN
ESTIMATE
SOLVE
EXAMINE

### LEARN ABOUT IT

Some problems have extra data that is not needed to solve the problem. You may have to sort through the data to find the facts you need.

> During September 155 doves, 3 owls, and 49 sparrows were brought to the Wildlife Shelter with injuries. How many more doves than sparrows were brought to the shelter?

I'll find only the data I need to solve the problem.

I'm ready to use the data to solve the problem.

Doves
155

Sparrows
49

$$\begin{array}{r} 155 \\ - 49 \\ \hline 106 \end{array}$$

106 more doves than sparrows were brought in with injuries.

### TRY IT OUT

Solve.

1. In May 725 animals were cared for at the shelter. In June 446 were cared for. In December only 57 were cared for. How many more animals were cared for in May than in December?

2. Maria checked in 8 crows at the shelter. She checked in 8 times as many sparrows as crows and 7 times as many mockingbirds as crows. How many mockingbirds were checked in?

3. Jan kept records of animals at the shelter. There were almost 13 times as many birds as mammals in one year. There were 676 birds and 49 mammals. What was the total number of animals Jan kept a record of?

4. Of the 676 birds Jan recorded, 152 were released in good health within 6 weeks. Of the 49 mammals, 23 were released within 6 weeks. How many animals were released within 6 weeks?

110

Solve. Use any problem solving strategy.

1. Last month 7 times as many squirrels as owls were brought to the shelter. Five owls were brought in. How many squirrels were brought in?

2. Approximately 2 out of every 8 animals cared for at the shelter are released in good health. How many animals would you expect to be released out of 40 animals cared for?

| Animals cared for | | | |
|---|---|---|---|
| Animals released | | | |

3. Three years ago, when Jess was 13, she volunteered 54 hours in 6 months at the Wildlife Shelter. She worked the same number of hours each month. How many hours did she volunteer each month?

4. In the 4 years from 1987 through 1990, how many animals have been cared for at the shelter?

| Year | Animals Cared For |
|---|---|
| 1987 | 2,886 |
| 1988 | 2,853 |
| 1989 | 3,350 |
| 1990 | 3,137 |

5. In 1990, 369 of the animals cared for at the shelter were mammals and the rest were birds. In 1991, 398 of the animals were mammals and 3,137 were birds. How many animals were cared for in 1991?

6. The shelter's cost for food for the animals was $1,280 for July. That cost was $268 less than the cost for June. What was the cost for June?

7. The animal shelter is open to visitors for 6 hours a day every day except Sunday and Monday. How many hours a week is the shelter open to visitors?

8. **Thinking About Your Solution**
The shelter cared for 88 more sea birds than sea mammals one month. The same month the shelter cared for 72 more land birds than sea mammals. Explain how you can tell without computing whether the shelter cared for more sea birds or more land birds that month.

# Data Collection and Analysis
## Group Decision Making

UNDERSTAND
ANALYZE DATA
PLAN
ESTIMATE
SOLVE
EXAMINE

**Doing a Simulation**
**Group Skill:**
Encourage and Respect Others

Herman is a little odd. He only wears red socks or blue socks. He bought 2 blue pairs and 4 red pairs on sale and stuffed them all in a dresser drawer. Each morning when he wakes up, he sleepily digs around in his drawer and pulls out the first two socks he finds without turning on the lights. Do you think he will get a blue pair, a red pair, or a mismatched pair more often? A **simulation,** in which you act out the situation to see what is likely to happen, will help you answer this question.

## Collecting Data

1. Work with your group to cut out 6 pairs of sock shapes. Color 2 pairs blue and 4 pairs red. The socks should all be the same size and shape.

2. Put all of the socks in a paper bag and mix them. Take turns drawing out two socks. Record each "pair" in a table like the one shown. Then put the socks back into the bag. Do this 50 times.

|  | Number of "Pairs" | Total |
|---|---|---|
| Red Pairs | JHT II | |
| Blue Pairs | JHT IIII | |
| Mismatched Pairs | III | |

3. Count the number of red pairs, blue pairs, and mismatched pairs you drew. Write the totals in your table.

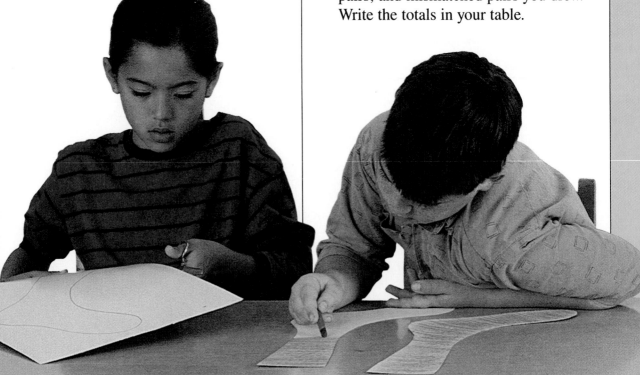

## Organizing Data

**4.** Make a bar graph using the data in the table. Make the scale longer or shorter to suit the data in your table.

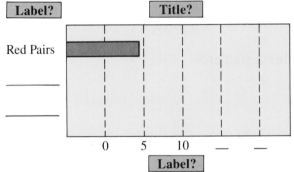

**Label?**

**Title?**

Red Pairs

_____

_____

0   5   10   __   __

**Label?**

**5.** Did you label and title your graph?

## Presenting Your Analysis

**6.** Did your predictions about whether Herman would draw more red pairs, blue pairs or mismatched pairs come close to the results of your simulation?

**7.** Write three or four sentences to tell what happened in your simulation. Why do you think you got the results you did?

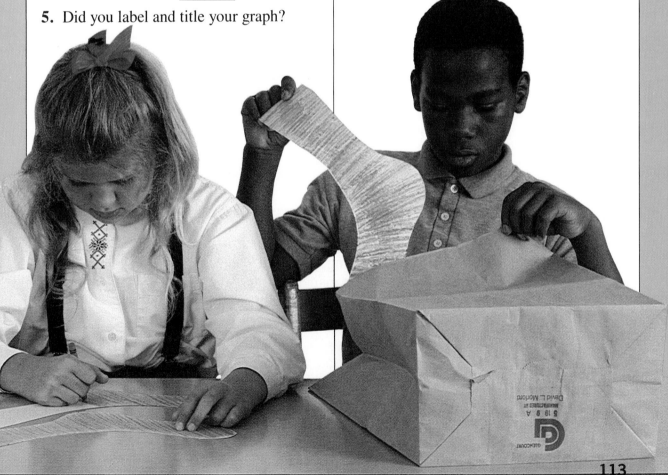

# WRAP UP

## Word Scavenger Hunt

Each word described below can be found in this chapter. Write the word.

1. a 5-letter word for the vertical and horizontal number lines on graphs

2. a 13-letter word for an instrument to collect data

3. an 8-letter word for the distance between two numbers on a scale

4. a 3-letter word that shows what number a picture represents on a pictograph

## Sometimes, Always, Never

Complete each statement by writing **sometimes**, **always**, or **never**. Explain your choice.

5. In a pictograph, you __?__ need a key to tell you what quantity each picture represents.

6. The numbers used in graphs are __?__ estimates.

7. Graphs are __?__ used to predict future events.

8. You can __?__ draw bar graphs for the same data that look different by changing the scale.

## Project

Survey your classmates about a topic of special interest to you. For example, you might ask, "For a vacation, would you rather go camping, go to an amusement park, go to the beach, or visit historic places?" Organize your responses in a table. Show the results of your survey in a bar graph.

# POWER PRACTICE/TEST

## Part 1   Understanding

1. What does each picture represent in the pictograph?

2. How many trees were planted in 1988?

3. Make a line graph that shows someone's test scores for 5 math quizzes. Write a story about your graph.

Number of Trees Planted

| | |
|---|---|
| 1988 | ⟑⟑⟑⟑⟑⟑⟑ |
| 1989 | ⟑⟑⟑⟑⟑⟑⟑⟑ |
| 1990 | ⟑⟑⟑⟑⟑⟑⟑⟑⟑⟑⟑⟑ |

⟑ represents 100 trees

## Part 2   Skills

4. Draw a double bar graph for the data in this chart.

**Magazines Sold**

| Week | Grade 5 | Grade 6 |
|------|---------|---------|
| 1 | 145 | 152 |
| 2 | 160 | 163 |
| 3 | 157 | 158 |

5. How many more magazines did Grade 6 sell than Grade 5?

6. How many magazines were sold in all during Week 1?

Find each of the following for this set of data:
151, 210, 176, 185, 164, 164, 175

7. mean          8. mode          9. median          10. range

Use compatible numbers to estimate each sum or difference.

11. $856 − $305.24          12. 341 + 53 + 98          13. 77 + 123 + 198

## Part 3   Applications

14. A charter bus can carry 50 people. The music club has 80 members who will need to ride on the bus. Tickets cost $4 each. How many buses are needed?

15. **Challenge**   The Odd Folks Library lets you take out 3 books on each visit, but you must give one back immediately. How many visits will it take you to have 10 books?

**115**

# ENRICHMENT
## Organizing Data to Make Comparisons

A table can be used to organize data so that you can compare. How you make the table depends on what you want to compare.

Look at this set of data.

Make a table that you can use to compare the number of people who like each game show. Use your table to answer these questions.

| Name | Grade | Male/Female | Favorite Game Show |
|---|---|---|---|
| Melinda | 5 | F | *Target Wheel* |
| Joe | 4 | M | *Turn Around* |
| Paul | 5 | M | *Roll Again* |
| Mimi | 5 | F | *Turn Around* |
| Ursula | 4 | F | *Roll Again* |
| Erin | 4 | F | *Buzz* |
| Elsie | 5 | F | *Turn Around* |
| Judy | 4 | F | *Turn Around* |
| Jimenez | 5 | M | *Roll Again* |
| Pablo | 5 | M | *Roll Again* |
| Amanda | 4 | F | *Target Wheel* |
| Alisa | 5 | F | *Turn Around* |
| Jamal | 5 | M | *Roll Again* |
| Pam | 4 | F | *Turn Around* |
| Jolene | 4 | F | *Target Wheel* |
| Jane | 4 | F | *Turn Around* |
| Gerald | 5 | M | *Buzz* |
| Toby | 5 | F | *Roll Again* |
| Mason | 5 | M | *Turn Around* |
| Harold | 4 | M | *Target Wheel* |

1. How many people were surveyed?

2. What are the names of the shows in order from the most liked to the least liked?

3. How many more people chose *Roll Again* than chose *Target Wheel*?

Make a table that you can use to compare the fourth graders' favorite shows with the fifth graders' favorite shows. Use your table to answer these questions.

4. How many in each grade were surveyed?

5. What is each grade's favorite show?

6. Which grade liked *Target Wheel* more? By how many more students was it chosen in that grade than in the other?

Make a table that you can use to compare the girls' favorite shows with the boys' favorite shows. Use the table to answer these questions.

7. How many girls were surveyed? how many boys?

8. Which show did the greatest number of girls like best? the greatest number of boys?

# Cumulative Review

**1.** What is 8,426,744 rounded to the nearest thousand?

   A. 8,400,000     B. 8,430,000

   C. 8,000,000     D. 8,427,000

**2.** Which number is between 7.321 and 7.330?

   A. 7.327     B. 7.320

   C. 7.331     D. 7.319

**3.** What is the standard form of 700,000 + 3,000 + 40 + 6?

   A. 7.346     B. 70,346

   C. 703,046     D. 73,046

**4.** Which number is less than 385,271?

   A. 385,283     B. 385,309

   C. 385,268     D. 386,004

**5.** Which number rounds to 4?

   A. 4.7   B. 3.98   C. 3.49   D. 4.6

Add or subtract.

**6.** 3.56 + 1.56

   A. 5.18   B. 5.12   C. 6.22   D. 6.18

**7.** 3.22 − 1.15

   A. 2.07   B. 1.02   C. 2.17   D. 3.37

**8.** Leah and Owen have 24 goldfish in all. Leah has 4 more than Owen. How many goldfish does she have?

   A. 12   B. 14   C. 16   D. 20

**9.** How you would group the numbers to find $4 \times 10 \times 25 \times 87$ mentally?

   A. $(4 \times 10) \times 25 \times 87$

   B. $(4 \times 25) \times 87 \times 10$

   C. $(10 \times 87) \times 25 \times 4$

   D. $(10 \times 25) \times 87 \times 4$

**10.** To find 8,516 + 394 using compensation:

   A. Add 400 to 8,516, then subtract 4.

   B. Add 400 to 8,516, then subtract 6.

   C. Add 4 to 8,516, then subtract 394.

   D. Subtract 6 from 8,516, then add 6 to 394

**11.** After solving a problem you should:

   A. Plan what to do

   B. Understand the situation

   C. Analyze the data

   D. Examine the answer

**12.** Which question can be asked about the following data? Seth has $12. Team shirts cost $5 each.

   A. How much change did he receive?

   B. How much are three ties?

   C. Can he buy two shirts?

   D. Can he buy a new hat?

# 5

**M**ATH AND SCIENCE

DATA BANK

Use the Science Data Bank on page 470 to answer the questions.

1  Which of the listed household electrical appliances costs the most to use per hour? Which of the listed appliances costs the least to use per hour?

# MULTIPLICATION: WHOLE NUMBERS AND DECIMALS

**THEME: ENERGY SOURCES**

**2** Find out how much power a Wind Wizard windmill produces at optimum wind speed. At that speed, how much power will 2 Wind Wizards produce? How much power will 3 produce?

**3** Which is greater, the cost of using an electric iron for 3 hours or the cost of using the color television set for 6 hours? How great is the difference in the two costs?

**4** **Using Critical Thinking** Jay studied the list of electricity costs and said, "The clothes dryer costs more to use each month than any other appliance." Do you agree with Jay? Explain.

A supervisor carefully records data registered on meters in the control room of a large utilities plant.

# Mental Math
## Special Products

**EXPLORE** **Discover a Pattern**

A small Elektro windmill produces 50 watts of power. Windmills are often placed in groups in windy places. Copy and complete the table to show how much power is produced by the larger groups of windmills.

| Number of windmills | Power output in watts |
|---|---|
| 10 | 500 |
| 20 | |
| 30 | |
| 40 | |
| 50 | |
| 60 | |

**TALK ABOUT IT**

1. What multiplication was needed to find the amount of power produced by 10 windmills? by 20 windmills? by 60 windmills?

2. A single Eagle III windmill can produce 3 kilowatts of power, so 2 of these windmills could produce 6 kilowatts of power. How can you use this fact to find the amount of power that 20 of these windmills could produce?

To multiply two multiples of 10 or 100, multiply the front digits in each factor. Attach as many zeros as there are in both factors.

■ **Here is how to do it.**

| | |
|---|---|
| Problem: | $90 \times 40$ |
| Multiply the front digits. | $9 \times 4$ |
| Write the product. | 36 |
| Attach the zeros. | 3,600 |

■ **Here is why it works.**

$90 \times 40 = (9 \times 10) \times (4 \times 10)$
$(9 \times 4) \times (10 \times 10)$ ← Using the
$36 \times 100$    commutative
$3,600$    and the associative properties.

**Other Examples**    $80 \times 50 = 4,000$    $40 \times 600 = 24,000$    $200 \times 500 = 100,000$

**TRY IT OUT**

Use mental math to find the products.

**1.** $30 \times 40$    **2.** $60 \times 50$    **3.** $30 \times 700$    **4.** $80 \times 500$    **5.** $900 \times 800$

1. $30 \times 90$    2. $80 \times 60$    3. $40 \times 800$    4. $80 \times 500$    5. $60 \times 200$

6. $70 \times 100$    7. $400 \times 900$    8. $70 \times 600$    9. $60 \times 40$    10. $70 \times 80$

11. $50 \times 60$    12. $30 \times 900$    13. $50 \times 600$    14. $60 \times 900$    15. $40 \times 700$

16. $80 \times 100$    17. $50 \times 90$    18. $70 \times 10$    19. $90 \times 700$    20. $300 \times 400$

21. $20 \times 30 \times 20$    22. $10 \times 400 \times 20$    23. $60 \times 200 \times 10$

24. $100 \times 20 \times 50$    25. $40 \times 10 \times 10 \times 60$    26. $300 \times 20 \times 200$

**APPLY**

### MATH REASONING

27. Show as many different ways as you can to write multiples of 10 or 100 in place of the variables to complete the equation.
$a \times b = 2{,}400$

### PROBLEM SOLVING

28. Each farmer in a group of 20 farmers is thinking of buying 10 windmills that can be used to pump water. If the cost of each windmill is $500, what would be the cost for all the windmills the farmers are thinking of buying?

29. **Science Data Bank**   How many watts of power would a group of 20 Wind Titan windmills produce when they are running at optimum wind speed? See page 470.

30. **Missing Data**   Tell what other data you need to solve this problem. Each Wind Wizard windmill can produce 600 watts of power. How many watts of power can be produced by the Wind Wizards located at the Galestorm Gap windmill farm?

▶ **COMMUNICATION   Writing to Learn**

31. Write a statement explaining how you can use the product in equation A to find the product in equation B.

   **A.** $47 \times 5 = 235$   **B.** $47 \times 50 = $ ▨

*More Practice, page 504, set B*

# Estimating Products Using Rounding

**EXPLORE  Solve to Understand**

Use the data about Murtle the Dolphin's food to answer these questions:

- About how many pounds of fish does Murtle eat in a year?

- What is Murtle's approximate weight?

**TALK ABOUT IT**

1. Explain how you found estimates for the questions above.

2. Make up another question using data about Murtle that can be answered by estimating.

> **MURTLE THE DOLPHIN**
> **Food Data**
>
> 1. Murtle eats about 19 pounds (lb) of fish each day.
> 2. Murtle's weight stays at about 20 times the weight of the food she eats daily.
> 3. Murtle likes fish. Her favorite fish cost 35¢ per pound. There are about 7 of the fish in a pound.
> 4. Murtle will jump 20 ft out of the water to get her food. She eats 4 times a day.

One way to estimate products is to round the factors to their highest place and use mental math to find the product. Here is how to do it.

Round each factor to its highest place. $\longrightarrow$ | Round to the nearest 10. | Round to the nearest 100. |

$$19 \times 365$$
$$\downarrow \qquad \downarrow$$

Use mental math to multiply. $\longrightarrow$ $20 \times 400 = 8,000$

---

## Other Examples

Round both factors to the nearest 10. $\longrightarrow 146 \times 12$
$$\downarrow \qquad \downarrow$$
$$150 \times 10 = 1,500$$

Round only the greater factor. $\longrightarrow 9 \times 398$
$$\downarrow$$
$$9 \times 400 = 3,600$$

**TRY IT OUT**

Use rounding and mental math to estimate the products.

**1.** $78 \times 37$    **2.** $11 \times 155$    **3.** $93 \times 89$    **4.** $287 \times 9$    **5.** $42 \times 517$

122

Estimate by rounding.

**1.** 72 × 8     **2.** 55 × 8     **3.** 49 × 7     **4.** 28 × 75     **5.** 17 × 36

**6.** 84 × 47    **7.** 486 × 28   **8.** 678 × 45   **9.** 216 × 90   **10.** 986 × 9

**11.** 219 × 6   **12.** 370 × 10  **13.** 495 × 316 **14.** 21 × 58   **15.** 67 × 415

**APPLY**

**MATH REASONING**

| Number List | | |
|---|---|---|
| 7 | 5 | 39 |
| 98 | 69 | 27 |
| 36 | 65 | 812 |
| 4 | 43 | 24 |
| 89 | 370 | 54 |
| 41 | 86 | 615 |
| 6 | 729 | 18 |

**16.** Use estimation to pick two numbers from the list whose product is close to 3,200. Then use a calculator to find the actual products. Which two factors give a product closest to 3,200?

**PROBLEM SOLVING**

**17.** Feed for dolphins costs only 5¢ for 2 bags. What would 12 bags cost? Copy and complete the table below to find out.

**18.** A college student earned $8.75 an hour helping at Murtle's sea animal show. About how much will she earn in 32 hours?

| bags | 2 | 4 | 6 | 8 | 10 | 12 |
|---|---|---|---|---|---|---|
| cost | | | | | | |

**MIXED REVIEW**

Round each number to the place of the underlined digit.

**19.** 2̲85     **20.** 9̲8̲7     **21.** 1,1̲18     **22.** 20.0̲7     **23.** 7̲32     **24.** 4̲,810

Write each number in words.

**25.** 84.21     **26.** 948,571     **27.** 7.981

Use place value to tell what the digit **6** in each number means.

**28.** 6,897,112,020     **29.** 877.006     **30.** 4,367,870

*More Practice, page 504, set C*

# Reviewing Whole Number Multiplication

**LEARN ABOUT IT**

The examples below will help you review whole number multiplication.

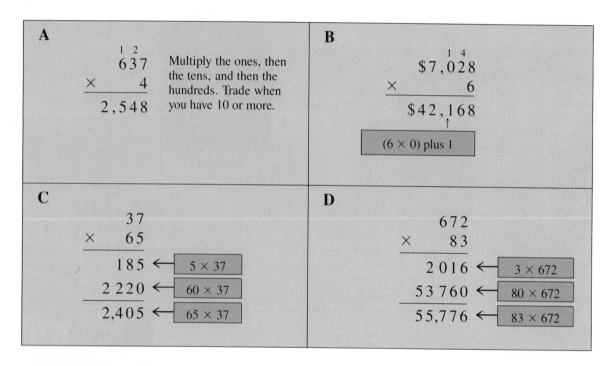

**A**

$$\begin{array}{r} \overset{1\ \ 2}{637} \\ \times \qquad 4 \\ \hline 2{,}548 \end{array}$$

Multiply the ones, then the tens, and then the hundreds. Trade when you have 10 or more.

**B**

$$\begin{array}{r} \overset{1\ 4}{\$7{,}028} \\ \times \qquad 6 \\ \hline \$42{,}168 \end{array}$$

(6 × 0) plus 1

**C**

$$\begin{array}{r} 37 \\ \times \quad 65 \\ \hline 185 \\ 2220 \\ \hline 2{,}405 \end{array}$$

185 ← 5 × 37
2220 ← 60 × 37
2,405 ← 65 × 37

**D**

$$\begin{array}{r} 672 \\ \times \quad 83 \\ \hline 2016 \\ 53760 \\ \hline 55{,}776 \end{array}$$

2016 ← 3 × 672
53760 ← 80 × 672
55,776 ← 83 × 672

**TRY IT OUT**

Multiply.

| | | | | |
|---|---|---|---|---|
| **1.** $\begin{array}{r}33\\ \times\ 8\\ \hline\end{array}$ | **2.** $\begin{array}{r}486\\ \times\ \ 3\\ \hline\end{array}$ | **3.** $\begin{array}{r}590\\ \times\ \ 9\\ \hline\end{array}$ | **4.** $\begin{array}{r}1{,}962\\ \times\ \ \ 6\\ \hline\end{array}$ | **5.** $\begin{array}{r}3{,}480\\ \times\ \ \ 4\\ \hline\end{array}$ |
| **6.** $\begin{array}{r}56\\ \times 23\\ \hline\end{array}$ | **7.** $\begin{array}{r}49\\ \times 48\\ \hline\end{array}$ | **8.** $\begin{array}{r}89\\ \times 56\\ \hline\end{array}$ | **9.** $\begin{array}{r}96\\ \times 24\\ \hline\end{array}$ | **10.** $\begin{array}{r}27\\ \times 79\\ \hline\end{array}$ |
| **11.** $\begin{array}{r}302\\ \times\ 94\\ \hline\end{array}$ | **12.** $\begin{array}{r}567\\ \times\ 32\\ \hline\end{array}$ | **13.** $\begin{array}{r}489\\ \times\ 86\\ \hline\end{array}$ | **14.** $\begin{array}{r}638\\ \times\ 55\\ \hline\end{array}$ | **15.** $\begin{array}{r}972\\ \times\ 73\\ \hline\end{array}$ |

Multiply.

| | | | | | | | | | |
|---|---|---|---|---|---|---|---|---|---|
| **1.** | 79 ×5 | **2.** | 436 ×8 | **3.** | 207 ×9 | **4.** | 3,509 ×7 | **5.** | 6,327 ×6 |
| **6.** | 96 ×54 | **7.** | 38 ×77 | **8.** | 83 ×69 | **9.** | 90 ×80 | **10.** | 75 ×75 |
| **11.** | 176 ×24 | **12.** | 263 ×57 | **13.** | 926 ×43 | **14.** | 869 ×78 | **15.** | 375 ×66 |

**16.** Find the product of 75 and 25.

**17.** Five times $126 is what amount?

Estimate each product.

**18.** 4 × 89      **19.** 3 × 298      **20.** 51 × 65      **21.** 42 × 79

**MATH REASONING**

For the exercises below, estimate whether the exact product is less than or greater than the given number. Find the exact answer to check.

**22.** 134 × 23    Less than or greater than 2,000?
**23.** 68 × 78     Less than or greater than 5,000?

**PROBLEM SOLVING**

**24.** In 1990, a small theater presented 12 performances of a play called *You Can't Take It with You.* If 145 people attended each of the performances, what was the total number who saw the show?

**25. Extra Data**   Tell which data is not needed. Then solve. Barry worked 7 hours Monday, 8 Tuesday, 6 Wednesday, and 8 Thursday. He earns $6 per hour. What were his total earnings for the first three days?

▶ **MENTAL MATH**

Choose a mental math technique to solve each problem.

**26.** 3 × 50        **27.** 68 + 3        **28.** 40 × 80

**29.** 24 + 71 + 26    **30.** 724 + 199    **31.** 5.25 + 4.75

| **Mental Math Techniques** |
|---|
| Counting On/Back Choosing Compatible Numbers Using Compensation |

*More Practice, page 504, Set D*

# Problem Solving
## Multiple-Step Problems

UNDERSTAND
ANALYZE DATA
PLAN
ESTIMATE
SOLVE
EXAMINE

**LEARN ABOUT IT**

Some problems can be solved using two or more of the operations **addition, subtraction, multiplication,** and **division.** These problems are called **multiple-step problems.**

Nikki works part time at a clothing store. She put price tags on 15 pairs of jeans that cost $32 each. She put price tags on 16 pairs that cost $24 each. What was the total value of the jeans Nikki tagged?

First I'll find the value of the first set of jeans.

$15 \times \$32 = \$480$

Then I'll find the value of the second set of jeans.

$16 \times \$24 = \$384$

To find the total value, I'll add the value of both sets.

$\$480 + \$384 = \$864$

The total value of the jeans Nikki tagged was $864.

**TRY IT OUT**

1. Julia had $32.79 left in her clothing budget. She saw a sweatshirt for $16.98 and a pair of jeans for $23.75. How much more money does she need to buy both items?

2. Kai bought one pair of jeans for $21.95 and another pair that had been priced at $23.89 but were on sale at $4.78 off. How much did he pay in all?

3. When some new jeans arrived, Rudi filled 12 shelves with 25 pairs of jeans on each shelf. He filled 6 racks with 45 pairs of jeans on each rack. How many jeans did he put on shelves and racks?

4. Geri bought 2 pairs of jeans for $23.99 each. She used the $16.98 in cash she got back from returning a shirt. She also had a $50 bill with her. How much of the $50 bill did she spend?

126

Solve. Use any problem solving strategy.

1. Rico's great grandfather was 22 years old when he panned for gold in 1853. That was the year that the first jeans were made. By 1990 how many years had passed since jeans were first made?

2. Bergland's Department Store received a new shipment of 60 jeans. Each pair had a value of $30. What was the value of the whole shipment?

3. Ralph put back on shelves the jeans people had left in 8 different dressing rooms. The same number of jeans had been left in each room. He put back 32 jeans in all. How many jeans were in each room?

4. At Roy's school 2 out of 5 students usually wear jeans. How many students would you expect to wear jeans in a class of 30 students?

| jeans | 2 | 4 | 6 | 8 | 10 | 12 |
|---|---|---|---|---|---|---|
| students | 5 | | | | | |

Use the table below for problems 5−7.

| Results of Rub Test for Jeans | | |
|---|---|---|
| Material | Weight | Number of rubs before material tore |
| A  cotton | 12 oz | 596 |
| B  cotton | 14 oz | 2,558 |
| C  cotton polyester | 14 oz | 2,863 |
| D  cotton polyester nylon | 12 oz | 2,873 |

5. Which material lasted for 174 more rubs than 4 times the number of rubs on material A?

6. How many more rubs did the strongest material allow than the weakest?

7. How many fewer rubs were there before material B tore than before material D tore?

8. **Write Your Own Problem**   Write a problem about jeans that can be solved by using multiplication.

# Problem Solving
## Solve a Simpler Problem

| UNDERSTAND |
| ANALYZE DATA |
| PLAN |
| ESTIMATE |
| SOLVE |
| EXAMINE |

## LEARN ABOUT IT

Sometimes you can find the answer to a problem by solving a problem that is like it but has smaller numbers. This problem solving strategy is called **Solve a Simpler Problem.**

Roger is helping to set up 20 small tables for an exhibit of Eskimo sculpture at his school. Each table can have one sculpture on each side. If Roger pushes all the tables together to make one long table, how many sculptures can he display?

> Instead of drawing 20 tables, I'll solve a simpler problem using 2, 3, and 4 tables. That may help me solve the more difficult problem.

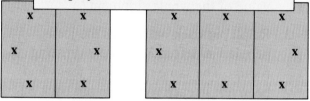

> I see! Two sculptures can be displayed at each of the 20 tables. Then 2 more sculptures can be placed at each end.

$2 \times 20 = 40$ $\qquad$ $40 + 2 = 42$

42 sculptures can be displayed.

## TRY IT OUT

Thelma was in charge of planning a dinner for visiting students from Anchorage, Alaska. She made a large square table from 25 small square tables. Each small table can seat one person on a side. How many students can sit at the large table? (Hint: Try 4 small tables. Then try 9.)

- How many students can sit on each side of a small square table?

- What shape does Thelma want the large table to be?

- Copy and complete the drawings to solve the problem.

## PRACTICE

Solve a simpler problem to help you solve each problem.

1. Bobby Lee told Thelma to put the 25 tables in one long row instead of in a square. How many seats would there be using Bobby Lee's idea?

2. At the dinner for Alaskan students, Tana made 15 cuts across each meat loaf. How many pieces did she get from each loaf?

## MIXED PRACTICE

Choose a strategy from the strategies list or use other strategies you know to solve these problems.

| Some Strategies | |
| --- | --- |
| Act Out | Guess and Check |
| Use Objects | Make a Table |
| Choose an Operation | Solve a Simpler |
| Draw a Picture | Problem |

3. At the dinner for Alaskan students, Pete wanted to cut a long loaf of bread into 36 slices. How many cuts did he need to make?

4. How many miles is the shortest route from Fairbanks to Anchorage?

5. Barb bought patches as souvenir gifts from her trip to Alaska. The cost of the patches was $4 for 5. How many patches could she buy with $16?

6. Jeff and his family are driving on the Alaskan Highway to Dawson Creek, British Columbia. They have driven about 600 miles. The entire drive will be about 900 miles. About how far do they still have to go?

7. Mrs. Vasquez saw an advertisement for a trip called "Sailing the Inside Passage." The cost is $148 a day. How much would a 12-day trip cost altogether?

8. The Alaskan oil pipeline is buried for 345 miles. The whole pipeline is 109 miles longer than twice the number of miles that are buried. How long is the whole pipeline?

# Mental Math
## Breaking Apart Numbers

This lesson introduces another number property that can help you use mental math to solve problems.

**EXPLORE** **Solve to Understand**
Find each product in column A. Find the value of each expression in column B.

| A | B |
|---|---|
| $2 \times 32$ | $(2 \times 30) + (2 \times 2)$ |
| $5 \times 21$ | $(5 \times 20) + (5 \times 1)$ |
| $4 \times 42$ | $(4 \times 40) + (4 \times 2)$ |

**TALK ABOUT IT**

1. What did you discover about the values in each row?
2. $30 + 2$ is another way of writing what 2-digit number?
3. In the last row, how was 42 broken apart into two numbers?

The **distributive property** can help you mentally multiply a 2-digit number by a 1-digit number, such as $4 \times 23$. This property involves both multiplication and addition.

- **Here is how to do it.**
  Problem: **$4 \times 23$**
  Break apart 23: 20 and 3
  Multiply: $4 \times 20 = 80$
  $\qquad\quad 4 \times 3 = 12$
  Add: $80 + 12 = 92$
  $\qquad\quad$ **$4 \times 23 = 92$**

- **Here is why it works.**

  $$\begin{array}{r} 23 \\ \times\ 4 \\ \hline \end{array} \qquad \begin{array}{r} 20 + 3 \\ \times \qquad 4 \\ \hline 80 + 12 = 92 \end{array}$$
  $\qquad\qquad\qquad\quad \uparrow \qquad \uparrow$
  $\qquad\qquad\quad \boxed{20 \times 4} \quad \boxed{3 \times 4}$

**TRY IT OUT**

Use the distributive property and mental math to find the products.

**1.** $2 \times 12$  **2.** $3 \times 13$  **3.** $2 \times 14$  **4.** $4 \times 12$  **5.** $3 \times 23$

**6.** $2 \times 34$  **7.** $3 \times 42$  **8.** $4 \times 23$  **9.** $2 \times 16$  **10.** $4 \times 24$

**11.** $2 \times 23$  **12.** $3 \times 43$  **13.** $16 \times 4$  **14.** $53 \times 2$  **15.** $6 \times 32$

*More Practice, page 504, set E*

# POWER PRACTICE/QUIZ

Use mental math to find the products.

**1.** 20 × 70
**2.** 60 × 50
**3.** 800 × 90
**4.** 900 × 40
**5.** 300 × 700

**6.** 500 × 200
**7.** 30 × 6,000
**8.** 80 × 70
**9.** 40 × 80
**10.** 70 × 7,000

**11.** 20 × 30 × 600
**12.** 90 × 90 × 10
**13.** 50 × 10 × 200 × 10

Round so you can estimate using mental math.

**14.** 64
× 9

**15.** 47
× 18

**16.** 279
× 85

**17.** 841
× 37

**18.** 625
× 73

Multiply.

**19.** 103
× 7

**20.** 68
× 25

**21.** 630
× 8

**22.** 496
× 39

**23.** 567
× 79

**24.** 54
× 45

**25.** 2,605
× 6

**26.** 907
× 88

**27.** 146
× 24

**28.** 4,352
× 7

## PROBLEM SOLVING

**29.** Andrew has 6 quarters, 8 nickels, and 5 dimes. How much money does Andrew have?

**30.** Luanna has 80 pictures to put in her photo album. The album holds 4 photos on each page. There are 18 pages. How many pictures will be left over?

**31.** Carole is pasting pictures in her scrapbook. Six of the pages will each hold 6 pictures and 8 of the pages will each hold 4 larger pictures. How many pictures can she fit in the scrapbook?

**32.** Julia wants to cut a 36-inch submarine sandwich into 20 pieces. How many cuts will she make if she makes all cuts in the same direction?

**33.** Vito has a display of 5 Great American Women stamps on each page of a 48-page album. How many stamps does he have in his album:

**34.** Guy bought fifteen 25¢ postage stamps. He gave the clerk a $10 bill. How much change should the clerk give Guy?

131

# Multiplying Decimals
## Making the Connection

**10 columns**

**10 rows**

Each row is 0.1 of the square.
Each column is also
0.1 of the square.

**LEARN ABOUT IT**

We can use graph paper to show some
decimal products.

**EXPLORE**  **Use a Graph Paper Model**
Work with a partner.

- Use 10 by 10 sections of graph paper.

- One partner shades one or more (but not *all*) of the rows
  using a crayon or a colored pencil. Name the decimal
  that tells what part of the square is shaded.

- The other partner then shades one or more (but not *all*)
  of the columns using a crayon or pencil of a different
  color. Again, name the decimal that tells what part of
  the square is shaded.

- Decide together what decimal names the part of the
  square that is shaded with both colors.

- Repeat this activity several times.

**TALK ABOUT IT**

1. Suppose you shaded 6 rows
   and 4 columns. What
   decimals would you write to
   record the parts of the square
   that you shaded?

2. Suppose you shaded 3 rows and 5 columns. What decimal
   would you write to record the part of the square that was
   shaded with both colors?

3. Suppose one student shades 3 rows with no space between
   them. Another student also shades 3 rows but leaves space
   between the rows. Both students then shade 4 columns
   with no space between columns. Would the decimal that
   the students record to tell what part of the square is
   shaded twice be the same for each student? Use graph
   paper to explain.

132

You have shaded rows and columns on graph paper and named the decimals for the parts that were shaded. You also gave the decimal for the parts that were shaded twice. Now you will learn how to record what you have done. This will help you understand how to find the product of two decimals such as 0.7 and 0.6.

**What You Do**                    **What You Record**

Show 7 tenths by shading 7 columns.          $0.7$

Show 6 tenths of 7 tenths by shading 6 rows.     $0.6$ of $0.7$
                                           or $0.6 \times 0.7$

How many small squares are shaded twice?

$0.6 \times 0.7 = 0.42$

**42 out of 100 squares are shaded twice.**

0.42 of the large square is shaded twice.

The product of 0.7 and 0.6 is 0.42.

---

**TRY IT OUT**

Use 10 by 10 sections of graph paper to show each product. Record your work using symbols.

**1.** $0.4 \times 0.8$     **2.** $0.5 \times 0.7$     **3.** $0.1 \times 0.1$     **4.** $0.9 \times 1$

# Multiplying Decimals

**EXPLORE**  Solve to Understand

A potato is an underground stem of a potato plant. Each potato is about 0.8 water. How many pounds of water are in a potato that weighs 0.7 pounds (lb)?

To solve this problem multiply 0.8 and 0.7.

| Multiply as with whole numbers. | Write the product so that it has as many decimal places as the sum of the decimal places in the factors. |
|---|---|
| $\begin{array}{r} 0.7 \\ \times 0.8 \\ \hline 56 \end{array}$ | $\begin{array}{r} 0.7 \leftarrow \text{1 decimal place} \\ \times 0.8 \leftarrow \text{1 decimal place} \\ \hline 0.56 \leftarrow \text{2 decimal places} \end{array}$ |

**TALK ABOUT IT**

1. In the second step why was the decimal point placed in front of the 5?
2. Is it reasonable that the product is less than 1? Why?
3. Give the answer to the Explore problem in a complete sentence.

## Other Examples

**A**
$$\begin{array}{r} 0.83 \leftarrow \text{2 decimal places} \\ \times 0.4 \leftarrow \text{1 decimal place} \\ \hline 0.332 \leftarrow \text{3 decimal places} \end{array}$$

**B**
$$\begin{array}{r} 5.3 \\ \times 1.4 \\ \hline 212 \\ 53\phantom{2} \\ \hline 7.42 \end{array}$$

**C**
$$\begin{array}{r} 0.073 \\ \times \quad 8 \\ \hline 0.584 \end{array}$$

Multiply.

1. $\begin{array}{r} 0.8 \\ \times 0.7 \end{array}$

2. $\begin{array}{r} 5.8 \\ \times 0.4 \end{array}$

3. $\begin{array}{r} 0.046 \\ \times \quad 7 \end{array}$

4. $\begin{array}{r} 9.67 \\ \times 1.8 \end{array}$

5. $\begin{array}{r} 0.75 \\ \times 9.3 \end{array}$

Multiply.

| | | | | |
|---|---|---|---|---|
| **1.**  3.2<br>$\times 0.3$ | **2.**  5.03<br>$\times\ 0.7$ | **3.**  5.02<br>$\times\ 0.1$ | **4.**  24<br>$\times 0.2$ | **5.**  0.509<br>$\times\ \ \ 6$ |
| **6.**  1.2<br>$\times 0.6$ | **7.**  7.4<br>$\times 0.05$ | **8.**  0.94<br>$\times\ 0.2$ | **9.**  4.02<br>$\times\ 0.4$ | **10.**  4.5<br>$\times 2.7$ |
| **11.**  424<br>$\times 7.2$ | **12.**  0.67<br>$\times\ \ \ 6$ | **13.**  40<br>$\times 2.3$ | **14.**  1.9<br>$\times\ 7$ | **15.**  12.8<br>$\times 0.01$ |

**16.** $0.2 \times 1.74$   **17.** $5.5 \times 0.3$   **18.** $0.011 \times 90$   **19.** $300 \times 0.001$

Copy the product. Write the decimal point in the correct place.

| | | | | |
|---|---|---|---|---|
| **20.**  24.6<br>$\times\ \ 3.5$<br>8610 | **21.**  11.3<br>$\times 0.3$<br>339 | **22.**  7.5<br>$\times 0.3$<br>225 | **23.**  1.5<br>$\times 0.4$<br>060 | **24.**  12<br>$\times 0.06$<br>072 |

**25.** Find the product of 6.9 and 0.64.

**26.** If the factors are 0.8 and 7.6, what is the product?

**MATH REASONING**

27. Write two numbers whose product is 0.48.
28. Write two numbers whose product is 2.4.

**PROBLEM SOLVING**

**29.** If a potato is 0.8 water, what is the weight of the water in a giant potato that weighs 2.87 lb?

**30.** If each potato is 0.8 water, how much more water is there in a 0.8 lb potato than there is in a 0.6 lb potato?

▶ **USING CRITICAL THINKING**   **Analyze the Evidence**

**31.** Who am I??????
  ■ I am a multiple of 5 and a multiple of 7.
  ■ I am not an odd number.
  ■ I am less than 100.

**32.** If you double me and add 12, you get 44. Who am I?

**33.** 8 more than 4 times me is 112. Who am I?

*More Practice, page 505, set A*

# Estimating with Decimals

**EXPLORE** **Evaluate an Answer**

It takes 8.79 hours (h) of work to make 1 minute
(min) of music on a compact disk. How many hours
of work would it take to make a 26.5 min disc?
Ava's answer is shown on the calculator at the right.

**TALK ABOUT IT**

1. Is the calculator answer reasonable? Explain.
2. How would you round the decimals to estimate
   the answer?
3. Can you think of another way to estimate the product?

- Sometimes you can replace the given numbers with
  **compatible numbers** to estimate products. For example:

Problem: $24.3 \times 4.78$
Replace the factors with
compatible numbers.     $\rightarrow 24.3 \times 4.78$
                                         $\downarrow$      $\downarrow$
                                    $25 \times 4 = 100$      $24.3 \times 4.78$ is about 100.

- Sometimes sums can be estimated using **clustering.** We
  can use this technique when each addend is close to (or
  "clusters around") a number that is easy to compute
  with mentally. For example:

Problem: Estimate $24.6 + 26.6 + 25 + 24.85$.
Replace each addend with 25.     $25 + 25 + 25 + 25 = 4 \times 25 = 100$
$24.6 + 26.6 + 25 + 24.85$ is about 100.

**TRY IT OUT**

Round or substitute compatible numbers to estimate each product.

**1.** $46.3 \times 57.9$      **2.** $23.4 \times 58.78$      **3.** $35.62 \times 54.89$      **4.** $67.76 \times 83.45$

Estimate each sum. Use clustering.

**5.** $9.75 + 10.3 + 11.1$      **6.** $81.3 + 78.96 + 80.05 + 82$      **7.** $905 + 908 + 897$

Estimate each product. Use any estimation technique you choose.

**1.** $3.87 \times 4.19$    **2.** $4.23 \times 8.76$    **3.** $872 \times 614$    **4.** $0.968 \times 6.45$

**5.** $12.7 \times 3.216$    **6.** $15.386 \times 1.89$    **7.** $43.28 \times 3.14$    **8.** $9.013 \times 6.872$

Estimate each sum. Use clustering.

**9.** $9.82 + 10.04 + 10.1 + 9.79$          **10.** $304 + 297 + 308 + 287$

**11.** $0.94 + 1.05 + 1.1 + 0.9$          **12.** $2,020 + 1,988 + 2,016$

## APPLY

### MATH REASONING

Use **estimation** to find the missing factor. In each case, the product must be not less than 40 or greater than 50.

**13.** $0.8 \times$ ▦ $= \underline{\ ?\ }$    **14.** $1.5 \times$ ▦ $= \underline{\ ?\ }$    **15.** $2.06 \times$ ▦ $= \underline{\ ?\ }$

**16.** $0.06 \times$ ▦ $= \underline{\ ?\ }$    **17.** $0.2 \times$ ▦ $= \underline{\ ?\ }$    **18.** $8.04 \times$ ▦ $= \underline{\ ?\ }$

### PROBLEM SOLVING

**19.** Darel worked 18.5 h at the recording studio last week. He earns $5.75 an hour. About how much did he earn last week working at the recording studio?

**20.** The record store is having a sale on old 45 rpm records. The records cost $0.25 each, but for every three a customer buys, the store gives 1 free record. Justine spent $1.50 on these records. How many did she get?

### ▶ CALCULATOR

Tell which of the key codes below will give the correct answer to the problem. Find the incorrect key code and tell why it will not give the correct answer.
Problem: Ben had $73 in the bank. Then he earned $6 a day for 24 days. How much money does he now have altogether?

**21.** [ON/AC] 73 [M+] 6 [X] 24 [M+] [MR]

**22.** [ON/AC] 73 [+] 6 [X] 24 [=]

**23.** [ON/AC] 6 [X] 24 [+] 73 [=]

*More Practice, page 505, set B*

# More About Multiplying Decimals

**EXPLORE  Analyze the Process**

Deena and her mother used a new recipe for sweet potato pie. It had to bake for 45 minutes. Electricity for the oven costs $0.0018 per minute. What was the cost of the electricity used to bake the pie?

To solve the problem, multiply $0.0018 by 45. Here is how to do it.

| Multiply as with whole numbers. | Write the product so that it has as many decimal places as the sum of the decimal places in the factors. |
|---|---|
| $0.0018 <br> × 45 <br> ——— <br> 90 <br> 72 <br> ——— <br> 810 | $0 0018 <br> × 45 <br> ——— <br> 90 <br> 72 <br> ——— <br> $0 0810 |

*Sometimes you need to write zeros in the product.*

**TALK ABOUT IT**

1. What would be the product if both factors were whole numbers?
2. Why was a zero added to the right of the decimal point in the final product?

**Other Examples**

| **A**   0.09 | **B**   0.2 | **C**   0.003 | **D**   37 |
|---|---|---|---|
| × 0.6 | × 0.04 | × 2 | × 0.002 |
| ——— | ——— | ——— | ——— |
| 0.054 | 0.008 | 0.006 | 0.074 |

Multiply. Write in zeros when necessary.

| **1.** 0.4 | **2.** 5.03 | **3.** 0.009 | **4.** 0.05 | **5.** 6.2 |
|---|---|---|---|---|
| 0.3 | × 0.7 | × 8 | × 0.3 | × 0.01 |

Multiply. Write in zeros when necessary.

| 1. | 0.006<br>× 3 | 2. | 0.008<br>× 6 | 3. | 0.09<br>× 0.6 | 4. | 0.2<br>×0.04 |
|---|---|---|---|---|---|---|---|
| 5. | 0.06<br>× 0.8 | 6. | 2.6<br>×0.04 | 7. | 0.9<br>×0.06 | 8. | 0.18<br>× 0.5 |
| 9. | 1.2<br>×0.06 | 10. | 7.4<br>×0.05 | 11. | 0.94<br>× 0.2 | 12. | 0.02<br>× 0.4 |

**13.** $4.1 \times 0.003$ **14.** $0.05 \times 0.3$ **15.** $0.4 \times 0.02$

**MATH REASONING**

Use **estimation** to decide in which box each decimal product belongs.

**16.** $0.5 \times 0.062$ **17.** $16 \times 0.15$ **18.** $0.03 \times 0.042$

**19.** $0.024 \times 0.060$ **20.** $0.81 \times 1.17$ **21.** $0.07 \times 0.42$

A
0.001 – 0.010

B
0.020 – 0.20

C
0.30 – 3.00

DATA BANK

**PROBLEM SOLVING**

**22.** A clothes dryer uses $0.006 worth of electricity each minute it is running. What would be the cost of running the dryer for 15 minutes?

**23.** **Science Data Bank** What would be the cost of the electricity for a color television set turned on for 5 hours a day every day of one week? See page 470.

**MIXED REVIEW**

Add.

| 24. | 8.92<br>+9.87 | 25. | 9.53<br>+5.80 | 26. | 55.94<br>+67.09 | 27. | $12.58<br>+ 8.65 | 28. | $155.50<br>+ 75.88 |
|---|---|---|---|---|---|---|---|---|---|

Multiply.

**29.** $792 \times 8$ **30.** $84 \times 17$ **31.** $346 \times 24$ **32.** $866 \times 70$

# Problem Solving
## Using a Calculator

UNDERSTAND
ANALYZE DATA
PLAN
ESTIMATE
SOLVE
EXAMINE

## LEARN ABOUT IT

When you use a calculator to solve multiple-step problems, it is helpful to use **memory** keys.

Tony and his mother want to buy 3 sleeping bags, 2 lanterns, and a camp stove at sale prices. Tony's mother has saved $250 to buy these items. Tony wants to know how much money they will have left.

## SALE

| | Regular | Sale |
|---|---|---|
| sleeping bag | $49.95 | $39.99 |
| camp stove | $34.95 | $29.99 |
| 80-quart cooler | $69.95 | $55.99 |
| lantern | $37.95 | $32.99 |
| backpack | $28.95 | $23.99 |

This is how Tony used the memory keys to solve the problem.

[ON/AC] 250 [M+] 3 [×] 39.99 [=] [M−] 2 [×] 32.99 [=] [M−] 29.99 [M−] [MR]

↑ Added to memory

↑ Subtracted from memory

↑ Subtracted from memory

↑ Subtracted from memory

Tony and his mother will have $34.06 left after buying the items.

| Memory Key | |
|---|---|
| [ON/AC] clears the memory. | [M−] subtracts from the total in memory. |
| [M+] adds to the total in memory. | [MR] recalls the total in memory. |

## TRY IT OUT

1. How much would 4 sleeping bags and 3 lanterns cost at the sale price?

2. Mr. Peterson is buying 2 coolers, 3 backpacks, and 1 lantern on sale. He has three $100 bills. How many of the bills will he need to give the clerk?

3. Martha's father gave the clerk $150 for 2 sleeping bags and a cooler at the sale price. How much change did he get?

4. If Jeff's aunt buys 3 sleeping bags, 2 backpacks, and a stove at sale prices, how much will she spend?

Solve. Use any problem solving strategy.

1. Each camper at Firebird Camp had to pay $25 for the overnight campout. If there were 64 campers, how much money did they pay in all?

2. The 64 campers were split up into 8 different campsites. If each campsite had the same number of campers, how many were at each campsite?

3. A 3-person tent costs $77.98, a 5-person costs $105.89, and an 8-person costs $205.89. How much more does the largest tent cost than the smallest?

4. For firewood on the camping trip, Kia chopped a fallen tree trunk into 25 pieces. All chops were straight across the trunk. How many cuts did she make?

Use this table for problems 5-7.

| Sale price | | |
|---|---|---|
| parka | $31.98 | (regularly $39.50) |
| woolen shirt | $24.98 | (regularly $26.50) |
| winter vest | $42.98 | (regularly $45.50) |
| hiking boots | $36.98 | (regularly $42.50) |

5. Fara Asad's father bought the family some clothing for winter camping. How much would he pay for a woolen shirt and a pair of hiking boots if he buys them on sale?

6. Mr. Asad has $225. How much will he have left if he buys 4 woolen shirts and 3 pairs of hiking boots on sale?

7. How much less would Mr. Asad pay for 4 pairs of hiking boots at the sale price than at the regular price?

8. **Missing Data** This problem has missing data. Tell what data is needed to solve the problem. Mrs. Kato bought backpacks for Michiko and her brothers. The backpacks cost $39.99 each. How much did she pay?

# Mental Math
## Multiplying Decimals by 10, 100, and 1,000

### EXPLORE  Find a Pattern

Use a calculator. Copy and complete the
table. Then select four other decimals.
Show the products when each decimal is
multiplied first by 10, then by 100 and
then by 1,000.

| Decimal | 3.142 | | | | |
|---------|-------|---|---|---|---|
| × 10 | | | | | |
| × 100 | | | | | |
| × 1000 | | | | | |

### TALK ABOUT IT

Look for patterns in your table. Complete the following
statements.

1. To multiply a decimal by **10,** "move" the decimal point
   __?__ places to the __?__ .
2. To multiply a decimal by **100,** "move" the decimal point
   __?__ places to the __?__ .
3. To multiply a decimal by **1,000,** "move" the decimal
   point __?__ places to the __?__ .
4. Suppose you multiply 4.5 by 100. Explain how you find
   and write the product.

When you multiply by 10, 100, or 1,000, the number of
zeros tells you how many places to move the decimal point.
To see why this works, think about $10 \times 2.45$. This is the
same as the sum of ten addends of 2.45.

$10 \times 2.45 = 2.45 + 2.45 + 2.45 + 2.45 + 2.45 + 2.45$
$+ 2.45 + 2.45 + 2.45 + 2.45 = 24.5.$

The decimal point in the factor 2.45 is one place to the
right in the product 24.5.

Use mental math to find these products.

1. $10 \times 3.678$
2. $100 \times 16.89$
3. $1,000 \times 4.629$
4. $6.782 \times 100$

5. $10 \times 73.2$
6. $100 \times 5.43$
7. $1,000 \times 0.545$
8. $10 \times 0.378$

142

Use mental math to solve these equations.

1. $3.4 \times 10$
2. $5.23 \times 100$
3. $1,000 \times 0.132$
4. $100 \times 2.856$

5. $10 \times 0.56$
6. $1,000 \times 0.2$
7. $3.175 \times 100$
8. $0.531 \times 10$

9. $4.23 \times 1,000$
10. $100 \times 5.68$
11. $0.713 \times 10$
12. $100 \times 1.1$

13. $6.82 \times 10$
14. $2.19 \times 100$
15. $7.9 \times 1,000$
16. $10 \times 0.053$

## APPLY

### MATH REASONING

In each problem below, the same shape stands for the same number. Tell what numbers should be placed in each shape to keep the scales in balance.

17.

18.

### PROBLEM SOLVING

19. Dana has two types of coin collector wrappers for pennies. One holds 10 pennies and the other holds 100 pennies. She has 4 of the smaller packages and 6 of the larger ones full of pennies. How many pennies does she have in these wrappers?

▶ CALCULATOR

20. Choose a 3 place decimal. Use the constant multiplier on your calculator to multiply the decimal by 10. Keep using the constant key to multiply by 10. How many times must you multiply by 10 to produce the same result as multiplying by 100? by 1,000?

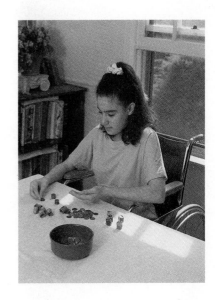

*More Practice, page 505, set D*

# Applied Problem Solving
## Group Decision Making

UNDERSTAND
ANALYZE DATA
PLAN
ESTIMATE
SOLVE
EXAMINE

**Group Skill:**
Listen to Others

Next month is National Peanut Month. Your class is in charge of setting up a peanut butter snack bar for one lunch during the month. What kinds of peanut butter snacks will you offer? How many of each kind will you prepare?

### Facts to Consider

■ Your class conducted a survey to help you in your planning. The survey results are shown below.

Survey Question: *What is your favorite peanut butter snack?*

| | |
|---|---|
| Peanut butter on crackers | JHT JHT JHT |
| Peanut butter on apple slices | JHT II |
| Peanut butter balls rolled in sesame seeds | JHT |
| Peanut butter on celery sticks | JHT JHT JHT II |
| Peanut butter and honey on crackers | IIII |
| Peanut butter on banana | JHT II |

■ You have 1 small, 1 medium, and 2 large jars of peanut butter to use.
■ Each kind of snack you will prepare uses 2 tablespoons of peanut butter per serving.

**Snappy Peanut Butter**
Net Weight 510 grams
Serving Size: 2 TBSP (32 g)
Servings per
Container ...... 15
Calories ....... 190
Protein ........ 9 g
Carbohydrates ... 5 g
Fat ........... 16 g
Cholesterol ..... 0 mg
Sodium ........ 140 mg

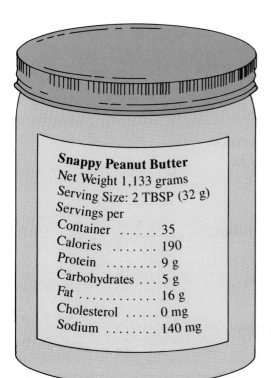

**Snappy Peanut Butter**
Net Weight 793 grams
Serving Size: 2 TBSP (32 g)
Servings per
Container ...... 24
Calories ....... 190
Protein ........ 9 g
Carbohydrates ... 5 g
Fat ........... 16 g
Cholesterol ..... 0 mg
Sodium ........ 140 mg

**Snappy Peanut Butter**
Net Weight 1,133 grams
Serving Size: 2 TBSP (32 g)
Servings per
Container ...... 35
Calories ....... 190
Protein ........ 9 g
Carbohydrates ... 5 g
Fat ........... 16 g
Cholesterol ..... 0 mg
Sodium ........ 140 mg

### Some Questions to Answer

1. How many students in the survey chose each snack?

2. Which data on the labels could help you figure out how many snacks could be made from the amount of peanut butter available? How many snacks can be made in all?

3. How could you make use of the survey to decide how many of each snack to prepare?

### What Is Your Decision?

Make a table for the students who will be preparing the snacks. Show how many of each snack they should make. Explain how you decided on these quantities?

# WRAP UP

## Sentence Completion

Complete each sentence by matching Part I and Part II.

Part I

**1.** To multiply 4.627 by 1,000,

**2.** The product of 8.47 and 0.8

**3.** The product of 4.12 and 2.03

**4.** To multiply 0.143 by 10,

Part II

A. move the decimal point one place to the right.

B. is less than 8.

C. move the decimal point three places to the right.

D. is greater than 8.

## Sometimes, Always, Never

Complete each statement by writing **sometimes**, **always**, or **never**. Explain your choice.

**5.** When you multiply hundredths by tenths, the product is __?__ hundredths.

**6.** When you multiply a whole number by 100, the product __?__ will have exactly two zeros.

**7.** To multiply a decimal by 10, __?__ move the decimal point one place to the left.

## Project

You can use **lattice multiplication** to find products such as 25 × 34. Start with a blank lattice like this one. Place the factors as shown. Use one factor for columns and the other for rows.

Multiply the column and row values for each box.

Start at the right. Find the sum for each diagonal. Regroup to the next diagonal when necessary.
25 × 34 = 850

Find these products using the lattice. Tell how many boxes you will need.

**1.** 237 × 42    **2.** 45 × 482    **3.** 139 × 476

2, 5, 3, 4
4 digits →
4 boxes

2   5

3

4

2   5

$5 \times 3 = 15$
$2 \times 3 = 6$
$5 \times 4 = 20$
$2 \times 4 = 8$

$5 + 2 + 8 = 15$

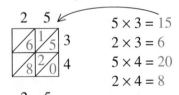

Write 5.
Regroup 1.

# POWER PRACTICE/TEST

## Part 1  Understanding

1. Which one uses rounding to estimate 42 × 672?

   A. 50 × 700 = 35,000
   B. 50 × 600 = 30,000
   C. 40 × 600 = 24,000
   D. 40 × 700 = 28,000

2. Which one uses clustering to estimate
   83.2 + 76.8 + 81.04 + 79?

   A. 83 + 77 + 81 + 79 = 320
   B. (83 + 81) + (77 + 79) = 320
   C. 4 × 80 = 320
   D. (80 + 75) + (80 + 75) = 320

3. If you use mental math to find 83 × 77, you would probably break the factor 83 into

   A. 60 + 23          B. 80 + 3
   C. 70 + 13          D. 90 − 7

4. Which one uses compatible numbers to estimate 23.04 × 4.27?

   A. 25 × 4 = 100   B. 23 × 4 = 92
   C. 23 × 5 = 115   D. 25 × 5 = 125

## Part 2  Skills

Use mental math to find each product.

5. 700 × 40          6. 800 × 600          7. 6 × 48

Multiply.

8. 1,075
   × 6

9. 148
   × 54

10. 6.7
    × 3.4

11. 3.71
    × 0.52

12. 0.03
    × 2.4

## Part 3  Applications

13. Tina returned an art book and got a $15.47 credit. Then she bought a music book for $12.86 and a dictionary for $36.89. How much change does she get from $40?

14. 8 friends love to talk on the phone. One night, each friend talked to each of the others once. How many phone calls did the friends make in all?

15. **Challenge.** Use the digits 2, 3, 4, and 5 to give the number for each ▥.
    ▥ × ▥ × ▥ + ▥ = 34

147

# ENRICHMENT
## Exponents

When a number is used as a factor several times, we can write it using an **exponent**. The exponent tells how many times the number, called the **base**, is used as a factor.

$2 \times 2 \times 2 \times 2 = 2^4$ ← exponent
← base

$2^4$ is read "two to the fourth power."

Exponents are very helpful for writing powers (products of multiplying the number by itself) of 10.

Look at this chart.

**Powers of Ten**

| | | |
|---|---|---|
| $10^1$ | 10 | = 10 |
| $10^2$ | $10 \times 10$ | = 100 |
| $10^3$ | $10 \times 10 \times 10$ | = 1,000 |
| $10^4$ | $10 \times 10 \times 10 \times 10$ | = 10,000 |
| $10^5$ | $10 \times 10 \times 10 \times 10 \times 10$ | = 100,000 |

**1.** Do you notice a pattern involving the exponent and the number of zeros in the product?

Astronomers and other scientists use powers of 10 to write very large numbers.

The planet Neptune is about 3,000,000,000 miles from Earth. To make it easier to work with such a large number, astronomers write $3 \times 10^9$.

$3,000,000,000 = 3 \times 1,000,000,000 = 3 \times 10^9$

Write these numbers the way an astronomer would.

**2.** 5,000,000          **3.** 20,000          **4.** 800 million

**5.** You can write 59,237 in expanded form using powers of 10. Write each term using powers of 10. For example, $50,000 = (5 \times 10^4)$.

$59,237 = (5 \times 10^4) + (9 \times 10^3) + (2 \times 10^2) + (3 \times 10^1) + 7$

Write these numbers in expanded form using powers of 10.

**6.** 3,457          **7.** 146,230          **8.** 43,625,700

# CUMULATIVE REVIEW

Add or subtract.

**1.** $324.16
    − 99.58

   A. $375.42
   B. $224.58
   C. $215.58
   D. $324.58

**2.** 854 + 563 + 27 + 106

   A. 1,550     B. 1,793
   C. 1,530     D. 1,451

**3.** 4.2 + 18.75 + 21.04 + 1.006

   A. 91.85     B. 60.27
   C. 59.17     D. 44.996

Use this graph for questions 4 and 5.

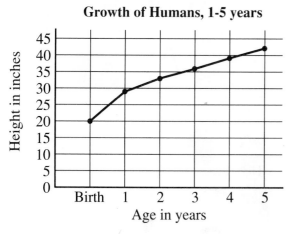

**Growth of Humans, 1-5 years**

(y-axis: Height in inches; x-axis: Age in years — Birth, 1, 2, 3, 4, 5)

**4.** Between what two ages does the most growth occur?

   A. 3 and 4     B. birth and 1
   C. 1 and 2     D. 2 and 3

**5.** Predict the average height for age 6.

   A. 43 in.     B. 48 in.
   C. 45 in.     D. 50 in.

**6.** Harry has a part-time job stuffing envelopes. He can stuff 65 in 5 minutes. How many can he stuff in an hour? Make a table.

   A. 780    B. 520    C. 450    D. 585

**7.** Which number has a 6 in the hundredths place?

   A. 604.12     B. 163.45
   C. 506.87     D. 806.06

**8.** Which number is between 27.045 and 30.047?

   A. 27.04     B. 30.05
   C. 27.1     D. 30.048

Use these numbers for items 10–12:
14, 26, 35, 19, 22, 26, 24.

**9.** The range of the numbers is

   A. 12    B. 35    C. 21    D. 26

**10.** The median is

   A. 26    B. 24    C. 23.6    D. 21

**11.** The mode is

   A. 26    B. 24    C. 21    D. 23.6

**12.** In 1513, Juan Ponce de Leon explored the coast of Florida. Francis Drake landed in California 66 years later, and 28 years after that, Captain John Smith started the first English colony at Jamestown. In what year was Jamestown settled?

   A. 1541     B. 1579
   C. 1592     D. 1607

# 6

# METRIC MEASUREMENT

**THEME: COMPETITIVE SPORTS**

**M**ATH AND
HEALTH AND FITNESS

DATA BANK

Use the Health and
Fitness Data Bank on
page 475 to answer
the questions.

1 In which of the listed
years was the fastest time
recorded for the Olympic
women's 800-meter race? In
which year was the slowest time
recorded for that race?

**2** In 1984 Kim Gallagher won the silver medal for the Olympic women's 800-meter run with a time of 1 minute, 58.63 seconds. How much slower than the winning time was she?

**3** In 1984 the bronze medal winner (third-place finish) was 1.23 seconds slower than the gold medal winner. How long did it take the bronze medal winner to run the race?

**4** **Using Critical Thinking** Compare the times for the women's 800-meter winners in the 1960s with those in the 1980s. Can you make a general statement about what you observe?

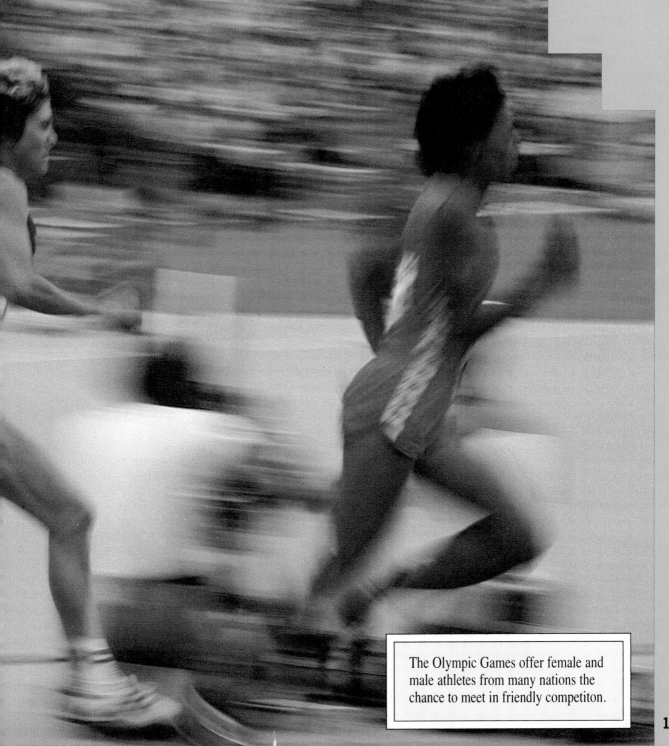

The Olympic Games offer female and male athletes from many nations the chance to meet in friendly competiton.

# Estimating Length

You can use what you know about **meters (m),** **decimeters (dm),** and **centimeters (cm)** to estimate lengths.

1 m = 10 dm = 100 cm
1 dm = 10 cm

## EXPLORE  Analyze the Process

Estimate in centimeters the width of your open math book.

## TALK ABOUT IT

1. How does thinking about the width of one page help you think about the total width of both pages?
2. If you knew the width of half a page, how could you find the width of your open book?

**Unitizing** is a method of estimating by dividing an object into smaller equal parts and then using the estimated length of one part to estimate the total length of the object. For example, you can estimate the length of a chalkboard by visually dividing it into smaller parts.

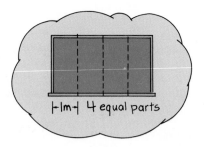

## TRY IT OUT

Use the unitizing method to make the estimates described below.

1. the length of your pencil in centimeters
2. the width of your desk top in decimeters
3. the length of a chalkboard in meters

Use the unitizing method to make each estimate. Then measure to check your estimates. Record in a table as shown.

| Object | Estimate | Actual |
|---|---|---|
| 1. notebook width | _____ | _____ |

1. **A.** notebook width in centimeters
   **B.** notebook length in centimeters

2. **A.** shoe width in centimeters
   **B.** shoe length in centimeters

3. **A.** door width in decimeters
   **B.** door height in decimeters

4. **A.** bulletin board width in decimeters
   **B.** bulletin board height in decimeters

**APPLY**

**MATH REASONING**

Write **reasonable** or **not reasonable** for each statement.

5. The width of my little finger is about 1 cm. So the width of my hand is about 10 dm.

6. The width of a piece of notebook paper is about 23 cm. So the length is about 28 cm.

**PROBLEM SOLVING**

7. Devra's bedroom is a rectangle with a width of about 3 m and a length of about 4.5 m. About how many meters is the perimeter of her room?

8. A carpenter makes 3-legged stools and 4-legged stools. This week she made a total of 35 stools and she used a total of 125 legs. How many of each type did she make?

▶ **USING CRITICAL THINKING** Analyze the Situation

9. In the story about David and the giant Goliath, Goliath's height was given as "6 cubits and a span." How could you find the length of a string as close to Goliath's actual height as possible?

1 span

1 cubit

*More Practice, page 506, Set A*

# Meters and Centimeters

## EXPLORE  Use a Meter Stick

Work in groups. List some objects whose length, width, height, or perimeter you estimate to be between 1 m and 2 m. Measure the objects to the nearest centimeter to check. Record your measurements in centimeters.

## TALK ABOUT IT

1. Should any of your measurements be less than 100 cm or more than 200 cm? Explain why or why not.
2. Use both meters and centimeters to express each measurement.
3. Do you think a table 1.5 m long would be more than or less than 100 cm long? more than or less than 200 cm?

Measurements with meters and centimeters can be written using meters and centimeters (3 m 58 cm), using only centimeters (358 cm), or using only meters (3.58 m— 1 cm = 0.01 m, so 58 cm = 0.58 m).

■ To change from centimeters to meters, think of the number of hundreds. Each 100 cm is 1 m.

$$247 \text{ cm} = ? \text{ m}$$

2 m 47 cm  ( 200 cm = 2 m )
247 cm = 2.47 m

■ To change from meters to centimeters, first think how many centimeters are in the whole number part and then how many are in the decimal part.

$$4.08 \text{ m} = ? \text{ cm}$$

4 m 8 cm  ( 4 m = 400 cm )
4.08 m = 408 cm

## TRY IT OUT

Write each measurement two ways, in centimeters and in meters.

**1.** 2 m 83 cm    **2.** 6 m 50 cm    **3.** 1 m 6 cm    **4.** 3 m 8 cm    **5.** 1 m 94 cm

Give the missing numbers.

**6.** 435 cm = ▓ m          **7.** 826 cm = ▓ m          **8.** 7.84 m = ▓ cm

Change each measure to meters.

1. table length
2. table width
3. table height

4. door height
5. door width
6. door thickness

Change each measure to centimeters.

7. bed length
8. bed width
9. bed height

10. bookcase height
11. bookcase width
12. bookcase depth

APPLY

**MATH REASONING**

Look for patterns in the table. Complete statements 13 and 14.

| | | | |
|---|---|---|---|
| 324.0 cm ......... 3.24 m | 5.43 m ......... 543.0 cm |
| 120.0 cm ......... 1.20 m | 7.08 m ......... 708.0 cm |
| 75.0 cm ......... 0.75 m | 0.54 m ......... 54.0 cm |

13. To change centimeters to meters, move the decimal point ___?___ .
14. To change meters to centimeters, move the decimal point ___?___ .

**PROBLEM SOLVING**

15. Robert Seagren's Olympic gold medal winning pole vault in 1968 was 5.40 m. Would a vault of 550 cm be higher or lower than Seagren's jump?

16. **Health and Fitness Data Bank** In the 1984 Olympics how much higher would Mike Tully have had to jump in order to have tied the jump made by the gold medal winner? See page 475.

▶ **ESTIMATION**

Give the best estimate for each length.

17. South wall    **A.** 4 m  **B.** 5 m  **C.** 7 m
18. West wall     **A.** 1 m  **B.** 2 m  **C.** 3 m
19. East wall     **A.** 3 m  **B.** 4 m  **C.** 5 m

*More Practice, page 506, set B*

155

# Centimeters and Millimeters

Decimals can be used to record **millimeters** (mm) as parts of a centimeter.

**1 cm = 10 mm**
**1 mm = 0.1 cm**

**EXPLORE** **Examine the Data**
During a storm, Josh read his homemade rain gauge every hour to see how much rain had fallen since the storm started. He recorded the amounts using millimeters only.

**TALK ABOUT IT**

1. Why would 7 mm be a more accurate measurement than 1 cm for the 9:00 a.m. reading?
2. How do you think Josh decided that the reading for 11:00 a.m. was 25 mm?
3. If Josh had used decimals for the noon reading, would 3.2 cm be a reasonable amount to record? Explain your reasoning.

To change from millimeters to centimeters, think of tens. Each ten millimeters is 1 centimeter.

To change from centimeters to millimeters, think how many millimeters are in the whole number part and then how many are in the decimal part.

24 mm = ? cm
2 cm 4 mm ( 20 mm = 2 cm )
24 mm = 2.4 cm

4.8 cm = ? mm
4 cm 8 mm ( 4 cm = 40 mm )
4.8 cm = 48 mm

Write each measurement two ways. First use only centimeters. Then use only millimeters.

**1.** 5 cm 7 mm      **2.** 3 cm 9 mm      **3.** 4 cm 0 mm      **4.** 6 cm 4 mm

Give the missing numbers.

**5.** 24 mm = ▓ cm      **6.** 7.8 cm = ▓ mm      **7.** 9 mm = ▓ cm

Give each rainfall amount in millimeters.

**1.** 8:00 a.m.

**2.** 9:00 a.m.

**3.** 10:00 a.m.

**4.** 11:00 a.m.

**5.** 12:00 noon

Give each rainfall amount in centimeters using decimals.

**6.** 4:00 p.m.

**7.** 5:00 p.m.

**8.** 6:00 p.m.

**9.** 7:00 p.m.

**10.** 8:00 p.m.

**APPLY**

### MATH REASONING

Select the best unit (m, cm, or mm) for each measure.

**11.** tree height: 3.8 __?__

**12.** ruler thickness: 2 __?__

**13.** photograph height: 15.4 __?__

**14.** drawer depth: 10 __?__

### PROBLEM SOLVING

**15.** Last Monday, Josh made this graph to show rainfall during a storm. Was the total rainfall more or less than 4 cm?

**16.** About how many millimeters of rain fell from 10:00 a.m. to 2:00 p.m.?

**17.** **Extra Data** About 3 mm of rain fell between noon and 1 p.m. The greatest amount fell between 10:00 a.m. and 11:00 a.m. About how much fell during that hour?

### MIXED REVIEW

Find these products mentally.

**18.** 50 × 60    **19.** 20 × 80    **20.** 30 × 400    **21.** 70 × 30    **22.** 9 × 600

Multiply.

Estimate by rounding.

**23.** 7.5
×0.3

**24.** 0.77
× 6.5

**25.** 7.45
×3.11

**26.** 223
× 89

**27.** 881
× 91

# Area of a Rectangle

The **area** of a figure is the number of **square units** that cover it exactly. In the figure shown, the square unit is 1 square centimeter ($cm^2$). The area of the larger square is 4 square centimeters (4 $cm^2$).

**1 square centimeter (cm²)**

**EXPLORE  Look for a Pattern**

Draw some rectangles of different sizes on centimeter graph paper. Make a table and record the length, width, and area of each rectangle. Look for a pattern in the table.

| rectangle | length | width | area |
|---|---|---|---|
| A | 6 cm | 4 cm | 24 cm² |
| B | | | |
| C | | | |
| D | | | |

**TALK ABOUT IT**

1. What method did you use to find the area of each rectangle?
2. If you had only the length and width measurements written in the table, how could you find the area of each rectangle?

One way to find the area of a rectangle is to use a **formula.**

$$\begin{array}{ccc} \text{Area} & \text{length} & \text{width} \\ A & = \quad l & \times \quad w \end{array}$$

**Example**    $A = 13 \times 8 = 104$

The area of the rectangle is 104 $cm^2$.

The formula for the area of a square is side $\times$ side.
$A = s \times s$

8 cm

13 cm

Use the formula to find the area of each rectangular figure.

1.

42.8 cm

65.3 cm

2.

14 m

12 m

3.

35 cm

54 cm

158

Use the area formula to find each area.

**1.** Table top area in square meters (m²)

**2.** Window area in square centimeters (cm²)

**3.** Mirror area in square centimeters

**4.** Area of the top of the counter in square meters

**MATH REASONING**

Guess and check to find the missing length or width for each rectangle.

**5.** Area = 156 cm²
length = 13 cm
width = ?

**6.** Area = 225 cm²
length = 15 cm
width = ?

**7.** Area = 1,200 m²
length = ?
width = 30m

**PROBLEM SOLVING**

**8.** Marjo needs to know the area of her bedroom floor so that she can order a new carpet. The room is rectangular. The width is 3.4 m and the length is 4.7 m. What is the area in square meters?

**9. Data Hunt** Measure the length and width of each object to the nearest centimeter. Then find each area in square centimeters.
**A.** front cover of your math book
**B.** piece of notebook paper
**C.** the top of your desk

▶ **USING CRITICAL THINKING   Give an Example**

**10.** Draw a picture and give the dimensions of a rectangle with an area of 24 square units. Give another example of a rectangle with the same area but a different perimeter.

*More Practice, page 506, Set D*

# Kilometers

**LEARN ABOUT IT**

You can use what you know about meters to help you think about a longer unit of length, the **kilometer** (km).

> 1 km = 1,000 m
> 1 m = 0.001 km

**EXPLORE** Solve to Understand

Imagine you are planning a 5-km race through Shady Grove Park. Find at least one route that would be 5 km long. Trace the map and show the route.

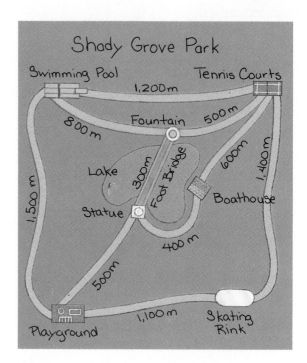

Shady Grove Park

**TALK ABOUT IT**

1. What distances written on the map are greater than 1 km?
2. If 100 m can be written as 0.1 km, how would you write 200 m as a kilometer measure?

**TRY IT OUT**

For items 1−4, express each distance in kilometers. Use decimals as needed.

1. from the swimming pool to the tennis courts
2. from the playground to the swimming pool
3. from the statue to the boathouse
4. from the fountain across the footbridge to the statue
5. Which places in the park are 0.5 km from each other?
6. Which places in the park are 1 km from each other?

Are these distances more than, less than, or the same as 2.5 km?

7. from the swimming pool to the tennis courts to the skating rink
8. from the boathouse to the statue to the fountain to the swimming pool

**160**

*More Practice, page 506, set E*

# POWER PRACTICE/QUIZ

Estimate using the unitizing method. Then measure to check.

**1.** height of a doorknob in decimeters    **2.** length of a book page in centimeters

Copy and complete the table below to show each measurement three ways.

| Dining Room Table | | | |
|---|---|---|---|
| | | m and cm | cm | m |
| **3.** | height | | 75 cm | |
| **4.** | width | | | 1.2 m |
| **5.** | length | 2 m 5 cm | | |

A plant's height was measured each day for one week.

**6.** Write the plant's height each day in millimeters.

**7.** Write the plant's height each day in centimeters, using decimals.

Find the area of each surface.

**8.** desk top

71.5 cm
73 cm

**9.** kitchen floor

3.1 m
2.7 m

## PROBLEM SOLVING

**10.** As a warm up, the players on the baseball team jog around the entire field twice. How far does each player jog?

73 m
81.2 m
81.2 m
121.7 m
121.7 m

**11.** When Shana walks fast, she travels about 3 m with every 4 steps. She counted 36 fast steps from her house to the end of the block. About how many meters is that?

161

# Capacity and Volume

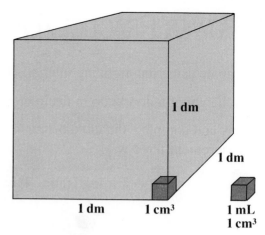

1 dm

1 dm

1 dm    1 cm³    1 mL
                 1 cm³

## LEARN ABOUT IT

Decimals can be used to record amounts
of capacity with the **liter** (L) and
**milliliter** (mL). These units are closely
related to the cubic decimeter (dm³) and
cubic centimeter (cm³) units of volume.

1 L of water will exactly fill a box that has a volume of 1 dm³.
1 mL of water will exactly fill a box that has a volume of 1 cm³.

> **1 L = 1,000 mL**      **1 mL = 0.001 L**

## EXPLORE  Make a Liter Model

Work in groups. Select a container that you think holds
more than 1 L. Then pour 100 mL of water into the
container. Mark that water level. Next, find a way to mark
the 1L water level on the container.

## TALK ABOUT IT

**1.** How does knowing the number of milliliters in a liter
help you make your own liter container?

**2.** Where on your container would you mark the level for 0.5 L?

■ To change milliliters to liters, think
of the number of thousands. Each
1,000 mL is 1 L.

$$3,285 \text{ mL} = ? \text{ L}$$
$$\swarrow \quad \downarrow$$
$$3 \text{ L } 285 \text{ mL} \quad 3,000 \text{ mL} = 3 \text{ L}$$
$$3,285 \text{ mL} = 3.285 \text{ L}$$

■ To change liters to milliliters, think how
many milliliters in the whole number
part and how many in the decimal part.

$$4.75 \text{ L} = ? \text{ mL}$$
$$\swarrow \downarrow$$
$$4 \text{ L } 750 \text{ mL} \quad 4 \text{ L} = 4,000 \text{ mL}$$
$$4.75 \text{ L} = 4,750 \text{ mL}$$

## TRY IT OUT

Give the missing numbers.

**1.** 500 mL = ▨ L    **2.** 2,064 mL = ▨ L **3.** 6,280 mL = ▨ L **4.** 1.5 L = ▨ mL

Change each measure to liters.

1. mustard

2. mayonnaise

3. salad dressing

**mustard
1,360 mL**

**mayonnaise
950 mL**

**Salad dressing
237 mL**

Change each measure to milliliters.

4. fruit punch

5. apple juice

6. tomato juice

**fruit punch
0.946 L**

**apple juice
3.78 L**

**tomato juice
1.892 L**

**APPLY**

**MATH REASONING**

Tell whether each statement is **true** or **false.**

7. $250 \text{ mL} = 250 \text{ cm}^3$

8. $500 \text{ mL} = 50 \text{ cm}^3$

9. $15 \text{ L} = 15 \text{ dm}^3$

**PROBLEM SOLVING**

10. Your recipe for fruit punch calls for 750 mL of orange juice. If you buy a bottle of juice labeled 0.65 L, will you have enough? If not, how much more will you need?

12. You want to make 4 loaves of bread. For each loaf you need 350 mL of milk. You have 1.5 L of milk. Will that be enough?

11. How could you pour from one container into another so that each would have 0.25 L of liquid?

A      B      C

400 mL    50 mL    300 mL

**MIXED REVIEW**

Multiply.

13.    0.008
    ×    2

14.    0.005
    ×    9

15.    0.007
    ×  2.8

16.    0.003
    × 3.87

17.    0.004
    × 2.07

Solve using mental math.

18. $704 - 5$

19. $34 \times 2 \times 5$

20. $37 + 14 + 3$

21. $42 \times 5 \times 2$

*More Practice, page 507, set A*

# Kilograms and Grams

**LEARN ABOUT IT**

You can use what you know about thousands and thousandths to help you record masses in **grams** (g) and **kilograms** (kg).

**about 1 kg**

**1 kg = 1,000 g**

**about 1 g**

**1 g = 0.001 kg**

**EXPLORE**  Use a Metric Scale

Work in groups. Estimate in grams the masses of different amounts of water. Try some amounts more than 1 L and some less than 1 L. Check your estimates by finding each amount in grams. Record in a table.

| Amount of water in mL | Estimated mass | Actual mass |
|---|---|---|
|  |  |  |

**TALK ABOUT IT**

1. Did the amounts of water more than 1 L have masses greater than 1 kg? Did the amounts less than 1 L have masses less than 1 kg?

2. In the metric system, 1 L of water has a mass of 1 kg and 1 mL of water has a mass of 1 g. What do you think the mass of 1.5 L of water should be?

To change grams to kilograms, think of the number of thousands. Each 1,000 g is 1 kg.

$$2,400 \text{ g} = ? \text{ kg}$$
$$2 \text{ kg } 400 \text{ g} \quad (2,000 \text{ g} = 2 \text{ kg})$$
$$2,400 \text{ g} = 2.4 \text{ kg}$$

To change kilograms to grams, think how many grams are in the whole number part and how many are in the decimal part.

$$3.75 \text{ kg} = ? \text{ g}$$
$$3 \text{ kg } 750 \text{ g} \quad (3 \text{ kg} = 3,000 \text{ g})$$
$$3.75 \text{ kg} = 3,750 \text{ g}$$

**TRY IT OUT**

Give the missing numbers.

1. 500 g = ▦ kg

2. 1,764 g = ▦ kg

3. 2,810 g = ▦ kg

4. 1.5 kg = ▦ g

5. 7.514 kg = ▦ g

6. 0.25 kg = ▦ g

Change each measure to kilograms.

1. cheese
2. bread
3. olives
4. sliced turkey

cheese
950 g

bread
900 g

olives
595 g

sliced turkey
72 g

Change each measure to grams.

5. ham
6. sausage
7. sliced beef
8. chicken

ham
2.534 kg

sausage
0.45 kg

sliced beef
1.3 kg

chicken
1.08 kg

APPLY

**MATH REASONING**

Copy and complete the table.

| | amount of water | mass in g | mass in kg |
|---|---|---|---|
| **9.** | 250 mL | ——— g | ——— kg |
| **10.** | ——— mL | 500 g | ——— kg |
| **11.** | ——— mL | ——— g | 0.75 kg |

**PROBLEM SOLVING**

12. Rhonda bought 50 g of sliced cheese and 50 g of sliced ham. If she needs 0.5 kg of each, did she get enough?

13. Vann wants to make 4 meat loaves. The recipe calls for 750 g of ground beef and 250 g of ground pork for each loaf. How many kg of ground beef should he buy?

▶ **COMMUNICATION   Writing to Learn**

14. Kathy said there had to be a mistake on these box weights because boxes that hold the same amount also have to weigh the same amount. Write several sentences explaining why you agree or disagree with Kathy's statement.

rice
2.481 kg

detergent
1.452 kg

cereal
0.875 kg

*More Practice, page 507, set B*

 **165**

# Problem Solving
## Make an Organized List

UNDERSTAND
ANALYZE DATA
PLAN
ESTIMATE
SOLVE
EXAMINE

## LEARN ABOUT IT

To solve some problems, you may need to write down all the possibilities in a planned way. This problem solving strategy is called **Make an Organized List.**

At swimming practice, Art, Bob, Carlos, David, and Egon raced against each other 2 at a time. How many races were there if everyone raced everyone else?

> First I'll list all the races that Art was in. I'll use initials for the boys' names.

A-B
A-C
A-D
A-E

> Then I'll write the races that Bob, Carlos, David, and Egon were in. I'll cross out any repeats. B-A is the same as A-B, C-A is the same as A-C, and so on.

| | | | | |
|---|---|---|---|---|
| A-B | ~~B-A~~ | ~~C-A~~ | ~~D-A~~ | ~~E-A~~ |
| A-C | B-C | ~~C-B~~ | ~~D-B~~ | ~~E-B~~ |
| A-D | B-D | C-D | ~~D-C~~ | ~~E-C~~ |
| A-E | B-E | C-E | D-E | ~~E-D~~ |

There were 10 races in all.

## TRY IT OUT

At the swim meet, Jenna will be swimming in one freestyle race. She can swim in the 50 m, 100 m, or 200 m freestyle. She will be swimming in Heat 1, Heat 2, or Heat 3 for her freestyle event. How many different races could her coach assign her to?

- What are the different freestyle races Jenna could swim in?
- What are the different heats she could swim in?
- Copy and complete the organized list below to help solve the problem.

  50 m—Heat 1
  50 m—Heat 2
  50 m—Heat 3

Make an organized list to help solve each problem.

**1.** Jamie can swim in lanes 1 through 4. She can do the breaststroke, butterfly, backstroke, or freestyle. How many possible choices does she have?

**2.** In the spring, Mark is busy with both swim team and baseball. The baseball jackets for his team each have 2 digits on them. Each digit is a 1, 2, 3, or 4. What are all the possible numbers for Mark's jacket?

**MIXED PRACTICE**

Choose a strategy from the strategies list or other strategies you know to solve these problems.

| Some Strategies | |
| --- | --- |
| Act Out | Guess and Check |
| Use Objects | Make a Table |
| Choose an Operation | Solve a Simpler Problem |
| Draw a Picture | Make an Organized List |

**3.** In the 1984 Olympic finals, Gaines swam the 100 m freestyle in 49.80 seconds (s). In the finals of the 1988 Olympics, Biondi swam the same event in 48.63 s. This was 0.21 s slower than Biondi's world record in the event. How much faster was Biondi than Gaines in the Olympic finals?

**4.** Maya practices 25 days each month. Each day she swims freestyle for 850 m and backstroke for 625 m. How many meters does she swim per month?

**5.** For the swim team awards dinner, 30 square tables were pushed into one long table. One person can be seated on each side of a square table. How many people can be seated at the long table?

**6.** Yoshio's long armspan of 1.52 m helps him swim faster in school meets. Matt Biondi's armspan is 1.4 times as long as Yoshio's. What is Biondi's armspan?

**7.** Tina needs to decorate the sports shop window with one of the new swimsuits and swimcaps for competition. There are black, blue, red, and purple suits. There are gold, silver, white, gray, and green caps. How many different combinations can she choose from?

**8.** In the 1988 Olympics, Janet Evans weighed 47.73 kg. One of her opponents was 34.09 kg heavier. How much did the heavier swimmer weigh?

# Time

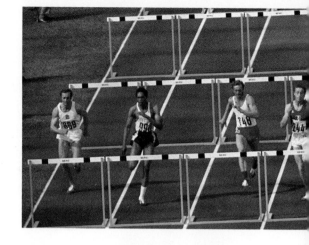

**LEARN ABOUT IT**

Many Olympics and other sports records are measures of the best time recorded for a given event.

**EXPLORE** Use a Calculator

Work with a partner and use a calculator to estimate how long 1 minute (min) is. Press [ON/AC] and [+] 1 on your calculator. Have your partner use a watch or timer. When your partner says "Start" begin to press = on your calculator and press once for each second you think has passed. Stop when your calculator shows 60. Was your estimated minute longer or shorter than 1 minute on the watch?

**TALK ABOUT IT**

**1.** How many seconds long was your estimate of 1 minute?

**2.** Was your estimate too short, too long, or just right?

Lengths of time can be recorded using only one unit or using two or more units.

1 unit: 83 s      2 units: 1 min 23 s

You can change a measurement from one time unit to another.

| Units of Time |
| --- |
| 1 day (d) = 24 hours (h) |
| 1 hour = 60 minutes (min) |
| 1 minute = 60 seconds (s) |

200 s → 3 min 20s
200 − 60 = 140
    − 60 =   80
    − 60 =   20

You can subtract 3 groups of 60 from 200 with 20 remaining.

4 h 8 min → 248 min
Find the number of minutes in 4 h. Then add minutes.
    4 × 60 = 240
and 8 more make 248.

**TRY IT OUT**

Give the missing numbers.

**1.** 110 s = ▦ min ▦ s

**2.** 304 s = ▦ min ▦ s

**3.** 25 h = ▦ d ▦ h

**4.** 5 min 9 s = ▦ s

**5.** 2 h 30 min = ▦ min

**6.** 2 d 12 h = ▦ h

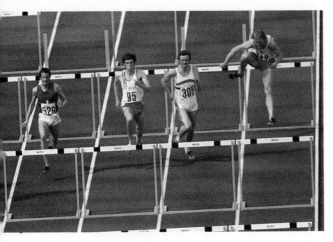

Give time in seconds only.

### River Road Race

| Name | Time |
|------|------|
| **1.** Enders | 2 min 23 s |
| **2.** Fong | 1 min 54 s |
| **3.** Gates | 3 min 18 s |
| **4.** Hastings | 4 min 2 s |

Give time in minutes and seconds.

### Lucky Lake Race

| Name | Time |
|------|------|
| **5.** Andrews | 118 s |
| **6.** Brown | 135 s |
| **7.** Conway | 152 s |
| **8.** Diaz | 184 s |

Give time in hours and minutes.

### Fun Run

| Name | Time |
|------|------|
| **9.** Ito | 115 min |
| **10.** Jacobs | 183 min |
| **11.** Klein | 139 min |
| **12.** Lopez | 242 min |

Give time in minutes only.

### Run in the Sun

| Name | Time |
|------|------|
| **13.** Moore | 3 h 14 min |
| **14.** Nawaz | 2 h 37 min |
| **15.** Olson | 4 h 1 min |
| **16.** Paris | 1 h 59 min |

## APPLY

### MATH REASONING

Which of these amounts of time—1 day, 2 days, or 3 days—is the best approximation for these numbers of hours?

**17.** 50 hours    **18.** 27 hours    **19.** 40 hours    **20.** 75 hours

### PROBLEM SOLVING

**21.** Gregory's time in last year's cross country race was 123 min. This year his time for the race was 1 h 59 min. Did he beat his old time?

**22. Health and Fitness Data Bank** In what years were the winning Olympic times less than 120 s in the women's 800 m run? See page 475.

### ▶ MENTAL MATH

Use mental math to find the amount of **elapsed time.**

**23.** While training for a marathon race, Peggy ran from 8:35 a.m. until 11:50 a.m. How long did she run in hours and minutes?

**24.** Peggy stayed with her grandparents from 11:10 a.m. to 5:30 p.m. How long was she there?

DATA BANK

*More Practice, page 507, set C*

# Problem Solving
## Using Data from a Thermometer

UNDERSTAND
ANALYZE DATA
PLAN
ESTIMATE
SOLVE
EXAMINE

### LEARN ABOUT IT

Scientists use degrees Celsius (0°C) to record temperatures above and below zero. The temperature 15°C is read "fifteen degrees Celsius above zero." The temperature −11°C is read "eleven degrees Celsius below zero."

Scientists in very cold places often use thermometers with ethyl alcohol in them instead of mercury. Ethyl alcohol freezes at −150°C. How do you read and write the temperature at which mercury freezes?

boiling point of water (100° C)

Barrow, AK 11 a.m. (5° C)
Freezing point of water (0° C)
Barrow, AK 2 p.m. (⁻9° C)
Barrow, AK 8 p.m. (⁻25° C)
Barrow, AK 11 p.m. (⁻33° C)

freezing point of mercury (⁻40° C)

above zero

zero

below zero

First I'll find zero on the thermometer.

Then I'll find how many degrees above or below zero.

Mercury freezes at −40°C.

Zero is the freezing point.

Mercury freezes at forty degrees Celsius below zero. I can write ⁻40°C.

### TRY IT OUT

1. Lorraine recorded the temperatures in one day in Barrow, Alaska. Some of her measurements are shown on the thermometer above. What was the temperature at 2 p.m.?

2. What was the temperature in Barrow at 8 p.m.?

3. What temperature did Lorraine record at 11 p.m.?

4. What was the highest temperature Lorraine recorded? When did she record it?

Solve. Use any problem solving strategy.

**1.** Nitrogen gas becomes a liquid at about −147°C. To study liquid nitrogen, Mr. Dodge divided his class of 35 students into 7 groups. There were the same number of students in each group. How many students were in each group?

**2.** One day in January, the temperature in Singapore was 3.3 degrees hotter than 10 times the temperature in Moscow. The temperature in Moscow was 2.75°C. What was the temperature in Singapore?

**3.** Geri made ice cubes of different colors and shapes for her party. She froze blue, green, red, yellow, and purple ice cubes. The shapes were square, hearts, and spheres. How many choices of different ice cubes did she have?

**4.** The thermometer shows the average summer temperature in Florida. This is 3 times higher than the average summer temperature in Iceland. What is the average summer temperature in Iceland?

**5.** One freezing weekend, Jeremy skied at two different ski areas. The first area had mountains as high as 1,981 m. The second had mountains 976 m higher. About what was the height of the mountains at the second ski area?

**6.** The Garcia family's medical thermometer measures temperatures as high as 41°C. Their scientific thermometer can measure temperatures about 9.75 times as high. About how many degrees can the scientific thermometer measure?

**7.** Jong lives in Dallas, Texas. He kept track of the high temperature for the first day of the month for 4 months. How many degrees difference was there between the high temperatures August 1 and November 1?

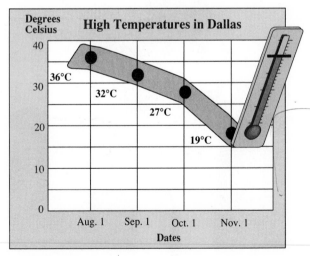

**8. Thinking About Your Solution** The temperature at 6:00 a.m. was 10°C. It rose 32 degrees by noon. It rose another 17 degrees by 2 p.m. It dropped 59 degrees by 8 p.m. What was the temperature at 8 p.m.?

**A.** Solve.

**B.** Write your answer in a complete sentence.

**C.** Write a description of how you solved the problem.

**D.** Name the strategy or strategies you used to solve it.

# Data Collection and Analysis
## Group Decision Making

UNDERSTAND
ANALYZE DATA
PLAN
ESTIMATE
SOLVE
EXAMINE

**Doing an Investigation**
**Group Skill:**
Explain and Summarize

### Investigation

Can you predict how high a ball will bounce if it is dropped from 1 meter or 3 meters? You can do an **investigation** to find out if there is a relationship between how far a ball is dropped and how high it bounces.

### Collecting Data

1. You are going to drop a ball from different heights and measure how high it bounces. Your group will need a ball and a measuring tape or stick. Discuss with your group how you will measure the height the ball is dropped and the height of the bounce.

2. Drop the ball from at least six different heights and measure how high it bounces. You may want to find the average of two bounces from each height and round to the nearest whole unit. Record the data in a table like the one below.

| Height Dropped | Height Bounced (average of two tries) |
|---|---|
| 50 cm | 12 cm |
| 100 cm | 28 cm |
| 150 cm | 37 cm |

**3.** You and your group make a line graph using the data in your table. Adjust the scales on the graph so that the largest and smallest measurements in your table fit on the graph. Show a point on your graph for each pair of measurements in your table.

**4.** Write a summary of your investigation procedures and your results. Include a description of any pattern you observed. How did you make your measurements? What do you notice about your graph?

**5.** Make some predictions. Do you think there is a maximum height the ball will bounce? How high do you think the ball would bounce if you dropped it 10 m? Be prepared to tell how you made your predictions.

_____Title_____

Height of Bounce in Centimeters

40 30 20 10 0

50  100  150  __  __  __

Height Dropped in _____

# Wrap Up

## Choosing Metric Units

Choose answers from the list at the right.

1. Write three units that measure length in order from least to greatest.

2. Write two units that measure volume.

3. Write two units that measure area.

4. Write two units that measure mass.

square meter
centimeter
cubic meter
kilogram
meter
cubic centimeter
gram
kilometer
square centimeter

## Sometimes, Always, Never

Complete each statement by writing **sometimes, always,** or **never.** Explain your choice.

5. When you change from a smaller metric unit to a larger one, the number of units __?__ increases.

6. If two rectangles have the same perimeter, they __?__ have the same area.

7. To change a larger unit of time to a smaller unit, you __?__ multiply twice.

## Project

Choose a model that you think represents a volume of about 1 cm$^3$. Then find an object that is about ten times greater in length, width, and height. What is its approximate volume? Find and list some objects that you estimate to have this volume.

Try to find some larger objects that are about ten times greater than this in length, width, and height. What is their approximate volume? Find and list some objects that you estimate to have this volume.

# POWER PRACTICE/TEST

## Part 1   Understanding

Select the most appropriate unit for each measure.
**mm, cm, m, km, mL, L, g, kg**

1. Mass of a turkey: 7 __?__

2. Amount of ink in a pen: 2 __?__

3. Width of tip of shoelace: 2 __?__

4. Height of a giraffe: 6.4 __?__

5. Length of 12 city blocks: 1 __?__

6. Mass of a nickel: 5 __?__

7. Width of index finger: 1 __?__

8. Amount of water a sink will hold: 10 __?__

About how many hours is:

9. 135 min?

10. 350 min?

## Part 2   Skills

Give the missing numbers.

11. 324 cm = ▓ m

12. 42.6 cm = ▓ mm

13. 500 m = ▓ km

14. 6.7 L = ▓ mL

15. 3.6 kg = ▓ g

16. 164 s = ▓ min ▓ s

17. 468 mL = ▓ L

18. 3,125 g = ▓ kg

19. 4 m 28 cm = ▓ cm

20. 387 min = ▓ h ▓ min

## Part 3   Applications

21. Greg asked Marilyn for change for a half dollar. How many different coin combinations are possible? Do not use pennies.

22. **Challenge.** The highest temperature ever recorded was in North Africa. The temperature was 1°C hotter than 2 times the temperature on an average summer day. The temperature on an average summer day is 28.4°C. What was the highest recorded temperature?

# ENRICHMENT
## Time Zones

Because the earth rotates on its axis, the sun is overhead at different times for different parts of the earth. The earth has been divided into 24 different standard time zones, since there are 24 hours in a day. The time in each zone is one hour more or one hour less than the time in the next time zone.

This map shows the six time zones of the United States. Use the map to answer the questions below.

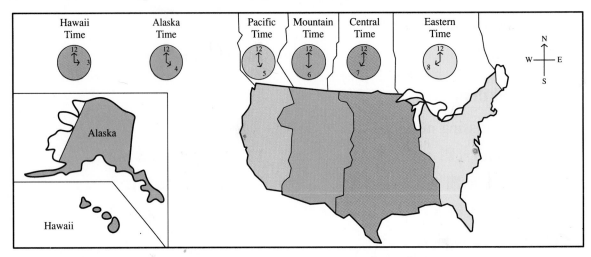

1. What happens to time as you travel east across the time zones?

2. What happens to time as you travel west across time zones?

Suppose it is noon Alaska Time.

3. What is the Central Time?

4. What is the Mountain Time?

5. What is the Pacific Time?

6. What is the Hawaii Time?

Suppose it is 3:30 p.m. Mountain Time.

7. What is the Eastern Time?

8. What is the Alaska Time?

9. What is the Pacific Time?

10. What is the Central Time?

11. A plane left Washington, D.C., at 11 a.m. Eastern Time and arrived in Los Angeles at 1 p.m. Pacific Time. How long did the flight take?

12. A flight from New Orleans to Honolulu takes 7 hours. If the plane leaves at 10 a.m. Central Time, what would be the time in Hawaii when it arrives?

176

# CUMULATIVE REVIEW

Use rounding to estimate.

**1.** 5,827 − 1,216

   **A.** 5,000 − 1,000 = 4,000

   **B.** 6,000 − 2,000 = 4,000

   **C.** 5,000 − 2,000 = 3,000

   **D.** 6,000 − 1,000 = 5,000

**2.** 1.247 + 6.8 + 15.91

   **A.** 1 + 7 + 16 = 24

   **B.** 1 + 6 + 15 = 22

   **C.** 2 + 6 + 16 = 24

   **D.** 1 + 7 + 15 = 23

Use this graph for questions 3–4.

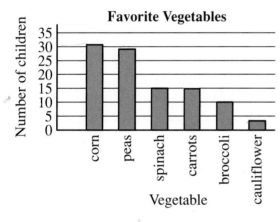

**3.** Which two vegetables are liked the most?

   **A.** spinach and carrots

   **B.** corn and peas

   **C.** peas and spinach

   **D.** carrots and broccoli

**4.** About how many children were questioned?

   **A.** 50  **B.** 100  **C.** 150  **D.** 200

Multiply.

**5.** 600 × 500

   **A.** 3,000     **B.** 30,000

   **C.** 300,000   **D.** 3,000,000

**6.**   542
   ×   4

   **A.** 546

   **B.** 2,068

   **C.** 2,168

   **D.** 20,168

**7.**   27
   × 85

   **A.** 2,295

   **B.** 351

   **C.** 112

   **D.** 2,315

**8.** Estimate using compatible numbers.

   246 + 98 + 51 + 107 + 62 + 41

   **A.** 400  **B.** 500  **C.** 600  **D.** 700

**9.** To multiply 476 × 8 using the distributive property and mental math:

   **A.** multiply the 4 by 8, add 76.

   **B.** multiply 400, 70, and 6 by 8, then add.

   **C.** multiply 476 by 10, and subtract 16.

   **D.** round 476 to 500 and multiply by 8.

**10.** Each of 8 teams in a volleyball tournament is scheduled to play every other team once. How many games are scheduled?

   **A.** 64  **B.** 28  **C.** 56  **D.** 15

# 7

## DIVISION: WHOLE NUMBERS AND DECIMALS

**THEME: TRANSPORTATION**

**M**ATH AND SOCIAL STUDIES

**DATA BANK**

Use the Social Studies Data Bank on page 482 to answer the questions.

1 What was the total cost of building the National Road from Cumberland, Maryland, to Wheeling, West Virginia?

**2** About how long would it have taken a stagecoach in 1870 to travel from Cumberland to Wheeling on the National Road?

**3** During which 30-year period did the traveling speed of a car increase the most? How much greater was the speed per hour at the end of that period than at the beginning of the period?

**4** **Using Critical Thinking** Compare the line graphs showing traveling speeds on railroads and on highways. How are the graphs different for the years after 1960? What may have caused the difference?

Thanks to recent advances in railroad technology, some of today's passenger trains can reach speeds of 170 mph.

179

# Mental Math
## Special Quotients

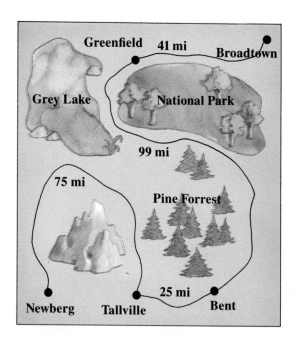

### LEARN ABOUT IT

Quotients that involve basic division facts are usually easy to find using mental math.

**EXPLORE** **Solve to Understand**

The Pedalpushers Bike Club was planning a 4-day tour from Newberg to Broadtown. How many miles would they have to ride each day to get to Broadtown if they rode the same distance each day?

### TALK ABOUT IT

1. How can you use mental math to find the total distance from Newberg to Broadtown?

2. Since the bikers will travel the same distance each day, what operation should be used to find the distance each day?

You can use basic division facts to find larger quotients.

**■ Here is how to do it.**

Problem: 240 ÷ 4
Look for a basic fact.        **240 ÷ 4**
Solve the basic fact.        24 ÷ 4 = 6
Attach the zeros.        60

**■ Here is why it works.**

240 is 24 tens. ("tens" means 1 zero)
24 tens ÷ 4 = 6 tens
6 tens is 60.

You can use multiplication to check. 60 × 4 = 240
The club would have to travel 60 miles each day.

## Other Examples

$24 ÷ 4 = 6$
$2,400 ÷ 4 = 600$

$40 ÷ 5 = 8$
$4,000 ÷ 5 = 800$

### TRY IT OUT

Use mental math to find these quotients.

**1.** 420 ÷ 6     **2.** 80 ÷ 2     **3.** 3,200 ÷ 8     **4.** 300 ÷ 5     **5.** 7,200 ÷ 8

Use mental math to find the quotients.

| | | | |
|---|---|---|---|
| **1.** $210 \div 3$ | **2.** $540 \div 6$ | **3.** $160 \div 8$ | **4.** $350 \div 7$ |
| **5.** $1,200 \div 3$ | **6.** $5,400 \div 9$ | **7.** $4,200 \div 6$ | **8.** $3,000 \div 5$ |
| **9.** $16,000 \div 4$ | **10.** $32,000 \div 8$ | **11.** $27,000 \div 9$ | **12.** $48,000 \div 8$ |

**13.** Find the quotient of 420 and 7.  **14.** What is 6,400 divided by 8?

**APPLY**

**MATH REASONING**

Write $>$, $<$, or $=$ for each ▦.

**15.** $2,800 \div 4$ ▦ $10 \times 70$

**16.** $30 \times 20$ ▦ $480 \div 6$

**17.** $8,000 \div 8$ ▦ $800 \times 10$

**18.** $3,500 \div 7$ ▦ $100 \times 50$

**PROBLEM SOLVING**

**19.** The Great Outdoors Bike Club made a 300-mile trip in 6 days. They rode the same number of miles each day. How far did they ride each day?

**20.** When Leroy, Rick, and Gwen left school one day, each was wearing a bicycle helmet that belonged to one of the others. Each was also wearing a jacket that belonged to someone other than the owner of the helmet. Rick had on Gwen's helmet. Copy and complete the table at the right.

| | helmet | jacket |
|---|---|---|
| Leroy | | |
| Rick | Gwen's | |
| Gwen | | |

▶ **USING CRITICAL THINKING   Discover a Pattern**

**21.** Look for patterns in Set A. Copy and complete Set B.

Set A: $28 \div 4 = 7$, $280 \div 4 = 70$, $2,800 \div 4 = 700$, $28,000 \div 4 = 7,000$

Set B: $32 \div 8 = 4$, $320 \div 8 =$ ▦ , $3,200 \div 8 =$ ▦ , $32,000 \div 8 =$ ▦

Look at the number of zeros in the dividend and the number of zeros in the quotient in the examples above. Can you make a **generalization** (a statement that holds true in many cases) about the number of zeros in the dividend and the number of zeros in the quotient? Do you think your generalization works for all cases?

*More Practice, page 507, set D*

# Estimating Quotients
## Rounding and Compatible Numbers

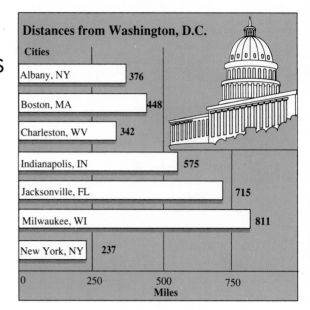

**Distances from Washington, D.C.**

| Cities | Miles |
|---|---|
| Albany, NY | 376 |
| Boston, MA | 448 |
| Charleston, WV | 342 |
| Indianapolis, IN | 575 |
| Jacksonville, FL | 715 |
| Milwaukee, WI | 811 |
| New York, NY | 237 |

You can substitute compatible numbers to estimate quotients.

**EXPLORE** **Examine the Data**

In the early 1800s travelers often rode on stagecoaches. On good roads stagecoaches could travel 8 miles per hour. Think about how many hours it would take a stagecoach to travel from Washington, D.C., to Charleston, W.V.

### TALK ABOUT IT

1. What data from the paragraph above and what data from the graph do you need in order to find about how long it would take a stagecoach to travel from Washington to Charleston?

2. Can you easily use rounding and mental math to estimate the number of hours the trip would take?

Rounding 342 to the nearest ten or the nearest hundred would not be very helpful, because $340 \div 8$ and $300 \div 8$ are not easily solved using mental math. You can more easily solve this problem by replacing 342 with a number that can easily be divided by 8.

■ Here is one way to estimate $342 \div 8$.

Substitute a compatible number for 342.

$$\downarrow$$
$$320 \div 8 = 40$$

The trip would take a stagecoach about 40 hours.

### TRY IT OUT

Estimate how many hours it would take a stagecoach to travel from Washington to:

1. Albany          2. Boston          3. Indianapolis          4. Jacksonville

Which would be a better choice for estimating the quotient?

1. 138 ÷ 8     **A.** 80 ÷ 8     **B.** 160 ÷ 8

2. 168 ÷ 5     **A.** 150 ÷ 5     **B.** 200 ÷ 5

3. 405 ÷ 7     **A.** 350 ÷ 7     **B.** 420 ÷ 7

Estimate each quotient by substituting compatible numbers.

4. 147 ÷ 3     **5.** 254 ÷ 5     **6.** 556 ÷ 7     **7.** 244 ÷ 6

8. 163 ÷ 2     **9.** 362 ÷ 4     **10.** 636 ÷ 8     **11.** 4,849 ÷ 6

12. 1,243 ÷ 3     **13.** 3,152 ÷ 4     **14.** 7,241 ÷ 9     **15.** 535 ÷ 9

16. 6,279 ÷ 9     **17.** 4,854 ÷ 7     **18.** 4,189 ÷ 7     **19.** 5,598 ÷ 6

**MATH REASONING**

Write > or < to show whether the exact quotient is greater than or less than the given estimate.

20. 3,473 ÷ 5    Estimate: 3,500 ÷ 5 = 700
21. 367 ÷ 7    Estimate: 350 ÷ 7 = 50
22. 6,575 ÷ 8    Estimate: 6,400 ÷ 8 = 800

**PROBLEM SOLVING**

23. Annie took a train from Washington to New York. The train made a few stops but got to New York in 3 hours. About how many miles per hour did the train travel?

24. **Social Studies Data Bank** About how many hours would it take to travel the 342 miles from Washington to Charleston in a Model T car of 1930? See page 482.

DATA BANK

Give the unit—**mm, cm, dm,** or **m**—that is most reasonable.

25. length of an ant: 6 __?__    **26.** height of a tree: 7 __?__    **27.** width of your foot: 6 __?__

Give the number for each ▦ .

28. 265 cm = ▦ m     **29.** 6.95 m = ▦ cm     **30.** 11 mm = ▦ cm

# Dividing Whole Numbers
## Making the Connection

We can understand the steps in division by using place value blocks and thinking about division as sharing.

**EXPLORE** **Use Place Value Blocks**
Work with a partner.
- One partner uses place value blocks (tens and ones) to show a two-digit number greater than 50.
- The other partner chooses 2, 3, 4, or 5 as the number of groups into which the blocks are to be divided.
- Together the partners divide the blocks into the chosen number of groups so that each group has the same number. Record the number in each group and the number left over.
- Repeat this activity several times. Try it once using blocks with the value of a three-digit number.

**TALK ABOUT IT**

1. Did you start with the tens or the ones blocks when you divided them into groups? Does it make a difference? Explain.
2. When did you have to trade? Give an example that shows when you have to trade.
3. When you divide blocks into groups, is it possible that you may not be able to place all of the blocks you started with in one of the groups?

You have divided blocks into groups and recorded the number in each group and the number left over. Now you will learn how to use symbols to record those steps. Here is how to divide 72 into 3 groups.

| **What You Do** | **What You Record** |
| --- | --- |

Show 72 as 7 tens and 2 ones. Show 3 groups.

$3\overline{)72}$

How many tens can be placed in each group?

$$\begin{array}{r} 2 \\ 3\overline{)72} \\ 6 \\ \hline 1 \end{array}$$

← 2 tens in each group

← 6 tens shared in all

← 1 ten left

Can you trade 1 ten so that it can be divided into 3 groups?

$$\begin{array}{r} 2 \\ 3\overline{)72} \\ 6 \\ \hline 12 \end{array}$$

← Bring down the ones.

How many ones can be placed in each group?

$$\begin{array}{r} 24 \\ 3\overline{)72} \\ 6 \\ \hline 12 \\ 12 \\ \hline 0 \end{array}$$

← 4 ones in each group

← 12 in all groups

← 0 left to be shared

**TRY IT OUT**

Find each quotient using place value blocks. Record your work using symbols.

**1.** 24 ÷ 2     **2.** 36 ÷ 2     **3.** 45 ÷ 3     **4.** 24 ÷ 4

Each picture shows the result *after* dividing. Use the multiplication fact to give the original division problem.

**5.**   　$2 \times 24 = 48$

**6.**  　$3 \times 12 = 36$

185

# Dividing
## 2- and 3-digit Quotients

Detroit to
Philadelphia
580 mi

**EXPLORE** **Analyze the Process**

Jamie flew the distance in 4 h. She traveled the
same number of miles each hour. How many
miles did she travel each hour?

She traveled the same distance each hour, so we divide.

| Divide hundreds. | Divide tens. | Divide ones. |
|---|---|---|
| $\begin{array}{r} 1 \\ 4\overline{)580} \\ -4 \\ \hline 1 \end{array}$ ■ Divide. ■ Multiply. ■ Subtract. ■ Compare. | $\begin{array}{r} 14 \\ 4\overline{)580} \\ 4\downarrow \\ \hline 18 \\ 16 \\ \hline 2 \end{array}$ ■ Bring down. ■ Divide. ■ Multiply. ■ Subtract. ■ Compare. | $\begin{array}{r} 145 \\ 4\overline{)580} \\ 4 \\ \hline 18 \\ 16\downarrow \\ \hline 20 \\ 20 \\ \hline 0 \end{array}$ ■ Bring down. ■ Divide. ■ Multiply. ■ Subtract. ■ Compare. |

**TALK ABOUT IT**

1. In the first step of the solution, where did the 4, written
   below the 5, come from?
2. In the second step, what number was divided by 4 to get
   the 4 in the quotient?

**Other Examples**

**A** $\begin{array}{r} 16\ R2 \\ 5\overline{)82} \\ 5 \\ \hline 32 \\ 30 \\ \hline 2 \end{array}$

**B** $\begin{array}{r} 21 \\ 4\overline{)84} \\ 8 \\ \hline 04 \\ 4 \\ \hline 0 \end{array}$

**C** $\begin{array}{r} 47\ R1 \\ 2\overline{)95} \\ 8 \\ \hline 15 \\ 14 \\ \hline 1 \end{array}$

Divide.

**1.** $3\overline{)413}$     **2.** $6\overline{)71}$     **3.** $3\overline{)827}$     **4.** $7\overline{)935}$     **5.** $2\overline{)768}$

Divide.

1. $3\overline{)69}$
2. $5\overline{)55}$
3. $2\overline{)48}$
4. $4\overline{)84}$
5. $3\overline{)93}$

6. $4\overline{)64}$
7. $2\overline{)93}$
8. $6\overline{)87}$
9. $7\overline{)91}$
10. $4\overline{)87}$

11. $4\overline{)57}$
12. $3\overline{)53}$
13. $8\overline{)90}$
14. $4\overline{)925}$
15. $8\overline{)976}$

16. $4\overline{)648}$
17. $3\overline{)639}$
18. $3\overline{)648}$
19. $8\overline{)915}$
20. $3\overline{)711}$

21. Find the quotient when 675 is the dividend and 5 is the divisor.

Use mental math to find each quotient:

22. $2\overline{)80}$
23. $4\overline{)3,200}$
24. $3\overline{)270}$
25. $5\overline{)3,000}$
26. $7\overline{)490}$

## APPLY

### MATH REASONING

Without dividing, tell which quotient is greater.

27. $4\overline{)684}$ or $4\overline{)864}$
28. $4\overline{)684}$ or $2\overline{)684}$
29. $5\overline{)810}$ or $6\overline{)576}$

### PROBLEM SOLVING

30. Rosita sailed her boat and swam a total of 12 h. She sailed twice as many hours as she swam. How long did she sail?

31. Renaldo flew 720 miles in 2 days. He flew the same distance each day. How many miles did he fly each day?

▶ **MENTAL MATH**

You can break apart a number to find the quotient. Use the method shown at the right to find these quotients.

$126 \div 3$
Think: $120 \div 3$ plus $6 \div 3$
$\downarrow$         $\downarrow$
$40$   plus   $2$   is 42.

32. $155 \div 5$
33. $184 \div 2$
34. $248 \div 4$
35. $189 \div 3$

*More Practice, page 508, set A*

# Dividing
## Deciding Where to Start

### EXPLORE  Analyze the Process

Sharif and 3 friends took a bus to summer camp. The total cost of the 4 tickets was $392. The price of each ticket was the same. How much did each ticket cost?

Since each ticket costs the same amount, we can divide to find the cost of each. Here is how.

| Decide where to start. | Divide the tens. | Divide the ones. |
|---|---|---|
| $4\overline{)392}$ <br><br> 4 > 3  Not enough hundreds <br> 4 > 39  Divide the tens first. | $\begin{array}{r} 9 \\ 4\overline{)392} \\ 36 \\ \hline 3 \end{array}$  ■ Divide. <br> ■ Multiply. <br> ■ Subtract. <br> ■ Compare. | $\begin{array}{r} 98 \\ 4\overline{)392} \\ 36\downarrow \\ \hline 32 \\ 32 \\ \hline 0 \end{array}$  ■ Bring down. <br> ■ Divide. <br> ■ Multiply. <br> ■ Subtract. <br> ■ Compare. |

### TALK ABOUT IT

1. If you have three $100 bills, can you divide them into 4 groups without trading?
2. What two numbers can be multiplied to get the 36 in the second step?

### Other Examples

**A**
$$\begin{array}{r} 58 \text{ R4} \\ 8\overline{)468} \\ 40 \\ \hline 68 \\ 64 \\ \hline 4 \end{array}$$

**B**
$$\begin{array}{r} 13 \text{ R2} \\ 5\overline{)67} \\ 5 \\ \hline 17 \\ 15 \\ \hline 2 \end{array}$$

Check by multiplying:

$$\begin{array}{r} 13 \\ \times\ 5 \\ \hline 65 \end{array} \qquad \begin{array}{r} 65 \\ +\ 2 \\ \hline 67 \end{array} ✔$$

Divide. Check by multiplying.

1. $8\overline{)168}$      2. $3\overline{)435}$      3. $5\overline{)467}$      4. $6\overline{)296}$

Where do you start dividing? Answer **hundreds** or **tens.**

1. $6\overline{)347}$    2. $3\overline{)474}$    3. $4\overline{)228}$    4. $6\overline{)770}$    5. $4\overline{)295}$

Divide. Check by using multiplication.

6. $5\overline{)425}$    7. $9\overline{)327}$    8. $6\overline{)411}$    9. $3\overline{)257}$    10. $7\overline{)119}$

11. $6\overline{)176}$    12. $5\overline{)184}$    13. $3\overline{)179}$    14. $4\overline{)476}$    15. $8\overline{)296}$

16. $5\overline{)423}$    17. $7\overline{)371}$    18. $5\overline{)197}$    19. $8\overline{)539}$    20. $8\overline{)227}$

Use mental math to find each quotient.

21. $7\overline{)147}$    22. $5\overline{)520}$    23. $3\overline{)927}$    24. $8\overline{)324}$    25. $6\overline{)234}$

**APPLY**

**MATH REASONING**

26. Make up a division problem where the quotient is 75.

27. Make up a division problem where the divisor is 4 and the remainder is 1.

**PROBLEM SOLVING**

28. Camp supplies for 4 girls cost $272. Each paid the same. What was the cost for each girl?

29. **Data Hunt**   Find the cost of a tent that would hold five people. If the total cost was shared by five people how much would each pay?

30. **Unfinished Problem**   Write a question that you can solve using the data below. Then answer your question. At camp 168 girls were placed in 7 cabins. Each cabin could hold no more than 25 girls.

▶ **ALGEBRA**

We can write **numerical expressions** that name the same number as equations. For example, since $23 + 15$ and $40 - 2$ are both names for 38, we can write $23 + 15 = 40 - 2$. An equation means that both sides of the equal sign name the same number.

Copy and give the number for each ▦ .

31. $42 - 12 = 6 \times$ ▦    32. $18 \times 3 = 85 -$ ▦    33. $36 \div 6 =$ ▦ $\div 8$

*More Practice, page 508, Set B*

# Dividing
## Special Cases

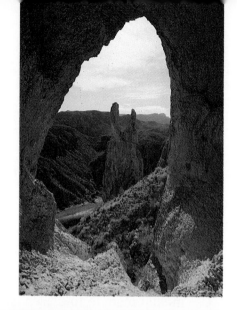

**EXPLORE** Analyze the Process

Ramon and his family are planning a trip to Big Bend National Park. They are allowing 6 days to make the 1,248 mile trip. If they travel the same distance each day, how many miles will they travel per day?

| Decide where to start. | Divide the hundreds. | Divide the tens. | Divide the ones. |
|---|---|---|---|
| $6\overline{)1,248}$ | $\begin{array}{r} 2\phantom{000} \\ 6\overline{)1,248} \\ \underline{12}\phantom{00} \\ 0\phantom{00} \end{array}$ ■ Divide.<br>■ Multiply.<br>■ Subtract.<br>■ Compare. | $\begin{array}{r} 20\phantom{0} \\ 6\overline{)1,248} \\ \underline{12}\!\downarrow\phantom{0} \\ 04\phantom{0} \\ \underline{0}\phantom{00} \\ 4\phantom{00} \end{array}$ ■ Bring down.<br>■ Divide.<br>■ Multiply.<br>■ Subtract.<br>■ Compare. | $\begin{array}{r} 208 \\ 6\overline{)1,248} \\ \underline{12}\phantom{00} \\ 04\phantom{0} \\ \underline{0}\!\downarrow\phantom{0} \\ 48 \\ \underline{48} \\ 0 \end{array}$ ■ Bring down.<br>■ Divide.<br>■ Multiply.<br>■ Subtract.<br>■ Compare |

$6 > 1$   Not enough thousands
$6 < 12$ Divide the hundreds.

**TALK ABOUT IT**

1. Why is the first digit in the quotient above the 2?
2. Use estimation to check the computed quotient.

**Other Examples**

A
$\begin{array}{r} 308 \\ 6\overline{)1,848} \\ \underline{18}\phantom{00} \\ 04\phantom{0} \\ \underline{0}\phantom{0} \\ 48 \\ \underline{48} \\ 0 \end{array}$

B
$\begin{array}{r} 316 \\ 7\overline{)2,212} \\ \underline{21}\phantom{00} \\ 11\phantom{0} \\ \underline{7}\phantom{0} \\ 42 \\ \underline{42} \\ 0 \end{array}$

C
$\begin{array}{r} 860 \text{ R5} \\ 9\overline{)7,745} \\ \underline{72}\phantom{00} \\ 54\phantom{0} \\ \underline{54}\phantom{0} \\ 05 \\ \underline{0} \\ 5 \end{array}$

Divide.

1. $6\overline{)1,836}$
2. $4\overline{)1,280}$
3. $3\overline{)1,390}$
4. $5\overline{)4,047}$

190

Divide. Check using multiplication.

**1.** $3\overline{)618}$ **2.** $4\overline{)432}$ **3.** $3\overline{)213}$ **4.** $5\overline{)205}$ **5.** $7\overline{)721}$

**6.** $4\overline{)363}$ **7.** $5\overline{)402}$ **8.** $6\overline{)965}$ **9.** $9\overline{)920}$ **10.** $4\overline{)835}$

**11.** $7\overline{)2,128}$ **12.** $8\overline{)6,456}$ **13.** $9\overline{)2,727}$ **14.** $7\overline{)2,660}$ **15.** $2\overline{)1,004}$

**16.** 1,632 divided by 4 is what number?

Find each quotient using **mental math.**

**17.** $150 \div 3$ **18.** $540 \div 6$ **19.** $2,400 \div 8$ **20.** $48,000 \div 6$ **21.** $42,000 \div 7$

APPLY

**MATH REASONING**

Use **estimation** to tell whether the exact quotient is less than or greater than the given number.

**22.** $6\overline{)1,920}$ <300 or > 300? **23.** $5\overline{)2,040}$ < 400 or > 400?

**PROBLEM SOLVING**

**24.** Francine traveled with her family to Olympic National Park. The 1,664-mile trip took them 8 days. If they traveled the same distance each day, how many miles did they travel per day?

**25. Social Studies Data Bank** Casey rode his bike along the original route of the National Road, from Cumberland to Wheeling and back. He was on the road for 5 days. How many miles per day did he ride? See page 482.

▶ **CALCULATOR**

On a calculator $3,789 \div 8$ gives 473.625. The remainder is shown as a decimal. Some calculators have a special key that gives the remainder as a whole number. For other calculators you can use this method to find the remainder.

- Multiply the quotient, 473, by the divisor, 8: $473 \times 8 = 3,784$.
- Subtract this product from the dividend, 3,789: $3,789 - 3,784 = 5$. The remainder is 5.

Find the quotient and whole number remainder using a calculator.

**26.** $6\overline{)4,965}$ **27.** $9\overline{)6,721}$ **28.** $7\overline{)5,529}$ **29.** $8\overline{)2,231}$

# Finding Averages

**LEARN ABOUT IT**

**EXPLORE  Use a Paper Model**

Work in groups. Cut out four strips of paper. Use these lengths: 5 in., 5 in., 6 in., 8 in. Tape all four pieces together end to end. Fold the long strip in half. Then fold it in half again. Now open the strip. The fold lines show four new sections, each the same length. Measure the length of one of the new sections.

**TALK ABOUT IT**

1.  What is the length of each new section?

2.  Is the length of the new section less than 8 in.? Is the length greater than 5 in.?

3.  Could the length of a new section be less than 5 in.? Explain your answer.

The length of each new section above is the average of the four numbers. Here is how to find the **average** of a group of numbers.

Problem: Find the average of 385, 402, and 416.

| | | | |
|---|---|---|---|
| Add. | 385<br>402<br>+416<br>1,203 | → | Divide the sum by the number of addends. | → | $\dfrac{401}{3\overline{)1,203}}$ | The quotient is the average. |

**TRY IT OUT**

Find the average of each set of numbers.

1.  26; 22; 33

2.  456; 275; 382

3.  17; 24; 28; 31; 20

4.  762; 849; 693; 804

5.  2,064; 3,488; 4,656; 7,624

6.  3; 6; 4; 5; 9; 9

7.  39; 58; 76; 43; 67; 77

8.  511; 584; 652; 871; 702

9.  46; 35; 54; 40; 60

10. 535; 410; 613; 512; 485

11. 1,273; 1,477; 975; 833; 1,002

192

# POWER PRACTICE/QUIZ

Divide using mental math.

**1.** $360 \div 9$    **2.** $280 \div 7$    **3.** $4,500 \div 5$    **4.** $5,600 \div 8$

**5.** $4,000 \div 8$    **6.** $420 \div 6$    **7.** $2,400 \div 3$    **8.** $490 \div 7$

**9.** $560 \div 7$    **10.** $2,500 \div 5$    **11.** $810 \div 9$    **12.** $6,400 \div 8$

**13.** $2,700 \div 9$    **14.** $720 \div 8$    **15.** $630 \div 7$    **16.** $2,000 \div 4$

Estimate each quotient.

**17.** $465 \div 6$    **18.** $217 \div 5$    **19.** $199 \div 3$    **20.** $739 \div 8$

**21.** $800 \div 9$    **22.** $550 \div 7$    **23.** $327 \div 4$    **24.** $113 \div 2$

**25.** $445 \div 5$    **26.** $315 \div 8$    **27.** $411 \div 7$    **28.** $261 \div 9$

Divide. Use multiplication or estimation to check.

**29.** $2\overline{)86}$    **30.** $3\overline{)376}$    **31.** $8\overline{)890}$    **32.** $4\overline{)324}$    **33.** $5\overline{)377}$

**34.** $8\overline{)108}$    **35.** $3\overline{)211}$    **36.** $7\overline{)274}$    **37.** $5\overline{)615}$    **38.** $8\overline{)700}$

**39.** $6\overline{)624}$    **40.** $8\overline{)875}$    **41.** $9\overline{)926}$    **42.** $7\overline{)85}$    **43.** $3\overline{)325}$

## PROBLEM SOLVING

**44.** David used place value blocks to show each of these division problems. For which of the problems did he have to trade tens for ones?

> **A.** $3\overline{)96}$    **B.** $7\overline{)42}$
> **C.** $4\overline{)52}$    **D.** $3\overline{)84}$

**45.** How can 32 students be divided into teams so that each team has either 5 or 6 players?

**46.** Saka and 2 friends washed 12 cars. They earned $5 for each car. If they shared the money equally, how much does each of them receive?

**47.** Paula's goal is to jog a total of 25 mi each week. She plans to reach her goal by jogging the same number of miles on each of the remaining days of the week. How many miles will she jog on each of those days?

| Paula's Jogging Record | | | | | | |
|---|---|---|---|---|---|---|
| Mon | Tues | Wed | Thu | Fri | Sat | Sun |
| 4 | 3 | 3 | 3 | ? | ? | ? |

193

# Problem Solving
## Interpreting Remainders

UNDERSTAND
ANALYZE DATA
PLAN
ESTIMATE
SOLVE
EXAMINE

**LEARN ABOUT IT**

Sometimes division does not give you the full answer to a problem. You may need to understand the meaning of a remainder. Think about the different ways you must interpret the remainders in the problems below.

There are 125 campers going to River Rafters Camp. They are riding to the camp in vans. Each van holds 9 campers. How many vans are needed?

At the rafting supplies store, Jeff put together some sets of life jackets. He had 119 jackets. He needed 8 jackets for each raft. For how many rafts could he put together a full set of life jackets?

$$
\begin{array}{r}
13 \text{ R8} \\
9\overline{)125} \\
9\phantom{0} \\
\hline
35 \\
27 \\
\hline
8 \\
\end{array}
$$

13 full vans are needed, but another is needed for the 8 remaining campers.

14 vans are needed.

$$
\begin{array}{r}
14 \text{ R7} \\
8\overline{)119} \\
8\phantom{0} \\
\hline
39 \\
32 \\
\hline
7 \\
\end{array}
$$

The remaining 7 jackets are not enough to make a full set.

He could put together a full set of life jackets for 14 rafts.

**TRY IT OUT**

1. Joel has $102 to buy rubber patch kits for the rafts. Each patch kit costs $9. How many patch kits can he buy?

2. At camp, no more than 7 rafting students ride with an instructor on each raft. How many rafts are needed for 131 students?

3. Each lunch table seats 14 campers. There were 158 campers for lunch one day. How many tables were needed?

4. The owner of the camp had $692 to spend for T-shirts for the campers. Each shirt cost $6. How many shirts could he buy?

Solve. Use any of the strategies.

1. There are 5 sessions at rafting camp. What was the average number of campers per session?

| Sessions at Camp | |
| --- | --- |
| Session | Attendance |
| 1 | 128 |
| 2 | 158 |
| 3 | 176 |
| 4 | 180 |
| 5 | 203 |

2. Mary has saved $80 for a rafting trip that costs $140. How much more money does she need?

3. Grip rope for the sides of a raft costs $4 for 10 ft. How much would 40 feet of grip rope cost?

4. Kerry, one of the campers, used up 12 rolls of film taking pictures of campers during the summer. There are 24 shots in each roll. One roll costs $4.79. How many pictures did she take?

5. In the display case at the rafting store, there are 42 stickers that cost $0.80 each and 28 stickers that cost $1.50 each. What would be the total cost of all of them?

6. One of the instructors bought juice for the rafting students. That day there were 203 students. The drinks came in 6-packs. How many packs did he need to get?

7. The rafting store has 136 sports caps for sale. The store manager wants to display as many as possible on the wall in rows of 9. How many rows of sports caps can there be?

8. **Thinking About Your Solution** Bev needs sneakers and socks. There are 3 colors of each: white, blue, and red. How many possible combinations of sneakers and socks can Bev buy?

   A. Solve.
   B. Write your answer in a complete sentence.
   C. Name the strategy or strategies you used to solve it.

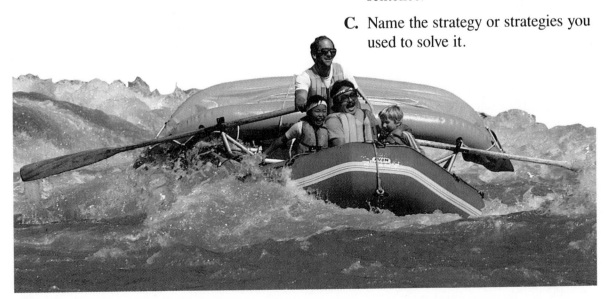

# Problem Solving
## Work Backward

UNDERSTAND
ANALYZE DATA
PLAN
ESTIMATE
SOLVE
EXAMINE

LEARN ABOUT IT

Some problems can be solved by
starting with a given number and
reversing the actions in the problem.
This problem solving strategy is
called **Work Backward.**

It often helps to make a flowchart
and a reverse flowchart for the problem.

Bo asked Deena how many inches long
Deena's pet iguana is. She said, "If you
subtract 10 from its length and then
double that difference, you will get 28."
How long is the iguana?

I can use what I know to make a flowchart.

Now I can work backward using a reverse flowchart.

Flowchart

Length? → -10 → x2 → 28

Reverse flowchart

Length 24 ← +10 ← ÷2 ← 28

The iguana is 24 in. long.

TRY IT OUT

Gabriela spent half of her money at the zoo's gift shop. She
spent half of what she had left on food at the zoo. She had
$1.06 left. How much money did she start out with?

- What part of her money did she spend
  at the zoo's gift shop?

- What part of the money she had left did
  she spend on food?

- Copy and complete the flowchart and
  reverse flowchart to help solve the
  problem.

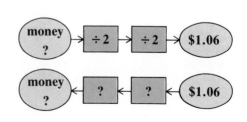

money ? → ÷2 → ÷2 → $1.06

money ? ← ? ← ? ← $1.06

196

Work backward to solve each problem.

1. Gino asked the woman who fed the puma at the zoo how old the puma was. She said, "If you multiply the puma's age in years by 12 and divide by 3, you get 44." How old is the puma?

2. When Jeremy's white mice had babies, he gave away half of them. Then he sold 6 to the pet store. He had 7 left. How many mice did he have to begin with?

## MIXED PRACTICE

Choose a strategy from the strategies list or use other strategies you know to solve these problems.

| Some Strategies | |
|---|---|
| Act Out | Guess and Check |
| Use Objects | Make a Table |
| Choose an Operation | Solve a Simpler Problem |
| Draw a Picture | Make an Organized List |
| Work Backward | |

3. Jake had 4 snakes. What was the average length of his snakes?

| Snake | Length (in.) |
|---|---|
| Boa Constrictor | 73 |
| Boa Constrictor | 68 |
| Rainbow Boa | 37 |
| Python | 66 |

4. An elephant's heart beats 25 times per minute. How many times does it beat in 24 hours?

5. Donna has a total of 30 pet fish and birds. She has 8 more fish than birds. How many birds does she have?

6. If you add the speed of a cheetah to the speed of a wildebeest and then divide by 2, you get 60. What is the speed of a cheetah?

| Animal | Speed (mph) |
|---|---|
| Human | 27.89 |
| Coyote | 43 |
| Greyhound | 39.45 |
| Wildebeest | 50 |

7. How much faster in miles per hour is a greyhound than a human?

8. A rabbit's heart beats about 200 times per minute. It lives for about 5 years. About how many times does its heart beat in an hour?

# Dividing Decimals
## Making the Connection

**LEARN ABOUT IT**

You can use play money to show that the steps you use to divide decimals make sense.

### EXPLORE  Use Play Money
- Work with a partner.
- One partner uses play money to show a number greater than $0.50 but less than $25.
- The other partner chooses a number of groups—2, 3, 4, 5, or 6. Together the partners divide the money into the chosen number of groups and then record the number in each group.
- Repeat this activity several times.

### TALK ABOUT IT

1. When you divided the play money into groups, did you start with the largest value of money or the smallest? Could you do it either way?

2. When did you have to trade dollars or dimes? Explain how you did it.

3. Did any of your activities end with money left over? Could this happen when you share real money among some friends?

You have divided play money into groups and recorded the amount in each group. You can use symbols to record the steps you followed. The steps are the same as when you divide with whole numbers. Here is how you divide $9.42 into 3 groups.

| **What You Do** | **What You Record** |
|---|---|

Show $9.42 as 9 ones, 4 dimes, 2 pennies.
Show 3 groups.

$$3\overline{)\$9.42}$$

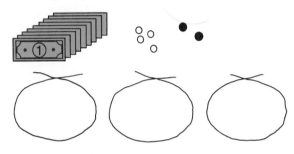

How many ones can be placed in each group?

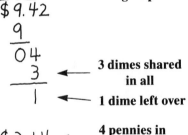

3 ones in each group

9 ones shared in all

How many dimes can be placed in each group?

1 dime in each group

3 dimes shared in all

1 dime left over

Regroup 1 dime as 10 pennies.
How many pennies can be placed in each group?

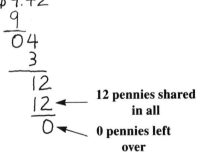

4 pennies in each group

12 pennies shared in all

0 pennies left over

**TRY IT OUT**

Divide. Use play money.

**1.** $10.24 ÷ 4        **2.** $9.56 ÷ 2        **3.** $12.50 ÷ 5        **4.** $0.65 ÷ 5

199

# Dividing Decimals

LEARN ABOUT IT

**EXPLORE  Analyze the Process**

What is the length of each side of the square shown at the right?

Because each side of a square has the same length, we divide.

**Perimeter: 35.32 cm**

| Divide the whole number part. | Place the decimal point. Divide the tenths. | Divide the hundredths. |
|---|---|---|
| $\begin{array}{r} 8\phantom{00} \\ 4)\overline{3\ 5.3\ 2} \\ \underline{3\ 2}\phantom{0} \\ 3\phantom{0} \end{array}$ | $\begin{array}{r} 8.8\phantom{0} \\ 4)\overline{3\ 5.3\ 2} \\ \underline{3\ 2}\phantom{0} \\ 3\ 3\phantom{0} \\ \underline{3\ 2}\phantom{0} \\ 1\phantom{0} \end{array}$ | $\begin{array}{r} 8.8\ 3 \\ 4)\overline{3\ 5.3\ 2} \\ \underline{3\ 2}\phantom{00} \\ 3\ 3\phantom{0} \\ \underline{3\ 2}\phantom{0} \\ 1\ 2 \\ \underline{1\ 2} \\ 0 \end{array}$ |

**TALK ABOUT IT**

1. Where does the 3 below the 2 come from in the first step?
2. How does the position of the decimal point in the dividend compare to its position in the quotient?

**Other Examples**

**A**
$$\begin{array}{r} 2\ 6.5\phantom{0} \\ 7)\overline{1\ 8\ 5.5} \\ \underline{1\ 4}\phantom{0000} \\ 4\ 5\phantom{00} \\ \underline{4\ 2}\phantom{00} \\ 3\ 5\phantom{0} \\ \underline{3\ 5}\phantom{0} \\ 0 \end{array}$$

**B**
$$\begin{array}{r} 0.5\ 3\ 7 \\ 2)\overline{1.0\ 7\ 4} \\ \underline{1\ 0}\phantom{000} \\ 0\ 7\phantom{0} \\ \underline{6}\phantom{0} \\ 1\ 4 \\ \underline{1\ 4} \\ 0 \end{array}$$

**C**
$$\begin{array}{r} 0.1\ 6\ 4 \\ 6)\overline{0.9\ 8\ 4} \\ \underline{6}\phantom{000} \\ 3\ 8\phantom{0} \\ \underline{3\ 6}\phantom{0} \\ 2\ 4 \\ \underline{2\ 4} \\ 0 \end{array}$$

**D**
$$\begin{array}{r} 0.0\ 0\ 7 \\ 4)\overline{0.0\ 2\ 8} \\ \underline{2\ 8} \\ 0 \end{array}$$

TRY IT OUT

Divide.

1. $3)\overline{8.52}$   2. $5)\overline{0.875}$   3. $2)\overline{1.672}$   4. $5)\overline{3.205}$

Divide and check.

**1.** $2\overline{)3.16}$     **2.** $3\overline{)1.095}$     **3.** $4\overline{)18.48}$     **4.** $5\overline{)41.5}$     **5.** $6\overline{)14.94}$

**6.** $4\overline{)7.28}$     **7.** $3\overline{)73.08}$     **8.** $7\overline{)16.8}$     **9.** $5\overline{)23.25}$     **10.** $4\overline{)2.348}$

**11.** $8\overline{)0.984}$     **12.** $9\overline{)34.56}$     **13.** $7\overline{)3.822}$     **14.** $5\overline{)31.45}$     **15.** $4\overline{)0.852}$

**16.** Find 0.7654 divided by 2.     **17.** Find the quotient of 16.048 and 4.

Use **mental math** to find each quotient.

**18.** $32.08 \div 8$     **19.** $448 \div 4$     **20.** $9.54 \div 9$     **21.** $2.50 \div 5$

**APPLY**

**MATH REASONING**

**22.** Copy and complete the following statement.

To check a division problem, multiply the __?__ by the __?__ . Add the __?__ .

**23.** Why is the remainder in this problem not a whole number?

**PROBLEM SOLVING**

**24.** Tara put a wire fence around her square garden. When she finished, she had 8.5 m of wire fence left. She started with a total of 40.5 m of fence. How long was each side of the garden?

**25.** The perimeter of the square below is shown. What is the length of each side?

P: 5.44 cm

**MIXED REVIEW**

Use mental math and the distributive property to find the products.

**26.** $7 \times 14$     **27.** $3 \times 45$     **28.** $2 \times 54$     **29.** $6 \times 24$     **30.** $3 \times 43$

Give the missing measure for each rectangle.

**31.** length: 3.5 cm
width: 3 cm
area: ▨

**32.** length: 4 cm
width: ▨
area: 8 cm²

**33.** length: ▨
width: 8 m
area: 128 m²

*More Practice, page 509, set A*

# Problem Solving
## Determining Reasonable Answers

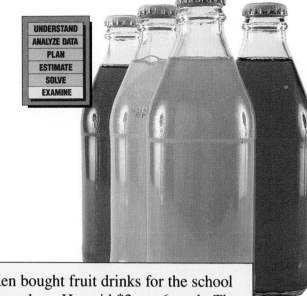

UNDERSTAND
ANALYZE DATA
PLAN
ESTIMATE
SOLVE
EXAMINE

A very important part of evaluating your thinking and your work when you solve problems is checking your work. The chart below shows some ways you can do this.

| Check Your Work |
| --- |
| ■ Is the arithmetic correct?<br>■ Did you use strategies correctly?<br>■ Is your answer reasonable? |

Ken bought fruit drinks for the school Round-up. He paid $2 per 6-pack. The total cost was $228. How many 6-packs did Ken buy?

Miriam used her calculator and got this answer:

Is the answer reasonable?

> I can use multiplication to check division. I can round to estimate the product.

> My check shows a total cost much less than the total given in the problem.

38

38 x 2 is about
40 x 2, or $80.

The answer is
not reasonable.

**TRY IT OUT**

Do not solve the problems. Decide whether the answer shown on the calculator is reasonable. If it is not reasonable, tell why not.

1. It takes 0.24 kilowatt hours (kwh) of energy to make a biodegradable milk carton. How much energy is needed to make 150 cartons?

   Tina's answer

   24

2. The energy needed to make 6 aluminum cans is 7.68 kwh. How much energy is needed to make 1 can? Joel's answer

   1.28

   MRC  M−  M+  ON/AC

Solve. Use any problem solving strategy.

1. It takes 5.04 kwh to make 6 paper cups. How many kilowatt hours does it take to make 1 paper cup?

2. One kilowatt hour is equal to 860 food calories. How many food calories would it take to equal 2.5 kwh?

Use data from the table below for problems 3, 4, and 5.

| Type of container | Energy needed to make container |
|---|---|
| milk carton | 0.24 kwh |
| steel can | 0.58 kwh |
| returnable glass bottle | 1.42 kwh |
| nonreturnable glass bottle | 0.85 kwh |

3. What is the difference in the number of kilowatt hours it takes to make a returnable glass bottle and a nonreturnable glass bottle?

4. The tomato juice Melanie drinks for her lunch 3 times a week comes in a steel can. How many kilowatt hours does it take to make the cans in a 6-pack of tomato juice?

5. What is the total number of kilowatt hours needed to make 100 steel cans and 100 returnable glass bottles?

6. Jon bought a 6-pack of apple juice for $1.88. About how much did he pay for each can of juice?

7. Julio said, "If you divide the number of returnable glass bottles of juice I bought for the party by 3 and add 13 to the quotient, you get 25." How many bottles did Julio buy?

8. Janet paid $89.00 for 100 cartons of milk for the day camp. What was the cost per carton?

9. **Understanding the Operations** Name the operation you would use. Show with objects or drawings why that operation makes sense for the problem.

Teresa had 39 recyclable paper cups to use at the party. That was 3 times the number of guests who were going to attend. How many guests were going to attend the party?

# Applied Problem Solving
## Group Decision Making

UNDERSTAND
ANALYZE DATA
PLAN
ESTIMATE
SOLVE
EXAMINE

### Group Skill:
Disagree in an Agreeable Way

Your school is having a pancake breakfast to raise money for a field trip. You will be offering a short stack of 2 pancakes and a tall stack of 3 pancakes. How much will you charge for each?

### Facts to Consider

- To the right are the prices of items you will need.

| Item | Cost/Information |
|------|------------------|
| Pancake mix | $1.79 |
| | 8 cups of mix per box. |
| Milk | $0.42 per quart |
| Syrup | $2.89 per bottle |
| | 1 bottle serves about 20 people. |
| Butter | $1.29 for 4 sticks |
| | 1 stick contains 8 tablespoons. |
| Orange juice | $0.95 for 1 quart |
| | 1 quart makes 8 servings. |
| Paper plates | $1.49 for 100 |
| Plastic forks | $0.45 for 24 forks |
| Paper cups | $1.15 for 50 cups |
| Napkins | $0.92 for 100 napkins |

- The recipe for pancakes calls for the following ingredients:

|  | Pancake mix | Milk |
|---|---|---|
| For 16 pancakes: | 2 cups | 2 cups |

- Juice will be included with each pancake breakfast.
- You will give 1 tablespoon of butter per pancake.

Some Questions to Answer

1. How many pancakes can you make from a box of mix? What is the cost per pancake?
2. How much would the butter for a short stack cost?
3. When a customer orders a short stack, how much does it cost you altogether to serve it to him or her?
4. How much profit do you want to make on each breakfast you serve? Is your price reasonable?

What Is Your Decision?

Make a poster advertising the pancake breakfast. Include all prices. On a separate paper, show how you decided on your prices.

205

# WRAP UP

## Sharing Equally

Tell the place of the first digit in these quotients:
**thousands, hundreds, tens,** or **ones.**

**1.** $7\overline{)578}$      **2.** $6\overline{)49}$      **3.** $4\overline{)2,108}$      **4.** $8\overline{)9,305}$

Without dividing, tell whether the given quotient is
**reasonable** or **not reasonable.**

**5.** $9\overline{)365}$ 8 R4      **6.** $7\overline{)79}$ 10 R9      **7.** $5\overline{)467}$ 93 R2      **8.** $4\overline{)315}$ 177 R7

## Sometimes, Always, Never

Complete each statement by writing **sometimes,
always,** or **never.** Explain your choices.

**9.** To find the average of six numbers you can __?__
find their sum and divide by 2.

**10.** Compatible numbers can __?__ be used to find an
exact quotient.

**11.** If $a - b = c$, then we can __?__ say that
$b + c = a$.

**12.** You __?__ can find a product mentally by
"breaking apart" the dividend.

**13.** The number of zeros in the dividend __?__ equals
the number of zeros in the quotient.

**14.** If the dividend has 3 digits and the divisor has 1
digit, the quotient will __?__ have 2 digits.

## Project

Find four books of different sizes. Find the length of
each book. What is the average length of the group
of books? What would happen if one book were 6 in.
longer? What would happen if you added a fifth
book that was 5 inches shorter than the average?

# POWER PRACTICE/TEST

## Part 1    Understanding

1. How would you use mental math to find
   $368 \div 4$?

2. Which gives an estimate of $4,729 \div 7$ by using
   compatible numbers?

   A. $4,600 \div 7$      B. $4,700 \div 7$

   C. $4,800 \div 7$      D. $4,900 \div 7$

## Part 2    Skills

In which place do you start dividing? Write **hundreds**
or **tens**.

3. $5\overline{)342}$      4. $8\overline{)165}$      5. $4\overline{)630}$      6. $7\overline{)921}$

Divide and check.

7. $6\overline{)705}$      8. $3\overline{)127}$      9. $4\overline{)883}$      10. $5\overline{)8,024}$

11. $7\overline{)2,156}$      12. $4\overline{)21.72}$      13. $6\overline{)0.450}$      14. $8\overline{)5.672}$

Give the average of each set of numbers.

15. 27, 31, 22, 28      16. 168, 142, 182      17. 14, 17, 25, 19, 30

## Part 3    Applications

18. Elena went shopping. She spent
    half of her money on groceries.
    Then she spent $9.63 at the
    bakery. She had $3.21 left. How
    much did she start with?

19. When Carlos was 7, his mother
    was four times as old as he was.
    Carlos is now 16. Is it reasonable
    to think that his mother is now
    64 years old?

20. Elliot has 200 photographs. The
    photo album he wants can hold 4
    photos on each page. If each
    album has 12 pages, how many
    albums does Elliot need for all of
    his photographs?

21. **Challenge.** A company claims
    that the average annual salary of
    its employees is $50,000. There
    are 10 employees. 9 of them earn
    $20,000 a year each. What is the
    salary of the other employee?

# ENRICHMENT
## Short Division

Since he started his baseball card collection 6 years ago, Richard has collected 3,068 cards. His younger sister, Rita, is helping him put the cards in plastic sheets that have 8 pockets in each sheet. How many sheets will Richard need? He used **short division** to solve the problem.

A.
$$8)\overline{3,068} \rightarrow$$

$$\begin{array}{r} 3 \\ 8)\overline{3,0\,^68} \end{array} \rightarrow$$

B.
$$\begin{array}{r} 3\ 8 \\ 8)\overline{3,0\,^6\,6\,^28} \end{array} \rightarrow$$

C.
$$\begin{array}{r} 3\ 8\ 3\ \text{R4} \\ 8)\overline{3,0\,^6\,6\,^28} \end{array}$$

Answer the questions about Richard's work.

1. What is the meaning of the small 6 between the 0 and the 6 in step A.

2. What is the meaning of the small 2 between the 6 and the 8 in step B?

3. What numbers did Richard divide in step C?

Use short division to divide.

4. $8)\overline{675}$      5. $4)\overline{258}$      6. $6)\overline{2,439}$      7. $5)\overline{4,762}$

8. $9)\overline{2,881}$      9. $7)\overline{5,235}$      10. $3)\overline{1,962}$      11. $4)\overline{3,473}$

12. $3)\overline{2,956}$      13. $8)\overline{6,739}$      14. $6)\overline{1,848}$      15. $3)\overline{4,760}$

# CUMULATIVE REVIEW

1. To estimate
   41.3 + 39.21 + 40.15 + 41.47
   using clustering,
   
   A. round to tenths, then add.
   
   B. add only the whole numbers.
   
   C. add whole numbers, round decimals.
   
   D. multiply 4 × 40.

2. Which expression is shown by the model?
   
   A. 0.7 × 0.1
   
   B. 0.4 × 0.8
   
   C. 0.7 × 0.4
   
   D. 0.6 × 0.3

3. Find the area of a rectangular room 14.8 m by 12.6 m.
   
   A. 54.8 m$^2$          B. 186.48 m$^2$
   
   C. 745.92 m$^2$        D. 27.4 m$^2$

Multiply.

4. 8.6 × 0.12
   
   A. 0.258              B. 2.472
   
   C. 1.022              D. 1.032

5. 14.28 × 100
   
   A. 0.1428            B. 1.428
   
   C. 142.8             D. 1,428

6. A flower shop sells 4 different kinds of plants in 3 types of pots. How many different combinations are there?
   
   A. 7        B. 12        C. 4        D. 3

7. A double bar graph
   
   A. shows trends in data.
   
   B. is used to make predictions.
   
   C. compares two sets of data.
   
   D. uses pictures to show data.

8. Which interval would you use on the scale of a line graph to show the number of campers?

   | Year | Campers |
   |------|---------|
   | 1987 | 185 |
   | 1988 | 193 |
   | 1989 | 208 |
   | 1990 | 214 |

   A. 5
   
   B. 50
   
   C. 100
   
   D. 1991

Choose the missing numbers.

9. 2,647 m = ▧ km
   
   A. 2.647 km          B. 26.47 km
   
   C. 264.7 km          D. 0.2647 km

10. 543 s = ▧ min ▧ s
    
    A. 22 min 15 s       B. 12 min 3 s
    
    C. 9 min 3 s         D. 90 min 3 s

11. 4 d 15 h = ▧ h
    
    A. 111    B. 255    C. 63    D. 100

12. To estimate the height of a door using the unitizing method,
    
    A. compare it to a known measurement.
    
    B. estimate larger parts.
    
    C. estimate smaller equal parts.
    
    D. mark off 100 cm, then estimate.

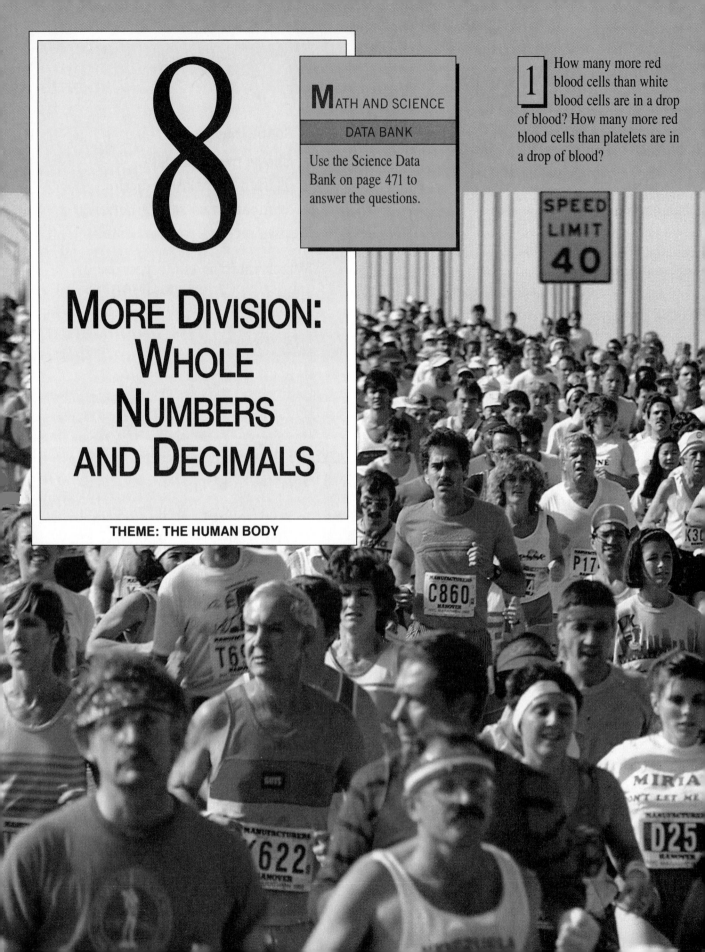

# 8

## MORE DIVISION: WHOLE NUMBERS AND DECIMALS

**THEME: THE HUMAN BODY**

**M**ATH AND SCIENCE

DATA BANK

Use the Science Data Bank on page 471 to answer the questions.

1 How many more red blood cells than white blood cells are in a drop of blood? How many more red blood cells than platelets are in a drop of blood?

SPEED LIMIT 40

**2** About how many liters of blood does the heart of an average person pump per hour when the person is at rest?

**3** About how many milliliters of air does the average person breathe in per minute? How many liters of air is this?

**4** **Using Critical Thinking** Compare the amount of air a person at rest breathes in with the amount after hard exercise. What can you say about hard exercise and your body's need for oxygen?

Women and men of all ages turn out to share the pleasure of running in long-distance races.

# Mental Math
## Special Quotients

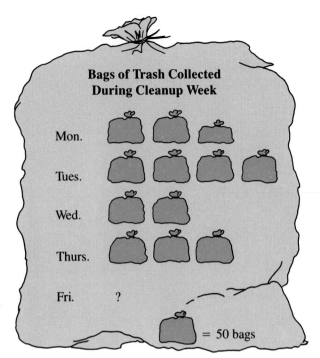

**Bags of Trash Collected During Cleanup Week**

Mon.

Tues.

Wed.

Thurs.

Fri.   ?

= 50 bags

### LEARN ABOUT IT

You can use basic facts and properties to find quotients like 350 ÷ 50.

### EXPLORE  Solve to Understand

Suppose you are making this pictograph to show the number of bags of trash your class collected. On Friday, your class collected 350 bags. How many bags should be shown on the graph for Friday?

### TALK ABOUT IT

1. What data do you need to calculate the number of cans for Friday?
2. How can you use guess and check to find a number you can multiply mentally by 50 to get 350?

When both the dividend and the divisor are divided by the same number, the resulting numbers will have the same quotient.

**To find**   **350 ÷ 50**

**Think**   **35 ÷ 5 = 7**    Divide both the dividend and the divisor by 10.

**So**   **350 ÷ 50 = 7**    Check: $7 \times 50 = 350$, so the quotient 7 is correct.

## Other Examples

**A** 2,800 ÷ 40.    Think about dividing each number by 10.
   **2,80**0 ÷ **4**0
   2,800 ÷ 40 = 70

**B** 4,900 ÷ 70.    Think about dividing each number by 10.
   **4,90**0 ÷ **7**0
   4,900 ÷ 70 = 70

### TRY IT OUT

Use mental math to find each quotient. Check by multiplying.

**1.** 540 ÷ 60    **2.** 2,000 ÷ 20    **3.** 3,500 ÷ 70    **4.** 6,300 ÷ 90    **5.** 2,500 ÷ 50

212

Divide and check.

1. 42 ÷ 6
   420 ÷ 60

2. 64 ÷ 8
   640 ÷ 80

3. 35 ÷ 7
   350 ÷ 70

4. 56 ÷ 8
   560 ÷ 80

5. 72 ÷ 9
   720 ÷ 90

6. 45 ÷ 5
   450 ÷ 50

7. 36 ÷ 4
   360 ÷ 40

8. 49 ÷ 7
   490 ÷ 70

9. 30 ÷ 6
   300 ÷ 60

10. 81 ÷ 9
    810 ÷ 90

Divide and check.

11. 80 ÷ 10

12. 60 ÷ 30

13. 40 ÷ 20

14. 90 ÷ 10

15. 100 ÷ 50

16. 210 ÷ 70

17. 160 ÷ 80

18. 150 ÷ 30

19. 180 ÷ 20

20. 240 ÷ 40

21. $30\overline{)1,200}$

22. $50\overline{)1,500}$

23. $60\overline{)2,400}$

24. $70\overline{)5,600}$

25. $80\overline{)400}$

26. $10\overline{)200}$

27. $90\overline{)2,700}$

28. $10\overline{)1,000}$

29. $70\overline{)6,300}$

30. $80\overline{)4,800}$

## APPLY

### MATH REASONING

Write two multiplication equations and two division equations for each family of numbers.

31. 40; 2,400; 60

32. 30; 2,100; 70

33. 70; 3,500; 50

34. 90; 4,500; 50

$40 \times 70 = 2,800$     $2,800 \div 70 = 40$
$70 \times 40 = 2,800$     $2,800 \div 40 = 70$

### PROBLEM SOLVING

35. Recycling carts hold 240 aluminum cans. One carton holds 40 cans. How many cartons can be placed on a cart?

36. Use the pictograph on page 212. How many fewer cans were collected on Monday than on Tuesday?

▶ **USING CRITICAL THINKING   Give a Counterexample**

37. Bill noticed that the factors of 8 are 1, 2, 4, and 8 and the factors of 10 are 1, 2, 5, and 10. He concluded, "All numbers have an even number of factors." Can you find and give the factors of a number that would show that Bill's statement is not correct?

*More Practice, page 509, set B*

**213**

# Estimating Quotient Digits

Front-end estimation and compatible number estimation can help you estimate quotient digits.

**EXPLORE  Study the Data**

A clothing store manager has decided to spend $375 per week on television advertising. Here are the ad costs.

| Time of Day | Cost of a 30-Second Television Ad |
|---|---|
| Morning | $ 40 |
| Midday | $ 70 |
| Late afternoon | $ 90 |
| Evening news | $300 |
| Evening | $200 |

**TALK ABOUT IT**

1. What operation can you use to find how many morning ads the store manager can buy for $375?

2. How can you use guess and check to estimate the number of midday ads the manager can buy for $375?

The example below shows one way to estimate the number of midday ads that could be bought for $375.

- **To estimate the quotient digit,**    $70\overline{)375}$

  **look at front-end digits and divide.**    $70\overline{)375}^{\,5}$

  > The compatible numbers 7 and 35 help you estimate the quotient.

- **Check the estimate by multiplying.**    $5 \times 70 = 350$

You can buy about 5 midday ads for $375.

Copy these exercises and underline the front-end digits you would use to estimate the quotient digit.

1. $40\overline{)258}$    2. $60\overline{)438}$    3. $80\overline{)743}$    4. $50\overline{)421}$

5. Rewrite exercises 1−4 to show how you would substitute compatible numbers to find the estimated quotient digit.

Estimate the number of these ads you could buy with $375.

6. morning    7. late afternoon    8. evenings news    9. evening

Copy these exercises. Underline the front-end digits you would use to estimate the quotient digit.

1. $50\overline{)328}$     2. $30\overline{)249}$     3. $60\overline{)308}$     4. $40\overline{)252}$     5. $70\overline{)363}$

6. $90\overline{)281}$     7. $20\overline{)88}$     8. $40\overline{)230}$     9. $30\overline{)281}$     10. $80\overline{)273}$

Estimate the quotient. Multiply to check.

11. $20\overline{)152}$     12. $40\overline{)291}$     13. $70\overline{)432}$     14. $30\overline{)195}$     15. $60\overline{)248}$

16. $80\overline{)340}$     17. $50\overline{)464}$     18. $90\overline{)385}$     19. $40\overline{)218}$     20. $70\overline{)578}$

21. $30\overline{)286}$     22. $60\overline{)382}$     23. $20\overline{)170}$     24. $80\overline{)660}$     25. $90\overline{)288}$

APPLY

**MATH REASONING**

Tell which estimate is closest to the exact answer.

26. $40\overline{)2,783}$   7, 70, or 700       27. $60\overline{)495}$   8, 80, or 800

28. $30\overline{)9,105}$   3, 30, or 300       29. $70\overline{)2,216}$   3, 30, or 300

**PROBLEM SOLVING**

Use the data on page 214 as needed.

30. Suppose you have $1,250. About how many 30-second ads can you buy during the evening news?

31. Suppose you have $1,850. About how many 30-second ads can you buy during the evening?

▶ **ALGEBRA**

Choose the correct meaning (A or B) of each algebraic expression.

32. $X - 5$    **A.** 5 more than a number    **B.** a number less 5

33. $H \div 4$    **A.** 4 divided by a number    **B.** a number divided by 4

34. $12M$    **A.** 12 times a number    **B.** 21 more than a number

35. $Y - 23$    **A.** 23 less than a number    **B.** 23 take away a number

# Dividing
## 1-Digit Quotients

**EXPLORE**  **Analyze the Process**

Alcott Middle School has 238 students. How many homerooms are needed if no homeroom can have more than 28 students?

Since the maximum number of students for each room is the same, we divide.

To solve this problem, divide 238 by 28. Here is how to do it.

| Decide where to start. | Estimate the first quotient digit. | Divide the ones. |
|---|---|---|
| $28\overline{)238}$ | $28\overline{)238}$ | $\begin{array}{r} 8\ \text{R}14 \\ 28\overline{)238} \\ \underline{224} \\ 14 \end{array}$ ■ Divide. ■ Multiply. ■ Subtract. ■ Compare. |
| 28 > 2 <br> 28 > 23 <br> 28 < 238 <br> Divide the ones. | Think $30\overline{)240}$ | Check: $\begin{array}{r} 28 \\ \times\ 8 \\ \hline 224 \\ +\ 14 \\ \hline 238 \end{array}$ |

## TALK ABOUT IT

1. Why is the first digit in the quotient in the ones place?
2. What two numbers are multiplied to give 224?
3. Why is 240 ÷ 30 a better estimate of the first digit in the quotient than 210 ÷ 30?

**Other Examples**

A  $\begin{array}{r} \phantom{30)}6\ \text{R}9 \\ 31\overline{)195} \\ \underline{186} \\ 9 \end{array}$  (30)

B  $\begin{array}{r} \phantom{78)}4\ \text{R}9 \\ 78\overline{)321} \\ \underline{312} \\ 9 \end{array}$  (80)

C  $\begin{array}{r} \phantom{44)}8 \\ 44\overline{)352} \\ \underline{352} \\ 0 \end{array}$  (40)

Divide and check.

1. $41\overline{)85}$  2. $22\overline{)156}$  3. $57\overline{)191}$  4. $42\overline{)175}$  5. $63\overline{)189}$

Divide and check.

1. $37\overline{)89}$    2. $22\overline{)66}$    3. $43\overline{)90}$    4. $51\overline{)162}$    5. $32\overline{)160}$

6. $12\overline{)49}$    7. $26\overline{)78}$    8. $45\overline{)207}$    9. $63\overline{)174}$    10. $82\overline{)328}$

11. $57\overline{)248}$    12. $73\overline{)511}$    13. $88\overline{)225}$    14. $94\overline{)190}$    15. $31\overline{)254}$

16. $212 \div 41$    17. $354 \div 68$    18. $600 \div 74$    19. $382 \div 39$    20. $809 \div 81$

21. Find the quotient of 262 divided by 91.    22. 482 divided by 59 is what number?

## APPLY

### MATH REASONING

23. Jered solved $341 \div 42$ and checked his work. It checked. Did Jered solve the problem correctly? If not, what did he do wrong?

$$
\begin{array}{r}
7\text{R}47 \\
42\overline{)341} \\
294 \\
\hline
47
\end{array}
\qquad
\begin{array}{r}
\text{Check:}\quad 42 \\
\times\ 7 \\
\hline
294 \\
47 \\
\hline
341
\end{array}
$$

### PROBLEM SOLVING

24. About how many students are in grades 5 through 8 at Lincoln School?

25. How many 5th grade homerooms are needed if each homeroom is to have no more than 24 students?

26. **Data Hunt**  How many students are in your grade at your school? How many homerooms are needed if each homeroom is to have no more than 23 students?

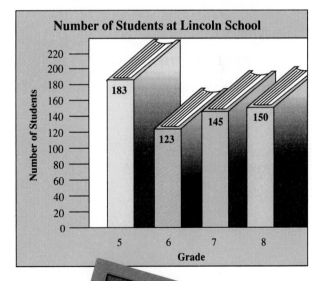

### CALCULATOR

27. Solve the problem $192 \div 24$ on your calculator by using any number keys but only the [−] operations key.

28. Solve the problem $5 \times 28$ on your calculator by using any number keys but only the [+] operations key.

*More Practice, page 509, Set D*

# Changing Estimates

## EXPLORE  Analyze the Process

At rest, an adult takes about 14 breaths per minute. If you take 28 breaths a minute while jogging slowly, how many minutes have you run by the time you have taken 168 breaths?

| Decide where to start. | Estimate the first quotient digit. | Estimate again if necessary. |
|---|---|---|
| $28\overline{)168}$ <br><br> Think $30\overline{)150}$ | $\begin{array}{r} 5 \\ 28\overline{)168} \\ \underline{140} \\ 28 \end{array}$    5 is not correct. This difference must be less than 28. | $\begin{array}{r} 6 \\ 28\overline{)168} \\ \underline{168} \end{array}$ |

## TALK ABOUT IT

1. Why is the first quotient digit in the ones place?

2. How can you tell that the estimate of 5 is not correct?

3. Give an answer to the Explore problem in a complete sentence.

## Other Examples

**A**
$$\begin{array}{r} 3 \\ 28\overline{)117} \\ \underline{84} \\ 33 \end{array} \rightarrow \begin{array}{r} 4 \\ 28\overline{)117} \\ \underline{112} \\ 5 \end{array}$$

Try $30\overline{)100}$.     3 is too low.

**B**
$$\begin{array}{r} 7 \\ 51\overline{)344} \\ \underline{357} \end{array} \rightarrow \begin{array}{r} 6 \\ 51\overline{)344} \\ \underline{306} \\ 38 \end{array}$$

Try $50\overline{)350}$.     7 is too high.

Decide which estimates must be changed. Give the correct estimates for the ones that need to be changed.

1. $\overset{4}{18\overline{)89}}$     2. $\overset{6}{83\overline{)490}}$     3. $\overset{5}{25\overline{)161}}$     4. $\overset{2}{94\overline{)201}}$     5. $\overset{6}{54\overline{)318}}$

Divide and check.

**1.** $31\overline{)96}$     **2.** $20\overline{)180}$     **3.** $18\overline{)161}$     **4.** $30\overline{)255}$     **5.** $14\overline{)104}$

**6.** $53\overline{)315}$     **7.** $60\overline{)500}$     **8.** $29\overline{)105}$     **9.** $32\overline{)275}$     **10.** $43\overline{)354}$

**11.** $22\overline{)156}$     **12.** $43\overline{)330}$     **13.** $70\overline{)452}$     **14.** $51\overline{)427}$     **15.** $25\overline{)169}$

**16.** $298 \div 75$     **17.** $628 \div 80$     **18.** $835 \div 91$     **19.** $529 \div 67$     **20.** $594 \div 82$

**21.** Find the quotient when 874 is divided by 38.

## APPLY

### MATH REASONING

Use **estimation** to decide whether the exact quotient is less than ($<$) or greater than ($>$) the given number.

**22.** $476 \div 66$   $< 7$ OR $> 7$?       **23.** $592 \div 71$   $< 8$ OR $> 8$?

**24.** $361 \div 81$   $< 5$ OR $> 5$?       **25.** $228 \div 39$   $< 6$ OR $> 6$?

### PROBLEM SOLVING

**26.** Homeroom 7 collected money for a science field trip from a walkathon. They made the same amount the next week with a pledge run. After paying $25 for expenses, they had $225. How much did they make from the walkathon?

**27.** Homeroom 12 sold $425 worth of adult tickets and $183 worth of children's tickets for the science fair. Each of the 32 members sold tickets worth the same amount. What was the value of the tickets sold by each student?

**28. Science Data Bank** If you take 35 breaths a minute after hard exercise, about how much air would you be taking in with each breath? See page 471.

### ► CALCULATOR

Use a calculator to find the missing numbers.

**29.** $n \div 21 = 4$ R2       **30.** $n \div 40 = 6$ R22

**31.** $n \div 37 = 5$ R10       **32.** $358 \div n = 7$ R8

# Finding Larger Quotients

| Area 11,070 ft² | Area 11,316 ft² | Area 10,947 ft² |
|---|---|---|
| Lot 16 | Lot 17 | Lot 18 |
| ←— 90 ft —→ | ←— 92 ft —→ | ←— 89 ft —→ |

**EXPLORE  Analyze the Process**

The lots on the north side of Elm Street are rectangular. Mr. and Mrs. Sanchez bought lot 17. How long is their lot?

To solve this problem, divide 11,316 by 92. Here is how to do it.

| Decide where to start. | Divide the hundreds. | Divide the tens. | Divide the ones. |
|---|---|---|---|
| $92\overline{)11{,}316}$  $92 > 11$ Not enough thousands. $92 < 113$ Divide the hundreds. | (90) $\begin{array}{r}1\phantom{00}\\92\overline{)11{,}316}\\\underline{92}\phantom{00}\\21\phantom{0}\end{array}$  ■ Divide. ■ Multiply. ■ Subtract. ■ Compare. | (90) $\begin{array}{r}12\phantom{0}\\92\overline{)11{,}316}\\\underline{92}\downarrow\phantom{0}\\211\phantom{}\\\underline{184}\phantom{}\\27\phantom{}\end{array}$  ■ Bring down. ■ Divide. ■ Multiply. ■ Subtract. ■ Compare. | $\begin{array}{r}123\\92\overline{)11{,}316}\\\underline{92}\phantom{00}\\211\phantom{}\\\underline{184}\downarrow\\276\\\underline{276}\\0\end{array}$  ■ Bring down. ■ Divide. ■ Multiply. ■ Subtract. ■ Compare. |

## TALK ABOUT IT

1. What do the words "Not enough thousands" mean?
2. Give the answer to the Explore problem in a complete sentence.

**Other Examples**

A $\begin{array}{r}58\text{ R}3\\41\overline{)2{,}381}\\\underline{205}\phantom{0}\\331\\\underline{328}\\3\end{array}$

B $\begin{array}{r}435\text{ R}10\\53\overline{)23{,}065}\\\underline{212}\phantom{00}\\186\phantom{}\\\underline{159}\phantom{}\\275\\\underline{265}\\10\end{array}$

Divide and check.

1. $31\overline{)458}$     2. $52\overline{)3{,}796}$     3. $23\overline{)14{,}763}$     4. $62\overline{)1{,}954}$

220

Divide and check. Remember to estimate the quotient first.

**1.** $68\overline{)775}$     **2.** $44\overline{)977}$     **3.** $21\overline{)319}$     **4.** $24\overline{)534}$

**5.** $45\overline{)560}$     **6.** $36\overline{)1,476}$     **7.** $50\overline{)2,872}$     **8.** $18\overline{)1,574}$

**9.** $35\overline{)1,166}$     **10.** $53\overline{)1,863}$     **11.** $82\overline{)1,776}$     **12.** $45\overline{)2,000}$

**13.** $3,422 \div 27$     **14.** $5,891 \div 76$     **15.** $2,335 \div 37$     **16.** $8,626 \div 54$

**17.** $5,579 \div 54$     **18.** $5,300 \div 63$     **19.** $3,237 \div 67$     **20.** $6,549 \div 85$

**APPLY**

**MATH REASONING**

Copy the problems and show what digit should be placed in each ▦.

**21.** ▦▦ )1,950 ... 450 ... 0

**22.** 4▦ )▦,6▦3 ... 4▦ ... 4▦ ... 36 ... 3 ... 84 ... 9 ... 18▦ R▦

**PROBLEM SOLVING**

**23.** How many rectangles with sides that are a whole number of units in length have an area of 1,155 square units?

**24.** What is the width of a rectangle with an area equal to 7,260 in.² and a length of 165 in.?

**MIXED REVIEW**

Give the number of units for each ▦.

**25.** 2,354 mL = ▦ L   **26.** 3.2L = ▦ mL   **27.** 54L = ▦ mL   **28.** 698 ml = ▦ L

Find the quotient.

**29.** $975 \div 8$    **30.** $592 \div 9$    **31.** $321 \div 3$    **32.** $719 \div 2$    **33.** $227 \div 6$

*More Practice, page 510, set B*

# Problem Solving
## Choosing a Calculation Method

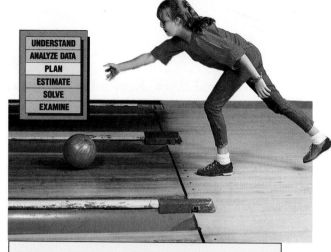

UNDERSTAND
ANALYZE DATA
PLAN
ESTIMATE
SOLVE
EXAMINE

### LEARN ABOUT IT

Look carefully at the numbers in a problem. The size of the numbers and the kinds of numbers help you to choose a calculation method.

**Calculation Methods**

- Paper and Pencil
- Calculator
- Mental Math

Sharon scored 1,050 in 10 games. What was her average score?

*Since the divisor is 10, I can use mental math to solve this.*

### TRY IT OUT

Choose an appropriate calculation method and tell why. Then solve.

1. 475 ÷ 25
2. 235 ÷ 7
3. 560 ÷ 7
4. 1,137 ÷ 6

5. 2,700 ÷ 90
6. 128 ÷ 4
7. 546 ÷ 9
8. 1,720 ÷ 42

9. 490 ÷ 70
10. 1,248 ÷ 6
11. 640 ÷ 8
12. 436 ÷ 4

13. Sharon and her dad are in a parent-child bowling league. Sharon scored 85, 117, and 104 in 3 games. What was her average score?

14. A night of bowling (5 games) costs $7.50 for Sharon's father and only $2.75 for Sharon. They usually spend another $5 on refreshments. What does it cost them for a night of bowling?

15. A regular game of bowling costs $1.75 at a certain bowling alley. About how many games could you bowl if you had $10?

16. Suppose you bowled 5 games that cost $2.15 per game. You rented shoes for $0.75. What did it cost you to bowl?

17. The manager told Sharon he used 5,100 bowling pins in 5 years. There are 15 lanes in this bowling alley. What was the average number of pins used per lane?

**222**

*More Practice, page 510, set C*

# POWER PRACTICE/QUIZ

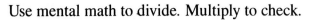

Use mental math to divide. Multiply to check.

**1.** $80 \div 40$     **2.** $360 \div 60$     **3.** $600 \div 20$     **4.** $2{,}400 \div 30$     **5.** $630 \div 70$

**6.** $240 \div 60$     **7.** $3{,}500 \div 70$     **8.** $4{,}800 \div 60$     **9.** $900 \div 30$     **10.** $2{,}700 \div 90$

**11.** $90\overline{)540}$     **12.** $60\overline{)4{,}200}$     **13.** $80\overline{)800}$     **14.** $90\overline{)3{,}600}$     **15.** $80\overline{)1{,}600}$

Estimate each quotient. Multiply to check whether the estimate is reasonable.

**16.** $30\overline{)256}$     **17.** $5\overline{)263}$     **18.** $80\overline{)177}$     **19.** $70\overline{)496}$     **20.** $9\overline{)463}$

**21.** $40\overline{)372}$     **22.** $7\overline{)445}$     **23.** $20\overline{)164}$     **24.** $50\overline{)264}$     **25.** $60\overline{)497}$

**26.** $40\overline{)290}$     **27.** $90\overline{)756}$     **28.** $60\overline{)561}$     **29.** $30\overline{)159}$     **30.** $70\overline{)588}$

Divide and check.

**31.** $54\overline{)267}$     **32.** $78\overline{)310}$     **33.** $44\overline{)386}$     **34.** $32\overline{)4{,}000}$     **35.** $80\overline{)700}$

**36.** $72\overline{)3{,}520}$     **37.** $26\overline{)9{,}224}$     **38.** $67\overline{)563}$     **39.** $15\overline{)8{,}935}$     **40.** $44\overline{)9{,}855}$

## PROBLEM SOLVING

**41.** During a two-week vacation, Andrew's family drove a total of 2,700 km. About how many kilometers per day was that?

**42.** A hamster's heart beats about 450 times in 1 minute. About how many times is that per second?

**43.** Boston's average rainfall about 110 cm per year. About how many centimeters is that per month?

**44.** A queen termite can lay about 350 eggs in 1 hour. About how many eggs is that per minute?

**45.** Maya jogged 83 km in 9 days. Estimate the average number of kilometers she jogged each day.

# Dividing
## Special Cases

**EXPLORE** **Analyze the Process**

The heart of an adult elephant may be as heavy as 15,912 g. This is about 52 times as heavy as the heart of a human. About how heavy is the heart of a human?

To solve the problem, we find $15{,}912 \div 52$.

| Decide where to start. | Divide the hundreds. | Divide the tens. | Divide the ones. |
|---|---|---|---|
| $52\overline{)15{,}912}$ | $\begin{array}{r} 3 \\ 52\overline{)15{,}912} \\ \underline{15\ 6} \\ 3 \end{array}$ ■ Divide. ■ Multiply. ■ Subtract. ■ Compare. | $\begin{array}{r} 30 \\ 52\overline{)15{,}912} \\ \underline{15\ 6\downarrow} \\ 31 \\ \underline{0} \\ 31 \end{array}$ | $\begin{array}{r} 306 \\ \overline{)15{,}912} \\ \underline{15\ 6} \\ 31 \\ \underline{0\downarrow} \\ 312 \\ \underline{312} \\ 0 \end{array}$ |
| $52 > 15$ Not enough thousands. $52 < 159$ Divide the hundreds. | | Remember! Every time you bring down, you must divide. | |

**TALK ABOUT IT**

1. Why is a 0 written below the 31 in the third step?
2. How could you estimate that the answer is about 300?

## Other Examples

**A**
$$\begin{array}{r} 4\,0\,0 \text{ R5} \\ 56\overline{)2\,2{,}4\,0\,5} \\ \underline{2\,2\,4} \\ 0\,0 \\ \underline{0} \\ 0\,5 \\ \underline{0} \\ 5 \end{array}$$

**B**
$$\begin{array}{r} \$2.4\,6 \\ 3\,2\overline{)\$7\,8.7\,2} \\ \underline{6\,4} \\ 1\,4\,7 \\ \underline{1\,2\,8} \\ 1\,9\,2 \\ \underline{1\,9\,2} \\ 0 \end{array}$$

> Divide as with whole numbers. Show dollars and cents, so the answers make sense.

Divide and check.

1. $42\overline{)8{,}736}$
2. $60\overline{)12{,}250}$
3. $78\overline{)47{,}270}$
4. $38\overline{)15{,}314}$

224

Divide and check.

**1.** $18\overline{)546}$    **2.** $23\overline{)478}$    **3.** $32\overline{)1,283}$    **4.** $48\overline{)5,113}$

**5.** $52\overline{)6,780}$    **6.** $60\overline{)12,540}$    **7.** $22\overline{)13,308}$    **8.** $56\overline{)16,820}$

**9.** $31\overline{)2,114}$    **10.** $72\overline{)30,275}$    **11.** $91\overline{)6,211}$    **12.** $44\overline{)15,928}$

**13.** $47,651 \div 68$    **14.** $33,708 \div 54$    **15.** $65,271 \div 81$    **16.** $59,290 \div 77$

Estimate each quotient.

**17.** $82\overline{)3,296}$    **18.** $33\overline{)13,472}$    **19.** $85\overline{)5,952}$    **20.** $47\overline{)19,500}$    **21.** $60\overline{)36,360}$

## APPLY

### MATH REASONING

**22.** Copy and complete the problem to give the quotient shown. Use each of the numbers in the box exactly one time.

$$4 \,\text{▇}\,\overline{)3\,\text{▇},\,\text{▇▇▇}} \quad \begin{array}{c} 7\ 0\ 5 \end{array}$$

$$\boxed{0\ 2\ 3\ 4\ 6}$$

### PROBLEM SOLVING

**23.** During its lifetime a red blood cell makes 75,000 trips between lungs and body cells at a rate of 625 trips per day. How many days is the lifetime of a red blood cell?

**24. Science Data Bank** How many times more platelets than white blood cells are there in a drop of blood? See page 471.

DATA BANK

▶ **MENTAL MATH**

Use one or more of the mental math techniques you have learned to complete the exercises below.

| Mental Math Techniques |
| --- |
| ■ Counting On/Back |
| ■ Breaking Apart Numbers |
| ■ Choosing Compatible Numbers |
| ■ Using Compensation |

**25.** $198 + 327$    **26.** $216 \div 4$    **27.** $278 - 99$

**28.** $19 + 58 + 81$    **29.** $23 \times 5$    **30.** $324 \div 3$

**31.** $541 - 302$    **32.** $6 \times 54$    **33.** $4 \times 9 \times 25$

# Problem Solving
## Look for a Pattern

UNDERSTAND
ANALYZE DATA
PLAN
ESTIMATE
SOLVE
EXAMINE

## LEARN ABOUT IT

You may find a pattern in the data to help you solve some problems. Making a table may help you discover the pattern. This problem-solving strategy is called **Look for a Pattern.**

Tom's soccer coach believes drills are very important. She divided the players into groups of 7. Each player in the group has to do the dribbling drill with every other player in the group. How many drills does each group do in all?

I'll start with a simpler problem.

2 players → 1 drill.

3 players → 3 drills.

4 players → 6 drills.

| Players | Drills |
|---------|--------|
| 2 | 1 |
| 3 | 3 |
| 4 | 6 |

I can continue a table and look for a pattern. I see! Each time the difference increases by 1.

| Players | Drills |
|---------|--------|
| 2 | 1 |
| 3 | 3 |
| 4 | 6 |
| 5 | 10 |
| 6 | 15 |
| 7 | 21 |

In Tom's group, they did 21 drills in all.

## TRY IT OUT

When Hari and her father practice soccer, she wants to score 1 goal the first day, 3 goals the second day, 5 goals the third day, and so on. After the sixth day, how many goals would she have scored in all?

| Day | Goals | Total Goals |
|-----|-------|-------------|
| 1 | 1 | 1 |
| 2 | 3 | 4 |
| 3 | 5 | 9 |
| 4 | 7 | — |
| 5 | — | — |
| 6 | — | — |

- How many goals did Hari want to score the second day?

- What was the total number of goals Hari should have scored after 2 days?

- Copy the table. Look for patterns to complete the table and solve the problem.

226

Look for a pattern to help you solve each problem.

**1.** At the end-of-season soccer tournament, all teams play each other once. There are 8 teams. How many games are played in all?

**2.** At their soccer games, the Booters scored 2 goals their first game, 4 their second, and 6 their third. If they continue to score at this rate, how many goals will they have scored in all after 5 games?

## MIXED PRACTICE

Choose a strategy from the strategies list or use other strategies you know to solve these problems.

**3.** Nina's mother is one of 49 soccer referees. There are 98 parents serving as coaches. There are 15 times as many players as coaches. How many players are there?

**4.** The banner for the Kicking Kings soccer team shows soccer balls in a pyramid shape. There is 1 ball in the top row, 2 in the second row, 4 in the third row, and 7 in the fourth row. There were 7 rows. How many balls does the banner show?

**5.** The banner for the Fleet Feet team cost $2.48 for edging and $11.98 for felt. The coach's gift cost $45.50. How much were all the expenses?

**6.** The printing shop had the following digits available for the Fleet Feet's jerseys: 1, 3, 5, and 7. How many different 2-digit numbers can Kimo choose from for his soccer jersey?

**7.** The Fleet Feet scored 103 points during the 1989 season. They scored 121 points during the 1990 season. How many more points did they score in 1990?

| Some Strategies | |
|---|---|
| Act Out | Make a Table |
| Use Objects | Solve a Simpler Problem |
| Choose an Operation | Make an Organized List |
| Draw a Picture | Work Backward |
| Guess and Check | Look for a Pattern |

**8.** Use the graph to find about how many players signed up for soccer in the 10 and 11 year old age groups altogether.

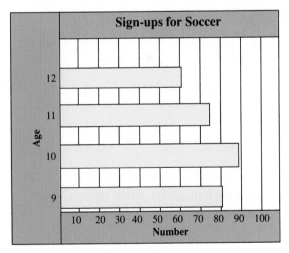

**9.** Last year 274 children signed up to play soccer. There had to be 15 players on each team. How many full teams could be formed?

**10.** The Tri-County League had 10 teams. There were 20 players on each team. How many players were there in the league?

*More Practice, page 525, set A*

# Mental Math
## Dividing Decimals by 10, 100, and 1,000

**EXPLORE  Discover a Pattern**

Work in groups and use a calculator to try the following.

- Choose several decimals such as 534.6 and divide them first by 10, then by 100, and then by 1,000.

- Make a table and record the results. The table should show each decimal you choose and the quotients that result when the decimal is divided by 10, 100, and 1,000.

**TALK ABOUT IT**

Look for patterns in your table. How would you complete the following statements?

1. To divide a decimal by 10 mentally, "move" the decimal point __?__ places to the __?__ .
2. To divide a decimal by 100 mentally, "move" the decimal point __?__ places to the __?__ .
3. To divide a decimal by 1,000 mentally, "move" the decimal point __?__ places to the __?__ .

The pattern explored above shows that the number of zeros in a divisor of 10, 100, or 1,000 tells us how many places we need to "move" the decimal point in the dividend in order to show the correct quotient. For example, to solve $34.5 \div 100$ we move the decimal point two places to the left of where it is in 34.5. So, $34.5 \div 100 = 0.345$.

Use mental math to find the missing number in each equation.

1. $34.69 \div 10 = n$  2. $57.83 \div 100 = b$  3. $687.2 \div 1,000 = y$  4. $879 \div 100 = x$

5. $56.4 \div 100 = a$  6. $298 \div 10 = c$  7. $0.76 \div 10 = z$  8. $436.6 \div 100 = w$

Use mental math to find the missing number in each equation.

**1.** $276.8 \div 10 = a$

**2.** $109.5 \div 100 = b$

**3.** $0.47 \div 10 = n$

**4.** $764.5 \div 1{,}000 = x$

**5.** $1{,}050 \div 100 = c$

**6.** $62.75 \div 1{,}000 = n$

**7.** $5.68 \div 10 = y$

**8.** $43.89 \div 100 = z$

**9.** $95.7 \div 10 = l$

**10.** $553.4 \div 1{,}000 = r$

**11.** $22.2 \div 100 = s$

**12.** $0.05 \div 10 = d$

**13.** $3{,}176 \div 1{,}000 = f$

**14.** $990.9 \div 100 = t$

**15.** $41.4 \div 10 = v$

**16.** $0.37 \div 100 = p$

**APPLY**

## MATH REASONING

Tell whether the divisor in each is 10, 100, or 1,000.

**17.** $456.6 \div n = 45.66$   **18.** $1{,}234.2 \div n = 1.2342$   **19.** $24.5 \div n = 0.0245$

**20.** $265.6 \div n = 2.656$   **21.** $0.01 \div n = 0.0001$   **22.** $51.7 \div n = 0.0517$

## PROBLEM SOLVING

**23.** How many dimes (10¢) could you get if you had 450 pennies?

**24.** How many dollar bills (100¢) could you get if you had 34,200 pennies?

**25.** A package of 10 computer disks cost $47.50. Each disk costs the same amount. What is the cost of each disk?

**26.** A census taker can put 100 names on a page. How many pages will be needed for 27,500 names?

## MIXED REVIEW

Give the number for each ▦ .

**27.** $850 \text{ g} = $ ▦ $\text{ kg}$

**28.** $3{,}240 \text{ g} = $ ▦ $\text{ kg}$

**29.** $2.3 \text{ kg} = $ ▦ $\text{ g}$

**30.** $0.5 \text{ kg} = $ ▦ $\text{ g}$

Divide.

**31.** $24.9 \div 6$   **32.** $312.9 \div 3$   **33.** $50.44 \div 4$   **34.** $67.27 \div 7$   **35.** $329.4 \div 9$

*More Practice, page 510, set E*

# Problem Solving
## Estimating the Answer

| UNDERSTAND |
|---|
| ANALYZE DATA |
| PLAN |
| ESTIMATE |
| SOLVE |
| EXAMINE |

Before solving a problem, it is important to decide what would be a reasonable answer. You can do this by estimating the answer.

|           | Atlanta | Chicago | Dallas | Miami | New York | San Francisco | Washington |
|-----------|---------|---------|--------|-------|----------|---------------|------------|
| Atlanta   | —       | 722     | 800    | 688   | 896      | 2,515         | 672        |
| Chicago   | 722     | —       | 933    | 1,410 | 831      | 2,205         | 753        |
| Dallas    | 800     | 933     | —      | 1,348 | 1,576    | 1,761         | 1,352      |
| Miami     | 688     | 1,410   | 1,348  | —     | 1,352    | 3,147         | 1,128      |
| New York  | 896     | 831     | 1,576  | 1,352 | —        | 2,996         | 224        |
| San Fran. | 2,515   | 2,205   | 1,761  | 3,147 | 2,996    | —             | 2,922      |
| Wash., D.C.| 672    | 753     | 1,352  | 1,128 | 224      | 2,922         | —          |

> Stephie and her father took a bike trip from New York to Washington, D.C. They rode 32 miles (mi) each day. How many days did it take?

Before solving the problem, estimate the answer.

I'll start by rounding 32 miles.

$$32 \rightarrow 30$$

I'll substitute a compatible number for the distance from New York to Washington, D.C.

$$224 \rightarrow 210$$

I'll use these numbers to estimate how many days the trip took.

$$210 \div 30 = 7$$

Now I'll solve the problem.

$$224 \div 32 = 7$$

7 is a reasonable answer because it is the same as my estimate.

Before solving each problem, estimate the answer. Then solve the problem and decide whether your answer is reasonable.

1. Jack's mother bicycled from Atlanta to Washington, D.C. Her average speed was 12 miles per hour (mph). How many hours did the trip take?

2. Maria's mother took 44.1 hours to drive from one city to another. Her average speed was 50 mph. What two cities did she travel between?

3. What is the distance from Miami to Dallas and back to Miami?

4. Jeannie wants to jog from Dallas to Atlanta to raise money for her favorite charity. She plans to jog about 21 mi each day. How many full days should she plan to be jogging?

Solve. Use any problem solving strategy.

1. How much farther is it from Dallas to New York than from Miami to New York?

2. Carlos took a trip in the family camper that was 654 miles farther than 3 times the distance from New York to Chicago. What two cities did they travel between?

3. Tony, who had a kidney transplant when he was very young, walked from Chicago to Washington, D.C., to raise money for kidney research. He walked at a speed of 3 mph. How many hours did it take him?

4. Julie's family took a trip from Dallas to Atlanta. The gasoline cost $0.92 per gallon. They drove 16 hours. On the average, how many miles did they travel per hour?

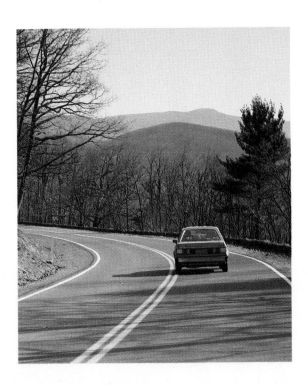

5. On a bike trip from Cincinnati to Cleveland, Yang rode at a speed of 10.5 mph. He rode for 24.5 hours. How far is it from Cincinnati to Cleveland?

6. Tom made a map showing the distances between 9 different cities. He connected every city to every other city. How many lines did he draw?

7. How far did Ms. Fraser travel when she drove from New York to Chicago to San Francisco to Dallas and back to New York?

8. Mr. Golden drove from San Francisco to Miami at an average speed just above 50 mph. About how many hours of driving time was that?

9. Five students had a bicycle race. Dan finished ahead of Carmen, but Carmen was not last. Betty finished far ahead of Carmen, and Ed finished just behind Betty. If Ralph finished last, who finished next to last?

10. **Understanding the Operations**
Tell what operation you would use. Explain why. Then solve the problem.

Jane traveled to 42 cities. This is 3 times the number of cities she had seen before the trip. How many cities had Jane seen before the trip?

*More Practice, page 525, set B*

**231**

# Data Collection and Analysis
## Group Decision Making

UNDERSTAND
ANALYZE DATA
PLAN
ESTIMATE
SOLVE
EXAMINE

### Doing a Questionnaire
### Group Skill:
Encourage and Respect Others

All of the members of your group are on a committee to choose older students to give help to others in an after-school program. Prepare a questionnaire for the older students to answer.

### Collecting Data

1. Have a brainstorming discussion about the kind of person a good student helper should be. Make a list of at least ten qualities a good helper should have.
2. Use your list to make a questionnaire that asks students to rate their personal qualities. Some examples are given below.

### Questionnaire

How would you rate yourself on the following personal qualities?

|  | very low | low | average | high | very high |
|---|---|---|---|---|---|
| 1. Patience | 1 | 2 | 3 | 4 | 5 |
| 2. Helpfulness | 1 | 2 | 3 | 4 | 5 |
| 3. Self-confidence | 1 | 2 | 3 | 4 | 5 |

3. Give your questionnaire to at least 3 or 4 students. Make changes if they find that it is unclear in any way.
4. Distribute the revised questionnaire to at least 10 students.

**Organizing Data**

5. One way your group can decide which students would make the best tutors is to find out who rated themselves highest on the questionnaire. You can do this by adding the ratings given by each student to get a total rating for each one. Make a list of the students in order from the one with the highest rating to the one with the lowest rating.

**Presenting Your Analysis**

6. Write a paragraph explaining why you think this is or is not a fair way to evaluate students for the job of helping others.

7. Be ready to tell what else your group could do to find out which students would be good student helpers.

233

# WRAP UP

## Division Time

**1.** Write these steps for dividing 8,976 by 5 in order.

    A. Bring down tens.

    B. Divide thousands, multiply, subtract, compare.

    C. Divide ones, multiply, subtract, compare.

    D. Write the remainder.

    E. Bring down hundreds.

    F. Divide tens, multiply, subtract, compare.

    G. Bring down ones.

    H. Divide hundreds, multiply, subtract, compare.

## Sometimes, Always, Never

Complete each statement by writing **sometimes, always,** or **never.** Explain your choices.

**2.** The quotient is __?__ larger than the divisor.

**3.** When both the dividend and the divisor are divided by the same number, the quotient of the new numbers is __?__ the same as the quotient of the original numbers.

**4.** When dividing, you __?__ work from right to left.

**5.** The quotient is __?__ smaller than the dividend.

**6.** To divide a decimal by 100, you should __?__ move the decimal point two places to the left.

## Project

Use the digits 1, 2, 4, 5, and 6 to make a 5-digit number. Divide it by 9 and record the remainder. Do this at least 5 times. What do you notice? Can you explain why it happens?

Try to find 5 other digits that give the same results.

# POWER PRACTICE/TEST

## Part 1    Understanding

What compatible numbers could you use to estimate
each quotient?

**1.** $70\overline{)586}$

**2.** $47\overline{)246}$

**3.** $32\overline{)251}$

Which method would you choose: paper and pencil,
calculator, or mental math? Explain.

**4.** $2,465 \div 57$

**5.** $1,632 \div 8$

**6.** $759 \div 8$

## Part 2    Skills

Use mental math to find each quotient.

**7.** $4,200 \div 70$   **8.** $3,600 \div 40$   **9.** $527.04 \div 10$   **10.** $0.073 \div 10$

Is the first estimate correct? Give the correct
estimate for exercises that need a second estimate.

**11.** $36\overline{)168}^{\,4}$

**12.** $89\overline{)530}^{\,6}$

**13.** $35\overline{)321}^{\,8}$

Divide.

**14.** $47\overline{)294}$

**15.** $62\overline{)506}$

**16.** $28\overline{)701}$

**17.** $71\overline{)15,416}$

**18.** $94\overline{)19,275}$

**19.** $39\overline{)\$327.60}$

## Part 3    Applications

**20.** A mail carrier drove 4,820 km in
83 working days. Is it reasonable
to estimate that the carrier drove
600 km per day? If not, find a
reasonable estimate.

**21. Challenge.** This large triangle is
made up of small triangles. How
many small triangles are in the
large triangle? How is the number
of small triangles related to the
number of rows?

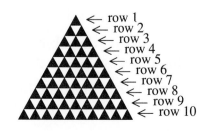

← row 1
← row 2
← row 3
← row 4
← row 5
← row 6
← row 7
← row 8
← row 9
← row 10

# ENRICHMENT
## Divisibility

We say 624 is **divisible** by 2 because the remainder is 0 when 624 is divided by 2. Look for patterns to discover some **divisibility tests.**

- *Divisibility test for 2.* Here are some numbers that are divisible by 2: 24; 316; 1,508; 570; and 92.

1. Find 5 other numbers that are divisible by 2.

2. Copy and complete the following:
   "A number is divisible by 2 if its last digit is __?__."

- *Divisibility test for 5.* Here are some numbers that are divisible by 5: 30; 635; 75; 320; and 5,125.

3. Find 5 other numbers that are divisible by 5.

4. Copy and complete the following:
   "A number is divisible by 5 if its last digit is __?__."

- *Divisibility test for 3.* Here are some numbers that are divisible by 3: 84; 72; 126; 513; 1,302; and 3,351.

5. Find 5 other numbers that are divisible by 3.

6. Copy and complete the following:
   "A number is divisible by 3 if the sum of its digits is __?__."

### Discover a Rule!

Find some examples to help you discover the number that should be written in place of the variable to make a divisibility rule.

7. A number is divisible by $x$ if twice the tens digit plus its ones digit is divisible by $x$.

8. A number is divisible by $y$ if it is divisible by 2 and 3.

236

# CUMULATIVE REVIEW

Solve using mental math.

**1.** 400 × 80 × 20

    A. 32,000        B. 640,000

    C. 160,000     D. 1,280,000

**2.** 23 × 8

    A. 40           B. 180

    C. 160         D. 184

**3.** 5,400 ÷ 9

    A. 600         B. 60

    C. 6            D. 6,000

**4.** 8.46 × 100

    A. 846         B. 0.846

    C. 84.6       D. 8,460

Give the missing numbers.

**5.** 82.4 m = ▥ cm

    A. 8.24        B. 824

    C. 0.824     D. 8,240

**6.** 397 mm = ▥ cm

    A. 3.97        B. 397

    C. 39.7       D. 3,970

**7.** 4,521 mL = ▥ L

    A. 45.21      B. 452.1

    C. 4.521     D. 4,521

**8.** 0.47 kg = ▥ g

    A. 4.7         B. 470

    C. 47         D. 4,700

**9.** What would be the best choice for estimating the quotient of 2,286 ÷ 3?

    A. 2,000 ÷ 3    B. 1,800 ÷ 3

    C. 3,000 ÷ 3    D. 2,100 ÷ 3

**10.** In which place do you start dividing to find the quotient of 824.6 ÷ 7?

    A. hundreds    B. ones

    C. tens       D. tenths

Divide.

**11.** 4)2,129

    A. 53 R9      B. 53

    C. 532 R1    D. 532 R3

**12.** 8)3,685

    A. 46 R5     B. 410 R5

    C. 461       D. 460 R5

**13.** Jennifer scored 87, 82, 92, 84, and 90 on her last five math tests. What was her average score for these tests?

    A. 85         B. 87

    C. 86         D. 88

**14.** There are 464 campers staying at Camp Whynot this summer. There are 8 campers and 2 counselors in each cabin. How many cabins are occupied?

    A. 46         B. 57

    C. 50         D. 58

# 9

# UNDERSTANDING FRACTIONS AND MIXED NUMBERS

**THEME: ARTS AND CRAFTS**

**M**ATH AND FINE ARTS

**DATA·BANK**

Use the Fine Arts Data Bank on page 477 to answer the questions.

1 How many equal parts are there in the Sioux Beadwork Mountain design? How many of the parts are blue? How many are yellow?

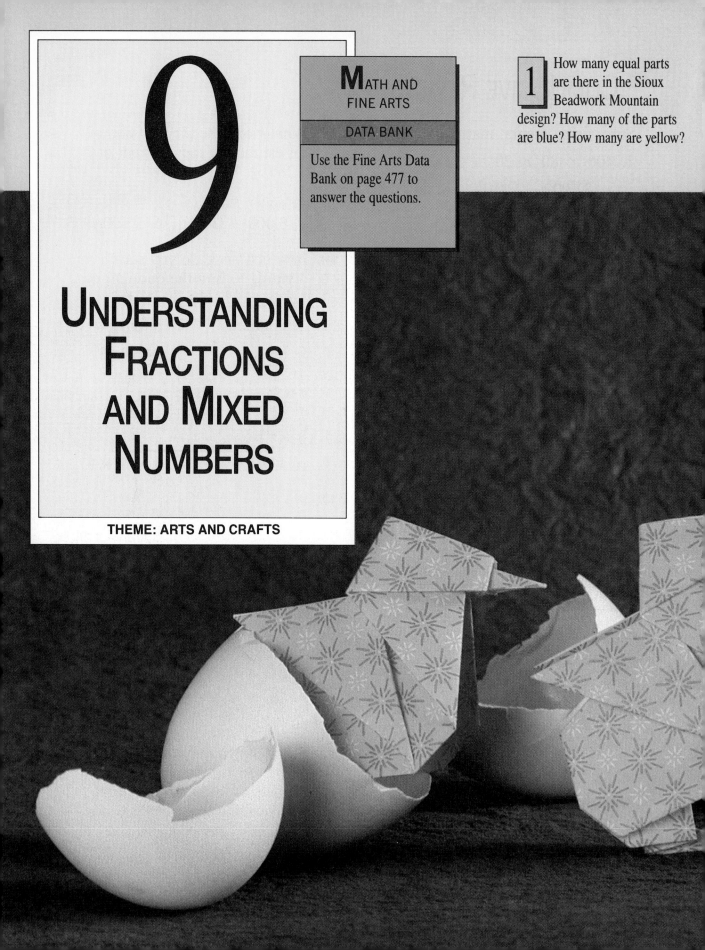

**2** Which of the Origami Basic Forms show folds into equal parts? How many equal parts are there in Basic Form 4?

**3** In the Sioux Beadwork Dragonfly design the number of yellow parts is how many times greater than the number of black parts?

**4** **Using Critical Thinking** Suppose the color pattern in the Sioux Horse Track design is continued so that there are a total of 3 tracks. How many of all the equal parts will be blue? Explain.

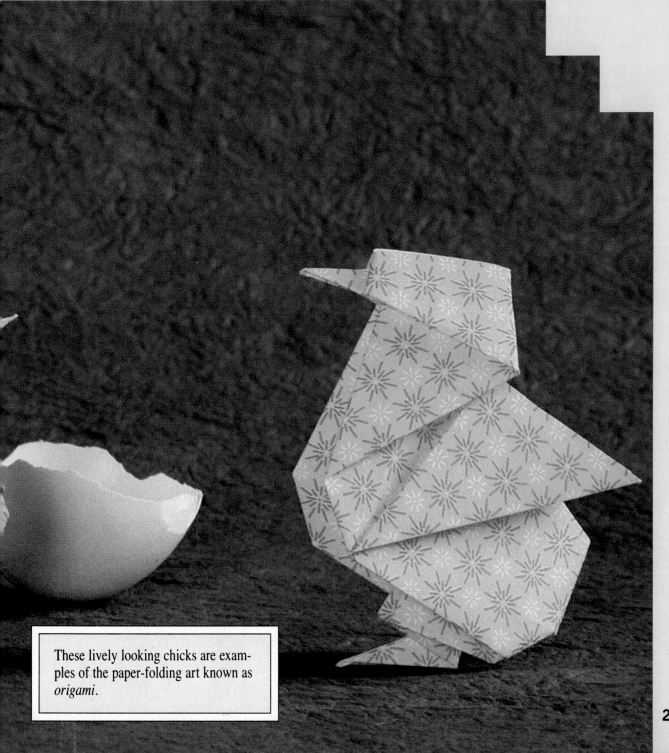

These lively looking chicks are examples of the paper-folding art known as *origami*.

# Reviewing the Meaning of Fractions

You can use fractions to tell about parts of a region or parts of a set.

**EXPLORE** **Consider the Examples**

Mosaic is an art form that uses small pieces of colored stone, glass, or other material to make pictures. You can use fractions to describe the mosaic region and the sets of mosaic pieces shown at the right.

Bright mosaics decorate the outer walls of Mexico's University Library, near Mexico City.

**TALK ABOUT IT**

1. In box A, is each part of the region the same size? How many parts are blue? red?
2. In box B, are the mosaic pieces all the same size? How many are green? How many are tan? How many are there in all?
3. How many sets are shown by the string and color?

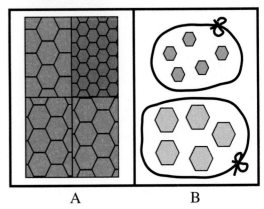

A          B

Remember how we read and write fractions. 3 of the 4 equal parts of the region are red.

We say: "three fourths"    We write: $\dfrac{3}{4}$    numerator
denominator

$\dfrac{3}{4}$ of the region is red. $\dfrac{1}{4}$ is blue.

1. What fraction of all the pieces in box B above are green?

2. Write the fraction that is colored.

  **A.**     **B.**     **C.**     **D.**

**240**

Give the fraction of the region that is colored.

**1.**     **2.**     **3.**     **4.**

Give the fraction of each set that is colored.

**5.**     **6.**     **7.**     **8.**

Write the fractions.

**9.** two thirds    **10.** three fourths    **11.** one half    **12.** two fifths

Write the word name for each fraction.

**13.** $\frac{7}{10}$    **14.** $\frac{9}{12}$    **15.** $\frac{6}{8}$    **16.** $\frac{1}{6}$    **17.** $\frac{3}{7}$

**MATH REASONING**

Show each fraction as part of a region and as part of a set.

**18.** $\frac{3}{5}$    **19.** $\frac{2}{6}$    **20.** $\frac{3}{8}$    **21.** $\frac{7}{10}$    **22.** $\frac{5}{12}$

**PROBLEM SOLVING**

**23.** A bag of 250 mosaic pieces cost $2.25. There were 100 green pieces in the bag. What fraction of the pieces were green?

**24.** Elena spent $1\frac{1}{2}$ h putting 75 mosaic pieces in place. Then she spent 30 min drawing another design. What fraction of the total time did she spend drawing?

▶ **ESTIMATION**

Estimate the fraction of each figure that is shaded.

**25.**     **26.**     **27.**     **28.**    **29.**

*More Practice, page 511, set A*

# Equivalent Fractions

**EXPLORE** Use Fraction Pieces

- Work in groups. Use fraction pieces to find different ways to cover $\frac{1}{2}$ exactly.

- Use fraction pieces to find different ways to cover $\frac{3}{4}$ exactly.

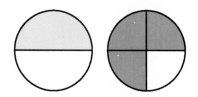

**TALK ABOUT IT**

1. What fractions did you find that show the same amount as $\frac{1}{2}$?

2. What fractions did you find that show the same amount as $\frac{3}{4}$?

Fractions that name the same amount of a region or set are called **equivalent fractions.**

We use an equal sign to show that two fractions are equivalent. The pictures below show that $\frac{2}{3} = \frac{6}{9}$.

**2 out of 3 boxes are colored.**          **6 out of 9 bulbs are colored.**

Use fraction pieces to show each of the following.

**1.** $\frac{1}{4} = \frac{2}{8}$       **2.** $\frac{3}{5} = \frac{6}{10}$       **3.** $\frac{5}{6} = \frac{10}{12}$       **4.** $\frac{2}{4} = \frac{1}{2}$

Use fraction pieces to help you find the missing numerator or denominator.

**5.** $\frac{1}{2} = \frac{\rule{0.6em}{0pt}}{6}$       **6.** $\frac{1}{2} = \frac{4}{\rule{0.6em}{0pt}}$       **7.** $\frac{2}{3} = \frac{\rule{0.6em}{0pt}}{6}$       **8.** $\frac{3}{4} = \frac{6}{\rule{0.6em}{0pt}}$

242

Write two fractions that name the shaded part of each region or set.

**1.**

**2.**

**3.**

**4.**

**5.**

**6.**

Use fraction pieces to show each of the following.

**7.** $\frac{1}{5} = \frac{2}{10}$

**8.** $\frac{1}{3} = \frac{2}{6}$

**9.** $\frac{3}{4} = \frac{6}{8}$

**10.** $\frac{5}{6} = \frac{10}{12}$

Use counters of two colors to show each of the following.

**11.** $\frac{1}{2} = \frac{3}{6}$

**12.** $\frac{3}{4} = \frac{6}{8}$

**13.** $\frac{2}{3} = \frac{4}{6}$

**14.** $\frac{2}{5} = \frac{4}{10}$

**APPLY**

**MATH REASONING**

Use fraction pieces to find the missing number.

**15.** $\frac{2}{4} = \frac{4}{\text{||||}}$

**16.** $\frac{1}{\text{||||}} = \frac{2}{12}$

**17.** $\frac{1}{\text{||||}} = \frac{4}{12}$

**18.** $\frac{2}{5} = \frac{4}{\text{||||}}$

**PROBLEM SOLVING**

**19.** Out of 16 sections in a basketball arena, 4 sections are for reserved seats. Todd said $\frac{4}{16}$ of the seats are reserved. Gail said only $\frac{1}{4}$ are reserved. Who is correct?

**RESERVED**

**MIXED REVIEW**

Divide. Check by using multiplication.

**20.** $1,864 \div 8$

**21.** $3,246 \div 6$

**22.** $2,395 \div 5$

**23.** $2,427 \div 3$

**24.** $1,624 \div 4$

**25.** $4,501 \div 7$

**26.** $7,515 \div 9$

**27.** $3,070 \div 5$

# Finding Equivalent Fractions

## LEARN ABOUT IT

**EXPLORE** **Solve to Understand**

Keith bought paper for making origami figures. He bought 2 packages of orange paper and 3 packages of yellow paper. What fraction of the papers were orange?

**TALK ABOUT IT**

1. How many packages of each color did Keith buy?

2. How many papers are in each package?

3. How many papers did Keith buy altogether?

2 of the 5 packages were orange. $\frac{2}{5}$ of the packages were orange.

6 of the 15 papers were orange. $\frac{6}{15}$ of the papers were orange.

orange
3
sheets

yellow
3
sheets

**6 sheets in all**

**9 sheets in all**

You can find a fraction that is equivalent to another fraction by multiplying or dividing the numerator and denominator by the same nonzero number.

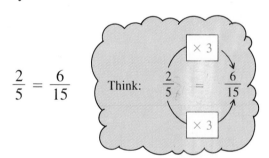

$\frac{2}{5} = \frac{6}{15}$  Think: $\frac{2}{5}$ $\xrightarrow{\times 3}$ $=$ $\frac{6}{15}$ $\xleftarrow{\times 3}$

$\frac{9}{12} = \frac{3}{4}$  Think: $\frac{9}{12}$ $\xrightarrow{\div 3}$ $=$ $\frac{3}{4}$ $\xleftarrow{\div 3}$

## TRY IT OUT

Find equivalent fractions by multiplying the numerator and denominator by 2.

1. $\frac{1}{2} = \frac{||||||}{||||||}$  2. $\frac{1}{6} = \frac{||||||}{||||||}$  3. $\frac{2}{3} = \frac{||||||}{||||||}$  4. $\frac{1}{8} = \frac{||||||}{||||||}$  5. $\frac{3}{5} = \frac{||||||}{||||||}$

Find the equivalent fractions by multiplying the numerator and denominator by 3.

6. $\frac{5}{8} = \frac{||||||}{||||||}$  7. $\frac{1}{5} = \frac{||||||}{||||||}$  8. $\frac{5}{6} = \frac{||||||}{||||||}$  9. $\frac{3}{4} = \frac{||||||}{||||||}$  10. $\frac{3}{8} = \frac{||||||}{||||||}$

Find equivalent fractions by multiplying the numerator and denominator by 4.

**1.** $\frac{1}{4} = \frac{\phantom{||}}{\phantom{||}}$    **2.** $\frac{3}{4} = \frac{\phantom{||}}{\phantom{||}}$    **3.** $\frac{2}{5} = \frac{\phantom{||}}{\phantom{||}}$    **4.** $\frac{1}{10} = \frac{\phantom{||}}{\phantom{||}}$    **5.** $\frac{5}{12} = \frac{\phantom{||}}{\phantom{||}}$

Tell what number the numerator and denominator were multiplied or divided by to get the equivalent fraction.

**6.** $\frac{5}{6} = \frac{15}{18}$    **7.** $\frac{3}{7} = \frac{9}{21}$    **8.** $\frac{12}{30} = \frac{2}{5}$    **9.** $\frac{4}{5} = \frac{12}{15}$    **10.** $\frac{16}{36} = \frac{4}{9}$

Give the next three equivalent fractions. What pattern did you use to find them?

**11.** $\frac{1}{2} = \frac{\phantom{||}}{\phantom{||}}, \frac{\phantom{||}}{\phantom{||}}, \frac{\phantom{||}}{\phantom{||}}$    **12.** $\frac{1}{3} = \frac{\phantom{||}}{\phantom{||}}, \frac{\phantom{||}}{\phantom{||}}, \frac{\phantom{||}}{\phantom{||}}$    **13.** $\frac{1}{6} = \frac{\phantom{||}}{\phantom{||}}, \frac{\phantom{||}}{\phantom{||}}, \frac{\phantom{||}}{\phantom{||}}$    **14.** $\frac{2}{3} = \frac{\phantom{||}}{\phantom{||}}, \frac{\phantom{||}}{\phantom{||}}, \frac{\phantom{||}}{\phantom{||}}$

**MATH REASONING**

Look for a pattern. Use a calculator to find the next three fractions.

**15.** $\frac{36}{97}, \frac{72}{194}, \frac{144}{388}, \frac{\phantom{||}}{\phantom{||}}, \frac{\phantom{||}}{\phantom{||}}, \frac{\phantom{||}}{\phantom{||}}$    **16.** $\frac{17}{23}, \frac{51}{69}, \frac{153}{207}, \frac{\phantom{||}}{\phantom{||}}, \frac{\phantom{||}}{\phantom{||}}, \frac{\phantom{||}}{\phantom{||}}$

**PROBLEM SOLVING**

**17.** Stan Wilson made 12 baskets out of 20 shots in last night's basketball game. What fraction of his shots did he make? Give two fractions equivalent to this, one of which has a denominator of 100.

**18. Fine Arts Data Bank**   What fraction of the origami figures show a single fold into two halves? Give an equivalent fraction. See page 477.

DATA BANK

▶ **USING CRITICAL THINKING    Discover a Relationship**

You can find the **cross products** by multiplying the red numbers and by multiplying the black numbers. Look for a relationship between the red numbers and the black numbers in the equivalent fractions. Complete the following sentence.

**19.** "If two fractions are equivalent, then the   ?     ?   are   ?  ."

Equivalent fractions

$\frac{5}{8} = \frac{10}{16}$    $\frac{3}{4} = \frac{6}{8}$

Not equivalent fractions

$\frac{2}{3} \neq \frac{6}{8}$    $\frac{1}{6} \neq \frac{6}{32}$

*More Practice, page 511, set B*

# Greatest Common Factor

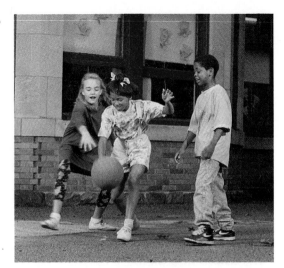

**LEARN ABOUT IT**

**EXPLORE  Analyze the Process**

There are 18 fifth graders and 24 sixth graders on the playground. The leader wants to divide the students from each grade into teams. She wants all the teams to be the same size and have as many players as possible. How can she do it?

**TALK ABOUT IT**

1. What are some sizes the teams might be? Explain.
2. Have you found the greatest possible number of players for each team? Try to prove it.

A number is a **factor** of another number if it divides into the number with remainder zero. In the problem above, the answer, 6, is the **greatest common factor (GCF)** of 18 and 24 because it the largest number that is a factor of both numbers. Here is how to find the GCF of 24 and 36.

| List the factors of each number. | List the common factors (the factors in both lists). | Find which common factor is the greatest. |
|---|---|---|
| 24: 1, 2, 3, 4, 6, 8, 12, 24<br><br>36: 1, 2, 3, 4, 6, 9, 12, 18, 36 | 1, 2, 3, 4, 6, 12 | 12 |

You can also use a **Venn diagram** to think about the greatest common factor.

Factors of 24     Factors of 36

8  1 2  9
3 4  18
24  6
12  36

GCF

Common Factors

**TRY IT OUT**

List the factors of each number. Then give the GCF.

1. $\frac{28}{42}$    2. $\frac{18}{27}$    3. $\frac{9}{12}$    4. $\frac{14}{25}$

List the factors of each number. Then give the greatest common factor.

1. $\frac{9}{12}$    2. $\frac{8}{20}$    3. $\frac{9}{15}$    4. $\frac{7}{13}$    5. $\frac{10}{14}$    6. $\frac{9}{27}$

7. $\frac{40}{50}$    8. $\frac{20}{25}$    9. $\frac{16}{24}$    10. $\frac{15}{18}$    11. $\frac{15}{25}$    12. $\frac{8}{14}$

13. $\frac{18}{24}$    14. $\frac{9}{10}$    15. $\frac{18}{30}$    16. $\frac{10}{30}$    17. $\frac{3}{21}$    18. $\frac{15}{21}$

Try a Shortcut!
- List only the factors of the smaller number.
- Find the largest of these that is a factor of the other number.

19. $\frac{12}{15}$    20. $\frac{18}{45}$    21. $\frac{28}{16}$    22. $\frac{42}{18}$    23. $\frac{16}{36}$    24. $\frac{18}{32}$

APPLY

**MATH REASONING**

25. Brian said, "If 6 is a factor of a number, then 2 and 3 are also factors of the number." Do you think Brian is right? Why or why not?

**PROBLEM SOLVING**

26. One hundred campers made a list of 145 camp songs they knew. They decided to sing each song once during the 12 days they would be at camp. How many did they need to sing each day if they sang about the same number each day?

▶ **ALGEBRA**

Algebraic expressions involving multiplication can be written in different ways. $5 \times n$, $5 \cdot n$, $5(n)$, and $5n$ all mean "five times a number."

> Remember, if an algebraic expression involves multiplication together with addition or subtraction, multiply first, then add or subtract.

Evaluate each expression.

27. $6m - 4$ when $m = 2$    28. $8 + 3g$ when $g = 4$    29. $12 - 5y$ when $y = 0$

30. $5 \times n$ when $n = 3$    31. $28 \div z$ when $z = 7$    32. $6w + 4$ when $w = 2$

# Lowest-Terms Fractions

**EXPLORE** **Solve to Understand**

Mrs. DeGroat weaves rugs in her spare time. One rug she wove has 6 rows of squares with 4 squares in each row. It has 18 brown squares and 6 green squares. The brown squares and green squares are divided evenly among the rows. What fraction of the squares in each row are brown?

**TALK ABOUT IT**

1. What two operations could you use to find the total number of squares in the blanket? What is the total number?

2. What fraction of all the squares are brown?

3. What operation can you use to find how many squares in each row are brown? What fraction of all squares in the row is this?

A fraction is in **lowest terms** when the greatest common factor of the numerator and the denominator is 1. Here are two ways to find an equivalent fraction in lowest terms.

- Divide both terms by common factors until the greatest common factor is 1.

$$\frac{18 \div 2}{24 \div 2} = \frac{9}{12} = \frac{9 \div 3}{12 \div 3} = \frac{3}{4} \quad \leftarrow \text{lowest-terms fraction}$$

- Divide both terms by their greatest common factor.

$$\frac{18 \div 6}{24 \div 6} = \frac{3}{4} \quad \boxed{\text{6 is the greatest common factor of 18 and 24.}}$$

## Other Examples

**A** $\frac{2}{6} = \frac{1}{3}$   Think: $\frac{2}{6} \overset{\div 2}{=} \frac{1}{3} \underset{\div 2}{}$

**B** $\frac{70}{100} = \frac{7}{10}$

Reduce to lowest terms when not already in lowest terms.

1. $\frac{12}{30}$    2. $\frac{4}{12}$    3. $\frac{4}{15}$    4. $\frac{9}{27}$    5. $\frac{7}{24}$    6. $\frac{12}{18}$

**248**

Tell whether the fraction is in lowest terms. Write **yes** or **no**.

1. $\frac{1}{5}$     2. $\frac{2}{66}$     3. $\frac{5}{10}$     4. $\frac{3}{12}$     5. $\frac{12}{18}$     6. $\frac{4}{9}$

7. $\frac{3}{8}$     8. $\frac{6}{8}$     9. $\frac{9}{15}$     10. $\frac{8}{20}$     11. $\frac{6}{13}$     12. $\frac{6}{18}$

Reduce to lowest terms when not already in lowest terms.

13. $\frac{6}{8}$     14. $\frac{9}{12}$     15. $\frac{18}{45}$     16. $\frac{3}{15}$     17. $\frac{7}{8}$     18. $\frac{8}{20}$

19. $\frac{3}{24}$     20. $\frac{12}{15}$     21. $\frac{2}{18}$     22. $\frac{2}{3}$     23. $\frac{35}{42}$     24. $\frac{8}{14}$

Use **mental math** to reduce each fraction to lowest terms.

25. $\frac{5}{10}$        26. $\frac{6}{60}$        27. $\frac{10}{35}$        28. $\frac{8}{400}$        29. $\frac{4}{100}$

APPLY

## MATH REASONING

Write **true** or **false** for each of the following statements.

30. If the numerator of a fraction is 1, the fraction is in lowest terms.

31. If the numerator of a fraction is not 1, the fraction can always be reduced to lowest terms.

## PROBLEM SOLVING

32. In the Explore problem on page 248, what fraction names the part of the total squares that are green? What is this fraction reduced to lowest terms?

33. **Fine Arts Data Bank**    What fraction in lowest terms names the part of the total squares in the Sioux Horse Tracks design that is yellow? See page 477.

DATA BANK

▶ **ESTIMATION**

Replace the terms of the fractions with **compatible numbers** to give an estimate for each fraction.

**Example:** $\frac{11}{23}$ is about $\frac{12}{24}$ or $\frac{1}{2}$.

34. $\frac{15}{22}$          35. $\frac{4}{26}$          36. $\frac{7}{27}$          37. $\frac{12}{35}$

*More Practice, page 511, set D*

# Exploring Algebra
## More About Variables

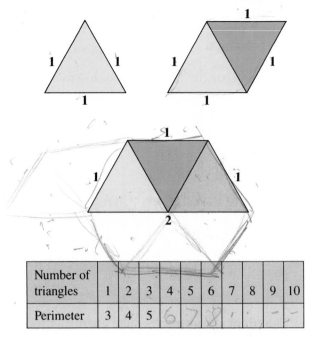

You have learned that a **variable** can stand for a single unknown number. A variable can also be used to stand for a **range of numbers.**

LEARN ABOUT IT

Work in groups.
Copy and complete the table at the right.
Make or draw triangles if you find that helpful. Look for patterns.

| Number of triangles | 1 | 2 | 3 | 4 | 5 | 6 | 7 | 8 | 9 | 10 |
|---|---|---|---|---|---|---|---|---|---|---|
| Perimeter | 3 | 4 | 5 | 6 | 7 | 8 | | | | |

**TALK ABOUT IT**

1. What is the perimeter when there are 6 triangles?

2. What is the perimeter when there are 10 triangles?

3. If you know the number of triangles, how can you find the perimeter?

In the table above, the number of triangles varies from 1 to 10. The perimeter varies from 3 to 12. Suppose $N$ stands for the number of triangles and $P$ stands for the perimeter. $N$ and $P$ are variables.

**TRY IT OUT**

Copy the tables. Look for patterns you can use to complete them. Describe the patterns you use.

1.

| B | 1 | 2 | 3 | 4 | 5 | 6 |
|---|---|---|---|---|---|---|
| C | 6 | 12 | 18 | | | |

2.

| A | 1 | 2 | 3 | 4 | 5 | 6 |
|---|---|---|---|---|---|---|
| B | 3 | 6 | 9 | | | |

3.

| A | 1 | 2 | 3 | 4 | 5 | 6 |
|---|---|---|---|---|---|---|
| S | 1 | 3 | 5 | | | 11 |

4.

| W | 10 | 20 | 30 | 40 | 50 | 60 |
|---|---|---|---|---|---|---|
| B | 21 | 41 | | | | 121 |

# POWER PRACTICE/QUIZ

Write two fractions to name the part that is colored. Write
two fractions to name the part that is not colored.

**1.**

**2.**

**3.**

Decide whether the fractions are equivalent. Write **yes** or **no.**

**4.** $\frac{3}{8} \overset{?}{=} \frac{6}{16}$

**5.** $\frac{1}{2} \overset{?}{=} \frac{5}{8}$

**6.** $\frac{2}{3} \overset{?}{=} \frac{4}{9}$

**7.** $\frac{4}{6} \overset{?}{=} \frac{6}{9}$

**8.** $\frac{4}{5} \overset{?}{=} \frac{6}{10}$

**9.** $\frac{7}{8} \overset{?}{=} \frac{14}{16}$

**10.** $\frac{1}{3} \overset{?}{=} \frac{4}{12}$

**11.** $\frac{6}{9} \overset{?}{=} \frac{3}{4}$

**12.** 6
8

**13.** 5
9

**14.** 12
4

**15.** 10
15

**16.** 18
12

Is the fraction in lowest terms? Write **yes** or **no.**

**17.** $\frac{3}{10}$

**18.** $\frac{5}{15}$

**19.** $\frac{10}{12}$

**20.** $\frac{2}{7}$

**21.** $\frac{3}{24}$

Reduce each fraction to lowest terms.

**22.** $\frac{4}{6}$

**23.** $\frac{5}{15}$

**24.** $\frac{9}{24}$

**25.** $\frac{2}{14}$

**26.** $\frac{6}{9}$

## PROBLEM SOLVING

**27.** "I am a fraction. My numerator is 6 less than my
denominator. In lowest terms, I reduce to $\frac{3}{5}$. What
fraction am I?"

**28.** Mario practiced piano 45 minutes. Brian practiced
trumpet 40 minutes. Write the lowest-term fractions
to show what part of an hour each boy practiced.

# Problem Solving
## Use Logical Reasoning

| UNDERSTAND |
| ANALYZE DATA |
| PLAN |
| ESTIMATE |
| SOLVE |
| EXAMINE |

To solve some problems, you may need to write what you know in a table. Then you can reason logically to complete the table. This problem solving strategy is **Use Logical Reasoning.**

Abe, Ben, Carol, and Dino each wrote a report on a different kind of whale. The reports were about blue whales, fin whales, humpbacks, and bowheads. Carol and Dino did not write about humpbacks. Ben wrote about fin whales. Abe did not write about blue whales, and Dino did not write about bowheads. Who wrote about each type of whale?

*First I'll make a table of what I know.*

*I can use what I know to find more information.*

*Hmmm...Now I know!*

| | Blue | Fin | Hump | Bow |
|------|------|------|------|------|
| Abe | no | | | |
| Ben | | yes | | |
| Carol | | | no | |
| Dino | | | no | no |

| | Blue | Fin | Hump | Bow |
|------|------|------|------|------|
| Abe | no | no | yes | no |
| Ben | no | yes | no | no |
| Carol | | no | no | |
| Dino | | no | no | no |

| | Blue | Fin | Hump | Bow |
|------|------|------|------|------|
| Abe | no | no | yes | no |
| Ben | no | yes | no | no |
| Carol | no | no | no | yes |
| Dino | yes | no | no | no |

Abe: humpbacks; Ben: fins; Carol: bowheads; Dino: blue

Ed and Nita each did two reports on animals. They did not write about any of the same animals. The animals were the elephant, bobcat, leopard, and gorilla. Ed did not write about the elephant. Nita did not write about the gorilla. The person who wrote about the gorilla did not write about the leopard. Which animal did each write about?

| | Ed | Nita |
|----------|------|------|
| Elephant | no | yes |
| Bobcat | | |
| Leopard | | |
| Gorilla | yes | no |

- Which animal did Ed not write about? Which did Nita not write about?

- Copy and complete the table. Use logical reasoning to solve the problem.

252

Use logical reasoning to help you solve these problems.

1. At Renaldo's house each person is in charge of recycling something different. One person recycles cans, another recycles newspapers, another bottles, and another boxes. Renaldo recycles cans. Maria does not recycle newspapers. Juanita does recycle bottles. What does Tina recycle?

2. Lee and Ron found information about conservation of wildlife, trees, energy, and water. Each boy chose two topics different from the other boy's topics. Lee did not study energy. Ron did not study trees. The one who studied animals did not study energy. Which topics did each boy study?

## MIXED PRACTICE

Choose a strategy from the strategies list or use other strategies you know to solve these problems.

| Some Strategies | |
| --- | --- |
| Act Out | Make a Table |
| Use Objects | Solve a Simpler Problem |
| Choose an Operation | Make an Organized List |
| Draw a Picture | Work Backward |
| Guess and Check | Look for a Pattern |
| Use Logical Reasoning | |

3. For every ton of paper recycled, 17 small trees are saved. Tim's school recycled 336 tons of paper last year. How many small trees did they save?

4. Karen recycled 47 cans in January and February. She recycled 7 more in January than in February. How many did she recycle in February?

5. There were about 225 thousand blue whales before man started hunting them. There are only about 15 thousand now. About how many fewer blue whales are there now?

6. Each person makes about 4.5 lb of garbage a day. How many pounds does each person make in a year?

**Garbage Content**

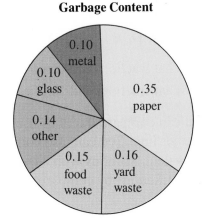

7. Use the circle graph above. What decimal part of the garbage is paper, yard waste, and food waste combined?

8. It takes 182 gallons of water to wash 12 loads of laundry. How many gallons of water does it take to wash 1 load?

9. Gwen, Sarah, Bob, and Nelda were the heads of 4 committees for Conservation Day. One was in charge of food, another drinks, another booths, and another cleanup. Gwen and Sarah did not do drinks or food. Sarah did not do booths. Bob did not do food. What committee was each person in charge of?

*More Practice, page 525, set C*

253

# Comparing and Ordering Fractions

**EXPLORE**  Use Fraction Pieces

Work with a partner.

- Use your fraction pieces. Find at least three fractions you can use to complete the statement. Write each statement using the "is less than" (<) symbol.

- Use the number line. Find at least three fractions you can use to complete the statement. Write each statement using the "is greater than" (>) symbol.

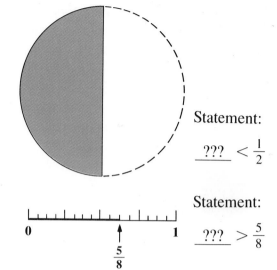

Statement:

$$\underline{???} < \frac{1}{2}$$

Statement:

$$\underline{???} > \frac{5}{8}$$

**TALK ABOUT IT**

1. What fractions did you find that are less than $\frac{1}{2}$?
2. What fractions did you find that are greater than $\frac{5}{8}$?

You can compare fractions using fraction pieces or the number line. You can also compare fractions by finding equivalent fractions with a common denominator. You can order fractions by comparing them two at a time.

| Look at the denominators. | Write equivalent fractions with a common denominator. | Compare the numerators. | The fractions compare the same way the numerators compare. |
|---|---|---|---|
| $\frac{3}{8}$ Not the same $\frac{2}{3}$ | $\frac{3}{8} = \frac{9}{24}$ The same $\frac{2}{3} = \frac{16}{24}$ | $9 < 16$ | $\frac{9}{24} < \frac{16}{24}$ so $\frac{3}{8} < \frac{2}{3}$ |

**TRY IT OUT**

Give the correct sign (<, >, or =) for each ▥.

**1.** $\frac{1}{2}$ ▥ $\frac{3}{7}$     **2.** $\frac{10}{12}$ ▥ $\frac{5}{6}$     **3.** $\frac{4}{5}$ ▥ $\frac{3}{4}$     **4.** $\frac{5}{8}$ ▥ $\frac{2}{3}$     **5.** $\frac{3}{4}$ ▥ $\frac{7}{10}$

Give the correct sign ($<$, $>$, or $=$) for each  .

1. $\frac{1}{5}$  $\frac{1}{4}$      2. $\frac{3}{4}$  $\frac{5}{6}$      3. $\frac{1}{2}$  $\frac{2}{3}$      4. $\frac{4}{5}$  $\frac{5}{8}$      5. $\frac{7}{8}$  $\frac{7}{10}$

6. $\frac{3}{10}$  $\frac{9}{30}$      7. $\frac{1}{3}$  $\frac{1}{2}$      8. $\frac{5}{6}$  $\frac{7}{8}$      9. $\frac{7}{12}$  $\frac{2}{3}$      10. $\frac{7}{10}$  $\frac{3}{4}$

11. $\frac{1}{4}$  $\frac{1}{3}$      12. $\frac{3}{5}$  $\frac{2}{3}$      13. $\frac{1}{3}$  $\frac{3}{8}$      14. $\frac{1}{5}$  $\frac{20}{100}$      15. $\frac{8}{10}$  $\frac{79}{100}$

Compare the fractions two at a time. Then write them in order from least to greatest.

16. $\frac{1}{2}, \frac{3}{8}, \frac{2}{5}$      17. $\frac{5}{8}, \frac{3}{5}, \frac{2}{3}$      18. $\frac{3}{4}, \frac{2}{3}, \frac{7}{12}$      19. $\frac{2}{3}, \frac{3}{4}, \frac{2}{5}$

**MATH REASONING**

20. **True** or **False**? If the numerators of the fractions are the same, the fraction with the larger denominator is the smaller of the two.

**PROBLEM SOLVING**

21. In 1989, $\frac{5}{8}$ of the fifth grade students at Mott school said they plan to go to college. In 1987, $\frac{7}{12}$ of the students said they plan to go to college. In which year did the greater fraction of students say they plan to go to college?

22. The Wildcats won $\frac{3}{4}$ of their games. The Owls won $\frac{5}{6}$ of their games. The Dolphins won $\frac{7}{8}$ of their games. Which team won the greatest fraction of their games? the least?

▶ **CALCULATOR**

We can read a fraction like $\frac{3}{4}$ as "3 divided by 4." We can change a fraction to a decimal by dividing the numerator by the denominator. (On a calculator, $3 \div 4 = 0.75$.)

Use a calculator to compare these fractions. Change each fraction to a decimal, rounded to the nearest hundredth. Then compare the decimals. Give the correct sign ($<$, $>$, or $=$) for each  .

23. $\frac{3}{8}$  $\frac{4}{7}$      24. $\frac{2}{3}$  $\frac{3}{5}$      25. $\frac{3}{4}$  $\frac{5}{6}$      26. $\frac{4}{5}$  $\frac{5}{8}$      27. $\frac{1}{3}$  $\frac{3}{9}$

# Improper Fractions and Mixed Numbers
## Using Manipulatives

Fractions can be used for amounts greater than 1.

**EXPLORE  Use Fraction Pieces**

Work in groups. Find fraction pieces to match the pictures.

Mr. Verga had 2 full wheels and $\frac{5}{8}$ of a wheel of Romano cheese in the display case. He cut the whole amount into eighths for packaging.

**TALK ABOUT IT**

1. How many pieces of cheese does Mr. Verga get from each full wheel?

2. How many pieces of cheese does Mr. Verga have after he cuts all the cheese into eighths?

Fractions with a numerator greater than or equal to the denominator are called **improper fractions.** Examples of improper fractions are $\frac{5}{3}$ and $\frac{5}{2}$. A whole number and a fraction make up a **mixed number.** Examples of mixed numbers are $1\frac{2}{3}$ and $2\frac{1}{2}$.

Mixed number: $2\frac{5}{8}$ (two and five eighths)

Improper fraction: $\frac{21}{8}$ (twenty-one eighths)

**TRY IT OUT**

Use fraction pieces or draw pictures to show each equation.

1. $1\frac{1}{5} = \frac{6}{5}$

2. $\frac{11}{4} = 2\frac{3}{4}$

3. $3 = \frac{9}{3}$

4. $4\frac{1}{2} = \frac{9}{2}$

5. $\frac{11}{6} = 1\frac{5}{6}$

6. $3\frac{1}{2} = \frac{7}{2}$

7. $\frac{8}{4} = 2$

8. $1\frac{1}{8} = \frac{9}{8}$

**PRACTICE**

Write the improper fraction and mixed number for the colored part of each picture.

1.

2.

3.

4.

5.

6.

Write each as an improper fraction. Use objects or pictures if necessary.

7. $1\frac{1}{5}$    8. $3\frac{1}{2}$    9. $4\frac{1}{5}$    10. $2\frac{1}{4}$    11. $6\frac{2}{3}$    12. $4\frac{1}{3}$

Write each as a mixed number. Use objects or pictures if necessary.

13. $\frac{15}{6}$    14. $\frac{10}{3}$    15. $\frac{9}{2}$    16. $\frac{23}{6}$    17. $\frac{17}{5}$    18. $\frac{33}{8}$

**APPLY**

**MATH REASONING**

19. Draw a picture that shows the improper fraction for $2\frac{5}{6}$.

20. Draw a picture that shows the mixed number for $\frac{18}{5}$.

**PROBLEM SOLVING**

21. Ann, Don, Bo, and Gina each like one kind of cheese. One likes Brie, one likes Swiss, one likes Cheddar, and one likes Edam. Ann does not like Edam. Bo and Gina do not like Swiss. Don likes Brie. Gina dislikes Cheddar. Who likes which kind of cheese?

▶ **COMMUNICATION   Writing to Learn**

22. Write a sentence that describes how to change a mixed number to an improper fraction.

23. Write a sentence that describes how to change an improper fraction to a mixed number.

*More Practice, page 512, set B*

**257**

# More Improper Fractions and Mixed Numbers

**EXPLORE** **Examine the Picture**

The amount of grapefruit in the picture at the right can be named using an improper fraction or a mixed number.

**TALK ABOUT IT**

1. How many whole grapefruits are shown?
2. Each grapefruit is made up of how many "half" grapefruits?
3. What mixed number can be used to name the amount of grapefruit?
4. What improper fraction can be used to name the amount of grapefruit?

Here is how to change improper fractions to mixed numbers and mixed numbers to improper fractions.

| To change an improper fraction to a mixed number: | To change a mixed number to an improper fraction: |
|---|---|
| Divide the numerator by the denominator. | Multiply the denominator by the whole number and add the numerator. |

$$\frac{9}{2} \rightarrow 2\overline{)9} \begin{array}{c} 4 \\ \underline{8} \\ 1 \end{array} \rightarrow 4\frac{1}{2}$$

$$4\frac{1}{2} \rightarrow \begin{array}{c} 4 \text{ times } 2 \\ \text{plus } 1 \end{array} \rightarrow \frac{9}{2}$$

## Other Examples

**A** $\frac{11}{4} = 2\frac{3}{4}$      **B** $\frac{12}{3} = 4$      **C** $1\frac{7}{10} = \frac{17}{10}$      **D** $15\frac{1}{2} = \frac{31}{2}$

Rename mixed numbers as improper fractions. Rename improper fractions as mixed numbers in lowest terms.

1. $\frac{10}{3}$      2. $3\frac{1}{2}$      3. $\frac{15}{4}$      4. $7\frac{5}{6}$      5. $\frac{17}{5}$      6. $6\frac{3}{10}$

Copy and complete.

**1.** $2 = \dfrac{\text{||||}}{3}$      **2.** $4 = \dfrac{\text{||||}}{5}$      **3.** $3 = \dfrac{\text{||||}}{3}$      **4.** $5 = \dfrac{\text{||||}}{2}$      **5.** $1 = \dfrac{\text{||||}}{4}$

Rename each as a whole number or mixed number. Reduce to lowest terms.

**6.** $\dfrac{27}{3}$    **7.** $\dfrac{8}{2}$    **8.** $\dfrac{15}{4}$    **9.** $\dfrac{18}{3}$    **10.** $\dfrac{13}{10}$    **11.** $\dfrac{4}{3}$

**12.** $\dfrac{46}{10}$    **13.** $\dfrac{20}{4}$    **14.** $\dfrac{25}{8}$    **15.** $\dfrac{28}{6}$    **16.** $\dfrac{17}{3}$    **17.** $\dfrac{24}{5}$

Rename each mixed number as an improper fraction.

**18.** $8\dfrac{1}{10}$    **19.** $3\dfrac{1}{2}$    **20.** $4\dfrac{1}{5}$    **21.** $2\dfrac{1}{4}$    **22.** $6\dfrac{2}{3}$    **23.** $4\dfrac{1}{3}$

**24.** $9\dfrac{3}{8}$    **25.** $12\dfrac{2}{5}$    **26.** $8\dfrac{1}{5}$    **27.** $2\dfrac{3}{4}$    **28.** $7\dfrac{5}{6}$    **29.** $11\dfrac{1}{4}$

**APPLY**

**MATH REASONING**

Give a mixed number and an improper fraction for the points.

**30.**

**31.**

**PROBLEM SOLVING**

**32.** A box of eggs contains 4 cartons. Each carton holds 1 dozen eggs. Rob has $3\dfrac{1}{2}$ boxes. How many cartons of 1 dozen does he have? How many eggs does he have?

**MIXED REVIEW**

Use mental math to find the quotients.

**33.** $720 \div 8$      **34.** $200 \div 40$      **35.** $2,100 \div 7$      **36.** $5,400 \div 6$

Find the quotients and remainders.

**37.** $42\overline{)2,852}$      **38.** $63\overline{)5,495}$      **39.** $57\overline{)3,876}$      **40.** $29\overline{)2,387}$

# Problem Solving
## Using Data from a Table

### LEARN ABOUT IT

To solve some problems you have to locate the data you need in a table.

> How many times longer is Daniel's boot size than Joey's?

| Jackson Family Rental of Skis, Boots, and Poles | | | | | | |
|---|---|---|---|---|---|---|
| | Skis (cm) | Wt. (lb) | Age/Ht. | Boot Size (mm) | Pole Size (cm) | Binding Setting |
| Julia | 140 | 98 | 41 yr 5 ft 2 in. | 270 | 42 | $3\frac{1}{2}$ |
| Michele | 130 | 82 | 11 yr 4 ft 6 in. | 290 | 40 | 2 |
| Tom | 120 | 59 | 8 yr 4 ft 2 in. | 260 | 36 | 2 |
| Daniel | 180 | 177 | 40 yr 6 ft 2 in. | 330 | 50 | $6\frac{1}{2}$ |
| Joey | 90 | 35 | $3\frac{1}{2}$ yr 3 ft 8 in. | 110 | no | 1 |

I'll find the data I need from the table.

Now I can solve the problem.

Daniel's boot size    330 mm

Joey's boot size    110 mm

$$110\overline{)330} \quad \begin{array}{r} 3 \\ \underline{330} \\ 0 \end{array}$$

Daniel's boot size is 3 times longer than Joey's.

### TRY IT OUT

Solve.

1. How much heavier is the person whose bindings are set at $6\frac{1}{2}$ than the person whose bindings are set at $3\frac{1}{2}$?

2. Daniel's brother Larry rented boots that are 1.2 times as long as Tom's. How long are Larry's boots?

260

Solve. Use any problem solving strategy.

1. The longest run at Birkwood Valley ski resort is 3.5 miles. The longest run at Snow Haven is 1.8 times as long. How many miles is the longest run at Snow Haven?

2. How much would the Jacksons pay for ski-lift tickets for a half day?

| | Lift Tickets | |
| --- | --- | --- |
| | Full Day | Half Day |
| Adult | $24 | $16 |
| Child (under 12) | $12 | $ 8 |

3. Julia, Michele, Tom, and Daniel each like different ski resorts. One likes White Cliffs, one likes Snow Haven, one likes Birkwood, and one likes Mountain Land. Daniel does not like Birkwood. Tom and Michele do not like Snow Haven. Julia likes White Cliffs. Tom does not like Birkwood. Who likes each resort?

Use the table below for problems 4-6.

| Snow Haven Chair Lifts | | |
| --- | --- | --- |
| Chair Lift | Minutes | Rise (ft) |
| West Bowl | 9 | 1,836 |
| Champion | 4 | 375 |
| Powder Run | 6 | 1,132 |
| Boulder | 10 | 1,498 |

4. Jeff got in line for the West Bowl chair at 3:25 p.m. He waited in line for 43 minutes before getting onto the lift. When did he get to the top of the chair lift?

5. How much higher does the West Bowl chair lift go than the Champion chair lift?

6. Suzu starts skiing down Powder Run at 1:45 p.m. She takes 9 minutes. Then she waits in line at Boulder chair for 24 minutes. When does she get to the top of Boulder chair?

7. The Jacksons rented skis, boots, and poles for 3 days. Each adult's set of equipment cost $18 per day. Each child's set of equipment cost $12 per day. Instead of renting by the day, they got a group rate that cost them $86 in all. How much did they save by getting the group rate?

8. **Suppose** Tell which of the following facts would change the solution to problem 7.

   A. The prices will be going up next year.

   B. Mike has a $\frac{1}{2}$-off coupon.

   C. The Jacksons paid with a credit card.

   D. They decided to rent the equipment for 1 day.

# Applied Problem Solving
## Group Decision Making

UNDERSTAND
ANALYZE DATA
PLAN
ESTIMATE
SOLVE
EXAMINE

**Group Skill:**
Listen to Others

The world you are growing up in today is much different from the world of 50, 20, or even just 10 years ago. Many of the big differences have been brought about by advances in technology. As shown in the graph below, there is a growing demand for workers who have been trained to use computers and other technical equipment.

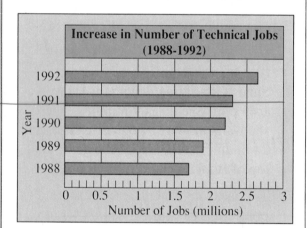

**Increase in Number of Technical Jobs (1988-1992)**

Do you know people whose jobs involve working with computers or other complex equipment such as copiers or recorders? Do you think you might like to work at a technical job after you finish school?

**Facts to Consider**

To help her decide whether it would be a good idea to plan for a career in technology after finishing high school, Jay's older sister, Miriam, made a list of what she thought were the main advantages and disadvantages of a technology career. She gave a point rating of 5, 4, 3, 2, or 1 to each advantage or disadvantage she listed. A rating of 5 meant "very important" and a rating of 1 meant "not important at all."

| Advantages | Rating |
|---|---|
| Good salary and benefits | 4 |
| College degree not required | 3 |
| Many jobs available, usually | 4 |
| Suits my abilities | 5 |
| No hard physical labor | 2 |
| **Disadvantages** | |
| Some special training needed | 2 |
| Usually work alone | 1 |
| Sometimes sudden layoffs | 3 |
| Limited chances for management jobs | 4 |
| Little chance for creativity | 2 |

## Some Questions to Answer

1. How many rating points did Miriam give to advantages of a technology career? to disadvantages?

2. If you were trying to make a decision about a job, what point rating would you give to each of the items in the list Miriam made?

3. Can you name some other things you think would be important in trying to make a career decision?

## What Is Your Decision?

Using your own point ratings for the advantages and disadvantages in Miriam's list, do you think a career in technology would be a good idea for you? Explain your decision.

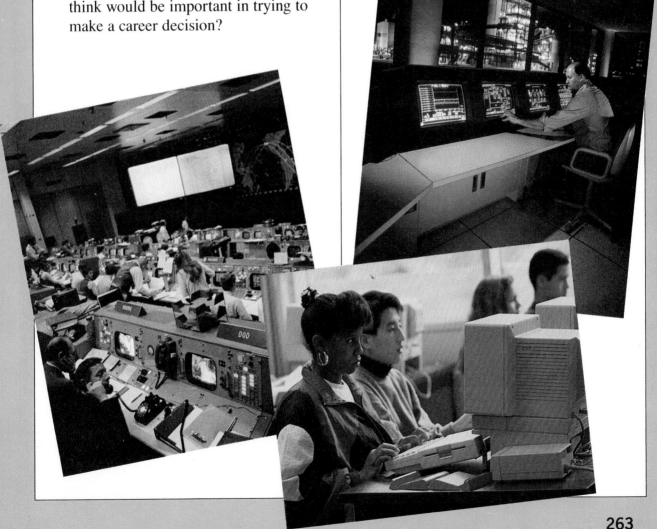

# WRAP UP

## What Is It?

Find the correct match for each term.

1. fraction
2. lowest terms fraction
3. improper fraction

4. terms of a fraction
5. equivalent fractions
6. greatest common factor

A. fractions that name the same amount

B. a fraction in which the greatest common factor of the numerator and denominator is 1

C. the numerator and the denominator of a fraction

D. a number that names a part compared to a whole unit

E. the largest number that is a factor of both the numerator and denominator

F. a fraction in which the numerator is equal to or greater than the denominator

## Sometimes, Always, Never

Complete each statement by writing **sometimes, always,** or **never.** Explain your choices.

7. The numerator of a fraction is __?__ smaller than the denominator.

8. If two fractions have the same nonzero numerator, the fraction with the smaller denominator is __?__ the larger fraction.

9. You can __?__ use cross products to find whether or not two fractions are equivalent.

## Project

Give the lowest-terms fraction for the part of all the whole numbers from 1 to 50 that are:

10. even numbers
11. odd numbers
12. factors of 18
13. multiples of 4
14. multiples of 5

# POWER PRACTICE/TEST

## Part 1    Understanding

Draw pictures to show the fractions in items 1–5.

**1.** $\frac{2}{3}$ of a set                    **2.** $\frac{1}{8}$ of a region

**3.** $\frac{3}{5} = \frac{9}{15}$        **4.** $3\frac{2}{3} = \frac{11}{3}$        **5.** $\frac{19}{4} = 4\frac{3}{4}$

**6.** Complete the table. Describe the pattern.

Give the number for each variable.

**7.** $\frac{5}{12} = \frac{n}{36}$        **8.** $\frac{3}{4} = \frac{a}{20}$

| $x$ | 4 | 5 | 6 | 7 | 8 | 9 |
|---|---|---|---|---|---|---|
| $y$ | 16 | 20 | 24 | | | |

## Part 2    Skills

Give the greatest common factor.

**9.** $\frac{15}{25}$        **10.** $\frac{18}{36}$

Reduce to lowest terms.

**11.** $\frac{8}{12}$        **12.** $\frac{15}{21}$

Write as a mixed number.

**13.** $\frac{11}{4}$        **14.** $\frac{23}{8}$

Write as an improper fraction.

**15.** $4\frac{2}{3}$        **16.** $8\frac{4}{5}$

**17.** Order $\frac{2}{3}$, $\frac{5}{8}$, and $\frac{3}{4}$ from greatest to least.

## Part 3    Applications

**18.** Dennis, Rachel, Mia, and Craig each wrote down one of these numbers: 394; 9,892; 56,146; 2,473. Use the clues to find the number each person wrote.

- Dennis's number does not have 4 digits.

- Rachel's number has more even digits than odd digits.

- If you multiply Mia's number by 4, you get Craig's number.

**19.** Which person has about twice as many goldfish as George?

| Person | Number of Goldfish |
|---|---|
| Suzanne | 29 |
| George | 15 |
| Eve | 7 |
| Stan | 10 |

**20. Challenge.** Draw 24 small squares. Color $\frac{1}{8}$ of the squares red, $\frac{1}{3}$ blue, and $\frac{1}{2}$ yellow. How many squares are not colored?

# ENRICHMENT
## Finding Prime Factors

*Problem:* How many ways can you find to express 60 as a product of two or more factors?

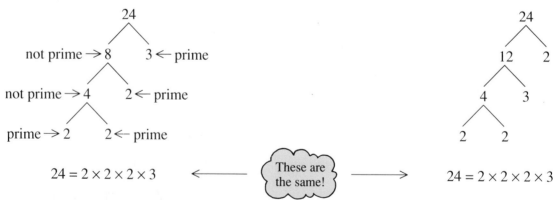

Hey Khala! I found two ways to use multiplication to get a product of 60!... 3×20 and 4×3×5.

There are more ways than that!

---

**Some Facts**
- A **prime number** is a whole number that has exactly two factors.
- The 2 factors of a prime number are the number itself and 1.
  Examples: 7 is a prime number. Its two factors are 7 and 1.
  6 is not a prime number. Its factors are 1, 2, 3, and 6.
- A number greater than 1 that is not prime is a **composite number.**
- A composite number can be expressed as a product of only one set of prime numbers. This expression is the **prime factorization** of the number.

---

You can use a **factor tree** to find the prime factorization of a number. Here are two factor trees for 24.

$$24 = 2 \times 2 \times 2 \times 3$$

These are the same!

$$24 = 2 \times 2 \times 2 \times 3$$

Make a factor tree to find the prime factors of each number. If the number given is prime, write **prime.**

**1.** 20  **2.** 30  **3.** 45  **4.** 23  **5.** 60  **6.** 1,000

# CUMULATIVE REVIEW

1. Find the area of a rectangle that is 23.4 cm long and 12.2 cm wide.

   A. 71.2 cm$^2$    B. 285.48 cm$^2$
   C. 35.6 cm$^2$    D. 142.74 cm$^2$

2. Which estimate must be changed?

   A. $34\overline{)177}$ (6)    B. $61\overline{)446}$ (7)
   C. $75\overline{)659}$ (8)    D. $93\overline{)375}$ (4)

Give the missing numbers.

3. 12.74 m = ▦ m ▦ cm

   A. 127 m 4 cm    B. 1 m 274 cm
   C. 1,274 m 0 cm    D. 12 m 74 cm

4. 4,627 mL = ▦ L

   A. 4.627    B. 46.27
   C. 462.7    D. 0.4627

5. The picture shows the result after dividing. Choose the original division problem.

   A. 36 ÷ 3    B. 72 ÷ 3
   C. 96 ÷ 3    D. 108 ÷ 3

Divide.

6. $6\overline{)44.4}$

   A. 74    B. 0.74
   C. 7.4    D. 0.074

Divide.

7. 7,200 ÷ 80

   A. 9    B. 90
   C. 900    D. 9,000

8. 527.6 ÷ 100

   A. 52.76    B. 5.276
   C. 0.5276    D. 5,276

9. $37\overline{)227}$

   A. 6 R5    B. 5 R42
   C. 5 R5    D. 6 R4

10. $86\overline{)42,507}$

    A. 424 R43    B. 49 R4
    C. 424 R23    D. 494 R23

11. When Maria's dog had a litter of puppies, Maria sold half the litter to the pet store. Then she gave half of the rest to her uncle and half of what was left to Sue. She had one puppy left for herself. How many puppies were in the original litter?

    A. 16    B. 4    C. 8    D. 12

12. Suppose you tear a piece of paper in half and give half to another person. Then each person with paper tears it in half and passes half on to another person. How many people would have a piece of paper after 10 rounds of tearing and passing?

    A. 320    B. 256    C. 512    D. 1,024

# 10

## ADDITION AND SUBTRACTION: FRACTIONS AND MIXED NUMBERS

THEME: PROSE AND POETRY

**M**ATH AND LANGUAGE ARTS

### DATA BANK

Use the Language Arts Data Bank on page 469 to answer the questions.

1 Is the fractional part of the content of Reading Series A that is poetry greater than or less than the part that is poetry in Reading Series B?

**2** List the poems on Side 2 of the *Treasury of Great Poems* that you can listen to in $1\frac{1}{2}$ minutes or less.

**3** Order the fractions for the types of writing in Reading Series A from least to greatest. Order those in Reading Series B from greatest to least.

**4** **Using Critical Thinking** Pat said, "It's easy to estimate that the total playing time for Side 1 of the record is longer than the time for Side 2." Do you agree with that conclusion? Explain.

Students sharpen communication skills as they record readings from a book of poems by Nikki Giovanni.

269

# Adding and Subtracting Fractions
## Like Denominators

### EXPLORE  Analyze The Process

The contents of the reading book used by Mr. Emerson's class are $\frac{3}{5}$ prose fiction and $\frac{1}{5}$ poetry. How much greater is the part that is fiction than the part that is poetry?

| Look at the denominators. | Subtract the numerators. Write the difference over the common denominator. |
|---|---|
| the same $\frac{3}{5} - \frac{1}{5}$ | $3 - 1$ $\frac{3}{5} - \frac{1}{5} = \frac{2}{5}$ |

### TALK ABOUT IT

1. What do you do to the numerators when subtracting fractions with like denominators?
2. What do you do to the denominators?
3. Write the answer to the Explore problem in a complete statement.

## Other Examples

**A** $(1 + 3)$

$\frac{1}{6} + \frac{3}{6} = \frac{4}{6} = \frac{2}{3}$

**B**

$\frac{7}{8} - \frac{3}{8} = \frac{4}{8} = \frac{1}{2}$

**C**

$\frac{3}{4} + \frac{2}{4} = \frac{5}{4} = 1\frac{1}{4}$

Add or subtract. Reduce to lowest terms.

1. $\frac{5}{6} - \frac{1}{6}$
2. $\frac{7}{8} + \frac{3}{8}$
3. $\frac{12}{8} - \frac{10}{8}$
4. $\frac{4}{12} + \frac{6}{12}$
5. $\frac{7}{10} - \frac{3}{10}$

Add. Reduce sums to lowest terms.

**1.** $\frac{1}{5} + \frac{2}{5}$     **2.** $\frac{1}{3} + \frac{1}{3}$     **3.** $\frac{1}{10} + \frac{7}{10}$     **4.** $\frac{3}{8} + \frac{3}{8}$

**5.** $\begin{array}{r} \frac{1}{8} \\ + \frac{3}{8} \\ \hline \end{array}$     **6.** $\begin{array}{r} \frac{5}{10} \\ + \frac{3}{10} \\ \hline \end{array}$     **7.** $\begin{array}{r} \frac{2}{4} \\ + \frac{1}{4} \\ \hline \end{array}$     **8.** $\begin{array}{r} \frac{5}{12} \\ + \frac{1}{12} \\ \hline \end{array}$     **9.** $\begin{array}{r} \frac{2}{6} \\ + \frac{2}{6} \\ \hline \end{array}$

Subtract. Reduce differences to lowest terms.

**10.** $\frac{2}{3} - \frac{1}{3}$     **11.** $\frac{5}{12} - \frac{1}{12}$     **12.** $\frac{4}{5} - \frac{2}{5}$     **13.** $\frac{9}{10} - \frac{3}{10}$

**14.** $\begin{array}{r} \frac{3}{8} \\ - \frac{2}{8} \\ \hline \end{array}$     **15.** $\begin{array}{r} \frac{13}{15} \\ - \frac{4}{15} \\ \hline \end{array}$     **16.** $\begin{array}{r} \frac{7}{8} \\ - \frac{5}{8} \\ \hline \end{array}$     **17.** $\begin{array}{r} \frac{11}{12} \\ - \frac{4}{12} \\ \hline \end{array}$     **18.** $\begin{array}{r} \frac{15}{16} \\ - \frac{9}{16} \\ \hline \end{array}$

**19.** Find the sum of $\frac{4}{10}$ and $\frac{6}{10}$.     **20.** Subtract $\frac{1}{6}$ from $\frac{5}{6}$.

**MATH REASONING**

Evaluate each expression when the variable has the given value.

**21.** $x + \frac{3}{5}$ when $x = \frac{4}{5}$     **22.** $m - \frac{1}{4}$ when $m = \frac{5}{4}$     **23.** $h + \frac{3}{10}$ when $h = \frac{5}{10}$

**PROBLEM SOLVING**

**24.** Ogden Nash's poem, "The Octopus," took up $\frac{1}{4}$ of the page in a reading book. A picture took up $\frac{3}{4}$ of the page. How much greater was the fraction of the page taken up by the picture?

**25. Language Arts Data Bank** How much greater is the fraction of the contents that are stories in Reading Series B than the fraction that are stories in Reading Series A? See page 469.

DATA BANK

▶ **ALGEBRA**

Write the algebraic expression. Use the letter $n$ for the unknown number.

**26.** a number increased by $\frac{1}{2}$     **27.** $\frac{3}{5}$ less than a number

**28.** 5 times a number     **29.** the sum of a number and $\frac{4}{5}$

# Least Common Multiple

**EXPLORE** **Solve to Understand**

Kara collects payments from her morning newspaper customers every 6 days. She collects from her afternoon customers every 8 days. Today she collected payments from all of her customers. How many days will it be before she again collects from her morning and afternoon customers on the same day?

**TALK ABOUT IT**

1. On what days will she collect from her morning customers?
2. On what days will she collect from her afternoon customers?
3. When is the first day she will collect from morning and afternoon customers on the same day?

The numerical part of the answer to the problem above is the **least common multiple (LCM)** of 6 and 8. Here is how to find the least common multiple of 4 and 6.

| List some multiples of each number. (Do not list 0.) | List the common multiples (the numbers in both lists). | Choose the smallest of these common multiples. |
|---|---|---|
| **4:** 4, 8, 12, 16, 20, 24 <br> **6:** 6, 12, 18, 24, 30, 36 | → **12, 24** | **12** |

The least common multiple of 4 and 6 is 12.
For the fractions $\frac{1}{4}$ and $\frac{1}{6}$, the **least common denominator** is 12.

## Other Examples

multiples of 4: 4, 8, 12  
multiples of 8: 8, 16, 24   LCM is 8.

multiples of 5: 5, 10, 15, 20  
multiples of 3: 3, 6, 12, 15, 18   LCM is 15.

Find the least common multiple for each pair of numbers.

**1.** 3 and 4        **2.** 3 and 5        **3.** 4 and 12        **4.** 8 and 10        **5.** 6 and 10

272

Find the least common multiple (LCM) for each pair of numbers.

**1.** 8 and 12 **2.** 4 and 5 **3.** 2 and 3 **4.** 6 and 8 **5.** 3 and 8

**6.** 6 and 9 **7.** 5 and 6 **8.** 4 and 6 **9.** 8 and 10 **10.** 9 and 12

Find the least common denominator (LCD) for each pair of fractions.

**11.** $\frac{1}{2}, \frac{2}{3}$ **12.** $\frac{2}{5}, \frac{5}{10}$ **13.** $\frac{1}{4}, \frac{1}{2}$ **14.** $\frac{2}{3}, \frac{5}{6}$ **15.** $\frac{5}{8}, \frac{7}{16}$

**APPLY**

**MATH REASONING**

■ Try a shortcut! Start a list of multiples of the larger
number of a pair whose LCM you want to find. Check
each number to see if it is also a multiple of the smaller
number. The smallest multiple of each is the LCM.

Use the shortcut to find the LCD for these fractions.

**16.** $\frac{1}{8}, \frac{5}{6}$ **17.** $\frac{2}{3}, \frac{3}{4}$ **18.** $\frac{3}{5}, \frac{1}{6}$ **19.** $\frac{1}{4}, \frac{5}{12}$ **20.** $\frac{5}{6}, \frac{49}{100}$

**PROBLEM SOLVING**

**21.** Myra collects from her morning newspaper customers
every 5 days. She collects from her afternoon
customers every 8 days. Today is February 1, and she
collected from both customers today. Is there another
day in February when she will again collect from both
customers on the same day?

▶ **CALCULATOR**

You can use the counting constant on a calculator to find the
LCM of two numbers. For example: Find the LCM of 24
and 18.

Find 5 or 6 multiples of the larger number:
[ON/AC] [+] 24 [=] [=], and so on.
Find multiples of 18: [ON/AC] [+] 18 [=] [=], and so on.
The first multiple on the display that is also a multiple of 24
is the LCM of 18 and 24.

Find the LCM of these numbers.

**22.** 24 and 26 **23.** 48 and 64 **24.** 18 and 48 **25.** 36 and 20

*More Practice, page 512, set E*

# Adding and Subtracting Fractions
## Making the Connection

**EXPLORE  Use Fraction Pieces**

Work with a partner.

- Pick a pair of fractions from those in the box.
- One partner shows each fraction using fraction pieces.
- The other partner puts together the two groups.
- Trade fraction pieces for equivalent pieces. Write the fraction that names the total.
- Write a number sentence that shows what you did.
- Repeat this several times changing roles and using different pairs of fractions.

| $\frac{1}{6}$ and $\frac{1}{3}$ | $\frac{1}{2}$ and $\frac{1}{4}$ |
|---|---|
| $\frac{3}{5}$ and $\frac{1}{10}$ | $\frac{1}{3}$ and $\frac{5}{12}$ |
| $\frac{1}{2}$ and $\frac{3}{8}$ | $\frac{1}{6}$ and $\frac{7}{12}$ |
| $\frac{1}{4}$ and $\frac{3}{8}$ | $\frac{5}{12}$ and $\frac{1}{2}$ |

**TALK ABOUT IT**

1. Use one of the pairs of fractions above. Tell what trade had to be made to write the total.

2. Why do you have to rename one of the fractions for each of the pairs above?

3. Use fraction pieces to find the total for $\frac{1}{2}$ and $\frac{1}{3}$. Explain any trades that had to be made.

You have put fraction pieces together, traded, and found the fraction that names the total. Now you will see a way to record what you have done. We can use fraction pieces to show $\frac{1}{4} + \frac{5}{8}$.

**What You Do**

Show each fraction.

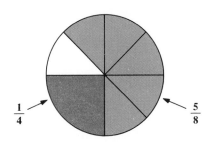

$\frac{1}{4}$          $\frac{5}{8}$

**What You Record**

$$\begin{array}{r} \frac{1}{4} \\ + \frac{5}{8} \\ \hline \end{array}$$

Can you change the fractions so they have the same denominator?

Change $\frac{1}{4}$ to an equivalent fraction.

$$\begin{array}{r} \frac{1}{4} = \frac{2}{8} \\ + \frac{5}{8} = \frac{5}{8} \\ \hline \end{array}$$

How many eighths are there altogether?

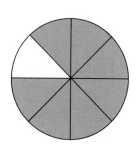

Add the numerators. Write the sum over the common denominator.

$$\begin{array}{r} \frac{2}{8} \\ + \frac{5}{8} \quad 2+5=7 \\ \hline \frac{7}{8} \end{array}$$

**TRY IT OUT**

Use fraction pieces to find each sum or difference. Rename one fraction so they both have the same denominator. Record what you did.

1. $\frac{1}{2} - \frac{1}{4}$

2. $\frac{2}{5} + \frac{3}{10}$

3. $\frac{2}{3} - \frac{1}{6}$

4. $\frac{2}{6} + \frac{3}{12}$

5. $\frac{1}{4} + \frac{3}{8}$

6. $\frac{1}{4} - \frac{1}{8}$

7. $\frac{1}{2} + \frac{1}{4}$

8. $\frac{5}{6} - \frac{2}{3}$

9. $\frac{4}{5} + \frac{1}{10}$

10. $\frac{3}{4} - \frac{1}{8}$

# Adding and Subtracting Fractions
## Unlike Denominators

**EXPLORE** Estimate Using Objects

Work in groups. Use fraction pieces to estimate each sum.

- $\frac{1}{2}$ and $\frac{1}{3}$ is about ___?___ .
- $\frac{3}{5}$ and $\frac{1}{2}$ is about ___?___ .
- $\frac{3}{4}$ and $\frac{5}{8}$ is about ___?___ .

Here is how to add fractions with unlike denominators.

| Look at the denominators. | Find the least common denominator. | Write equivalent fractions with this denominator. | Add the fractions. |
|---|---|---|---|
| $\frac{1}{4}$ ← Not the $+\frac{3}{8}$ ← same | Multiples of 4: 4, 8 Multiples of 8: 8 | $\frac{1}{4} = \frac{2}{8}$ $+\frac{3}{8} = \frac{3}{8}$ | $\frac{2}{8}$ $+\frac{3}{8}$ $\frac{5}{8}$ |

**TALK ABOUT IT**

1. Will the LCD always be one of the denominators in the given fraction?
2. How could you estimate that the sum will be less than 1?

**Other Examples**

A  $\frac{2}{3} = \frac{8}{12}$
$+\frac{3}{4} = \frac{9}{12}$
Rename → $\frac{17}{12} = 1\frac{5}{12}$

B  $\frac{5}{6} = \frac{20}{24}$
$-\frac{3}{8} = \frac{9}{24}$
$\frac{11}{24}$

C  $\frac{3}{5} = \frac{12}{20}$
$-\frac{1}{4} = \frac{5}{20}$
$\frac{7}{20}$

Add or subtract.

1. $\frac{1}{8}$
$+\frac{3}{4}$

2. $\frac{1}{3}$
$+\frac{2}{5}$

3. $\frac{2}{3}$
$-\frac{1}{4}$

4. $\frac{7}{8}$
$-\frac{5}{10}$

5. $\frac{2}{3}$
$+\frac{3}{5}$

Add or subtract. Reduce answers to lowest terms.

**1.** $\dfrac{2}{5}$
$+\dfrac{3}{10}$

**2.** $\dfrac{4}{5}$
$-\dfrac{1}{2}$

**3.** $\dfrac{1}{6}$
$+\dfrac{1}{3}$

**4.** $\dfrac{3}{4}$
$+\dfrac{1}{2}$

**5.** $\dfrac{5}{6}$
$-\dfrac{2}{3}$

**6.** $\dfrac{1}{4}$
$+\dfrac{3}{8}$

**7.** $\dfrac{2}{3}$
$-\dfrac{1}{12}$

**8.** $\dfrac{7}{8}$
$-\dfrac{3}{4}$

**9.** $\dfrac{1}{5}$
$+\dfrac{1}{2}$

**10.** $\dfrac{1}{3}$
$+\dfrac{3}{4}$

**11.** $\dfrac{9}{10} + \dfrac{3}{100}$

**12.** $\dfrac{3}{4} - \dfrac{2}{3}$

**13.** $\dfrac{3}{10} + \dfrac{9}{20}$

**14.** $\dfrac{1}{6} - \dfrac{1}{8}$

**15.** $\dfrac{3}{10} + \dfrac{49}{100}$

**16.** $\dfrac{4}{5} - \dfrac{3}{10}$

**17.** $\dfrac{9}{100} + \dfrac{9}{10}$

**18.** $\dfrac{83}{100} + \dfrac{7}{10}$

**19.** What is the sum of $\dfrac{5}{6}$ and $\dfrac{5}{8}$?

**20.** What is $\dfrac{4}{5}$ less than $\dfrac{7}{8}$?

## APPLY

### MATH REASONING

Evaluate each expression for the values given.

**21.** $m + \dfrac{2}{3}$ for $m = \dfrac{3}{5}$ and for $m = \dfrac{1}{8}$

**22.** $n - \dfrac{1}{4}$ for $n = \dfrac{4}{5}$ and for $n = \dfrac{3}{10}$

### PROBLEM SOLVING

**23.** Plant C grew $\dfrac{2}{3}$ in. more than Plant D in a science experiment. Plant D grew $\dfrac{7}{8}$ in. How much did Plant C grow?

**24.** Plant B grew $\dfrac{1}{2}$ in. more than Plant A. Plant C grew $\dfrac{2}{3}$ in. less than Plant B. Plant D grew $\dfrac{1}{2}$ in. more than Plant C. Plant D grew $\dfrac{9}{10}$ in. How much did each plant grow?

### MIXED REVIEW

Divide.

**25.** $72 \div 23$  **26.** $587 \div 68$  **27.** $629 \div 74$  **28.** $388 \div 54$  **29.** $471 \div 49$

Give the next three equivalent fractions.

**30.** $\dfrac{1}{3}$  **31.** $\dfrac{3}{5}$  **32.** $\dfrac{1}{10}$  **33.** $\dfrac{2}{7}$

*More Practice, page 513, set A*

# Problem Solving
## Problems Without Solutions

UNDERSTAND
ANALYZE DATA
PLAN
ESTIMATE
SOLVE
EXAMINE

**LEARN ABOUT IT**

All the problems you have seen
so far have had solutions. Some
problems do not have solutions.

> Danielle's father bought her 5 coins for her collection
> of American coins. None of the coins was a half dollar.
> Could the total face value of the coins be $1.00?

> I can make an organized list to
> help me find the possibilities. I'll
> use Q for quarter, D for dime, and
> N for nickel.

| Q | D | N | Face Value |
|---|---|---|---|
| 5 | 0 | 0 | $1.25 |
| 4 | 1 | 0 | $1.10 |
| 4 | 0 | 1 | $1.05 |
| 3 | 1 | 1 | $ .90 |
| 2 | 3 | 0 | $ .80 |

None of the possibilities adds
up to $100.

This problem has no solution.

You cannot get exactly $1.00 with 5 coins if one is not a
half dollar.

**TRY IT OUT**

If the problem has a solution, find it. If it has no solution,
explain why not.

**1.** Ray has a collection of old U.S. coins.
He bought 4 more old coins. Their face
value is 75¢. None is a quarter. What
coins did he buy?

**2.** Rosa was looking at two facing pages
in a book about old Spanish "pieces of
eight." Just for fun, she quickly added
the numbers of the pages and got 24.
Did she add correctly?

**3.** At the coin show, Jeff's father set up a
rectangular table to sell coins. The
perimeter of the table was 210 in. One
side was 52 in. What was the length of
the other side?

**4.** Tommy just bought 5 coins for his
collection. They were all pennies,
nickels, or quarters. When he added
their face values, he got 55¢ as the
total. Did he add correctly?

Solve. Choose a strategy from the list or use other strategies that you know.

| Some Strategies | |
| --- | --- |
| Act Out | Make a Table |
| Use Objects | Solve a Simpler Problem |
| Choose an Operation | Make an Organized List |
| Draw a Picture | Work Backward |
| Guess and Check | Look for a Pattern |
| Use Logical Reasoning | |

1. Denise has $\frac{1}{2}$ page of Lincoln pennies and $\frac{2}{3}$ page of buffalo nickels. How many pages does she have altogether?

2. Divers who discovered a Spanish ship that was wrecked in 1622 found two chests. One weighed 137 pounds and contained 2,516 coins. Another weighed 124 pounds and contained 7,139 coins. How many coins did the divers find?

3. Jim bought 10 Greek coins for $27.50. Each coin cost the same amount. How much did each coin cost?

4. How much do you save by buying the off-center coins together instead of one at a time?

| Off-center Lincoln penny | $ 0.99 |
| --- | --- |
| Off-center Jefferson nickel | $ 3.95 |
| Off-center Roosevelt dime | $ 3.95 |
| Off-center Washington quarter | $ 9.95 |
| A complete set of 4 (one of each) | $16.95 |

5. Elsa keeps her coin collection in a special case. The area of the case's cover is 17 in.². The width and the length are both a whole number of inches. What are the length and the width of the case?

6. Martin gave $\frac{1}{5}$ of his collection of old coins to his brother. He gave $\frac{3}{4}$ to his friend Sam. What part of his collection did he give away altogether?

7. Elena could get 3 half-dimes for $13. How much would 15 half-dimes cost her?

8. Ms. Braun has a large collection of coins. She has 48 coins in one book, 54 in another book, 45 in a third book, and 57 in a fourth book. About how many coins does Ms. Braun have altogether in the four books?

9. **Talk About Your Solution** Jennifer spent $\frac{1}{2}$ of her money on Washington quarters. Then she spent $3 on coin books. She had $2.12 left. How much did she have to start with? Explain your solution to a classmate. Compare your solutions.

# Estimating Fraction Sums and Differences

**LEARN ABOUT IT**

**EXPLORE  Examine the Map**

Roberto made a map to show some distances between several cities in the United States and Mexico. He wrote his measurements on the map.

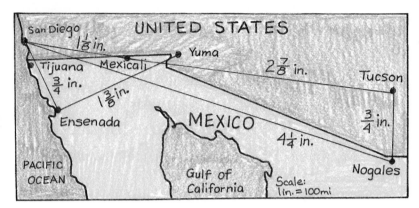

## TALK ABOUT IT

1. What whole number of inches on the map is closest to the distance between Tucson and Mexicali?

2. How would you estimate the distance in miles between Tucson and Mexicali? between Nogales and San Diego?

   Estimate the sum: $\frac{3}{4} + 4\frac{5}{8} + 1\frac{3}{8} + 2\frac{7}{8}$

- **Using rounding**
  Round to whole numbers.          $1 + 5 + 1 + 3 = 10$

  Round **down** if the fraction part is less than $\frac{1}{2}$. Round **up** if the fraction part is greater than or equal to $\frac{1}{2}$.

- **Using compatible numbers**
  Substitute whole numbers or $\frac{1}{2}$.          $1 + 4\frac{1}{2} + 1\frac{1}{2} + 3 = 10$

**TRY IT OUT**

Use the estimation method of your choice.

1. $6\frac{1}{4} - 2\frac{5}{6}$    2. $12\frac{1}{8} - 4\frac{3}{4}$    3. $2\frac{3}{5} + 1\frac{1}{2} + 5\frac{3}{8}$

4. $1\frac{7}{8} + \frac{9}{16} + 3\frac{4}{9}$    5. $7\frac{5}{6} - 2\frac{2}{3}$    6. $3\frac{1}{8} + \frac{3}{4} + 4\frac{1}{6}$

7. Estimate the distance in miles between Ensenada and Yuma.

8. Estimate the distance in miles if you travel from Tucson to Ensenada through Mexicali and San Diego.

# POWER PRACTICE/QUIZ

Find the least common multiple (LCM) for each pair of numbers.

**1.** 2, 3      **2.** 8, 4      **3.** 18, 6      **4.** 9, 5      **5.** 10, 4      **6.** 3, 7

Suppose you showed these four problems using fraction pieces.

**7.** For which problems can you rename the fractions using sixths to find the answer?

**A.** $\frac{2}{3} + \frac{5}{6}$      **B.** $\frac{1}{2} + \frac{1}{3}$

**C.** $\frac{7}{8} - \frac{1}{8}$      **D.** $\frac{5}{9} - \frac{1}{6}$

**8.** For which problems can the final answer be reduced?

Add or subtract. Reduce answers to lowest terms.

**9.** $\frac{3}{5} + \frac{1}{5}$      **10.** $\frac{5}{12} + \frac{5}{12}$      **11.** $\frac{1}{6} + \frac{1}{4}$      **12.** $\frac{2}{3} + \frac{1}{6}$

**13.** $\frac{3}{8} + \frac{5}{8}$      **14.** $\frac{5}{6} - \frac{1}{6}$      **15.** $\frac{7}{9} - \frac{5}{18}$      **16.** $\frac{9}{10} - \frac{3}{8}$

**17.** $\begin{array}{r} \frac{9}{10} \\ -\frac{3}{10} \\ \hline \end{array}$    **18.** $\begin{array}{r} \frac{3}{4} \\ -\frac{1}{4} \\ \hline \end{array}$    **19.** $\begin{array}{r} \frac{3}{5} \\ -\frac{1}{3} \\ \hline \end{array}$    **20.** $\begin{array}{r} \frac{5}{6} \\ +\frac{4}{15} \\ \hline \end{array}$    **21.** $\begin{array}{r} \frac{7}{12} \\ -\frac{5}{12} \\ \hline \end{array}$

**22.** $\begin{array}{r} \frac{3}{4} \\ +\frac{1}{2} \\ \hline \end{array}$    **23.** $\begin{array}{r} \frac{2}{3} \\ +\frac{3}{4} \\ \hline \end{array}$    **24.** $\begin{array}{r} \frac{5}{7} \\ +\frac{1}{7} \\ \hline \end{array}$    **25.** $\begin{array}{r} \frac{7}{8} \\ -\frac{5}{6} \\ \hline \end{array}$    **26.** $\begin{array}{r} \frac{11}{12} \\ -\frac{1}{4} \\ \hline \end{array}$

## PROBLEM SOLVING

Solve the fraction riddles. If there is no solution, tell how you know.

**27.** "My numerator is 3 less than my denominator. When you add me to $\frac{3}{4}$, my sum is 1."

**28.** "My denominator is 6 more than my numerator. When you subtract me from $\frac{7}{12}$, the difference is $\frac{1}{4}$."

**29.** "I am equivalent to $\frac{3}{8}$. When you double my numerator you get my denominator."

**30.** "I am in lowest terms. When you double my numerator and my denominator the result is $\frac{10}{15}$."

# Adding and Subtracting Mixed Numbers
## Making the Connection

### EXPLORE  Use Fraction Pieces

Work with a partner.

- Pick a pair of mixed numbers from those at the right.
- One partner shows each mixed number using fraction pieces.
- The other partner puts together the two groups to find the total.
- Pick another pair of mixed numbers.
- One partner shows only the larger of the two numbers using fraction pieces.
- The other partner takes away an amount represented by the smaller mixed number.

$$1\frac{1}{4} \qquad 2\frac{1}{4} \qquad 3\frac{1}{4}$$

$$2\frac{1}{2} \qquad 1\frac{1}{2} \qquad 2\frac{3}{4}$$

$$3\frac{3}{4} \qquad 3\frac{1}{2} \qquad 1\frac{3}{4}$$

### TALK ABOUT IT

1. Use one pair of mixed numbers. What trades had to be made when the two groups were put together?
2. Use one pair of mixed numbers. What trades had to be made when taking the smaller amount away from the larger amount?
3. Explain how 1 whole unit can be traded for fraction pieces.

You have put together and taken away fraction pieces to find sums and differences. Now you will see a way to record what you have done. We can use fraction pieces to show $3\frac{1}{4} - 1\frac{3}{4}$.

|  **What You Do**  |  **What You Record**  |

Show the greater mixed number.

$$3\frac{1}{4}$$
$$-1\frac{3}{4}$$

— switch everything to impropers

— get common denominator

Can you take away $\frac{3}{4}$?  If not, trade.

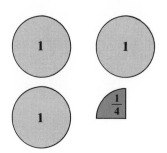

Trade

$$3\frac{1}{4} = 2\frac{5}{4}$$
$$-1\frac{3}{4} = 1\frac{3}{4}$$

Take away the fraction part. Take away the whole number part.

$$2\frac{5}{4}$$  Subtract the fractions.
$$-1\frac{3}{4}$$  Subtract the whole numbers.
$$\overline{1\frac{2}{4}} = 1\frac{1}{2}$$

---

**TRY IT OUT**

Use fraction pieces to find each sum or difference. Record what you do.

**1.** $3\frac{2}{3} - 1\frac{1}{3}$  **2.** $1\frac{1}{5} + 1\frac{3}{5}$  **3.** $3\frac{1}{6} - 1\frac{5}{6}$  **4.** $1\frac{4}{5} + 1\frac{3}{5}$

**5.** $2\frac{1}{2} + 2\frac{1}{4}$  **6.** $1\frac{5}{8} + 1\frac{3}{4}$  **7.** $4\frac{2}{3} - 1\frac{1}{6}$  **8.** $3\frac{1}{5} - 1\frac{7}{10}$

# Adding Mixed Numbers

**EXPLORE** **Analyze the Process**

Jan and Dean spent $1\frac{3}{4}$ h decorating a valentines box. They spent $2\frac{1}{2}$ h making valentines. Altogether, how much time did they spend on these jobs?

Here is how to find the answer.

| Look at the denominators. | Find equivalent fractions with like denominators. | Add the fractions. | Add the whole numbers. |
|---|---|---|---|
| $1\frac{3}{4}$ ← Not the same <br> $+2\frac{1}{2}$ | $1\frac{3}{4} = 1\frac{3}{4}$ <br> $+2\frac{1}{2} = 2\frac{2}{4}$ | $1\frac{3}{4}$ <br> $+2\frac{2}{4}$ <br> $\frac{5}{4}$ | $1\frac{3}{4}$ <br> $+2\frac{2}{4}$ <br> $3\frac{5}{4} = 4\frac{1}{4}$ <br> Rename |

**TALK ABOUT IT**

1. How do you know that the LCD was 4?
2. Why are the fractions added first?

**Other Examples**

A
$$12\frac{1}{5} = 12\frac{3}{15}$$
$$+17\frac{2}{3} = 17\frac{10}{15}$$
$$29\frac{13}{15}$$

B
$$7\frac{1}{2} = 7\frac{10}{20}$$
$$5\frac{4}{5} = 5\frac{16}{20}$$
$$+2\frac{3}{4} = 2\frac{15}{20}$$
$$14\frac{41}{20} = 16\frac{1}{20}$$

Add. Reduce sums to lowest terms.

1. $4\frac{4}{5}$
$+2\frac{3}{5}$

2. $5\frac{5}{6}$
$+8\frac{1}{3}$

3. $9\frac{3}{4}$
$+14\frac{5}{6}$

4. $34\frac{5}{6}$
$+25\frac{4}{5}$

5. $8\frac{3}{4}$
$+5\frac{1}{3}$
$+6\frac{1}{6}$

Add. Reduce sums to lowest terms.

**1.** $3\frac{2}{3}$

$+6\frac{2}{3}$

**2.** $8\frac{5}{6}$

$+2\frac{4}{6}$

**3.** $11\frac{5}{7}$

$+7\frac{6}{7}$

**4.** $4\frac{7}{12}$

$+8\frac{5}{6}$

**5.** $19\frac{1}{2}$

$+2\frac{3}{4}$

**6.** $92\frac{3}{5}$

$88\frac{3}{5}$

$+9\frac{3}{5}$

**7.** $27\frac{1}{4}$

$46\frac{3}{4}$

$+50\frac{1}{2}$

**8.** $27\frac{1}{2}$

$18\frac{5}{8}$

$+12\frac{1}{4}$

**9.** $48\frac{1}{10}$

$65\frac{3}{5}$

$+74\frac{1}{2}$

**10.** $40\frac{4}{5}$

$23\frac{5}{6}$

$+8\frac{10}{15}$

Estimate each sum.

**11.** $5\frac{4}{5}+12\frac{1}{8}$ **12.** $9\frac{4}{5}+8\frac{3}{10}$ **13.** $4\frac{3}{10}+7\frac{7}{8}$ **14.** $8\frac{2}{3}+7\frac{1}{8}$

APPLY

### MATH REASONING

**15.** Give the number for each ▦.  ▦$\frac{3}{5}+8\frac{5}{▦}=14\frac{13}{▦}$

### PROBLEM SOLVING

**16.** Jan and Dean used $3\frac{1}{4}$ yd of red ribbon and $3\frac{5}{8}$ yd of white ribbon for their valentine box. How many yards of ribbon did they use altogether?

**17.** Three boxes full of valentines were weighed. Their weights were $1\frac{1}{2}$ lb, $2\frac{1}{8}$ lb, and $1\frac{3}{4}$ lb. What was the total weight of these boxes?

▶ **MENTAL MATH**

You can use **compatible numbers** to add mixed numbers.
For example:

$4\frac{4}{5}+2\frac{1}{2}+3\frac{1}{5}$     $4\frac{4}{5}+3\frac{1}{5}$ are easy to add mentally:

$$4+3+1=8; \quad 8+2\frac{1}{2}=10\frac{1}{2}$$

Decide which you can solve using mental math. Find those sums only.

**18.** $8\frac{1}{4}+4\frac{1}{2}+1\frac{3}{4}$ **19.** $1\frac{7}{8}+2\frac{3}{4}+4\frac{1}{2}$ **20.** $6\frac{5}{6}+7\frac{3}{4}+3\frac{1}{6}$

# Subtracting Mixed Numbers

**EXPLORE  Analyze the Process**

Mortimer Mouse won the high jump with a jump of $9\frac{1}{4}$ in. Miranda Mouse jumped $7\frac{1}{2}$ in. How much higher was Mortimer's jump?

Here is how to find the answer.

| Look at the denominators. | Find equivalent fractions with like denominators. | Rename if necessary. Subtract the fractions. | Subtract the whole numbers. |
|---|---|---|---|
| $9\frac{1}{4}$ ← Not the same $-7\frac{1}{2}$ | $9\frac{1}{4} = 9\frac{1}{4}$ $-7\frac{1}{2} = 7\frac{2}{4}$ | $9\frac{1}{4} = 8\frac{5}{4}$ $7\frac{2}{4} = 7\frac{2}{4}$ $\frac{3}{4}$ | $8\frac{5}{4}$ $-7\frac{2}{4}$ $1\frac{3}{4}$ |

**TALK ABOUT IT**

1. Why was $9\frac{1}{4}$ renamed?
2. How could you have estimated the difference?
3. Give the answer to the Explore problem in a complete sentence.

**Other Examples**

**A**
$$14 = 13\frac{3}{3}$$
$$-12\frac{2}{3} = 12\frac{2}{3}$$
$$1\frac{1}{3}$$

**B**
$$12\frac{1}{3} = 12\frac{2}{6} = 11\frac{8}{6}$$
$$-9\frac{5}{6} = 9\frac{5}{6} = 9\frac{5}{6}$$
$$2\frac{3}{6} = 2\frac{1}{2}$$

Subtract.

1. $6\frac{1}{3}$
$-3\frac{2}{3}$

2. $11$
$-6\frac{3}{5}$

3. $7\frac{2}{5}$
$-3\frac{7}{10}$

4. $9\frac{2}{3}$
$-6\frac{5}{6}$

5. $11\frac{3}{4}$
$-5\frac{3}{8}$

Subtract. Reduce answers to lowest terms.

**1.** $6\frac{1}{5}$
$-\ 3\frac{5}{10}$

**2.** $8\frac{1}{4}$
$-\ 3\frac{3}{4}$

**3.** $10\frac{1}{3}$
$-\ 4\frac{2}{3}$

**4.** $22$
$-\ 9\frac{5}{8}$

**5.** $32\frac{1}{6}$
$-\ 10\frac{5}{12}$

**6.** $47\frac{5}{8}$
$-\ 11\frac{3}{4}$

**7.** $41\frac{1}{2}$
$-\ 7\frac{1}{10}$

**8.** $86\frac{1}{3}$
$-\ 38\frac{3}{4}$

**9.** $60\frac{1}{6}$
$-\ 7\frac{4}{5}$

**10.** $52\frac{3}{8}$
$-\ 27\frac{4}{5}$

Estimate each difference.

**11.** $67\frac{3}{5} - 48\frac{1}{3}$ **12.** $60\frac{3}{4} - 26$ **13.** $87\frac{1}{5} - 16\frac{9}{10}$ **14.** $43\frac{1}{4} - 29\frac{5}{8}$

**MATH REASONING**

Use **mental math** to write the number for each ▓.

**15.** $5\frac{3}{8} + 7\frac{1}{6} = 12\frac{13}{24} \rightarrow 5\frac{3}{8} + 5\frac{1}{6} = $ ▓

**16.** $8\frac{4}{5} - 3\frac{1}{2} = 5\frac{3}{10} \rightarrow 10\frac{4}{5} - 3\frac{1}{2} = $ ▓

**PROBLEM SOLVING**

**17.** Mortimer Mouse set a new pole vault record of 15 in. The old record was only $8\frac{1}{4}$ in. By how much did he break the record?

**18.** Miranda Mouse broke the old record for the long jump event by a length of $3\frac{3}{4}$ in. The old record was $18\frac{5}{8}$ in. How far did Miranda jump?

Give the correct sign ($>$, $<$, or $=$) for each ▓.

**19.** $\frac{2}{4}$ ▓ $\frac{2}{4}$ **20.** $\frac{3}{4}$ ▓ $\frac{2}{5}$ **21.** $\frac{7}{8}$ ▓ $\frac{14}{16}$ **22.** $\frac{4}{16}$ ▓ $\frac{2}{4}$

Divide and check.

**23.** $24,805 \div 41$ **24.** $22,790 \div 53$ **25.** $12,749 \div 61$ **26.** $\$329.67 \div 37$

*More Practice, page 513, set C*

# More Adding and Subtracting
## Whole Numbers, Fractions, and Mixed Numbers

## LEARN ABOUT IT

### EXPLORE  Analyze the Process

On a recording of readings of popular poems, "Gunga Din" lasts $4\frac{1}{2}$ min, "The Owl and the Pussycat" lasts $1\frac{3}{4}$ min, and "The Highwayman" lasts 7 min. What is the total time needed for listening to these three poems?

To solve the problem, add 7, $1\frac{3}{4}$, and $4\frac{1}{2}$. Here is how.

| Look at the denominators. | Find equivalent fractions with like denominators. | Add or subtract the fractions. | Add or subtract the whole numbers. |
|---|---|---|---|
| $4\frac{1}{2}$ ← Not the same $1\frac{3}{4}$ ←  $+7$ | $4\frac{1}{2} = 4\frac{2}{4}$ $1\frac{3}{4} = 1\frac{3}{4}$ $+7\ \ = 7$ | $4\frac{2}{4}$ $1\frac{3}{4}$ $+7$ $\overline{\frac{5}{4}}$ | $4\frac{2}{4}$ $1\frac{3}{4}$ $+7$ $\overline{12\frac{5}{4} = 13\frac{1}{4}}$ |

### TALK ABOUT IT

1. What is the least common denominator for the fractions?
2. Give the answer to the Explore problem in a complete sentence.

### Other Examples

A
$$\frac{5}{6} = \frac{25}{30}$$
$$+3\frac{1}{5} = 3\frac{6}{30}$$
$$\overline{3\frac{31}{30} = 4\frac{1}{30}}$$

B
$$8 = 7\frac{3}{3}$$
$$-4\frac{2}{3} = 4\frac{2}{3}$$
$$\overline{3\frac{1}{3}}$$

C
$$16 = 15\frac{5}{5}$$
$$-\ \frac{4}{5} = \frac{4}{5}$$
$$\overline{15\frac{1}{5}}$$

## TRY IT OUT

Add or subtract. Reduce answers to lowest terms.

1. $\frac{3}{4}$ $+6\frac{5}{8}$

2. $23$ $-4\frac{7}{10}$

3. $30\frac{4}{5}$ $-12\frac{5}{6}$

4. $9\frac{3}{5}$ $+\ \frac{9}{10}$

5. $12\frac{1}{2}$ $+\ \frac{7}{8}$

Add or subtract. Reduce answers to lowest terms.

**1.** $9\frac{1}{3}$
$+4\frac{1}{6}$

**2.** $6\frac{7}{8}$
$-\frac{2}{4}$

**3.** $12$
$-7\frac{1}{5}$

**4.** $14\frac{2}{5}$
$+8$

**5.** $26\frac{5}{6}$
$+14\frac{1}{6}$

**6.** $32\frac{1}{3}$
$-16\frac{5}{15}$

**7.** $62$
$+34\frac{4}{12}$

**8.** $\frac{9}{12}$
$+\frac{3}{8}$

**9.** $48$
$-31\frac{7}{10}$

**10.** $28$
$-2\frac{5}{8}$

**11.** $37\frac{2}{3}$
$+68\frac{3}{5}$

**12.** $\frac{21}{4}$
$+\frac{55}{8}$

**13.** $\frac{13}{8} - \frac{2}{3}$

**14.** $26\frac{4}{8} + 4 + \frac{3}{5}$

**15.** $73 - 6\frac{3}{8}$

**16.** $13\frac{4}{5} + 20\frac{2}{3} + 10$

Estimate each sum or difference.

**17.** $49\frac{7}{8} + 24\frac{6}{12}$

**18.** $38\frac{2}{3} - 27\frac{5}{6}$

**19.** $14\frac{1}{8} + 11\frac{9}{10}$

**20.** $28\frac{1}{4} - 5\frac{5}{6}$

**MATH REASONING**

Write a mixed number that will give a sum or difference in the given range.

**21.** $5\frac{5}{8} + x\frac{y}{z}$ is between 9 and 10.

**22.** $12\frac{1}{3} - x\frac{y}{z}$ is between 6 and 7.

**PROBLEM SOLVING**

**23.** A public reading of two poems at the library took 15 min. When Luis read the same two poems silently it took him only $8\frac{1}{4}$ min. How much less was the silent reading time?

**24. Language Arts Data Bank** On the recording *A Treasury of Great Poems*, how much less time does the poem by Lear take than the poem by Poe? How much less time than the poem by Hay? See page 469.

DATA BANK

▶ **USING CRITICAL THINKING**  Discover a Pattern

Give the missing numbers.

**25.** $4\frac{1}{2}$, 6, $7\frac{1}{2}$, ▨▨, ▨▨

**26.** $3\frac{1}{3}$, 5, $6\frac{2}{3}$, ▨▨, ▨▨

**27.** ▨▨, ▨▨, $32\frac{1}{2}$, 25, $17\frac{1}{2}$

**28.** $\frac{1}{8}$, $\frac{1}{4}$, $\frac{3}{8}$, ▨▨, ▨▨

**29.** $1\frac{1}{4}$, $2\frac{1}{2}$, $3\frac{3}{4}$, ▨▨, ▨▨

**30.** 6, $4\frac{7}{8}$, $3\frac{3}{4}$, ▨▨, ▨▨

# Problem Solving
## Choosing a Calculation Method

UNDERSTAND
ANALYZE DATA
PLAN
ESTIMATE
SOLVE
EXAMINE

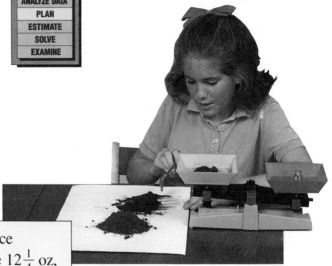

**LEARN ABOUT IT**

Before using paper and pencil to add or subtract fractions, look carefully at the fractions. Some fractions can be added or subtracted easily using mental math.

Three soil samples were collected for a science experiment. The weights of the samples were $12\frac{1}{4}$ oz, $7\frac{1}{2}$ oz, and $10\frac{3}{4}$ oz. What was the total weight of the soil samples?

I need an exact answer. Here's what I need to find.

$$12\frac{1}{4} + 7\frac{1}{2} + 10\frac{3}{4}$$

$\frac{1}{4}$ and $\frac{3}{4}$ are compatible fractions. I can use mental math.

Think: $12\frac{1}{4} + 10\frac{3}{4}$
is $12 + 10 + 1$, or $23$.
$23$ and $7\frac{1}{2}$ is $30\frac{1}{2}$.

The total weight of the soil samples was $30\frac{1}{2}$ oz.

**TRY IT OUT**

Solve. Explain your choice of calculation method.

1. Tamara started an experiment with 12 oz. of water. At the end she had $2\frac{1}{2}$ oz. How much water did she use for her experiment?

2. The rectangular lid of a soil sample box is $3\frac{1}{4}$ in. long and $2\frac{1}{2}$ in. wide. What is its perimeter?

3. A half an orange weighs $7\frac{1}{4}$ oz. When it has been dried out completely, it weighs $2\frac{2}{5}$ oz. How heavy was the water in the orange slice?

4. The total weight of two soil samples is $10\frac{3}{4}$ oz. One sample weighs $7\frac{1}{4}$ oz. What is the weight of the other sample?

290

Solve. Use any problem solving strategies to solve the problems. Use data from the table as needed.

| Sizes of Mice | | |
|---|---|---|
| | Length in Inches | |
| Mouse | Head and Body | Tail |
| White-footed | $3\frac{3}{4}$ | $3\frac{1}{5}$ |
| Grasshopper | $2\frac{1}{2}$ | $1\frac{7}{10}$ |
| Meadow | $6\frac{7}{8}$ | $3\frac{1}{4}$ |

1. How much longer is the head and body of the white-footed mouse than the head and body of the grasshopper mouse?

2. Hamsters take 75 breaths per minute. A hamster's heart beats 260 to 600 times per minute. How many breaths do hamsters take in an hour?

3. Terry, Roger, and Amy Bolt bought the supplies for their guinea pig. They each paid the same amount. How much was that?
   $3.99 water bottle    $2.19 vegetables
   $2.99 dish            $1.78 pellet food

4. A guinea pig's normal temperature is 99.5°F. A human's temperature is 98.6°F. How many degrees less is a human's normal temperature?

5. About how much shorter is the head and body of the white-footed mouse than the head and body of the meadow mouse?

6. Alice, Bunky, Marv, and Rick have rodents for pets. One has a mouse, one a hamster, one a rat, and one a guinea pig. Bunky does not have a mouse. Rick has a rat. The name of the kind of pet Marv has does not start with the letter **g**. Alice would not like to own a hamster or a mouse. What pet does each person have?

7. What is the total length of the grasshopper mouse from head to tail?

8. Anita's golden hamster eats 16 oz of dry food in a month. Anita has 68 oz of that food at home. How many full months of food is this?

9. **Finishing the Solution** Linda's white-footed mouse's total length was 4 in. when she bought it. It grew $\frac{1}{2}$ in. the first month she had it and $\frac{1}{8}$ in. less than that during the second, third, and fourth months. What was its total length at the end of the fourth month? Copy and complete the table.

| | Start | 1st Month | 2nd Month | 3rd Month | 4th Month |
|---|---|---|---|---|---|
| Length at beginning of month | 4 in. | 4 in. | $4\frac{1}{2}$ in. | | |
| Growth during month | 0 | $\frac{1}{2}$ in. | $\frac{3}{8}$ in. | | |
| Length at end of month | 4 in. | $4\frac{1}{2}$ in. | | | |

# Data Collection and Analysis
## Group Decision Making

UNDERSTAND
ANALYZE DATA
PLAN
ESTIMATE
SOLVE
EXAMINE

**Doing a Survey**
**Group Skill:**
Check for Understanding

In your school, who would like to have a dog as a pet, more girls or more boys? Who thinks dogs are hard to take care of, girls or boys? Make some predictions and then conduct a survey to find out.

### Collecting Data

1. Work with your group to think of two questions to ask in a survey about dogs as pets. Write the questions so that the answer is a rating from 1 to 10.

   *Sample Question:*
   On a scale from 1 to 10, how much do you like playing with a dog? (1 means **not at all** and 10 means **very much**.)

2. You will need at least 15 girls and 15 boys so that you can compare these groups. Talk about how to make sure that your sample fairly represents the students in your school.

3. Conduct your survey. Make a table to record your results, as in the sample shown.

| Survey Results | |
|---|---|
| Question 1 | Boys' Ratings:<br>2, 9, 9, 5, 6, 10, 7, 5, 5, 3, 9, 10, 8, 6, 8<br>Girls' Ratings:<br>4, 6, 10, 4, 8, 1, 7, 6, 7, 3, 9, 2, 3, 6, 5, 4 |
| Question 2 | Boys' Ratings:<br>_____<br>Girls' Ratings:<br>_____ |

292

**4.** Find the sums of the boys' ratings for each question and the sums of the girls' ratings for each question. Make a double bar graph to show the sums.

*Question 1*    Sum of the boys' ratings: 102
Sum of the girls' ratings: 85

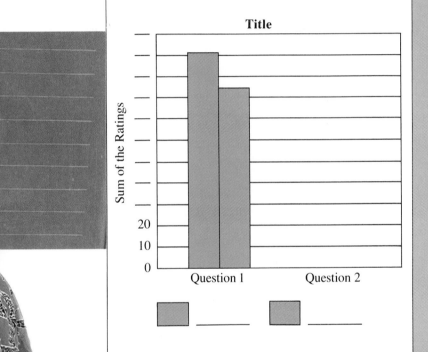

**Presenting Your Analysis**

**5.** Write a summary to tell about your survey. Be sure to include the questions you asked, how you selected your sample, and what you found.

**6.** Give two or three reasons that you think led to the results that you found.

293

# WRAP UP

## Come to Terms with Fractions

Choose the term that correctly completes each sentence.

1. To add or subtract fractions with like denominators, add or subtract the numerators and write the answer over the __?__.

2. To find the least common denominator for two fractions, find the __?__ of the denominators.

3. To add or subtract fractions with unlike denominators, first rename the fractions as __?__ with common denominators.

4. When adding mixed numbers, if the sum of the fractional parts is greater than 1 you should __?__.

A. rename

B. least common multiple

C. common denominator

D. equivalent fractions

## Sometimes, Always, Never

Complete each statement by writing **sometimes, always,** or **never.** Explain your choices.

5. A problem __?__ has a solution.

6. If two fractions have the same denominator, their sum is __?__ the sum of the numerators over the sum of the denominators.

7. The least common denominator (LCD) of two fractions is __?__ the same as the least common multiple (LCM) of the two denominators.

8. You __?__ need to rename a mixed number before subtracting.

## Project

Find these sums. What pattern do you notice? What are the next three sums?

A. $\frac{1}{2} + \frac{1}{4}$

B. $\frac{1}{2} + \frac{1}{4} + \frac{1}{8}$

C. $\frac{1}{2} + \frac{1}{4} + \frac{1}{8} + \frac{1}{16}$

D. $\frac{1}{2} + \frac{1}{4} + \frac{1}{8} + \frac{1}{16} + \frac{1}{32}$

E. $\frac{1}{2} + \frac{1}{4} + \frac{1}{8} + \frac{1}{16} + \frac{1}{32} + \frac{1}{64}$

# POWER PRACTICE/TEST

## Part 1   Understanding

1. Show how to estimate $3\frac{1}{8} + 4\frac{11}{12} + 2\frac{3}{5}$ using compatible numbers. Substitute whole numbers or $\frac{1}{2}$.

2. Show how to estimate $8\frac{7}{8} - 3\frac{1}{4}$ using front-end digits and adjusting.

Use fraction pieces to find each sum or difference. Record what you did. Reduce answers to lowest terms.

3. $\frac{7}{12} - \frac{2}{6}$

4. $3\frac{1}{2} + 4\frac{5}{6}$

5. $8\frac{1}{2} - 5\frac{3}{8}$

## Part 2   Skills

Find the least common multiple for each set of numbers.

6. 3 and 7

7. 5 and 8

8. 2 and 15

Add or subtract. Reduce answers to lowest terms.

9. $\frac{5}{4} + \frac{1}{2}$

10. $\frac{5}{12} - \frac{1}{12}$

11. $\frac{3}{8} + \frac{3}{6}$

12. $\frac{7}{10} - \frac{1}{6}$

13. $\quad 15\frac{1}{3}$
    $+\; 23\frac{1}{2}$

14. $\quad 8$
    $+\; 4\frac{2}{3}$

15. $\quad 50\frac{7}{8}$
    $-\; 41\frac{2}{3}$

16. $\quad 7$
    $-\; 2\frac{1}{9}$

## Part 3   Applications

17. Marsha's dog weighed $67\frac{1}{4}$ lb. It now weighs $72\frac{5}{6}$ lb. How much weight did it gain.

18. Byron needs $4\frac{3}{8}$ ft of blue ribbon and $2\frac{1}{2}$ ft of white ribbon. How much ribbon does he need in all?

19. If the problem has a solution, give it. If it has no solution, explain why not.
    Eva spent exactly $4.35 on stamps. She bought only $0.25 stamps. How many stamps did she buy?

20. **Challenge.** A unit fraction is a fraction with a numerator of 1. $\frac{1}{6}$ and $\frac{1}{2}$ are unit fractions. All fractions can be written as the sum of unit fractions. Find two unit fractions that have a sum of $\frac{7}{12}$. Try some others on your own.

# ENRICHMENT
## Fractions Between Fractions

You can make rulers to find numbers between numbers. To find a number halfway between 3 and 8, label a paper ruler as shown and fold it so the 8 falls on the 3.

Where is the fold?

Think: $3 + 2\frac{1}{2} = 5\frac{1}{2}$

$8 - 2\frac{1}{2} = 5\frac{1}{2}$

$5\frac{1}{2}$ is halfway between 3 and 8, so the fold is at about $5\frac{1}{2}$.

There is always another fraction between any two fractions. You can make fraction rulers to find fractions halfway between fractions. To find a number halfway between $\frac{1}{4}$ and $\frac{2}{3}$, label a paper ruler as shown and fold it so $\frac{2}{3}$ falls on $\frac{1}{4}$. Where is the fold?

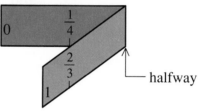

To find the name of the fraction halfway between $\frac{1}{4}$ and $\frac{2}{3}$:

**Step 1**
Write equivalent fractions using the least common denominator, 12.
$\frac{1}{4} = \frac{3}{12}$   Can you tell what is
$\frac{2}{3} = \frac{8}{12}$   halfway between? No.

**Step 2**
Try another pair of equivalent fractions. Multiply both fractions by $\frac{2}{2}$.

$\frac{3}{12} \times \frac{2}{2} = \frac{6}{24}$   $6 + 5 = 11$

$\frac{8}{12} \times \frac{2}{2} = \frac{16}{24}$   $16 - 5 = 11$

$\frac{11}{24}$ is halfway between $\frac{1}{4}$ and $\frac{2}{3}$.

Find a fraction halfway between each pair of fractions.

**1.** $\frac{5}{9}$ and $\frac{6}{9}$

**2.** $\frac{6}{15}$ and $\frac{7}{15}$

**3.** $\frac{1}{9}$ and $\frac{2}{3}$

**4.** $\frac{2}{3}$ and $\frac{4}{5}$

**5.** $\frac{3}{4}$ and $\frac{4}{5}$

**6.** $\frac{1}{2}$ and $\frac{1}{3}$

# CUMULATIVE REVIEW

1. Which fraction is equivalent to $\frac{9}{12}$?

   A. $\frac{6}{9}$   B. $\frac{2}{3}$   C. $\frac{10}{13}$   D. $\frac{6}{8}$

2. Rename $4\frac{5}{9}$ as an improper fraction.

   A. $\frac{36}{9}$   B. $\frac{41}{9}$   C. $\frac{36}{5}$   D. $\frac{41}{5}$

3. What pattern can you use to complete this table?

   | B | 5 | 10 | 15 | 20 | 25 | 30 |
   |---|---|----|----|----|----|----|
   | W | 17 | 32 | 47 | 62 | | |

   A. $W = B - 12$
   B. $W = (3 \times B) + 2$
   C. $W = B + 22$
   D. $W = (2 \times B) + 7$

Divide.

4. $4,800 \div 80$

   A. 6   B. 60   C. 600   D. 6,000

5. $37\overline{)1,999}$

   A. 54 R1          B. 540 R1
   C. 49 R5          D. 495 R1

6. Choose the greatest common factor of 32 and 24.

   A. 12   B. 6   C. 4   D. 8

7. What improper fraction names the shaded part?

   A. $\frac{8}{5}$   B. $\frac{10}{8}$   C. $\frac{8}{2}$   D. $\frac{8}{10}$

8. Reduce $\frac{32}{72}$ to lowest terms.

   A. $\frac{16}{36}$          B. $\frac{8}{18}$
   C. $\frac{4}{9}$           D. $\frac{5}{6}$

9. Find the average of this set of data:
   4,252; 5,016; 358; 7,914.

   A. 7,556          B. 2,305
   C. 17,540         D. 4,385

10. What compatible numbers would you use to divide 5,745 by 8?

    A. $5,700 \div 8$     B. $5,600 \div 8$
    C. $6,400 \div 10$    D. $4,800 \div 8$

11. Which answer is reasonable? A truck delivered 625 watermelons to the supermarket. If the average weight of each melon is 20 lb, about how many pounds of melons were delivered?

    A. 120            B. 1,200
    C. 12,000         D. 120,000

12. Eileen, Joyce, Ray, and Dawn are two sets of twins. One is a veterinarian, one a computer operator, one a musician, and one a truck driver. The musician is not female. Eileen and Joyce have lunch every week with the computer operator. Joyce's sister is her cat's veterinarian. Who is the truck driver?

    A. Eileen         B. Joyce
    C. Ray            D. Dawn

# 11

## CUSTOMARY MEASUREMENT

**THEME: SEA CREATURES**

### Math and Science

**DATA BANK**

Use the Science Data Bank on page 472 to answer the questions.

1. Look at the graph showing the sizes of full-grown whales. Which would be the better estimate of the length of a full-grown right whale, 60 feet or 80 feet?

Conservation efforts of recent decades have led to population increases for some endangered species of whales.

**2** What kind of full-grown whale is 12 times the length of a young dolphin that is only 5 feet long?

**3** On an average day about how many waves per hour strike the beach described in the article on the movement of beach sands?

**4** **Using Critical Thinking** Julio said, "I can see that 2 grown fin whales would have a total weight greater than that of 1 grown blue whale." Do you believe Julio is correct? Explain your answer.

# Customary Units of Length

## EXPLORE  Make a Measurement

Work in groups. Measure each of your
heights to the nearest inch. What different
units can you use to record your height—
inches, feet, yards?

1 foot (ft)  =  12 inches (in.)
1 yard (yd)  =  3 ft  =  36 in.

## TALK ABOUT IT

1. How many inches tall are you?
2. Give your height in feet and inches.
3. Is your height closest to 4 ft, 5 ft, or 2 yd?
   Explain your answer.

Sometimes we use two units instead of one to give a
measure. It is usually easier to think about a person's height
as 5 ft 2 in. rather than 62 in. Here is how to change units
like these.

To change smaller units to larger units,
divide.

Example: Change 59 in. to feet and
inches.

12 in. = 1 ft

$$\begin{array}{r} 4\ R11 \\ 12\overline{)59} \\ 48 \\ \hline 11 \end{array}$$ ← extra inches

So 59 in. = 4 ft 11 in.

To change larger units to smaller units,
multiply.

Example: Change 6 ft 5 in. to inches.

$$\begin{array}{r} 12 \\ \times\ 6 \\ \hline 72 \end{array}$$  12 in. = 1 ft  $$\begin{array}{r} 72 \\ +\ 5 \\ \hline 77 \end{array}$$ ← extra inches

So 6 ft 5 in. = 77 in.

Change the units in each measurement.

1. 97 in. = ▓ ft ▓ in.
2. 114 in. = ▓ ft ▓ in.
3. 50 in. = ▓ ft ▓ in.
4. 7 ft 4 in. = ▓ in.
5. 3 ft 5 in. = ▓ in.
6. 4 ft 7 in. = ▓ in.

Change each measure to inches.

1. refrigerator height
2. refrigerator width
3. refrigerator depth

4. dresser width
5. dresser depth
6. dresser height

Change each measure to feet and inches.

7. TV width
8. TV height
9. TV depth

10. van width
11. van length
12. van height

**MATH REASONING**

Does this make sense? Write **yes** or **no.** Tell why or why not.

13. A basketball player 7 ft 4 in. tall has a bed 78 in. long.

14. A curtain 54 in. wide covers a window 4 ft 3 in. wide.

15. An extension cord 3 yd long is used to reach a distance of 8 ft 6 in.

**PROBLEM SOLVING**

16. Mary needed 100 in. of ribbon. She bought a roll with 9 ft of ribbon. Was there enough ribbon? If so, how much will she have left over?

17. **Suppose** Tell which of the following items of information would change the solution to problem 16.
   A. Mary needed 75 in. of ribbon.
   B. The package had 10 ft of ribbon.
   C. The ribbon was 1 inch wide.

▶ **MENTAL MATH**

You can often use mental math to add measurements given in feet and inches. First think how many feet and how many inches. Then change units if necessary.

Try this method to add these measurements.

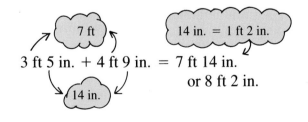

3 ft 5 in. + 4 ft 9 in. = 7 ft 14 in.
or 8 ft 2 in.

18. 4 ft 8 in. + 2 ft 8 in.
20. 7 ft 2 in. + 2 ft 10 in.

19. 1 ft 10 in. + 3 ft 6 in.
21. 6 ft 3 in. + 7 ft 8 in.

*More Practice, page 514, set C*

# Length
## Parts of an Inch

**EXPLORE** **Examine the Data**

Paul recorded the length of the horseshoe crab, with
and without its tail, in 4 different ways.

| | Whole crab (with tail) | Crab's body |
|---|---|---|
| Nearest inch | 4 in. | 2 in. |
| Nearest $\frac{1}{2}$ inch | $3\frac{1}{2}$ in. | $2\frac{1}{2}$ in. |
| Nearest $\frac{1}{4}$ inch | $3\frac{1}{2}$ in. | $2\frac{1}{2}$ in. |
| Nearest $\frac{1}{8}$ inch | $3\frac{5}{8}$ in. | $2\frac{3}{8}$ in. |

**TALK ABOUT IT**

1. Why can different measurements be given for the length
   of the whole crab?
2. Why are some of the measurements for the body length
   the same?
3. For each length, which measurement is the most
   accurate?

The smaller the part of a unit in a measurement, the more
precise the measurement. In the data above, $3\frac{5}{8}$ in. is a
more precise measurement than $3\frac{1}{2}$ in.

**TRY IT OUT**

Measure your math book cover to the nearest inch or the
given part of an inch.

Width

1. nearest inch
2. nearest $\frac{1}{2}$ inch
3. nearest $\frac{1}{4}$ inch
4. nearest $\frac{1}{8}$ inch

Length (height)

5. nearest inch
6. nearest $\frac{1}{2}$ inch
7. nearest $\frac{1}{4}$ inch
8. nearest $\frac{1}{8}$ inch

Which of the objects shown at the right measure

1. between 2 in. and 3 in. long?

2. 2 in. long to the nearest inch?

3. $2\frac{1}{2}$ in. long to the nearest $\frac{1}{2}$ inch?

4. 3 in. long to the nearest $\frac{1}{2}$ inch?

5. $2\frac{3}{4}$ in. long to the nearest $\frac{1}{4}$ inch?

6. $3\frac{3}{8}$ in. long to the nearest $\frac{1}{8}$ inch?

**APPLY**

**MATH REASONING**

Which is the more precise measurement for each length?
Explain why.

7.

    **A.** $1\frac{7}{8}$ in.   **B.** 2 in.

8.

    **A.** $2\frac{5}{8}$ in.   **B.** $2\frac{3}{4}$ in.

DATA
BANK

**PROBLEM SOLVING**

9. Paul is building a frame for a model of a tidepool. He cut a board $34\frac{1}{2}$ in. long from a board 4 ft long. How long was the piece that was left over?

10. **Science Data Bank**  Do you think that lengths listed for the whales on this graph are measurements to the nearest one foot, five feet, or ten feet? See page 472.

▶ **ALGEBRA**

Remember, the formula for finding the area of a rectangle is
$A = l \times w$.

11. Find the length of a rectangle if $A = 240$ in.$^2$ and $w = 12$ in.

12. Find the width of a rectangle if $A = 144$ in.$^2$ and $l = 14.4$ in.

13. Find the area of a rectangle if $l = 20$ in. and $w = 16$ in.

# Length
## Feet, Yards, and Miles

### LEARN ABOUT IT

You have worked with the foot as a unit of measurement.
Here you will work with larger units.

**EXPLORE  Make Some Estimates**

A 1-inch segment is shown at the right.
Use this to help you make the following
estimates.

← 1 inch →

- My math book is about ▦ inches long.
- A baseball bat is about ▦ inches long.
- A baseball bat is about ▦ math books long.

### TALK ABOUT IT

1. Explain how you made your decisions for each situation.
2. Which of your estimates do you think is closest to the
   actual length? Explain why you think so.
3. Which estimate was most difficult to make? Why?

The **yard (yd)** is a customary unit of
length.

The **mile (mi)** is a customary unit of
length used for measuring long distances.

A baseball bat is about a yard long.
**1 yd = 3 ft = 36 in.**

15 football fields laid end to end would be
about 1 mile long.
**1 mi = 1,760 yd = 5,280 ft**

### TRY IT OUT

Which unit would you use? Write in., ft, yd, or mi.

1. An airplane might fly 6 __?__ high.
2. An automobile is about 14 __?__ long.
3. A long step might be about 1 __?__ long.

Write the unit (in., ft, yd, mi) you would use to measure the following.

1. the length of your classroom
2. the length of a train track
3. the length of a city block
4. the distance of an hour's bike ride
5. the height of a flagpole
6. the distance across a river
7. the height of a skyscraper
8. the perimeter of your school building
9. the distance you walk each week
10. the distance between two cities

**APPLY**

**MATH REASONING**

Use mental math to give the number for each ▦ .

11. 6 yd = ▦ ft
12. 2 yd = ▦ in.
13. 10 mi = ▦ ft
14. 24 ft = ▦ yd
15. 100 yd = ▦ ft
16. 10 yd = ▦ in.

**PROBLEM SOLVING**

Tell whether the distance described in problems 17 and 18 is **more than, less than,** or **about** 1 mile.

17. distance around your school playground

18. distance around a large city park

19. **Data Hunt**  About how many fifth grade students standing fingertip to fingertip with arms stretched out would it take to make 1 mi?

Rename each mixed number as an improper fraction.

20. $4\frac{2}{3}$
21. $3\frac{3}{8}$
22. $7\frac{4}{5}$
23. $3\frac{1}{3}$
24. $2\frac{5}{6}$
25. $3\frac{3}{10}$

Subtract. Reduce to lowest terms.

26. $\frac{5}{6}$ $-\frac{1}{6}$
27. $\frac{7}{10}$ $-\frac{4}{10}$
28. $\frac{7}{12}$ $-\frac{5}{12}$
29. $\frac{5}{6}$ $-\frac{2}{6}$
30. $\frac{4}{5}$ $-\frac{3}{5}$
31. $\frac{5}{8}$ $-\frac{3}{8}$

# Problem Solving
## Problems with More Than One Answer

UNDERSTAND
ANALYZE DATA
PLAN
ESTIMATE
SOLVE
EXAMINE

## LEARN ABOUT IT

Some problems have more than one answer. After you find one answer to a problem, ask yourself if other answers are possible.

> I could use guess and check to find an answer.

> I should check for other answers. I can organize my work in a table.

The floor of the rabbit hutch Rick is building is 48 ft². Each side is a whole number of feet. What is the perimeter of the floor?

Try

20 ft

2 ft

$20 \times 2 = 40 \text{ft}^2$ Too low.

Try

24 ft

2 ft

$24 \times 2 = 48 \text{ft}^2$ That works!

| length | width | area | perimeter |
|--------|-------|------|-----------|
| 1 | 48 | 48 | 98 |
| 2 | 24 | 48 | 52 |
| 3 | 16 | 48 | 38 |
| 4 | 12 | 48 | 32 |
| 5 | (will not work) | | |
| 6 | 8 | 48 | 28 |
| 7 | (will not work) | | |
| 8 | 6 (same as 6 and 8) | | |

There are 5 possible answers for the perimeter of the floor.
The perimeter could be 98 ft, 52 ft, 38 ft, 32 ft, or 28 ft.

## TRY IT OUT

Solve. Find as many answers as possible.

1. To make a coaster car, Gretchen used a piece of plywood with an area of 24 ft². The length of each side of the plywood is a whole number of feet. What is the perimeter of the piece?

2. The workbench Adam and Marti made had a perimeter of 20 ft. Each side was a whole number of feet. How wide and how long was the workbench?

3. Rico entered a coaster car in a race. There were 3-wheeled cars and 4-wheeled cars. He counted 26 wheels in all. How many 3-wheeled and 4-wheeled cars did he see?

4. The raft Harry built is 35 ft². The length of each side is a whole number of feet. What is the perimeter?

Solve. Choose any of the listed strategies or use any other strategy you know.

| Some Strategies | |
|---|---|
| Act Out | Make a Table |
| Use Objects | Solve a Simpler Problem |
| Choose an Operation | Make an Organized List |
| Draw a Picture | Work Backward |
| Guess and Check | Look for a Pattern |
| Use Logical Reasoning | |

**1.** The following people got on the raft Harry built:

| Name | Weight | Age |
|---|---|---|
| Mingel | 102 lb | 10 years old |
| Ben | 127 lb | 11 years old |
| Tommy Lee | 132 lb | 9 years old |
| Ben's father | 212 lb | 41 years old |
| Margy | 113 lb | 10 years old |

What was the average weight of the children on the raft?

**2.** What is the total height of one of the stilts that Rudy built?

5 ft $\frac{3}{4}$ in.

1 ft $\frac{1}{2}$ in.

**3.** Gail spent a total of $35 for lumber to build a workbench and a raft. She spent $9 more on the lumber for the raft. How much did she pay for the lumber for the workbench?

**4.** Joe had a piece of lumber 3 ft 5 in. long. He sawed off a piece 9 in. long to make a sign. How long was the piece of lumber that was left?

**5.** Peter made a set of blocks for his little brother Mo. He sawed a piece of wood 8 in. long into pieces of a whole number of inches of the same length. How many pieces did he saw the wood into?

**6.** Peter built Mo some steps with blocks. It took 1 block to make 1 step, 3 blocks to make 2 steps, and so on. How many steps did he make with 36 blocks?

**7.** Chris needed a piece of wood $5\frac{3}{4}$ ft long for his puppet theater. About how much wood will he have left from a piece of lumber that is $8\frac{1}{12}$ long?

**8. Developing a Plan**   Tell what steps you could follow to solve this problem. Find all of the correct choices. Sandra bought 12 pieces of lumber at $2.99 each. Sandra and 3 of her friends split the cost equally. How much did each pay?
   **A.** Divide $2.99 by 4. Multiply by 12.
   **B.** Multiply 12 times $2.99. Divide by 4.
   **C.** Divide $2.99 by 12. Multiply by 4.

*More Practice, page 526, set B*

# Temperature
## Degrees Fahrenheit

### EXPLORE  Study the Situation

When Joni didn't feel well on Sunday night, her father took
her body temperature. The thermometer her father used
shows a mark for every 0.2 degrees.

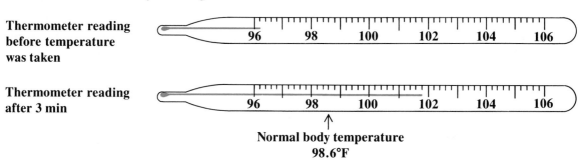

**Thermometer reading
before temperature
was taken**

**Thermometer reading
after 3 min**

Normal body temperature
98.6°F

### TALK ABOUT IT

1. What did the thermometer read before Joni's
   temperature was taken?
2. What was her temperature at the end of 3 min?
3. How much above normal is Joni's temperature?

**TRY IT OUT**

Joni's temperature readings for two days are shown below.
Give each temperature to the nearest tenth of one degree.

Monday           Tuesday

8:00 a.m.    1.            2.

1:00 p.m.    3.            4.

7:00 p.m.    5.            6.

7. Give the day and the time that Joni's temperature was
   the highest.

**308**

# POWER PRACTICE/QUIZ

Change each measure to feet and inches.

**1.** 72 in.  **2.** 40 in.  **3.** 27 in.  **4.** 50 in.

**5.** Which of the measures in exercises 1−4 are longer than a yard?

Measure each side of the triangle.

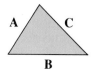

**6.** What is the measure of side A to the nearest inch?

**7.** What is the measure of side B to the nearest half inch?

**8.** What is the measure of side C to the nearest quarter inch?

Decide which unit—in., ft, yd, or mi—would be most reasonable to use to measure the following lengths or distances.

**9.** from your desk to the door

**10.** your walking step

**11.** a 1-hour bike ride

**12.** length of your foot

**13.** from your home to school

**14.** from Florida to Iowa

**15.** length of a football field

**16.** width of your notebook

## PROBLEM SOLVING

Solve. Find as many solutions as you can.

**17.** Stuart measured a board and found that its surface area was 48 in². The board's length and width were both a whole number of inches. What are the possible measures of the length and the width?

**18.** Connie owed her sister 75¢. She repaid her with 5 coins. What coins might Connie have given to her sister?

**19.** The top of a bookcase that Ms. Kelley built has a perimeter of 16 ft. The top is a whole number of feet in length and width. What might its area be in square feet?

# Customary Units of Capacity

## LEARN ABOUT IT

You often need to use multiplication or division to help you change customary units of capacity.

### EXPLORE  Solve to Understand

Arlene needs to put 6 gal (gallons) of water in her fish tank. She is using a quart jar to put the water into the tank. How many times will she need to fill the jar to get enough water?

### TALK ABOUT IT

**1.** How many quarts are in one gallon?

**2.** What operation did you use to find how many times Arlene needed to fill the quart jar?

**3.** If Arlene told you she had put 16 qt into the tank, how could you find how many gallons that was?

| Units of Capacity |
|---|
| 2 tablespoons (tbsp) = 1 fluid ounce (fl oz) |
| 8 fl oz = 1 cup (c) |
| 2 c = 1 pint (pt) |
| 2 pt = 1 quart (qt) |
| 2 qt = $\frac{1}{2}$ gallon (gal) |
| 4 qt = 1 gal |

To change smaller units to larger units, you can divide.

Example: Change 8 pt to gallons.

8 pt = 4 qt

$\quad$ First change to quarts.
$\quad$ 8 ÷ 2 = 4

4 qt = 1 gal

So 8 pt = 1 gal

To change larger units to smaller units, you can multiply.

Example: Change 3 gal to cups.

3 gal = 12 qt $\quad$ First change to quarts. 3 × 4 = 12

12 qt = 24 pt $\quad$ Next change to pints. 2 × 12 = 24

24 pt = 48 c $\quad$ Next change to cups. 2 × 24 = 48

So 3 gal = 48 c

## TRY IT OUT

Give the number for each ▦ .

**1.** $\frac{1}{2}$ gal = ▦ c

**2.** 3 qt = ▦ c

**3.** 16 fl oz = ▦ pt

**4.** 32 c = ▦ qt

**5.** $\frac{1}{2}$ pt = ▦ fl oz

**6.** 1 c = ▦ tbsp

Give the number for each ▦ .

1. ▦ tablespoons of vanilla extract

2. ▦ cups of bottled water

3. ▦ fluid ounces of juice

4. ▦ pints of milk

Juice
1 qt 14 oz

Milk
1 gal

Vanilla extract
14 fl oz

Bottled water
1 gal

Do the pictures show the correct amount for items 5–8?
Explain why or why not.

5. 1 pt sour cream

6. 1 gal milk

7. 1 pt salad dressing

8. 3 c vinegar

vinegar
1 pt

salad dressing
8 fl oz

milk
1 qt

milk
1 qt

sour cream
16 fl oz

milk
1 qt

**APPLY**

**MATH REASONING**

Do the statements below make sense? Tell why or why not.

9. A quart jar holds $\frac{1}{2}$ gallon of milk.

10. A gallon jug holds 7 pints of lemonade.

**PROBLEM SOLVING**

11. Millie and Jose have put 6 qt of water into their fish tank. It holds 4 gal. How many more quarts of water do they need to put into the tank?

12. **Science Data Bank** Ben wants to buy these tropical fish: 1 velvet swordtail, 2 neon tetras, and 2 angelfish. How many gallons of water will he need in a tank for these fish? See page 472.

DATA
BANK

▶ **CALCULATOR**

13. Imagine that you have a leaky faucet that drips 2 fl oz of water each hour. About how many gallons of water would you lose from the faucet in 1 week? in 1 month? in 1 year?

# Customary Units of Weight

The **ounce** (oz), **pound** (lb), and **ton** (T) are frequently used customary units of weight.

about 1 oz

about 1 lb
16 oz = 1 lb

about 1 T
2,000 lb = 1 T

### EXPLORE  Make Some Estimates

Work in groups. Find some objects that you estimate weigh about 1 oz, about 1 lb, or about 5 lb. Then weigh the objects.

### TALK ABOUT IT

**1.** Were your estimates too high, too low, or about right?
**2.** Describe your method for estimating weights.

Sometimes we use two units instead of one to give a measure. For instance, we would usually state a baby's weight as 10 lb 3 oz rather than 163 oz.

To change a smaller unit to a larger unit, you can divide.
Example: Change 36 oz to pounds and ounces.

$$16 \text{ oz} = 1 \text{ lb} \quad \begin{array}{r} 2 \text{ R4} \\ 16\overline{)36} \\ \underline{32} \\ 4 \leftarrow \text{remaining oz} \end{array}$$

So 36 oz = 2 lb 4 oz

To change a larger unit to a smaller unit, you can multiply.
Example: Change 8 lb 11 oz to ounces.

$$\begin{array}{r} 16 \leftarrow 16 \text{ oz} = 1 \text{ lb} \\ \times \quad 8 \\ \hline 128 \end{array} \qquad \begin{array}{r} 128 \\ + \quad 11 \leftarrow \text{extra oz} \\ \hline 139 \end{array}$$

So 8 lb 11 oz = 139 oz

---

Give the number for each ▦ .

**1.** 35 oz = ▦ lb ▦ oz

**2.** 50 oz = ▦ lb ▦ oz

**3.** 3 lb 4 oz = ▦ oz

**4.** 2 lb 8 oz = ▦ oz

**5.** 3 T = ▦ lb

**6.** 2,500 lb = ▦ T ▦ lb

Give the number for each  .

1. pancake mix: ▒ lb ▒ oz
2. baked beans: ▒ lb ▒ oz
3. relish: ▒ lb ▒ oz
4. bread: ▒ lb ▒ oz
5. peanut butter: ▒ oz
6. rice: ▒ oz
7. applesauce: ▒ oz
8. cereal: ▒ oz

APPLY

### MATH REASONING

Do you have enough? Tell why or why not.

9. You need 1 lb of grapes.
   You have 26 oz.

10. You need 1 T of cement.
    You have four 200-lb bags.

### PROBLEM SOLVING

11. How much less does the small bunch of grapes weigh than the large bunch of grapes?

12. **Missing Data** Make up the missing data, then solve. Four students in Mrs. Sutton's class divided a bag of clay equally among them. How much clay did each student get? Give your answer in pounds and ounces.

MIXED REVIEW

Rename each improper fraction as a whole number or as a mixed number in lowest terms.

13. $\frac{16}{4}$    14. $\frac{7}{3}$    15. $\frac{12}{3}$    16. $\frac{10}{4}$    17. $\frac{7}{2}$    18. $\frac{32}{10}$

Add. Reduce to lowest terms.

19. $\frac{2}{3}$   20. $\frac{1}{4}$   21. $\frac{2}{9}$   22. $\frac{5}{8}$   23. $\frac{5}{6}$   24. $\frac{7}{12}$
   $+\frac{2}{3}$      $+\frac{3}{4}$      $+\frac{4}{9}$      $+\frac{1}{8}$      $+\frac{5}{6}$      $+\frac{1}{12}$

# Problem Solving
## Deciding When to Estimate

| |
|---|
| **UNDERSTAND** |
| **ANALYZE DATA** |
| **PLAN** |
| **ESTIMATE** |
| **SOLVE** |
| **EXAMINE** |

UNDERSTAND
ANALYZE DATA
PLAN
ESTIMATE
SOLVE
EXAMINE

### LEARN ABOUT IT

Chad's class did a social studies project on "Human Rights Leaders." As they worked on the project, they needed to find some lengths and areas. The purpose of the measurement helped them decide whether to estimate or make an actual measurement.

Portrait stamps honor the leadership of Abraham Lincoln, Susan B. Anthony, Mahatma Gandhi, and Martin Luther King, Jr.

> **Problem 1**  Chad needs to get enough paper to cover the bulletin boards that will display data about the leaders. Should he estimate or measure the bulletin board area?

Chad needs to know whether 1 roll of paper will be enough. An estimate is ok.

> **Problem 2**  To buy frames for pictures of the leaders, should Jean estimate or measure the pictures' dimensions?

Since Jean needs to get frames that fit the pictures, she needs to measure.

### TRY IT OUT

Explain whether you would estimate or measure.

1. Carl is using a map of India to find how far Gandhi traveled on one of his trips. Should he measure or estimate?

2. Lita is cutting some rolls of crepe paper to make borders for the bulletin boards. Should she measure or estimate the length of paper needed?

3. Mindy is making a scale model of the Lincoln Memorial in Washington, D.C. Should she estimate or measure to mark the dimensions of her model?

4. Should Joel estimate or measure to find how many miles of highway are named for Martin Luther King, Jr. in his state?

**314**

Solve. Use any problem solving strategy.

1. The project bulletin board display showed this information on some of the leaders. How many years did each live?

> Abraham Lincoln (1809–1865)
> Susan B. Anthony (1820–1906)
> Mahatma Gandhi (1869–1948)
> Martin Luther King (1929–1968)

2. Gandhi once fasted for 21 days to help bring freedom to India. For how many hours did his fast last?

3. In 1868 Susan B. Anthony issued a publication that demanded voting rights for women. The 19th Amendment, which guaranteed women's right to vote, became law 52 years later. In what year did the amendment become law?

4. Martin Luther King once spent 5 days in a Birmingham jail because he led a nonviolent demonstration supporting racial justice. How many hours did he spend in jail?

5. Kerry had 175 copies of a sheet with data about the leaders made at the copy shop. The cost for copying was $0.07 per sheet. What was the total cost?

6. Leilani wrote 3 paragraphs of her project report on Monday, 5 on Tuesday, 7 on Wednesday, and so on. At this rate, how many paragraphs in all will she have written by the end of Saturday?

7. On Friday, 47 people attended the open house and came to see the project display. Geraldo told his friend that 6 more than twice that number came to see the project on Saturday. How many people visited the project during those two days?

8. **Developing a Plan** Class committees worked on the project for 43 h in all. The displays committee worked 3 times as long as the publicity committee. The reports committee worked 3 h more than the other two committees combined. How many hours did each committee work?

   A. List two or more strategies you think might help you solve this problem.

   B. Solve the problem.

   C. Look back at your solution. What strategies did you use?

# Applied Problem Solving
## Group Decision Making

UNDERSTAND
ANALYZE DATA
PLAN
ESTIMATE
SOLVE
EXAMINE

**Group Skill:**
Check for Understanding

Your class is going to build a puppet theater for the children's wing of the hospital near your school. One of your classmates brought in the plans for the theater. Your group is to look over the plans and decide what lumber to buy.

### Facts to Consider

■ This diagram shows the different parts of the theater.

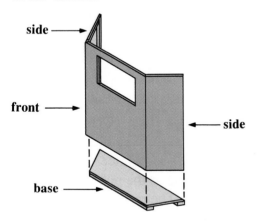

■ The diagrams below show the measurements of the large pieces of wood and of the narrow framing pieces needed to make the theater.

**View from the front**

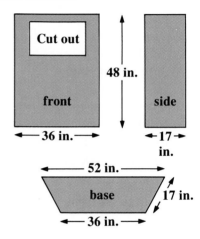

**View from the back showing narrow framing pieces**

- The front and sides of the theater will be made from hardwood. Hardwood comes in sheets that are 4 ft wide and 8 ft long.
- The base will be made from plywood. Plywood comes in sheets that are 4 ft wide and 8 ft long.
- The framing pieces are used to reinforce the hardwood and the plywood. They are narrow strips of wood 1 in. high, 2 in. wide, and 8 ft long.

1. Will one piece of hardwood be enough to build the front and sides of the theater?

2. How many 4 foot long framing pieces will you need? How much lumber will you buy to cut these pieces from?

3. How could drawing a picture or a diagram help you figure out the total number of 8 foot long framing pieces you will need?

**What Is Your Decision?**

Make a list of the kinds and sizes of lumber you will need to buy.

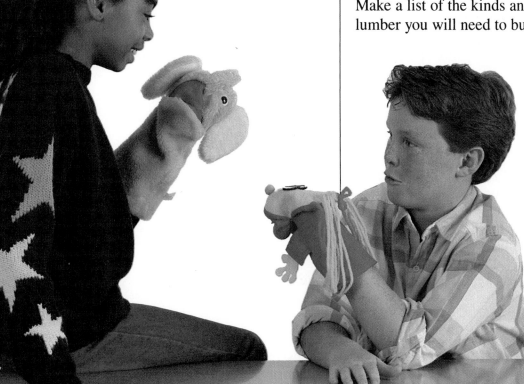

# WRAP UP

## Unit/Number Match

Match the words and numbers.

1. inches in a foot
2. quarts in a gallon
3. inches in a yard
4. yards in a mile
5. cups in a pint
6. pounds in a ton
7. ounces in a pound
8. fluid ounces in a cup
9. feet in a mile
10. feet in a yard

A. 3   B. 2,000   C. 36   D. 2   E. 1,760   F. 8   G. 4   H. 16   I. 12   J. 5,280

## Sometimes, Always, Never

Complete each statement by writing **sometimes**, **always**, or **never**. Explain your choices.

11. When you change from a smaller customary unit to a larger one, the number __?__ gets larger.

12. 6 pints of sour cream will __?__ fit in a quart container.

13. To change from smaller units to larger units, you can __?__ multiply by a whole number.

## Project

Choose a model that you think has a volume of about 1 in.$^3$ Use it to try to find larger objects, such as boxes, that are about 12 times the length, width, and height of the cubic inch. What would be the approximate volume of the larger objects?

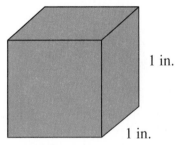

1 in.

1 in.

1 in.

Now try to find some objects that are about 3 times as long, wide, and high as the boxes. What would be the approximate volume of these objects? List as many objects as you can find in school or in your neighborhood that you estimate to have this volume. How can you check your estimates?

# POWER PRACTICE/TEST

## Part 1   Understanding

Give the most appropriate customary unit of measure for each.

1. Heat of boiling water

2. Weight of a white mouse

3. Distance from Chicago to Houston

4. Length of a football field

5. Amount of flour in a loaf of bread

6. Amount of water in a bathtub

## Part 2   Skills

Give the missing numbers.

7. 15 ft 6 in. = ▥ in.

8. 150 in. = ▥ ft ▥ in

9. 2 c = ▥ tbsp

10. 3 gal = ▥ qt

11. 40 fl oz = ▥ qt ▥ fl oz

12. 4 T = ▥ lb

Measure the line segment.

13. to the nearest $\frac{1}{4}$ inch

14. to the nearest $\frac{1}{8}$ inch

Give each temperature to the nearest tenth of one degree.

15.

16.

## Part 3   Applications

17. Duane built a rectangular deck with an area of 48 yd$^2$. The length of each side is a whole number. What could the perimeter of the deck be?

18. **Challenge.** In liquid measures, 1 gal contains 231 in.$^3$ How many cubic inches are in a quart?

**319**

# ENRICHMENT
## Estimating Length

Pia is estimating the length of her arm from her shoulder to her fingertips.

Hand, about 5 inches
Wrist to elbow, about 7 inches
Elbow to shoulder, about 9 inches

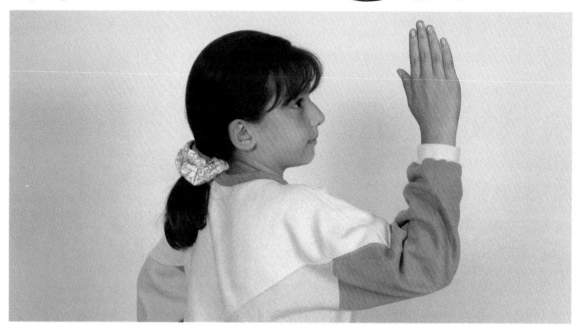

1. Use Pia's estimates. What is the length of her arm?

2. Describe the method Pia used to estimate her arm length.

3. This method of estimating lengths, heights, and distances is called **chunking**. Why do you think it was given such a name?

Use the chunking method to make each estimate.

4. height in feet of your classroom wall

5. height in inches of your chair

6. height in inches of a door

7. length in feet of your classroom

8. length in feet of the chalkboard

9. length of your leg from your heel to your hipbone

10. length in inches of your teacher's desk

11. height in inches of a window

12. length of the hall outside your classroom

# CUMULATIVE REVIEW

1. What fraction of the region is shaded?

A. $\frac{3}{8}$    B. $\frac{5}{3}$    C. $\frac{5}{8}$    D. $\frac{3}{5}$

2. Rename $\frac{15}{4}$.

A. 4    B. $3\frac{3}{4}$    C. $3\frac{1}{2}$    D. $4\frac{1}{4}$

3. By what was $\frac{5}{12}$ multiplied to get $\frac{20}{48}$?

A. $\frac{5}{4}$    B. $\frac{3}{4}$    C. $\frac{4}{6}$    D. $\frac{4}{4}$

Divide.

4. $68\overline{)435}$

A. 60 R27      B. 6 R27

C. 5 R12      D. 51 R27

5. $74\overline{)\$446.22}$

A. $603.00      B. $60.30

C. $0.603      D. $6.03

6. $381.62 \div 100$

A. 38.162      B. 3,816.2

C. 3.8162      D. 0.38162

7. Mai is reading two facing pages in her English book. The product of the page numbers is 42. What are the numbers of the pages she is reading?

A. 6 and 8      B. 7 and 8

C. 8 and 9      D. 6 and 7

Add or subtract. Reduce answers to lowest terms.

8. $14 - 6\frac{1}{3}$

A. $7\frac{2}{3}$   B. $8\frac{2}{3}$   C. $7\frac{1}{3}$   D. $8\frac{1}{3}$

9. $26\frac{3}{4} + 35\frac{1}{12}$

A. $61\frac{1}{3}$   B. $61\frac{10}{12}$   C. $61\frac{5}{6}$   D. 62

10. $6\frac{2}{3} + 2\frac{2}{5}$

A. $9\frac{1}{15}$   B. $8\frac{11}{15}$   C. $8\frac{1}{15}$   D. $9\frac{4}{15}$

11. $41\frac{1}{8} - 27\frac{5}{6}$

A. $13\frac{7}{24}$   B. $14\frac{17}{24}$   C. $13\frac{1}{6}$   D. $14\frac{7}{24}$

12. How many more points did Andrea score than Rae? Use the table.

| Player | Andrea | Mia | Rae |
|--------|--------|-----|-----|
| Points | 62 | 59 | 48 |

A. 3    B. 11    C. 14    D. 110

13. Gail drank $8\frac{1}{4}$ oz of water in the morning, $7\frac{5}{8}$ oz in the afternoon, and $12\frac{3}{4}$ oz in the evening. What method would you use to find out how much water Gail drank?

A. estimation

B. calculator

C. mental math

D. paper and pencil

# 12

### MATH AND FINE ARTS

### DATA BANK

Use the Fine Arts Data Bank on page 478 to answer the questions.

1. What fraction of all the musical instruments shown in the diagram of an orchestra are brass instruments? What fraction are woodwinds?

# MULTIPLICATION AND DIVISION OF FRACTIONS

**THEME: MUSIC**

The fractional parts of an orchestra that are strings, woodwinds, brass, or percussion vary from group to group.

**2** Violins are what fraction of all the string instruments in the orchestra?

**3** What fraction of all the violins in the orchestra are first violins? Give the fraction in lowest terms.

**4** **Using Critical Thinking** Do you think it would be easier to find a job as a violin player or as a tuba player in a large orchestra? Explain your thinking.

323

# Multiplying a Fraction and a Whole Number

### LEARN ABOUT IT

You can use what you know about division of whole numbers to help you think about finding a fraction of a whole number.

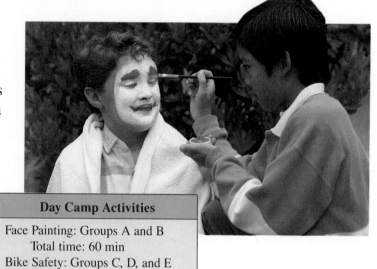

### EXPLORE  Make a Decision

Work in groups. Your group is in charge of planning activities at a day camp for young children. Use the data to decide how many minutes each group will spend on each activity if the time is shared equally.

| Day Camp Activities |
|---|
| Face Painting: Groups A and B |
| Total time: 60 min |
| Bike Safety: Groups C, D, and E |
| Total time: 60 min |
| Nature Study: Groups F, G, H, and I |
| Total time: 60 min |

### TALK ABOUT IT

The situation above shows one way to think about finding a fraction of a number. The pictures below also show how to think about finding a fraction of a whole number.

$\frac{1}{3}$ of 18

**1 out of 3 equal groups**

$\frac{2}{3}$ of 18

**2 out of 3 equal groups**

$\frac{1}{3} \times 18 = 6$   ( Divide 18 by 3. )

$\frac{2}{3} \times 18 = 12$   ( Divide 18 by 3. Multiply by 2. )

## Other Examples

**A** $\frac{1}{2} \times 20 = 10$  **B** $\frac{2}{5} \times 30 = 12$  **C** $\frac{5}{8} \times 16 = 10$

### TRY IT OUT

Multiply.

**1.** $\frac{1}{2} \times 18$  **2.** $\frac{3}{4} \times 12$  **3.** $\frac{1}{5} \times 40$  **4.** $\frac{2}{3} \times 24$

Multiply.

**1.** $\frac{1}{2} \times 8$      **2.** $\frac{1}{3} \times 15$      **3.** $\frac{2}{3} \times 12$      **4.** $\frac{1}{4} \times 16$      **5.** $\frac{2}{5} \times 10$

**6.** $\frac{3}{4} \times 20$      **7.** $\frac{1}{8} \times 32$      **8.** $\frac{3}{5} \times 30$      **9.** $\frac{1}{6} \times 42$      **10.** $\frac{2}{3} \times 21$

**11.** $\frac{1}{10} \times 50$      **12.** $\frac{5}{6} \times 18$      **13.** $\frac{3}{8} \times 40$      **14.** $\frac{4}{5} \times 35$      **15.** $\frac{3}{7} \times 14$

**16.** Find three fifths of twenty-five.      **17.** Find nine tenths of one hundred.

## APPLY

### MATH REASONING

Tell the value for the variable that will make the equation true.

**18.** $\frac{1}{x} \times 20 = 10$      **19.** $\frac{1}{n} \times 16 = 2$      **20.** $\frac{2}{m} \times 12 = 8$

### PROBLEM SOLVING

**21.** Last month 60 students came to day camp. $\frac{2}{3}$ of the students signed up for art. How many of the students signed up for art?

**22.** This year 40 students signed up for swimming. Only 15 of these had lessons last year. $\frac{1}{5}$ of those who did not have lessons last year said they were not afraid of the water. How many are not afraid of the water?

### ► USING CRITICAL THINKING    Discover a Relationship

$3 \times 4 = 4 + 4 + 4$

Use this way to think about multiplication to find each of the following.

**23.** $5 \times \frac{2}{15}$      **24.** $6 \times \frac{1}{12}$      **25.** $8 \times \frac{3}{4}$      **26.** $4 \times \frac{9}{10}$

# Estimating a Fraction of a Number

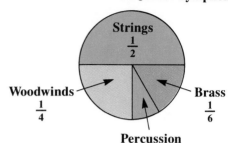

## LEARN ABOUT IT

### EXPLORE  Study a Graph

Melissa's class did some research on the instruments in the Junior Symphony. They made a circle graph to show the results.

### TALK ABOUT IT

1. Suppose the Junior Symphony has 50 members. How many of the instruments are played by the members of the strings section?

2. Suppose the Junior Symphony has 60 members. How many of the instruments would be played by members of the brass section?

3. Suppose the Junior Symphony has 40 members. What number close to 40 is divisible by 6? Can you use this fact to estimate the number of instruments in the brass section?

You can estimate a fraction of a whole number by substituting compatible numbers. For example, estimate $\frac{1}{6} \times 52$.

*Betsy's estimate:*

$\frac{1}{6}$ of 54 is 9, so $\frac{1}{6}$ of 52 is about 9.

*Todd's estimate:*

$\frac{1}{5}$ of 50 is 10, so $\frac{1}{6}$ of 52 is about 10.

Both are reasonable ways to estimate the product.

## TRY IT OUT

Substitute compatible numbers to estimate each.

1. $\frac{1}{3} \times 23$

2. $\frac{1}{5} \times 33$

3. $\frac{1}{4} \times 30$

4. $\frac{1}{8} \times 43$

5. $\frac{1}{12} \times 86$

6. $\frac{1}{6} \times 50$

7. $\frac{2}{3} \times 19$

8. $\frac{3}{4} \times 34$

Substitute compatible numbers to estimate each.

**1.** $\frac{1}{5} \times 38$    **2.** $\frac{1}{2} \times 17$    **3.** $\frac{1}{3} \times 236$    **4.** $\frac{2}{3} \times 118$

**5.** $\frac{2}{3} \times 29$    **6.** $\frac{1}{4} \times 41$    **7.** $\frac{3}{4} \times 35$    **8.** $\frac{1}{2} \times 27$

**9.** $\frac{2}{3} \times 53$    **10.** $\frac{1}{10} \times 57$    **11.** $\frac{5}{6} \times 19$    **12.** $\frac{3}{4} \times 57$

Estimate each. Write **+** if the exact answer is greater than your estimate.

**13.** $\frac{2}{5} \times 53$    **14.** $\frac{1}{2} \times 67$    **15.** $\frac{1}{4} \times 43$    **16.** $\frac{3}{10} \times 73$

**17.** $\frac{1}{3} \times \$61.89$    **18.** $\frac{4}{5} \times \$27.95$    **19.** $\frac{3}{4} \times \$53.21$    **20.** $\frac{1}{2} \times \$32.75$

**APPLY**

**MATH REASONING**

Write a fraction or whole number that could replace the variable.

**21.** $x$ of 27 is about 4.    **22.** $y$ of 67 is about 11.    **23.** $z$ of 143 is about 14.

**24.** $m$ of 27 is about 21.    **25.** $\frac{3}{5}$ of $a$ is about 36.    **26.** $\frac{3}{4}$ of $b$ is about 21.

**PROBLEM SOLVING**

**27.** One year the Junior Symphony had 56 members. About how many of the members played brass instruments that year? See the graph on page 326.

**28. Fine Arts Data Bank**   What fraction of all the instruments in a typical symphony orchestra are the violins? See page 478.

DATA
BANK

▶ **CALCULATOR**

You can find a fraction of a whole number using a calculator. Example:

Find $\frac{3}{4} \times 120$. Key code: [ON/AC] 3 [×] 120 [÷] 4 [=]  $\boxed{90}$

Use a calculator to find each.

**29.** $\frac{5}{6} \times 78$    **30.** $\frac{1}{2} \times 62$    **31.** $\frac{1}{3} \times 42$    **32.** $\frac{2}{3} \times 72$

# Multiplying Fractions
## Making the Connection

**LEARN ABOUT IT**

**EXPLORE** **Draw to Understand**

Work with a partner.

- One partner divides a square into any number of equal vertical sections like the one at the right, then shades and names the fraction.
- The other partner divides the same square into any number of equal horizontal sections, then shades and names the fraction.
- Together, the partners decide how many small rectangles are in the original square and name the fraction of the square that is shaded twice.

**TALK ABOUT IT**

1. Is the fraction represented by the region shaded twice greater than or less than each of the original fractions?

2. How can you find the total number of rectangles the square will be divided into by thinking about the denominators of the original fractions?

3. How can you find the number of squares shaded twice by looking at the numerators of the original fractions?

**328**

You have drawn pictures to find a fraction of a fraction. Here you will see how to record what you have done. Here is how to find $\frac{2}{3} \times \frac{6}{8}$.

| **What You Do** | **What You Record** |
|---|---|

Show $\frac{6}{8}$.

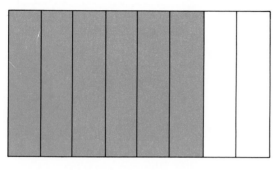

$$\frac{2}{3} \times \frac{6}{8}$$

Can you divide $\frac{6}{8}$ into thirds?

$$\frac{2}{3} \times \frac{6}{8}$$

How much is $\frac{2}{3}$ of $\frac{6}{8}$?

$$\frac{2}{3} \times \frac{6}{8} = \frac{12}{24}$$

**TRY IT OUT**

Draw pictures to show each product.

**1.** $\frac{1}{2} \times \frac{4}{8}$  **2.** $\frac{1}{3} \times \frac{3}{5}$  **3.** $\frac{1}{2} \times \frac{5}{8}$  **4.** $\frac{3}{4} \times \frac{1}{6}$

# Multiplying Fractions

In the previous lesson, you drew pictures to multiply fractions. Here you will learn how to do this using only symbols.

**EXPLORE  Analyze the Process**

Suppose you have to spray the grass in the Huff's yard with a weed killer. Their yard is $\frac{2}{3}$ grass. What part of an acre do you need to spray?

Tell why multiplication is the operation needed to solve this problem. Here is how to find the answer.

| Multiply the numerators. | Multiply the denominators. | Reduce if possible. |
|---|---|---|
| $\frac{2}{3} \times \frac{3}{8} = \frac{6}{}$ | $\frac{2}{3} \times \frac{3}{8} = \frac{6}{24}$ | $\frac{2}{3} \times \frac{3}{8} = \frac{6}{24} = \frac{1}{4}$ |

**TALK ABOUT IT**

1. Could you multiply denominators before the numerators?
2. Do you need to have like denominators to multiply two fractions?
3. Give the answer to the Explore problem in a complete sentence.

## Other Examples

**A** $\frac{1}{2} \times \frac{3}{4} = \frac{3}{8}$

**B** $\frac{3}{4} \times \frac{5}{2} = \frac{15}{8} = 1\frac{7}{8}$

**C** $\frac{2}{3} \times 5 = \frac{2}{3} \times \frac{5}{1} = \frac{10}{3} = 3\frac{1}{3}$

Multiply.

1. $\frac{3}{5} \times \frac{2}{3}$

2. $8 \times \frac{1}{3}$

3. $\frac{3}{10} \times \frac{7}{10}$

4. $\frac{4}{9} \times 9$

Multiply. Reduce to lowest terms.

**1.** $\frac{1}{4} \times \frac{2}{5}$      **2.** $\frac{6}{1} \times \frac{3}{4}$      **3.** $\frac{3}{2} \times \frac{1}{4}$      **4.** $\frac{1}{3} \times \frac{5}{8}$

**5.** $\frac{5}{6} \times \frac{1}{2}$      **6.** $9 \times \frac{2}{3}$      **7.** $\frac{2}{3} \times \frac{3}{8}$      **8.** $\frac{1}{5} \times \frac{3}{10}$

**9.** $16 \times \frac{5}{8}$      **10.** $\frac{3}{4} \times \frac{4}{3}$      **11.** $\frac{2}{5} \times 12$      **12.** $8 \times \frac{9}{10}$

## APPLY

### MATH REASONING

Using each number only once, write 1, 2, 3, or 4 for each ▦ to make:

**13.** the largest product possible.
**14.** the smallest product possible.
**15.** a product close to 1.

$$\frac{▦}{▦} \times \frac{▦}{▦} = ?$$

Write $+$, $-$, or $\times$ for each ▦ .

**16.** $\frac{1}{2} \ ▦ \ \frac{1}{2} = 0$      **17.** $\frac{1}{2} \ ▦ \ \frac{1}{2} = \frac{1}{4}$      **18.** $\frac{1}{2} \ ▦ \ \frac{1}{2} = 1$      **19.** $\frac{3}{4} \ ▦ \ \frac{2}{3} = 1\frac{5}{12}$

### PROBLEM SOLVING

**20.** How many acres of yard do the Bradys and Changs have together? Use the graph on page 330.

**21.** The Smiths have a 1-acre yard. How much larger is this than the Bradys' yard?

**22.** The Changs live next to the Huffs. Together their yards are $\frac{3}{4}$ grass. How many acres of grass is this?

**23. Unfinished Problem** Write and answer a question about this data. The Jones family have $\frac{1}{8}$ acre more yard than the Huff family. The yard is $\frac{7}{8}$ grass.

### MIXED REVIEW

**24.** $\begin{array}{r} \frac{3}{4} \\ + \frac{1}{8} \\ \hline \end{array}$      **25.** $\begin{array}{r} \frac{2}{3} \\ + \frac{1}{2} \\ \hline \end{array}$      **26.** $\begin{array}{r} \frac{5}{6} \\ + \frac{1}{3} \\ \hline \end{array}$      **27.** $\begin{array}{r} \frac{3}{8} \\ + \frac{5}{12} \\ \hline \end{array}$      **28.** $\begin{array}{r} \frac{7}{10} \\ + \frac{3}{5} \\ \hline \end{array}$

# Exploring Algebra
## Informal Algebra in Problem Solving

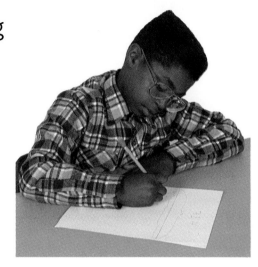

You can guess and check, draw pictures, or use objects to help you solve many problems.

Solve.

One more than twice Sal's age is 25. How old is Sal?

$$\boxed{?} + \boxed{?} + 1 \rightarrow 25$$

Try 8:  8+8+1=17    Too low!
Try 12: 12+12+1=25  Correct!

**TALK ABOUT IT**

1. What do the question marks represent? Why are there two of them?

2. Give a guess that Sal might have made that is too high.

3. Give the answer to the problem above in a complete sentence.

**TRY IT OUT**

Draw pictures, use objects, or guess and check to help you solve each.

1. Bob's parrot is 6 years older than Bob. The parrot is 21 years old. How old is Bob?

2. If you add Donna's and Wanda's ages you get 21. If you multiply their ages you get 110. What age is each girl?

3. In 7 more years, Marie will be 21. How old is Marie now?

4. 2 less than 3 times Turk's weight is 178 pounds. How much does Turk weigh?

5. Tom's weight is 2 times his brother's weight. Tom weighs 54 pounds. How much does his brother weigh?

6. If you add Yolanda's age and Teresa's age you get 54. If you subtract their ages you get 14. What age is each?

7. Terri is half as old as her sister. Terri is 13. How old is her sister?

8. 5 more than half Paul's age is 13. How old is Paul?

# POWER PRACTICE/QUIZ

Multiply.

**1.** $\frac{1}{9} \times 45$      **2.** $\frac{3}{8} \times 24$      **3.** $\frac{4}{5} \times 20$      **4.** $\frac{2}{7} \times 42$

**5.** $\frac{1}{3} \times 18$      **6.** $\frac{3}{4} \times 12$      **7.** $\frac{2}{5} \times 10$      **8.** $\frac{1}{6} \times 30$

Substitute compatible numbers to estimate each. Write +
after an estimate if the exact answer is greater than your
estimate.

**9.** $\frac{2}{3} \times 17$      **10.** $\frac{1}{5} \times 46$      **11.** $\frac{1}{8} \times 50$      **12.** $\frac{3}{4} \times 29$

**13.** $\frac{1}{4} \times 11$      **14.** $\frac{2}{3} \times 25$      **15.** $\frac{1}{6} \times 35$      **16.** $\frac{3}{8} \times 15$

Multiply. Write each product in lowest terms.

**17.** $\frac{1}{2} \times \frac{2}{3}$      **18.** $\frac{2}{3} \times \frac{3}{5}$      **19.** $\frac{3}{4} \times \frac{4}{9}$      **20.** $\frac{1}{3} \times \frac{6}{8}$

**21.** $\frac{1}{6} \times \frac{8}{9}$      **22.** $\frac{2}{3} \times \frac{2}{3}$      **23.** $\frac{7}{10} \times 15$      **24.** $\frac{2}{5} \times \frac{3}{8}$

**25.** $\frac{3}{5} \times \frac{1}{4}$      **26.** $\frac{2}{3} \times \frac{3}{4}$      **27.** $\frac{5}{6} \times \frac{3}{5}$      **28.** $\frac{3}{8} \times \frac{2}{3}$

## PROBLEM SOLVING

**29.** A recipe calls for $\frac{3}{4}$ lb of butter. How many ounces of
butter are needed? (1 lb = 16 oz)

**30.** Gayle walked $\frac{1}{3}$ mi and then jogged 9 times that
distance. What is the distance she jogged?

**31.** Gretchen ran $\frac{1}{3}$ the distance Gayle jogged. What is the
distance Gretchen ran?

**32.** Grace rides her bike between home and school 8 times
a week. The distance is $\frac{3}{4}$ mi. How many miles does
she ride in a week?

# Problem Solving
## Multiple-Step Problems

UNDERSTAND
ANALYZE DATA
PLAN
ESTIMATE
SOLVE
EXAMINE

### LEARN ABOUT IT

Some problems can be solved using two or more operations (addition, subtraction, multiplication, and division). These problems are called **multiple-step** problems.

The student council decided to sell school T-shirts and sweatshirts. $\frac{2}{5}$ of the fifth graders and $\frac{1}{6}$ of the sixth graders bought shirts the first week. What was the total number of fifth and sixth graders who bought T-shirts the first week?

Fifth grade:    65 students enrolled
Sixth grade:    72 students enrolled

First I'll find out how many fifth graders bought T-shirts.

$$\frac{2}{5} \times 65 = 26$$

Next I'll find out how many sixth graders bought T-shirts.

$$\frac{1}{6} \times 72 = 12$$

Then I'll add them together.

$$26 + 12 = 38$$

38 fifth and sixth graders bought T-shirts the first week.

### TRY IT OUT

Solve. Use the T-shirt cost data table as needed.

1. Jack ordered 80 T-shirts for the school store the first month. The second month he ordered only $\frac{1}{4}$ that number. What was the cost of the shirts he ordered the second month?

2. How much would the student council save by buying one batch of 100 T-shirts instead of buying 2 different batches of 50 T-shirts each?

| Cost for One T-Shirt or Sweatshirt | | | | | |
|---|---|---|---|---|---|
| Number of shirts | 1−24 | 25−60 | 61−96 | 97−144 | 145−200 |
| T-shirts | $6.90 | $6.45 | $6.05 | $5.65 | $5.25 |
| Sweatshirts | $7.70 | $7.20 | $6.75 | $6.35 | $5.85 |

334

Use any strategy to solve the problems.

1. The students at Penrose Elementary voted on what symbol to use on their school T-shirts. $\frac{1}{2}$ of the students who wanted the bulldog also wanted a black T-shirt. What part of the students who voted wanted a bulldog on a black shirt?

**Symbol Survey**
**Fifth and Sixth Grade Voting Results**

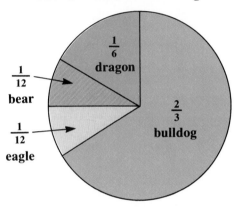

2. There are 96 fifth and sixth graders at Penrose. How many voted for the bulldog and the dragon altogether?

3. Ari works at the school store. He sold $\frac{1}{2}$ of the T-shirts at the store in the first month. He sold 27 more the second month. At that point he had 12 shirts left. How many T-shirts did he start out with?

4. What part of the students voted for the bear and the eagle altogether?

5. Marta collected $27.75 when she sold 3 sweatshirts. How much would she collect if she sold 4 sweatshirts at the same price per shirt?

6. Tops T-Shirt Store has been open for 3 days. $\frac{2}{3}$ of the T-shirts they ordered have arrived. $\frac{1}{3}$ of those shirts have been priced and put on the shelves. What part of the T-shirts that have been ordered are priced and on the shelves?

7. How much would 21 T-shirts cost on sale?

**The Tops Sale**
**3 for $11**

8. **Finding Another Way**  The following digits could be used for the backs of the Bear Cubs' baseball shirts: 2, 4, 7, 9. Each player will have a 2-digit number. How many different numbers can be put on the shirts? Corita solved this problem by drawing a picture. Find, and show another way to solve the problem.

# Multiplying Mixed Numbers

You can use what you know about multiplying fractions to help you multiply mixed numbers.

**EXPLORE** **Analyze the Process**

A city architect is planning a new housing and parklands project. It will cover a rectangular section of land $2\frac{1}{3}$ mi long and $1\frac{1}{4}$ mi wide. What is its area?

Why is multiplication the operation needed to solve this problem?

Here is how to find the exact answer.

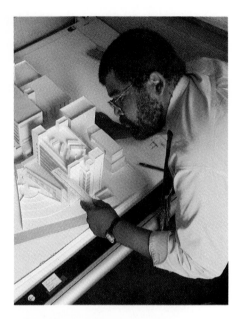

| Write the mixed numbers as improper fractions. | Multiply the fractions. Reduce to lowest terms. |
|---|---|
| $2\frac{1}{3} \times 1\frac{1}{4} = \frac{7}{3} \times \frac{5}{4}$ | $\frac{7}{3} \times \frac{5}{4} = \frac{35}{12} = 2\frac{11}{12}$ |

**TALK ABOUT IT**

1. What steps did you follow to multiply the fractions?
2. What might you have estimated the product to be?
3. Give a reasonable answer to the Explore problem in a complete sentence.

## Other Examples

**A** $3\frac{1}{3} \times 1\frac{3}{4} = \frac{10}{3} \times \frac{7}{4} = \frac{70}{12} = 5\frac{5}{6}$

**B** $\frac{1}{3} \times 3\frac{2}{5} = \frac{1}{3} \times \frac{17}{5} = \frac{17}{15} = 1\frac{2}{15}$

**C** $2\frac{1}{4} \times 5 = \frac{9}{4} \times \frac{5}{1} = \frac{45}{4} = 11\frac{1}{4}$

**D** $5 \times 4\frac{3}{8} = \frac{5}{1} \times \frac{35}{8} = \frac{175}{8} = 21\frac{7}{8}$

Multiply.

**1.** $3\frac{2}{3} \times 1\frac{2}{5}$    **2.** $1\frac{3}{8} \times 6$    **3.** $1\frac{5}{6} \times 3\frac{7}{8}$    **4.** $8 \times 2\frac{1}{4}$

Multiply. Reduce to lowest terms.

**1.** $1\frac{1}{3} \times 2\frac{1}{2}$      **2.** $2\frac{1}{3} \times 1\frac{1}{4}$      **3.** $\frac{3}{4} \times 1\frac{1}{2}$      **4.** $5 \times 1\frac{2}{5}$

**5.** $2\frac{1}{5} \times 1\frac{1}{4}$      **6.** $10 \times 2\frac{1}{2}$      **7.** $1\frac{1}{3} \times \frac{2}{3}$      **8.** $2\frac{1}{8} \times \frac{1}{4}$

**9.** $1\frac{3}{4} \times 1\frac{2}{3}$      **10.** $8\frac{1}{2} \times 4$      **11.** $1\frac{2}{3} \times 12$      **12.** $2\frac{1}{2} \times 1\frac{3}{4}$

**MATH REASONING**

**13.** Use the digits 1, 2, 3, 4, 5, or 6 in place of each ▦ to make a problem with a product close to 8.

**PROBLEM SOLVING**

**14.** A new park band shell has a stage that is 60 ft long and $40\frac{1}{2}$ ft wide. What is the area of the stage?

**15.** The symphony gave 6 free concerts in the park. The concerts lasted an average of $2\frac{3}{4}$ h each. What was the total number of hours of free concerts?

**16. Fine Arts Data Bank** Suppose half of the second violin players in a typical orchestra are women. How many women would that be? See page 478.

DATA BANK

▶ **ESTIMATION**

Use one or more of the techniques you have learned to estimate these products.

**17.** $4\frac{1}{3} \times 5\frac{5}{8}$      **18.** $12\frac{1}{5} \times 7\frac{1}{8}$

**19.** $\frac{2}{3} \times 3\frac{1}{2}$      **20.** $4\frac{1}{5} \times 2\frac{2}{3}$

| Estimation Techniques |
| --- |
| ■ Front-end |
| ■ Rounding |
| ■ Compatible numbers |
| ■ Clustering |

# Problem Solving
## Using a Calculator

UNDERSTAND
ANALYZE DATA
PLAN
ESTIMATE
SOLVE
EXAMINE

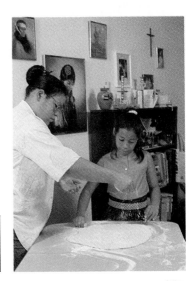

**LEARN ABOUT IT**

Toni's mother has taught her how to make many traditional American Indian dishes. Toni also likes to try out traditional recipes of other cultures.

> Toni uses $2\frac{1}{2}$ c of flour to make bread for 4 people. How many cups would she use to make bread for 14 people?

She can use a calculator that does fraction computations to solve the problem.

> Since I know $2\frac{1}{2}$ c are enough for 4 people, I'll divide $2\frac{1}{2}$ by 4 to find how much I need for 1 person.

[ON/AC] 2 [Unit] 1/2 [÷] 4 [=] 5/8

> Now I can multiply $\frac{5}{8}$ c by 14 to find how much I need to use to make enough for 14 people.

[×] 14 [=] 70/8

[Ab/c] 8 u 6/8 [Simp] [=] 8 u 3/4

Toni would use $8\frac{3}{4}$ c of flour.

**TRY IT OUT**

Solve. Use a fraction calculator.

1. Paul brought some Cajun food to a picnic. His chicken recipe called for using $2\frac{1}{4}$ lb of chicken for 8 people. How many pounds would he need for 6 people?

2. Yee's recipe for Chinese almond cookies calls for $2\frac{1}{4}$ c of flour. He needs to use only $\frac{2}{3}$ of that amount. How many cups of flour does he need?

3. Audra is using an African recipe for Injera bread that calls for 5 c of flour. The recipe makes enough bread to serve 8 people. How much flour should Audra use to make enough for 12 people?

4. Simca made a Malaysian dessert that has $\frac{3}{4}$ lb of grated coconut. If coconut costs $5.96 per pound, what would be the cost of $\frac{3}{4}$ lb?

**338**

Solve. Use the data in the recipe and any of the strategies.

**AFRICAN YAM FRITTERS**

*Ingredients*

$1\frac{1}{2}$ lb yams, boiled and mashed

1 egg, beaten

$\frac{1}{2}$ tsp salt

$\frac{1}{4}$ tsp black pepper

$\frac{1}{4}$ tsp thyme

pinch of cayenne pepper

$\frac{1}{2}$ green chili, seeded and minced

1 medium onion, chopped fine

1 medium tomato, chopped fine

$\frac{1}{2}$ c bread crumbs

peanut oil for frying

*Makes 4 servings.

**Some Strategies**

| | |
|---|---|
| Act Out | Make a Table |
| Use Objects | Solve a Simpler Problem |
| Choose an Operation | Make an Organized List |
| Draw a Picture | Work Backward |
| Guess and Check | Look for a Pattern |
| | Use Logical Reasoning |

1. Carla wants to make 12 servings of fritters. How many pounds of yams should she use? How many green chilis should she use?

2. What is the total amount of salt, thyme, and black pepper Terri needs to use to make 8 servings of fritters?

3. Yams cost $0.68 per pound at the market where Aaron shops. What will the yams cost if Aaron buys enough to make 10 servings of fritters?

4. Leona bought 3 whole green chilis. She used enough of the chilis to make 8 servings of fritters. How many chilis does she have left?

5. Harriet has 72 recipe cards in a box. Each is for a dessert or a main dish. She has twice as many dessert recipes as main dish recipes. How many of each type does she have?

6. Tom used half as many eggs in one recipe as he used in another recipe. He dropped 3 eggs and could not use them. There are 3 eggs left in the carton. If the carton had 2 dozen eggs to begin with, how many eggs did he use in each recipe?

7. **Data Hunt**   Find a recipe that has been a favorite of your family or relatives. How much of each item would you use to make $2\frac{1}{2}$ times the amount called for in the recipe?

# Dividing Fractions
## Using Objects and Pictures

### LEARN ABOUT IT

You can think about what it means to divide whole numbers to help you divide fractions. For example, $15 \div 3$ can mean, "How many threes are in 15?" $2 \div \frac{1}{2}$ can mean, "How many halves are in 2?"

### EXPLORE  Solve to Understand
Work in groups.

- The pictures below show how to use fraction pieces to find how many halves are in 2, or $2 \div \frac{1}{2}$.

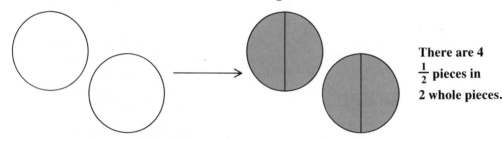

There are 4 $\frac{1}{2}$ pieces in 2 whole pieces.

- Draw a picture to show how many eighths are in $\frac{3}{4}$, that is, $\frac{3}{4} \div \frac{1}{8}$.

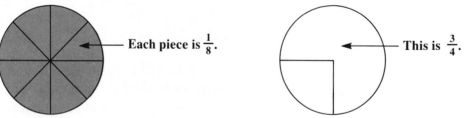

Each piece is $\frac{1}{8}$.

This is $\frac{3}{4}$.

### TALK ABOUT IT

1. How many $\frac{1}{2}$ pieces are in 2?   What is $2 \div \frac{1}{2}$?
2. How many $\frac{1}{8}$ pieces are in $\frac{3}{4}$?   What is $\frac{3}{4} \div \frac{1}{8}$?

### TRY IT OUT

Use fraction pieces or draw pictures to find each.

1. How many thirds in 2?   $2 \div \frac{1}{3} = $ ▓▓▓

2. How many thirds in $\frac{2}{3}$?   $\frac{2}{3} \div \frac{1}{3} = $ ▓▓▓

**340**

Find the quotients. Check by multiplying.

**1.** How many fourths are in 2?

$$2 \div \frac{1}{4} = n$$

**2.** How many sixths are in $\frac{2}{3}$?

$$\frac{2}{3} \div \frac{1}{6} = n$$

Use fraction pieces or draw pictures to find each quotient.
Check by multiplying.

**3.** How many halves are in 2?

$$2 \div \frac{1}{2} = n$$

**4.** How many fourths are in 3?

$$3 \div \frac{1}{4} = n$$

**5.** How many eighths are in $\frac{1}{2}$?

$$\frac{1}{2} \div \frac{1}{8} = n$$

**6.** How many eighths are in $\frac{1}{4}$?

$$\frac{1}{4} \div \frac{1}{8} = n$$

**7.** How many thirds are in 3?

$$3 \div \frac{1}{3} = n$$

**8.** How many fourths are in $\frac{1}{2}$?

$$\frac{1}{2} \div \frac{1}{4} = n$$

## APPLY

### MATH REASONING

Look for a **pattern** in the pairs of problems. Copy and
complete the next two pairs of problems.

**9.** $\frac{1}{2} \div \frac{1}{8} = 4$ $\qquad \frac{1}{2} \times \frac{8}{1} = 4$

$\frac{5}{6} \div \frac{2}{3} = 1\frac{1}{4}$ $\qquad \frac{5}{6} \times \frac{3}{2} = 1\frac{1}{4}$

$\frac{1}{2} \div \frac{3}{8} = 1\frac{1}{3}$ $\qquad \frac{1}{2} \times \text{▮▮▮} = \text{▮▮▮}$

**10.** $\frac{3}{4} \div \frac{1}{4} = 3$ $\qquad \frac{3}{4} \times \frac{4}{1} = 3$

$\frac{3}{4} \div \frac{3}{8} = 2$ $\qquad \frac{3}{4} \times \frac{8}{3} = 2$

$\frac{1}{6} \div \frac{1}{3} = \frac{1}{2}$ $\qquad \frac{1}{6} \times \text{▮▮▮} = \text{▮▮▮}$

### PROBLEM SOLVING

**11. Write Your Own Problem** Write a division question
using this data. Jan was making a snack for her friends.
She cut 4 oranges into sixths.

### ▶ ALGEBRA

You can write algebraic expressions involving division. The
expression for "a number divided by 5" is $n \div 5$ or $\frac{n}{5}$.

The "bar" means
*divided by.*

Write an algebraic expression for each.

**12.** six and one half plus a number

**13.** twelve divided by a number

**14.** three fourths of a number

**15.** a number divided by 5

*More Practice, page 517, set A*

# Data Collection and Analysis
## Group Decision Making

UNDERSTAND
ANALYZE DATA
PLAN
ESTIMATE
SOLVE
EXAMINE

### Making a Questionnaire
### Group Skill:
Encourage and Respect Others

Are there household jobs that you now do or could do? Helping with chores around the house gives you the satisfaction of knowing you are doing your part as a member of your family. It also helps to prepare you for many responsibilities you will have later in your life. Do most of the students in your school do things to help out around the house? Make a questionnaire to find out.

### Collecting Data

1. Work with your group to make a list of at least ten things you now do or could do to help out at home.

2. Use the items in your list to prepare a questionnaire that will help you find out what kinds of chores students do and how often they do them.

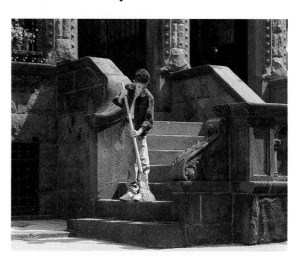

### Questionnaire

How often do you help out at home by doing any of the listed items? Check the box that best applies.

|  | Daily | Sometimes | Never |
|---|---|---|---|
| 1. Help in kitchen | ☐ | ☐ | ☐ |
| 2. Care for pets | ☐ | ☐ | ☐ |
| 3. Make bed | ☐ | ☐ | ☐ |
| 4. Take out garbage | ☐ | ☐ | ☐ |
| 5. Help with cleaning | ☐ | ☐ | ☐ |
| 6. Run errands | ☐ | ☐ | ☐ |
| 7. Care for younger children | ☐ | ☐ | ☐ |
| **Others (List below.)** | | | |
| _____ | ☐ | ☐ | ☐ |
| _____ | ☐ | ☐ | ☐ |

**3.** Check your questionnaire by having two or three people fill it out. Make sure each person who answers your questionnaire will understand how to complete it properly. Revise your questionnaire if necessary.

**4.** Make copies of the questionnaire for each person in your group. Find at least 25 students in your school who will be willing to provide responses.

### Organizing Data

**5.** Sort the completed questionnaires into groups according to responses:
1) students who do some of the listed activities daily
2) students who never do any of the activities daily but sometimes do some of the activities
3) students who never do any of the activities

**6.** Count the number of students in each of the three groups. Make a pictograph that shows how many students are in each group. Design your own symbol to use on the graph.

### Presenting Your Analysis

**7.** Write a short paragraph describing how you decided which students to ask to complete the questionnaire. Was your sample selected randomly?

**8.** Tell how you decided on the design for the symbol to use in your graph.

**9.** Prepare a short summary of your results to share with the class.

# WRAP UP

## Fraction Fill-In

Choose the word from the box that completes each
sentence. Some words will not be used.

| | | |
|---|---|---|
| less | greater | divide |
| sixths | compatible | five |
| multiply | thirds | four |

1. You can estimate a fraction of a whole number by
   substituting __?__ numbers.

2. To find $\frac{3}{5}$ of 40, __?__ 40 by 5, then __?__ by 3.

3. Two thirds of one half is two __?__.

4. Five eighths of 32 is __?__ than two sixths of 54.

## Sometimes, Always, Never

Complete each statement by writing **sometimes**,
**always**, or **never**. Explain your choices.

5. When you multiply two fractions between 0 and
   1, the product is __?__ smaller than either fraction.

6. When you divide one fraction by another, the
   quotient is __?__ a fraction.

7. To multiply two mixed numbers, you should __?__
   multiply the whole numbers, multiply the
   fractions, then add the two products.

## Project

Use the digits 1 through 8 as often as
you like to write two fractions with
the given product and sum. Make up
four others to exchange with a
partner.

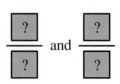

8. Product: $\frac{1}{5}$
   Sum: $\frac{9}{10}$

9. Product: $\frac{1}{10}$
   Sum: $\frac{13}{20}$

10. Product: $\frac{1}{9}$
    Sum: $\frac{5}{6}$

11. Product: $\frac{5}{8}$
    Sum: $1\frac{7}{12}$

# POWER PRACTICE/TEST

## Part 1  Understanding

Use the digits 4, 5, 6, and 7 only once in each ▦ to make:   $\frac{▦}{▦} \times \frac{▦}{▦}$

**1.** the largest possible product

**2.** the smallest possible product

Draw a picture for each. Give the answer.

**3.** $\frac{1}{2} \times \frac{3}{5}$

**4.** The number of eighths in $\frac{3}{4}$
$$\frac{3}{4} \div \frac{1}{8}$$

## Part 2  Skills

Multiply.

**5.** $\frac{3}{4} \times 16$

**6.** $\frac{2}{3} \times 27$

**7.** $\frac{1}{4} \times 36$

**8.** $\frac{6}{7} \times \frac{5}{12}$

**9.** $\frac{5}{8} \times \frac{3}{10}$

**10.** $\frac{7}{8} \times \frac{4}{5}$

**11.** $2\frac{5}{6} \times 1\frac{7}{8}$

**12.** $8\frac{1}{2} \times 4\frac{2}{3}$

**13.** $2\frac{1}{3} \times 3\frac{3}{7}$

Estimate each.

**14.** $\frac{1}{2} \times 19$

**15.** $\frac{2}{3} \times 25$

**16.** $\frac{4}{5} \times 48$

**17.** $\frac{1}{5} \times 24$

**18.** $\frac{3}{4} \times 29$

**19.** $\frac{3}{8} \times 15$

Find the quotients. Check by multiplying.

**20.** How many thirds are in 1?

$1 \div \frac{1}{3} = n$

**21.** How many fifths are in 2?

$2 \div \frac{1}{5} = n$

## Part 3  Applications

**22.** If you add Jim's and Kara's ages, you get 26. If you multiply their ages, you get 168. What are their ages?

**23.** Kee had 56 books. He donated $\frac{3}{8}$ of them to the hospital library and $\frac{1}{4}$ of them to the school library. How many books did he keep for himself?

**24. Challenge** A $1 bill is $2\frac{5}{8}$ in. wide and about $6\frac{1}{8}$ in. long. How many stacks of $1 bills will fit into a briefcase that is 14 in. wide and 22 in. long?

# ENRICHMENT
## Following Flow Chart Directions

Find the missing numbers.

**1.**

Enter
?

Add
314

Subtract
68

556

**2.**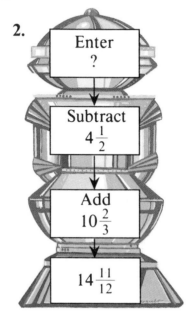

Enter
?

Subtract
$4\frac{1}{2}$

Add
$10\frac{2}{3}$

$14\frac{11}{12}$

**3.**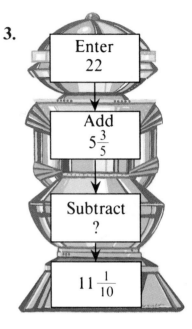

Enter
22

Add
$5\frac{3}{5}$

Subtract
?

$11\frac{1}{10}$

**4.**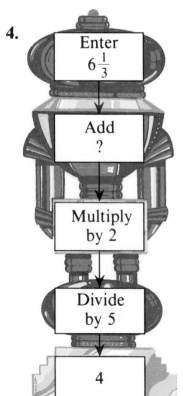

Enter
$6\frac{1}{3}$

Add
?

Multiply
by 2

Divide
by 5

4

**5.**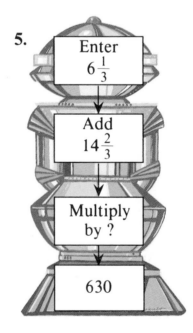

Enter
$6\frac{1}{3}$

Add
$14\frac{2}{3}$

Multiply
by ?

630

**6.**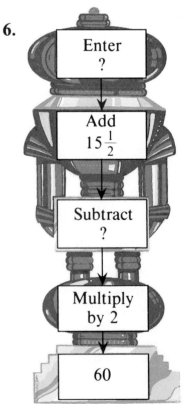

Enter
?

Add
$15\frac{1}{2}$

Subtract
?

Multiply
by 2

60

# CUMULATIVE REVIEW

**1.** What fraction of the set is shaded?

   A. $\frac{7}{12}$    B. $\frac{5}{7}$    C. $\frac{5}{12}$    D. $\frac{7}{5}$

**2.** Which unit would you use to measure the length of your backyard?

   A. inch              B. pound
   C. yard              D. mile

Add or subtract. Reduce answers to lowest terms.

**3.** $\frac{11}{12} - \frac{5}{12}$

   A. $\frac{1}{2}$    B. $\frac{16}{12}$    C. $1\frac{1}{3}$    D. $\frac{7}{12}$

**4.** $\frac{2}{5} + \frac{3}{4}$

   A. $1\frac{3}{20}$    B. $\frac{9}{20}$    C. $\frac{7}{20}$    D. $\frac{5}{9}$

**5.** $86\frac{1}{5} - 27\frac{1}{3}$

   A. $58\frac{8}{15}$              B. $58\frac{13}{15}$
   C. $62\frac{8}{15}$              D. $62\frac{13}{15}$

**6.** Which answer is *not* a possible answer for this problem?

Angela counted 44 wheels. Some belonged to bicycles and some to tricycles. How many bicycles and tricycles did she see?

   A. 4 and 12          B. 11 and 7
   C. 10 and 8          D. 16 and 4

**7.** Which line measures $1\frac{3}{4}$ in. to the nearest $\frac{1}{4}$ inch?

   A. _____

   B. _____

   C. _____

   D. _____

**8.** Which fraction is equivalent to $\frac{5}{6}$?

   A. $\frac{15}{12}$    B. $\frac{10}{18}$    C. $\frac{15}{36}$    D. $\frac{20}{24}$

**9.** Which fraction is less than $\frac{2}{3}$?

   A. $\frac{4}{5}$    B. $\frac{8}{9}$    C. $\frac{9}{12}$    D. $\frac{5}{8}$

Give the missing numbers.

**10.** 85 in. = ▨ ft ▨ in.

   A. 6 ft 13 in.       B. 7 ft 5 in.
   C. 8 ft 5 in.        D. 7 ft 1 in.

**11.** 1 gal = ▨ c

   A. 16    B. 8    C. 4    D. 2

**12.** 5 lb 12 oz = ▨ oz

   A. 80    B. 92    C. 86    D. 98

**13.** Which would you be most likely to estimate?

   A. the length of drapes for a window

   B. the length of rope for a clothesline

   C. the length of a picture frame for a special picture

   D. the length of your foot when buying shoes

**347**

# 13

## GEOMETRY

**M**ATH AND
HEALTH AND FITNESS

### DATA BANK

Use the Health and
Fitness Data Bank on
page 476 to answer
the questions.

**1** Which of the sports playing areas has sides that
are all the same length?
Which area is only half as wide
as it is long?

**THEME: PLAYING FIELDS**

**2** Most sports are played on fields that have rectangular shapes. Which sport uses playing fields that are not rectangular?

**3** Is the diamond on a baseball field the same shape as a boxing ring? Is a boxing ring the same shape as a karate area?

**4** **Using Critical Thinking** Use the clues to solve the riddle. "It is more than 3 yards long. It is less than 40 feet wide. It is not a square. Which sports playing area is it?"

Football is an action-packed sport whose beginnings can be traced back to games played in ancient Egypt.

# Analyzing Solid Figures

Geometric solid figures are used to make many useful objects.

**EXPLORE  Make a Model**
Trace this figure on your paper. Then cut it out, fold on dashed lines, and tape the edges together to make a solid figure.

**TALK ABOUT IT**

1. A straight edge of a solid is a **line segment.** How many line segments can you find on your solid?

2. The flat surfaces of your model are its **faces.** Each of its faces is a **polygon.** What kinds of polygons are the faces of your model?

3. A corner of a solid is a **point,** or **vertex.** How many vertices does your solid have?

Here are some of the different types of solid figures.

**Pattern for a square pyramid**

cylinder

sphere

rectangular prism

triangular prism

cone

rectangular pyramid

**TRY IT OUT**

1. Name a solid figure above that has the figure named below as one or more of its flat surfaces.

   **A.** square          **B.** triangle          **C.** rectangle

2. A **cube** is a rectangular prism with square faces. How many faces, edges, and vertices does a cube have?

Name a real object that is shaped like each solid figure below.

**1.**  **2.**  **3.**  **4.**

Name a solid figure that has these flat surfaces.

**5.** 2 circles　　　　　　**6.** 2 squares, 4 rectangles　**7.** 4 triangles

**8.** no flat surfaces　　　**9.** 2 triangles, 3 rectangles　**10.** 1 circle

**11.** Copy and complete this chart for faces, edges, and vertices of solid figures.

| Solid Figure | Faces | Edges | Vertices |
|---|---|---|---|
| Rectangular Prism | | | |
| Triangular Pyramid | | | |
| Triangular Prism | | | |

**MATH REASONING**

**12.** Do you see a pattern in the table above? (Hint: Add the number of faces to the number of vertices.) How many edges would there be on a solid that has 7 faces and 10 vertices?

**PROBLEM SOLVING**

**13.** The cup shaped like a cylinder holds 3 times as much as the cup shaped like a cone. If the cone-shaped cup holds 198 mL, how much does the other cup hold?

**14.** A tent floor is 4 yd long and 3 yd wide. If twice the area of the floor is needed to set up the tent, how many square yards of ground are needed?

▶ **USING CRITICAL THINKING　Analyze the Situation**

**15.** What figure do you predict will appear on the screen? What if the cylinder is replaced with the sphere? the cone?

# Exploring Triangles

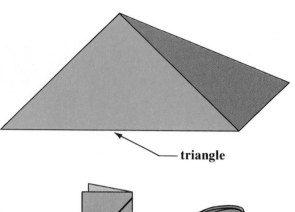

triangle

You have seen that the face of a pyramid is a triangle. In this lesson you will explore the properties of triangles.

**EXPLORE  Construct Models**

Work in groups. Fold a sheet of paper. Make a triangle by cutting twice on the folded side. Can you cut a triangle that has

**A.** exactly 2 sides the same length?

**C.** a square corner?

**B.** all 3 sides the same length?

**D.** a triangle with no sides the same length?

**TALK ABOUT IT**

1. Which of the triangles above cannot be cut from folded paper? Why?

2. How many angles does a triangle have?

3. Use this picture and your cutout triangles to show a **line of symmetry** of each of the triangles. Can you cut a triangle from folded paper so that the triangle has no line of symmetry?

angle of a triangle

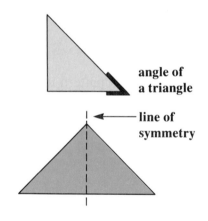

line of symmetry

Three types of triangles are shown below.

**scalene triangle**
(no sides the same)

**isosceles triangle**
(at least two sides the same)

**equilateral triangle**
(three sides the same)

1. Draw a picture to show the lines of symmetry for each triangle above.

2. Can every triangle be divided by a line into 2 "square corner" triangles? Draw a picture of each type of triangle to explain.

Is the triangle **equilateral, isosceles,** or **scalene?**

1.

2.

3.

4.

5.

6.

APPLY

## MATH REASONING

Complete the following with **equilateral, scalene,** or **isosceles.**

7. Every __?__ triangle is also an isosceles triangle.
8. No __?__ triangle is also an isosceles triangle.
9. Some __?__ triangles are also equilateral triangles.

## PROBLEM SOLVING

10. Draw an isosceles triangle and show a line of symmetry.

11. Use this figure to trace an equilateral, a scalene, and an isosceles triangle. Tell which type each triangle is.

12. How many triangles can you find in this figure? There are more than 6.

▶ **USING CRITICAL THINKING** Evaluate the Assumptions

Jim said, "You can draw straight lines and divide any figure into triangles." "I'm not so sure," said Jeryl. "It depends on what you mean by *figures.*"

13. What might Jim have assumed about "figures"? What other assumptions might be made?

14. Is Jim's statement true for all polygons? Draw some pictures to support your conclusion.

*More Practice, page 517, set C*

# Measuring Angles

The size or amount of opening of an angle is measured using a unit called a **degree.** Each of the red angles has a **measure** of 90°.

### EXPLORE  Analyze a Diagram

∠*XYZ* is an **acute** angle. Acute angles have measures less than 90°.

∠*PQR* is an **obtuse** angle. Obtuse angles have measures greater than 90°.

### TALK ABOUT IT

1. An angle with a measure of 90° is called a **right** angle. Where would *X* be in ∠*XYZ* if ∠*XYZ* were a right angle?
2. What is the measure of ∠*XYZ*? How did you decide?
3. What is the measure of ∠*PQR*? How did you decide?

We use a **protractor** to measure angles. Steps 1, 2, and 3 tell how to use a protractor.

③ Read the measure of the angle.

The measure of ∠*ABC* is 47°

② Place the zero edge of the protractor along one side of the angle.

① Place the arrow on the vertex of the angle.

### TRY IT OUT

Draw 4 angles, 2 acute and 2 obtuse. First estimate, then measure each angle. Record your results in a table.

| Estimate | Measure | Difference |
|---|---|---|
|  |  |  |
|  |  |  |

First **estimate** the measure of each angle. Then use a protractor to check your estimate. Trace the angle and draw longer sides if necessary.

**1.** **2.** **3.** **4.**

### MATH REASONING

Tell if the angle is **right, acute,** or **obtuse.** Choose the best estimate for its measure. Then measure with a protractor. Was your estimate reasonable?

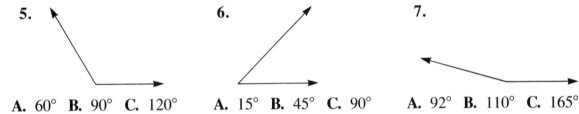

**5.** **A.** 60° **B.** 90° **C.** 120°   **6.** **A.** 15° **B.** 45° **C.** 90°   **7.** **A.** 92° **B.** 110° **C.** 165°

### PROBLEM SOLVING

**8.** Explain why the hands of a clock do *not* form a right angle at 12:15 p.m.

**9.** Give two times when the hands of a clock *do* form a right angle.

### ▶ ESTIMATION

Estimate whether each angle is closest to 15°, 30°, 45°, 60°, or 90°. Use a protractor to check your estimates.

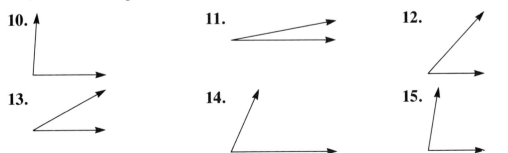

**10.**   **11.**   **12.**

**13.**   **14.**   **15.**

# Quadrilaterals

**EXPLORE**  **Make a Figure**

Trace and cut out 4 copies of this right triangle. How many 4-sided figures of different shapes can you make by putting two triangles together? four triangles together? Draw pictures to show your figures.

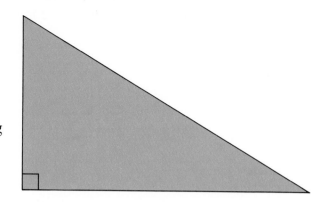

**TALK ABOUT IT**

1. Can you name your figures? Do some figures have more than one name?
2. Do you think you have made all the possible 4-sided figures? Explain.
3. Can all 4-sided figures be divided into two triangles? Draw pictures to justify your answer.

Four-sided polygons are called **quadrilaterals.**
Here are some different types of quadrilaterals.

**Square**

All sides the same length
All angles right angles

**Rhombus**

All sides the same length

**Rectangle**

Two pairs of sides the same length
All angles right angles

**Parallelogram**

Two pairs of sides the same length
Two pairs of parallel sides

**Trapezoid**

Exactly one pair of
parallel sides

**Kite**

Two pairs of touching sides the
same length

**TRY IT OUT**

Copy and complete each statement.

1. A square is also a __?__ .

2. A rhombus is also a __?__ .

Write the name that best describes each figure: **square, rectangle, parallelogram, rhombus, trapezoid,** or **kite.**

**1.**

**2.**

**3.**

**4.**

**5.**

**6.**

### MATH REASONING

Which quadrilateral has

**7.** all sides the same length and four right angles?

**8.** only one pair of parallel sides?

**9.** no right angles, but two pairs of parallel sides?

### PROBLEM SOLVING

**10.** How many *different* rectangles can be found on a 5 by 5 geoboard? Here are some rules and hints.

- Sides do not have to be parallel to the sides of the geoboard.

- The same rectangle in a different position does not count as different.

- There are more than 10 but less than 20.

- Squares are a type of rectangle.

### ▶ USING CRITICAL THINKING    Test a Conjecture

**11.** Myron said, "Every rectangle is a square." Barry said, "No, you're wrong. Every square is a rectangle." Write a paragraph supporting the statement you think is correct.

*More Practice, page 518, set A*

# More About Quadrilaterals

## LEARN ABOUT IT

A jai alai court is a quadrilateral. It is also a rectangle. In this lesson you will learn more about other quadrilaterals.

### EXPLORE  Try Some Paper-Folding

Work in groups. Fold a sheet of paper and cut out a piece like this. What kind of a figure will it be when you unfold it? Try to cut out pieces that unfold to make

**A.** a square.

**B.** a rectangle.

**C.** a rhombus.

**D.** a trapezoid.

**E.** a kite.

**F.** a parallelogram that is not a square, a rectangle, or a rhombus.

## TALK ABOUT IT

1. Which quadrilaterals did you find cannot be cut from a folded piece of paper?

2. Can all of the quadrilaterals that you were able to cut out be folded so that two halves match exactly? Explain.

A quadrilateral has a **line of symmetry** if it can be folded so that the two halves match exactly. Some quadrilaterals have no lines of symmetry. Others have more than one line of symmetry.

## TRY IT OUT

1. Tell what this figure will be when cut out and unfolded.

2. Give the total number of lines of symmetry for the unfolded figure.

Give the number of lines of symmetry for each geometric shape. Trace and fold the shape if necessary.

**1.**

**2.**

**3.**

**4.**

**5.**

**6.**

**APPLY**

### MATH REASONING

Draw what you would cut from the folded paper in order to get a figure that when unfolded would be

**7.** a long thin rectangle

**8.** a square folded on the diagonal

**9.** a thin rhombus

**10.** a trapezoid with one very short side

### PROBLEM SOLVING

**11.** Here is a horizontally symmetric word and a vertically symmetric word. Give another example of each.

**12. Health and Fitness Data Bank** How many lines of symmetry are drawn on a basketball court? Find another line of symmetry on the court. See page 476.

**MIXED REVIEW**

Multiply. Reduce answers to lowest terms.

**13.** $\frac{2}{3} \times \frac{1}{5}$

**14.** $\frac{3}{8} \times \frac{2}{4}$

**15.** $\frac{5}{7} \times \frac{3}{5}$

**16.** $\frac{2}{7} \times \frac{3}{4}$

**17.** $\frac{5}{6} \times \frac{1}{2}$

**18.** $\frac{3}{4} \times \frac{1}{8}$

**19.** $\frac{1}{2} \times \frac{2}{3}$

**20.** $\frac{3}{5} \times \frac{3}{4}$

**21.** $\frac{2}{3} \times 1\frac{1}{4}$

**22.** $1\frac{1}{2} \times 3\frac{1}{3}$

**23.** $\frac{3}{4} \times 2\frac{1}{5}$

**24.** $2\frac{1}{4} \times 1\frac{1}{3}$

# Using Critical Thinking

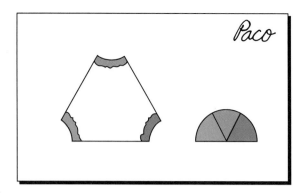
Paco

Paco made a poster to show something he discovered about the angles of a triangle. "I cut off the corners of an equilateral triangle," he explained. "Since the three angles fill half a circle and it can be folded to form two right angles, I've proved that the sum of the angles of a triangle is 180°. The angles fit into a **straight angle!**"

"But look at the triangles on my poster," said Sally. "You used an equilateral triangle. My triangles aren't equilateral, so I'm not sure you've proved what you say you did."

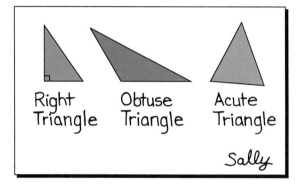
Right Triangle    Obtuse Triangle    Acute Triangle

Sally

**TALK ABOUT IT**

1. Do you think Sally has a good point? Explain.

2. How could you help support the conclusion that the sum of the measures of the angles of any triangle is 180°?

**TRY IT OUT**

Try an experiment that helps support Paco's conclusion. Measure the angles and find the sum of the angle measures of each triangle. Do the results agree with your earlier conclusion?

**1.**　　　**2.**　　　**3.**

4. A triangle has a 47° angle and a 26° angle. What is the measure of the other angle?

# POWER PRACTICE/QUIZ

**1.** Name each figure.

**2.** What shapes are the faces in in figure **A**?

**3.** How many faces, edges, and vertices are in figure **B**?

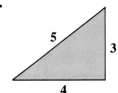

A      B      C      D

Which of the triangles below are

**4.** scalene?

**5.** equilateral?

**6.** isosceles?

**A.**

**B.**

**C.**

**D.**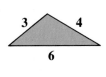

Which of the triangles above have

**7.** a right angle?

**8.** an acute angle?

**9.** an obtuse angle?

Estimate the angle measure each angle is closest to: 15°, 30°, 45°, 60°, or 90°. Then use a protractor to check.

**10.**

**11.**

**12.**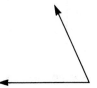

## PROBLEM SOLVING

**13.** A triangle has a right angle. What is the sum of the measures of its other angles?

**14.** A triangle has an obtuse angle and two sides that are the same length. Are the two sides that are the same length longer than or shorter than the third side?

**15.** A certain prism is 3 inches tall. The bottom face is in the shape of this hexagon. What is the shape of the top?

3 in.

1 in.      1 in.

1 in.      1 in.

3 in.

**361**

# Congruent Figures and Motions

LEARN ABOUT IT

Two figures are **congruent** to each other if they have the same size and shape. In sports, rules require that certain playing fields be congruent. For example, every football field is congruent to other football fields and every professional soccer field is congruent to other professional soccer fields.

### EXPLORE  Make a Figure

Draw a scalene triangle on the left half of a sheet of paper.

### TALK ABOUT IT

How can you use tracing paper to help you draw a figure on the right half that is

1. congruent to the top figure, but **turned** in a different direction?
2. congruent to the top figure, but **flipped** over?
3. a figure that has been neither turned nor flipped?

Two figures are **congruent** if you can slide, flip, or turn (rotate) one to make it fit exactly on the other.

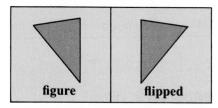

TRY IT OUT

Use your tracing paper to decide whether figure A must be **slid, slid and turned,** or **slid and flipped** to fit on figure B.

362

Is figure A congruent to figure B? Use tracing paper to test. Then tell which you had to do: **slide, slide and turn,** or **slide and flip.**

**1.**

**2.**

**3.**

**4.**

**5.**

**6.**

## APPLY

### MATH REASONING

**7.** Copy this figure on graph paper. Draw the reflection image of the triangle by flipping it across line *a*. Draw the reflection image of the new triangle by flipping it across line *b*. What single motion would move the original triangle onto the final triangle?

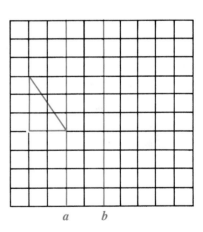

### PROBLEM SOLVING

**8. Health and Fitness Data Bank**  In professional baseball, what part of the field is congruent to the same part of other fields? Can you find two stadiums that seem to have congruent outfields? See page 476.

▶ **USING CRITICAL THINKING**   Give a Counterexample

Do you agree with the statement?
If not, give an example that shows that it is not true.

**9.** Dorcas said "All right angles are congruent."

**10.** Martin said "All right triangles are congruent."

# Problem Solving
## Using Data from a Picture

UNDERSTAND
ANALYZE DATA
PLAN
ESTIMATE
SOLVE
EXAMINE

To solve some
problems, you must
find the data
you need in
a picture.

The Sea Rovers are going on a sailing trip on an old ship
named the *C. A. Thayer*. Dawn is making a model of the
ship. She needs to know the measure of ∠C on the
mizzenmast.

Tonnage (weight): 452 tons
Total area of canvas (sails): 7,292 ft

I'll find the data I need in the picture.

Now I can use the fact that the sum of
the angles of a triangle is 180°.

I can add the angles I know. Then I
can subtract from 180°.

Angle A is 30°.
Angle B is a right angle. It is 90°

30° + 90° = 120°
180° − 120 = 60°

The measure of ∠C is 60°.

**TRY IT OUT**

1. How much greater is the overall length of the ship than
   the length of the hull?

2. What is the area of the top of the rectangular
   deckhouse?

Solve. Use any of the strategies. You may need data from page 364.

| Some Strategies | |
| --- | --- |
| Act Out | Make a Table |
| Use Objects | Solve a Simpler Problem |
| Choose an Operation | Make an Organized List |
| Draw a Picture | Work Backward |
| Guess and Check | Look for a Pattern |
| Use Logical Reasoning | |

**1.** The *C. A. Thayer* has 6 sails. The total area of the sails is about 7,292 ft². Another ship, the *Bowdoin,* has 4 sails with 2,566 ft² of sail area. About how much greater is the area of the sails on the *C. A. Thayer?*

**2.** What is the area of the rectangular mainsail on the *C. A. Thayer?*

**3.** Suppose the *Thayer's* mizzensail had been cut in one piece from a rectangular piece of canvas. What would the area of that piece of canvas have been?

**4.** What is the area of the *Thayer's* mizzensail? (You can use your answer to problem 3 to help you.)

**5.** The *Balclutha* weighs about 3.7 times as much as the *C. A. Thayer.* How much does the *Balclutha* weigh?

**6.** What is the perimeter of the deckhouse on the *C. A. Thayer?*

**7.** For the trip on the *C. A. Thayer,* the 65 Rovers are divided into crews. There are 13 in each crew. How many crews are there?

**8.** Roddy practiced knot tying for 5 minutes the first day, 10 minutes the second day, 15 minutes the third day, and so on. How many minutes would he have practiced in all at the end of the fifth day?

**9.** Janice needs to decide which one of the following crews she wants to be on: galley, linehandler, deckhand, fishing, rigger. She also needs to decide if she wants to be a sailor or an officer on her crew. How many different choices does she have?

**10.** On Eric's model of a ship, the hull is 10 in. long. The hull of the actual ship is 240 times as long. How many feet long is the hull of the actual ship?

**11. Write Your Own Problem** Use the given data to write a problem about a model of a sailing ship. The hull is 3 in. shorter than the overall length of the ship. The beam is only a third the length of the hull. The overall length is 36 in.

*More Practice, page 527, set A*

# Other Polygons
## Tessellations

### EXPLORE  Examine a Pattern

Cathy's neighbor liked to make quilts.
Here are two of her patterns.

**Pattern A**

**Pattern B**

**TALK ABOUT IT**

1. What type of polygon was used to make pattern A? How many of these fit around point P?
2. Describe the types of polygons and their arrangements in pattern B.
3. How are patterns A and B alike? How are they different?

In geometry, quilt patterns of polygons like those above are called **tessellations.** Some **regular polygons** (polygons with all sides congruent and all angles congruent) can be used to make tessellations. Equilateral triangles, squares, hexagons, and octagons (with another polygon) can be used, but pentagons cannot.

**pentagon
(5 sides)**

**hexagon
(6 sides)**

**octagon
(8 sides)**

**TRY IT OUT**

1. Look for examples of tessellations in your school and other places. Describe the kinds of polygons used.
2. Trace copies of the hexagon to make a tessellation that covers a square at least 3 in. on a side.

A

B

1. Name the polygons used to make tessellation A.
2. Name the polygons used to make tessellation B.
3. What polygon is on each side of every hexagon in A?
4. What polygon is on each side of every hexagon in B?

**APPLY**

**MATH REASONING**

5. Here is another tessellation. How is it like tessellations A and B? How is it different from tessellations A and B?

**PROBLEM SOLVING**

6. Lyle made a floor design using a square and an octagon. The design was a tessellation. Use tracing paper and draw a tessellation that covers a square 4 in. on a side.

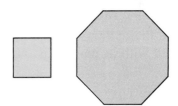

**MIXED REVIEW**

Give the number for each ▨.

7. $\frac{1}{2}$ gal = ▨ qt

8. 3 qt = ▨ pt

9. 32 fl oz = ▨ c

Multiply. Reduce to lowest terms.

10. $3\frac{1}{4} \times 2\frac{1}{3}$

11. $2\frac{1}{2} \times 3\frac{1}{3}$

12. $1\frac{1}{8} \times 2\frac{3}{4}$

13. $3\frac{1}{2} \times \frac{2}{3}$

14. $\frac{3}{8} \times 4$

*More Practice, page 518, Set D*

# Circles

We see circles every day. Circles are useful in making a great many things, from tractor tires to colorful decorative designs.

**EXPLORE** **Make Circular Designs**

- Can you use a compass to make this design?

- Make a circular design of your own and color it.

**TALK ABOUT IT**

1. When you draw a circle with a compass, the compass tip is at the **center** of the circle. How are the points on the circle related to the center of the circle?

2. Draw a line segment with endpoints on the circle and which passes through the center. How does the length of the total segment compare to the length from the center to one of the endpoints? Do you think this is always true?

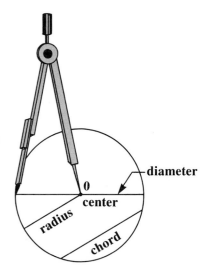

The distance the compass is open when you use it to draw a circle is the **radius** of the circle. The distance across the circle through the center is the **diameter.** A **chord** is a line segment with its endpoints on the circle.

**TRY IT OUT**

1. Draw several circles, each with a different radius. Measure with a centimeter ruler to complete a table like this.

| Circle | radius (cm) | diameter (cm) |
|--------|-------------|---------------|
| 1 | ? | ? |
| 2 | ? | ? |

Look for a pattern to help you complete these statements.

2. The length of the diameter of a circle is __?__ the length of the radius.

3. The length of the radius of a circle is __?__ the length of the diameter.

Measure the diameter or radius shown in red to the nearest centimeter. Use this measure to find the other.

1.

2.

3.

Use a compass and a centimeter ruler to draw a circle with

**4.** radius 5 cm.     **5.** diameter 6 cm.    **6.** diameter 4 cm.    **7.** radius 3 cm.

**MATH REASONING**

**8.** Draw a circle in which the diameter is equal to the radius multiplied by itself.

**PROBLEM SOLVING**

**9.** How many circles can you make with a radius of 1 unit on the dot paper at the right? A unit is the vertical or horizontal distance between 2 dots. Copy the dot paper and show your circle.

▶ **ESTIMATION**

**10.** A circular pool has a diameter of 6 m. About what distance would you go if you walked all the way around it?

Choose the best estimate.

    **A.** 6 m        **B.** 12 m

    **C.** 18 m      **D.** 24 m

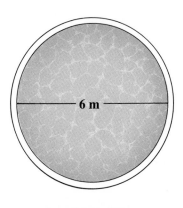

6 m

*More Practice, page 518, set E*

# Circumference

The **circumference** of a circle is the distance around the circle.

**EXPLORE  Discover a Relationship**
Work in groups.

- Use a string and a ruler to find the circumference ($C$) and the diameter ($d$) of a can to the nearest millimeter. Record your measurements in a table like the one at the right.

- Divide the circumference by the diameter. Use a calculator to find the quotient to the nearest tenth. Record the quotient in the table.

- Repeat this activity with at least four other objects.

| Object | $C$ | $d$ | $\frac{C}{d}$ |
|--------|-----|-----|---------------|
|        |     |     |               |
|        |     |     |               |
|        |     |     |               |

## TALK ABOUT IT

1. Is there a number around which your quotients appear to cluster?

2. Do you think this ratio $\left(\frac{C}{d}\right)$ will be the same regardless of the circular object you measure?

The ratio $\frac{C}{d}$ is the same for all circles. We call this ratio *pi* (symbol $\pi$). We know:

$$\pi = \frac{C}{d} = 3.1415926 \text{ (to seven decimal places)}$$

We can also write $C = \pi \times d$ (or $C = \pi d$). Since the diameter is twice the radius ($d = 2r$), we can also write $C = 2\pi r$. As approximations for $\pi$, we often use $3.14$ or $3\frac{1}{7} = \frac{22}{7}$.

## TRY IT OUT

Find the circumference. Use 3.14 for $\pi$.

1. $d = 12$ cm    2. $r = 8$ mm    3. $r = 8.5$ cm    4. $d = 12.1$ m

**370**

Find the circumference.

1.

Marker: $d = 1.8$ cm

2.

Quarter: $r = 12$ mm

3.

Glass: $d = 6.5$ cm

**Estimate** the circumference of each.

4.

Dime: $d = 17$ mm

5.

Cup: $r = 7.2$ cm

6.

Saucer: $d = 3.9$ cm

**APPLY**

### MATH REASONING

Use a calculator to find the missing measurement to the nearest tenth.

7. $C = 85$ cm, $d = $ ▥

8. $C = 63$ cm, $r = $ ▥

9. $C = 6.28$ cm, $d = $ ▥

### PROBLEM SOLVING

10. A playing field has the shape shown at the right. The ends of the field are half circles. Find the perimeter of the entire playing field.

25 m

50 m

▶ **USING CRITICAL THINKING    Make a Conjecture**

11. Suppose the diameter of a circular memorial garden is doubled. Make a conjecture (general statement) about how this would change the circumference of the garden. Make up several examples to test your conjecture.

12. Suppose the radius of a circular garden is doubled. How would this change the circumference of the garden? Make a conjecture and test it.

# Coordinate Geometry

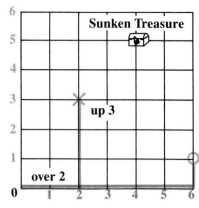

A mathematician named Descartes (1596–1650) invented a way to use pairs of numbers to show points on a grid. This idea has been used in mathematics and science ever since.

**EXPLORE** **Learn from a Game**

- Try a game with a partner.

  Make a copy of the Sunken Treasure grid. Roll number cubes and use the pair of numbers to mark a point on the grid as shown with an **X.** Then your partner rolls the number cubes and marks the point with an **O.**

- The first person to land on the sunken treasure wins the game. Repeat the game several times.

To find where to mark the point, start at 0 and go **over** 2 and **up** 3.

**Your Roll**

**Your Partner's Roll**

**TALK ABOUT IT**

1. Does the number pair (3, 5) have the same location on the grid as (5, 3)? Explain.

2. What if you found a location for a number pair by going up first and then over? Would the location of the pair (2, 3) change? Explain.

Pairs of numbers like (3, 5) are called **coordinates** or **ordered pairs.** When you mark a point for the coordinates, you are **graphing the point.**

**TRY IT OUT**

1. Mark 4 points on a grid that form a trapezoid when the points are connected. Give the coordinates of the points.

2. Give a partner the coordinates for 3 points that form an isosceles triangle and ask him or her to graph the points and connect them.

Start with point *A* and give the coordinates of the vertices of each polygon in order. Name each polygon.

**1.**

**2.**

**3.**

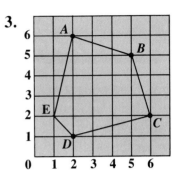

## MATH REASONING

Graph these points. Connect them in order and name the polygon.

**4.** (1, 3), (3, 8), (5, 2), (1, 3)

**5.** (1, 6), (5, 10), (9, 6), (7, 1), (3, 1), (1, 6)

**6.** (3, 4), (3, 7), (6, 9), (9, 7), (9, 4), (6, 2), (3, 4)

**7.** (3, 9), (6, 9), (8, 7), (8, 4), (6, 2), (3, 2), (1, 4), (1, 7), (3, 9)

Graph these sets of points. Connect the points and show the lines of symmetry on the figures.

**8.** (7, 5), (5, 9), (1, 7), (3, 3), (7, 5)

**9.** (1, 1), (1, 3), (6, 3), (6, 1), (1, 1)

## PROBLEM SOLVING

**10.** How many different squares can you find on a 5-by-5 geoboard? You may count congruent squares as different if their positions on the board are different.

## ▶ ALGEBRA

**11.** Use numbers less than 10 and show 5 more cards this machine would produce. Graph the coordinates on each card. What do you discover?

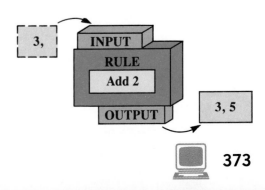

*More Practice, page 519, set A*

# Applied Problem Solving
## Group Decision Making

UNDERSTAND
ANALYZE DATA
PLAN
ESTIMATE
SOLVE
EXAMINE

**Group Skill:**
Disagree in an Agreeable Way

You have bought a new chair and have decided to rearrange your living room. Work with your group to copy on graph paper the outline of the room and each piece of furniture. Cut out the pieces of furniture.

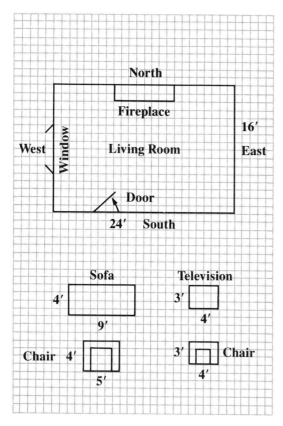

**Facts to Consider**

- You want to arrange the furniture so that someone sitting on the sofa or a chair can see the television set.
- You do not want any furniture directly in front of the fireplace.
- As you try different arrangements, you may want to record them so that you can remember which ones you have tried.
- There is a window in the west wall that you like to gaze through as you are sitting on the sofa or chair.

**374**

## Some Questions to Answer

1. Is there enough room on the west wall to put the two chairs and the television?

2. Will the sofa fit against the south wall without getting hit by the opening door?

3. Can the television and the sofa be on the same side of the room?

4. How many different arrangements can you make?

## What Is Your Decision?

Use graph paper to make a drawing of the arrangement that your group decided to use. Tell why you chose that arrangement.

# WRAP UP

## Word Scavenger Hunt

Each word described below can be found in this chapter. Give the word.

**1.** A 13-letter word that means four sided.

**2.** 10 letters that name an instrument used to measure angles.

**3.** A 9-letter word that describes a triangle with at least two equal sides.

## Sometimes, Always, Never

Complete each statement by writing **sometimes**, **always**, or **never**. Explain your choices.

**4.** Solid figures __?__ have straight edges.

**5.** A rectangle __?__ is a special parallelogram.

**6.** An isosceles triangle __?__ has three acute angles.

## Project

Benny sometimes sees models of geometric ideas that remind him of situations he observes in everyday life. For example, a circle has points that continue in a repeating sequence again and again. The circle reminds him of the phases of the moon—new moon, quarter moon, half moon, three quarters moon, full moon—that occur regularly month after month. What other examples from everyday life can you think of that occur regularly over a period of time?

Parallel lines remind Amelia of events that happen at the same time but that are not really related. For example, she remembers an article she read about county fairs that were being held in Texas and Oklahoma during the same two weeks in August. What examples from your own experience suggest the idea of events that take place at the same time but are not related in other ways?

# POWER PRACTICE/TEST

## Part 1  Understanding

Name a solid figure that has exactly these flat surfaces.

**1.** 2 triangular surfaces     **2.** 1 circular surface     **3.** 2 circular surfaces

Draw an example of each quadrilateral.

**4.** parallelogram          **5.** trapezoid          **6.** rhombus

**7.** A triangle has angles that measure 45° and 37°. What is the measure of the third angle?

**8.** Draw a triangle. Use slide and flip to produce a congruent triangle.

**9.** Name the polygons used to make this tessellation.

**10.** Draw and label a scalene, an isosceles, and an equilateral triangle.

**11.** Mark 5 points on a grid that form a pentagon. Give the coordinates of the points.

## Part 2  Skills

**12.** Draw a square. Then draw all of its lines of symmetry.

**13.** Use a compass and ruler to draw a circle with a diameter of 16 cm.

**14.** Find the circumference of a circle with radius 6.3 cm. Use 3.14 for $\pi$.

**15.** What is the measure of angle $A$?

A

## Part 3  Applications

**16.** Mrs. Herrera wants to fence in her garden. How much fencing does she need in addition to a 4-ft gate?

**17.** **Challenge** Which requires more fencing to go around it, a square garden plot with a side of 4 units or a circular garden plot with a radius of 2 units?

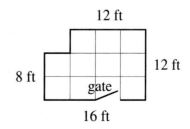

12 ft

12 ft

8 ft

gate

16 ft

# ENRICHMENT
## Top, Bottom, Front, and Side Views

Most space figures look different when viewed from different places.

Make a model of a triangular prism. Draw pictures to show what it would look like if you looked at it from the top, from the bottom, and from the front.

Make or use models of the following shapes. For each shape, draw the top view, bottom view, front view, and side view.

**1.** triangular pyramid

**2.** cube

**3.** hexagonal prism

**4.** cylinder

**5.** rectangular prism

**6.** square pyramid

**7.** Which figure has four and only four identical views?

**8.** How are the top view of the triangular pyramid and the top view of the square pyramid alike?

# CUMULATIVE REVIEW

Multiply.

**1.** $\frac{2}{3} \times 30$

    A. 20    B. 2    C. 15    D. 4

**2.** $\frac{5}{8} \times \frac{1}{4}$

    A. $\frac{1}{12}$    B. $\frac{3}{4}$    C. $\frac{5}{32}$    D. $\frac{2}{5}$

**3.** $15 \times \frac{3}{4}$

    A. $4\frac{1}{2}$    B. $11\frac{1}{4}$    C. $7\frac{1}{2}$    D. 20

**4.** $2\frac{3}{4} \times 1\frac{2}{3}$

    A. $4\frac{7}{12}$    B. $2\frac{2}{7}$    C. $3\frac{1}{2}$    D. 2

**5.** There are 40 people on the editorial staff of a local newspaper. $\frac{5}{8}$ are reporters and $\frac{1}{5}$ are photographers. How many people are *neither* reporters *nor* photographers?

    A. 33    B. 25    C. 8    D. 7

**6.** Which would you use to estimate this sum?

$$8\frac{1}{4} + 4\frac{7}{15} + 7\frac{9}{10}$$

    A. $9 + 4\frac{1}{2} + 8$    B. $9 + 5 + 8$

    C. $8 + 4\frac{1}{2} + 8$    D. $8 + 4 + 7$

Choose the missing numbers.

**7.** 65 oz = ▊▊ lb ▊▊ oz

    A. 4, 1  B. 5, 5  C. 8, 1  D. 16, 1

**8.** 8 ft 5 in. = ▊▊ in.

    A. 29  B. 293  C. 101  D. 74

**9.** 4 gal = ▊▊ c

    A. 32  B. 16  C. 48  D. 64

**10.** Which is the least common multiple of 3 and 7?

    A. 7  B. 21  C. 14  D. 28

**11.** To estimate $\frac{3}{8} \times 58$ using compatible numbers, find

    A. $\frac{1}{10}$ of 60, then multiply by 3

    B. $\frac{1}{7}$ of 56, then multiply by 3

    C. $\frac{1}{8}$ of 48, then multiply by 3

    D. $\frac{1}{8}$ of 56, then multiply by 3

**12.** What common denominator would you use to find the difference between $3\frac{1}{3}$ and $1\frac{3}{4}$?

    A. sixths    B. twelfths

    C. eighths    D. tenths

**13.** Rafe is 5 more than 3 times Wesley's age. If Rafe is 17, how old is Wesley?

    A. 4    B. 2

    C. 32    D. 7

# 14

## MATH AND SCIENCE

### DATA BANK

Use the Science Data Bank on page 473 to answer the questions.

## RATIO AND PERCENT

**THEME: WEATHER**

1 What was the average number of degrees Fahrenheit that the temperature fell each hour between noon and midnight in Fairfield, Montana, on December 24, 1924?

**2** How many degrees did the temperature rise in Spearfish, South Dakota, between 7:30 am and 7:32 am? About how many degrees per minute was this?

**3** At an altitude of 15,000 feet above sea level, about how many degrees colder would the air be than the air at sea level?

**4** **Using Critical Thinking** Study the graph of temperatures on the day of a storm. At what time do you think the storm began? About how long do you think the storm lasted?

Weather forecasters base predictions on data from land-based stations, ships at sea, and weather satellites.

# Ratio

## EXPLORE Look for a Pattern

Work in groups. Use dot paper to draw ladders with different numbers of steps and 2 pegs for each step. Copy and complete the table. Then graph the ordered pairs (steps, pegs) on a coordinate grid.

**1 step, 2 pegs**    **2 steps, 4 pegs**

| Steps | 1 | 2 | 3 | 4 | 5 | 6 | 7 | 8 |
|-------|---|---|---|---|---|---|---|---|
| Pegs  | 2 | 4 |   |   |   |   |   |   |

## TALK ABOUT IT

1. What patterns do you see in the table?
2. If you connect the points for the ordered pairs, what would the new graph look like?
3. If there were 50 steps, how many pegs would there be? How do you know?

Two numbers can be compared by a **ratio.** A ratio can be written in three ways. The ratio of the number of steps to the number of pegs can be written:

| In words | Colon notation | Fraction notation |
|----------|----------------|-------------------|
| 1 to 2   | 1:2            | $\frac{1}{2}$     |

## TRY IT OUT

Use the double ladder at the right to find each ratio. Write each ratio in three ways.

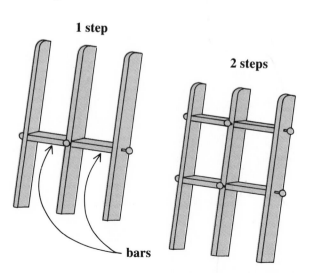

**1 step**    **2 steps**

bars

1. number of steps to the number of pegs

2. number of steps to the number of bars

3. number of bars to the number of pegs

4. number of pegs to the number of bars

**382**

Write the ratio suggested by each picture in three ways.

1.

packs to cans

2.

tires to bicycles

3.

balls to cans

4.

oranges to glasses

5. Bananas: 89 cents for 3 pounds.

cents to pounds

6. 3 apples for 60 cents

cents to apples

### MATH REASONING

Write three different ratios for each picture or set of data.

7.

8.

9.
| Smith | 10 pts |
|---|---|
| Denman | 12 pts |
| Clark | 6 pts |
| Ball | 8 pt |
| Total | 36 pts |

### PROBLEM SOLVING

10. Out of 29 students 11 listed soccer as their favorite sport. What ratio will compare the number of students who did not pick soccer to the total number of students?

11. How many different ratios can be formed using the numbers 8, 9, and 10? Each ratio must use 2 different numbers. Write the ratios.

### ▶ ESTIMATION

12. What ratio could be used to compare the size of rectangle A to rectangle B?

# Ratio Tables

The same ratio may be shown by different fractions.

**EXPLORE  Study the Situation**

An LP record makes 5 complete turns every 9 seconds.

**TALK ABOUT IT**

1. What ratio compares the number of turns to the number of seconds?
2. How long would it take to make 10 complete turns? What is this ratio of turns to seconds?
3. Give one other ratio that compares turns to seconds for LP records.

Since 5 turns take 9 seconds, 10 turns would take 18 seconds, 15 turns would take 27 seconds, and so on. A **ratio table** can be used to record the ratios. Here is an example using the data about LP records.

|  | $5 \times 1$ | $5 \times 2$ | $5 \times 3$ | $5 \times 4$ | $5 \times 5$ | $5 \times 6$ |
|---|---|---|---|---|---|---|
| Number of turns | 5 | 10 | 15 | 20 | 25 | 30 |
| Number of seconds | 9 | 18 | 27 | 36 | 45 | 54 |
|  | $9 \times 1$ | $9 \times 2$ | $9 \times 3$ | $9 \times 4$ | $9 \times 5$ | $9 \times 6$ |

The ratios $\frac{5}{9}$, $\frac{10}{18}$, $\frac{15}{27}$, $\frac{20}{36}$, $\frac{25}{45}$, and $\frac{30}{54}$ are **equal ratios.** They are named by equivalent fractions.

**TRY IT OUT**

Copy and complete the ratio table to solve this problem.

A record makes 3 turns every 4 seconds. How many seconds will it take to make 15 turns?

|  | $3 \times 1$ | $3 \times 2$ | $3 \times 3$ | $3 \times 4$ | $3 \times 5$ |
|---|---|---|---|---|---|
| Turns | 3 | 6 | 9 | 12 | 15 |
| Seconds | 4 |  |  |  |  |
|  | $4 \times 1$ | $4 \times 2$ | $4 \times 3$ | $4 \times 4$ | $4 \times 5$ |

384

Copy and complete each ratio table.

**1.**

| 1 | 2 | 3 | 4 | 5 | 6 |
|---|---|---|---|---|---|
| 8 | 16 |  |  |  |  |

**2.**

| 2 | 4 | 6 | 8 | 10 | 12 |
|---|---|---|---|---|---|
| 7 | 14 |  |  |  |  |

**3.**

| 8 | 16 | 24 | 32 | 40 | 48 |
|---|---|---|---|---|---|
| 3 | 6 |  |  |  |  |

**4.**

| 1 | 2 | 3 | 4 | 5 | 6 |
|---|---|---|---|---|---|
| 25 |  |  |  |  |  |

Write = or ≠ (not equal) for each pair of ratios. Use a ratio
table if necessary.

**5.** $\frac{2}{3}$ ▥ $\frac{6}{10}$    **6.** $\frac{4}{12}$ ▥ $\frac{1}{4}$    **7.** $\frac{2}{5}$ ▥ $\frac{14}{35}$    **8.** $\frac{1}{10}$ ▥ $\frac{10}{100}$

**9.** $\frac{5}{6}$ ▥ $\frac{25}{36}$    **10.** $\frac{3}{10}$ ▥ $\frac{2}{5}$    **11.** $\frac{7}{8}$ ▥ $\frac{24}{32}$    **12.** $\frac{400}{800}$ ▥ $\frac{1}{2}$

**MATH REASONING**

**13.** Make a ratio table with the data given
in the bar graph. What two items are
being compared?

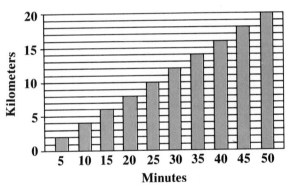

**PROBLEM SOLVING**

**14.** A cup of milk provides 2 mg
(milligrams) of vitamin C. Make a
ratio table that shows the vitamin C in
1, 2, 3, 4, and 5 cups of milk.

**15.** Samantha earned $19 by working 3
hours. About how many hours must
she work to earn $100?

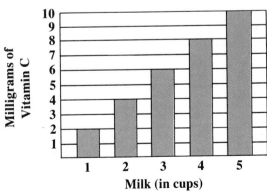

▶ **ALGEBRA**

**16.** Which expression can be used to find
equal ratios when any nonzero
number replaces the number $n$?

**A.** $\frac{2 + n}{3 + n}$    **B.** $\frac{2 \times n}{3 \times n}$

# Proportions

**EXPLORE  Study the Information**

A thunderstorm was raging near Gary's house. Gary's sister told him that for every 1 mile between him and the lightning, there would be a 5-s gap between lightning and thunder. Gary counted 20 s between the time he saw lightning and the time he heard thunder.

**TALK ABOUT IT**

1. What ratio compares the distance from the lightning strike to the seconds counted?
2. How many seconds did Gary count?

If you know the ratio of distance in miles to seconds passed, you can find how far away lightning is. You can use a ratio table, or you can write and solve a proportion. An equation showing that two ratios are equal is called a **proportion.** Here is how to solve a proportion.

Let $n$ equal the miles between Gary and the thunder. Write an equation of equal ratios.

$$\frac{1}{5} = \frac{n}{20}$$

Since $5 \times 4 = 20$,
$1 \times 4 = n$.
So, $n = 4$.
The lightning is
4 mi away.

## Other Examples

**A** $\frac{3}{5} = \frac{n}{40}$

$5 \times 8 = 40$
$3 \times 8 = 24$
$n = 24$

**B** $\frac{4}{9} = \frac{n}{45}$

$9 \times 5 = 45$
$4 \times 5 = 20$
$n = 20$

**TRY IT OUT**

Solve.

**1.** $\frac{5}{6} = \frac{n}{24}$

**2.** $\frac{1}{4} = \frac{n}{20}$

**3.** $\frac{9}{10} = \frac{n}{50}$

**4.** $\frac{2}{3} = \frac{n}{18}$

**5.** $\frac{4}{3} = \frac{n}{9}$

**6.** $\frac{3}{4} = \frac{n}{20}$

**7.** $\frac{4}{7} = \frac{n}{28}$

**8.** $\frac{3}{8} = \frac{n}{48}$

386

Solve.

**1.** $\frac{9}{10} = \frac{n}{50}$  **2.** $\frac{5}{2} = \frac{n}{10}$  **3.** $\frac{1}{4} = \frac{n}{28}$  **4.** $\frac{4}{5} = \frac{n}{25}$  **5.** $\frac{7}{3} = \frac{n}{18}$

**6.** $\frac{7}{9} = \frac{n}{72}$  **7.** $\frac{1}{2} = \frac{n}{60}$  **8.** $\frac{2}{5} = \frac{n}{30}$  **9.** $\frac{5}{12} = \frac{n}{48}$  **10.** $\frac{3}{2} = \frac{n}{100}$

**11.** $\frac{6}{9} = \frac{n}{45}$  **12.** $\frac{7}{6} = \frac{n}{42}$  **13.** $\frac{1}{3} = \frac{n}{45}$  **14.** $\frac{10}{9} = \frac{n}{27}$  **15.** $\frac{9}{10} = \frac{n}{1000}$

APPLY

**MATH REASONING**

**16.** To find the ratio of the number of hits to the total times at bat, Kelly solved $\frac{1}{3} + \frac{2}{3}$. Did Kelly find the correct ratio? Explain. Draw pictures if you wish.

| Kelly's Batting Record | | |
|---|---|---|
| | Game 1 | Game 2 |
| hits | 1 | 2 |
| times at bat | 3 | 3 |

**PROBLEM SOLVING**

**17.** In Becky's town, it rains 3 out of every 10 days during the spring. About how many rainy days should Becky expect out of 60 spring days?

**18.** Stormydale has thunderstorms 22 out of every 30 days. About how many days with thunderstorms could Stormydale expect to have out of 90 summer days?

**19. Science Data Bank** What city has rain or snow about 1 out of every 10 days of the year? See page 473.

▶ **USING CRITICAL THINKING** Make a Generalization

**20.** Find the products for the red numbers and the black numbers in each proportion. These products are called the **cross products.** Complete the statement below.

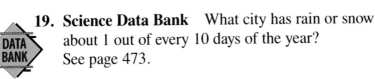

$$\frac{2}{3} = \frac{6}{9} \qquad \frac{4}{5} = \frac{12}{15} \qquad \frac{15}{24} = \frac{5}{8} \qquad \frac{3}{10} = \frac{30}{100}$$

"When two ratios are equal, their cross products are ___?___."

# Problem Solving
## Using Data from a Scale Drawing

UNDERSTAND
ANALYZE DATA
PLAN
ESTIMATE
SOLVE
EXAMINE

### LEARN ABOUT IT

Maps, blueprints, and floor plans are examples of scale drawings. In this map, 1 cm on the map represents an actual distance of 10 km.

Jeremiah and his family went to Yellowstone National Park. They drove from Mammoth Hot Springs to Norris. How far did they drive?

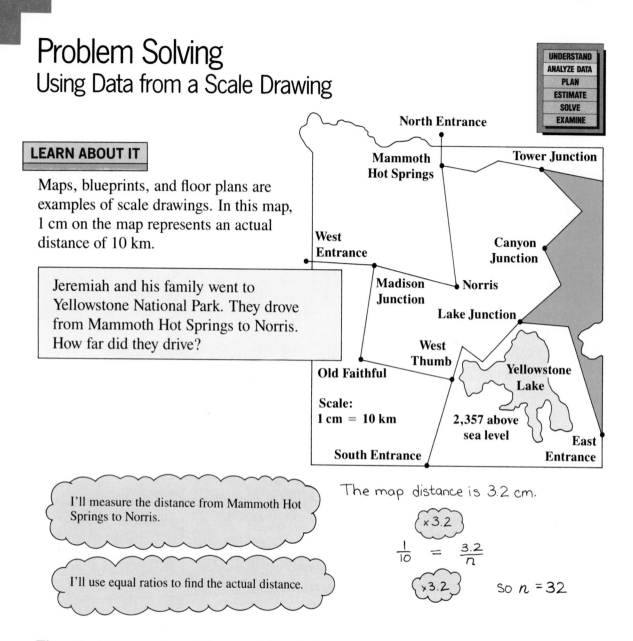

North Entrance

Mammoth Hot Springs

Tower Junction

West Entrance

Canyon Junction

Madison Junction

Norris

Lake Junction

West Thumb

Old Faithful

Yellowstone Lake

Scale:
1 cm = 10 km

2,357 above sea level

East Entrance

South Entrance

I'll measure the distance from Mammoth Hot Springs to Norris.

I'll use equal ratios to find the actual distance.

The map distance is 3.2 cm.

$\times 3.2$

$$\frac{1}{10} = \frac{3.2}{n}$$

$\times 3.2$

So $n = 32$

The actual distance from Mammoth Hot Springs to Norris is 32 km.

### TRY IT OUT

1. Bart's family drove from the West Entrance to Madison Junction. How many kilometers did they drive?

2. Roman hiked along the road from Norris to Old Faithful Geyser. How long was the hike?

3. It is 20 km from Canyon Junction to Norris. How many centimeters would this road be on the map?

4. Nelly biked from Lake Junction to Tower Junction. How far did she bike?

388

Solve. Use any of the strategies.

1. How far would you drive if you made a trip from Old Faithful to West Thumb and back?

2. It took Marge $5\frac{1}{2}$ h to walk from Canyon Junction to Lake Junction. It took Grecia $4\frac{3}{4}$ h to walk the same distance. How much longer did Marge take?

3. Abe, Babs, Carol, and Don each like a different national park. One likes Rocky Mountain, another Yellowstone, another Acadia, and another Grand Canyon. Abe's favorite is not Yellowstone or Rocky Mountain. Babs likes Acadia. Don's favorite does not start with the letter Y. Which national park does each like best?

4. How much farther is it from Lake Junction to West Thumb than from Lake Junction to Canyon Junction?

5. Julie biked from Mammoth Hot Springs to Tower Junction. How far did she bike?

6. From Madison Junction to Canyon Junction is about 40 km. How many centimeters should this be on the map?

7. Yellowstone National Park, the oldest national park, became a park in 1872. How old was the park in 1990?

8. When Ted came in the North Entrance and Tom came in the East Entrance, they were 138 km apart. They are both traveling toward Canyon Junction. Ted has gone 34.2 km and Tom has gone 27.9 km. How far apart are they now?

9. Jake's family drove from West Thumb to the East Entrance. Their average speed was 58 kilometers per hour. How far did they drive?

10. To reach the park, Julio drove 8 times as far as the distance between the West Entrance and Madison Junction. How far did Julio drive?

11. **Write Your Own Problem** Write a problem that can be solved using equal ratios. Use data from the map on page 388.

# Understanding Percent

**EXPLORE  Make a Model**

Use your finger to trace a path through the maze from "Start" to "End." Is there more than one path?

Design a maze of your own. Shade squares on a 10 by 10 grid of paper to form a path from "Start" to "End." Trade mazes with classmates for some "a-maze-ment."

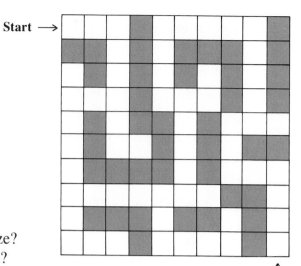

Start →

↑
End

**TALK ABOUT IT**

1. How many total squares are in your maze?
2. How many of the squares did you shade?
3. What ratio compares the shaded squares to all squares?
4. What ratio compares the unshaded squares to all squares?

To make the maze shown above, 41 out of 100 squares in the grid were shaded.

A ratio that compares a number to 100 can be expressed as a **percent.**
41 percent means 41 out of 100.
The word "percent" means "per hundred."

The symbol **%** is used with numbers as a symbol for percent. $41\% = \frac{41}{100}$

---

## Other Examples

**A** 20% means 20 out of 100. $20\% = \frac{20}{100}$   **B** 1% means 1 out of 100. $1\% = \frac{1}{100}$

**TRY IT OUT**

Write as percents.

**1.** 3 out of 100     **2.** $\frac{19}{100}$          **3.** 66 to 100          **4.** $\frac{100}{100}$

Write each percent as a ratio in fraction form.

**5.** 9%          **6.** 33%          **7.** 75%          **8.** 43%

Write a ratio as a fraction and a percent for the part of the region that is shaded.

1.   2.   3. 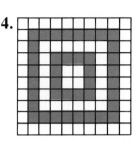  4.

Write each ratio as a percent. Write each percent as a fraction.

**5.** 3 to 100    **6.** $\frac{58}{100}$    **7.** 79 to 100    **8.** $\frac{85}{100}$    **9.** 1 to 100

**10.** 16%    **11.** 29%    **12.** 48%    **13.** 20%    **14.** 15.2%

**MATH REASONING**

Estimate the percent for each point labeled on the number line.

**15.**

**16.**

**PROBLEM SOLVING**

**17.** If you have 35 cents in change, what percent of a dollar do you have in change? What additional percent would you need in order to have a dollar?

**18.** Jenny had $1. She spent 79¢. What percent of the dollar did she spend? What percent of a dollar does she have left?

Tell whether $+$, $-$, or $\times$ should be written in the �.

**19.** $\frac{3}{4} \ \text{◍} \ \frac{3}{4} = 1\frac{1}{2}$    **20.** $\frac{5}{6} \ \text{◍} \ \frac{2}{3} = \frac{1}{6}$    **21.** $\frac{2}{5} \ \text{◍} \ \frac{1}{2} = \frac{2}{10}$    **22.** $\frac{6}{8} \ \text{◍} \ 3\frac{2}{4} = 4\frac{1}{4}$

Write the number of sides for each polygon.

**23.** quadrilateral    **24.** octagon    **25.** triangle    **26.** pentagon

# Percents as Decimals or Fractions

LEARN ABOUT IT

When computing with percents, a fraction or a decimal is used for the percent.

**EXPLORE** **Examine a Picture**

Have you ever tried to solve a cross-number puzzle? Examine this example.

**TALK ABOUT IT**

1. How many squares are in the grid? What part of the total grid is shaded?

2. What decimal names the part of the grid that is shaded?

3. What percent of the grid is shaded?

In the picture above, 22 out of 100 squares are shaded. We can write a percent as a fraction and as a decimal.

$$22\% = \frac{22}{100} = 0.22$$

| 1 | 5 | 7 | 2 |   |   |   | 6 | 3 | 8 | 4 |
|---|---|---|---|---|---|---|---|---|---|---|
| 6 | 3 |   | 5 | 8 | 4 | 7 |   | 9 | 2 |   |
| 2 | 9 | 6 | 4 |   | 9 | 5 | 6 | 1 | 7 |   |
| 3 |   | 9 | 7 |   | 3 | 2 | 9 |   | 3 |   |
|   | 7 | 8 | 9 | 5 | 6 |   | 8 | 5 |   |   |
|   | 1 | 3 |   | 4 | 2 | 9 | 3 | 7 |   |   |
| 7 |   | 5 | 8 | 2 |   | 7 | 1 |   | 4 |   |
| 3 | 5 | 7 | 6 | 9 |   | 2 | 4 | 7 | 8 |   |
| 9 | 8 |   | 1 | 7 | 3 | 6 |   | 6 | 3 |   |
| 5 | 2 | 7 | 4 |   |   | 8 | 1 | 3 | 6 |   |

## Other Examples

**A** $38\% = \frac{38}{100} = 0.38$      **B** $100\% = \frac{100}{100} = 1.00$      **C** $47\% = \frac{47}{100} = 0.47$

TRY IT OUT

Write a fraction and decimal for each percent.

**1.** 25%          **2.** 60%          **3.** 10%          **4.** 75%          **5.** 50%

Write as a percent.

**6.** 0.15          **7.** $\frac{33}{100}$          **8.** 0.07          **9.** $\frac{83}{100}$          **10.** 0.57

**11.** $\frac{105}{100}$          **12.** $\frac{35}{100}$          **13.** 0.19          **14.** $\frac{28}{100}$          **15.** 0.99

Write a fraction, a decimal, and a percent that tells what part of each 10 by 10 grid is shaded.

**1.**   **2.**   **3.**   **4.**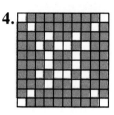

Write each ratio as a percent and as a decimal.

**5.** 3 to 100          **6.** 23 to 100          **7.** 79 to 100          **8.** 94 to 100

**9.** $\frac{37}{100}$          **10.** $\frac{58}{100}$          **11.** $\frac{17}{100}$          **12.** $\frac{85}{100}$

Write each percent as a fraction and as a decimal.

**13.** 2%          **14.** 49%          **15.** 95%          **16.** 9%          **17.** 30%

Write a percent for each decimal.

**18.** 0.45          **19.** 0.07          **20.** 0.61          **21.** 0.01          **22.** 0.5

**MATH REASONING**

**23.** Which is greater, 0.08 or 80%?

**24.** Which number is the same as 100%?
**A.** 0.01 **B.** 100 **C.** 1.0 **D.** 0.100

**PROBLEM SOLVING**

**25.** Jill's batting average was 0.320. What percent of her times at bat did Jill get a hit?

**26.** In his last 75 times at bat, Garo has 20 hits. He expects to be at bat 25 more times this season. How many more hits does he need to have hits 30% of his times at bat?

▶ **MENTAL MATH**

What percent of 1 dollar is each of these U.S. coins?

**27.** penny          **28.** nickel

**29.** dime          **30.** quarter

*More Practice, page 520, set B*

# Percents and Lowest-terms Fractions

**EXPLORE  Examine a Graph**

Mrs. Alba's class made a circle graph to show how many days last year Austin had some rain or snow and how many days it had none.

**TALK ABOUT IT**

1. What fraction of the circle represents days with rain or snow?

2. What fraction of the circle represents days without rain or snow?

3. What percent of days do not have rain or snow?

To write a fraction as a percent, find an equivalent fraction with a denominator of 100.

**Rainy or Snowy Days in Austin**

 Days with rain or snow

 Days without rain or snow

$$\overset{\times 10}{\frac{3}{10} = \frac{30}{100}} \text{ and } \frac{30}{100} = 30\% \qquad \overset{\times 20}{\frac{4}{5} = \frac{80}{100}} \text{ and } \frac{80}{100} = 80\%$$

Percents can also be expressed as lowest-terms fractions.

$$40\% = \overset{\div 20}{\frac{40}{100} = \frac{2}{5}} \qquad 25\% = \frac{25}{100} = \frac{1}{4} \qquad 50\% = \frac{50}{100} = \frac{1}{2}$$

**TRY IT OUT**

Give the percent for each fraction.

1. $\frac{1}{10}$     2. $\frac{3}{5}$     3. $\frac{7}{10}$     4. $\frac{11}{25}$     5. $\frac{19}{20}$

Give the lowest-terms fraction for each percent.

6. 60%     7. 12%     8. 2%     9. 45%     10. 64%

*More Practice, page 520, set C*

# POWER PRACTICE/QUIZ

Gracie's math class has 6 boys for every 5 girls.
Copy and complete the ratio table.

| Boys | 6 | 12 | | | |
|------|---|----|--|--|--|
| Girls | 5 | 10 | | | |

1. Write the ratio of boys to girls in three ways.

2. If there are 12 boys, how many students are in the class?

Are these ratios equal? **3.** $\frac{6}{5}, \frac{15}{18}$   **4.** $\frac{30}{25}, \frac{24}{15}$   **5.** $\frac{10}{12}, \frac{30}{36}$

Solve for $n$.   **6.** $\frac{2}{3} = \frac{n}{9}$   **7.** $\frac{7}{4} = \frac{n}{28}$   **8.** $\frac{8}{9} = \frac{n}{900}$

9. What fraction of the square is shaded?

10. What percent of the square is shaded?

11. Write a fraction and a decimal for the part that is not shaded.

Write a percent for each.

**12.** $\frac{15}{100}$   **13.** 0.03   **14.** $\frac{80}{100}$   **15.** 0.20

**16.** 0.05   **17.** $\frac{1}{2}$   **18.** $\frac{4}{5}$   **19.** $\frac{2}{50}$

Write a lowest-terms fraction for each.

**20.** 25%   **21.** 64%   **22.** 90%   **23.** 6%

## PROBLEM SOLVING

One centimeter on this map represents an actual distance of 20 km.

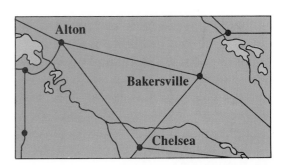

24. Find the map distance and the actual distance between:
    **A.** Alton and Bakersville
    **B.** Bakersville and Chelsea

25. Julio can ride his bike 16 km in 1 h. At that rate, how long will it take him to bike from Alton to Bakersville and back?

| kilometers | 16 | 32 | |
|------------|----|----|--|
| hours | 1 | 2 | |

**395**

# Mental Math and Estimation with Percents

**EXPLORE  Draw a Picture**

You can use mental math to find some percents of numbers by substituting fractions for the percents before computing. Copy the dot pictures below. Draw a ring around dots to show the answers.

| Percents | | Fractions | |
|---|---|---|---|
| $10\% = \frac{1}{10}$ | | $20\% = \frac{1}{5}$ | |
| $25\% = \frac{1}{4}$ | | $33\frac{1}{3}\% = \frac{1}{3}$ | |
| $50\% = \frac{1}{2}$ | | $75\% = \frac{3}{4}$ | |

Find 50% of 30.

Find 10% of 60.

**TALK ABOUT IT**

1. How did you find 50% of 30? 10% of 60?

2. How does thinking about 50% as $\frac{1}{2}$ help you find 50% of 30 mentally?

You can estimate a percent of a number by substituting one of the percents given in the chart at the top of the page. You can also substitute compatible numbers.

**Estimate:**  27% of 48 is about 25% of 48, or $\frac{1}{4}$ of 48.
27% of 48 is about 12.

21% of 19 is about 20% of 20, or $\frac{1}{5}$ of 20.
21% of 19 is about 4.

Solve. Use mental math, and estimation when appropriate.

1. 19% of 25          2. 50% of 18          3. 27% of 80          4. $33\frac{1}{3}\%$ of 15

Solve. Use mental math.

**1.** 10% of 30  **2.** 20% of 45  **3.** 25% of 8  **4.** 50% of 400

**5.** 25% of 40  **6.** $33\frac{1}{3}$% of 24  **7.** 75% of 20  **8.** 10% of 1,000

Estimate.

**9.** 24% of 32  **10.** 50% of 61  **11.** 32% of 21  **12.** 11% of 50

**13.** 9% of 80  **14.** 26% of 44  **15.** 10% of 199  **16.** $33\frac{1}{3}$% of 31

**APPLY**

**MATH REASONING**

Give 2 numbers that could replace each variable.

**17.** 23% of $x$ is about 20.  **18.** 73% of $y$ is between 40 and 50.

**PROBLEM SOLVING**

**19.** In Los Angeles, 10% of the days in a year have some rain. Is this number of days more than or less than the number of days in a 30-day month?

**20. Science Data Bank**  What fraction of the days in a year have rain or snow in Juneau, Alaska? About what percent is this? See page 473.

**MIXED REVIEW**

Write **oz, lb,** or **T** for the unit you would use to weigh each item.

**21.** a feather  **22.** a large ship  **23.** a truck  **24.** a jar of cinnamon

**25.** a sack of potatoes  **26.** yourself  **27.** a TV set  **28.** a tulip

Complete each sentence.

**29.** The distance across a circle is the ___?___ .
**30.** The distance around a circle is the ___?___ .
**31.** The distance from the center of a circle to a point on the circle is the ___?___ .
**32.** The symbol $\pi$ represents the ratio of the ___?___ to the diameter of a circle.

*More Practice, page 520, set D*

# Finding a Percent of a Number

**EXPLORE** **Analyze a Situation**

The members of the Sky Searchers Club want to buy a small telescope. They decided to buy the telescope shown in this advertisement in a local newspaper.

**TALK ABOUT IT**

1. What is the regular price of the telescope in the advertisement?

2. What is the meaning of the term "20% off"?

3. How can you use mental math to find 20% of $400?

Bring the heavens 200 times closer!

Regularly $395.00

Quality TELESCOPE NOW

**20%** OFF

You can multiply to find a percent of a number. Write percents as fractions or as decimals to multiply. Here is how to find 20% of $395.

20% of $395 is the same as 0.20 × $395.

$$\begin{array}{r} \$395 \\ \times\ 0.20 \\ \hline \$79.00 \end{array}$$

> You can use the percent key on a calculator.
> 20 [%] [×] 395 [=]

## Other Examples

**A** 25% of $128
$\frac{1}{4} \times 128 = 32$
25% of $128 is $32.

**B** 30% of $60
$0.30 \times 60 = 18.00$
30% of $60 is $18.

**C** 85% of $120
$0.85 \times 120 = 102.00$
85% of $120 is $102.

Find the percent of each number or amount.

1. 16% of 800

2. 80% of $64.95

3. 23% of 2,000

4. 75% of 400

5. 15% of 200

6. 60% of 150

7. 45% of 160

8. 30% of 600

Find the percent of each amount. Round answers to the nearest cent if necessary.

**1.** 15% of $90.00    **2.** 25% of $400.00    **3.** 75% of $160.00    **4.** 8% of $2,300

**5.** 3% of $72.00    **6.** 19% of $85.00    **7.** 11% of $72.85    **8.** 66% of $66.66

Find the amount saved.

**9.**

$210—30% off

**10.**

$49.95—40% off

**11.**

$75.00—33% off

**12.**

$9.95—5% off

**13.**

$72.00—18% off

**14.**

$28.00—15% off

APPLY

**MATH REASONING**

**15.** A video camera that usually costs $800 is on sale for 20% off. What is the sale price of the camera? (Hint: The new price will be what percent of the original price?)

**PROBLEM SOLVING**

**16.** A high-power flashlight regularly costs $29.95. It is on sale for 30% off. Is the sale price more or less than $25?

**17.** Jean correctly answered 85% of the 60 questions on a science test. On the same test Teresa correctly answered 95% of the items. How many fewer questions did Jean answer correctly?

▶ **USING CRITICAL THINKING**   Support Your Conclusion

**18.** The regular price of a junior telescope was $120.00. At a sale it was marked 25% off. When the telescope was not sold, it was marked, "Take 10% off the reduced price." Is this the same as taking 35% off the original price of $120.00? Explain.

*More Practice, page 520, set E*

# Problem Solving
## Finding Related Problems

UNDERSTAND
ANALYZE DATA
PLAN
ESTIMATE
SOLVE
EXAMINE

When you are solving a problem, sometimes it helps to think about a related problem.

Here are two related problems. They can both be solved using the same strategy.

> At Bud's Safety Gear Shop, hockey helmets come in 4 colors: white, black, blue, and yellow. They come in 3 brands: Racer, Brock, and Safe-T. How many different helmets can Ralph choose from?

| white-Racer | black-Racer | blue-Racer | yellow-Racer |
| white-Brock | black-Brock | blue-Brock | yellow-Brock |
| white-Safe-T | black-Safe-T | blue-Safe-T | yellow-Safe-T |

Ralph can choose from 12 different helmets.

> The players on Jan's team have 2-digit numbers on their jerseys. They used the digits 3, 4, and 5. How many different numbers could they make?

33 34 35     43 44 45     53 54 55

They could make 9 different 2-digit numbers.

---

**TRY IT OUT**

Solve. Tell which two problems are related.

1. Ms. Wong bought two hockey helmets—one for Sam and one for John. She paid $63 in all. Sam's helmet cost $11 more than John's. How much did John's cost?

2. Elvira spent 50% of her money for a bike helmet. Then she spent $2.19 on a water bottle. She had $3.55 left. How much money did she have before she bought those items?

3. On Monday 69 students rode bikes to school. 5 more of them wore helmets than rode without helmets. How many wore helmets?

Choose a strategy from the strategies list or use other strategies to solve these problems.

Use the circle graph to solve problems 1 and 2.

| Some Strategies | |
|---|---|
| Act Out | Make a Table |
| Use Objects | Solve a Simpler Problem |
| Choose an Operation | Make an Organized List |
| Draw a Picture | Work Backward |
| Guess and Check | Look for a Pattern |
| Use Logical Reasoning | |

**Causes of Bicycle Injuries**
**(200 Injuries)**

Running into Fixed Objects 23%

Falling 33%

Colliding with Moving Object 44%

**1.** How many of the 200 injuries in the circle graph were from falls?

**2.** How many of the injuries were from running into a fixed object?

**3.** Jan bought her helmet at school. How much did she pay for it?

$32.95 regular price
**20% off** if you buy it at your school this week

**4.** Gina spent 25% of the $16 she had saved in order to buy a bicycle light. How much did the light cost?

**5.** Almost 9 out of 10 adults who do serious bicycle racing wear helmets. Out of 90 serious adult bikers, how many would probably wear helmets?

**6.** In which two age groups do about 56% of the bike injuries occur?

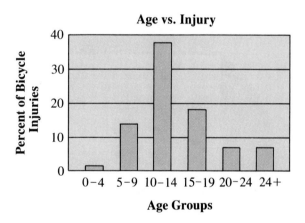

Age vs. Injury

**7.** 126 students from all the elementary schools met to discuss bicycle safety. They split into committees of 14 students. How many committees were there?

**8.** On Friday 75 students rode their bikes to school. 40% wore helmets. Only 14 bikes had current licenses. How many students wore helmets?

# Data Collection and Analysis
## Group Decision Making

UNDERSTAND
ANALYZE DATA
PLAN
ESTIMATE
SOLVE
EXAMINE

### Doing an Investigation
**Group Skill:**
Explain and Summarize

A minute can seem like a very short time when you are playing a video game, or it can seem like a long time if you are waiting for a bus. Do you think you can estimate a minute? Conduct an investigation to see how well you can estimate a minute to find out whether you can improve your estimation skills with practice.

### Collecting Data

1. Each person in your group will take turns estimating a minute. You will need a watch which gives time in seconds and a person to watch the time. Your group's timer says when to start, and the estimator says when he or she thinks a minute has gone by. The actual number of seconds is recorded in a table. Each person in your group gets three trials, one right after the other.

2. Compute the average number of seconds estimated by your group for trial 1, for trial 2, and for trial 3. Round each average to the nearest whole second.

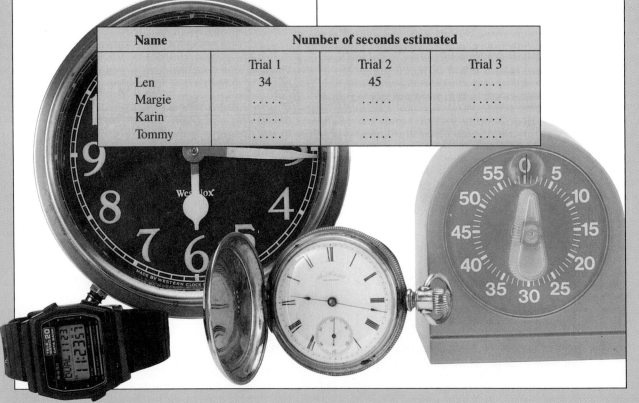

| Name | Number of seconds estimated | | |
|---|---|---|---|
| | Trial 1 | Trial 2 | Trial 3 |
| Len | 34 | 45 | . . . . . |
| Margie | . . . . . | . . . . . | . . . . . |
| Karin | . . . . . | . . . . . | . . . . . |
| Tommy | . . . . . | . . . . . | . . . . . |

**3.** Make a bar graph to show the average number of seconds estimated by the members of your group for each trial.

Title

Average Number of Seconds Estimated by Our Group

30
20
10
0

Trial 1

**4.** Write a paragraph about your results. Did your group's average improve with practice?

**5.** Tell why you think your results turned out as they did. If you did the investigation again, what would you do differently?

# WRAP UP

## How Do You Do?

In your own words, tell how you do each of the following.

1. Find the missing number in $\frac{5}{6} = \frac{n}{30}$.

2. Write 60% as a fraction in lowest terms.

3. Use mental math to find 75% of 40.

4. Make a ratio table for the ratio 4:7.

5. Estimate 28% of 300.

6. Write $\frac{4}{5}$ as a percent.

## Sometimes, Always, Never

Complete each statement by writing **sometimes**, **always**, or **never**. Explain your choices.

7. Percent is a special ratio that __?__ compares a number to a cent.

8. To change a fraction to a percent, you can __?__ divide the numerator by the denominator, then write the % sign.

9. The first number in a ratio is __?__ smaller than the second.

10. A ratio can __?__ be written as a percent.

## Project

Draw the letters of the alphabet from $A$ to $Z$ in block letters on graph paper. Compare the areas of at least 5 different pairs of letters and express the ratios as fractions. Some pairs you can compare are:

$E$ to $F$    $O$ to $P$    $S$ to $T$

404

# POWER PRACTICE/TEST

## Part 1    Understanding

1. Write the ratio that compares the number of triangles to the number of squares in three ways.

2. Write the ratio 9 out of 100 as a percent.

Write each as a percent.

3. 0.5          4. 0.41          5. $\frac{2}{5}$          6. $\frac{3}{10}$

Write a lowest-terms fraction for each.

7. 12%          8. 4%          9. 80%          10. 75%

What strategy would you use to solve? Write a related problem.

11. Pablo walked south 6 blocks, east 4 blocks, and north 3 blocks. How far north and west does he have to walk to get back where he started?

## Part 2    Skills

Solve.

12. $\frac{5}{6} = \frac{n}{30}$          13. $\frac{3}{4} = \frac{n}{36}$          14. 22% of 450

15. 35% of $65.40          16. $33\frac{1}{3}$% of 96          17. 75% of 80

## Part 3    Applications

18. On the floor plan for Bart's room, 2 cm represents 1 m. How wide is the room if the floor plan width is 14 cm?

19. A recipe for 6 bran muffins calls for 2 teaspoons baking powder. Make a ratio table that shows teaspoons of baking powder needed for 12, 18, 24, and 36 muffins.

20. **Challenge** When a piece of clothing arrives at Rainy Day Discounts, the date and full price are marked on it. After 1 week, the price goes down 25%. After 2 weeks, another $33\frac{1}{3}$% is taken off the last price. After 3 weeks, 50% is taken off the last price. Give examples to show that the final price is $\frac{1}{4}$ of the original price.

# ENRICHMENT
## Percent Patterns Using Mental Math

If you know 10% of a number, you can find or estimate other percents of the number. Ms. Evans wanted to find 15% of $24, so she thought

> 10% is $2.40.
> 5% is $1.20.
> 15% is $3.60.

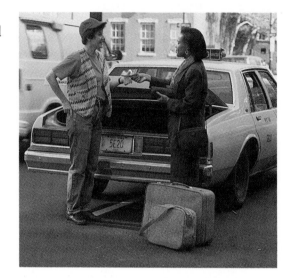

Study each of the problems below. Do you see a pattern?

$$
\begin{array}{r} 60 \\ \times\,0.10 \\ \hline 6 \end{array}
\qquad
\begin{array}{r} 240 \\ \times\,0.10 \\ \hline 24 \end{array}
\qquad
\begin{array}{r} 160 \\ \times\,0.10 \\ \hline 16 \end{array}
\qquad
\begin{array}{r} 3{,}400 \\ \times\,0.10 \\ \hline 340 \end{array}
$$

Use the products above to find each of these percents of a number.

**1.** 5% of 60　　　**2.** 5% of 240　　　**3.** 5% of 160　　　**4.** 5% of 3,400

**5.** 1% of 60　　　**6.** 1% of 240　　　**7.** 1% of 160　　　**8.** 1% of 3,400

Use reasoning and your answers above to find these.

**9.** 15% of 60　　**10.** 11% of 60　　**11.** 15% of 240　　**12.** 11% of 240

**13.** 15% of 160　　**14.** 11% of 160　　**15.** 15% of 3,400　　**16.** 11% of 3,400

Use 10%, 5%, and 1% to find the percent of each number.

**17.** 15% of 80　　**18.** 15% of 800　　**19.** 15% of 200　　**20.** 6% of 200

**21.** 25% of 60　　**22.** 30% of 70　　**23.** 70% of 20　　**24.** 15% of 360

# CUMULATIVE REVIEW

**1.** Which line segment measures $2\frac{1}{4}$ inches to the nearest $\frac{1}{4}$ inch?

   A. _____

   B. _____

   C. _____

   D. _____

**2.** What does this picture show?

   A. $\frac{1}{4} \times \frac{5}{6} = \frac{5}{24}$

   B. $\frac{3}{4} \times \frac{5}{6} = \frac{5}{8}$

   C. $\frac{1}{4} \times \frac{5}{24} = \frac{5}{96}$

   D. $\frac{5}{24} \times \frac{5}{6} = \frac{25}{144}$

**3.** The diameter of a circle is

   A. 3 times the radius

   B. $\frac{1}{2}$ the radius

   C. 3.14 times the radius

   D. 2 times the radius

**4.** Which solid figure has two faces that are circles?

   A. sphere   B. cone

   C. cylinder   D. triangular pyramid

**5.** Find the number of twelfths in 2.

   A. 24   B. 6   C. 36   D. 8

**6.** A triangle has a 52° angle and a right angle. What is the measure of the third angle?

   A. 90°   B. 142°   C. 180°   D. 38°

**7.** Which is the most likely temperature of a hot drink?

   A. 32°F         B. 70°F

   C. 105°F      D. 306°F

**8.** Which describes an isosceles triangle?

   A. All three sides are equal.

   B. No two sides are equal.

   C. Two sides have equal length.

   D. One angle measures 90°.

**9.** What is the first step in measuring an angle with a protractor?

   A. Read the measure of the angle.

   B. Place the point of the arrow on the vertex of the angle.

   C. Place the zero edge along one side of the angle.

   D. Follow one ray to the protractor.

**10.** Multiply $\frac{3}{4} \times 24$.

   A. 72   B. 6   C. 18   D. 32

**11.** How much larger is the area of the barn than the area of the coop?

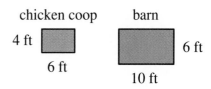

   A. 24 ft$^2$       B. 60 ft$^2$

   C. 20 ft$^2$       D. 36 ft$^2$

# 15

## PROBABILITY

**THEME: AMERICAN INDIAN GAMES**

MATH AND SOCIAL STUDIES

DATA BANK

Use the Social Studies Data Bank on page 483 to answer the questions.

1 Len and Barry are playing Stick Game 1. There are 51 sticks in the pile. Len takes out 23 sticks. Barry gets the rest. Who has more sticks? Who wins the game?

The sport of blanket tossing began as a hunting skill developed by Native Alaskans.

**2** Naomi is playing the Hidden Bean Game. How many ways can she make a wrong guess about where the bean is hidden? How many ways can she make a right guess?

**3** Maria scored a total of 9 points in 3 turns while she was playing Stick Game 2. How could she have scored that total for 3 turns?

**4** **Using Critical Thinking** Think carefully about the rules for Stick Game 1. Why do you think the players always began with an odd number of sticks in the pile?

# Fair and Unfair Games

### EXPLORE Learn from a Game

Play the game Odd-Even Products with a partner. You will need two number cubes with faces numbered 1 through 6. Follow these rules:

- One player is Odd and the other is Even.
- Each player takes a turn tossing the cubes and finding the product of the two numbers tossed.
- If the product is odd, the Odd player scores 1 point. If it is even, the Even player scores 1 point.
- The first player to get 10 points wins the game.
- Play the game at least 3 times.

**5 × 3 = 15. Odd**

### TALK ABOUT IT

1. Who won more games, Odd or Even? Were the scores close?
2. Is the game of Odd-Even Products a fair or unfair game? Explain.
3. Make up a table of the possible products for this game. Explain how it can be used to decide whether this is a fair game.

**4 × 2 = 8. Even**

A game in which each of two players has the same chance of winning is a **fair game.** Otherwise it is an **unfair game.** The Odd-Even Products game is not a fair game. The person choosing the even numbers has a better chance of winning.

Change the rules of the game so that the **sum** instead of the product of the two numbers is used for Odd and Even. Play the game several times. Does this seem like a fair game?

**410**

Play each game with a classmate. Use a spinner divided into red and blue sections as shown. Decide whether each game is fair or unfair.

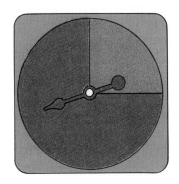

1. **Two-color Spinner Game**  *Rules:* One team is Red, the other Blue. Spin the spinner. The Red team scores 3 points if the pointer stops on red. The Blue team scores 1 point if it stops on blue. 24 points wins!

2. **Five-to-One Game**  *Rules:* The rules are the same as for the two-color spinner game except that the Red team gets 5 points when the spinner stops on red. The Blue team still gets 1 point when the spinner stops on blue.

**MATH REASONING**

3. Make up point values for the sections in the spinner shown above so that the Spinner Game is fair. Make up other values so that it is unfair. How did you decide?

**PROBLEM SOLVING**

4. **Play a Strategy Game**  Place 15 dots in a straight line. Player 1 draws an X through any dot. Player 2 then circles any other dot on the line. The first player to mark a dot so that there are three consecutive marked dots is the winner. Try to find a winning strategy.

▶ **USING CRITICAL THINKING**  Analyzing a Game

5. **2-Chip Match Game**
   *Materials:* 2 chips. One chip is labeled "heads" on both sides. The other chip is labeled "heads" on one side and "tails" on the other.

   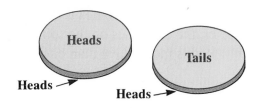

   *Rules:* One team is the Match team. The other is the No-Match team. Toss both chips at once. If both chips come up heads, then the Match team scores one point. Otherwise, the No-Match team scores a point. 10 points wins!

   A. Which team would you want to be on, Match or No-Match? Why?

   B. Tell why the game is fair or unfair.

411

# Equally Likely Outcomes

## LEARN ABOUT IT

American Indians played many tossing games with 2-sided sticks, shells, and bone pieces. When they tossed one of these, it landed on a decorated side or a plain side, so there were 2 possible equally likely results. When you toss a coin you have the same number of results, or **outcomes.**

### EXPLORE  Try an Experiment

Work in groups. Toss a coin 20 times. Keep a record of the outcomes.

| Heads | |
|-------|--|
| Tails | |

## TALK ABOUT IT

1. Did you get about the same number of heads as tails in the 20 tosses? Do you think that heads and tails have the same chance of coming up?
2. Predict how many times you would get heads in 50 tosses of a coin. Try tossing a coin 50 times. How close was your prediction?
3. Suppose you have tossed a fair coin 3 times and it came up tails each time. Do you think it is more likely to come up heads on the next toss than tails?

A head is just as likely to come up as a tail when a fair coin is tossed. The two outcomes are said to be **equally likely.** However, the outcomes on the spinner are not equally likely. Red is more likely than blue or yellow.

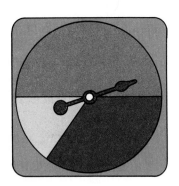

## TRY IT OUT

Give all the outcomes for each experiment. Tell if they are equally likely or not.

1. Toss a number cube.

2. Spin the spinner.

3. Spin the spinner.

Try each activity. Decide if the outcomes are equally likely.

1. Toss a number cube 50 times. Keep a record of the number of times each outcome occurs.

2. Toss a paper cup 50 times. Keep a record of the way it lands.

Up    Down    Side

3. Toss 2 number cubes 50 times. An outcome is the sum of the 2 numbers tossed. Keep a record of the number of times each sum occurs.

4. Spin a spinner like this 50 times. Keep a record of the outcomes.

**MATH REASONING**

5. Make up a game using three numbers cubes where each outcome is equally likely.

DATA BANK

**PROBLEM SOLVING**

6. Local telephone numbers have seven digits, for example, 555-6842. What is the greatest sum possible for the last 4 digits? the smallest sum? Are all sums in between possible?

7. **Social Studies Data Bank**   Give the name of a game played by American Indians that has the same number of outcomes as tossing a coin. See page 483.

▶ **ALGEBRA**

8. Toss a thumb tack many times (at least 25).
   Let **U** = number of times it lands with point **up.**
   Let **D** = number of times it lands point **down.**
   Let **T** = the number of **tosses.**

   Write the ratios $\frac{U}{T}$ and $\frac{D}{T}$.

   Which ratio is greater? Do you think the two outcomes are equally likely?

Up              Down

413

# Probability of Outcomes

**EXPLORE** **Analyze a Situation**
The spinner is divided into four parts of
equal size. The four outcomes, 1, 2, 3,
and 4, are equally likely to happen.
Suppose you spin the spinner 100 times.

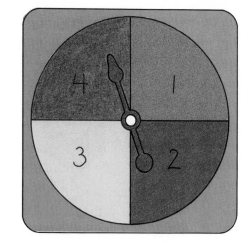

**TALK ABOUT IT**

1. Which describes your chances of spinning a 3?
   **A.** 1 chance in 100      **B.** 1 chance in 10
   **C.** 1 chance in 4        **D.** 1 chance in 2

2. What are your chances of spinning the number 5?

3. What are your chances of spinning a number less than 5?

There is **1 chance in 4** of spinning the number 3 on the
spinner. The **probability** of spinning a 3 is $\frac{1}{4}$.

We write:    $P(3) = \frac{1}{4}$.

We say:      The probability of 3 is $\frac{1}{4}$.

There are **3 chances in 4** of **not** spinning        $P(\text{not } 2) = \frac{3}{4}$.
a 2.

There are **0 chances in 4** of spinning a 5.          $P(5) = \frac{0}{4} = 0$

There are **4 chances in 4** of spinning a            $P(\text{number} > 0) = \frac{4}{4} = 1$.
number greater than 0.

**The probability of any outcome is always a number from
0 through 1.**

Give the probability of each outcome.

1. Toss a coin.
   $P(\text{heads}) = $ ▦

   $P(\text{tails}) = $ ▦

2. Toss a number cube (1−6).
   $P(1) = $ ▦    $P(4) = $ ▦

   $P(2) = $ ▦    $P(5) = $ ▦

   $P(3) = $ ▦    $P(6) = $ ▦

**414**

Give the probability of the outcome.

**1.** Spin the spinner.

$P(4) = $ ▒

**2.** Toss a coin.

$P(\text{Tails}) = $ ▒

**3.** Toss a number cube.

$P(3) = $ ▒

**4.** Spin the spinner.

$P(C) = $ ▒

**5.** Toss a number cube.

$P(9) = $ ▒

**6.** Spin the spinner.

$P(\text{even number}) = $ ▒

APPLY

**MATH REASONING**

Use the spinner at the right to complete Exercises 7−10.

**7.** $P(5) = $ ▒

**8.** $P(2) = $ ▒

**9.** $P(\text{odd number}) = $ ▒

**10.** $P(\text{even number}) = $ ▒

**PROBLEM SOLVING**

**11.** Laurie bought 5 tickets for a door prize. A total of 175 tickets were sold. What is the probability that Laurie will win the door prize?

**12.** You can win a large teddy bear if on one toss of a fair number cube, you get a 1 or a 6. What is the probability of **not** winning the bear?

MIXED REVIEW

Change the measures to pounds and ounces.

**13.** 54 oz  **14.** 49 oz  **15.** 29 oz  **16.** 24 oz  **17.** 63 oz

Solve each proportion.

**18.** $\frac{2}{3} = \frac{x}{9}$  **19.** $\frac{4}{10} = \frac{x}{30}$  **20.** $\frac{3}{6} = \frac{x}{42}$  **21.** $\frac{3}{12} = \frac{x}{48}$

*More Practice, page 521, set A*

# Experimental and Mathematical Probabilities

LEARN ABOUT IT

When American Indians played games of chance such as tossing 2-sided sticks or other objects, they often tossed more than one at a time. If you toss more than one coin at a time, you can do coin-tossing experiments faster.

**EXPLORE  Try an Experiment**

Work in groups. If you toss a penny 100 times, how many heads and how many tails do you think you will get? Try it.

**TALK ABOUT IT**

1. How many heads did your group get in 100 tosses?

2. Write the ratio: **number of heads to number of tosses.** Is this ratio close to $\frac{1}{2}$? Should it be close to $\frac{1}{2}$?

3. Combine your results with those of other groups and find the ratio of heads to tosses. Is this ratio closer to $\frac{1}{2}$?

We can compare the **experimental probability** for the penny tossing with the **mathematical probability.**

**Mathematical Probability**

$$P(\text{heads}) = \frac{50}{100} \quad \begin{array}{l} \leftarrow \text{ expected number of heads} \\ \leftarrow \text{ total tosses} \end{array}$$

$$= \frac{1}{2}$$

**Experimental Probability**

$$P(\text{heads}) = \frac{47}{100} \quad \begin{array}{l} \leftarrow \text{ actual number of heads} \\ \leftarrow \text{ total tosses} \end{array}$$

The experimental probability is close to the mathematical probability, because $\frac{47}{100}$ is close to $\frac{1}{2}$.

TRY IT OUT

1. Find the experimental and mathematical probabilities of tossing an even number with one number cube. Use at least 40 tosses.

2. Find the experimental and mathematical probabilities of getting a match of numbers when you toss two cubes numbered 1-6. Use at least 25 tosses.

Complete each probability activity. Give the experimental and the mathematical probabilities.

**1.** Spin the spinner 60 times.

$P(\text{number} < 4)$

**2.** Toss a number cube 60 times.

$P(6)$

**3.** Spin the spinner 100 times.

$P(\text{even number})$

## MATH REASONING

**4.** Estimate how many times you might have to roll a number cube before all 6 numbers have come up at least once each. Try the experiment several times. What is the least number of rolls you took?

**5.** Estimate how many times you might have to toss a coin before you get 3 heads in a row or 3 tails in a row. Then try the experiment and compare the actual number with your estimate.

## PROBLEM SOLVING

**6. Social Studies Data Bank**   How many outcomes are possible in the American Indians' Stick Game 2? Do you think each of the outcomes is equally likely? See page 483.

## ▶ CALCULATOR

**7.** Jeff and Jenny used a computer program to simulate tossing a coin 15,000 times. Then they used their calculators to find whose result was closer to the mathematical probability. Jeff's simulation gave heads 7,119 times. Jenny's gave heads 7,804 times. Whose simulation gave a result closer to the mathematical probability?

# Using Critical Thinking

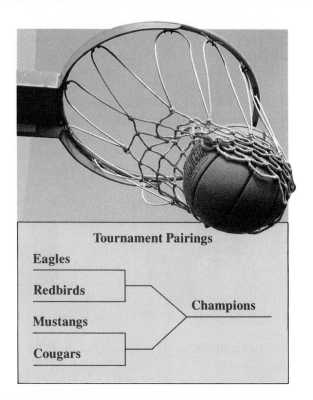

"Well," said the Redbirds' coach, "It looks like a tough tournament." "It really does," agreed the assistant coach. "Do you think we can beat the Eagles in the first round? If we do, what team do you predict we will play for the championship?"

The coach looked at the tournament pairings and the information sheet shown below. Then he whispered his prediction to the assistant coach.

**Tournament Pairings**

Eagles

Redbirds

Mustangs

Cougars

Champions

| Scores for Season Games | | | | Tournament Data |
|---|---|---|---|---|
| Redbirds | 68 | Cougars | 67 | The tournament is being played on the Redbirds' home court. |
| Eagles | 75 | Mustangs | 58 | |
| Redbirds | 94 | Mustangs | 61 | Freddie Flash, the Cougars' best player, will not be able to play. The Eagles are a young team, with no tournament experience. |
| Cougars | 59 | Eagles | 57 | |
| Eagles | 74 | Redbirds | 73 | |
| Cougars | 68 | Mustangs | 60 | |

## TALK ABOUT IT

1. How can the scores help the coach make his prediction?

2. How can the Tournament Data help the coach to make his prediction?

3. Is the probability of winning the tournament $\frac{1}{4}$ for each team? Why or why not?

4. Which team do you predict will win the tournament? Explain.

Choose a sports league you are interested in. Predict which team will win or have the best record. Give reasons for your predictions.

# POWER PRACTICE/QUIZ

Use pictures A, B, and C for review items 1–4.

A

B

C

1. List the possible outcomes for each toss of the number cube or spin of a spinner. Tell whether the outcomes are equally likely.

2. Find these probabilities for the toss of the number cube.

   **A.** $P(3)$        **B.** $P(\text{odd number})$        **C.** $P(\text{number} < 7)$        **D.** $P(7)$

3. For spinners B and C, which outcomes have a probability of $\frac{1}{4}$?

4. After 1,000 spins of spinner C, would you expect
   **A.** more 10s or more 20s?        **B.** more 20s or more 30s?

This spinner was spun 100 times and produced the outcomes shown.

> **r** means the spinner pointed in the red area and **b** means it pointed in the blue.
>
> b b r r b b b r b b b b b b r r b r b b
> b b r b b r b r b b b r r b b r b r r b
> b b r r b b b r b b b r b b r b b b r b
> r b b b r b b r r b r b b b b b r b r b
> b b b r b r r b b b b r b b r b r r b b

5. What is the mathematical probability of $P(\text{red})$? of $P(\text{blue})$?

6. What was the experimental probability of each outcome?

## PROBLEM SOLVING

Suppose you play games in which you and another player take turns spinning the red and blue spinner and score points only when you spin your chosen color. Blue begins. Decide which seem to be fair games.

7. Game 1: Blue scores 1 for each **b**; Red scores 2 for each **r**.

8. Game 2: Blue scores 1 for each **b**; Red scores 1 for each **r** and spins again.

419

# Problem Solving
## Using Data from an Order Form

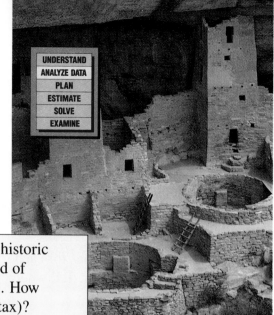

| | |
|---|---|
| UNDERSTAND | |
| ANALYZE DATA | |
| PLAN | |
| ESTIMATE | |
| SOLVE | |
| EXAMINE | |

**LEARN ABOUT IT**

Joan and her family went on a tour of some historic sites. Afterward, they had pictures developed of themselves visiting places of special interest. How much did the 11 × 14 photos cost (without tax)?

| Historic Sites Photographs | | | | | |
|---|---|---|---|---|---|
| **Date** | **Site** | **Frame #** | **Size (in.)** | **Quantity** | **Amount** |
| 5/21/90 | San Jacinto | 27 | 8 × 10 | 2 | $28.00 |
| 5/21/90 | The Alamo | 32 | **11 × 14** | **3** | ? |
| 5/21/90 | Mesa Verde | 42 | 16 × 20 | 1 | ? |

Prices

| | | | |
|---|---|---|---|
| 8 × 10 | $14.00 each | Subtotal | ? |
| **11 × 14** | **$19.50** each | | |
| 16 × 20 | $39.50 each | Tax (6%) | ? |
| 20 × 24 | $59.50 each | | |
| proofsheet | $12.00 each | Total Cost | ? |

> I'll find the data I need on the order form.

> Now I'll multiply to find the answer.

11 x 14 photos cost $19.50 each. They bought 3 photos this size.

$19.50
×    3
$58.50

The cost of the 11 × 14 photos was $58.50.

**TRY IT OUT**

1. How much will the photos cost altogether before tax is added on?

2. How much tax must Joan and her friends pay in all? What is the total cost of the order?

Solve. Use a strategy from the strategies list or other strategies you know to solve these problems.

1. Barbara decided to buy one tour picture for $39.50. Is the area of her photo more or less than the area of two dozen 3 × 5 photos? How much more or less? Use the data on page 420.

| Some Strategies | |
|---|---|
| Act Out | Make a Table |
| Use Objects | Solve a Simpler Problem |
| Choose an Operation | Make an Organized List |
| Draw a Picture | Work Backward |
| Guess and Check | Look for a Pattern |
| Use Logical Reasoning | |

2. Bonita had two $50 bills. How much tax would she pay on an order of tour photos whose total cost is $95?

3. Joan's mother had twenty 8 × 10 photos of the tour lined up side-by-side in a row. What was the perimeter of the photo display?

4. Jon wanted a photo whose width was $\frac{4}{5}$ its length. Which sizes might he have bought?

5. Bob arranged some photos in squares of increasing size. How many photos did he need to make the fifth square?

6. How much would a dozen 11 × 14 photos cost before tax? Use the data on page 420.

7. Is the area of these two photos a little more or a little less than 55 in²?

5 in.

3 in.

7 in.

5 in.

first    second    third    fourth    fifth
?    ?    ?

8. **Developing a Plan** A photo was enlarged so that each side of the new photo was double the length of the original. How many times larger was the area of the new photo than the original?

   A. List 2 or more strategies you think might help you solve this problem.

   B. Solve the problem.

   C. Look back at your solution. What strategies did you use?

# Making Estimates by Sampling

**LEARN ABOUT IT**

**EXPLORE  Analyze the Situation**

Suppose the drawing represents a photograph of a cluster of stars. What is your estimate of the total number of stars in the drawing?

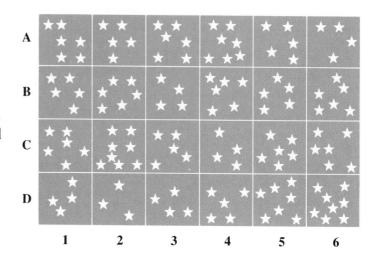

**TALK ABOUT IT**

1. How did you make your estimate?

2. How can the squares help you make your estimate?

3. Section **D1** contains 4 stars. If all sections contained 4 stars, how many stars would be in the photograph?

4. Section **D1** is a **sample** of the stars in the photograph. If you were asked to choose one section as a sample, which section would you choose? Why?

To make estimates of a large number of objects that are not easily counted, we can take **random samples.** For example, to choose one of the squares in the grid as a random sample, we could use a spinner with parts A, B, C, and D and toss a number cube with numbers 1 through 6.

Outcome: B5

The spinner and number cube show an outcome of B5. Section B5 contains 5 stars. There are 24 sections.
Estimate: $5 \times 24 = 120$

**TRY IT OUT**

Estimate the number of stars using these sections.

1. C4          2. D1          3. A3          4. B6          5. D2

Use a spinner and a number cube like the ones shown on page 422 to choose 5 random samples of stars from the picture. Record the section and number of stars in a table.

1. What is the mean (or average) number of stars in your sample?

2. Estimate the total number of stars using the mean from your samples.

3. Count the number of stars in the picture. How close was your estimate?

|  | Section | Number of stars |
|---|---|---|
| Sample 1 |  |  |
| Sample 2 |  |  |

Remember: The **mean** of a list of numbers is the total divided by the number in the list.

## APPLY

### MATH REASONING

4. Estimate what fraction of the pages in this book have a photograph. Then randomly select 20 pages and find the fraction of those that have photographs. How does this compare to your estimate? Randomly select 40 pages and find the fraction. Which number of pages is likely to give an estimate closer to the actual fraction for the entire book? Explain.

### PROBLEM SOLVING

5. An overhead photograph of 1 mi² of forest is divided into 20 equal sections. You count the number of trees in 5 randomly chosen sections. You get these results: 53, 57, 60, 51, 59. What would be your estimate of the total number of trees in the square mile?

▶ COMMUNICATION   Writing to Learn

6. Find some ways to estimate the number of people in the photograph. Write a description of your method and why you think your estimate is a good one.

# Simulations

## LEARN ABOUT IT

Carlos had a 10-item true-false quiz in his French class. He wondered what he might score if he just guessed at all of the items (even though he would not really do it!). What would you predict?

### EXPLORE  Try a Simulation

Toss a coin 10 times, once for each test item. Let heads = true, tails = false. Check your outcomes against the answers shown in the box at the right. How many answers did you get correct?

| True-False Quiz Answers | | | | |
| --- | --- | --- | --- | --- |
| **1.** T | **2.** T | **3.** F | **4.** T | **5.** F |
| **6.** F | **7.** F | **8.** F | **9.** F | **10.** F |

## TALK ABOUT IT

1. Do you think you would get at least half of the items correct by guessing? Why?

2. How likely are you to get all 10 correct just by guessing?

3. How many might you expect to get correct if there were 20 items rather than 10?

To decide the possible result in certain situations, you can make a model or **simulation** of the situation. The coin-tossing activity above was a simulation of guessing the answer to each item.

## TRY IT OUT

1. Try the simulation described above 3 more times. Record the number of correct answers for each. Compare your results with those of your classmates. What is the greatest number of correct answers anyone found? What is the least number of correct answers anyone found?

2. Combine your number of correct answers with other students' results. Find the average number of correct answers for all the students in your class.

424

Guess          Answer

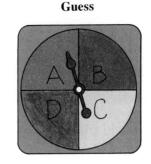

1. Work with a partner and try this simulation. Use a "Guess" spinner and an "Answer" spinner like the ones shown. One partner spins the "Guess" spinner 12 times and the other spins the "Answer" spinner 12 times. Keep a record of the outcomes. Then find out how many times the Guess outcome matches the Answer outcome. How many matches did you get out of 12 tries?

**APPLY**

**MATH REASONING**

2. A multiple-choice quiz has 12 questions. There are four choices of answers: A, B, C, and D. Suppose you just guessed at the answer to all 12 items. Estimate how many answers you would get correct. Use your results from exercise 1 to help you decide.

**PROBLEM SOLVING**

3. Combine the results of your simulation in Practice, Exercise 1, with the results obtained by 5 of your classmates. Find the average number of correct answers.

 MIXED REVIEW

Write each ratio as a percent.

**4.** 4 to 100          **5.** 36 to 100          **6.** 44 to 100          **7.** 12 to 100

**8.** $\frac{85}{100}$          **9.** $\frac{61}{100}$          **10.** $\frac{10}{100}$          **11.** $\frac{73}{100}$

Write each percent as a lowest-terms fraction.

**12.** 45%          **13.** 60%          **14.** 30%

**15.** 75%          **16.** 15%          **17.** 25%

# Applied Problem Solving
## Group Decision Making

UNDERSTAND
ANALYZE DATA
PLAN
ESTIMATE
SOLVE
EXAMINE

### Group Skill:
Check for Understanding

Your class is planning a field trip to the Museum of Natural History. Your group must make a schedule for the day that lists the starting and ending time for each of the day's activities.

### Facts to Consider

- Your class cannot leave school before 8:30 a.m. and must be back by 3:30 p.m.
- The bus trip from your school to the museum takes 30 minutes.
- You must allow time in the schedule for lunch.
- You must allow time for afternoon or morning refreshments, washing up, and getting from one section of the museum to another.
- You and your classmates have already decided that you want to visit these sections of the museum:
  Hall of the Ancient Egyptians
  Hall of Chinese Jades
  Hall of Equatorial Africa
  Hall of American Indians
- You do not need to spend equal time in each hall, so you may want to do a brief survey to find out which exhibits are most interesting to your classmates.

### Some Questions to Answer

1. About how much time is needed to go to and from the museum? (Be sure to allow time for getting on and off the bus and getting into and out of the museum.)

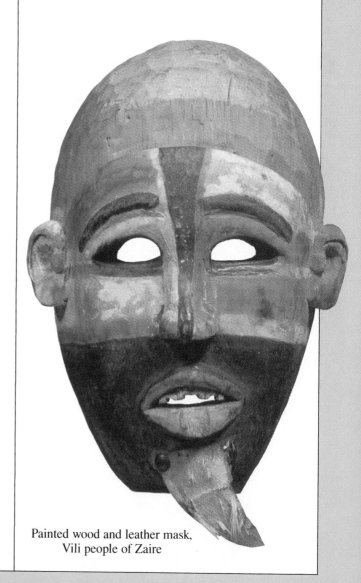

Painted wood and leather mask,
Vili people of Zaire

**2.** How much time should you allow for lunch? Do you want to allow time for a morning or afternoon refreshment break?

**3.** About how much extra time, if any, should you allow for unexpected delays?

**4.** How much time will be left for you to visit the exhibits? How will you divide this time among the four halls?

**What Is Your Decision?**

Use your decisions about times to make a possible schedule for the day. Get reactions from your classmates, and revise the schedule if necessary.

Wood mask,
Luba people of Zaire

Coming-of-age mask,
Biombo people of Zaire

# WRAP UP

## Word Choice

Complete each sentence with the correct word or words from the box. Not all words will be used.

| mathematical |
| unfair |
| one |
| fair |
| zero |
| simulation |

1. A game in which all players have the same chance of winning is called __?__.

2. The probability of picking 1 blue marble from a bag of 6 red marbles is __?__.

3. The probability of picking 1 blue marble from a bag of 6 blue marbles is __?__.

4. A model of a situation is called a __?__.

## Sometimes, Always, Never

Complete each statement by writing **sometimes**, **always**, or **never**. Explain your choices.

5. If an outcome is impossible, the probability is __?__ 1.

6. If an outcome is certain, the probability is __?__ 1.

7. If there are only two possible outcomes and both are equally likely, the probability of one of them occurring is __?__ $\frac{1}{2}$.

## Project

Suppose you have 1 red cube, 1 blue cube, and 1 white cube. Predict how many different ways you can arrange them in a row. Try it! Use colored cubes or cut-out squares. Compare your prediction with your trial using models.

Try the same activity with 2 red cubes and 1 blue cube. First predict, then use models. What was your prediction? What was the result of your trial with models?

Make up your own predict-and-try problem. Give it to a classmate to do.

# POWER PRACTICE/TEST

## Part 1   Understanding

Explain why each game is fair or unfair.

**1. Vowel-Consonant** A bag contains 6 cards. Each card has one of these letters on it: A, E, I, B, O, U. A player chooses a card without looking. If it is a vowel, that player gets 1 point. If it is a consonant, the other player gets 1.

**2. Odd-Even** One player is *Odd* and the other is *Even*. Toss two number cubes that both have 1, 2, 2, 3, 3, and 4 on them. If the sum of the numbers is even, *Even* gets 1 point. If the sum is odd, *Odd* gets 1 point.

## Part 2   Skills

Use the activities above. Find the probability of each.

**Vowel-Consonant:**   **3.** $P(A)$   **4.** $P(\text{consonant})$   **5.** $P(z)$

**Odd-Even:**   **6.** $P(5)$   **7.** $P(4)$   **8.** $P(2)$

**9.** Would you be more likely to roll a 4 or a 7 in an **Odd-Even** game?

**10.** Find the experimental and mathematical probability of tossing a 7 in the **Odd-Even** game. Use 60 tosses.

## Part 3   Applications

**11.** Estimate the number of dots using B4.

**12.** An order form states that Style 203 notebooks cost $1.50 each. There is a handling charge of $2.50 for each order. What payment must Myrna make for 6 notebooks?

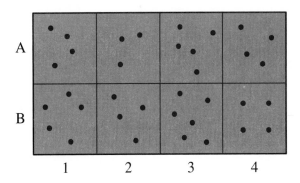

**13. Challenge** Suppose you took a multiple-choice test with 100 questions. There are 5 choices for each question. You decide to guess at every answer. How could you simulate this situation to estimate how many answers you would get correct?

**429**

# ENRICHMENT
## Combinations

Mindy, Charles, Leah, Sean, and Penny are all running for president of the student council. The person with the most votes will be president. The person with the second most votes will be vice president.

One way to find and show the different possible election results is by drawing a tree diagram. Here is the tree diagram if Mindy were elected president.

| *President* | *Vice President* | *Combination* |
|---|---|---|
| | Charles | Mindy—Charles |
| | Leah | Mindy—Leah |
| Mindy | Sean | Mindy—Sean |
| | Penny | Mindy—Penny |

**1.** Make similar tree diagrams in which Charles, Leah, Sean, and Penny are each elected president.

**2.** How many combinations are possible with Mindy as president? with Charles as president? with Leah? Sean? Penny? How many combinations are there in all? Can you see a pattern? Explain.

# CUMULATIVE REVIEW

1. What compatible numbers would you use to estimate $\frac{1}{4} \times 39$?

   A. $\frac{3}{4} \times 36$　　　　B. $\frac{1}{4} \times 36$

   C. $\frac{3}{4} \times 40$　　　　D. $\frac{1}{4} \times 40$

2. Multiply $2\frac{2}{3} \times 3\frac{1}{4}$. Reduce to lowest terms.

   A. $6\frac{1}{6}$　　　　　　　B. $8\frac{2}{3}$

   C. 8　　　　　　　　D. $6\frac{2}{3}$

3. Which is *not* a correct way to write a ratio?

   A. 4 to 7　　　　　　B. $\frac{4}{7}$

   C. $\frac{4}{7}\%$　　　　　　D. 4:7

4. Write 36% as a lowest-terms fraction.

   A. $\frac{36}{100}$　　　　　　B. $\frac{9}{25}$

   C. $\frac{1}{4}$　　　　　　　D. $\frac{18}{50}$

5. Write 16:100 as a percent.

   A. 100%　　　　　　B. $\frac{16}{100}\%$

   C. 16%　　　　　　D. 25%

6. Which of the following is *not* a quadrilateral?

   A. rhombus　　　　B. parallelogram

   C. trapezoid　　　　D. octagon

7. Murray got 9 out of every 10 math problems correct. The test had a total of 40 problems. How many problems did Murray answer correctly?

   A. 9　　B. 18　　C. 27　　D. 36

8. Find the circumference of a circle with a diameter of 6.8 cm. Use 3.14 for $\pi$.

   A. 42.704 cm　　　　B. 21.352 cm

   C. 10.676 cm　　　　D. 64.056 cm

9. Solve $\frac{2}{3} = \frac{n}{24}$ for $n$.

   A. 16　　B. 14　　C. 12　　D. 18

10. Which regular polygon *cannot* be used in a tessellation?

    A. pentagon　　　　B. triangle

    C. hexagon　　　　D. octagon

11. Write 27% as a decimal.

    A. 2.70　　　　　　B. 27.00

    C. 0.27　　　　　　D. 0.027

12. Which number pair completes the ratio table?

    | 3 | 6 | 9 | 12 | 15 | ▓ |
    |---|---|---|----|----|---|
    | 8 | 16 | 24 | 32 | 40 | ▓ |

    A. 18, 48　　　　　　B. 18, 44

    C. 17, 44　　　　　　D. 17, 48

13. Wanda is one third as old as her brother. Wanda is 6. How old is her brother?

    A. 2　　B. 3　　C. 12　　D. 18

14. Ian sliced 3 whole pizzas into equal sixths. How many sixths did he get altogether?

    A. 6　　B. 18　　C. 3　　D. 12

# 16

## PERIMETER, AREA, AND VOLUME

**M**ATH AND
FINE ARTS

### DATA BANK

Use the Fine Arts Data
Bank on page 479 to
answer the questions.

**1** What is the length of the
base of the Parthenon to
the nearest meter? What
is the width of the base to the
nearest meter?

**THEME: FAMOUS STRUCTURES**

**2** Suppose you took a walk all the way around the base of the Parthenon. About how many meters would you have walked? About how many meters less than a kilometer is that?

**3** Would a walk around the base of the Great Pyramid be longer or shorter than the walk around the Parthenon? About how many meters longer or shorter would it be?

**4** **Using Critical Thinking** Leslie studied the Parthenon facts and said, "I can add the number of columns on each side to find how many outside columns there are in all." Do you agree?

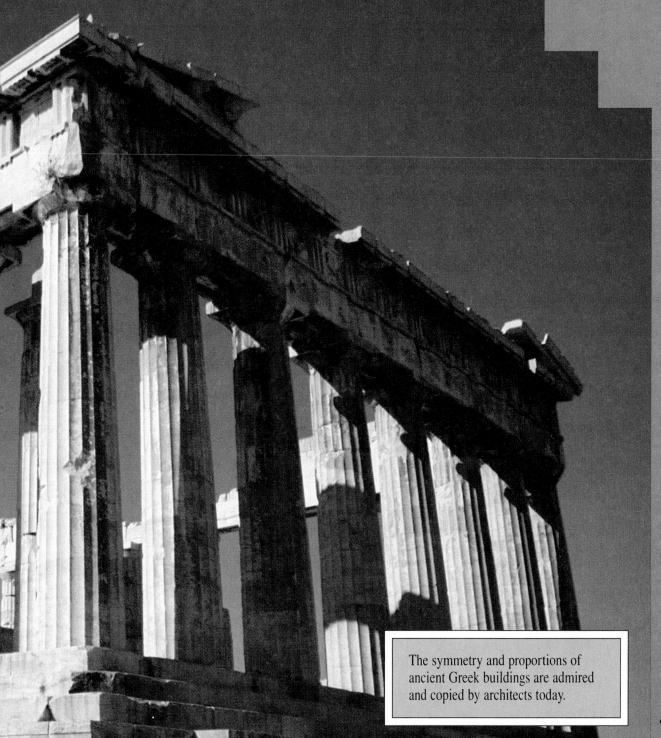

The symmetry and proportions of ancient Greek buildings are admired and copied by architects today.

# Perimeter

Many buildings and other structures have rectangular bases. You can use what you know about parallel sides of rectangles to help you find the perimeter of a rectangle.

## EXPLORE  Find How Many Ways

Work in groups. How many different rectangles with a perimeter of 24 units can you draw on graph paper? Each side should be a whole number of units.

## TALK ABOUT IT

1. How could you find the perimeter of a rectangle without adding all four sides?
2. Are any of the rectangles you made squares? How can you find the perimeter of a square without adding?
3. If each side of a rectangle is a whole number, can the perimeter be an odd number?

One way to find the perimeter of a rectangle is to use a formula.

**Perimeter** $= (2 \times \textbf{length}) + (2 \times \textbf{width})$
$$P = 2l + 2w$$

The formula for the perimeter of a square is $P = 4l$.

Example: Find the perimeter of a rectangle 14 cm long and 4 cm wide.
$$P = (2 \times 14) + (2 \times 4)$$
$$= 28 + 8 = 36$$
$$P = 36 \text{ cm}$$

**TRY IT OUT**

Find the perimeter of each figure. Write **yes** if you can use a formula.

1.

738 m

294 m

2.

589 km

456 km

3.

42 cm   31 cm

35 cm

50 cm   48 cm

46 cm

37 cm

Find the perimeter of each figure. Write **yes** if you can use a formula.

**1.** basketball court

14 m

26 m

**2.** soccer field

90 m

120 m

**3.** table tennis

1.52 m

2.74 m

**4.** baseball field

**5.** baseball diamond

73.0 m

81.2 m          81.2 m

27.4 m

94.3 m          94.3 m

27.4 m     27.4 m

**MATH REASONING**

**Estimate** the width of these rectangular figures.

**6.** $P = 260$ cm
$l = 82$ cm

**7.** $P = 90$ m
$l = 24$ m

**8.** $P = 20$ m
$l = 6.8$ m

**PROBLEM SOLVING**

**9.** The North Stone Pyramid of Egypt has a height of 99 m. The perimeter of its square base is 880 m. What is the length of each side of the base?

**10.** The Pentagon Building in Washington, D.C., has 5 equal sides. The distance from one corner to the next is 281 m. What is the perimeter of the building?

**11. Fine Arts Data Bank**  What is the perimeter of the Lincoln Memorial in Washington, D.C.? See page 479.

DATA BANK

## MIXED REVIEW

Write a percent for each decimal.

**12.** 0.91      **13.** 0.45      **14.** 0.89      **15.** 0.63      **16.** 0.07      **17.** 0.39

Give the lowest-terms fraction for each percent.

**18.** 75%      **19.** 80%      **20.** 35%      **21.** 22%      **22.** 40%      **23.** 65%

# Problem Solving
## Estimating the Answer

| |
|---|
| UNDERSTAND |
| ANALYZE DATA |
| PLAN |
| ESTIMATE |
| SOLVE |
| EXAMINE |

### LEARN ABOUT IT

Before solving a problem, you often can estimate to decide what would be a reasonable answer.

> The action and comedy movies at Midcity Video are next to each other on the wall. The wall space they cover is 6.35 m long and 1.8 m high. What is the area of the wall space they cover?

I'll begin by rounding both dimensions.

$$6.35 \longrightarrow 6$$
$$1.8 \longrightarrow 2$$

Then I'll use the numbers to estimate the area of the wall space.

$$6 \times 2 \longrightarrow 12$$

Now I'll solve the problem.

$$6.35 \times 1.8 \longrightarrow 11.43$$

The answer 11.43 m² is reasonable because it is close to 12.

### TRY IT OUT

First estimate the answer. Then solve the problem and decide whether your answer is reasonable.

1. The narrow side of each videotape is 3.2 cm wide. Jan can fit exactly 39 tapes on a shelf. How long is each shelf?

2. The perimeter of the poster for foreign tapes is 298 cm. The length is 98 cm. What is the width?

3. Bing took some of his friends to a movie to celebrate his birthday. He paid $20.79 for 11 large lemonades. How much did each lemonade cost?

Solve. Choose a strategy from the list or use other strategies that you know.

1. The floor plan of Midcity Video is shown below. What is the area of the store?

Midcity Video

customer area

3.3 m

counter

1.4 m

4.6 m

7.2 m

| Some Strategies | |
|---|---|
| Act Out | Make a Table |
| Use Objects | Solve a Simpler Problem |
| Choose an Operation | Make an Organized List |
| Draw a Picture | Work Backward |
| Guess and Check | Look for a Pattern |
| Use Logical Reasoning | |

5. It costs $29.50 to become a member at Midcity Video. When you pay for membership, you get a packet of tickets that allows you to rent 9 movies free. Videotape rentals normally cost $2.50 each. If you subtract the amount you save on rental costs, what does it cost to become a member?

2. The owner of Midcity Video is going to enlarge his store by making it 3.2 m longer. What will its perimeter be then?

6. The floor of a movie theater is a square. Its area is 16 m² and its perimeter is 16 m. How long is each side of the floor?

3. About how many movies are there in all at Midcity Video?

| Midcity Video Movies | |
|---|---|
| **Type** | **Number** |
| Comedy | 182 |
| Children's | 192 |
| Drama | 321 |
| Horror | 125 |
| Science Fiction | 81 |
| Foreign | 192 |
| Action | 183 |

7. For the opening of the new theater, the manager put a giant balloon on each lamp post on the perimeter of the parking lot. The lamp posts are 22 m apart and the parking lot is 132 m on each side. How many balloons did she need?

8. The popcorn container shaped like a cylinder holds about 3 times as much popcorn as the container shaped like a cone. The cone-shaped holder holds 32.5 g of popcorn. About how much does the container shaped like a cylinder hold?

4. While looking over the foreign movies, Julie, Serena, and Ivan realized that they each can speak a different foreign language—Italian, Spanish, and Japanese. None of them speaks a language that starts with the first letter of his or her first name. Serena does not speak Japanese. Which language does each person speak?

# Area of Figures with Irregular Shapes

**LEARN ABOUT IT**

### EXPLORE  Analyze a Plan

When Carrie and David each found the
area of the floor shown in the plan, they
thought about it in different ways.

Carrie mentally divided the room into
these 2 rectangles and found their areas.

David mentally divided the room into
these 2 rectangles and found their areas.

### TALK ABOUT IT

1. How can Carrie and David find the total area for the room?
   Is the area the same or different for the two methods?
2. How could the floor plan for the room be divided into
   3 rectangles? Will you get the same total area?

This is one way to find the area of an irregular shape.
- Break the shape into rectangular parts.
- Find the area of each rectangle and add these areas to find
  the total area.

---

*Calculator Key Code*

To find the area of an irregular shape divided into two rectangles:
[ON/AC] length $a$ [×] width $a$ [=] [M+] length $b$ [×] width $b$ [=] [M+] [MR]

---

**TRY IT OUT**

Trace this figure twice. Show two different
ways to break the figure into 2 smaller
rectangles. Find the total area for the figure.

**438**

The students in room 5B want to paint only the walls of their classroom. Find the area of each wall to be painted.

1. North wall

2. East wall

3. South wall

4. West wall

## MATH REASONING

**Estimate** whether the area of each figure is a little more than or a little less than 24 m².

**5.**

**6.**

**7.**

## PROBLEM SOLVING

8. Carrie wants to buy carpet that costs $19.95 per square meter for this room. What is the area of the floor without the fireplace?

9. **Data Hunt** What is the area of your desk top or table top? Use a unit of measure of your choice.

## ▶ CALCULATOR

10. Use the **memory minus** [M−] key to find the area of the blue portion of this figure.

You can use this key code:

[ON/AC] length *a* [×] width *a* [=] [M+] length *b* [×] width *b* [=] [M−] [MR]

# Using Critical Thinking

**LEARN ABOUT IT**

Mrs. Manypets used Plan 1 to make two pens. "I've used the same length of fence for each pen," she told her two children. "You will each have the same amount of pen area to care for."

As time passed, one of the children complained that the jobs were not equal. "It will be easy to fix this," said Mrs. Manypets, "I can just rearrange the fence according to Plan 2 and the areas of the pens will then be exactly the same."

## TALK ABOUT IT

1. What two types of measures of figures are involved in deciding about the pens?

2. Do you agree with the conclusion Mrs. Manypets reached about Plan 1? Explain. Do you agree with the conclusion she reached about Plan 2? Explain.

3. What have you learned about perimeter and area of a rectangle from this story?

**TRY IT OUT**

1. Draw and label two rectangles, both with a perimeter of 24 ft, but with different areas.

2. Draw and label two rectangles, both with an area of 24 ft², but with different perimeters.

3. A rectangle has sides that are all whole numbers of units. Its area is 18 square units and its perimeter is 18 units. What are its length and width?

440

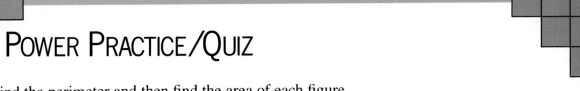

Find the perimeter and then find the area of each figure.

**1.**

9 yd
20 yd    20 yd
9 yd

perimeter = ▨
area = ▨

**2.**

2.7 m
1.5 m    1.5 m
2.7 m

perimeter = ▨
area = ▨

**3.**

6.03 m    6.03 m
6.03 m    6.03 m

perimeter = ▨
area = ▨

**4.**

18 m
14 m    10 m
12 m
4 m
6 m

perimeter = ▨
area = ▨

**5.**

1.4 m
2.4 m    2.4 m
2.4 m    2.4 m
1.4 m    1.4 m
2.4 m    2.4 m
2.4 m    2.4 m
1.4 m

perimeter = ▨
area = ▨

**6.**

70 cm
20 cm
50 cm
10 cm
10 cm

perimeter = ▨
area = ▨

## PROBLEM SOLVING

Gordon, Caryl, and Ann each planted rectangular gardens.

Gordon's Garden

3 m
8 m

Caryl's Garden

5 m
6 m

Ann's Garden

6 m
4 m

7. Which garden needs the least amount of fencing?

8. Which garden covers the greatest area?

9. Andy has 50 m of fencing for a garden. What is the greatest area he can fence in if his garden is rectangular and is a whole number of meters on each side?

10. Dawn used 36 m of fencing around her garden. Tim's garden covers an area of 56 m². Could both gardens be rectangular and have the same dimensions? Explain.

# Area of Right Triangles

**EXPLORE  Make a Model**

Work in groups. When you cut a rectangle along the diagonal, do the two right triangles you make always have the same area as each other? Try rectangles of different sizes to find out.

**TALK ABOUT IT**

1. What fractional part of the rectangle does each right triangle represent?
2. Is the area of each triangle the same as half the area of the rectangle? Explain.

You can find the area of a right triangle by first finding the area of a rectangle with the same base and height and then dividing by 2.

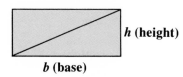

**Area of a right triangle $= \frac{1}{2} \times$ base $\times$ height**

$$A = \frac{1}{2} \times b \times h$$

Example:  $A = \frac{1}{2} \times 8 \times 4$

$$A = \frac{1}{2} \times 32 = 16$$

The area of the right triangle is 16 cm².

**TRY IT OUT**

Give the height and base of each right triangle. Then use the formula to find the area.

1.

$h = $ ▦ units
$b = $ ▦ units
$A = $ ▦ square units

2.

$h = $ ▦ units
$b = $ ▦ units
$A = $ ▦ square units

3.
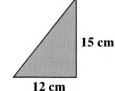

$h = $ ▦ cm
$b = $ ▦ cm
$A = $ ▦ cm²

Give the height, base, and area of each right triangle.

□ = 1 square unit

**1.**

**2.**

**3.**

**4.**

Find the area of each triangle.

**5.**

75 m

62 m

**6.** 125.5 m

98 m

**7.**

50 in.          50 in.

**MATH REASONING**

8. Does a right triangle with a base greater than the base of another right triangle always have the greater area? Give examples to support your reasoning.

**PROBLEM SOLVING**

9. What is the area of a triangular sail on a sailboat with height 42 m and base 2.4 m?

10. The city wants a park with an area of at least 1 km² but no more than 2 km². Which plan or plans could they use?

Plan 1    Plan 2    Plan 3

1.5 km

1.5 km

2.8 km

0.8 km

0.8 km

1.4 km

▶ **MENTAL MATH**

Study Julie's method for finding the area of a right triangle with height or base an even number. Use Julie's method to find the area of each figure.

Julie's Method

4 units

8 units

$\frac{1}{2}$ of 4 = 2

2 × 8 = 16
Area = 16 square units

**11.**

6 units

8 units

**12.**

7 units

4 units

**13.**

10 units

2 units

443

# More About Area of Triangles

The faces of the Pyramids at Giza are triangular, but are not right triangles.

**EXPLORE  Make a Model**

Use grid paper. Draw a rectangle of any size. Color a green triangle inside the rectangle as shown at the right. Cut out the rectangle and then the green triangle. Can you find a way to fit the 2 smaller white triangles exactly on top of the green triangle?

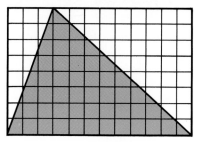

**TALK ABOUT IT**

1. What fractional part of the rectangle is the green triangle?
2. Is the area of any triangle the same as half the area of a rectangle with the same base and height? Why?

The area formula for a right triangle can be used to find the area of any triangle.

area of a rectangle

**Area of a triangle** $= \frac{1}{2} \times$ **base** $\times$ **height**

$$A = \frac{1}{2} \times b \times h$$

*Example:* Find the area of a triangle with base 8 cm and height 6 cm.

$$A = \frac{1}{2} \times 8 \times 6$$

$$A = \frac{1}{2} \times 48 = 24$$

The area of the triangle is 24 cm².

**TRY IT OUT**

Give the height and base of each triangle. Then use the formula to find the area for each.

1.

$h = $ ▓ units
$b = $ ▓ units
$A = $ ▓ square units

2.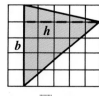

$h = $ ▓ units
$b = $ ▓ units
$A = $ ▓ square units

3.

$h = $ ▓ cm
$b = $ ▓ cm
$A = $ ▓ cm²

444

Give the height, base, and area of each triangle.

**1.**

**2.**

**3.**

**4.**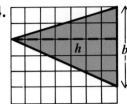

Find the area of each object.

**5.**   $h = 8$ m, $6.5$ m

**6.**   $h = 58$ in., $23$ in., COLORADO

**7.**   $0.3$ m, $0.4$ m, $0.4$ m

**MATH REASONING**

Give the height of a triangle with the same base as the triangle shown on the right but with

**8.** less area    **9.** more area

1.8 cm, 4.5 cm

**PROBLEM SOLVING**

**10.** Janet made a model of a pyramid. The height, base, and area measurement of each triangular face was the same number. What is the number?

**11. Fine Arts Data Bank**  What is the area of each triangular face of the 2nd Pyramid at Giza? See page 479.

DATA BANK

▶ **ALGEBRA**

If the base and height of a triangle are whole number measurements, give two different values for $b$ and $h$ that make each equation true.

**12.** $A = 12$ cm$^2$, $b = $ ▓ cm, $h = $ ▓ cm    **13.** $A = 48$ m$^2$, $b = $ ▓ m, $h = $ ▓ m

*More Practice, page 521, set D*

# Area of Parallelograms

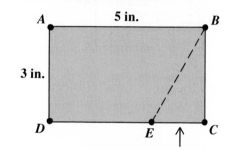

A parallelogram has 2 pairs of sides the same length and 2 pairs of parallel sides.

**EXPLORE  Make a Model**
Cut out a rectangle like the one shown at the right. Draw line segment *BE* on your rectangle. Cut along *BE*. Tape side *BC* to *AD* as shown.

**TALK ABOUT IT**

1.  What was the area of the original rectangle?

2.  What type of figure results from cutting and taping the triangle?

3.  What is the area of the new figure? How do you know?

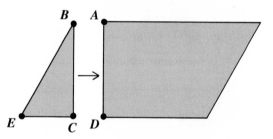

The activity above shows why the area formula for a parallelogram is related to the area formula for a rectangle.

**Area of parallelogram = base × height**

$A = b \times h$

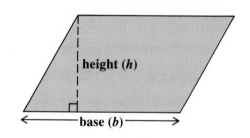

---

**TRY IT OUT**

Find the area of each parallelogram.

1.

2.  $b = 12.5$ m
    $h = 5.8$ m

3.

4.  $b = 2\frac{1}{2}$ ft
    $h = 5\frac{1}{4}$ ft

**446**

Find the area of each parallelogram.

**1.**

h = 8 ft
b = 23 ft

**2.**

h = 12 m

b = 5 m

**3.**

h = 4.8 cm
b = 10 cm

**4.**

h = 3$\frac{1}{2}$ ft

b = 8$\frac{3}{4}$ ft

**5.** $h = 12$ m, $b = 15$ m  **6.** $h = 2.86$ cm, $b = 5.5$ cm  **7.** $h = 120$ yd, $b = 10$ yd

**MATH REASONING**

**8.** Draw and label 3 different parallelograms, each with an area of 24 cm² and height and base an even number.

**PROBLEM SOLVING**

**9.** Suppose roofing material costs $1.95 per square foot. Estimate the cost of the material for the roof shown at the right. Remember to include both sides of the roof.

45 ft

24 ft

Write a percent for each fraction.

**10.** $\frac{3}{4}$    **11.** $\frac{4}{5}$    **12.** $\frac{6}{20}$    **13.** $\frac{1}{25}$    **14.** $\frac{8}{10}$    **15.** $\frac{8}{50}$

**16.** $\frac{19}{20}$    **17.** $\frac{16}{20}$    **18.** $\frac{2}{5}$    **19.** $\frac{20}{25}$    **20.** $\frac{1}{10}$    **21.** $\frac{15}{30}$

Find the perimeter of each rectangle.

**22.** 24 m × 12 m        **23.** 8 ft × 10 ft            **24.** 20 in. × 6 in.

# Volume

**EXPLORE**  **Make a Model**
Work in groups. How many different
rectangular prisms can you make with
24 cubes? with 25 cubes?

## TALK ABOUT IT

1. Can you make the same number of rectangular prisms
   with 25 cubes as with 24 cubes? Explain.

2. How can you find the number of cubes in a prism
   without counting each one?

Volume is the number of cubic units an object can hold. We
can use a formula to find the volume of a rectangular prism.

**Volume = length × width × height**

$$V = \quad l \quad \times \quad w \quad \times \quad h$$

number in a layer ⏟ number of layers ⏜

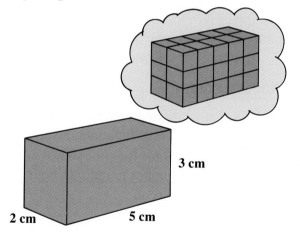

Example: $V = 5 \times 2 \times 3$
$V = 30$

The volume is 30 cm³ (cubic centimeters).

3 cm
2 cm    5 cm

## TRY IT OUT

Give the length, width, and height of each rectangular
prism. Then use the formula to find each volume.

**1.**

$h = $ ▥ units
$w = $ ▥ units
$l = $ ▥ units
$V = $ ▥ cubic units

**2.**

$h = $ ▥ cm
$w = $ ▥ cm
$l = $ ▥ cm
$V = $ ▥ cm³

6 cm
2 cm    8 cm

**448**

Give the length, width, height, and volume of each.

**1.**

**2.**

**3.**

8 cm

15 cm

20 cm

Find the volume of each box made by the EZ Box Company.

| | Box size | length | width | height | Volume |
|---|---|---|---|---|---|
| **4.** | A | | | | |
| **5.** | B | | | | |
| **6.** | C | | | | |
| **7.** | D | | | | |

A  17 cm  18 cm  15 cm

B  12 cm  27 cm  11 cm

C  26 cm  18 cm  9 cm

D  0.1 m  0.7 m  0.3 m

**MATH REASONING**

Give the height of each box.

**8.** $V = 30$ cm³

? 

2 cm    5 cm

**9.** $V = 192$ cm³

?

8 cm

2 cm

**PROBLEM SOLVING**

**10.** What would be the capacity (in milliliters) of a fish tank that is 40 cm long, 20 cm wide, and 30 cm high? Remember: 1 cm³ = 1 mL

**11. Use Objects** If cubes are used to build a rectangular prism that shows 4 cubes on each side, how many faces of the cubes do not form part of the surface of the prism?

▶ **USING CRITICAL THINKING    Use Visual Thinking**

**12.** Here are four views of the same cube. What figure is opposite the star?

# Surface Area

**EXPLORE  Make a Model**

When you fold a figure like this into a box, do you think the faces opposite each other will have the same or different areas? To check, trace and make the figure as shown.

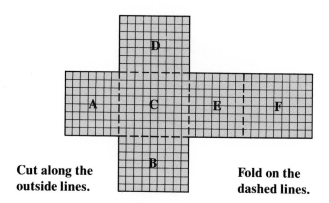

**Cut along the outside lines.**

**Fold on the dashed lines.**

**TALK ABOUT IT**

1. Give the area for each face in square units. Which faces are opposite? Do the opposite faces have the same area?

2. What is the total surface area of the box? How did you find your answer?

The formula for finding the area of a rectangle can be used to help find the **surface area** of a rectangular prism. Here is one method for finding the surface area of a rectangular prism.

- Find the area of the top face, front face, and an end face.

- Multiply each area by 2 since the opposite faces have the same area.

- Find the sum of the three products.

> Remember, for a rectangle, $A = l \times w$.

**TRY IT OUT**

Find the surface area of each box. Use a calculator if available.

1.

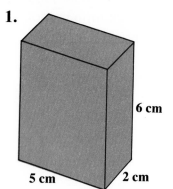

6 cm

5 cm    2 cm

2.

18 cm

3 cm

3 cm

3.

1.2 m

1.5 m    0.8 m

**450**

Find the surface area of each box. Use a calculator if possible.

**1.**
60 cm
90 cm
80 cm

**2.**
0.3 m
0.5 m
0.1 m

**3.**
2.2 m
0.8 m
1.1 m

Find the surface area of each object. Use a calculator if possible.

**4.** shoe box

12 cm
13 cm   20 cm

**5.** tool box

56 cm
95 cm   42 cm

**6.** suitcase

0.2 m
0.5 m
0.7 m

**7.** box for flowers

12 cm
15 cm   80 cm

**APPLY**

## MATH REASONING

Use **mental math** to find the surface area of these cubes.

**8.**
3 m
3 m
3 m

**9.**
5 cm
5 cm
5 cm

**10.**
10 cm
10 cm
10 cm

## PROBLEM SOLVING

**11.** If aluminum costs 8¢ a square meter, will a can company have to pay more than or less than 8¢ for enough aluminum to make this gasoline can?

GAS
0.5 m
0.4 m   0.2 m

**12.** Give the length, width, and height for two different boxes that have the same volume, but different surface areas.

▶ **COMMUNICATION   Write to Learn**

**13.** Write a paragraph to explain the difference between volume and surface area.

# Data Collection and Analysis
## Group Decision Making

UNDERSTAND
ANALYZE DATA
PLAN
ESTIMATE
SOLVE
EXAMINE

### Doing a Simulation
### Group Skill:
Disagree in an Agreeable Way

Every morning as you walk to school you have to cross three streets with stoplights. Each stop light has an equal chance of being either red or green. You usually wake up early enough to get to school on time, but this morning you slept a little longer than you should have. You need for all three stop lights to be green when you reach them. Do a simulation with your group to see what your chances are.

### Collecting Data

1. Your group will need three coins to represent the three stop lights. Decide what each side of the coin will represent, a red light or a green light.

2. Toss all three coins at once. Were they all green lights? Keep a record of your tosses. Toss at least 100 times.

| 3 green lights | Not 3 green lights |
|---|---|
|  |  |

### Organizing Data

3. Count the number of times you got 3 green lights and the number of times you did not get 3 green lights. Make a bar graph to show your results.

### Presenting Your Analysis

4. Write a paragraph to tell how you conducted your simulation and what your results were.

5. How many times out of 100 did you get all green lights and make it to school on time? Were you surprised? Explain.

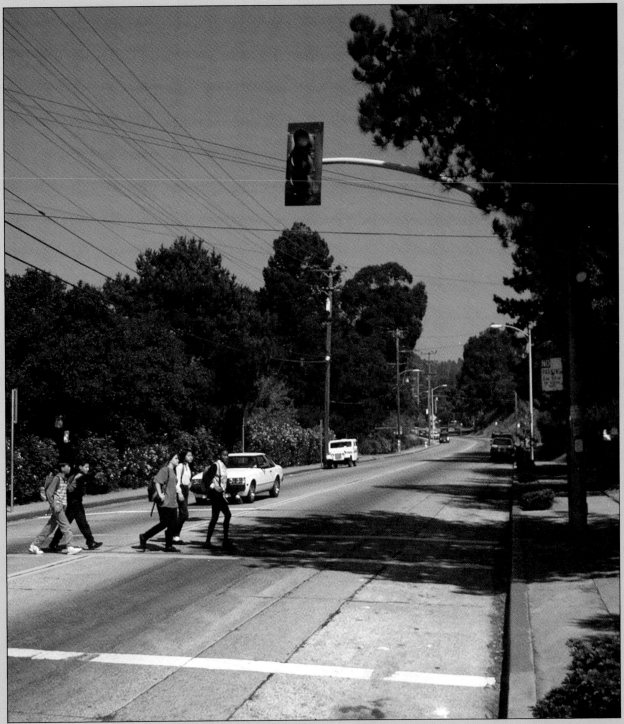

# WRAP UP

## Picture This

Use the pictures to help you explain.

1. How are the areas of this triangle and rectangle related?

2. How do you find the perimeter and the area of this rectangle? What units do you use for each?

3. What do finding the area of an irregular shape and finding the surface area of a box have in common?

4. How do you find the volume of a box? What units do you use?

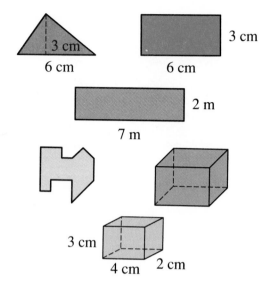

3 cm

6 cm

3 cm

6 cm

2 m

7 m

3 cm

4 cm    2 cm

## Sometimes, Always, Never

Complete each statement by writing **sometimes**, **always**, or **never**. Explain your choices.

5. You can __?__ use a formula to find perimeter.

6. Two rectangles with the same perimeter also __?__ have the same area.

7. The area of a rectangle is __?__ an even number.

8. The volume of a box is __?__ the number of cubic units it takes to "fill" it.

## Project

Make or draw a three-dimensional figure that is made up of 20 centimeter cubes. Record the surface area and volume of your figure.

Make several other figures using the same 20 centimeter cubes. Record the surface area and volume of each. What changes? What remains the same?

6 + 2 + 12 = 20 blocks

454

# POWER PRACTICE/TEST

## Part 1   Understanding

1. Draw and label two rectangles, both with a perimeter of 30 ft but with different areas.

2. Draw and label a rectangle with sides in whole units that has an area of 36 square units and the least possible perimeter.

What measures do you need to know in order to find the area or surface area?

3. square        4. triangle        5. parallelogram        6. rectangular prism

## Part 2   Skills

Find the perimeter of each.

7. square with side of 3 cm

8. rectangle with length 6 cm, width 5 cm

9. square with side of 10 cm

10. rectangle with length 9 cm, width 8 cm

Find the area of each figure.

11. right triangle with base measuring 3.4 cm and height 2.7 cm.

12. parallelogram with base measuring 3.9 cm and height of 2.1 cm.

Find the volume of each rectangular prism.

13. 9 cm by 4 cm by 5 cm

14. 5 cm by 8 cm by 6 cm

Find the surface area of each rectangular prism.

15. 20 cm by 30 cm by 40 cm

16. 6 cm by 7 cm by 9 cm

## Part 3   Applications

17. Joel has a box that measures 42 cm by 53 cm by 6 cm. He said that it would hold 133,560 $cm^3$. Estimate to decide whether his answer is reasonable.

18. **Challenge** What happens to the area if you enlarge a photo so that each side is double the length of the original? What happens to the area if you triple the length of each side?

**455**

# ENRICHMENT
## Estimating Area

1. Estimate the area covered by the hand. Tell what method you used. The area of each square is 1 square unit.

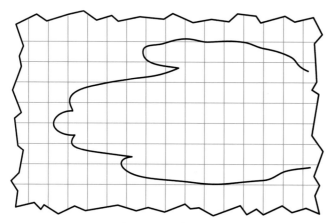

You can use averaging to estimate the area of any irregular shape such as a hand. Follow these steps to estimate the area of the hand.

- Count the full squares that are completely inside the outlines of the hand.

- Count all the squares used in covering the hand, those completely inside, and those only partly inside the hand.

- Find the average of those two numbers. (Add the two numbers and divide by 2.)

2. How does this estimate compare with your first estimate?

3. Trace the outline of your hand on graph paper. Use averaging to estimate its area.

4. Find 3 objects with irregular shapes. Trace them on graph paper. Use averaging to estimate their areas.

# CUMULATIVE REVIEW

Use this grid for exercises 1 and 2.

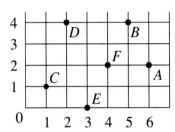

**1.** The coordinates for point *E* are

    **A.** (1,3)           **B.** (3,1)

    **C.** (0,3)          **D.** (3,0)

**2.** What point is at coordinate (4,2)?

    **A.** *F*            **B.** *D*

    **C.** *B*            **D.** *C*

**3.** Find the area of triangle *ABC* with a height of 8 cm and a base of 6 cm.

    **A.** 48 cm$^2$       **B.** 24 cm$^2$

    **C.** 30 cm$^2$       **D.** 40 cm$^2$

**4.** During the tennis season, Marcy won 15 out of 20 games, Kim won 18 out of 25 games, Lana won 37 out of 50 games, and Judy won 6 out of 10. Which player won the greatest percent of her games?

    **A.** Marcy       **B.** Kim

    **C.** Lana        **D.** Judy

**5.** Find the surface area of a box 12 in. long, 7 in. wide, and 2 in. high.

    **A.** 48 in.$^2$       **B.** 366 in.$^2$

    **C.** 122 in.$^2$      **D.** 244 in.$^2$

**6.** Find 88% of 25.

    **A.** 20     **B.** 21     **C.** 22     **D.** 23

Think of a number cube with 1, 2, 3, 4, 5, 6 on its faces for exercises 7–9.

**7.** If you were tossing this cube in a fair game, how many points should you give for tossing a number less than 3 if you give 4 points for tossing a number greater than 2?

    **A.** 2     **B.** 6     **C.** 4     **D.** 8

**8.** Find *P* (odd).

    **A.** $\frac{1}{6}$     **B.** $\frac{1}{2}$     **C.** $\frac{1}{3}$     **D.** $\frac{2}{3}$

**9.** If you toss the cube 100 times, how many times would you expect to get either 1 or 6?

    **A.** 60     **B.** 50     **C.** 33     **D.** 20

**10.** A printer's order form states that 1–10 copies cost 15¢ each, 11–25 copies cost 12¢ each, and more than 25 copies are 10¢ each. What would be the total cost of 20 copies?

    **A.** $3.00         **B.** $2.40

    **C.** $2.00        **D.** $2.70

**11.** If you have 2 red, 3 blue, 1 green, and 2 yellow chips in a bag, which colors are equally likely to be drawn?

    **A.** red, blue      **B.** red, green

    **C.** red, yellow    **D.** green, yellow

# RESOURCE
# BANK
# AND
# APPENDIX

## RESOURCE BANK

**Skills Review Bank**　　　460
Review some skills from
last year.

**Data Bank**　　　468
Use data for solving
problems related to
different subjects.

**Calculator Bank**　　　484
Learn and practice some
calculator skills.

**Computer Bank**　　　492
Use some computer
programs to solve problems.

**More Practice Bank**　　　500
Practice the computational
skills and problem solving
skills and strategies you
have learned.

# APPENDIX

**Table of Measures**          **528**

Refresh your memory
of measurement unit
relationships.

**Glossary**          **529**

Find definitions of important
math words used in your
book.

# Adding: Trading

School

There are two elementary schools in the Leland School district. Northeast has 349 students and Southwest has 276 students. What is the total number of elementary school students in the district?

School

Since we want to find the total number of students, we add.

| Add the ones. Trade if necessary. | Add the tens. Trade if necessary. | Add the hundreds. |
|---|---|---|
| $\overset{1}{3}49$ <br> $+\ 276$ <br> $\overline{\phantom{00}5}$ <br> *15 ones is 1 ten and 5 ones.* | $\overset{1\ 1}{3}49$ <br> $+\ 276$ <br> $\overline{\phantom{0}25}$ <br> *12 tens is 1 hundred and 2 tens.* | $\overset{1\ 1}{3}49$ <br> $+\ 276$ <br> $\overline{\phantom{0}625}$ |

The total number of students in the school district is 625.

## Other Examples

**1.** $\overset{1\ 1}{4{,}289}$
$+\ 2{,}186$
$\overline{6{,}475}$

**2.** $\overset{1\ 1}{3{,}094}$
$6{,}238$
$\overline{9{,}332}$

**3.** $\overset{1\ 1\ 1}{47{,}570}$
$26{,}933$
$\overline{74{,}503}$

**4.** $\overset{1\ 1\ 1\ 1}{66{,}495}$
$16{,}528$
$\overline{83{,}023}$

### TRY IT OUT

Decide if you have to make a trade. Find the answer.

**1.** $684$
$+\ \ 29$

**2.** $996$
$+\ 428$

**3.** $9{,}732$
$+\ 9{,}188$

**4.** $32{,}364$
$+\ 18{,}707$

**5.** $63{,}988$
$+\ 10{,}822$

# Subtracting: Trading

Look at the chart on the right. How many more days does it take for Mars to orbit the sun than it does for Mercury?

| Name of Planet | Time it takes to orbit the sun |
|---|---|
| Pluto | 248 years |
| Neptune | 165 years |
| Uranus | 84 years |
| Saturn | 29.5 years |
| Jupiter | 12 years |
| Mars | 687 days |
| Earth | 365 days |
| Venus | 225 days |
| Mercury | 88 days |

Since we want to compare the numbers, we subtract.

| Subtract the ones. Trade if necessary. | Subtract the tens. Trade if necessary. | Subtract the hundreds. |
|---|---|---|
| $\begin{array}{r} 7\ 17 \\ 6\ 8\ 7 \\ -\quad 8\ 8 \\ \hline 9 \end{array}$ | $\begin{array}{r} 5\ 17\ 17 \\ 6\ 8\ 7 \\ -\quad 8\ 8 \\ \hline 9\ 9 \end{array}$ | $\begin{array}{r} 5\ 17\ 17 \\ 6\ 8\ 7 \\ -\quad 8\ 8 \\ \hline 5\ 9\ 9 \end{array}$ |

Mars takes 599 days longer to orbit the sun than Mercury.

## Other Examples

$\begin{array}{r} 13\ 17 \\ 1\ 4\ 7 \\ -\quad 7\ 9 \\ \hline 6\ 8 \end{array}$
$\qquad$
$\begin{array}{r} 7\ 13\ 11 \\ 8\ 4\ 1 \\ -\ 7\ 9\ 5 \\ \hline 4\ 6 \end{array}$
$\qquad$
$\begin{array}{r} 8\ 14 \\ 8\ 9\ 4 \\ -\quad 8\ 6 \\ \hline 8\ 0\ 8 \end{array}$
$\qquad$
$\begin{array}{r} 1\ 15\ 16\ 12 \\ 2{,}6\ 7\ 2 \\ -\ 1{,}8\ 9\ 4 \\ \hline 7\ 7\ 8 \end{array}$
$\qquad$
$\begin{array}{r} 4\ 16\ 12\ 14\ 17 \\ 5\ 7{,}3\ 5\ 7 \\ -\ 1\ 9{,}5\ 9\ 8 \\ \hline 3\ 7{,}7\ 5\ 9 \end{array}$

### TRY IT OUT

Subtract. Check by adding.

1.  $\begin{array}{r} 211 \\ -\ 98 \end{array}$
2.  $\begin{array}{r} 864 \\ -\ 491 \end{array}$
3.  $\begin{array}{r} 474 \\ -\ 89 \end{array}$
4.  $\begin{array}{r} 592 \\ -\ 416 \end{array}$
5.  $\begin{array}{r} 2{,}161 \\ -\ 1{,}988 \end{array}$

# Subtracting: With Zeros

The Dallas Cowboys' Texas Stadium holds 65,000 fans. Candlestick Park, home of the San Francisco 49ers, holds 61,185. How many more fans does the Texas stadium hold?

Since we want to compare the two numbers, we subtract.

| Subtract the ones. Trade if necessary. | Subtract the tens. Trade if necessary. | Subtract the hundreds. Trade if necessary. | Subtract the thousands. |
|---|---|---|---|
| 4 9 9 10<br>6 5̶,0̶0̶0̶<br>− 6 1,1 8 5<br>5 | 4 9 9 10<br>6 5̶,0̶0̶0̶<br>− 6 1,1 8 5<br>1 5 | 4 9 9 10<br>6 5̶,0̶0̶0̶<br>− 6 1,1 8 5<br>8 1 5 | 4 9 9 10<br>6 5̶,0̶0̶0̶<br>− 6 1,1 8 5<br>3,8 1 5 |

The Dallas stadium holds 3,815 more fans than the San Francisco stadium.

## Other Examples

| 4 9 10<br>5̶0̶0̶<br>− 2 6 6<br>2 3 4 | 6 10<br>7̶0̶5<br>− 5 6 1<br>1 4 4 | 4 9 18 12<br>5̶,0̶9̶2̶<br>− 4,7 9 5<br>2 9 7 | 4 9 9 12<br>5̶,0̶0̶2̶<br>− 2,3 7 4<br>2,6 2 8 | 7 9 9 9 10<br>8̶0̶,0̶0̶0̶<br>− 2 9,8 6 1<br>5 0,1 3 9 |
|---|---|---|---|---|

**TRY IT OUT**

Subtract. Check by adding.

1.   600
  − 264

2.   904
  − 642

3.   8,071
  − 3,653

4.   9,001
  − 4,543

5.   60,000
  − 26,437

# Multiplying by a 1-Digit Factor

One golf ball has 336 dimples. What would be the total number of dimples on 5 golf balls?

Since we want to find the total for 5 equal amounts, we multiply.

| Multiply the ones. Trade if necessary. | Multiply the tens. Add any extra tens. Trade if necessary. | Multiply the hundreds. Add any extra hundreds. |
|---|---|---|
| 3<br>336<br>× 5<br>___<br>0 | 1 3<br>336<br>× 5<br>___<br>80 | 1 3<br>336<br>× 5<br>___<br>1,680 |

There are 1,680 dimples on 5 golf balls.

## Other Examples

$$\begin{array}{r} {\scriptstyle 2} \\ 94 \\ \times\ 6 \\ \hline 564 \end{array}$$
$$\begin{array}{r} {\scriptstyle 6\,6} \\ 189 \\ \times\ 7 \\ \hline 1,323 \end{array}$$
$$\begin{array}{r} {\scriptstyle 1} \\ 803 \\ \times\ 5 \\ \hline 4,015 \end{array}$$
$$\begin{array}{r} {\scriptstyle 1\ \ 1} \\ 8,726 \\ \times\ 2 \\ \hline 17,452 \end{array}$$

### TRY IT OUT

Multiply.

1. 28
× 3

2. 146
× 4

3. 407
× 6

4. 537
× 4

5. 75
× 9

# Multiplying by Multiples of 10 and 100

The loggers in Lake County are allowed to cut only 300 trees in each square mile. The area of the forest is 125 square miles. How many trees are the loggers allowed to cut down?

Since we want to find the total for a number of equal amounts, we multiply.

| Multiply by the ones. | Multiply by the tens. | Multiply by the hundreds. |
|---|---|---|
| 125<br>× 300<br>——<br>0 | 125<br>× 300<br>——<br>00 | 125<br>× 300<br>——<br>37,500 |

The loggers are allowed to cut down 37,500 trees.

## Other Examples

```
  1                1 3                1               2
 85              125              507             780             61
× 30            ×  60            × 200           × 300          × 700
─────           ─────           ───────         ───────        ──────
2,550           7,500           101,400         234,000        42,700
```

**TRY IT OUT**

Multiply.

1.   46      2.  143      3.   380      4.   970      5.   497
   × 60         ×  50        × 600         × 700         × 300

6.   35      7.  207      8.   170      9.   420     10.   760
   × 40         ×  60        × 500         × 400         × 800

# Multiplying by a 2-Digit Factor

The fifth grade class figures it will take about 47 pieces of tile for each square foot of the mosaic they plan to make. A mosaic that measures 16 square feet will take how many pieces?

Since we want to find the total of a number of equal amounts, we multiply.

| Multiply by the ones. | Multiply by the tens. | Add the products. |
|---|---|---|
| 47<br>× 16<br>282   6 × 47 | 47<br>× 16<br>282<br>470   10 × 47 | 47<br>× 16<br>282<br>470<br>752   16 × 47 |

The students will need about 752 pieces of tile to complete their mosaic.

## Other Examples

| 24 | 309 | 468 |
|---|---|---|
| × 53 | × 68 | × 23 |
| 72 | 2472 | 1404 |
| 1200 | 18540 | 9360 |
| 1,272 | 21,012 | 10,764 |

Multiply.

**1.**    69
       × 28

**2.**    92
       × 45

**3.**    67
       × 74

**4.**    26
       × 89

**5.**    67
       × 29

# Multiplying by a 3-Digit Factor

An average of 286 tourists visit Stonehenge in Wiltshire, England, each day. How many visit in a year? (Use 365 days in a year.)

To find the total for a number of equal amounts, we multiply.

| Multiply by the ones. | Multiply by the tens. | Multiply by the hundreds. | Add the products. |
|---|---|---|---|
| 286 <br> × 365 <br> 1430 <br> *5 × 286* | 286 <br> × 365 <br> 1430 <br> 17160 <br> *60 × 286* | 286 <br> × 365 <br> 1430 <br> 17160 <br> 85800 <br> *300 × 286* | 286 <br> × 365 <br> 1430 <br> 17160 <br> 85800 <br> 104,390 <br> *365 × 286* |

104,390 tourists visit Stonehenge in a year.

## Other Examples

$$
\begin{array}{r}
429 \\
\times\ 261 \\
\hline
429 \\
25740 \\
85800 \\
\hline
111,969
\end{array}
\qquad
\begin{array}{r}
327 \\
\times\ 650 \\
\hline
16350 \\
196200 \\
\hline
212,550
\end{array}
\qquad
\begin{array}{r}
258 \\
\times\ 600 \\
\hline
154,800
\end{array}
\qquad
\begin{array}{r}
628 \\
\times\ 543 \\
\hline
1884 \\
25120 \\
314000 \\
\hline
341,004
\end{array}
$$

Multiply.

1. 214 × 326
2. 138 × 248
3. 708 × 239
4. 285 × 500
5. 926 × 362

# Money: Making Change

Lisa works in the rental room of a roller skating rink. A customer rented skates for $3.09 and gave her a $5 bill. What change did Lisa give the customer?

Lisa starts with the cost of the skates and counts out enough coins and bills to bring the total to $5.00.

Count these coins and bills to see that the total amount of change given was $1.91. Then check by subtracting $3.09 from $5.00.

$$\begin{array}{r} {\scriptstyle 4\ 9\ 10} \\ \$\cancel{5}.\cancel{0}\cancel{0} \\ +\ 3.0\,9 \\ \hline \$1.9\,1 \end{array}$$

| Lisa says: | She gives the customer: | |
|---|---|---|
| "$3.09" | | |
| "$3.10" | penny |  |
| "$3.15" | nickel | |
| "$3.25" | dime | |
| "$3.50" | quarter | |
| "$4.00" | half dollar | |
| "$5.00" | dollar bill | |

**TRY IT OUT**

List in order each coin or bill you would count out as change. Use the fewest possible coins and bills.

**Example:** Cost $2.60. Customer paid with $5.00.
Answer: 5¢, 10¢, 25¢, $1, $1

1. Cost $0.77. Customer paid with $1.00.
2. Cost $0.49. Customer paid with $1.00.
3. Cost $3.24. Customer paid with $5.00.
4. Cost $4.45. Customer paid with $10.00.

# Math and Language Arts Data Bank

## Dewey Decimal Number Groups

| | |
|---|---|
| 000–099 | Encyclopedias, periodicals, journalism |
| 100–199 | Philosophy, psychology, logic |
| 200–299 | Religion |
| 300–399 | Social sciences |
| 400–499 | Language, grammar, dictionaries |
| 500–599 | Physical and life sciences, mathematics |
| 600–699 | Medicine, engineering, business, media |
| 700–799 | The arts |
| 800–899 | Novels, poetry, plays |
| 900–999 | Geography, history, biography |

## Egyptian Hieroglyphic Numerals

The Egyptians of long ago used pictures called hieroglyphics to represent numbers. They did not use place value, but simply added the value of each symbol to get the number. For example, ∩∩ ||| = 23.

| Stroke | Arch | Coiled Rope | Lotus Flower | Pointed Finger | Tadpole | Surprised Person |
|---|---|---|---|---|---|---|
| \| | ∩ | 𝓠 | ☽ | ⟋ | ⬯ | 大 |
| 1 | 10 | 100 | 1,000 | 10,000 | 100,000 | 1,000,000 |

## Braille Alphabet and Numerals

| a | b | c | d | e | f | g | h | i | j | k | l | m |
|---|---|---|---|---|---|---|---|---|---|---|---|---|

| n | o | p | q | r | s | t | u | v | w | x | y | z |
|---|---|---|---|---|---|---|---|---|---|---|---|---|

| 1 | 2 | 3 | 4 | 5 | 6 | 7 | 8 | 9 | 0 |
|---|---|---|---|---|---|---|---|---|---|

# Math and Language Arts Data Bank

## A Treasury of Great Poems
### (Recorded Readings)

| | Listening Time |
|---|---|
| (Side 1) | |
| 1. An Introduction: What is Poetry? | $3\frac{1}{4}$ min |
| 2. Paul Revere's Ride (Longfellow) | $6\frac{1}{4}$ min |
| 3. Gunga Din (Kipling) | $4\frac{1}{2}$ min |
| 4. The Highwayman (Noyes) | 7 min |
| (Side 2) | |
| 1. Lord Randal (Anon.) | $1\frac{1}{2}$ min |
| 2. Little Breeches (Hay) | $2\frac{1}{2}$ min |
| 3. Annabelle Lee (Poe) | 3 min |
| 4. I Never Saw a Moor (Dickinson) | 1 min |
| 5. The Eagle (Tennyson) | $1\frac{1}{4}$ min |
| 6. I Hear America Singing (Whitman) | 1 min |
| 7. Get Up and Bar the Door (Anon.) | 3 min |
| 8. The Fox and the Grapes (Untermeyer) | $1\frac{1}{4}$ min |
| 9. The Owl and the Pussycat (Lear) | $1\frac{3}{4}$ min |
| 10. The Last Leaf (Holmes) | $2\frac{1}{4}$ min |
| 11. Great Lines from Great Poems | $2\frac{1}{2}$ min |

## Comparison of Two Reading Series
### Types of Writing as Fractions of Total Content

Reading Series A

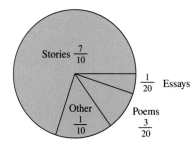

Reading Series B

# Math and Science Data Bank

## Household Electricity Use

| Appliance | Cost per Hour |
|---|---|
| Clothes dryer | $0.37 |
| Clothes washer | 0.03 |
| Color television | 0.04 |
| Hair dryer | 0.12 |
| Iron | 0.09 |
| Oven | 0.11 |
| Portable heater | 0.13 |
| Refrigerator | 0.02 |
| Toaster | 0.10 |

(based on average wattages and temperatures)

## Power Generated by Windmills

| Model | Wattage* |
|---|---|
| Elektro W50 | 50 watts |
| Wind Wizard | 600 watts |
| Wind Titan (10 ft) | 500 watts |
| Kedco 1205 | 1,900 watts |
| Dunlite 2000W | 2,000 watts |
| Eagle III | 3,000 watts |
| Merkham Machine (40 ft) | 45,000 watts |

*at optimum wind speed

# Math and Science Data Bank

### Circulatory System Facts

In a drop of blood there are about

- 5,400,000 red blood cells.

- 5,000 white blood cells.

- 340,000 platelets.

The average heartbeat is 72 beats per minute. At rest, the heart pumps about 4.7 L of blood per minute.

### Respiratory System Facts

The average person takes about 14 breaths per minute. Each breath takes in about 500 mL of air. After hard exercise, a person might take in as much as 118 L of air per minute.

# Math and Science Data Bank

## Does the Sand on a Beach Stand Still?

The action of the waves actually makes sand travel. Waves often strike a beach at an angle and create a longshore current. This current moves sand slowly along the shoreline. Each wave might move the grains of sand about ¼ inch. Scientists studying one beach found that on an average day, 14,000 waves struck the shore.

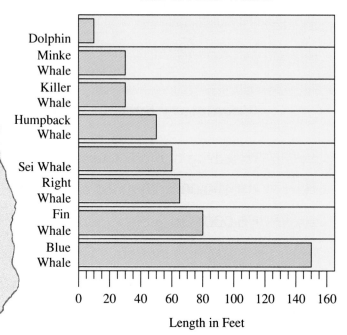

Size of Adult Whales

Length in Feet

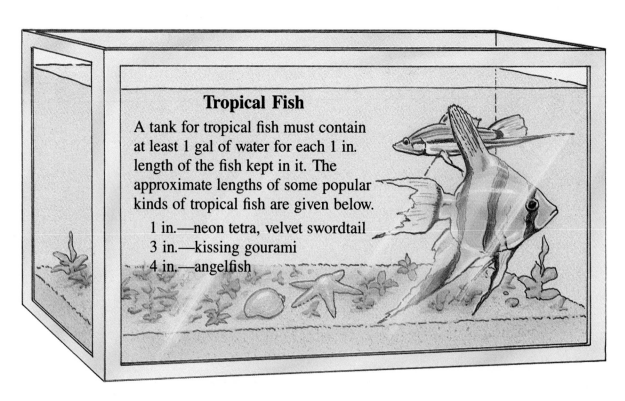

### Tropical Fish

A tank for tropical fish must contain at least 1 gal of water for each 1 in. length of the fish kept in it. The approximate lengths of some popular kinds of tropical fish are given below.

1 in.—neon tetra, velvet swordtail
3 in.—kissing gourami
4 in.—angelfish

# Math and Science Data Bank

## AMAZING CHANGES IN TEMPERATURE

**December 24, 1924, Fairfield, Montana**

The temperature fell 84° F in only 12 hours, from 63° F at noon to −21° F at midnight.

**January 22, 1943, Spearfish, South Dakota**

The temperature rose 49° F in only 2 minutes, from −4° F at 7:30 a.m. to 45° F at 7:32 a.m.

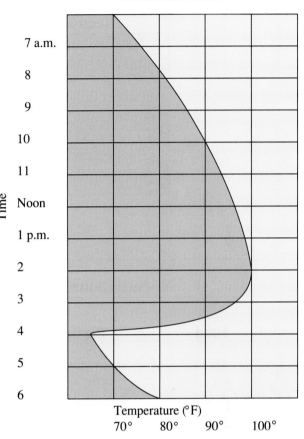

Temperatures on the Day of a Summer Storm

Time (vertical axis): 7 a.m., 8, 9, 10, 11, Noon, 1 p.m., 2, 3, 4, 5, 6

Temperature (°F): 70°  80°  90°  100°

## Days of Rain or Snow per Year

| City | Days having rain or snow | Percent of days with rain or snow |
| --- | --- | --- |
| Los Angeles, CA | 36 | 10% |
| San Antonio, TX | 81 | 22% |
| Tampa, FL | 107 | 29% |
| Chicago, IL | 127 | 35% |
| Buffalo, NY | 169 | 46% |
| Juneau, AK | 220 | 60% |

## Air Temperatures at High Altitudes

Air grows colder as the distance from sea level increases. For every 1,000 ft of altitude above sea level, the air temperature drops by 3° F. This is generally true for altitudes up to 40,000 feet.

# Math and Health and Fitness Data Bank

| Hours of Sleep per Day Needed by Average Humans | | |
|---|---|---|
| Age | Minimum hours | Maximum hours |
| newborn infant | 20 | 22 |
| 4 years | 10 | 14 |
| 10 years | 9 | 12 |
| 20–60 years | 7 | 9 |
| over 60 | 5 | 7 |

| Nutritional Values of Common Foods | | | | | | | | |
|---|---|---|---|---|---|---|---|---|
| | | | | | | Vitamins | | |
| Food | Portion | Calories | Protein (g) | Calcium (mg) | Iron (mg) | A (I.U.) | C (mg) | D (I.U.) |
| Apple, raw | 1 large | 117 | 0.6 | 12 | 0.6 | 180 | 9 | 0 |
| Banana, raw | 1 large | 176 | 2.4 | 16 | 1.2 | 860 | 20 | 0 |
| Beans, green, cooked | 1 cup | 27 | 1.8 | 45 | 0.9 | 830 | 18 | 0 |
| Beef, round, cooked | 1 serving | 214 | 24.7 | 10 | 3.1 | 0 | 0 | 0 |
| Broccoli, cooked | ⅔ cup | 29 | 3.3 | 130 | 1.3 | 3,400 | 74 | 0 |
| Butter | 1 tablespoon | 100 | 0.1 | 33 | 0.0 | 460 | 0 | 5 |
| Cabbage, cooked | ½ cup | 20 | 1.2 | 39 | 0.4 | 75 | 27 | 0 |
| Carrots, raw | 1 cup, shredded | 42 | 1.2 | 39 | 0.8 | 12,000 | 6 | 0 |
| Chicken, fried | ½ breast | 232 | 26.8 | 19 | 1.3 | 460 | 0 | 0 |
| Egg, boiled | 1 medium | 77 | 6.1 | 26 | 1.3 | 550 | 0 | 27 |
| Margarine, fortified | 1 tablespoon | 101 | 0.1 | 3 | 0.0 | 460 | 0 | 0 |
| Milk, whole, cow's | 1 glass | 124 | 6.4 | 216 | 0.2 | 293 | 2 | 4 |
| Orange, whole | 1 medium | 68 | 1.4 | 50 | 0.6 | 285 | 74 | 0 |
| Pork, shoulder, roasted | 2 slices | 320 | 19.2 | 9 | 2.0 | 0 | 0 | 0 |
| Tomatoes, raw | 1 large | 40 | 2.0 | 22 | 1.2 | 2,200 | 46 | 0 |
| Potatoes, white, baked | 1 medium | 98 | 2.4 | 13 | 0.8 | 20 | 17 | 0 |
| Rice, white, cooked | 1 cup | 201 | 4.2 | 13 | 0.5 | 0 | 0 | 0 |

g = grams; mg = milligrams; mcg = micrograms; I.U. = International Units; tr. = trace.

# Math and Health and Fitness Data Bank

| Olympic Gold Medal Winners Women's 800-Meter Run | | |
|---|---|---|
| 1928 | Lina Radke, Germany | 2 min 16.8 s |
| 1960 | Ljudmila Shevcova, USSR | 2 min 4.3 s |
| 1964 | Ann Packer, Great Britain | 2 min 1.1 s |
| 1968 | Madeline Manning, United States | 2 min 0.9 s |
| 1972 | Hildegard Falck, West Germany | 1 min 58.6 s |
| 1976 | Tatiana Kazankina, USSR | 1 min 54.94 s |
| 1980 | Nadezhda Olizarenko, USSR | 1 min 53.5 s |
| 1984 | Doina Melinte, Romania | 1 min 57.60 s |
| 1988 | Sigrun Wodars, East Germany | 1 min 56.10 s |

| Olympic Men's Pole Vault | Gold | Silver | Bronze |
|---|---|---|---|
| 1972 | Wolfgang Nordwig (GDR) 5.50m | Robert L. Seagren (USA) 5.40m | Jan E. Johnson (USA) 5.35m |
| 1976 | Tadeusz Slusarski (POL) 5.50m | Antti Kalliomaki (FIN) 5.50m | David Roberts (USA) 5.50m |
| 1980 | Wladyslaw Kozakiewicz (POL) 5.78m | Konstantin Volkov (URS) 5.65m | Tadeusz Slusarski (POL) 5.65m |
| 1984 | Pierre Quinon (FRA) 5.75m | Mike Tully (USA) 5.65m | Earl Bell (USA) 5.60m<br>Thierry Vigneron (FRA) 5.60m |
| 1988 | Sergey Bubka (USSR) 5.90m | Radion Gataoulline (USSR) 5.85m | Grigory Egorov (USSR) 5.80m |

# Math and Health and Fitness Data Bank

## Dimensions of Sports Playing Areas

| Sport | Length | Width |
|---|---|---|
| Table tennis surface | 9 ft | 5 ft |
| Boxing ring | 20 ft | 20 ft |
| Karate area | 26 ft | 26 ft |
| Tennis court (doubles) | 26 yd | 12 yd |
| Ice hockey rink | 200 ft | 100 ft |
| U.S. football field | 120 yd | 160 ft |
| Soccer field | 110 yd | 80 yd |

## Baseball Field Dimensions

All baseball fields have square areas called "diamonds" measuring 90 ft by 90 ft. The dimensions shown here are distances from home plate to outfield walls.

| Stadium | Left | Left-center | Center | Right-center | Right |
|---|---|---|---|---|---|
| Astrodome (Houston) | 330 | 375 | 400 | 375 | 330 |
| Candlestick (San Francisco) | 335 | 365 | 410 | 375 | 335 |
| Fenway (Boston) | 305 | 388 | 423 | 380 | 302 |
| Fulton Co. (Atlanta) | 330 | 375 | 400 | 375 | 330 |
| Jack Murphy (San Diego) | 380 | 370 | 420 | 370 | 380 |
| Memorial (Baltimore) | 309 | 378 | 405 | 378 | 309 |
| Royals (Kansas City, MO) | 330 | 385 | 410 | 385 | 330 |

## Outline of a Basketball Court

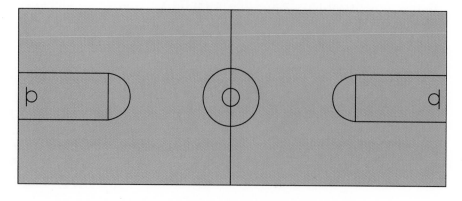

# Math and Fine Arts Data Bank

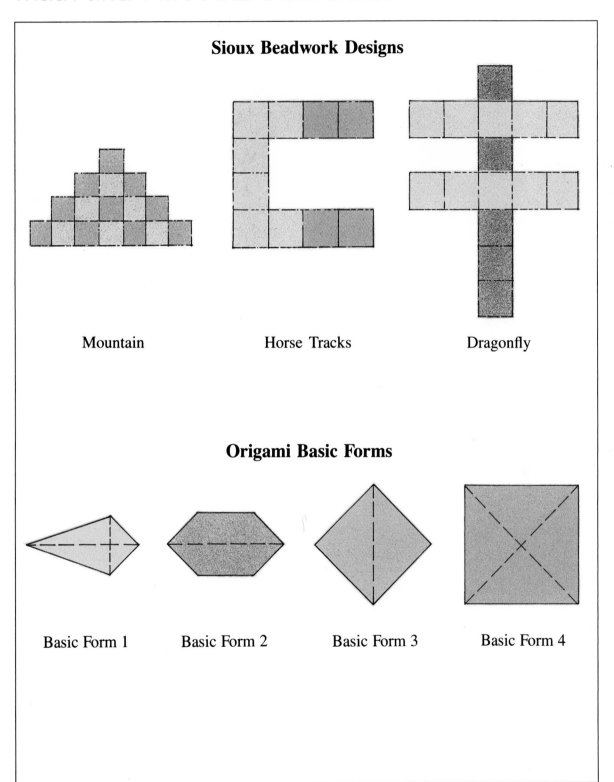

## Sioux Beadwork Designs

Mountain     Horse Tracks     Dragonfly

## Origami Basic Forms

Basic Form 1    Basic Form 2    Basic Form 3    Basic Form 4

# Math and Fine Arts Data Bank

**Seating Plan for a Typical Orchestra**

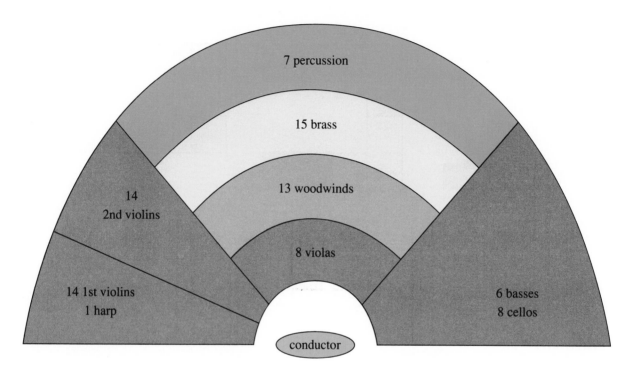

7 percussion

15 brass

13 woodwinds

14 2nd violins

8 violas

14 1st violins
1 harp

6 basses
8 cellos

conductor

Total instruments: 86

| Instrument Families | |
|---|---|
| Strings | |
| Woodwinds | |
| Brass | |
| Percussion | |

# Math and Fine Arts Data Bank

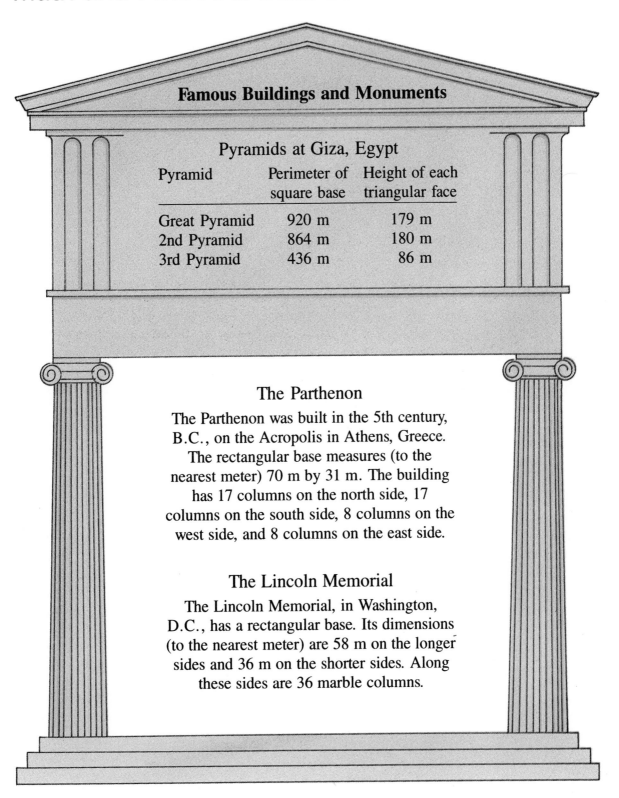

## Famous Buildings and Monuments

### Pyramids at Giza, Egypt

| Pyramid | Perimeter of square base | Height of each triangular face |
|---------|--------------------------|-------------------------------|
| Great Pyramid | 920 m | 179 m |
| 2nd Pyramid | 864 m | 180 m |
| 3rd Pyramid | 436 m | 86 m |

### The Parthenon

The Parthenon was built in the 5th century, B.C., on the Acropolis in Athens, Greece. The rectangular base measures (to the nearest meter) 70 m by 31 m. The building has 17 columns on the north side, 17 columns on the south side, 8 columns on the west side, and 8 columns on the east side.

### The Lincoln Memorial

The Lincoln Memorial, in Washington, D.C., has a rectangular base. Its dimensions (to the nearest meter) are 58 m on the longer sides and 36 m on the shorter sides. Along these sides are 36 marble columns.

# DATA BANK

# Math and Social Studies Data Bank

## Facts About the Original 13 States

| Original 13 States | Date of Entry into Union | Population 1780 | Population 1980 | Area in Square Miles (mi$^2$) | Population per Square Mile (1980) |
|---|---|---|---|---|---|
| Connecticut | Jan. 1788 | 207,000 | 3,153,000 | 5,009 | 629.47 |
| Delaware | Dec. 1787 | 45,000 | 602,000 | 2,057 | 292.66 |
| Georgia | Jan. 1788 | 56,000 | 5,639,000 | 58,876 | 95.78 |
| Maryland | Apr. 1788 | 246,000 | 4,265,000 | 10,577 | 403.23 |
| Massachusetts | Feb. 1788 | 269,000 | 5,781,000 | 8,257 | 700.13 |
| New Hampshire | June 1788 | 88,000 | 951,000 | 9,304 | 102.21 |
| New Jersey | Dec. 1787 | 140,000 | 7,438,000 | 7,836 | 949.21 |
| New York | July 1788 | 211,000 | 17,659,000 | 49,576 | 356.20 |
| North Carolina | Nov. 1789 | 270,000 | 6,019,000 | 52,586 | 114.46 |
| Pennsylvania | Dec. 1787 | 327,000 | 11,865,000 | 45,333 | 261.73 |
| Rhode Island | May 1790 | 53,000 | 958,000 | 1,214 | 789.13 |
| South Carolina | May 1788 | 180,000 | 2,203,000 | 31,055 | 70.94 |
| Virginia | June 1788 | 538,000 | 5,491,000 | 40,817 | 134.53 |

## Centuries and Decades

There are 100 years in a century.

| 16th Century | 17th Century | 18th Century | 19th Century | 20th Century |
|---|---|---|---|---|
| 1501–1600 | 1601–1700 | 1701–1800 | 1801–1900 | 1901–2000 |

There are 10 decades in a century.

20th Century

1900s  1910s  1920s  1930s  1940s  1950s  1960s  1970s  1980s  1990s

There are 10 years in a decade.

1990s

1991  1992  1993  1994  1995  1996  1997  1998  1999  2000

480

# Math and Social Studies Data Bank

## Inventions Timeline

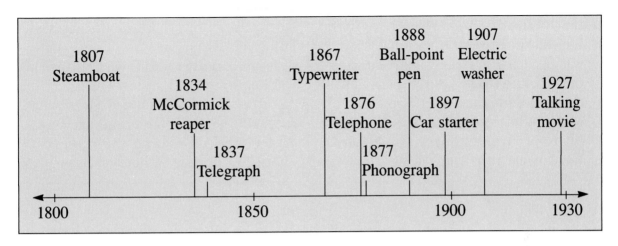

1807 Steamboat

1834 McCormick reaper

1837 Telegraph

1867 Typewriter

1876 Telephone

1877 Phonograph

1888 Ball-point pen

1897 Car starter

1907 Electric washer

1927 Talking movie

1800          1850          1900     1930

## Patents on Inventions, 1836–1840

| Year | Number of Patents Requested | Number of Patents Given |
|------|------|------|
| 1840 | 765 | 458 |
| 1839 | 800 | 404 |
| 1838 | 900 | 514 |
| 1837 | 650 | 426 |
| 1836 | 400 | 103 |

## Presidents of the U.S.

| Name | Year Inaugurated | Age When Inaugurated |
|------|------|------|
| George Washington | 1789 | 57 |
| John Adams | 1797 | 61 |
| Thomas Jefferson | 1801 | 57 |
| James Madison | 1809 | 57 |
| James Monroe | 1817 | 58 |
| John Quincy Adams | 1825 | 57 |
| Andrew Jackson | 1829 | 61 |
| Martin Van Buren | 1837 | 54 |
| William Henry Harrison | 1841 | 68 |

# Math and Social Studies Data Bank

### The National Road

One of the first good roads built in the United States was the National Road. It was made of stones broken into small pieces. The road was made highest in the middle so that water would run off to the sides. At the sides were gutters made of larger stones. The National Road was 130 miles long. It went from Cumberland, Maryland, on the Potomac River, to Wheeling, West Virginia, on the Ohio River. The work was begun in 1811 and was finished in 1818. Workers cleared a path for the road 66 feet wide. The road itself was 20 feet wide. Building the road cost about $13,000 per mile.

## Railroad and Highway Travel Speeds

Speeds on Railroads

Miles per Hour

1840, train   1870, train   1900, train   1930, train   1960, train   1990, train

Year, Vehicle

Speeds on Roads/Highways

Miles per Hour

1840, stage-coach   1870, stage-coach   1900, car   1930, car   1960, car   1990, car

Year, Vehicle

# Math and Social Studies Data Bank

## Games Played by American Indians

### Hidden-Bean Game (Papagos)

Use 4 hollow reeds. Hide a bean in one of them. The other players try to guess which reed the bean is hidden in.

### Which Hand?

About 100 different tribes played this game. Use two objects made of wood or bone. One of them is decorated. A player hides the objects, one in each hand. The other players try to guess which hand the decorated object is in.

### Stick Game 1 (Hurons)

Have an odd number of sticks in a pile. One player uses a dividing pole to separate out a group of sticks, which he keeps. The other player keeps the other sticks. They count the sticks. The player with the odd number of sticks wins.

### Stick Game 2 (Havasupais)

Play with 3 flat sticks. Each stick has a white side and a red side. Toss the sticks in the air and see how they land. Score like this:

| Outcome | Score |
| --- | --- |
| 3 white | 10 points |
| 2 white, 1 red | 2 points |
| 2 red, 1 white | 3 points |
| 3 red | 5 points |

# Basic Operations

To do arithmetic operations on your calculator, enter the key code just the way you say the problem. If you make an error, press CE/C to clear the last entry. Pressing CE/C CE/C clears the display and operation. Pressing ON/AC clears the memory as well as the display and the operation.

| Problem | Enter | Display |
|---|---|---|
| Seventy and one tenth minus thirteen | 70.1 − 13 = | 57.1 |
| Eight thousand two times fifteen | 8002 × 15 = | 120030 |
| Twelve million divided by four tenths | 12000000 ÷ .4 = | 30000000 |
| Two ten-thousandths divided by fifty thousand | .002 ÷ 50000 = | Error U |
| Nine hundred and four tenths divided by zero | 900.4 ÷ 0 = | Error A |

The last two problems create **Error** displays. When a number is too small, many calculators will show an **Underflow Error**. Division by zero is not allowed. It gives a **Logic,** or **Arithmetic, Error**.

The largest number most calculators can display is 99999999. What happens when you add one to this number? Enter 99999999 + 1 =. If the number is too large, many calculators show an **Overflow Error**.

With most calculators, the result of dividing 82 by 5 is 16.4. On the Math Explorer calculator, you can use the INT÷ key to find the quotient and remainder.

| Enter | Display | |
|---|---|---|
| 82 INT÷ 5 = | 16 | 2 |
| | Q | R |

## Activity

Find two numbers in the box with:

**1.** a sum of 892.04
**2.** a difference of 0.0488
**3.** a quotient of 17 R 450
**4.** a quotient too small for the display
**5.** a product too large for the display

| | | |
|---|---|---|
| 0.8 | 9800 | 550 |
| 70000 | 0.0012 | |
| 342.04 | 0.05 | |

# Counting and Counting Patterns

Make your calculator count by threes. Try these key codes.

[ON/AC] [+] 3 [Cons] [Cons] [Cons] [Cons] [Cons] . . .
[ON/AC] [+] 3 [=] [=] [=] [=] [=] . . .

Entering [+] 3 [Cons] or [+] 3 sets up a **constant,** a number that stays the same. Each time you press [Cons] or [=], the calculator adds 3 to the number in the display.

Use your calculator to count by 1.5. Start at 20. Your display should show 21.5, 23, 24.5, 26, 27.5, and so on.

Now **count backward** by 1.5, starting from 30. Your display should show 28.5, 27, 25.5, 24, and so on.

Use the **multiplication constant** to multiply 4, 5.5, and 9 by 5.

Enter [ON/AC] [×] 5 [Cons] 4 [Cons] 5.5 [Cons] 9 [Cons]
or     [ON/AC] 4 [×] 5 [=] 5.5 [=] 9 [=]

Your display should show 20, 27.5, and 45.

Use the **division constant** to divide 16, 64, and 88.8 by 8.

Enter [ON/AC] [÷] 8 [Cons] 16 [Cons] 64 [Cons] 88.8 [Cons]
or     [ON/AC] 16 [÷] 8 [=] 64 [=] 88.8 [=]

Your display should show 2, 8, and 11.1.

## Activity

Use your calculator to find the first 5 numbers in each pattern. Find the next two numbers mentally. Check with your calculator.

**1.** Start at 11011.
Count by 1001.

**2.** Start at 88888
Count back by 1001.

**3.** 234 × 1001
345 × 1001
456 × 1001
567 × 1001
678 × 1001
789 × 1001
890 × 1001

**4.** 20000 ÷ 1001
30000 ÷ 1001
40000 ÷ 1001
50000 ÷ 1001
60000 ÷ 1001
70000 ÷ 1001
80000 ÷ 1001

# Order of Operations: Memory Keys

To solve a problem involving more than one operation, perform operations within parentheses first. Next multiply and divide from left to right. Then add and subtract from left to right.

For 75 ÷ 15 + 3 × 21, first find 75 ÷ 15, then 3 × 21. Then add.

| | |
|---|---|
| ON/AC 75 ÷ 15 = | 5 |
| ON/AC 3 × 21 = | 63 |
| ON/AC 5 + 63 = | 68 |

You can use the **memory keys** on your calculator to make the calculator remember the result of one calculation while it does another calculation.

| | |
|---|---|
| M+ | Adds the display to the calculator's memory |
| M− | Subtracts the display from the calculator's memory |
| MR | Recalls the total in memory |

Find 5 × (12 − 6) − 3 × 8.

| | Enter | Display |
|---|---|---|
| ON/AC 12 − 6 = × 5 = M+ | | 30 |
| 3 × 8 = M− | | 24 |
| MR | | 6 |

The Math Explorer calculator follows order of operations. You can enter the problem just as it is written. To do the problem above, enter:

ON/AC 5 × (( 12 − 6 )) − 3 × 8 =

## Activity

Arrange the numbers and signs to make a true equation.

**1.** 4, 7, 9, 67, +, ×, =

**2.** 1, 4, 9, 45, −, ÷, =

**3.** 2, 3, 6, 10, 12, +, ×, ÷, ( ), =

**4.** 5, 6, 9, 10, 12, −, ×, ÷, ( ), =

# Fractions and Decimals

To find the decimal equivalent of a fraction, you can use your calculator to divide the numerator by the denominator. To find the decimal for $\frac{2}{5}$ enter ON/AC 2 ÷ 5 =. The display shows 0.4.

Find the decimal for $\frac{5}{8}$, $\frac{9}{4}$, and $\frac{2}{3}$.

The F⇄D key on the Math Explorer calculator changes a fraction to a decimal or a decimal to a fraction (if the decimal has 3 or fewer places). To change $\frac{19}{20}$ to the decimal 0.95, enter ON/AC 19 / 20 F⇄D.

Find the decimal for $\frac{7}{8}$, $\frac{13}{5}$, and $\frac{1}{6}$ using the F⇄D and / keys. (0.875, 2.6, and 0.1666667)

Now find the decimal for $\frac{12}{25}$.

| Enter | Display |
|---|---|
| ON/AC 12 / 25 F⇄D | 0.48 |
| Press F⇄D again. | 48/100 |

Pressing F⇄D the second time changes the decimal 0.48 back to a fraction. The N/D → n/d in the display means that the fraction is not in simplest form (lowest terms). To simplify the fraction, enter Simp = until N/D → n/d disappears from the display.

| | |
|---|---|
| Simp = | 24/50 |
| Simp = | 12/25 |

Find the simplest fraction for 1.45.

| Enter | Display |
|---|---|
| 1.45 F⇄D | 1 u 45/100 |
| Simp 5 = | 1 u 9/20 |

1 is the whole number or **unit** part of the mixed number.

## Activity

Write as many different fractions as you can from the numbers 12, 7, 5, and 1. Give the decimal equivalent of each fraction.

# Adding and Subtracting Fractions

To add or subtract fractions using a calculator, change them to decimals. Write down the decimal for each fraction or use memory keys.

Add $\frac{4}{5} + \frac{3}{4}$.

| Enter | Display |
|---|---|
| $\boxed{\text{ON/AC}}$ 4 $\boxed{\div}$ 5 $\boxed{=}$ | 0.8 |
| $\boxed{\text{ON/AC}}$ 3 $\boxed{\div}$ 4 $\boxed{=}$ | 0.75 |
| $\boxed{\text{ON/AC}}$ .8 $\boxed{+}$ .75 $\boxed{=}$ | 1.55 |

To add or subtract mixed numbers, first change the mixed number to an improper fraction. For example, $2\frac{1}{4} - 1\frac{5}{8} = \frac{9}{4} - \frac{13}{8}$.

$\boxed{\text{ON/AC}}$ 9 $\boxed{\div}$ 4 $\boxed{=}$ $\boxed{\text{M+}}$ 13 $\boxed{\div}$ 8 $\boxed{=}$ $\boxed{\text{M-}}$ $\boxed{\text{MR}}$

Display
0.625

To add or subtract fractions on the Math Explorer, enter the key code just the way you write the problem. Use the $\boxed{\text{Unit}}$ key to enter the whole number part of a mixed number.

| Problem | Key Code | Display |
|---|---|---|
| $\frac{11}{10} - \frac{1}{2}$ | 11 $\boxed{/}$ 10 $\boxed{-}$ 1 $\boxed{/}$ 2 $\boxed{=}$ <br> $\boxed{\text{Simp}}$ $\boxed{=}$ | 6/10 <br> 3/5 |
| $2\frac{1}{2} + 1\frac{3}{8}$ | 2 $\boxed{\text{Unit}}$ 1 $\boxed{/}$ 2 $\boxed{+}$ 1 $\boxed{\text{Unit}}$ 3 $\boxed{/}$ 8 $\boxed{=}$ | 3 u 7/8 |
| $\frac{7}{9} + \frac{2}{3}$ | 7 $\boxed{/}$ 9 $\boxed{+}$ 2 $\boxed{/}$ 3 $\boxed{=}$ <br> $\boxed{\text{Ab/c}}$ | 13/9 <br> 1 u 4/9 |
| $2\frac{3}{4} + \frac{1}{2}$ | 2 $\boxed{\text{Unit}}$ 3 $\boxed{/}$ 4 $\boxed{+}$ 1 $\boxed{/}$ 2 $\boxed{=}$ <br> $\boxed{\text{Ab/c}}$ | 2 u 5/4 <br> 3 u 1/4 |

Note that the $\boxed{\text{Ab/c}}$ key changes improper fractions to mixed numbers.

## Activity

Use these numbers: 1, 2, 3, 4, 5, 8, and 9. Make true equations.

1. $\frac{\text{||||}}{\text{||||}} + \frac{\text{||||}}{\text{||||}} = \frac{8}{9}$

2. $\text{||||}\frac{\text{||||}}{\text{||||}} + \text{||||}\frac{\text{||||}}{\text{||||}} = 6\frac{3}{10}$

3. $\frac{\text{||||}}{\text{||||}} - \frac{\text{||||}}{\text{||||}} = \frac{1}{8}$

4. $\text{||||}\frac{\text{||||}}{\text{||||}} - \text{||||}\frac{\text{||||}}{\text{||||}} = 2\frac{1}{8}$

# Multiplying and Dividing Fractions

You can multiply or divide fractions by multiplying or dividing their decimal equivalents. Multiply $\frac{5}{8} \times \frac{3}{4}$.

|  |  | Display |
|---|---|---|
| Enter | ON/AC 5 ÷ 8 × 3 ÷ 4 = | 0.46875 |
| or | ON/AC 5 ÷ 8 = M+ 3 ÷ 4 × MR = | 0.46875 |

Divide $\frac{15}{16}$ by $\frac{3}{4}$. Find the decimal for the divisor first.

| | Display |
|---|---|
| ON/AC 3 ÷ 4 = M+ | 0.75 |
| 15 ÷ 16 = | 0.9375 |
| ÷ MR = | 1.25 |

To multiply or divide mixed numbers, first change the mixed number to an improper fraction. For instance, $2\frac{1}{2} \times 3\frac{1}{4}$, $= \frac{5}{2} \times \frac{13}{4}$.

| | Display |
|---|---|
| ON/AC 5 ÷ 2 = M+ 13 ÷ 4 × MR = | 8.125 |

With the Math Explorer calculator, you can enter multiplication and division problems just the way they are written. Try these.

| Problem | Key Code | Display |
|---|---|---|
| $\frac{7}{9} \times \frac{3}{5}$ | 7 / 9 × 3 / 5 = Simp = | 7/15 |
| $1\frac{5}{6} \times 3\frac{2}{3}$ | 1 Unit 5 / 6 × 3 Unit 2 / 3 =  Ab/c | 121/18  6 u 13/18 |
| $\frac{3}{4} \div \frac{3}{10}$ | 3 / 4 ÷ 3 / 10 =  Ab/c | 30/12  2 u 6/12 |
| | Simp 6 = | 2 u 1/2 |

## Activity

Put these numbers in the boxes to make a true equation: 2, 3, 4, 5, 6, 8, 9, and 10.

$$\frac{\text{IIII}}{\text{IIII}} \times \frac{\text{IIII}}{\text{IIII}} = \frac{\text{IIII}}{\text{IIII}} \div \frac{\text{IIII}}{\text{IIII}}$$

# Percent

The percent key $\boxed{\%}$ converts the number in the display to a decimal by dividing it by 100 (or by multiplying it by 0.01).

Enter $\boxed{\text{ON/AC}}$ 63 $\boxed{\%}$. The display will show 0.63.

Find the decimal for each percent: 83%, 99%, 1%, and 192%. Your calculator should display 0.83, 0.99, 0.01, and 1.92.

On the Math Explorer calculator, you can find the fraction for a percent. Try this.

|  | Display |
|---|---|
| $\boxed{\text{ON/AC}}$ 85 $\boxed{\%}$ $\boxed{\text{F⇄D}}$ | 85/100 |
| $\boxed{\text{Simp}}$ $\boxed{=}$ | 17/20 |

Find the fractions for 20%, 5%, 150%, and .5%. Your calculator should display 1/5, 1/20, 1 u 1/2, and 1/200.

Multiply to find the percent of a number. For example, to find 15% of 175:

$\boxed{\text{ON/AC}}$ 175 $\boxed{\times}$ 15 $\boxed{\%}$ $\boxed{=}$     26.25

Find 190% of 310. Your display should show 589.

Find 6% of $12.90. Your display should show 0.774.

## Activity

This circle graph shows the computer use at Brown's Feed Company.

If the graph is based on a study of 3,600 hours of computer use, how many hours is the computer used for each job?

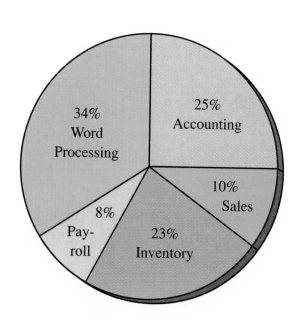

34% Word Processing
25% Accounting
10% Sales
23% Inventory
8% Payroll

# Squares and Square Roots

To square a number, that is, to multiply a number by itself, use the $\boxed{\times^2}$ key on your calculator. To find the area of a square 7 units on each side, find $7^2$.

|  | Display |
|---|---|
| $\boxed{\text{ON/AC}}$ 7 $\boxed{\times}$ 7 $\boxed{=}$ | 49 |
| or  $\boxed{\text{ON/AC}}$ 7 $\boxed{\times^2}$ | 49 |

Find $8^2$, $120^2$, and $2.2^2$. Your display should show 64, 14400, and 4.84.

Use the $\boxed{\sqrt{}}$ key on your calculator to find the square root of a number. The square root is a number that can be multiplied by itself to equal the number in the display. The $\boxed{\sqrt{}}$ key "undoes" the work of the $\boxed{\times^2}$ key. To find the length of the side of a square if its area is 49, find the square root of 49, which is written $\sqrt{49}$.

|  | Display |
|---|---|
| $\boxed{\text{ON/AC}}$ 49 $\boxed{\sqrt{}}$ | 7 |

Find the square root of 81, 14400, and 4.84. Your display should show 9, 120, and 2.2.

## Activity

Find the missing length or area in each figure below.

**1.**  l = 10   A = ?

**2.**  l = ?   A = 169

**3.**  l = 5.5   A = ?

**4.**  l = ?   A = 22,500

**5.**  l = 72   A = ?

**6.**  l = ?   A = 6,561

# Front-End Estimation

Vicki kept a record of how many
miles she rode her bicycle each week.
She wanted to estimate the total
distance she had ridden in 6 weeks.
She decided to use front-end
estimation to get a good estimate of
the sum.

**Bicycle Distances**

| | |
|---|---|
| Week 1 | 59 |
| Week 2 | 83 |
| Week 3 | 91 |
| Week 4 | 87 |
| Week 5 | 88 |
| Week 6 | 55 |

How far do you think she rode?

The computer program below will
give you practice in estimating sums
using the front-end method. You can
often make a better estimate with this
method than you can by rounding the
numbers.

```
10   PRINT"FRONT-END ESTIMATION":GOSUB 200
20   PRINT:INPUT"HOW MANY NUMBERS TO ADD?";N: DIM X(N)
30   S = 0:FOR I = 1 TO N:X(I) = INT (90*RND(1) + 10)
40   S = S+ X(I):NEXT I
50   PRINT"HERE IS YOUR ADDITION PROBLEM.":PRINT
60   FOR I = 1 TO N − 1
70   PRINT TAB(2)X(I):PRINT:NEXT I
80   PRINT"+";X(N)
90   PRINT"____"
100  PRINT:PRINT "WHAT IS THE ESTIMATED SUM OF THE TENS":INPUT
        "DIGITS?";T
110  PRINT"ABOUT HOW MANY MORE TENS DO YOU":INPUT"ESTIMATE FROM
        THE ONES SUM?";O
120  PRINT:PRINT"YOUR ESTIMATE IS";10*(T + O)
130  PRINT"THE EXACT SUM IS";S
140  PRINT:INPUT"WANT TO TRY ANOTHER PROBLEM?";Y$
150  IF LEFT$(Y$,1) = "Y" THEN GOTO 30
160  END
200  PRINT"USE THE FRONT-END METHOD TO ESTIMATE":PRINT "THE
        FOLLOWING SUMS. YOU CAN OFTEN MAKE"
210  PRINT"A BETTER ESTIMATE WITH THIS METHOD THAN":PRINT"YOU CAN
        BY ROUNDING THE NUMBERS."
220  RETURN
```

# Estimating Products

Manny wants to plant a small patch
of tomatoes. He has space for 23
rows and plans to put 38 plants in
each row. How many tomato plants
will he need?

Since there will be the same number of plants in
each row, you can find the total by multiplying.
First, try to estimate the number of plants. Then
find the exact number.

The computer program below will give you practice
in estimation skills in multiplication. It will also tell
you how close your estimate is to the exact product.

```
10   PRINT:PRINT:PRINT"ESTIMATING PRODUCTS"
20   F1 = INT (90*RND(1) + 1):F2 = INT (90* RND (1) + 1)
30   P = F1*F2
40   PRINT"ESTIMATE THIS PRODUCT."
50   PRINT:PRINT TAB(15 - LEN(STR$(F1)))F1:PRINT
60   PRINT TAB(12)"x";TAB(15 - LEN(STR$(F2)))F2
70   PRINT TAB(12)"____"
80   PRINT:INPUT"ESTIMATE =";P1
90   PRINT:PRINT"THE EXACT PRODUCT IS ";P
100 D = ABS (P - P1): IF D < 10 THEN GOTO 120
110 PRINT"YOUR ESTIMATE IS OFF BY";D:GOTO 130
120 PRINT P1;"IS A VERY GOOD ESTIMATE."
130 PRINT:INPUT"DO YOU WANT TO TRY ANOTHER PROBLEM?";Y$
140 IF LEFT$(Y$,1) = "Y" THEN GOTO 10
150 END
```

# Perimeter Problems

Mr. Johnson had 32 m of fencing. He wanted to use all of it to put a fence around a rectangular garden. He decided to make the length of the garden 3 times as long as the width.

Can you help Mr. Johnson find out how long and how wide his garden must be?

What strategies would you use to try to solve the problem above? Would you Draw a Picture? Would you use Guess and Check? The computer program below will help you develop your problem solving skills.

```
10   PRINT:PRINT:PRINT"PERIMETER PROBLEMS"
20   W = INT (10*RND(1) + 1):T = INT (5*RND (1) + 1):L = T*W
30   P = 2*(L + W)
40   PRINT"THE PERIMETER OF A RECTANGLE IS";P
50   PRINT"UNITS. THE LENGTH IS ";T;" TIMES THE":PRINT"WIDTH."
60   PRINT:INPUT "WHAT IS THE LENGTH?";L1
70   INPUT "WHAT IS THE WIDTH?";W1:PRINT
80   PRINT "THE PERIMETER IS 2 X";L1;" + 2X";W1;" = ";2*(L1 + W1);".":PRINT
       T;" TIMES THE WIDTH GIVES A LENGTH OF";T*W1;"."
90   IF L1 = T*W1 AND 2*(L1 + W1) = P THEN PRINT "CORRECT.":GOTO 130
100  PRINT "NOT CORRECT"
110  PRINT:INPUT"DO YOU WANT TO TRY AGAIN?";Y$
120  IF LEFT$(Y$,1) = "Y" THEN PRINT:GOTO 40
130  INPUT"DO YOU WANT TO TRY ANOTHER PROBLEM?";Y$
140  IF LEFT$(Y$,1) = "Y" THEN GOTO 10
150  END
```

# Finding Total Amounts

Kwang had $10 to spend at the electronics store. He wanted to buy as much as he could. There was a sales tax of 6 cents on each dollar to be added on. How close can Kwang come to spending his $10 if he chooses from the items shown here? Is $10 enough to buy all of the items?

| | |
|---|---|
| Videotape | $3.39 |
| Audiotape | 1.89 |
| Electrical outlet | 4.25 |
| AAA batteries | 0.89 |

Use the computer program below to help develop your addition estimation skills.

```
10  PRINT:PRINT:PRINT"FINDING TOTAL AMOUNTS":T = 0:1 = 0
20  A = INT(1000*RND(1) + 1)/100:B = INT(1000* RND(1) + 1)/100:IF ((A > = 1)
    AND (LEN(STR$(A)) < 4)) OR ((B > = 1) AND (LEN(STR$(B)) < 4)) THEN
    GOTO 20
30  C = INT(1000*RND(1) + 1)/100:D = INT(1000*RND(1)+ 1)/100:IF((C > = 1)
    AND (LEN(STR$(C)) < 4)) OR ((D > = 1) AND (LEN(STR$(D)) < 4)) THEN
    GOTO 30
40  PRINT"CHOOSE AS MANY OF THE FOLLOWING":PRINT"AMOUNTS AS YOU
    CAN TO FIND A TOTAL"
50  PRINT"UNDER $10.A 6% SALES TAX IS ADDED."
60  PRINT:PRINT"$"; TAB(6 - LEN(STR$(A)))A:PRINT"$"; TAB(6 -
    LEN(STR$(B)))B:PRINT"$"; TAB(6 - LEN(STR$(C)))C:PRINT"$";TAB(6 -
    LEN(STR$(D)))D
70  I = I + 1
80  PRINT:PRINT"TYPE AN AMOUNT WITHOUT THE DOLLAR":INPUT"SIGN.";X(I)
90  T = T + X(I)
100 PRINT:INPUT"WANT ANOTHER CHOICE?TYPE Y OR N.";Y$
110 IF LEFT$(Y$,1) = "Y" THEN GOTO 70
120 PRINT:Z = INT(100*T*.06)/100
130 FOR N = 1 TO I:PRINT TAB(15)"$";TAB(20 - LEN(STR$(X(N))))X(N):PRINT:
    NEXT N
140 PRINT TAB(10)"TAX +";TAB(20 - LEN(STR$(Z)))Z:PRINT TAB(14)"____":PRINT
150 IF T + Z = 10 THEN PRINT TAB(8)"TOTAL $10.00":PRINT:PRINT"YOU HAVE
    ENOUGH MONEY.":GOTO 180
160 IF T + Z > 10 THEN PRINT TAB(8)"TOTAL $"T + Z:PRINT;PRINT "YOU DO
    NOT HAVE ENOUGH MONEY.":GOTO 180
170 PRINT TAB(8)"TOTAL $";TAB(20 - LEN(STR$(T + Z)))T + Z:PRINT:PRINT"YOU
    HAVE ENOUGH MONEY."
180 INPUT"DO YOU WANT ANOTHER PROBLEM?";Y$
190 IF LEFT$(Y$,1) = "Y" THEN GOTO 10
200 END
```

# Guess and Check

Milly thought of two numbers. She told Lalo the sum of the two numbers was 30 and the difference of the two numbers was 6. Lalo tried to use the strategy of Guess and Check to find the two numbers.

He thought: $20 + 10 = 30$, but $20 - 10 = 10$, so 20 and 10 did not check. The sum was correct but the difference was too large. Lalo thought he must be close to the two numbers so he must guess again and then check his guess.

What do you think Milly's two numbers were?

You can use the computer program below to practice using the Guess and Check strategy.

```
10  PRINT:PRINT:PRINT"GUESS AND CHECK STRATEGY"
20  A = INT(20*RND(1) + 1):B = INT(20* RND(1) +)
30  IF A < = B THEN GOTO 20
40  PRINT"THE SUM OF TWO NUMBERS IS "A + B". THE"
50  PRINT"DIFFERENCE OF THE TWO NUMBERS IS "A - B"."
60  PRINT"GUESS THE TWO NUMBERS.LIST THE":PRINT"LARGEST ONE
        FIRST."
70  PRINT:INPUT"FIRST NUMBER = ";F:INPUT"SECOND NUMBER = ";S
80  PRINT:PRINT"SUM = ";F + S,"DIFFERENCE = ";F - S
90  IF A = F AND B = S THEN GOTO 120
100 PRINT:PRINT"NOT CORRECT":INPUT"DO YOU WANT TO TRY AGAIN?";Y$:IF
        LEFT$(Y$,1) = "Y" THEN PRINT:PRINT:GOTO 40
110 GOTO 130
120 PRINT:PRINT"YOU HAVE FOUND THE TWO NUMBERS."
130 INPUT"DO YOU WANT ANOTHER PROBLEM?";Y$
140 IF LEFT$(Y$,1) = "Y" THEN GOTO 10
150 END
```

# Probability Experiment

Joseph and Tami were tossing a number cube with faces numbered 1 through 6. Joseph thought if they tossed the cube 1,000 times, one of the faces would come up many more times than another. Tami thought each face would come up about the same number of times.

What do you think will happen in 1,000 tosses of the number cube?

Computers can be programmed to simulate probability problems. The program below can be used to simulate a spinner with any number of equal sectors. It can simulate the number cube by choosing the outcome for a spinner with 6 equal-size sectors. To simulate a coin toss, choose a spinner with 2 same-size sectors. You can choose any number of trials for the spinner.

```
10   PRINT"PROBABILITY SPINNER":PRINT"THIS IS AN EXPERIMENT IN
        PROBABILITY.":PRINT"CHOOSE A SPINNER WITH ANY NUMBER
        OF":PRINT"EQUAL PARTS. CHOOSE ANY NUMBER OF":PRINT"SPINS.
        THE COMPUTER WILL QUICKLY GIVE":PRINT"THE OUTCOME."
20   PRINT:INPUT"HOW MANY SECTORS OF EQUAL SIZE?";X
30   DIM D(X)
40   FOR N = 1 TO X:D(N) = 0:NEXT N
50   INPUT"HOW MANY SPINS DO YOU WANT?";Y:PRINT
60   FOR I = 1 TO Y:R = INT (X*RND (1)) + 1
70   LET D(R) = D(R) +1: NEXT I
80   PRINT:"NUMBER","FREQUENCY"
90   FOR N = 1 TO X:PRINT N,D(N):NEXT N
100 END
```

# Computer Graphs

Lisa wanted to make a simple pictograph of the data in the table. She decided to use stars, (*), to represent the meters in the table. She had to decide how many meters each star would represent in the graph. At first she was going to use 1 star for every 4 m, but she found that this would take too many stars.

| Highest Points (meters) | |
|---|---|
| Illinois | 376 |
| Indiana | 383 |
| Michigan | 804 |
| Minnesota | 701 |
| Ohio | 472 |
| Wisconsin | 595 |

She decided to use 1 star for every 15 m. How many stars would she need for each state?

You can use the computer program below to make a pictograph of the data. You must decide how much each symbol represents. Try the program with some data from the Data Bank (pages 468–483).

```
10   PRINT:PRINT:PRINT"COMPUTER GRAPHING":PRINT"ENTER THE
        FOLLOWING INFORMATION AND THE":PRINT"COMPUTER WILL CREATE A
        GRAPH."
20   PRINT:INPUT"HOW MANY NUMBERS FOR THE GRAPH?";N
30   DIM N$(N):DIM X(N)
40   PRINT"FOR EACH ITEM, TYPE THE NAME AND THE":PRINT"NUMBER
        SEPARATED BY A COMMA."
50   FOR I = 1 TO N:INPUT N$(I),X(I):NEXT I
60   S = 1:FOR Q = 1 TO N:S1 = INT (X(Q)/23 + 1):IF S1 > S THEN S =S1
70   NEXT Q:INPUT "TYPE THE NAME OF THE GRAPH.";G$
80   PRINT:PRINT TAB(20)G$
90   PRINT"_____"
100  FOR I = 1 TO N:PRINT N$(I),
110  FOR J = 1 TO INT (X(I)/S + .5):PRINT"*";:NEXT J
120  PRINT:NEXT I
130  PRINT"_____":PRINT
140  PRINT:"EACH*=";S
150  END
```

# Estimating Length

Estimate the length of your desk top or table in centimeters. Then estimate the width of your desk top or table. Use a centimeter ruler to check your estimates. Were they within 5 to 10 cm of the actual measures?

It is important to develop good estimation skills. In the computer program below you can practice estimating the lengths of objects using different units.

```
10   U = INT (6*RND (1) +3)
20   S = INT (78*RND (1) +1)
30   IF S < U THEN 10
40   L = INT (S/U*10)/10
50   PRINT:PRINT:FOR N = 1 TO U:PRINT"-";:NEXT N:PRINT"1
       UNIT":PRINT:PRINT:FOR N = 1 TO S:PRINT"-";:NEXT N
60   PRINT"?UNITS":PRINT:PRINT:GOSUB 150:PRINT:INPUT"WHAT IS YOUR
       ESTIMATE?";E
70   PRINT"LENGTH","EST.","DIFF."
80   PRINT L,E,ABS (L-E)
90   INPUT"TRY AGAIN? (Y/N)";Y$
100 IF LEFT$(Y$,1) = "Y"THEN 10
120 END
130 PRINT"ESTIMATING LENGTH":PRINT"USE THE UNIT SEGMENT SHOWN TO
       ESTIMATE":PRINT"THE LENGTH OF THE GIVEN SEGMENT TO
       THE":PRINT"NEAREST UNIT."
140 RETURN
```

**Set A   For use after page 5.**

Write each numerical expression using symbols.

**1.** nine divided by three

**2.** six more than one

**3.** eleven less two

**4.** the sum of five and two

**5.** twelve minus seven

**6.** two times ten

Choose the correct symbols for the math words.
More than one choice may be correct.

**7.** fifteen multiplied by eight
   **A.** $\frac{15}{8}$   **B.** $8 \times 15$   **C.** $15 + 8$

**8.** twelve less three
   **A.** $12 < 3$   **B.** $3 - 12$   **C.** $12 - 3$

**9.** eleven more than seven
   **A.** $11 + 7$   **B.** $11 > 7$   **C.** $7 + 11$

**10.** sixteen divided by four
   **A.** $16 \div 4$   **B.** $\frac{16}{4}$   **C.** $\frac{4}{16}$

**Set B   For use after page 7.**

Find the value of each expression.

**1.** $(35 \div 5) + 4$

**2.** $(3 + 5) + 8$

**3.** $14 - (3 \times 3)$

**4.** $(11 - 8) \times 5$

**5.** $4 + (5 + 4)$

**6.** $15 - (27 \div 3)$

**7.** $(14 \div 2) + 5$

**8.** $9 - (3 + 6)$

**9.** $8 \times (4 + 1)$

**Set C   For use after page 9.**

Show how you would change the order and grouping.
Then solve using mental math.

**1.** $25 + 18 + 75$

**2.** $5 \times 13 \times 20$

**3.** $120 + 98 + 80 + 2$

**4.** $4 \times 35 \times 25$

**5.** $525 + 19 + 75$

**6.** $50 \times 17 \times 2$

**7.** $95 + 137 + 5$

**8.** $25 \times 19 \times 4$

**9.** $75 + 97 + 25 + 3$

**Set D   For use after page 29.**

Use place value to tell what each red digit means.

**1.** 3,574

**2.** 6,384

**3.** 3,596

**4.** 23,329

**5.** 45,520

**6.** 72,521

**7.** 425

**8.** 197,600

**9.** 165,372

**10.** 24,819

**11.** 361,472

**12.** 910,345

# MORE PRACTICE BANK

**Set A   For use after page 31.**
Use place value to tell what each red digit means.

**1.** 59,876,476        **2.** 864,327,413        **3.** 362,470,198

**4.** 5,468,294,300        **5.** 42,385,297        **6.** 3,576,284

**Set B   For use after page 33.**
Write > (greater than) or < (less than) for each ⫴.

**1.** 251 ⫴ 261        **2.** 6,900 ⫴ 6,799        **3.** 5,055 ⫴ 5,505

Order from least to greatest.

**4.** 3,191; 3,011; 3,121; 3,111        **5.** 28,303; 29,003; 28,330; 28,033

**Set C   For use after page 35.**
Round to the nearest ten. Then round to the nearest hundred.

**1.** 841      **2.** 513      **3.** 1,458      **4.** 8,325      **5.** 5,899

Round to the nearest thousand. Then round to the nearest ten thousand.

**6.** 16,450      **7.** 8,674      **8.** 34,489      **9.** 27,510      **10.** 64,399

**Set D   For use after page 41.**
Write the word name for each decimal.

**1.** 16.1            **2.** 0.49

**3.** 12.15           **4.** 8.08

Write the decimal.

**5.** thirty-two hundredths    **6.** five and two tenths    **7.** seven hundredths

**Set E   For use after page 43.**
Write in standard form.

**1.** five hundredths        **2.** one and two tenths        **3.** forty-two thousandths

Write the word name for each decimal.

**4.** 0.323      **5.** 0.41      **6.** 1.21      **7.** 1.210      **8.** 8.62

## MORE PRACTICE BANK

**Set A   For use after page 45.**

Write >, <, or = for each ⫴.

**1.** 0.9 ⫴ 0.09     **2.** 3.2 ⫴ 3.32     **3.** 68.1 ⫴ 68.11     **4.** 0.303 ⫴ 0.033

Order the numbers from least to greatest.

**5.** 0.0312; 0.039; 0.0041; 0.0301;     **6.** 0.1043; 0.0976; 0.0909; 0.1100;
0.0049                                        0.1009

**Set B   For use after page 47.**

Round to the nearest tenth, then to the nearest hundredth.

**1.** 1.983     **2.** 6.0451     **3.** 0.057     **4.** 1.1192     **5.** 20.022

Round to the nearest whole number.

**6.** 8.5     **7.** 3.27     **8.** 16.0003     **9.** 54.587     **10.** 0.54

**Set C   For use after page 59.**

Estimate by rounding to the nearest thousand.

| 1. | 2. | 3. | 4. | 5. |
|---|---|---|---|---|
| 11,873 − 9,260 | 3,866 + 2,149 | 23,788 − 14,022 | 5,870 + 4,366 | 18,625 − 10,440 |

Estimate by rounding to the nearest dollar.

| 6. | 7. | 8. | 9. | 10. |
|---|---|---|---|---|
| $6.50 + 3.25 | $19.52 − 12.80 | $13.60 + 5.80 | $6.49 + 3.71 | $20.89 + 3.90 |

**Set D   For use after page 61.**

Add or subtract.

| 1. | 2. | 3. | 4. | 5. |
|---|---|---|---|---|
| 239 87 + 125 | 521 893 + 326 | 1,297 793 + 3,442 | 35,008 − 14,397 | $40.00 − 23.12 |

**Set E   For use after page 63.**

Estimate. Use the front-end method.

| 1. | 2. | 3. | 4. | 5. |
|---|---|---|---|---|
| 317 + 985 | 442 + 365 | 224 + 977 | $6.31 + 4.72 | $10.68 + 5.35 |

**Set A    For use after page 69.**
Add.

| | | | | |
|---|---|---|---|---|
| **1.** 4.7<br>+ 8.6 | **2.** 0.55<br>+ 0.78 | **3.** 47.5<br>+ 26.4 | **4.** 6.472<br>+ 1.131 | **5.** 0.082<br>+ 0.69 |
| **6.** 622.8<br>+ 67.3 | **7.** 0.045<br>+ 0.264 | **8.** 61.0<br>+ 9.71 | **9.** 172.61<br>+ 148.94 | **10.** 3.472<br>+ 2.5188 |
| **11.** 5.98<br>+ 27.15 | **12.** 12.64<br>+ 9.77 | **13.** 9.459<br>+ 0.571 | **14.** $37.68<br>+ 82.43 | **15.** $ 5.26<br>+ 94.99 |

**16.** 15.6 + 3.54 + 12.75  **17.** 9.08 + 1.743 + 8.5  **18.** $78.95 + $183.69

**Set B    For use after page 77.**
Subtract.

| | | | | |
|---|---|---|---|---|
| **1.** 9.2<br>− 2.6 | **2.** 0.61<br>− 0.17 | **3.** 4.63<br>− 3.55 | **4.** 0.518<br>− 0.245 | **5.** 7.546<br>− 2.485 |
| **6.** 0.73<br>− 0.42 | **7.** 2.585<br>− 2.499 | **8.** 0.7655<br>− 0.4645 | **9.** 1.42<br>− 1.265 | **10.** 4.7642<br>− 1.5887 |
| **11.** 7.83<br>− 6.09 | **12.** $56.70<br>− 16.80 | **13.** $80.35<br>− 37.28 | **14.** 3.54<br>− 1.467 | **15.** 6.0102<br>− 4.8213 |

**16.** 10.07 − 8.8          **17.** 0.9452 − 0.7643      **18.** $95.39 − $29.49

**Set C    For use after page 79.**
Use compensation to find the sums and differences
mentally.

**1.** 152 + 97      **2.** 202 + 349      **3.** 197 + 468      **4.** 584 + 196

**5.** 253 − 98      **6.** 312 − 202      **7.** 896 − 497      **8.** 388 − 198

**Set D    For use after page 103.**
Find the range, mean, median, and mode for each
set of numbers.

**1.** 43, 29, 38, 26, 19                    **2.** 17, 24, 34, 27, 18, 24

**3.** 20, 15, 24, 28, 31, 20, 30

**Set A    For use after page 109.**

Substitute compatible numbers to estimate each sum
or difference.

1. $198 - 96$

2. $\$81 + \$201 + \$19$

3. $576 - 174$

4. $592 + 24 + 78$

5. $\$76 + \$5 + \$194 + \$123$

6. $\$1.19 + \$4.98 + \$0.78 + \$15.04$

**Set B    For use after page 121.**

Find the products using mental math.

1. $10 \times 10$

2. $100 \times 10$

3. $10 \times 1,000$

4. $100 \times 100$

5. $90 \times 40$

6. $30 \times 70$

7. $60 \times 30$

8. $80 \times 60$

9. $20 \times 90$

10. $30 \times 500$

11. $200 \times 400$

12. $10 \times 500 \times 20$

**Set C    For use after page 123.**

Estimate these products by rounding 2-digit numbers
to the nearest ten and 3-digit numbers to the nearest
hundred.

1. $6 \times 72$

2. $4 \times 98$

3. $8 \times 53$

4. $5 \times 894$

5. $3 \times 456$

6. $7 \times 634$

7. $2 \times 279$

8. $9 \times 852$

9. $29 \times 74$

10. $38 \times 43$

**Set D    For use after page 125.**

Multiply.

1. $\begin{array}{r} 42 \\ \times\ 2 \\ \hline \end{array}$

2. $\begin{array}{r} 91 \\ \times\ 3 \\ \hline \end{array}$

3. $\begin{array}{r} 27 \\ \times\ 7 \\ \hline \end{array}$

4. $\begin{array}{r} 29 \\ \times 19 \\ \hline \end{array}$

5. $\begin{array}{r} 35 \\ \times 27 \\ \hline \end{array}$

6. $\begin{array}{r} 61 \\ \times 23 \\ \hline \end{array}$

7. $\begin{array}{r} 469 \\ \times\ 39 \\ \hline \end{array}$

8. $\begin{array}{r} 625 \\ \times\ 30 \\ \hline \end{array}$

9. $\begin{array}{r} 289 \\ \times\ 78 \\ \hline \end{array}$

10. $\begin{array}{r} 456 \\ \times\ 37 \\ \hline \end{array}$

**Set E    For use after page 130.**

Use the distributive property to find the products
mentally.

1. $3 \times 15$

2. $2 \times 18$

3. $4 \times 17$

4. $17 \times 3$

5. $6 \times 12$

6. $3 \times 52$

7. $4 \times 33$

8. $2 \times 26$

## MORE PRACTICE BANK

**Set A   For use after page 135.**
Multiply. Use models if necessary.

| | | | | | | | | | |
|---|---|---|---|---|---|---|---|---|---|
| **1.** | 3.4 $\times$ 0.6 | **2.** | 2.8 $\times$ 5.9 | **3.** | 0.35 $\times$ 6 | **4.** | 4.28 $\times$ 9 | **5.** | 26.5 $\times$ 0.46 |
| **6.** | 1.765 $\times$ 8 | **7.** | 3.46 $\times$ 2.9 | **8.** | 2.78 $\times$ 4.6 | **9.** | 437.9 $\times$ 26.4 | **10.** | 7.23 $\times$ 4.5 |
| **11.** | 4.5 $\times$ 2.8 | **12.** | 7.9 $\times$ 8.4 | **13.** | 0.23 $\times$ 5 | **14.** | 3.79 $\times$ 4 | **15.** | 1.29 $\times$ 0.27 |

**Set B   For use after page 137.**
Estimate the products by rounding so that you can
use a basic fact.

| | | | | | | | | | |
|---|---|---|---|---|---|---|---|---|---|
| **1.** | 4.8 $\times$ 3.2 | **2.** | 5.34 $\times$ 3 | **3.** | 9.26 $\times$ 3.44 | **4.** | $6.67 $\times$ 4.9 | **5.** | $214.85 $\times$ 8.7 |

Estimate each sum. Use clustering.

**6.** 411 + 395 + 407 + 394        **7.** 6,989 + 6,978 + 7,031 + 7,019

**8.** 0.96 + 1.1 + 0.98 + 0.9 + 1.11   **9.** $8.04 + $7.89 + $7.93 + $8.08

**Set C   For use after page 139.**
Multiply.

| | | | | | | | | | |
|---|---|---|---|---|---|---|---|---|---|
| **1.** | 0.2 $\times$ 0.9 | **2.** | 0.05 $\times$ 0.03 | **3.** | 6.8 $\times$ 0.7 | **4.** | 3.08 $\times$ 0.07 | **5.** | 12.26 $\times$ 0.005 |
| **6.** | 25.03 $\times$ 0.2 | **7.** | 5.79 $\times$ 0.06 | **8.** | 89.22 $\times$ 0.13 | **9.** | 0.062 $\times$ 0.07 | **10.** | 124.3 $\times$ 0.006 |
| **11.** | 3.07 $\times$ 0.08 | **12.** | 0.90 $\times$ 0.11 | **13.** | 0.05 $\times$ 0.02 | **14.** | 1.009 $\times$ 0.04 | **15.** | 2.3 $\times$ 0.008 |

**Set D   For use after page 143.**
Multiply. Write only the answers.

**1.** 8.51 $\times$ 10   **2.** 0.03 $\times$ 100   **3.** 10 $\times$ 5.921   **4.** 3.245 $\times$ 1,000

**5.** 100 $\times$ 0.45   **6.** 7.68 $\times$ 10   **7.** 1,000 $\times$ 0.399  **8.** 100 $\times$ 4.6

**Set A   For use after page 153.**

Choose the measure that is most reasonable.

1. length of a pencil
   19 mm      19 cm      19 dm

2. length of a housefly
   8 mm      8 cm      8 m

Which unit (m, cm, or mm) would you use to measure

3. the width of your book?

4. the length of a soccer field?

5. the thickness of a book cover?

6. the height of a flagpole?

**Set B   For use after page 155.**

Give the number for each ▥.

1. 3.64 m = ▥ cm

2. 9.68 m = ▥ cm

3. 0.86 m = ▥ cm

4. ▥ cm = 0.9 m

5. 79 cm = ▥ m

6. 3.4 m = ▥ cm

7. 1,000 cm = ▥ m

8. ▥ cm = 1.75 m

9. ▥ m = 550 cm

**Set C   For use after page 157.**

Give the number for each ▥.

1. 1 cm = ▥ mm

2. 1 mm = ▥ cm

3. 8.4 cm = ▥ mm

4. ▥ cm = 500 mm

5. 4.9 cm = ▥ mm

6. 150 mm = ▥ cm

**Set D   For use after page 159.**

Find the area of each rectangular region.

1. Kitchen floor
   $l$ = 6.4 m
   $w$ = 4.5 m

2. Lot for a house
   $l$ = 45 m
   $w$ = 36 m

3. Kitchen wall
   $l$ = 4.8 m
   $w$ = 2.5 m

4. Calendar
   $l$ = 29 cm
   $w$ = 26.5 cm

5. Envelope
   $l$ = 24 cm
   $w$ = 10.3 cm

6. Postage stamp
   $l$ = 38 mm
   $w$ = 25 mm

**Set E   For use after page 160.**

Give the number for each ▥.

1. 5.876 km = ▥ m

2. 7.8 km = ▥ m

3. 867 m = ▥ km

4. 98 m = ▥ km

5. 1,264 m = ▥ km

6. 2,876 m = ▥ km

**Set A   For use after page 163.**

Choose the best estimate for the capacity of each container.

1. goldfish tank
   40 mL   40 L

2. fruit juice glass
   200 mL   200 L

3. gas tank of a car
   65 mL   65 L

Give the number for each ▓.

4. 7 L = ▓ mL

5. 375 mL = ▓ L

6. ▓ L = 5,000 mL

7. 25 mL = ▓ L

8. 3.4 L = ▓ mL

9. ▓ L = 2,750 mL

**Set B   For use after page 165.**

Give the number for each ▓.

1. 5 kg = ▓ g

2. 0.250 kg = ▓ g

3. 8,346 g = ▓ kg

4. 750 g = ▓ kg

5. 5,243 g = ▓ kg

6. 0.41 kg = ▓ g

**Set C   For use after page 169.**

Give the number for each ▓.

1. 3 h = ▓ min   2. 120 s = ▓ min   3. 240 min = ▓ h   4. 2 min 30 s = ▓ s

5. 7 d = ▓ h   6. 120 h = ▓ d   7. ▓ h = 2 d 12 h   8. ▓ s = 8 min

**Set D   For use after page 181.**

Find the quotients. Use pencils for answers only

1. 210 ÷ 7

2. 180 ÷ 3

3. 560 ÷ 7

4. 2,700 ÷ 9

5. 4,800 ÷ 8

6. 45,000 ÷ 5

7. 4,000 ÷ 8

8. 8,100 ÷ 9

9. 1,800 ÷ 9

10. 2,100 ÷ 7

11. 720 ÷ 8

12. 30,000 ÷ 6

13. 630 ÷ 7

14. 54,000 ÷ 6

15. 28,000 ÷ 4

16. 32,000 ÷ 8

**Set E   For use after page 183.**

Estimate these quotients. Choose compatible numbers so that you can use a basic fact.

1. 284 ÷ 7

2. 555 ÷ 8

3. 535 ÷ 6

4. 398 ÷ 8

5. 268 ÷ 3

6. 295 ÷ 5

7. 475 ÷ 6

8. 809 ÷ 9

**Set A   For use after page 187.**
Divide and check.

1. $2\overline{)28}$     2. $6\overline{)84}$     3. $3\overline{)86}$     4. $5\overline{)59}$     5. $9\overline{)198}$     6. $7\overline{)164}$

7. $3\overline{)175}$    8. $8\overline{)576}$    9. $4\overline{)332}$    10. $3\overline{)139}$   11. $8\overline{)216}$   12. $7\overline{)96}$

13. $3\overline{)547}$   14. $6\overline{)278}$   15. $7\overline{)963}$   16. $2\overline{)587}$   17. $4\overline{)689}$

Use mental math to find each quotient.

18. $5\overline{)450}$   19. $8\overline{)640}$   20. $6\overline{)1,800}$   21. $9\overline{)540}$   22. $7\overline{)5,600}$

**Set B   For use after page 189.**
Divide and check.

1. $2\overline{)187}$    2. $4\overline{)283}$    3. $7\overline{)476}$    4. $5\overline{)207}$    5. $9\overline{)499}$

6. $8\overline{)987}$    7. $6\overline{)273}$    8. $2\overline{)197}$    9. $4\overline{)255}$    10. $3\overline{)907}$

11. $5\overline{)385}$   12. $9\overline{)972}$   13. $7\overline{)678}$   14. $6\overline{)726}$   15. $8\overline{)954}$

Use mental math to find each quotient.

16. $3\overline{)210}$   17. $5\overline{)305}$   18. $8\overline{)824}$   19. $4\overline{)364}$   20. $6\overline{)618}$

**Set C   For use after page 191.**
Divide.

1. $7\overline{)1,431}$   2. $4\overline{)2,121}$   3. $8\overline{)1,650}$   4. $6\overline{)2,450}$   5. $9\overline{)4,563}$

6. $5\overline{)4,511}$   7. $7\overline{)5,666}$   8. $6\overline{)3,047}$   9. $8\overline{)3,846}$   10. $4\overline{)3,630}$

11. $3\overline{)2,573}$  12. $9\overline{)3,762}$  13. $2\overline{)1,356}$  14. $5\overline{)4,217}$  15. $6\overline{)2,965}$

**Set D   For use after page 192.**
Find the average of these sets of numbers.

1. 76, 84, 96, 80     2. 98, 91, 86, 93     3. 99, 89, 82     4. 58, 70, 63, 49

5. 67, 74, 86, 92, 96     6. 71, 75, 86, 94, 82, 72     7. 84, 98, 79, 83, 76

8. 389, 373, 401, 361, 396          9. 2,105; 2,314; 1,921; 2,142; 1,973

# MORE PRACTICE BANK

**Set A   For use after page 201.**

Divide.

1. $2\overline{)7.24}$    2. $4\overline{)31.76}$    3. $3\overline{)17.52}$    4. $5\overline{)30.15}$    5. $7\overline{)63.84}$

6. $6\overline{)2.898}$    7. $8\overline{)8.344}$    8. $9\overline{)0.5733}$    9. $4\overline{)93.04}$    10. $3\overline{)168.6}$

11. $7\overline{)5.81}$    12. $5\overline{)13.30}$    13. $9\overline{)27.45}$    14. $4\overline{)121.6}$    15. $7\overline{)36.61}$

Use mental math to find the quotients.

16. $6\overline{)48.06}$    17. $8\overline{)16.16}$    18. $3\overline{)21.6}$    19. $5\overline{)45.5}$    20. $9\overline{)8.19}$

**Set B   For use after page 213.**

Find the quotients. Use pencils for answers only.

1. $420 \div 70$    2. $540 \div 60$    3. $3,600 \div 40$    4. $6,300 \div 90$

5. $18,000 \div 60$    6. $27,000 \div 30$    7. $210 \div 70$    8. $2,800 \div 40$

9. $180 \div 90$    10. $1,600 \div 20$    11. $3,500 \div 70$    12. $560 \div 80$

13. $7,200 \div 90$    14. $20,000 \div 50$    15. $36,000 \div 90$    16. $1,600 \div 40$

**Set C   For use after page 215.**

Estimate the quotients. Multiply to check.

1. $30\overline{)125}$    2. $60\overline{)427}$    3. $20\overline{)163}$    4. $50\overline{)306}$    5. $70\overline{)362}$

6. $80\overline{)337}$    7. $90\overline{)456}$    8. $50\overline{)462}$    9. $60\overline{)274}$    10. $70\overline{)508}$

11. $40\overline{)331}$    12. $20\overline{)172}$    13. $50\overline{)363}$    14. $80\overline{)652}$    15. $70\overline{)641}$

16. $90\overline{)550}$    17. $60\overline{)435}$    18. $30\overline{)254}$    19. $40\overline{)293}$    20. $80\overline{)582}$

**Set D   For use after page 217.**

Divide and check.

1. $42\overline{)381}$    2. $62\overline{)546}$    3. $23\overline{)218}$    4. $45\overline{)360}$    5. $72\overline{)655}$

6. $95\overline{)760}$    7. $59\overline{)413}$    8. $61\overline{)317}$    9. $75\overline{)450}$    10. $99\overline{)912}$

11. $54\overline{)417}$    12. $32\overline{)256}$    13. $43\overline{)303}$    14. $86\overline{)434}$    15. $65\overline{)392}$

16. $94\overline{)382}$    17. $29\overline{)261}$    18. $76\overline{)535}$    19. $63\overline{)504}$    20. $84\overline{)760}$

## MORE PRACTICE BANK

**Set A   For use after page 219.**
Divide. Watch for estimates that need to be changed.

**1.** $52\overline{)315}$    **2.** $58\overline{)563}$    **3.** $26\overline{)210}$    **4.** $53\overline{)368}$    **5.** $84\overline{)589}$

**6.** $36\overline{)183}$    **7.** $68\overline{)333}$    **8.** $43\overline{)426}$    **9.** $73\overline{)442}$    **10.** $56\overline{)506}$

**Set B   For use after page 221.**
Divide and check.

**1.** $23\overline{)1,035}$    **2.** $56\overline{)952}$    **3.** $61\overline{)1,586}$    **4.** $39\overline{)1,992}$    **5.** $54\overline{)1,404}$

**6.** $57\overline{)3,881}$    **7.** $35\overline{)4,486}$    **8.** $53\overline{)2,188}$    **9.** $86\overline{)3,637}$    **10.** $87\overline{)4,824}$

**11.** $64\overline{)5,196}$    **12.** $75\overline{)3,855}$    **13.** $19\overline{)2,784}$    **14.** $37\overline{)8,895}$    **15.** $93\overline{)2,604}$

**Set C   For use after page 222.**
Choose a calculation method and solve.

**1.** $360 \div 20$    **2.** $104 \div 8$    **3.** $552 \div 4$    **4.** $525 \div 5$

**5.** $2,580 \div 15$    **6.** $57 \times 8$    **7.** $1,600 \div 8$    **8.** $660 \div 55$

**9.** $416 \div 2$    **10.** $5 \times 198$    **11.** $498 \div 6$    **12.** $60 \times 102$

**Set D   For use after page 225.**
Divide.

**1.** $43\overline{)2,580}$    **2.** $67\overline{)6,045}$    **3.** $53\overline{)3,551}$    **4.** $32\overline{)6,562}$

**5.** $89\overline{)9,970}$    **6.** $74\overline{)7,548}$    **7.** $26\overline{)6,240}$    **8.** $20\overline{)1,030}$

**9.** $38\overline{)9,984}$    **10.** $22\overline{)8,866}$    **11.** $43\overline{)21,844}$    **12.** $67\overline{)13,738}$

**Set E   For use after page 229.**
Divide. Write only the answers.

**1.** $3.7 \div 10$    **2.** $12.19 \div 10$    **3.** $7.05 \div 10$    **4.** $61.9 \div 100$

**5.** $0.7 \div 100$    **6.** $652.3 \div 100$    **7.** $3.9 \div 1,000$    **8.** $4.22 \div 10$

Use mental math to find the missing numbers.

**9.** $43.75 \div 100 = a$    **10.** $11.17 \div 10 = b$    **11.** $56.3 \div 1,000 = c$

**Set A   For use after page 241.**

Write the fraction.

**1.** two fifths

**2.** four sixths

**3.** one third

**4.** seven twelfths

**5.** five sevenths

**6.** three tenths

Write the word name for each fraction.

**7.** $\frac{2}{3}$

**8.** $\frac{1}{10}$

**9.** $\frac{3}{4}$

**10.** $\frac{5}{8}$

**11.** $\frac{5}{6}$

**12.** $\frac{4}{5}$

**Set B   For use after page 245.**

Find equivalent fractions by multiplying the numerator and denominator by 2.

**1.** $\frac{1}{2} = \frac{||||}{||||}$

**2.** $\frac{3}{5} = \frac{||||}{||||}$

**3.** $\frac{3}{8} = \frac{||||}{||||}$

**4.** $\frac{2}{3} = \frac{||||}{||||}$

Find equivalent fractions by multiplying the numerator and denominator by 3.

**5.** $\frac{1}{3} = \frac{||||}{||||}$

**6.** $\frac{5}{6} = \frac{||||}{||||}$

**7.** $\frac{3}{10} = \frac{||||}{||||}$

**8.** $\frac{1}{4} = \frac{||||}{||||}$

Tell what number the numerator and denominator of the first fraction were multiplied or divided by to get the equivalent fraction.

**9.** $\frac{3}{5} = \frac{9}{15}$

**10.** $\frac{8}{12} = \frac{2}{3}$

**11.** $\frac{6}{8} = \frac{3}{4}$

**12.** $\frac{3}{8} = \frac{15}{40}$

Give the next three equivalent fractions.

**13.** $\frac{1}{5} = \frac{||||}{||||}, \frac{||||}{||||}, \frac{||||}{||||}$

**14.** $\frac{1}{8} = \frac{||||}{||||}, \frac{||||}{||||}, \frac{||||}{||||}$

**15.** $\frac{3}{4} = \frac{||||}{||||}, \frac{||||}{||||}, \frac{||||}{||||}$

**16.** $\frac{5}{6} = \frac{||||}{||||}, \frac{||||}{||||}, \frac{||||}{||||}$

**Set C   For use after page 247.**

Find the greatest common factor for each pair of numbers.

**1.** $\frac{8}{20}$

**2.** $\frac{6}{26}$

**3.** $\frac{20}{16}$

**4.** $\frac{35}{50}$

**5.** $\frac{16}{48}$

**6.** $\frac{7}{15}$

**7.** $\frac{21}{28}$

**8.** $\frac{6}{32}$

**9.** $\frac{8}{52}$

**10.** $\frac{21}{56}$

**11.** $\frac{24}{60}$

**12.** $\frac{18}{54}$

**Set D   For use after page 249.**

Write each fraction in lowest terms.

**1.** $\frac{6}{21}$

**2.** $\frac{9}{30}$

**3.** $\frac{8}{28}$

**4.** $\frac{25}{40}$

**5.** $\frac{15}{35}$

**6.** $\frac{14}{42}$

**7.** $\frac{12}{32}$

**8.** $\frac{18}{45}$

**9.** $\frac{20}{42}$

**10.** $\frac{36}{60}$

**11.** $\frac{16}{20}$

**12.** $\frac{24}{30}$

**Set A   For use after page 255.**

Compare the fractions two at a time. Then list them in order from least to greatest.

1. $\frac{3}{10}, \frac{2}{7}, \frac{2}{5}$
2. $\frac{4}{7}, \frac{1}{3}, \frac{9}{14}$
3. $\frac{2}{3}, \frac{5}{9}, \frac{4}{7}$
4. $\frac{1}{7}, \frac{7}{8}, \frac{1}{4}$

**Set B   For use after page 257.**

Write each improper fraction as a mixed number or whole number.

1. $\frac{10}{3}$
2. $\frac{22}{5}$
3. $\frac{22}{6}$
4. $\frac{33}{2}$
5. $\frac{56}{8}$
6. $\frac{67}{10}$

Write each mixed number as an improper fraction.

7. $2\frac{4}{5}$
8. $1\frac{7}{10}$
9. $5\frac{2}{9}$
10. $3\frac{4}{7}$
11. $5\frac{3}{8}$
12. $4\frac{1}{10}$

**Set C   For use after page 259.**

Write each improper fraction as a mixed number or whole number.

1. $\frac{37}{15}$
2. $\frac{29}{4}$
3. $\frac{28}{13}$
4. $\frac{44}{9}$
5. $\frac{95}{5}$
6. $\frac{49}{6}$

Write each mixed number as an improper fraction.

7. $9\frac{5}{8}$
8. $2\frac{7}{11}$
9. $7\frac{3}{5}$
10. $6\frac{5}{9}$
11. $7\frac{2}{3}$
12. $10\frac{1}{5}$

**Set D   For use after page 271.**

Add or subtract.

1. $\frac{5}{6} + \frac{1}{6}$
2. $\frac{3}{11} + \frac{2}{11}$
3. $\frac{4}{5} + \frac{3}{5}$
4. $\frac{9}{10} - \frac{3}{10}$
5. $10\frac{4}{5} - 3\frac{1}{5}$

6. $\frac{7}{8} - \frac{2}{8}$
7. $\frac{3}{5} + \frac{2}{5}$
8. $\frac{11}{12} - \frac{5}{12}$
9. $\frac{5}{6} - \frac{4}{6}$
10. $\frac{7}{10} + \frac{4}{10}$

**Set E   For use after page 273.**

Find the least common denominator of these fractions.

1. $\frac{3}{8}, \frac{1}{16}$
2. $\frac{5}{12}, \frac{1}{3}$
3. $\frac{3}{4}, \frac{2}{7}$
4. $\frac{1}{2}, \frac{3}{5}$
5. $\frac{5}{8}, \frac{1}{6}, \frac{2}{3}$
6. $\frac{3}{10}, \frac{3}{4}$
7. $\frac{1}{2}, \frac{3}{20}$
8. $\frac{5}{24}, \frac{7}{8}$
9. $\frac{4}{5}, \frac{3}{7}$
10. $\frac{2}{3}, \frac{7}{12}, \frac{4}{5}$

## MORE PRACTICE BANK

**Set A  For use after page 277.**

Add or subtract.

1. $\frac{3}{10}$
$+\frac{2}{5}$

2. $\frac{4}{5}$
$+\frac{1}{2}$

3. $\frac{2}{3}$
$+\frac{1}{2}$

4. $\frac{3}{2}$
$-\frac{1}{4}$

5. $\frac{3}{4}$
$-\frac{3}{8}$

6. $\frac{2}{3}$
$-\frac{1}{4}$

7. $\frac{1}{8}$
$+\frac{3}{4}$

8. $\frac{2}{3}$
$+\frac{1}{6}$

9. $\frac{1}{10}$
$+\frac{2}{5}$

10. $\frac{3}{4}$
$-\frac{7}{16}$

11. $\frac{4}{5}$
$-\frac{3}{4}$

12. $\frac{5}{6}$
$-\frac{5}{18}$

13. $\frac{5}{8}$
$-\frac{1}{4}$

14. $\frac{7}{10}$
$+\frac{1}{5}$

15. $\frac{5}{6}$
$-\frac{5}{12}$

16. $\frac{3}{4}$
$+\frac{7}{8}$

17. $\frac{2}{3}$
$-\frac{2}{9}$

18. $\frac{1}{2}$
$-\frac{3}{8}$

**Set B  For use after page 285.**

Find the sums.

1. $2\frac{3}{8}$
$+4\frac{3}{4}$

2. $3\frac{3}{4}$
$+5\frac{1}{2}$

3. $7\frac{1}{4}$
$+2\frac{1}{6}$

4. $14\frac{4}{5}$
$+\ 6$

5. $13\frac{2}{3}$
$+\ 4\frac{2}{5}$

6. $3\frac{1}{2}$
$+2\frac{3}{8}$

7. $10\frac{1}{6}$
$+\ 3\frac{1}{12}$

8. $1\frac{4}{5}$
$+3\frac{2}{15}$

9. $15\frac{1}{3}$
$41\frac{5}{6}$
$+29\frac{1}{6}$

10. $68\frac{2}{3}$
$9\frac{1}{4}$
$+10\frac{5}{12}$

**Set C  For use after page 287.**

Subtract.

1. $20\frac{11}{12}$
$-15\frac{3}{4}$

2. $16\frac{4}{9}$
$-\ 7\frac{1}{6}$

3. $12\frac{4}{5}$
$-12\frac{2}{3}$

4. $8\frac{3}{4}$
$-3\frac{2}{5}$

5. $9\frac{5}{6}$
$-7\frac{3}{4}$

6. $47\frac{5}{8}$
$-11\frac{1}{4}$

7. $41\frac{1}{2}$
$-27\frac{1}{10}$

8. $86\frac{1}{3}$
$-38\frac{3}{4}$

9. $60\frac{1}{6}$
$-\ 7\frac{4}{5}$

10. $52\frac{3}{8}$
$-27\frac{4}{5}$

**Set A   For use after page 289.**

Add or subtract. Give answers in lowest terms.

1. $\frac{5}{6}$
   $+\frac{1}{4}$

2. $\frac{5}{16}$
   $+\frac{7}{8}$

3. $\frac{2}{3}$
   $-\frac{1}{4}$

4. $\frac{1}{4}$
   $-\frac{1}{5}$

5. $2\frac{1}{4}$
   $+5\frac{1}{4}$

6. $7\frac{3}{8}$
   $-5$

7. $3\frac{4}{5}$
   $+5\frac{1}{5}$

8. $4\frac{1}{2}$
   $+6$

9. $13\frac{5}{6}$
   $-8\frac{3}{4}$

10. $9\frac{1}{8}$
    $+7\frac{3}{4}$

11. $15\frac{1}{2}$
    $-6\frac{1}{3}$

12. $12\frac{1}{4}$
    $-5\frac{3}{4}$

13. $5$
    $-4\frac{1}{3}$

14. $3\frac{1}{2}$
    $+4\frac{2}{3}$

15. $4\frac{1}{4}$
    $-2\frac{3}{8}$

16. $13\frac{5}{6}$
    $+5\frac{1}{3}$

17. $12$
    $-2\frac{5}{6}$

18. $7\frac{3}{4}$
    $+2\frac{5}{8}$

**Set B   For use after page 291.**

Solve. Use mental math when you can.

1. $1\frac{3}{4}$
   $+2\frac{1}{4}$

2. $9$
   $+2\frac{5}{8}$

3. $6\frac{3}{8}$
   $-4\frac{1}{8}$

4. $8\frac{1}{2}$
   $-3\frac{5}{8}$

5. $12\frac{1}{2}$
   $+8\frac{1}{2}$

6. $4\frac{5}{6}$
   $-2\frac{1}{3}$

7. $3$
   $-1\frac{1}{4}$

8. $4\frac{3}{8}$
   $+2\frac{1}{8}$

9. $6\frac{1}{4}$
   $-3\frac{3}{4}$

10. $2\frac{3}{8}$
    $+7\frac{5}{8}$

11. $7\frac{1}{2}$
    $-4\frac{2}{3}$

12. $5\frac{2}{3}$
    $+2\frac{1}{6}$

**Set C   For use after page 301.**

Give the number for each ▦.

1. 4 ft = ▦ in.

2. 24 in. = ▦ ft

3. $2\frac{1}{2}$ ft = ▦ in.

4. 3 ft = ▦ in.

5. 5 ft 4 in. = ▦ in.

6. 72 in. = ▦ ft

**Set D   For use after page 303.**

Measure each segment to the nearest $\frac{1}{2}$ in.

1. _____

2. _____

Measure each segment to the nearest $\frac{1}{4}$ in.

3. _____

4. _____

### Set A   For use after page 305.

Give the unit (**in., ft, yd, mi**) that would be most reasonable to use to measure each.

**1.** length of a ballpoint pen

**2.** length of a football field

**3.** length of a carrot

**4.** distance between two cities

**5.** width of a classroom

**6.** length of a river

### Set B   For use after page 308.

Give the temperature in Fahrenheit degrees (F°) to the nearest tenth of a degree.

**1.**

**2.**

**3.**

**4.**

### Set C   For use after page 311.

Give the number for each ▒.

**1.** 2 oz = ▒ tablespoons

**2.** 2 c = ▒ oz

**3.** 3 pt = ▒ c

**4.** 2 gal = ▒ qt

**5.** 1 gal = ▒ pt

**6.** 1 gal = ▒ c

### Set D   For use after page 313.

Give the number for each ▒.

**1.** 1 lb = ▒ oz

**2.** 1 T = ▒ lb

**3.** 4 T = ▒ lb

**4.** $\frac{3}{4}$ lb = ▒ oz

**5.** 32 oz = ▒ lb

**6.** 10,000 lb = ▒ T

### Set E   For use after page 325.

Multiply.

**1.** $\frac{1}{2} \times 20$

**2.** $\frac{3}{4} \times 36$

**3.** $\frac{1}{3} \times 12$

**4.** $\frac{1}{8} \times 32$

**5.** $\frac{3}{8} \times 32$

**6.** $\frac{1}{10} \times 40$

**7.** $\frac{3}{10} \times 60$

**8.** $\frac{1}{7} \times 28$

## MORE PRACTICE BANK

**Set A  For use after page 327.**

Substitute compatible numbers to estimate each of the following.

1. $\frac{1}{8} \times 23$    2. $\frac{1}{4} \times 35$    3. $\frac{1}{5} \times 97$    4. $\frac{5}{8} \times 42$

5. $\frac{2}{3} \times 11$    6. $\frac{5}{6} \times 19$    7. $\frac{1}{6} \times 32$    8. $\frac{9}{10} \times 48$

9. $\frac{1}{5} \times 26$    10. $\frac{3}{8} \times 15$    11. $\frac{7}{10} \times 29$    12. $\frac{1}{4} \times 27$

13. $\frac{5}{6} \times 11$    14. $\frac{1}{8} \times 65$    15. $\frac{3}{5} \times 31$    16. $\frac{2}{3} \times 28$

**Set B  For use after page 331.**

Give the product in lowest terms.

1. $\frac{2}{5} \times \frac{1}{3}$    2. $\frac{1}{2} \times \frac{1}{4}$    3. $\frac{3}{4} \times \frac{7}{8}$    4. $\frac{5}{6} \times \frac{2}{3}$

5. $\frac{2}{3} \times \frac{3}{5}$    6. $\frac{7}{4} \times \frac{3}{2}$    7. $\frac{4}{5} \times \frac{5}{4}$    8. $\frac{3}{4} \times \frac{1}{3}$

9. $\frac{1}{6} \times \frac{6}{7}$    10. $\frac{1}{10} \times \frac{9}{10}$    11. $\frac{7}{3} \times \frac{1}{2}$    12. $\frac{4}{3} \times \frac{5}{2}$

13. $\frac{3}{8} \times \frac{8}{3}$    14. $\frac{5}{6} \times \frac{3}{4}$    15. $\frac{5}{8} \times \frac{2}{3}$    16. $\frac{2}{5} \times \frac{3}{4}$

17. $\frac{2}{5} \times \frac{9}{3}$    18. $\frac{3}{10} \times 20$    19. $\frac{5}{6} \times \frac{3}{5}$    20. $15 \times \frac{2}{3}$

21. $\frac{3}{8} \times \frac{2}{3}$    22. $\frac{4}{5} \times \frac{5}{8}$    23. $16 \times \frac{3}{4}$    24. $\frac{3}{5} \times 30$

**Set C  For use after page 337.**

Give the product in lowest terms.

1. $1\frac{1}{3} \times 4\frac{1}{2}$    2. $1\frac{3}{8} \times 1\frac{3}{5}$    3. $2\frac{2}{3} \times 3$    4. $1\frac{5}{9} \times 3\frac{6}{7}$

5. $12 \times 1\frac{5}{6}$    6. $3\frac{1}{3} \times 1\frac{3}{5}$    7. $3\frac{3}{7} \times 3\frac{1}{2}$    8. $2\frac{1}{3} \times 1\frac{5}{28}$

9. $3\frac{4}{5} \times 2\frac{3}{8}$    10. $2\frac{1}{6} \times 1\frac{5}{8}$    11. $3\frac{2}{3} \times 2\frac{4}{5}$    12. $1\frac{5}{6} \times 3\frac{7}{8}$

13. $4\frac{1}{2} \times 7\frac{2}{3}$    14. $2\frac{1}{8} \times 1\frac{1}{6}$    15. $3\frac{1}{3} \times 2\frac{3}{4}$    16. $5\frac{1}{3} \times 1\frac{1}{8}$

**Set A   For use after page 341.**

Use fraction pieces or draw pictures to answer the questions.

**1.** How many halves are in 3?

**2.** How many fourths are in $\frac{5}{2}$?

**3.** How many sixths are in $\frac{2}{3}$?

**4.** How many fourths are in $2\frac{1}{4}$?

**5.** How many thirds are in 3?

**6.** How many eighths are in $\frac{3}{4}$?

**Set B   For use after page 351.**

Name the following solid figures.

**1.** **2.** **3.** **4.** **5.**

**Set C   For use after page 353.**

Tell whether the triangle is **scalene**, **isosceles**, or **equilateral**.

**1.**

38 mm   *Q*

*P*

21 mm

38 mm

*R*

**2.**

*B*

28 mm   28 mm

*A*   28 mm   *C*

**3.**

*D*   32 mm

21 mm   *E*

43 mm

*F*

**Set D   For use after page 355.**

Tell whether each triangle is **acute**, **right**, or **obtuse**.

**1.** **2.** **3.**

Draw angles (without using a protractor) which you estimate to have the measures given below. Then measure each angle to check your estimate.

**4.** 45°   **5.** 60°   **6.** 95°   **7.** 120°   **8.** 145°   **9.** 175°

**Set A   For use after page 357.**
Name the following quadrilaterals.

1.    2.    3.    4.    5.

**Set B   For use after page 359.**
Draw the following shapes. Then give the number of lines of symmetry for each shape.

**1.** parallelogram          **2.** rhombus          **3.** kite

**Set C   For use after page 363.**
Is figure **A** congruent to figure **B**? Write **yes** or **no**.

1.    2.    3.

A   B          A   B          A   B

**Set D   For use after page 367.**
Name each of these polygons.

1.    2.    3.    4.

**Set E   For use after page 369.**
Give the missing length.

**1.** Radius: 4 cm     **2.** Radius: 3.5 m     **3.** Diameter: 12 cm     **4.** Diameter: 4.6 mm

4 cm          3.5 m          12 cm          4.6 mm

Diameter: ▓     Diameter: ▓     Radius: ▓     Radius: ▓

**Set F   For use after page 371.**
Find the circumference for a circle with the given diameter or radius. Use 3.14 for $\pi$.

**1.** $d = 2.5$ cm     **2.** $r = 6$ mm     **3.** $d = 5.2$ cm     **4.** $r = 3.1$ m

## MORE PRACTICE BANK

**Set A   For use after page 373.**

On a piece of graph paper, graph the following figures. Give the coordinates of the vertices.

**1.** triangle          **2.** pentagon          **3.** rectangle          **4.** trapezoid

Graph and connect each point.

**5.** (1,1), (3,6), (6,3), (1,1)                    **6.** (2,2), (2,6), (8,6), (8,2), (2,2)

Name the figure formed by graphing and connecting the points.

**7.** (1,1), (3,6), (6,3), (1,1)                    **8.** (2,2), (2,6), (8,6), (8,2), (2,2)

**9.** (0,1), (2,3), (4,3), (6,1), (0,1)          **10.** (3,1), (1,4), (3,6), (5,4), (3,1)

**Set B   For use after page 383.**

Write each ratio in 2 other ways.

**1.** Bike flags: 2 for $5. What is the ratio of flags to dollars?

**2.** Arturo rode 47 km in 2 h. What is the ratio of kilometers to hours?

**3.** 4 to 5

**4.** 7:10

**5.** 3 out of 7

**6.** 3 for every 2

**Set C   For use after page 385.**

Copy and complete each ratio table.

**1.**

**2.**

**3.**

**4.**

**Set D   For use after page 387.**

Solve the proportions.

**1.** $\frac{1}{4} = \frac{n}{48}$    **2.** $\frac{4}{5} = \frac{n}{60}$    **3.** $\frac{3}{8} = \frac{n}{96}$    **4.** $\frac{2}{3} = \frac{n}{45}$    **5.** $\frac{4}{7} = \frac{n}{28}$

**6.** $\frac{3}{4} = \frac{n}{24}$    **7.** $\frac{1}{3} = \frac{n}{48}$    **8.** $\frac{3}{10} = \frac{n}{100}$    **9.** $\frac{5}{6} = \frac{n}{90}$    **10.** $\frac{6}{5} = \frac{n}{60}$

## MORE PRACTICE BANK

**Set A   For use after page 391.**
Write each ratio as a percent.

**1.** 24 to 100    **2.** 50 to 100    **3.** 10 to 100    **4.** 8 to 100    **5.** 1 to 100

Write each percent as a fraction.

**6.** 25%          **7.** 35%          **8.** 40%          **9.** 17%          **10.** 110%

**Set B   For use after page 393.**
Write each decimal or fraction as a percent.

**1.** 0.25    **2.** 0.67    **3.** $\frac{40}{100}$    **4.** 0.12    **5.** 0.10    **6.** $\frac{9}{100}$

Write each percent as a decimal.

**7.** 43%    **8.** 26%    **9.** 17%    **10.** 8%    **11.** 40%    **12.** 2%

**Set C   For use after page 394.**
Write a lowest-terms fraction for each percent.

**1.** 25%    **2.** 30%    **3.** 14%    **4.** 43%    **5.** 32%

**6.** 85%    **7.** 6%    **8.** 48%    **9.** 115%    **10.** 35%

**Set D   For use after page 397.**
Find the percent of each number using mental math.

**1.** 75% of 20    **2.** 21% of 200    **3.** $12\frac{1}{2}$% of 400    **4.** 15% of 300

**5.** 25% of 800    **6.** $33\frac{1}{3}$% of 60    **7.** 90% of 200    **8.** 40% of 300

Estimate the percent of the number.

**9.** 24% of 80    **10.** 34% of 300    **11.** 9% of 70    **12.** 19% of 50

**13.** 35% of 90    **14.** 32% of 150    **15.** 26% of 32    **16.** 76% of 400

**Set E   For use after page 399.**
Find the percent of each number or amount.

**1.** 19% of 26    **2.** 43% of 85    **3.** 76% of 95    **4.** 15% of 72

**5.** 31% of 90    **6.** 78% of 100    **7.** 25% of 240    **8.** 12% of 150

**9.** 20% of $180    **10.** 50% of $12.98   **11.** 30% of $115    **12.** 8% of $29.50

## MORE PRACTICE BANK

**Set A   For use after page 415.**
Give the probability of each outcome.

**1.** Toss a coin.
$P$ (Heads) = ▦

**2.** Toss a number cube (1–6).
$P$ (Odd number) = ▦

**3.** Toss a number cube (1–6).
$P$ (4) = ▦

**Set B   For use after page 435.**
Find the perimeter of each figure.

**1.**

339 km
Kansas
(Suppose it is a rectangle.)
626 km

**2.**

Pentagon Building Washington, D.C.
276.3 m

**3.**

72 m
72 m
72 m
Baseball Field
120 m
120 m

**Set C   For use after page 439.**
Find the area of each figure.

**1.**

5 m
3 m
2 m
2 m
3 m
1 m

**2.**

4 m
4 m
1.5 m
2.5 m
2.5 m
1.5 m

**3.**

1 m
1 m
1 m
1.5 m
2.5 m
1.5 m
3.5 m

**Set D   For use after page 445.**
Find the area of each figure.

**1.**

95 m
70 m

**2.**

25 cm
25 cm
25 cm

**3.**

60 m
47 m

**Set E   For use after page 447.**
Find the volume of each box.

**1.** $l$ = 15 cm
$w$ = 3.5 cm
$h$ = 10 cm

**2.** $l$ = 4 m
$w$ = 1.5 m
$h$ = 2 m

**3.** $l$ = 10.8 cm
$w$ = 7.0 cm
$h$ = 5.5 cm

**Set A  For use after page 449.**

Find the surface area of each box.

**1.**

4 m
4 m
4 m

**2.**

6 cm
6 cm  2 cm

**3.**

2 mm
3 mm
4 mm

**Set B  For use after page 17.**

Solve. Use the 5-Point Checklist.

**1.** Eddie went on 6 rides an hour for 5 hours. How many rides did he take?

**2.** Jenny rode 14 rides in the first 3 hours. Nan rode 6 less than this. How many rides did Nan take?

**Set C  For use after page 19.**

Decide whether to estimate or find an exact answer.

**1.** Someone asks you how far it is from your town to Montreal, Canada.

**2.** You receive 20 cents for every mile between your town and Montreal, Canada.

**Set D  For use after page 37.**

Solve by drawing a picture.

**1.** Five girls ran in a 100-m dash. Debbie finished ahead of Carmen, and Carmen was not last. Betty finished far ahead of Carmen, and Evelyn finished just behind Betty. If Darlene finished last, which girl finished next to last?

**2.** Derek has a ribbon 180 cm long. He wants to cut the ribbon into pieces 20 cm long. How many cuts will he have to make?

**Set E  For use after page 65.**

Solve by using the guess and check strategy.

**1.** A test had 10 questions worth 3 points and 10 worth 5 points. Scott had 15 correct answers and a total score of 57 points. How many questions of each kind did he answer correctly?

**2.** Paula is 6 years old. Her Uncle Steve is 4 times as old. How old will Paula be when she is half as old as her uncle?

**Set A   For use after page 73.**

Choose a calculation method. Then solve.

1. The total cost of having a magazine sent to you each week for 52 weeks is $51.75. Is this cost per copy more than or less than the newsstand cost of $1.25 per copy?

2. Which charge for developing 35-mm film is cheaper, 36 pictures for $7.56 or 24 pictures for $3.12?

**Set B   For use after page 111.**

Solve.

1. The cost of a fully equipped motorcycle is $1,050 more than the cost of a basic cycle for each of four models. The basic models cost $2,058, $2,575, $2,955, and $3,324. What is the cost of the least expensive fully equipped model you could buy?

2. A basic model of an electronic keyboard costs $153 less than each of three deluxe models. The deluxe models cost $710, $953, and $1,125. What is the cost of the least expensive basic model?

**Set C   For use after page 127.**

Solve.

1. A person's heart pumps about 5 L of blood every minute. How many liters is this per day?

2. The eyes of an average person blink 25 times per minute. How many blinks is this per day? per year?

**Set D   For use after page 141.**

Solve.

1. For their hiking trip Duffy's family needed to buy 4 backpacks, 4 sleeping bags, and a first aid kit. The backpacks cost $18 each, the sleeping bags cost $47 each, and the first aid kit cost $9. What was the total cost?

2. In June a ranger took 23 groups of visitors on hikes. There were 18 in each group. In July she took 38 groups on hikes, with 14 in each group. How many more did she take in one month than in the other?

**Set A    For use after page 167.**
Solve by making an organized list.

**1.** Shelly has white, tan, and gray shorts. She has brown, red, blue, and green shirts. How many different outfits can she wear?

**2.** How many different playing orders are possible for 4 players on a tennis team? (One possible order would be 1, 2, 3, 4.)

**Set B    For use after page 171.**
Solve.

**1.** At noon the temperature was 13°C. At midnight the temperature was 5°C lower. What was the temperature at midnight?

**2.** One day the hottest temperature was 8°C higher than the coldest. If the coldest was 12°C, what was the hottest?

**Set C    For use after page 195.**
Solve. Think carefully about the remainder.

**1.** The cook had 38 eggs. He needed 4 eggs for each cake. He made as many cakes as he could. How many cakes did he make?

**2.** The cook needed 430 rolls. Each package held 8 rolls. How many packages did the cook need to buy?

**Set D    For use after page 197.**
Solve by working backward.

**1.** Chuck bought some picture post cards for $0.29 and a ball point pen that cost 3 times as much as the cards. He has $3.18 left. How much did he have at the start?

**2.** Kate spent $6.75 of her paycheck on a tape. She spent twice that amount for a book. Then she had $9.75 left. What was the amount of her paycheck?

**Set E    For use after page 203.**
For each problem, tell whether the answer is reasonable. If it is not reasonable, tell why not.

**1.** Sean had $20 to use for party snacks. He spent $3.98 for fruit, $4.03 for crackers, and $9.89 for mix for punch. How much money did he have left? **Answer: $4.79**

**2.** Marian bought 6 new stamps for her stamp collection. The total cost was $19.08. What was the average cost for each stamp? **Answer: $3.18**

## MORE PRACTICE BANK

**Set A    For use after page 227.**
Solve by finding a pattern.

1. What is the greatest number of roads that can go through 8 cities if each road goes through exactly two of the cities?

2. If a job paid $1 the first day, $2 the second day, $3 the third day, and so on, how much would a worker earn for 14 days' work?

**Set B    For use after page 231.**
Before solving each problem, estimate the answer. Then solve.

1. Each shelf can hold 9 softball bats. How many shelves are needed for 108 bats?

2. A school paid $343 for 7 pairs of football shoes. What was the average cost of each pair?

**Set C    For use after page 253.**
Solve by using logical reasoning.

1. Nan, Fran, Dan, and Jan are two sets of twins. One is a doctor, one a lawyer, one a teacher, and one an engineer. The teacher is not female. Nan and Fran have lunch every week with the lawyer. Fran's sister is her doctor. Give the profession of each person.

2. Anna, Bob, Cathy, and Don have different favorite weekend activities. One likes hiking, one swimming, one bicycling, and one softball. Cathy and Don do not like bicycling. Bob thinks hiking is great fun. Don does not swim. What is each person's favorite weekend activity?

**Set D    For use after page 261.**
Solve.

1. The longest ski run at Blue Valley is 4.8 miles. The longest run at Rocky Mount is just 0.8 times that long. How long is the run at Rocky Mount?

2. One of the chair lifts at Snowy Heights rises 1,128 ft in 6 minutes. What is the average number of feet the lift rises in 1 minute?

3. At Blue Valley, $\frac{7}{10}$ of the students in the beginners class were children. At Rocky Mount $\frac{3}{5}$ of the students were children. Which place had the greater fraction of students who were children?

4. Carlo spent 5 h 15 min skiing at Rocky Mount. Angela spent 345 min skiing. Who spent more time skiing? How much more time was that?

**Set A**   **For use after page 291.**

Solve.

1. Bus 26 travels $5\frac{3}{4}$ miles on its morning route and $8\frac{3}{4}$ miles on its afternoon route. What is the total distance Bus 26 travels?

2. Bus 17 has an oil leak. On Monday the bus needed $2\frac{1}{4}$ quarts of oil. On Tuesday it needed $3\frac{3}{4}$ quarts of oil. What was the total amount of oil Bus 17 needed on those two days?

**Set B**   **For use after page 307.**

Solve. Be sure to check for more than one answer.

1. Tom had 8 cans of juice that he wanted to share with three of his friends. How many cans could each person get?

2. How many coins does it take to make 10 cents?

**Set C**   **For use after page 315.**

In which situation would you estimate? In which would you find an exact answer?

1. You are deciding how many quarts of soft drinks to buy for a party.

2. You are deciding how much to charge a customer who buys a $200 suit at 20% off.

**Set D**   **For use after page 339.**

Solve.

1. Art's T-Shirt Shop sells $\frac{1}{2}$ as many extra large shirts as large shirts. The shop sells $\frac{1}{2}$ as many large shirts as medium shirts. If the shop sells 88 medium shirts, how many extra large shirts does it sell?

2. Marlene worked $12\frac{1}{2}$ h last week. This week she worked $1\frac{1}{2}$ times as that. How many hours in all did Marlene work in the last two weeks?

3. A recipe for making tortillas for ten people calls for $1\frac{1}{4}$ cups of corn flour. Julio needs to make tortillas for 40 people. How much corn flour does he need to use?

4. Rusty is making a spicy sauce that calls for using $1\frac{1}{2}$ teaspoons of curry powder. It also calls for $\frac{2}{3}$ as much salt as curry powder and $\frac{1}{2}$ as much paprika as salt. How much paprika does she need to use?

**Set A   For use after page 365.**

Solve.

1. One of the angles of a ship's triangular sail has a measure of 35°. Another angle of the sail has a measure of 90°. What is the measure of the third angle?

2. A ship's triangular sail has a base that measures 30 ft. Its height is 44 ft. What is the area of the sail?

**Set B   For use after page 401.**

Solve.

1. Marcus deposited $50 in a savings account. The rate of interest was 8% per year. How much interest did he receive at the end of a year?

2. The bank paid Joan 10% interest on $280 she deposited in a savings account. How much money did the bank pay Joan for using her money for 1 year?

**Set C   For use after page 421.**

Solve.

1. One hiker weighed 56 kg. Her backpack weighed $\frac{1}{4}$ as much as she did. What was the total weight of the hiker and the backpack?

2. Yellowstone National Park has $\frac{3}{4}$ million hectares of land. Forest covers $\frac{4}{5}$ of this land. How many million hectares is covered by forest?

**Set D   For use after page 437.**

Draw a picture in order to solve the problems.

1. The width of a garden is 8.4 m. Its length is 16.8 m. What is the perimeter of the garden?

2. The width of a soccer field is 46 m. The length is 45 m greater than the width. What is the perimeter of the field?

First estimate the answer. Then solve the problem and check to be sure that your answer is reasonable.

3. The length of each side of a pentagon is 4.9 cm. The length of each side of an octagon is 3.9 cm. Which figure has the greater perimeter? How much greater is that?

4. A farmer has $10\frac{3}{4}$ acres planted with barley, $9\frac{1}{4}$ acres with oats, $11\frac{1}{2}$ acres with corn, and $5\frac{1}{2}$ acres with rye. How many acres does he have planted in all?

# TABLE OF MEASURES

**Metric System**                                    **Customary System**

### Length

| | | | |
|---|---|---|---|
| 1 centimeter (cm) | 10 millimeters (mm) | 1 foot (ft) | 12 inches (in.) |
| 1 decimeter (dm) | $\begin{cases} 100 \text{ millimeters (mm)} \\ 10 \text{ centimeters (cm)} \end{cases}$ | 1 yard (yd) | $\begin{cases} 36 \text{ inches (in.)} \\ 3 \text{ feet (ft)} \end{cases}$ |
| 1 meter (m) | $\begin{cases} 1{,}000 \text{ millimeters (mm)} \\ 100 \text{ centimeters (cm)} \\ 10 \text{ decimeters (dm)} \end{cases}$ | 1 mile (mi) | $\begin{cases} 5{,}280 \text{ feet (ft)} \\ 1{,}760 \text{ yards (yd)} \end{cases}$ |
| 1 kilometer (km) | 1,000 meters (m) | | |

### Area

| | | | |
|---|---|---|---|
| 1 square meter (m²) | $\begin{cases} 100 \text{ square} \\ \quad \text{decimeters (dm}^2) \\ 10{,}000 \text{ square} \\ \quad \text{centimeters (cm}^2) \end{cases}$ | 1 square foot (ft²) | 144 square inches (in.²) |

### Volume

| | | | |
|---|---|---|---|
| 1 cubic decimeter (dm³) | $\begin{cases} 1{,}000 \text{ cubic centimeters} \\ \quad \text{(cm}^3) \\ 1 \text{ liter (L)} \end{cases}$ | 1 cubic foot (ft³) | 1,728 cubic inches (in.³) |

### Capacity

| | | | |
|---|---|---|---|
| 1 teaspoon | 5 milliliters (mL) | 1 cup (c) | 8 fluid ounces (fl oz) |
| 1 tablespoon | 12.5 milliliters (mL) | 1 pint (pt) | $\begin{cases} 16 \text{ fluid ounces (fl oz)} \\ 2 \text{ cups (c)} \end{cases}$ |
| 1 liter (L) | $\begin{cases} 1{,}000 \text{ milliliters (mL)} \\ 1{,}000 \text{ cubic centimeters} \\ \quad \text{(cm}^3) \\ 1 \text{ cubic decimeter (dm}^3) \\ 4 \text{ metric cups} \end{cases}$ | 1 quart (qt) | $\begin{cases} 32 \text{ fluid ounces (fl oz)} \\ 4 \text{ cups (c)} \\ 2 \text{ pints (pt)} \end{cases}$ |
| | | 1 gallon (gal) | $\begin{cases} 128 \text{ fluid ounces (fl oz)} \\ 16 \text{ cups (c)} \\ 8 \text{ pints (pt)} \\ 4 \text{ quarts (qt)} \end{cases}$ |

**Mass**                                             **Weight**

| | | | |
|---|---|---|---|
| 1 gram (g) | 1,000 milligrams (mg) | 1 pound (lb) | 16 ounces (oz) |
| 1 kilogram (kg) | 1,000 grams (g) | 1 ton (T) | 2,000 pounds (lb) |

### Time

| | | | |
|---|---|---|---|
| 1 minute (min) | 60 seconds (s) | | |
| 1 hour (h) | 60 minutes (min) | 1 year (yr) | $\begin{cases} 365 \text{ days} \\ 52 \text{ weeks} \\ 12 \text{ months} \end{cases}$ |
| 1 day (d) | 24 hours (h) | | |
| 1 week (w) | 7 days (d) | 1 decade | 10 years |
| 1 month (mo) | about 4 weeks | 1 century | 100 years |

**a.m.** A way to indicate time from 12:00 midnight to 12:00 noon. See also **p.m.**

**acute angle** An angle that has a measure less than 90°.

**addend** One of the numbers to be added.

Example: $\begin{array}{r} 3 \\ + 5 \\ \hline 8 \end{array}$ addends

**addition** An operation that gives the total number when you put together two or more numbers.

**algebraic expression** An expression that contains at least one variable; for example, $n + 5$.

**angle** Two rays from a single point.

**area** The measure of a region, in square units.

**associative (grouping) property** The sum (or product) of three or more numbers is the same regardless of grouping.

Examples: $2 + (8 + 6) = (2 + 8) + 6$
$3 \times (4 \times 2) = (3 \times 4) \times 2$

**average** The quotient when the sum of a set of numbers is divided by the number of addends.

**bar graph** A diagram that uses vertical or horizontal bars to show information.

**benchmark** An object of known measure used to estimate the measure of another object.

**breaking apart** Breaking a number into addends or factors in order to make mental calculations easy.

Example: $7\frac{5}{8} - 3\frac{2}{8} = 7 - 3$ plus $\frac{5}{8} - \frac{2}{8}$

**capacity** The volume of a space figure given in terms of liquid measurement.

**center** The point from which all points on a circle are equally distant.

**chances** The probability that a particular event will occur.

**chord** A straight line with both endpoints on a circle.

**circle** A plane figure in which all the points are the same distance from a point called the center.

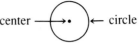

center →⊙← circle

**circle graph** A graph in the form of a circle that is divided into sectors showing how the whole is broken into parts.

**circumference** The distance around a circle.

**clustering** Finding addends or factors that are nearly alike in order to make estimating easy.

Example:
$28 + 31 + 29 + 32 \longrightarrow 4 \times 30 = 120$

**common factor** A number that is a factor of two different numbers is a common factor of those two numbers.

**common multiple** A number that is a multiple of two different numbers is a common multiple of those two numbers.

**commutative (order) property** The sum (or product) of any two numbers is the same regardless of the order in which they are added (or multiplied).

Examples: $17 + 13 = 13 + 17$
$5 \times 24 = 24 \times 5$

**compass** An instrument used to make circles.

**compatible numbers** Combinations of numbers that are easy to compute with mentally.

Examples: $25 + 175, 5 \times 20, 360 \div 9$

**composite number** Any whole number greater than 1 that has more than two different factors.

**cone** A space figure with one circular face and one vertex.

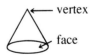

vertex
face

**congruent figures** Figures that have the same size and shape.

congruent triangles

**529**

**constant** A key on a calculator that allows you to use the same number over and over. For example, you can use the constant key to multiply different numbers by the same factor or to divide different numbers by the same divisor.

**coordinates** Number pair used in graphing.

**cross products** Products obtained by multiplying the numerator of one fraction by the denominator of a second fraction, and the denominator of the first fraction by the numerator of the second fraction.

**cube** A space figure whose faces are all squares.

**customary units of measure** See Table of Measures, page 528.

**cylinder** A space figure with two congruent circular faces.

**data bank** A place where information is stored.

**decimal** Any base-ten numeral written using a decimal point.

3.2 ← decimal
  ↑— decimal point

**degree** A unit of measure for angles.

**degree Celsius (°C)** A unit for measuring temperature in the metric system.

**degree Fahrenheit (°F)** A unit for measuring temperature in the customary system.

**denominator** The number below the line in a fraction.

$\frac{3}{4}$ ← denominator

**diagonal** A segment, other than a side, connecting two vertices of a polygon.

diagonal — vertex
vertex

**diameter** A segment containing two points of a circle and the center.

diameter
center

**difference** The number obtained by subtracting one number from another.

Example:  9
       − 4
        5 ← difference

**digits** The symbols used to write numerals: 0, 1, 2, 3, 4, 5, 6, 7, 8, and 9.

**distributive property** Multiplying a sum by a number is the same as multiplying each addend by the number and then adding the products.

Example: $3 \times (2 + 4) = 18$
        $(3 \times 2) + (3 \times 4) = 18$

**dividend** A number to be divided.

$\overset{4}{7)\overline{28}}$ ← dividend

**division** An operation that tells how many sets or how many in each set.

**divisor** The number by which a dividend is divided.

divisor → $\overset{4}{7)\overline{28}}$

**double bar graph** A bar graph that uses pairs of bars to compare information.

**edge** One of the segments making up any of the faces of a space figure.

 ← edge

**END** An instruction in a computer program that tells the computer to stop.

**equality** (equals, or =) A mathematical relation of being exactly the same.

**equally likely outcomes** Outcomes that have the same chance of occurring.

**equal ratios** Ratios that give the same comparison. $\frac{9}{27}$ and $\frac{1}{3}$ are equal ratios.

**equation** A number sentence that uses the equality symbol to show that two expressions have the same value.

Example: $9 + 2 = 11$

**equilateral triangle** A triangle with all 3 sides the same length and all angles the same measure.

**equivalent fractions** Fractions that name the same amount.

Example: $\frac{1}{2}$ and $\frac{2}{4}$

**estimate** To find an answer that is close to the exact answer.

**evaluate** To find the number that an algebraic expression names.

**even number** A whole number that has 0, 2, 4, 6, or 8 in the ones place.

**expanded form** A way to write numbers that shows the place value of each digit.

Example: $9,000 + 300 + 20 + 5$

**experimental probability** Probability based on the results of an experiment.

**exponent** A number that tells how many times another number is to be used as a factor.

$$5 \times 5 \times 5 = 5^3 \quad \substack{\leftarrow \text{ Exponent} \\ \leftarrow \text{ Base}}$$

**face** One of the plane figures (surfaces) making up a space figure.

**factors** Numbers that are combined in the multiplication operation to give a number called the product.

$$\text{factors} \longrightarrow 6 \times 7 = 42$$

**factor tree** A diagram used to find the prime factors of a number.

Example:
$$
\begin{array}{c}
42 \\
6 \quad \times \quad 7 \\
3 \times 2 \times 7
\end{array}
$$

**fair game** A game in which each player has the same chance of winning.

**flip** To turn a figure to its reverse side. A flip and a slide result in a reflection image.

**flowchart** A chart that shows a step-by-step way of doing something.

**formula** A general rule expressed by symbols. For example, the area ($A$) of any parallelogram with base $b$ and height $h$ is given by the formula $A = bh$.

**fraction** A number that expresses parts of a whole or a set.

Example: $\frac{3}{4}$

**front-end estimation** A method of estimating by adding or subtracting the digits with the greatest place value. Often the other digits are used to adjust the estimate.

**GOTO** An instruction in a computer program that causes the computer to skip to a specified line in the program.

**graph** A picture that shows information in an organized way.

**greater than (>)** The relationship of one number being larger than another number.

Example: $6 > 5$, read "6 is greater than 5."

**greatest common factor (GCF)** The greatest number that is a factor of each of two numbers.

**grouping property** See *associative property*.

**hexagon** A polygon with six sides.

**improper fraction** A fraction whose numerator is greater than or equal to the denominator.

**INPUT** An instruction in a computer program that causes the computer to stop and request data while running a program.

**integers** The whole numbers together with their opposites.

Examples: $^-5$, 0, 23

**interval** The number of units between spaces on a graph's scale.

**isosceles triangle** A triangle with at least 2 sides the same length and at least 2 angles the same measure.

**least common denominator (LCD)** The least common multiple of two denominators.

**least common multiple (LCM)** The smallest nonzero number that is a multiple of each of two given numbers.

**less than** (<) The relationship of one number being smaller than another number.

    Example: 5 < 6, read "5 is less than 6."

**line** A straight path that is endless in both directions.

**line graph** A diagram that uses a rising or falling line to show increases or decreases over a period of time.

**line of symmetry** A line on which a figure can be folded so that the two parts fit exactly.

line of symmetry

**line segment** Part of a line that extends from one point to another point.

**LIST** A copy of a set of instructions that tells a computer what to do.

**Logo** A computer language that can be used for computer graphics.

**lowest terms** A fraction is in the lowest terms if the numerator and denominator have no common factor greater than 1.

    Examples: $\frac{3}{8}, \frac{5}{6}, \frac{2}{3}$

**mass** The amount of matter that something contains.

**mathematical probability** The probability of a certain outcome if the number of trials is extended indefinitely.

**mean** The average of a set of numbers; found by dividing the sum of the numbers by the number of addends.

**median** The middle number when numbers are arranged in order. If there is no one middle number, then the median is the average of the two middle numbers.

**memory key** A key on a calculator that allows the calculator to store in its memory the result of one calculation while it performs another calculation.

**mental math** Performing calculations in your mind, without using pencil and paper or a calculator.

**metric units of measure** See Table of Measures, page 528.

**mixed number** A number that has a whole number part and a fraction part, such as $2\frac{3}{4}$.

**mode** The number or numbers that occur most often in a set of numbers.

**multiple** A number that is the product of a given number and a whole number.

**multiplication** An operation that combines two numbers, called factors, to give one number, called the product.

**negative number** A number that is less than zero.

**number line** A line that shows numbers in order.

```
7   8   9   10
```

**number pair** Two numbers that are used to give the location of a point on a graph.

    Example: (3,2)

**number properties** Number properties include the associative (grouping) property, the commutative (order) property, the distributive property, the one property of multiplication, the zero property of addition, and the zero property of multiplication.

**numeral** A symbol for a number.

**numerator** The number above the line in a fraction.

$$\frac{3}{4} \longleftarrow \text{numerator}$$

**numerical expression** An expression (name for a number) that contains two or more numbers. Example: 4 + 5

# GLOSSARY

**obtuse angle**   An angle with a measure greater than 90° and less than 180°.

**odd number**   A whole number that has 1, 3, 5, 7, or 9 in the ones place.

**one property**   In multiplication, when either factor is 1, the product is the other factor.

**order property**   See *commutative property*.

**ordered pairs**   See *coordinates*.

**ordinal number**   A number used to tell order.

   Examples: first, fifth

**outcome**   A possible result in a probability experiment.

**p.m.**   A way to indicate time from 12:00 noon to 12:00 midnight. See also **a.m.**

**parallel lines**   Two lines that lie in the same plane and do not intersect.

**parallelogram**   A quadrilateral with two pairs of parallel sides.

   parallelogram

**pentagon**   A polygon with five sides.

**percent**   Per 100; a way to compare a number with 100.

**perimeter**   The distance around a figure.

**period**   In large numbers, a group of three digits separated from other groups by commas.

**perpendicular lines**   Two lines that intersect at right angles.

**pi ($\pi$)**   The ratio of the circumference of a circle to its diameter. The decimal for $\pi$ is 3.141592... As approximations for $\pi$, we often use 3.14 or $3\frac{1}{7}$.

**pictograph**   A kind of graph that uses pictures or symbols to represent numbers.

**place value**   The value given to the place a digit occupies in a number.

   Example:        3 5 6

      hundreds place ⌐
        tens place ⌐
        ones place ⌐

**plane figure**   A figure that lies on a flat surface.

   Examples:

   square        triangle       circle

**point**   A single, exact location, often represented by a dot.

**polygon**   A closed figure formed by line segments.

**prediction**   An educated guess about what will happen.

**prime factorization**   Expressing a composite number as a product of prime factors.

**prime number**   A number that has exactly 2 factors (the number itself and 1).

**PRINT**   An instruction in a computer program that tells a computer to type something.

**prism**   A space figure whose bases are congruent polygons in parallel planes and whose faces are parallelograms.

**probability**   The probability that an event will occur in a set of equally likely outcomes is the number of ways the event can occur divided by the total number of possible outcomes.

**product**   The result of the multiplication operation.

   Example: $6 \times 7 = 42$
                              ↑
                           product

**program**   A set of instructions that tells a computer what to do.

**proportion**   An equation showing that two ratios are equal.

   Example: $\frac{6}{8} = \frac{3}{4}$

**protractor**   An instrument used for measuring angles.

**pyramid**   A space figure whose base is a polygon and whose faces are triangles with a common vertex.

**quadrilateral**   A polygon with four sides.

**quotient**   The number (other than the remainder) that is the result of the division operation.

Examples:

$$45 \div 9 = 5 \qquad 7\overline{)45}$$

quotient

6 ← quotient

$\dfrac{42}{3}$

**radius**   A segment from the center of a circle to a point on the circle.

radius

**range**   The difference between the highest and the lowest numbers in a set of numbers.

**ratio**   A pair of numbers used in making certain comparisons. The ratio of 3 to 4 can be written 3 to 4, 3:4, or $\frac{3}{4}$.

**ratio table**   A chart or table that displays a set of equal ratios.

**ray**   A part of a line, having only one end point.

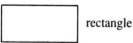

ray

**rectangle**   A quadrilateral that has four right angles.

rectangle

**reflection image**   The new figure obtained by sliding and flipping a figure.

**regular polygon**   A polygon with all sides the same length and all angles the same measure.

**remainder**   The number less than the divisor that remains after the division process is completed.

Example: $7\overline{)47}$

6

$\dfrac{42}{5}$ ← remainder

**rhombus**   A quadrilateral with all sides the same length.

rhombus

**right angle**   An angle that has a measure of 90 degrees.

right angle

**right triangle**   A triangle that has one right angle.

right triangle

**Roman numerals**   Numerals used by the Romans.

Examples:   I = 1
V = 5
VI = 6

**rotation image**   The new figure obtained by sliding and turning a figure.

**rounding**   Replacing specific numbers with numbers expressed in even units, such as tens, hundreds, or thousands.

Example: 23 rounded to the nearest 10 is 20.

**RUN**   A command that tells the computer to execute a program.

**sample**   A representative part of a larger group.

**scale**   Numbers along the side or bottom of a graph. Also, a ratio that shows the relationship between a scale drawing and the actual object or between distances on a map and actual distances.

**scalene triangle**   A triangle with no sides the same length and no angles the same measure.

**segment**   A straight path from one point to another.

**sequence**   A set of numbers in a particular pattern or order.

**similar figures**   Two figures that have the same shape.

similar figures

**simulation**   A way of acting out or creating a situation like one in the real world to see what is likely to happen in the real world.

# GLOSSARY

**skip counting**   Counting by a number other than 1.

>   Example: 0, 5, 10, 15
>           skip counting by fives

**slide**   To obtain another figure by moving a figure without flipping or turning it. A slide results in a translation image.

**space figure**   A figure that has volume.

>   Examples:

>   cube        cylinder

**sphere**   A space figure in which all the points are the same distance from a center point.

sphere

**square**   A quadrilateral with four right angles and all sides the same length.

square

**square of a number**   The product of a number and itself

**subtraction**   An operation that tells the difference between two numbers, or how many are left when some are taken away.

**sum**   The number obtained by adding numbers.

>   Example:   3
>             + 2
>            ———
>              5  ← sum

**surface area**   The sum of the areas of all the faces of a space figure.

**symmetric figure**   A plane figure that can be folded in half so that the two halves match.

**tally**   A mark used to keep track of items when counting. Tally marks are in groups of five, with the fifth in the group recorded as a slash.

>   Example: ⑪⑪ ⑪⑪ ‖

**trading**   To make a group of ten from one of the next highest place value, or one from ten of the next lowest place value. Examples: one hundred can be traded for ten tens; ten ones can be traded for one ten.

**translation image**   The new figure obtained by sliding a figure without flipping or turning it.

**trapezoid**   A quadrilateral with only one pair of parallel sides.

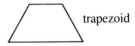

trapezoid

**triangle**   A polygon with three sides.

**turn**   To obtain a new figure by rotating a figure into a different position. The result of a turn is a rotation image.

**unit**   One of something. An amount or quality used as a standard of measurement. Set Table of Measures, page 528.

**unitizing**   Estimating size by visually dividing an object into smaller parts and using the estimated size of one part to estimate the total size.

**variable**   A symbol, usually a letter, used to represent a number or a range of numbers.

**vertex** (plural, **vertices**)   The point that the two rays of an angle have in common.

vertex →

**volume**   the number of cubic units of space that a space figure holds.

**zero property**   In addition, 0 added to any number does not change that number. In subtraction, 0 subtracted from any number gives the original number. In multiplication, the product of any number multiplied by 0 is 0.

**Acre,** 330-31

**Actions,** operations suggested by, in problem solving, 10-11

**Activities in lessons.** *See* Applied problem solving, Data hunt problems, Manipulatives.

**Acute angles,** 354

**Acute triangles,** 360

**Addends,** 6

**Addition.** *See also* Sums.
associative (grouping) property of, 6-7
commutative (order) property of, 6-7
computer and, 495
decimals, 66-69, 109
fractions, 270-71
calculator and, 448
multiple-step problems, 126
whole numbers, 60-61, 460
zero property of, 12

**Algebra**
area of a rectagle, 303
area of a triangle, 445
coordinates (ordered pairs), 372-73
equations, concept of, 15, 31, 121, 143, 181, 189, 256-57, 325, 332
expressions, 38, 189, 215, 247, 271, 341
patterns, functions, and relations, 14-15, 70, 181, 250, 373
problem solving and, 332, 388-389
proportions, 386-87
ratios, 384-85
variables, 12, 33, 250, 386-87

**Alternate approach,** 335.
*See also* Problem solving.

**Angles**
estimating measure, 354-55
measuring, 354-55, 360
of quadrilaterals, 356-57
of triangles, 352, 360

**Answers,** determining reasonable, 16, 63, 230

**Applications.** *See* Applied problem solving, Problem-solving applications.

**Applied problem solving,** 20-21, 82-83, 144-45, 204-5, 316-17, 426-27

**Area**
irregularly shaped figures, 438-39
and perimeter relationship, 440
rectangles, 158-59, 221, 303, 440
right triangles, 442-43
surface, 450-51
triangles, 444-45

**Arithmetic error** (calculator), 484

**Associative (grouping) property,** 6-7, 8-9

**Average (mean),** 102-3, 192, 222

**Bar graphs,** 90-91, 96-97, 107, 113

**"Betweenness" for fractions,** 296

**Billions,** place value, 30-31

**Broken-line graphs.** *See* Line graphs.

**Calculation methods,** choosing, 72-73, 222, 290

**Calculator-assisted problem solving,** 41, 69, 80-81, 100, 137, 140-41, 168, 191, 217, 219, 255, 273, 311, 338, 417, 438, 439

**Calculator bank,** 484-91

**Capacity,** 162-63
customary units, 310-11
metric units, 162-63

**Careers,** 28, 58, 88-89, 118-19, 170, 214, 256, 262-63, 304, 322-23, 336, 381-82, 418

**Celsius,** 170

**Center of a circle,** 368

**Centimeters,** 152, 154-57

**Century,** 480, 528

**Certain events,** 414

**Chance.** *See* Probability.

**Change making,** 467

**Chapter Power Practice/Tests,** 23, 53, 85, 115, 147, 175, 207, 235, 265, 295, 319, 345, 377, 405, 429, 455

**Choose the operation,** 16-17

**Choosing a calculation method,** 72, 222, 290

**Chord,** 368

**Circle graphs,** 253, 326-27, 394, 401, 490

**Circles,** 368-69, 370-371

**Circumference,** 370-371

**Classifying plane figures,** 356-57

**Classifying solid figures,** 350-51

**Clocks,** 168, 176

**Clustering,** 136-37, 337

**Collecting data,** *See* Data collection and analysis

**Combinations,** 430

**Common denominator,** 270-71

**Common factor,** 246-47

**Common multiple,** 272-73

**Communication,** problems, 73, 121, 165, 257, 423, 451

**Commutative (order) property,** 6-7, 8-9

**Comparing and ordering**
decimals, 44-45
fractions, 254-55
whole numbers, 32-33

**Compass,** 368-69

**Compatible numbers,** 8-9, 108-9, 249, 285

**Compensation,** 78-79

**Composite number,** 266

**Computer bank,** 492-99

**Computer careers,** 262-63

**Computer graphs,** 498

**Concrete materials.**
*See* Manipulatives.

**Cone,** 350-51

**Congruent figures,** 362-63

**Connecting concrete and symbolic,** 66, 132, 184, 198, 274, 282, 328

**Connections.** *See* Curriculum connectons.

**Constants,** 485

**Constructons.** *See* Geometric constructions.

**Consumer math.** *See* Problem solving applications.

**Cooperative learning groups.**
*See* Applied problem solving, Data collection and analysis.

**Coordinate geometry,** 372-73

**Counting on, counting back,** 9

**Create your own problem.**
*See* Write your own problem.

**Critical thinking,** 14-15, 29, 35, 63, 70, 93, 97, 98-99, 135, 153, 159, 181, 213, 245, 289, 325, 351, 353, 357, 360, 363, 371, 387, 399, 411, 418, 440, 449. *See also* Math reasoning

**Cross products,** 245, 387

**Cubits,** 153

**Cumulative review,** 25, 55, 87, 117, 149, 177, 209, 237, 267, 297, 321, 347, 379, 407, 431, 457

**Cups,** 310

**Curriculum connections,** 2-3, 4-5, 8-9, 26-27, 32-33, 44-45, 56-57, 58-59, 68-69, 88-89, 94-95, 102-3, 118-19, 120-21, 138-39, 150-51, 154-55, 168-69, 178-79, 182-83, 190-91, 210-11, 218-19, 224-25, 238-39, 244-45, 248-49, 268-69, 270-71, 288-89, 298-99, 302-3, 310-11, 322-23, 326-27, 336-37, 348-49, 358-59, 362-63, 380-81, 386-87, 396-97, 408-9, 412-13, 416-17, 432-33, 434-35, 444-45

**Customary units of measure.** *See* Measurement.

**Cylinder,** 350-51

**Data bank,** 468-83

**Data bank problems,** 5, 9, 33, 45, 59, 69, 95, 103, 121, 139, 155, 169, 183, 191, 219, 225, 245, 271, 289, 303, 359, 363, 387, 417, 435, 445

**Data collection and analysis,** 20-21, 50-51, 112-13, 172-73, 232-33, 292-93, 342-43, 402-3, 452-53

**Data hunt problems,** 17, 47, 97, 159, 189, 217, 305, 339, 439

**Day,** 168, 528

**Decade,** 27, 528

**Deciding when to estimate,** 18-19, 314-15

**Decimals**
  addition, 66-69, 109

  calculator and, 487
  comparing and ordering, 44-45
  division, 198-201
    by 10, 100, 1,000, 228
  estimating, 136-37
  multiplication, 132-135, 138-39, 142-43
  percents as, 392-93
  place value, 40-43
  rounding, 46-47
  subtraction, 74-77

**Decimeters,** 152, 528

**Decision making.** *See* Applied problem solving, Data collection and analysis.

**Degrees**
of an angle, 354-55, 360
Celsius, 70
Fahrenheit, 308

**Denominators**
  like, 270-71
  unlike, 276-77

**Dewey decimal system,** 9, 468

**Diagrams in problem solving.** *See* Problem solving skills and strategies.

**Diameter,** 368-69

**Differences.** *See* Subtraction.

**Digits,** 28, 39
  front-end in estimating, 62-63

**Discount,** 126, 140-41, 398-99, 401

**Distributive property,** 130

**Divisibility,** patterns and rules, 236

**Division.** *See also* Quotients.
  decimals, 198-201
  by 10, 100, 1,000, 228
  1-digit quotients, 216
  2- and 3-digit quotients, 186-87
  fractions, 340-41
    calculator and, 489
  interpreting remainders, 194-95
  in multiple-step problems, 126
  short, 208
  special cases, 190-91, 224
  special quotients, 180-81, 212-13
  where to start, 188-89
  whole numbers, 180-91, 212-21, 224-25, 228-29

**Division constant** (calculator), 485

**Double bar graphs,** 96-97

**Draw a diagram.** *See* Problem solving skills and strategies.

**Edge,** of a polyhedron, 350-51

**Egyptian hieroglyphic numerals,** 3, 5, 468

**Elapsed time,** 169

**Enrichment lessons,** 24, 54, 86, 116, 148, 176, 208, 236, 266, 320, 346, 378, 406, 430, 456

**Equal decimals,** 44-45

**Equal ratios,** 384-85, 386-87

**Equally likely outcomes,** 412-13

**Equations**
  area
    parallelogram, 446
    rectangle, 158-59
    right triangle, 442-43
    triangle, 303, 444-45
  circumference, 370
  concept of, 15, 31, 121, 143, 181, 189, 256-57, 325
  perimeter, 434
  volume, 448

**Equilateral triangles,** 352

**Equivalent fractions,** 242-45

**Error displays** (calculator), 484

**Estimation**
  angle measures, 355
  area, 439, 456
  chunking, 320
  circumference, 369
  clustering, 136-37, 337
  compatible numbers, 108-9, 249
  deciding when to use, 18-19, 314
  decimals, 43, 136-37, 139
  differences, 58-59, 61, 77, 280
  fractions, 241, 249, 280, 326
  front-end, 62-63
    computer and, 492
  graphs, 91
  length, 152-53, 155
    computer and, 498
  percents, 396-97
  problem solving, 18-19, 59, 63, 65, 72-73, 109, 153,

230, 290-91, 314-15, 436-37

products, 122-23, 326-27, 337, 493

quotient digits, 214-15

quotients, 182-83, 191, 218-19

ratios, 383

reasonable answers, 16, 63, 230

reference point (benchmark), 125, 137, 191, 305

rounding, 58-59, 122-23, 280

sampling, 422-23

sums, 77, 280

unitizing, 152-53, 161

**Even numbers,** 63

**Events.** *See* Outcomes, Probability.

**Expanded form numbers,** 28-31

**Experimental probability,** 416-17

**Experiments and outcomes,** 412-417

**Exponents,** 148

**Expressions**
algebraic, 38, 189, 215, 247, 271, 341

numerical, 4-5, 189

**Faces,** of solid figures, 350-51, 378

**Factor tree,** 266

**Factors**
greatest common, 246-47

prime, 266

**Fahrenheit,** 308

**Fair games,** 410-11

**Feet,** 304-5, 528

**Find a pattern,** 226

**Fine arts data bank,** 477-79

**Fine arts data bank problems,** 245, 249, 435, 445

**Flips,** 362-63

**Flow charts,** 196, 346

**Fluid ounces,** 310, 528

**Foot,** 300-1, 304-5, 528

**Formulas.** *See* Equations.

**Fraction pieces,** 242-43, 254, 340

**Fractions,** concept, 240-41
addition, 270-77, 280, 282-85, 288-89

calculator and, 255, 273, 327, 338, 486-89

comparing and ordering, 254-55

decimals, percents, and, 392-93

division, 340-41

equivalent, 242-45

estimation, 280, 326-27, 337

improper, 256-59

lowest-terms, 248-49
percents and, 394-95

multiplication, 324-25, 328-31

percents as, 392-93

subtraction, 270-77, 282-83, 286-89

**Freezing point,** 170

**Front-end estimation,** 62-63
computer and, 492

**Functions,** 14-15, 70, 250, 372-73

**Gallons,** 310, 528

**Games,** fair and unfair, 410-11

**Gather data.** *See* Data collection and analysis.

**Generalization,** 181

**Geoboard,** 357, 373

**Geometric constructions,** 352-53, 358-59, 362-63, 368-69, 370-71, 378, 448-51

**Geometric figures.** *See also* specific figures.
plane figures, 352-71

solid figures, 351-51, 378

**Geometry,** 350-378
coordinate, 372-73

**Glossary,** 529-35

**Grams,** 164-65, 528

**Graphing points,** 372-73

**Graphs**
bar, 90-91, 112-13, 331, 385, 402-03, 452-53

circle, 253, 326-27, 394, 401, 490

computer, 498

double bar, 96-97

interpreting, 90-91, 98-99, 100-1

line 90-91, 92-95, 98-99, 101, 172-73

pictograph, 98, 498

**Greater than (>) symbol,** 32, 69, 181, 183, 219, 254

**Greatest common factor,** 246-47

**Group decision making,** group skills, 20-21. *See also* Applied problem solving, Data collection and analysis.

**Grouping (associative) property,** 6-7, 8-9

**Health and fitness data bank,** 474-76

**Health and fitness data bank problems,** 59, 69, 359, 363

**Hexagons,** 366

**Horizontal axis,** 92, 94

**Hour,** 168, 528

**Hundred thousands,** 28-29

**Hundreds,** 28-29

**Hundredths,** 40-41

**Impossible events,** 414-15

**Improper fractions,** 256-59

**Inch,** 302-3, 528

**Inequalities.** *See* Comparing and ordering.

**Input/Output.** *See* Functions.

**Interpret graphs.** *See* Graphs.

**Interpret the remainder,** 194-95

**Interpreting data.** *See* Data collection and analysis.

**Inverse operations,** 16-17, 185, 188, 202, 212-13, 214-15

**Isosceles triangles,** 352

**Keys,** for pictographs, 90

**Kilograms,** 164-65

**Kilometers,** 160

**Kites,** 356-57, 358

**Labels,** of graphs, 90, 94

**Language arts data bank,** 468-69

**Language arts data bank problems,** 5, 9, 271, 289

**Lattice multiplication,** 146

**Least common denominator,** 272-73

**Least common multiple,** 272-73

**Length**
customary units, 300-1

estimation, 152-53, 155

feet, yards, and miles, 304-5

# INDEX

metric units, 152-57
parts of an inch, 302-3
**Less than ( < ) symbol,** 32-33, 69, 181, 183, 219, 254
**Like denominators,** 270-71
**Line graphs,** 92-95
**Line segment,** 350
**Line of symmetry,** 352, 358
**Liquid measure,** 162-63, 310-11
**Liters,** 162-63
**Logic errors** (calculator), 484
**Logical reasoning.** *See* Critical thinking.
**Lowest-terms fractions,** 248-49, 394-95

**Magic squares,** 86
**Making change,** 467
**Manipulatives,** 28, 40, 42, 66, 74, 112-13, 162, 184, 192, 198, 242-43, 254, 256, 274, 276, 282, 350, 352, 358, 372, 410, 412-13
**Map scale,** 388
**Mass,** 164-65
**Math history,** 24, 54, 86, 153
**Mathematical probability,** 416-17
**Math reasoning**
adding, 61
adding mixed numbers, 285, 289
adding and subtracting fractions, 271, 277
analyzing solid figures, 351
analyzing triangles, 353
area of an irregularly shaped figure, 439
area of a parallelogram, 447
area of a rectangle, 159
area of a right triangle, 443
area of a triangle, 445
circles, 369
circumferences, 371
comparing and ordering fractions, 255
compensation, 79
congruent figures, 363
coordinate geometry, 373
customary units of capacity, 311
customary units of length, 301, 303, 305

customary units of weight, 313
decimals, 41, 43, 45, 69
differences, 77
dividing, 189
dividing decimals by 10, 100, 1,000, 228
dividing fractions, 341
dividing special cases, 225
equally likely outcomes, 413
equivalent fractions, 243, 245
estimating, 59, 109, 123, 125, 137, 139
front-end, 63
estimating length, 153
estimating quotient digits, 215
estimating quotients, 183, 191, 219
estimating with percents, 397
estimating by sampling, 423
experimental and mathematical probability, 417
fair and unfair games, 411
finding larger quotients, 221
fractions, 241
grams and kilograms, 165
graphs, 91, 93, 95, 97
greatest common factor, 247
improper fractions, 257, 259
least common multiples, 273
measuring angles, 355
meters and centimeters, 155
milliliters and liters, 163
mixed numbers, 257, 259
multiplying, 121
multiplying decimals, 135
multiplying and dividing, 213
multiplying fractions, 331
multiplying fractions and whole numbers, 325
multiplying mixed numbers, 337
number frames, 29
number properties, 7, 9
numerical expressions, 5
1-digit quotients, 217
percent, 391
percent as decimal or fraction, 393
percent of a number, 399
perimeter, 435
place values, 31
polygons, 367
probability of outcomes, 415

proportions, 387
quadrilaterals, 357, 359
questionnaires, 104-5, 232-33, 342-43
quotients, 181
range, mode, and mean, 103
ratios, 383
ratio tables, 385
remainders, 201
rounding, 35
rounding decimals, 46-47
simulation, 112-13, 417, 424-25, 452-53
subtracting mixed numbers, 287, 289
surface area, 451
time, 169
2- and 3-digit quotients, 187
whole numbers, 33
volume, 449
**Math symbols,** 4-5 *See also* Algebra.
**Math words,** 4-5
**Mean,** 102-3
**Measurement**
angles, 354-55
area, 158-59, 438-39, 440, 442-45, 450-51
capacity, 162-63, 310-11, 528
customary units, 300-13, 528
estimation, 152-53, 164-65, 168-69, 174, 183, 305, 312-13, 318, 320, 436-37, 456, 499
length, 152-57, 160, 300-5
metric units, 152-67
table of measures, 528
temperature, 170-71, 308
time, 168-69, 176
**Median,** 102-3
**Memory keys,** 140, 439, 486
**Mental math**
adding mixed numbers, 285
adding and subtracting, 9
area of a right triangle, 443
breaking apart numbers, 130
as calculation method, 72
compatible numbers, 8-9
compensation, 78-79
customary units of length, 301
decimals, 45, 109
dividing decimals by 10, 100, 1,000, 228
estimating with percents, 396-97

lowest-terms fractions, 249
multiplying decimals by
  10, 100, 1,000, 142-43
percent as decimal or fraction,
  393
quotients, 180-81, 201, 212
special products, 120-21
subtracting mixed numbers,
  287
surface area, 451
techniques, 125, 225
time, 169
2- and 3-digit quotients, 187
**Meters,** 152, 154-55
**Metric units of measure.**
  *See* Measurement.
**Miles,** 304-5
**Milliliters,** 162-63
**Millimeters,** 156-57
**Millions,** place value, 30-31
**Minute,** 168, 528
**Mixed numbers**
  adding, 282-85, 288-89
  concept, 256-59
  multiplying, 336-37
  subtracting, 282-83, 286-89
**Mixed review,** 7, 15, 31, 47,
  59, 79, 95, 103, 123, 139,
  157, 163, 183, 201, 221,
  229, 243, 259, 277, 287,
  305, 313, 331, 359, 367,
  391, 397, 415, 425, 435, 447
**Mode,** 102-3
**Money**
  adding, 68
  dividing, 98-99
  making change, 467
  multiplying, 124
  subtracting, 76
**More practice bank,** 500-27
**Multiple,** least common,
  272-73
**Multiples,** 142, 228
**Multiple-step problems,**
  126-27
**Multiplication,** 213.
  *See also* Products.
  associative (grouping)
    property of, 6-7
  commutative (order) property
    of, 6-7
  decimals, 132-25, 138-39,
    142-43
  distributive property, 130
  fractions, 328-31

calculator and, 489
fractions and whole numbers,
  324-25
mental math and, 120-21
mixed numbers, 336-37
one property of, 12
whole numbers, 124-25
zero property of, 12
**Multiplication-addition
property.** *See* Distributive
property.
**Multiplication constant**
  (calculator), 485

**Number line,** 34, 46
**Number pairs,** 372-73
**Number patterns.** *See*
Patterns.
**Number properties**
  associative (grouping), 6-7
  commutative (order), 6-7
  distributive, 130
  one property of
    multiplication, 12
  zero property, 12
**Number relationships.**
  *See* Critical thinking,
  Math reasoning.
**Numbers**
  adding, 60-61
  comparing and ordering,
    32-33, 44-45, 254-55
  compatible, 8-9, 249, 285
  dividing, 184-85
  expanded form of, 28-29
  expressing, 4-5
  finding percent of, 398-99
  fractions of
    estimating, 326
    multiplying, 324-25
  mixed, 256-59
    adding, 282-85
    multiplying, 336-37
    subtracting, 286-87
  odd and even, 63
  prime factors of, 266
  range of, 250
  rounding, 34-35
  square, 24
  standard form of, 28-29, 39
  subtracting, 60-61
  triangular, 24
**Number scale,** 90
**Number sense,** *See* Critical
Thinking, Math Reasoning.

**Number sentences.**
  *See* Equations.
**Number theory.** *See also*
Comparing and ordering,
Factors, Multiples, Number
properties, Place value.
  even and odd numbers, 63
  prime and composite
    numbers, 266
  square numbers, 24
  triangular numbers, 24
**Numerals, Roman,** 54
**Numerator,** 240
**Numerical expressions,**
  4-5, 189

**Obtuse angles,** 354
**Obtuse triangle,** 360
**Octagon,** 366
**Odd numbers,** 63
**One property,** of
  multiplication, 12
**Ones,** place value, 28-30
**Operations.** *See also* Addition,
Division, Multiplication,
Subtraction.
  order of, 6-7, 486
  understanding, 10-11
**Order of operations,**
  6-7, 486
**Order (commutative)
property,** 6-7
**Ordered pairs,** 372-73
**Ordering.** *See* Comparing and
  ordering
**Organizing data,** 116,
  166-67, 260-61. *See also*
  Data collection and analysis.
**Ounces,** 312-13, 528
**Outcomes,** 412-15
**Overflow error** (calculator),
  484

**Parallelogram,** 356-57
  area, 446-47
**Parentheses,** order of
  operations and, 6
**Patterns**
  divisibility, 236
  geometric, 351, 366-67,
    368-69
  number, 14-15, 24, 86,
    341, 406
  in problem solving, 46-47,
    61, 108-9, 168-69

**Pentagons,** 366
**Percent,** 390-91
  calculator and, 490
  as decimal or fraction, 392-93
  estimating with, 396-97
  lowest-terms fractions and,
    394
  of a number, 398-99
**Perimeter problems,** 200-1,
  434-35, 436-37, 440
  computer and, 494
**Periods,** 28, 30
**Pi,** 370
**Pictographs,** 90-91, 212
**Pint,** 310, 528
**Place value**
  chart, 28, 30, 40
  decimal, 40-43
  expanded form, 28-31
  millions and billions, 30-31
  periods, 28, 30
  standard form, 28-31
  thousands, 28-29
**Plane figures,** 356-60, 368-69
**Points,** 350, 372-73
**Polygons,** 350-53, 356-360,
  366-367
**Polyhedron,** 350-351, 378
**Possible outcomes,** 412,
  414-15
**Pounds,** 312-13, 528
**Powers of ten,** 148
**Practice.** *See also* Mixed
  review, Skills review bank.
  more practice bank, 500-527
  power practice, 13, 23, 39,
    53, 71, 85, 101, 115, 131,
    147, 161, 175, 193, 207,
    223, 235, 251, 265, 281,
    295, 309, 319, 333, 345,
    361, 377, 395, 405, 419,
    429, 441, 455
**Pre-algebra.** *See* Algebra.
**Predictions,** 414-15. *See also*
  Estimation, Mental math.
**Prime factorization,** 266
**Prime numbers,** 266
**Prisms,** 350-51, 378, 450
**Probability,** 410-25
  chances, 414-15
  computer and, 497
  fair and unfair games,
    410-11
  equally likely outcomes,
    412-13

experimental probability,
  416-17
mathematical probability,
  416-17
outcomes, 414-15
prediction, 420
random sample, 422-23
simulation, 417, 424-25
**Problems,** *See also* Data bank
  problems, Data hunt
  problems.
  multiple-step, 126-27, 334
  one-step, 16
**Problem solving.** *See also*
  Applied problem solving,
  Calculator-assisted problem
  solving, Data collection and
  analysis, Problem solving
  applications, Problem solving
  skills and strategies.
  algebra in, 332
  understanding the operations,
    10-11, 13
  using tables, 7, 9
**Problem-solving applications**
  addition and subtraction, 61
  angles, measuring, 355
  area
    irregularly shaped figure, 439
    parallelogram, 447
    rectangle, 159
    right triangle, 443
    triangle, 445
  capacity, customary units of,
    311
  circles, 369
  circumferences, 371
  compensation, 79
  congruent figures, 363
  coordinate geometry, 373
  decimals 43, 60, 139, 201
    dividing by 10, 100, 1,000,
      228
    multiplying, 135
    rounding, 46-47
  differences, 77
  division, 189
    special cases, 225
  equally likely outcomes, 413
  estimation, 5, 18-19, 59, 109,
    123, 137
    front-end, 63
    of length, 153
    with percents, 397
    of quotient digits, 215

of quotients, 183, 219
  by sampling, 423
fractions 241
  adding and subtracting,
    271, 277
  comparing and ordering, 255
  dividing, 341
  equivalent, 243, 245
  improper, 257, 259
  lowest-terms, 249
  multiplying, 325, 331
games, fair and unfair, 411
grams and kilograms, 165
graphs, 91, 93, 95, 97
length
  customary units of, 303, 305
  estimating, 153
least common multiples, 273
meters and centimeters, 155
milliliters and liters, 163
millimeters, 157
mixed numbers, 257, 259
  adding, 285, 289
  multiplying, 337
  subtracting, 289-89
money, 18-19, 29, 47, 63, 65,
  72-73, 278, 467
multiplication, 121, 125
multi-step problems,
  126-27
percent, 391
  as decimal or fraction, 393
  of a number, 399
perimeter, 435
place values, 31
polygons, 367
probability
  experimental and
    mathematical, 417
  of outcomes, 415
proportions, 387
quadrilaterals, 357, 359
questionnaires, 104-5,
  232-33, 342-43
quotients, 181, 191
  finding larger, 221
  1-digit, 217
  2- and 3-digit, 187
range, mean, median, and
  mode, 103
ratios, 383
ratio tables, 385
rounding, 35, 46-47
simulation, 112-13, 417,
  424-25, 452-53

solid figures, analyzing, 351
surface area, 451
time, 169
triangles
 are of, 443, 445
 analyzing, 353
volume, 449
weight, customary units of, 313
whole numbers
 comparing, 33
 multiplying, 325
word problems, 39
**Problem-solving skills and strategies**
choose a calculation method, 72-73, 222
choose the operation, 16-17
deciding when to estimate, 18-19, 314
determining reasonable answers, 202-3
draw a picture, 36-37
estimating the answer, 230, 436
extra data, 110-11
finding related problems, 400
guess and check, 64-65
interpreting remainders, 194-95
look for a pattern, 226
make an organized list, 166-67
make a table, 106-7
multiple-step problems, 334
problems with more than one answer, 306-7
problems without solutions, 278
solve a simpler problem, 128-29
understanding the question, 48-49
use logical reasoning, 252-53
using a calculator, 81-81, 140-41, 338
using data from an order form, 420
using data from a picture, 364
using data from a scale drawing, 374-75, 388
using data from a thermometer, 170-71
work backward, 196-97

**Products,** 6. *See also* Multiplication.
 cross, 245, 387
 estimating, 122-23, 326-27, 493
**Properties of operations.** *See* Number properties.
**Proportions,** 386-88
**Protractor,** 354-55
**Pyramids,** 350-51, 352, 378

**Quadrilaterals,** 356-59

**Radius,** 368-69, 370-71
**Random samples,** 422-23
**Range,** 102-3
**Rates,** 106-7, 214-15. *See also* Ratio.
**Ratio,** 382-391
 concept, 382-83
 tables, 384-85
**Reasonable answers,** 11, 18, 19, 63, 153, 202
**Reasoning.** *See* Critical thinking, Math reasoning.
**Rectangles,** 356-57
 area, 158-59, 438-39, 440, 450
 perimeter, 200-1, 434-35, 436-37, 440
**Rectangular prisms,** 351
 surface area, 450
**Reflections,** 362-63
**Regrouping,** 6, 8-9, 66-67
**Regular polygons,** 366-67
**Remainders,** interpreting, 194-95
**Renaming,** 276
**Rhombus,** 356-57
**Right angles,** 354-55, 356, 364
**Right triangles,** 360, 442-43
**Roman numerals,** 54
**Rotation,** 362-63
**Rounding**
 decimals, 46-47
 in estimating
 differences, 58-59, 280
 products, 122-23, 326
 quotients, 182, 214, 218
 sums, 58-59, 280
 fractions, 280, 326
 whole numbers, 34-35

**Running totals** (calculator), 100

**Sampling,** 422-23
**Scale drawing,** 374-75, 388
**Scalene triangle,** 352
**Scales**
 on graphs, 90-97
 on maps, 388-89
**Science data bank,** 470-73
**Science data bank problems,** 219, 225, 303, 387
**Segment,** line, 350
**Sequence.** *See* Patterns.
**Short division,** 208
**Side of a figure,** 378
**Simulation,** 112-13, 417, 424-25, 452-53
**Situational problems.** *See* Applied problem solving, Data collection and analysis, Data hunt problems, Problem solving.
**Skills review bank,** 460-67
**Slide,** 362-63
**Slope,** on line graph, 92
**Social studies data bank,** 480-83
**Social studies data bank problems,** 33, 45, 95, 103, 183, 191, 413, 417
**Solid figures,** 350-51, 378
**Solution**
 finishing the, 291
 problems without, 278-79
 talk about your, 81, 279
 think about your, 11, 171, 195
**Space figures.** *See* Solid figures.
**Sphere,** 350-51
**Square**
 calculator and, 490
 figures, 356
 numbers, 24
 root, 490
**Square units,** 158-159, 440
**Standard form,** of numbers, 28-29, 31, 39
**Standard time,** 176
**Statistics.** *See* Data collection and analysis, Graphs, Probability.
**Subject integration.** *See* Curriculum connections.

# INDEX

**Subtraction**
decimals, 74-77
fractions, 270-77
calculator and, 488
estimating, 280
mixed numbers, 286-89
whole numbers, 60-61
zero property, 12
**Sums,** 6. *See also* Addition.
computer and, 495
decimals, estimating, 58
fractions, estimating, 280
**Surface area,** 450-51
**Survey,** 97, 116, 292
**Symbols,** math, 4-5. *See also*
Algebra.
**Symmetry,** line of, 352, 358

**Table of measures,** 528
**Tables**
problem solving using, 7, 9,
106-7
using data from, 61, 65, 69,
100-11, 123, 127, 195, 197,
203, 215, 226-27, 230-31,
260-61, 334-35
**Tablespoon,** 310, 528
**Technology.** *See* Calculator,
Calculator bank, Computer
bank.
**Temperature,** 170-71, 308
**Tens,** 28-30
**Ten thousands,** 28-30

**Tenths,** 40-41
**Tessellations,** 366-67
**Theoretical probability.**
*See* Probability.
**Thermometer,** 170-71, 308
**Thinking questions,** *See*
Critical thinking, Math
reasoning.
**Thousands,** place value, 28-29
**Thousandths,** 42-43
**Three-dimensional figures.**
*See* Solid figures.
**Time,** 168-69, 528
elapsed, 169
zones, 176
**Titles,** of graphs, 90-91, 94,
97, 113
**Tons,** 312, 528
**Transformations,** 362-63
**Translations,** 362-63
**Trapezoid,** 356-57
**Tree diagram,** 266, 430
**Triangles,** 352-53, 360
area, 303, 442-43, 444-45
**Triangular numbers,** 24
**Triangular prism,** 350-51,
378
**Triangular pyramid,** 350-51,
378
**Turn** (rotation), 362-63
**Two dimensional figures,**
352-371. *See also* specific
figures.

**Underflow error** (calculator),
484
**Unfair game,** 410-11
**Unfinished problems,**
198, 331
**Unitizing,** 152-153, 161
**Unlike fractions,** 276-277

**Variables,** 12, 33, 38, 250
**Vertex,** 350
**Vertical axis,** 92, 94
**Visual thinking,** 351, 355,
378, 440, 449
**Volume**
customary units, 310-11,
448-49
estimating, 174, 318
metric units, 162-63

**Weight**
customary units, 312-13
estimating, 164
metric units, 164-65
**Working together.** *See* Applied
problem solving, Data
collection and analysis.
**Write your own problem,** 10,
17, 127, 341, 365, 389. *See
also* Unfinished problems.

**Zero property,** 12

# ACKNOWLEDGMENTS

## Illustration Acknowledgments

**Alex Bloch** p. 404, 465, 467

**Barbara Counsellar** p. 58, 73, 132, 397, 442

**Tony Crnkovich** p. 376

**David Cunningham** p. 24a

**Marie DeJohn** p. 152, 153, 312, 313

**Simon Galkin** p. 114, 208, 430, 462

**Betty Gee** p. 468b, 469b, 471a, 472c

**Bill Gerhold** p. 84, 467

**Jeff Hukill** p. 70, 76, 472a, 472b, 477a, 479a, 481a

**Susan Jaekel** p. 63, 122, 123, 134

**Tom Leonard** p. 29

**Susan Lexa** p. 162, 163, 164, 165, 270, 304 b & c

**Rich Lo** p. 54

**Laurie Marks** p. 244

**Tim McWilliams** p. 266

**Judy Nostrant** p. 14, 32, 33, 34, 41, 46, 106, 197, 226, 258, 288, 308, 383

**Tim O'Toole** p. 148, 464, 494

**Rodney Pate** p. 12, 36, 37

**Alison Perreault** p, 346a, 463, 499

**Walter Porter** p. 72, 100, 105, 109, 124, 129, 130, 180, 182b, 183, 186, 187, 214, 215, 272, 335, 350, 351, 361, 364, 365, 369, 382, 388, 389, 395, 398, 446, 448, 451

**Rick Sams** p. 470a, 470b, 483a

**Margaret Sanfilippo** p. 30, 196, 259, 261, 304a, 334, 340, 410, 412, 416

**Seventeenth Street Studios, Valerie Winemiller** p. 280, 371

**Joel Snyder** p. 140, 141, 192

**Rosalind Solomon** p. 468a, 469a, 473a

**Andrea Tachiera** p. 69, 108, 260, 286, 287

**Karen Tafoya** p. 198a & c, 273

**Dave Taylor** p. 421f, 461

**Pat Traub** p. 59, 302, 303, 306

**Laslo Vespremi** p. 58, 157, 171, 182a, 217, 227, 330

**Nancy Lee Walters** p. 236

## Photo Acknowledgments

**Table of Contents:** iii Ken Karp*; iv Ken Karp*; v Lawrence Migdale*; vi Janice Sheldon*; vii Stephen Frisch*; viii Ken Karp*; ix Ken Karp*; x Janice Sheldon*; xi Ken Karp*; xii Ken Karp*.

**Chapter 1:** 2-3 Robert Caputo/Stock, Boston; 4 Janice Sheldon*; 6 Ken Karp*; 7 Ken Karp*; 8 Jeffry W. Myers/The Stock Market; 11 Ken Karp*; 16 Douglas L. Peck*; 17 Barbara Von Hoffmann/Tom Stack & Associates; 18 Ken Karp*; 20-21 Douglas L. Peck*.

**Chapter 2:** 26-27 Leif Skoogfors/Woodfin Camp & Associates; 28 Janice Sheldon*; 38 Janice Sheldon*; 44 Christiana Dittman/Rainbow; 48 James W. Kay/Bruce Coleman Inc.; 50-51 Erwin & Peggy Bauer/Bruce Coleman Inc.; 54 Janice Sheldon*.

**Chapter 3:** 56-57 Bob Daemmrich/Stock, Boston; 60 John Elk III/Stock, Boston; 61 Matt Bradley/Bruce Coleman Inc.; 62 Janice Sheldon*; 64 Janice Sheldon*; 66 Janice Sheldon*; 78 Douglas L. Peck*; 79 Douglas L. Peck*; 80 John Cancalosi/Tom Stack & Associates; 81 Ken Straiton/The Stock Market; 82-83 John Elk III/Stock, Boston; 86 Janice Sheldon*.

**Chapter 4:** 88-89 Eric Lars Bakke; 96 Jeff Persons/Stock, Boston; 98 Janice Sheldon*; 99 Hank Morgan/Rainbow; 102 Jon Feingersh/Stock, Boston; 103 Harry S Truman Library; 104 Janice Sheldon*; 110 Tim Davis; 111 M.A. Chappell/Animals, Animals; 112-113 Nick Pavloff*.

**Chapter 5:** 118-119 Robert Rathe/Stock, Boston; 120 Thomas Braise/The Stock Market; 121 David Madison/Bruce Coleman Inc.; 126 Lawrence Migdale*; 127 Janice Sheldon*; 138 Janice Sheldon*; 143 Ken Karp*; 144-145 Wayland Lee*/Addison-Wesley Publishing Company.

**Chapter 6:** 150-151 Bill Ross/West Light; 154 Wally McNamee/Woodfin Camp & Associates; 166 Norman Tomalin/Bruce Coleman Inc.; 167 David Madison; 168-169 Gerry Cranham/Photo Researchers; 172-173 Tim Davis*.

**Chapter 7:** 178-179 Michael Tamborrino/The Stock Market; 184 Janice Sheldon*; 188 Jeffry W. Myers/Stock, Boston; 190 Bob Daemmrich/Stock, Boston; 191 Wayland Lee*/Addison-Wesley Publishing Company; 194 Doug Greene/The Stock Market; 195 David Stoecklein/The Stock Market; 198 Janice Sheldon*; 202 Wayland Lee*/Addison-Wesley Publishing Company; 203 Larry Lefever/Grant Heilman; 204-205 Tim Davis*; 208 Lawrence Midgale*.

**Chapter 8:** 210-211 Gerd Ludwig/Woodfin Camp & Associates; 216 Barbara Kirk/The Stock Market; 217 Wayland Lee*/Addison-Wesley Publishing Company; 218 Ken Karp*; 222 Douglas L. Peck*; 224 David Madison; 231 Charles Feil/Stock, Boston; 232-233 Tim Davis*; 234 Janice Sheldon*.

**Chapter 9:** 238-239 Janice Sheldon*; 240 Dagmar Fabricius/Stock, Boston; 246 Ken Karp*; 248 Ken Karp*; 252 Vince Streano/The Stock Market; 256 Ken Karp*; 257 Ken Karp*; 262 Stephen Frisch*; 263A Stephen Frisch*; 263B Charles Thatcher/Tony Stone Worldwide; 263C NASA.

**Chapter 10:** 268-269 Stephen Frisch*; 274 Janice Sheldon*; 276 Wayland Lee*/Addison-Wesley Publishing Company; 278 Tim Davis*; 279 Tim Davis*; 282 Janice Sheldon*; 284 Tim Davis*; 290 Tim Davis*; 292-293 Tim Davis*.

**Chapter 11:** 298-299 Paul Chesley/All Stock; 300 Tim Davis*; 305 Janice Sheldon*; 310 Mark Tuschman*; 314 Ken Karp*; 315 Ken Karp*; 317 Nick Pavloff*; 320 Janice Sheldon*.

## ACKNOWLEDGMENTS

**Chapter 12:** 322-323 Richard Pasley/Stock, Boston; 324 Nick Pavloff*; 325 Joe McDonald/Bruce Coleman Inc.; 326 Menschenfreund/The Stock Market; 328 Janice Sheldon*; 332 Janice Sheldon*; 336 Janice Sheldon*; 337 Thomas Kitchin/Tom Stack & Associates; 338 Lawrence Migdale*; 339 Ken Karp*; 342-343 Ken Karp*.

**Chapter 13:** 348-349 Warren Morgan/West Light; 358 Focus On Sports; 362 David Madison; 366 Janice Sheldon*; 368 David Barnes/The Stock Market; 370 Janice Sheldon*; 374-375 Elliott Smith*.

**Chapter 14:** 380-381 Janice Sheldon*; 384 Tim Davis*; 386 Gary Milburn/Tom Stack & Associates; 387 Sandy Roessler/The Stock Market; 394 Kasz Maciag/The Stock Market; 399 Ken Karp*; 402-403 Wayland Lee*/Addison-Wesley Publishing Company; 406 Ken Karp*.

**Chapter 15:** 408-409 Lawrence Migdale; 410 Janice Sheldon*; 418 David C. Bitters; 420 E.R. Degginger/Bruce Coleman Inc.; 421B David Madison; 421T Terry Eiler/Stock, Boston; 423 David Madison; 426 Vatican, Museo Missionario Etnografico/Art Resource, New York; 427A Smithsonian Institution, Museum of African Art/Art Resource, New York; 427B New York, Museum of Primitive Art/Giraudon/Art Resource, New York.

**Chapter 16:** 432-433 David Hurn/Magnum Photos; 434 Brent Peters/The Stock Market; 444 Bill Gallery/Stock, Boston; 453 Janice Sheldon*.

*Photographed expressly for Addison-Wesley Publishing Company, Inc.

Special thanks to Shell Self-Serve Gas Station, The Alamada, Berkeley, California; Department of Geology, University of California, Berkeley, California; Black American West Museum, Denver, Colorado; Anshen & Allen, San Francisco, California; Berkeley Cycle, Berkeley, California; Desktop Products, Inc., Emeryville, California; Murray's Cheese Shop, New York, New York; Davidson Middle School, San Rafael, California; Rodney's Video Warehouse, White Plains, New York.